INSIGHT GUIDES

NORTHERN ITALY

INSIGHT GUIDE
NORTHERN ITALY

Editorial
Project Editor
Dorothy Stannard
Editorial Director
Brian Bell

Distribution
UK & Ireland
GeoCenter International Ltd
Meridian House, Churchill Way West
Basingstoke, Hampshire RG21 6YR
Fax: (44) 1256 817988
United States
Langenscheidt Publishers, Inc.
36–36 33rd Street 4th Floor
Long Island City, NY 11106
Fax: 1 (718) 784 0640
Australia
Universal Publishers
1 Waterloo Road
Macquarie Park, NSW 2113
Fax: (61) 2 9888 9074
New Zealand
Hema Maps New Zealand Ltd (HNZ)
Unit D, 24 Ra ORA Drive
East Tamaki, Auckland
Fax: (64) 9 273 6479
Worldwide
Apa Publications GmbH & Co.
Verlag KG (Singapore branch)
38 Joo Koon Road, Singapore 628990
Tel: (65) 6865 1600. Fax: (65) 6861 6438

Printing
Insight Print Services (Pte) Ltd
38 Joo Koon Road, Singapore 628990
Tel: (65) 6865 1600. Fax: (65) 6861 6438

First Edition 1999
Updated 2007

CONTACTING THE EDITORS
We would appreciate it if readers would alert us to errors or outdated information by writing to:
Insight Guides, P.O. Box 7910, London SE1 1WE, England.
Fax: (44) 20 7403 0290.
insight@apaguide.co.uk

www.insightguides.com
In North America:
www.insighttravelguides.com

About This Book

The first Insight Guide pioneered the use of creative full-colour photography in travel guides in 1970. Since then, we have expanded our range to cater for our readers' need not only for reliable information about their chosen destination but also for a real understanding of the culture and workings of that destination.

Now, when the internet can supply inexhaustible (but not always reliable) facts, our books marry text and pictures to provide those much more elusive qualities: knowledge and discernment. To achieve this, they rely heavily on the authority and experience of a team of locally based writers and photographers.

How to use this book

Insight Guide: Northern Italy has been carefully structured to convey a thorough understanding of the region and its culture, and to guide readers through its sights and attractions:

◆ The Features section, headed by a yellow colour bar, covers the country's history and culture in a series of lively and authoritative essays written by specialists.

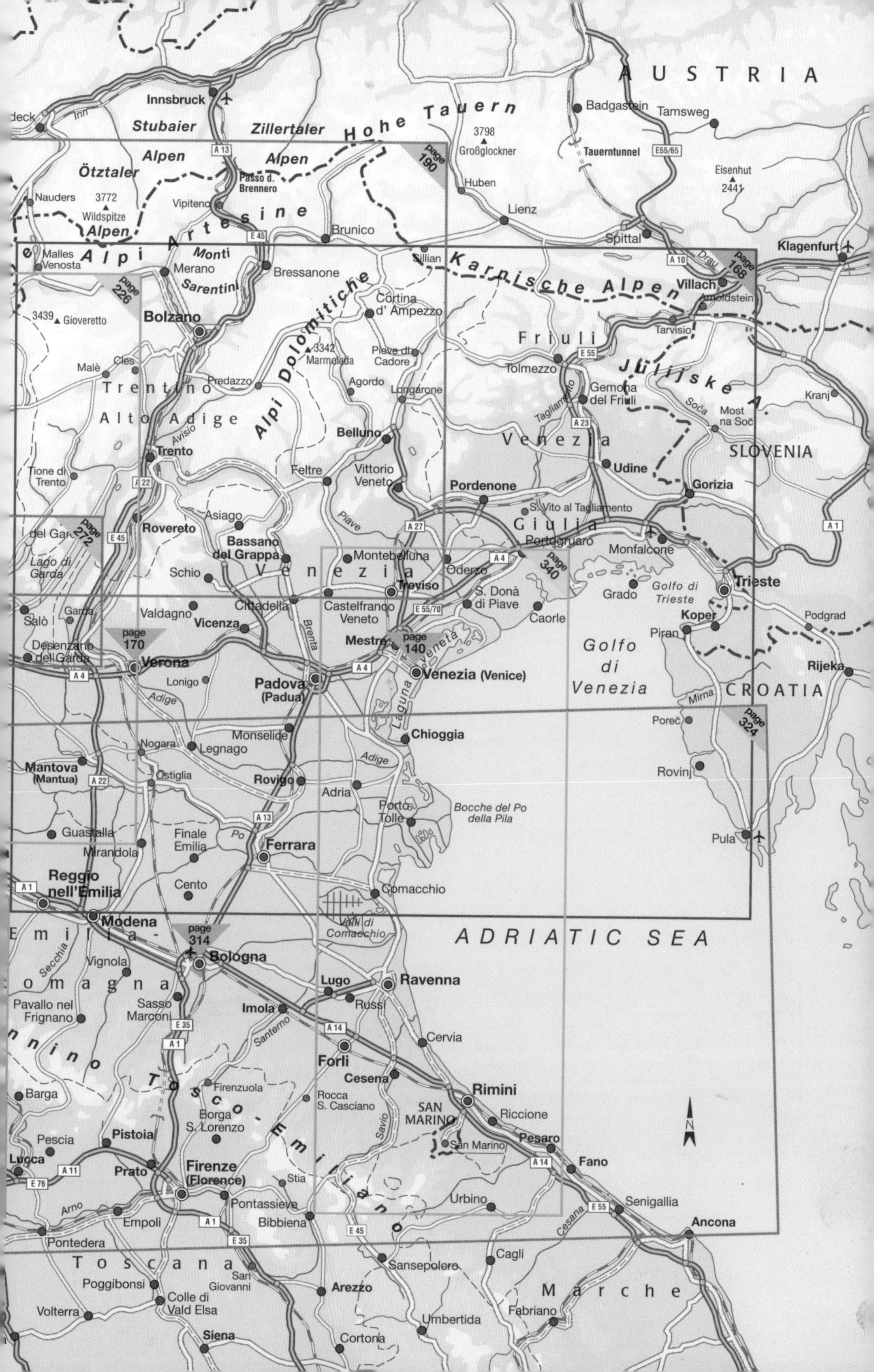
AUSTRIA
Innsbruck
Stubaier
Zillertaler
Alpen
Ötztaler
Alpen
Hohe Tauern
3798
Großglockner
Badgastein
Tamsweg
Tauerntunnel
E55/65
Eisenhut
2441
page 190
A 13
Passo d. Brennero
Vipiteno
Nauders
3772
Wildspitze
Alpen
Alpi Artesine
Huben
Lienz
Brunico
Spittal
Klagenfurt
Malles Venosta
Monti Sarentini
Merano
Bressanone
Sillian
Karnische Alpen
A 10
Drau
page 168
Villach
Arnoldstein
page 226
3439 Gioveretto
Bolzano
Alpi Dolomitiche
Cortina d'Ampezzo
Tarvisio
3342 Marmolada
Pieve di Cadore
Friuli
E 55
Tolmezzo
Julijske A.
Kranj
Malè
Cles
Predazzo
Agordo
Longarone
Gemona del Friuli
Tagliamento
Soča
Most na Soči
Trentino
Alto Adige
Avisio
Belluno
A 23
Venezia
SLOVENIA
Trento
Tione di Trento
A 22
Feltre
Vittorio Veneto
Udine
Pordenone
Gorizia
S. Vito al Tagliamento
Giulia
Asiago
Piave
A 27
A 1
Rovereto
page 272
del Garda
E 45
Bassano del Grappa
Montebelluna
Portogruaro
A 4
Monfalcone
Lago di Garda
Schio
Venezia
Oderzo
page 340
Treviso
Trieste
S. Donà di Piave
Grado
Golfo di Trieste
Salò
Garda
Valdagno
Cittadella
Castelfranco Veneto
E 55/70
Caorle
Koper
Podgrad
Vicenza
Piran
page 170
Mestre
page 140
Golfo di Venezia
Desenzano del Garda
Verona
A 4
Brenta
Rijeka
Padova (Padua)
Venezia (Venice)
Laguna veneta
Lonigo
Adige
Mirna
CROATIA
Poreč
page 324
Monselice
Chioggia
Nogara
Legnago
Mantova (Mantua)
A 22
Ostiglia
Rovigo
Adige
Rovinj
Adria
Porto Tolle
Bocche del Po della Pila
A 13
Guastalla
Finale Emilia
Po
Ferrara
Pula
Mirandola
Reggio nell'Emilia
A 1
Cento
Comacchio
Modena
Valli di Comacchio
ADRIATIC SEA
Emilia-
page 314
Secchia
Bologna
Vignola
Romagna
Lugo
Ravenna
Pavallo nel Frignano
Sasso Marconi
Imola
Russi
E 35
Santerno
A 14
A 1
Cervia
Appennino
Forlì
Cesena
Tosco-Emiliano
Firenzuola
Rimini
Barga
Rocca S. Casciano
SAN MARINO
Riccione
Borga S. Lorenzo
Savio
N
Pescia
Pistoia
San Marino
Pesaro
Lucca
A 11
Prato
Firenze (Florence)
A 14
Fano
E 76
Stia
Pontassieve
Urbino
Senigallia
Arno
E 55
Empoli
Bibbiena
Cesana
A 1
Ancona
E 35
E 45
Pontedera
Toscana
Cagli
Sansepolcro
San Giovanni
Poggibonsi
Colle di Vald Elsa
Arezzo
Marche
Volterra
Fabriano
Umbertida
Siena
Cortona

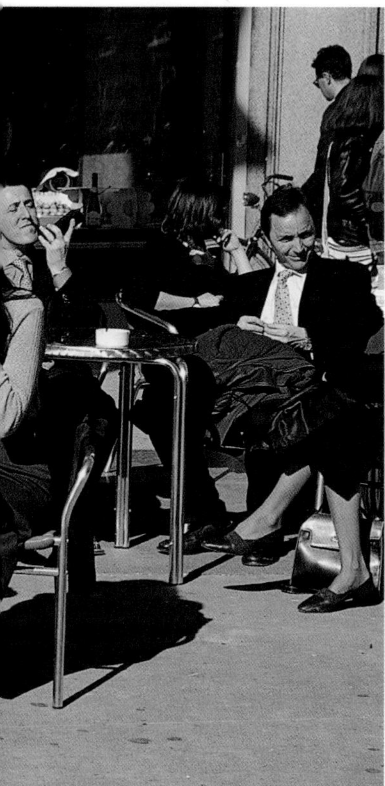

◆ The Places section, with a blue bar, provides full details of all the sights and areas worth seeing. The chief places of interest are coordinated by number with the corresponding maps.

◆ The Travel Tips section, headed by an orange bar, at the back of the book offers a convenient point of reference for information on travel, accommodation, restaurants, and other practical aspects of the country. Its contents are indexed on the back flap, which also serves as a convenient bookmark.

◆ The Photographs are chosen not only to illustrate the beauty and variety of the cities and landscapes but also to convey an impression of the everyday lives of the Northern Italians.

The contributors

Long-standing Italophile **Lisa Gerard-Sharp**, a writer and broadcaster who wrote the majority of this book, aims to convey the contemporary flavour of life in the north – from its guise as a café society and fashion showcase to its seminal role as an economic powerhouse and hot-bed of regionalism. **Adele Evans** thoroughly updated this guide as well as contributing new material.

Roger Williams, journalist, novelist and Insight Guide veteran, whose acclaimed novel *Lunch With Elizabeth David* was partly set in Italy, was a leading contributor to the book. He paints a refreshingly new picture of Turin, Piedmont, Valle d'Aosta, Friuli and Trieste. The other key member of the writing team was **Jonathan Keates**, an Italian expert and author of the wrily perceptive *Italian Journeys*, as well as being a regular contributor to the literary pages of the British press. Here, Keates turns his critical eye to the history section, as well as writing the chapter on art and architecture.

The Travel Tips were compiled by **Sibylle Geier** and **Nicky Swallow**. The principal photography was provided by **Bill Wassmann**, **John Heseltine** and **Michael Jenner**. Editing was completed by **Pam Barrett**, Roger Williams and **Dorothy Stannard**. The book was proofread by **Anne Esden** and indexed by **Laura Hicks**.

Map Legend

— · —	International Boundary
- - - -	Region Boundary
▪ • ▪	National Park/Reserve
- - - -	Ferry Route
Ⓜ	Metro
✈ ✈	Airport: International/ Regional
🚌	Bus Station
P	Parking
ℹ	Tourist Information
✉	Post Office
✝ ✝ ✝	Church/Ruins
✝	Monastery
☪	Mosque
✡	Synagogue
♜ ♜	Castle/Ruins
∴	Archaeological Site
∩	Cave
𝐢	Statue/Monument
★	Place of Interest

The main places of interest in the Places section are coordinated by number with a full-colour map (e.g. ❶), and a symbol at the top of every right-hand page tells you where to find the map.

INSIGHT GUIDE
NORTHERN ITALY

CONTENTS

Maps

Northern Italy **136**
Venice **140**
Veneto and Friuli-Venezia Giulia **168**
Verona **170**
Trentino-Alto Adige **190**
Milan **206**
Lombardy **226**
Valle d'Aosta and Piedmont **240**
Turin **254**
Eastern Lakes **272**
Como **279**
Western Lakes **280**
Genoa **292**
The Ligurian Riviera **300**
Bologna **314**
Emilia Romagna **324**
The Adriatic Coast **340**

Northern Italy **Inside front cover**
Venice Transport Network **Inside back cover**

Introduction

This Resonant Region **15**

People

The Northern Italians **17**

History

Decisive Dates **26**
Cultural Corridors **29**
City States and Dynasties **35**
Noble Courts to Nationhood .. **43**
The Tumultuous 20th Century **49**

Features

The Contemporary Scene **59**
Regionalism Rules **65**
Princes of Industry **71**
A Sense of Style.................... **79**
Art and Architecture **85**
Venetian Artists **90**
The Musical Tradition **93**
Rustic and Classic Cuisine **103**
Café Society **110**
Villas and Gardens **117**
Walking and Wildlife **123**

The Certosa di Pavia, Lombardy

Insight on ...

The Venetian Republic 40
Wine 112
Carnival 162
Design 220

Information panels

Football Fever 69
The Fiat Family 72
Textile Valley 83
Parmesan Cheese 109
Palladian Style 121
Venice's Jewish Ghetto 161
Italy with a German Soul 201
Alta Moda 219
Skiing 249
Gabriele D'Annunzio 287
Pavarotti 335
The Po Delta 342
San Marino 351

Places

Introduction 139
Venice 143
The Veneto 167
Friuli-Venezia Giulia 181
Trentino-Alto Adige 189
Milan 205
Lombardy 225
Valle d'Aosta 243
Turin 253
Piedmont 263
The Lakes 271
Genoa 291
The Ligurian Riviera 299
Bologna 313
Emilia Romagna 323
The Adriatic 339

Travel Tips

Getting Acquainted .. 354
Planning the Trip 354
Practical Tips 357
Getting Around 359
Where to Stay 362
Where to Eat 372
Culture 379
Nightlife 381
Festivals 381
Outdoor Activities ... 382
Sport 383
Shopping 384
Language 384
Further Reading 391

♦ **Full Travel Tips index is on page 353**

Polenta
farina di grano duro
farina 00
AGNESI
AGNESI

Dole

botaces
paîsc
paȥedins
DELBA
roc
es dei
CIANPEDÈL
POZA
pati
PERA
clavai
sác
béches
SPORT

THIS RESONANT REGION

Diverse landscapes, a wealth of cultural sites and a proud people make Northern Italy a distinctive region

Northern Italy has previously been ill-served by guidebooks, with a plethora of books on selected cities, notably Venice and Milan, yet a dearth of readable writing on the distinctiveness of northern society, complemented by its rural hinterland and historic cities. Apart from conveying the charm of the scenery, from country villas and gardens to national parks, this book hopes to redress the balance by highlighting the "minor" art cities, from Mantua to Trento, as well as covering the complex social scene. In this, as in all aspects of society, regional rivalry is an Italian characteristic writ large, taking the form of pride in local opera and architecture, dialects and dishes, festivals and football teams.

Moreover, even in standard tourist terms, few comparable regions can match northern Italy for sheer variety of scenery and linked leisure pursuits, from hiking along the Ligurian coast or lounging on the brash Adriatic beaches, to sailing on the melancholic northern lakes, wallowing in the sybaritic spas of the Euganean hills, or simply skiing or dog-sledding in the prestigious Dolomite mountain resorts.

Since the boundaries of northern Italy are disputed by the Italians themselves, we have arbitrarily decided to draw the line beneath Emilia Romagna. This resonantly artistic region was too rich to leave in the notional no-man's land of "central Italy". However, we rightly excluded Florence, Tuscany, Umbria and areas south, since these places are well served in their own right by other Insight Guides. ❑

PRECEDING PAGES: a Venetian gondolier; classic ingredients in the culinary heart of Europe; murals in the South Tyrol; the Alpine pastures of Trentino.
LEFT: the resort of Portovenere near La Spezia.

THE NORTHERN ITALIANS

"Italians are baffled by their own behaviour. The only people who have no doubt... are foreigners who streak through it in a few days" – Luigi Barzini

In northern Italy, geography is destiny, to a greater degree than elsewhere, simply because a citizen born in the wealthy north sees little need to move from the confines of his cosy world. Still less does the average citizen desire to shape his destiny in any but the most obvious economic ways. Why stray when one's status is already assured at home, when there is a ready-made support system to help one through the complex bureaucracy operated by a heartless state?

The price of peace

If the Faustian pact weighs inner life, exploration and stimulation against the safety and comfort of a known world, there is no contest. Which northerner does not want to eat decent food, stock home-made wine in a small cellar, dress smartly, drive an acceptable car, do up his home, and live in a small town unscarred by urban blight? This is a conservative society that half believes in the old saying, "*Moglie e buoi dei paesi tuoi.*" (Choose your wife and your cattle from your own backyard.) As the English writer Jonathan Keates says of the complacent citizens of Modena: "There is little anguish or doubt or stress because the *piccolo mondo moderno* they inhabit is so full of certainties."

When parochialism becomes self-perpetuating, regional differences remain as pronounced as ever. Mobility may have increased, but the Italian mindset tends to stay behind, comparing the new place unfavourably with the cherished home town. As the novelist Tim Parks says astutely: "When an Italian leaves a place it is almost always with the intention of returning victorious and vindicated."

According to the historian Valerio Lintner, the so-called northern Italian character emerged during the time of the medieval city states, creating "the relaxed, friendly and congenial atmosphere which we now associate with many Italian cities". Compared with the more feudal south, the north fostered the development of communities run with relative autonomy and respect for the rule of law, cities imbued with a sense of civic responsibility. The importance of commerce, finance and social mobility distinguished the north from the autocratic, landowning southern societies.

LEFT AND RIGHT: effortless elegance and a love of *"il mare"* – two very Italian traits.

The abiding northern values are regional pride and attachment to one's roots, compounded by complacency, conservatism and consumerism. A Christian work ethic justifies the pursuit of wealth and the passionate defence of the interests of the tribe. In case this all seems too cosy, the mixture is stirred with resentment of Roman bureaucracy and slurs on other regions, particularly with regard to perceived southern fecklessness.

Despite certain shared values, the regions have preserved their cultural distinctiveness. Even the Milanese metropolis is less cosmopolitan than comparable European capitals. Italians delight in the game of regional and city stereotyping: they are suspicious of the cool, secretive, contradictory Venetians but tacitly admiring of the materialistic, prosaic, rather joyless Milanese; the aloof, melancholic, patrician Piedmontese are compared with the mean, enterprising, independent Genoese, heirs to an equally noble tradition, and the bluff, hardy Trentini are the more Italianate neighbours of the Germanic South Tyroleans. Further south, the rough, rebellious Romagnoli are distinguished from the greedy, pampered, sensuous Emilians

STYLISH BIRTHRIGHT

"It helps to have been born in Milan: it's a graphic city, dedicated to good design, but also deeply surrealistic." – Fashion guru, Anna Piaggi.

and the smugly bourgeois Bolognese who run the regional capital. Only when describing southerners does the northern vocabulary suddenly shrink to a few choice insults.

Materialistic Milan

Milanese citizens see themselves as running the real capital of Italy, at odds with slothful and incompetent Rome. Even Cardinal Biffi of Bologna, once mooted as a candidate for the Papacy, sees no shame in declaring: "As a Milanese, I would be deeply unhappy if I had to go and live in Rome." The Milanese character is calibrated on its antipathy to Rome, and on a commitment to money-making, the sole passport to social mobility and conventional success. More than any other region, rich Lombardy feels treated as the milch cow for bloated southern bureaucracy. An entrepreneurial ethos is shared by immigrants and incomers drawn to Milan's economic success. Milan has long been a melting pot, a magnet for ambitious Italians from poorer regions. The Milanese pride themselves on their glamorous image as creative, stylish movers and shakers. Yet any journey on the city metro will reveal the myth of the Milanese as fashion plates. The city of silk suits is restricted to certain quarters and certain classes. In many ways Silvio Berlusconi, the brash media magnate, is the quintessential Milanese, a powerful, self-made man with a perma-tan and televisual blue suits; if he were a perfume, it would be Essence of Milan, a potent parvenu, packaged elegantly but swiftly passé.

Milan is often dismissed as a "prose capital", its citizens as rational and unromantic as the neon signs that light up the grey city centre. Yet the actress Veronica Pivetti is eager to dispel such notions: "As a real Milanese, I even love the fog and the drizzle on those sad November days." Socially, the Milanese Catholic hinterland can be as conformist as anywhere in southern Italy. Irene Pivetti, the actress's politician sister, is a high-profile product of such conservatism, with intransigent public views on such social issues as contraception and divorce.

Indeed, beyond the northern capital, Lombardy remains economically progressive but socially conservative. The Milanese metropolis, dedicated to shiny materialism, is no myth, but sophisticated Milan is shackled by its strait-laced hinterland and the dreary industrial foothills of the Alps. Despite an early and influential socialist movement, a countercurrent of Catholic paternalism still colours the regional character today, swelling the ranks of the northern separatist movement.

Scraping the glittering Latin surface of Lombardy reveals Longobard bluffness and the brutality of the Teutonic tribes who colonised the fat, rich plains in the 6th century. The loud, unsophisticated temperament lives on in Umberto Bossi, leader of the separatist Northern League (Lega Nord). As a born-again Lombard, he is a zealous demagogue who propounds a truculent racism in public but is a smoother operator in private. Marco Formentini, former Mayor of Milan, represents a slightly less brutish strand of northern federalism: "We believe in a united Europe of 50 regions like Lombardy, Bavaria or Wales – and not in the Europe of 12 nations."

Secretive Turin

The Milanese dismiss Turin as *grigio*: a grey city. Sometimes impressions may confirm Turin as a city populated by taciturn, reserved, hard-working Piedmontese. However, the citizens can be seen in a softer light during their festivals devoted to general gluttony, or in their cult of café life and *stuzzichini*, Turin tapas or *aperitivi*. Under the city arcades, moneyed *Torino-bene* (respectable citizens) sip coffee and nibble on *gianduiotti*, the city's hazelnut-studded chocolates.

Turin is still perceived by some as melancholic, old-fashioned and prey to provincialism, a view belied by the city's aristocratic past and its cutting-edge, avant-garde industrial present. The historian Denis Mack Smith notes: "The aristocracy of Turin belonged to a closed society in which pigtails and powdered wigs survived longer than elsewhere, where serfs and feudal prisons could be found." Today some of the old guard still maintain a snooty, almost French sangfroid, a haughtiness bred of rigid, stoical

LEFT: Gianfranco Ferré on Via Montenapoleone, Milan's designer street.
ABOVE: quintessential Milanese man, Silvio Berlusconi.

Piedmontese society with its blue-blooded lineage. Amadeo di Savoia, Duke of Aosta, is the last remaining emblem of monarchism in the Italian Republic. The monarchy was abolished by a referendum in 1946, and male descendants are still banned from settling permanently in Italy.

The spirit of public service is part of the Piedmontese ethos, one embodied by Count Camillo di Cavour (1810–61), the aristocratic patriot and prime minister. In dutifully rising to the challenge, Cavour was industrious, moderate, reasonable, tolerant: a typical Piedmontese of the old school. Yet he was equally Piedmontese in his political pragmatism and his forthright appreciation of good food.

FEED THE REVOLUTION

In 1860, after plotting the Risorgimento (Italian unification) in Turin's Il Cambio restaurant, Cavour said: "Today we've made history, now let's have dinner."

This sense of duty and (restaurant) service is shared by a number of individualistic contemporary politicians. Fausto Bertinotti, the dedicated but disruptive leader of the Communist Party *(Rifondazione Communista)*, is partial to chic suits and urban café life. Bertinotti, who grew up in a hotbed of trade unionism in Turin, continues to rattle the establishment with his suspicion of capitalism, and his plans to halt privatisation and abolish Nato. Often considered to be a radical leftist, he is also admired and respected by many on the right for his smartness and coherence. Emma Bonino, who was born north of Turin, is, like the classic Piedmontese politician, both an outsider and an insider. Her controversial role as Fisheries Commissioner in Brussels caused her to be dubbed "the Eva Peron of the halibut". Unlike most faceless Brussels bureaucrats, she is a forthright liberal and also an approachable, un-pompous member of the Radical Party.

The former Archbishop of Milan, Cardinal Martini, was a Piedmontese candidate for the papacy and spokesman for Milanese liberalism (now retired). Although a pillar of the establishment, he is also a modernist. However, his attitude to celibacy in the priesthood ("It will remain in force, but local adjustments may be made") can be seen as either sheer sophistry or a masterpiece of Piedmontese diplomacy. (Today's Archbishop is Cardinal Pappalasdo.)

Tyrolean twist

Trentino-Alto Adige has a split personality, with Austrian and Italian influences reflecting a dual cultural heritage. Germanic traits are evident in the citizens' law-abiding nature and environmentally aware approach to the lakes and mountains. As befits such a rugged region, the South Tyrol is proud of producing some of Italy's hardiest sportspeople, including Reinhold Meisner, a world-famous climber, and Alberto Tomba, the country's once most famous alpine skier (now it is Christian Ghedina from Contiva). Francesco Moser, a politician and former cycling world champion, is typical of hearty, Italianate Trentino folk: a bluff wine-lover who cultivates his vineyards of luscious red Marzemino wines.

The German-speaking community in Bolzano claims Lili Gruber, a celebrity television journalist. She was no Latin siren but a cool, direct interviewer who won popularity for her un-Italian toughness and professionalism.

Venetian subtlety

The Venetians are naturally courteous and tolerant, as befits a cosmopolitan people who have come to terms with the loss of empire. Their philosophical detachment is often mistaken for aloofness, with their calm and sanguine air likened to Anglo-Saxon aplomb. Still, the lingering image is of a cool and closed people, canny, cosmopolitan and conservative but concealing a sinister heart. The Republic was respected but not much loved, while widespread fear was engendered by its skilful spies. Yet there is a lighter side to the Venetians: a pronounced aesthetic sense, poetic sensibility and a playful nature sustained by pageantry, a pleasure-seeking image once matched by morals as slippery as the lagoon itself.

According to the historian Valerio Lintner, Marco Polo (1254–1324) best represents the Venetian character of old, "adventurous and daring in pursuit of profit, whilst financially conservative and prudent". The Venetians are also noted for their curiosity and spirit of intellectual enquiry, a disposition that led to empire-building. Yet this lofty outlook is tempered by a profound indifference to matters beyond the lagoon. It is a view personified by Marco Polo, who remained a home-town boy despite his exploits. "Every time I describe a city, I am saying something about Venice," he wrote.

LEFT: South Tyrol has a distinctly Austrian character – from its law-abiding citizens to its wooden chalets..
ABOVE: café society in sophisticated Portofino.

Genoese adventurers

As befits a former maritime state, Genoa is cosmopolitan, raffish and commercial in equal measures. The mercantile character of the city, and the citizens' skill at money-lending, have given the Genoese an undeserved reputation for meanness, much like the Jews elsewhere. However, as befits an erstwhile republic that pioneered such modern devices as bills of credit, cheques and insurance, Genoese banking and business skills are held in high regard. The people are reputed to be rugged individualists, shrewd, calculating, enterprising and independent. The great seafarer Christopher Columbus (1451–1506) is the city's most famous son. Giuseppe Mazzini (1805–72) was a romantic adventurer of the old school: the "father of the Italian nation" succeeded in putting a united Italy on the political agenda.

Renzo Piano, one of the world's most celebrated architects and urban planners, is as enterprising, cosmopolitan and chameleon as Genoa, his native city. Apart from designing the Pompidou Centre in Paris with Richard Rogers, the Potsdamerplatz in Berlin and Kansai airport in Osaka, he has also left his mark on northern Italy. Piano remodelled part of the historic Fiat Lingotto works in Turin, designed a new aquarium and congress centre in Genoa, and conceived a high-tech wind tunnel for the Ferrari test track at Maranello. He approaches every new challenge with typical Genoese pragmatism: "My rule is that if I have to build

THE NORTH-SOUTH DIVIDE

The north-south divide is as elusive yet definite as the Italian character itself. Racist northerners often joke that Garibaldi did not unify Italy but dismembered Africa. Angelo Maraini, an activist in the secessionist Northern League, declares: "Thank goodness we in the north were invaded by the Austrians, and the Habsburgs left good traces in our blood." Lombardy and the Veneto are Italy's richest regions, and 80 percent of the country's personal taxation comes from the north, which has some of the highest productivity rates in the European Union. In this culture of economic dependence, the financial burden is shouldered by the north, while the south receives the subsidies.

Commentators increasingly wonder whether the glue of national solidarity can continue to support a rich north and a poor south. The argument for fostering closer ties with regions north of the Alps has a clear appeal for northerners. After all, Milan is closer to Munich than to Messina, and Brescia does more business with Bavaria than with Bari. In federalist eyes, the banding together of the northern Italian regions would be a triumph, embracing the industrial triangle of Turin, Milan and Genoa as well as the wealth of small businesses in Emilia. This seductive logic has won many sympathisers. A federalist Europe represents the best hope for dissatisfied northern Italians.

a monastery, then I become a bit of a friar, and if I have to work for Ferrari, then I'm a mechanic."

The Ligurians of the Genoese hinterland are considered a proud, stubborn people with the ingenuity to make the most of humble resources. Liguria has long been a land of fishermen-sailors and merchant-wayfarers, although, with the development of such renowned resorts as Portofino, the population has looked for more profitable activities. Alfonso Scanio, a Green MP, even accuses the Ligurians of "going in for disposable tourism: the belief that if they ruin one thing, something else will come along".

MARRIAGE VOWS

"He might leave home for a plate of spaghetti, but for a woman, never." – Pavarotti's wife on first hearing the (accurate) rumours that the singer was about to leave her for his secretary.

Greedy Emilians

Given their superb cuisine and love of the good life, citizens of Emilia Romagna are routinely envied. In the eyes of fellow Italians, the Emilians are a soft, sensual, pampered people with a cosmopolitan outlook. Yet they are secretly admired for their pragmatism and public honesty, and for the smooth efficiency with which they run the prosperous cities of Italy's political "red belt". Luciano Pavarotti, the ultimate figure of a tenor, personifies the generosity, gregariousness and greed of Emilians. In the rarefied world of opera, Pavarotti is as earthy and pampered as his home town, Modena.

The Bolognese are considered the intellectual bourgeoisie personified: progressive, sociable, affable and open. The common criticism of these model citizens is that they are smugly superior, prescriptive about the world's wrongs, while dabbling in daring social experiments. As the capital of the former Papal States, Bologna became virulently anticlerical and still maintains a wary relationship with the Church. Pope John Paul II even condemned the region as the most degenerate in Italy, given its record divorce and abortion rates.

Liberals, however, praise such qualities as civic maturity and tolerant attitudes to sex and drugs. Yet Luciano Pignotti, a long-term city resident, finds the fabled Bolognese openness skin-deep, a form of conformity: "The Bolognese pride themselves on being open-minded so everyone else has to be open-minded, too."

Writers and film directors from Emilia Romagna are extraordinarily attuned to aesthetic concerns. Federico Fellini *(see page 349)* may be the god of the Emilian cinematic pantheon, but Antonioni and Bertolucci are also venerable names. When asked why his films always look so lush, Bernardo Bertolucci pointed to his upbringing in Parma: "Growing up in such a beautiful city is a kind of *dolce condanna*, a sweet prison sentence. Look at our local painter, Parmigiano, he was the most decorative of all the Mannerists, the least tortured. I think beauty is in my DNA."

Michelangelo Antonioni, the veteran film director, has always looked to his native Ferrara for inspiration. As an artist who deals in lush surface beauties, he lingers over shadowy encounters in Renaissance palaces, soft mists that rise over the Po Valley. His film *Beyond the Clouds* (1998) focused on unfulfilled erotic encounters in his secretive city, the black-magic capital of Italy. If planning any form of social, erotic or gastronomic encounters with northerners, one would do well to begin with the Emilians. ❑

LEFT: Genoese architect, Renzo Piano, outside the huge church he designed in Southern Italy dedicated to Padre Pio. **RIGHT:** Sophia Loren and Federico Fellini.

MAR DI PROVENZA
MARE DI GENOVA
MARE DI CORSICA
MARE DI TOSCANA
MARE DI SARDEGNA
MARE
MARE MEDIT
DELFINATO
DUC DI MANTOVA
DUC DI PARMA
GRANDUCATO DI TOSC
VESCOVATO DI TRENTO
MONFERATO
Conte d'Angera
Bocche di Bonifacio
PARMA
MANTOVA
GENOVA
MILANO
PIEMONTE
SAVOIE
MODENA
LUCCA
LIBERTAS
Miglia d'Italia
Leghe comuni di Francia
Leghe comuni di Spagna
Leghe comuni Todesche
Arcivescovato
Vescovato
Abbazie
Feudi Imperiali
Feudi della Chiesa
Bar. Baronia.
R.D.S. Re di Spagna.
G.D. Gran Duca.
A.M. Arciu. di Milano
V.P. Vescouo di Parma
V.N. Vescouo di Nouara
M. Modena.
Descritta da
Geografo del

L'ITALIA
Dedicata
CARNIOLA
Golfo di Trieste
Quarnero
MARE ET ISOLE DI DALMATIA
GOLFO DI VENETIA ouero MARE ADRIATICO
VENETIA
Ancona
Loreto
Marca d'Ancona
Vmbria
Abruzzo Vltra
Abruzzo Citra
Roma
Campagna di Roma
Capitanata
Co. di Molise
MAR DI PVGLIA
Terra di Bari
Principato Citra
Golfo di Napoli
Basilicata
Golfo di Taranto
Capo Rosito
Capo Trionto
Capo dell'Alice
Capo delle Colonne
Capo Risuto
Golfo di Squilaci
Capo di Palinuro
MARE DI NAPOLI
TIRENO
ISOLE DI LIPARI O DI VVLCANO
Stromboli I.
Panaria I.
Vulcano I.
Felicudi I.
TOSCANA
CHIESA
NAPO
Confine dello stato della Republica di Ragusi
Isole di Tremiti de C.R.L.
MAR IONI ouero MAR DI GRECI
RRA
NEO
MESSINA
Milazzo

Decisive Dates

1000–800 BC "Villanova" culture flourishes.
500 BC Etruscans rule Po valley from Bologna.
218 BC Carthaginian army under Hannibal crosses the Alps with his elephants.
27 BC–AD 14 Reign of Emperor Augustus.
307–337 Reign of Emperor Constantine. Christians no longer persecuted in the empire.
374 Saint Ambrose becomes Bishop of Milan.
410 Rome falls to the Goths.
489 Theodoric, King of the Ostrogoths, makes Verona his capital.

535 Ravenna is the chief city of Byzantine Italy.
568 The Longobards, led by Alboin, overrun northern Italy.
697 Paoluccio Anafesto elected first Doge of the Venetian Republic.
773 Invited by the Pope, Charlemagne seizes the Longobard domains.
1088 Foundation of Bologna University.
1176 Lombard League, formed to challenge Holy Roman Emperor Frederick Barbarossa, defeats his forces at Legnano.
1202–04 Fourth Crusade. The sack of Constantinople provides Venice with a springboard for a Mediterranean trading empire.
1320 The Visconti family rises to power in Milan.
1321 Death of Dante Alighieri, poet and author of *The Divine Comedy*, in exile at Ravenna.
1347 The Black Death ravages northern Italy.
1381 Venice wins the so-called War of Chioggia against its trade rival Genoa.
1402 Death of Gian Galeazzo Visconti.
1405 The Venetians conquer Verona and Padua.
1447 Francesco Sforza seizes power in Milan.
1485 Birth of Titian (Tiziano Vecellio), Europe's most admired painter of the 16th century.
1499 French army, led by Louis XII, attacks Milan and overthrows the Sforza dynasty.
1530 Charles V crowned Holy Roman Emperor at Bologna by Pope Clement VII. Lombardy becomes part of the Empire.
1545 Pier Luigi Farnese created first Duke of Parma and Piacenza by Pope Paul III. The First Council of Trent opens.
1556 Milan and Lombardy pass to Charles V's son Philip II, King of Spain.
1570 Venice loses Cyprus to the Turks. A Venetian naval victory over the Turks at Lepanto fails to halt the collapse of the trading empire.
1598 The Duchy of Ferrara, ruled for more than a century by the d'Este family, passes to the Papacy for lack of an heir. Illegitimate Cesare d'Este becomes first Duke of Modena.
1607 Claudio Monteverdi's *La Favola d'Orfeo* opens in Mantua and creates vogue for opera.
1627 Death of Vincenzo Gonzaga, Duke of Mantua, whose famous picture collection is sold to Charles I of England.
1630 Mantua sacked by the Imperial army during the Thirty Years War.
1683 Vittorio Amedeo II seizes power as Duke of Savoy.
1696 Birth of Giambattista Tiepolo, Venice's last great painter.
1713 Treaty of Utrecht. Austria becomes ruler of Lombardy and Mantua. Vittorio Amedeo II recognised as King of Piedmont and Sardinia.
1718 Venice surrenders Peloponnese to Turks.
1745 Popular uprising against an occupying Austrian army by the Genoese offers the earliest symbol of Italian dreams of unification.
1796 French forces invade Italy.
1797 Terrified by the French invasion, the Venetian Republic votes for its own abolition.
1800 Napoleon decisively defeats Austrian army at Marengo.
1813 Napoleon defeated at Leipzig. Italian states, except Genoa and Venice, restored to their former rulers.

1831 Ciro Menotti's abortive revolt in Modena. Giuseppe Mazzini founds Young Italy movement.
1840–42 Alessandro Manzoni publishes his novel *I Promessi Sposi* (The Betrothed).
1848 Revolutions in all Italian states. Venice expels Austrian garrison. King Charles Albert of Piedmont declares war on Austria.
1849 Failure of revolutions and defeat of Charles Albert. Austria re-establishes dominance in northern Italy.
1850 Giuseppe Verdi's *Rigoletto* first performed in La Fenice, Venice.
1859 Franco–Austrian war in northern Italy. French victories at Magenta and Solferino begin the process of unification under Victor Emmanuel II of Piedmont. In 1866 Austria cedes Venice and all of the Veneto to Italy.
1870 Unification of Italy completed.
1880–1900 Widespread social unrest in Italian cities. Rioting and street battles in Milan.
1904 Giovanni Giolitti becomes Prime Minister.
1912 Giovanni Agnelli begins mass production of Fiat automobiles in Turin.
1915 Italy enters World War I as ally of Britain and France.
1922 Fascists seize power in Italy.
1935 War against Ethiopia.
1938 Racial laws strike at Italy's Jewish communities.
1940 Italy enters World War II as ally of Nazi Germany.
1943 After Italy surrenders to the Allies, Mussolini flees to Salò and German armies occupy the north. Beginning of the Partisan Movement.
1945 Mussolini captured by Italians and executed in Milan.
1948–92 Parliamentary democracy introduced, dominated by Christian Democrats,though Lombardy and Emilia Romagna remain Communist.
1951 Italy joins the EEC as founder member.
1992–94 Elections see the rise of Umberto Bossi's Lega Nord (Northern League) and Silvio Berlusconi's Forza Italia as important political forces in northern Italy.
2001 Silvio Berlusconi is elected Prime Minister. Genoa hosts the June G8 Summit under maximum security.
2002 The euro becomes the official currency.
2003 Gianni Agnelli, head of Fiat, dies.
2004 Genoa is the European Cultural Capital.
2005 Pope John Paul II dies and is succeeded by Cardinal Joseph Ratzinger, Benedict XVI.
2006 Turin hosts the Winter Olympics. Giorgio Napolitano is elected president. ❑

PRECEDING PAGES: historical map of Italy.
LEFT: Isabella d'Este (1474–1539) by Caroto.
ABOVE: the Battle of Solferino, 1859.

VIRGILIVS POETARVM EXCELENTISSIMVS
VLTIMA CVMEI IAM VENIT CARMINIS ETAS
MAGNVS AB ETERNO SANCTORVM NASCITVR ORDO

CULTURAL CORRIDORS

The early tribes wandered in and out of the region, and though Rome long held sway, others, such as the Longobards, also had a lasting effect

The earliest known northern Italian turned up as late as 1991, when his 5,000-year-old corpse, perfectly preserved, was discovered by German tourists in the Tyrol. This body of a man in his mid-40s, lying where presumably he had fallen while seeking shelter in a mountain storm, retained everything from blue tattoo marks to the traces of a last meal, a quiverful of arrows carried for hunting and a cloak of woven grass, useless in the end against the bitter cold of the high peaks. Though found close to the Austrian frontier, "the Ice Man" (nicknamed *Ötzi*), has finally been judged to have been of Italian origin. The organic remains, the oldest known in Europe, continue to intrigue and puzzle the scientists.

Two thousand years later the Ice Man's descendants began leaving the mountains for the great plains below, in those days a terrain of forests and marshes between rivers such as the Po and the Ticino. Almost nothing is known of the people who scratched primitive hunting scenes and human figures on the surface of rocks in Valcamonica, north of Brescia. Settlers further south, however, known today as Villanovans (from a village in the Apennine foothills where their traces were first identified), left bronze weapons, jewellery and clay urns in the graves of their dead.

Arrival of the Etruscans

The biggest Villanovan settlement was based on the site of modern Bologna, the place chosen for their capital by the Etruscans, who swept northwards in the 5th century BC to claim the area as an outpost of a realm which included Tuscany and Lazio and stretched as far as Italy's eastern seaboard. Feline, as the Etruscan town was called, fell eventually to the Celtic tribes swarming across the Alps during the 4th century, but it was the Romans, triumphant after Hannibal's defeat in 202 BC, who finally became masters of the land they named Cisalpine Gaul (modern France being known as Transalpine Gaul).

Clearing the fertile river plains for farming, they laid their dead-straight roads between newly-built towns such as Piacenza, Cremona and Modena, whose historic city centres even today preserve the classic Roman grid pattern and traces of ramparts, baths, theatres or arenas. Prosperous and generally well-governed, Cisalpine Gaul benefited also from good schools, which fostered a lively literary culture. Some of the foremost Latin writers were native north Italians. The poet Gaius Valerius Catullus came from Verona and divided most of his short life (*circa* 84–54 BC) between Rome and a villa at Sirmione on Lake Garda. His verse, written in a racy, colloquial style, mingles scenes from daily life, letters to friends and satirical hits at well-known political figures with poems charting the course of a disastrous love affair with the aristocrat Clodia Metella. From nearby

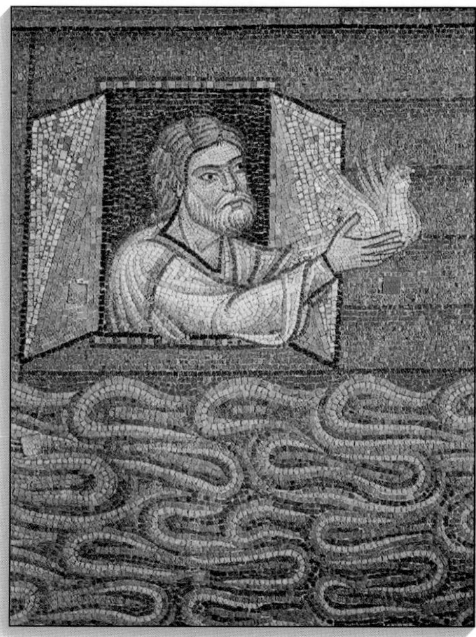

LEFT: Virgil, author of the *Aeneid*, was born in Mantua.
RIGHT: Noah sends out the dove; 13th-century mosaic at St Mark's Cathedral, Venice.

Padua (Patavium) came the historian Livy (Titus Livius), who began his huge *Story of Rome from Its Foundation* in 29 BC; issued in instalments, it achieved instant classic status and had a profound influence on later European historiography. Legends of pre-Roman Italy meanwhile inspired Virgil (Publius Vergilius Maro), born near Mantua, to write the *Aeneid*, which was unfinished at his death in 19 BC.

The decline of Rome

Racked by internal tensions between the army and successive emperors, as well as facing increased unrest along its frontiers, the Roman Empire, around the end of the 3rd century AD, began entering a slow spiral of decline. Interested watchers of this protracted imperial collapse included the Germanic people known as the Goths, scattered over a wide area around the basin of the River Danube. Seizing his moment, their king, Alaric, led them westwards into Greece and Italy, and Rome itself was finally surrounded and sacked in 410. Though Roman generals drove the Goths back across the Alps, the seat of imperial rule had already shifted to the eastern city of Byzantium, or Constantinople, and fresh barbarian hordes, including the Huns under their leader Attila,

swept into northern Italy. By the beginning of the 6th century almost all of Italy lay under the sway of the Gothic warlord Theodoric, with the city of Verona as his capital.

When Theodoric died in 526, the Byzantine Emperor Justinian, a Bulgarian peasant's son, was possessed of an iron resolve to snatch back the lost Roman dominions, he invaded Italy and began a process of reconquest lasting nearly 30 years. While Justinian continued to govern from Constantinople, the Italian provinces were administered by his proconsul, known as the *exarch*, from the coastal city of Ravenna. Once the headquarters of Rome's Adriatic fleet, this was the spot Theodoric had marked for his burial

CURTAIN UP ON AMBROSIA

Northern Italy was among the first areas of the Roman Empire to accept Christianity. It was in Milan (Mediolanum) in 313 that the Emperor Constantine granted Christians freedom of worship. A former governor, Ambrosius (340–397), was named archbishop by popular acclaim, giving his private fortune to charity. With powerful connections at court, Ambrosius became the moral guardian of the empire, mounting a massive propaganda campaign against heresy. His feast day (Sant'Ambrogio), on 7 December, traditionally marks the beginning of the opera season at Milan's Teatro alla Scala, the high point in the city's social calendar.

place with an impressive domed mausoleum. The Byzantine presence in Ravenna renewed the tradition of pictorial mosaic decoration in the city's churches, which had been so strikingly established here a century earlier in Empress Galla Placidia's memorial chapel.

Settlement of the Longobards

Northern Italy was not allowed to remain at peace for long. In 568, only a few years after the last Goths had been driven out, another barbarian people began the march southwards. Within a decade the Longobards, leaving their tribal homeland of north Germany, had achieved almost complete mastery over the Po valley and the northeastern area between the Dolomites and the Adriatic coast, known as Friuli. As their chief cities they chose Pavia, southwest of Milan, and Brescia, which had been an important trading centre under the Romans. Though the Longobards soon embraced Christianity and accepted the surviving imperial forms of law and civil administration, they never lost their pride in their ancient north European ancestry and warlike ancestral traditions. This powerful warrior aristocracy eventually gave the name "Lombardia" to the whole region between the northern lakes and the River Po.

An uneasy balance of forces now existed between the Byzantine Empire, clinging to what remained of the exarchate around Ravenna, and the Longobards, determined to gain full control of Italy. In 751 Ravenna yielded to Longobard King Aistulf, and it seemed as if Rome would fall to the victorious northerners. In 754 Pope Stephen II secured a promise of help from King Pepin of the Franks, and accorded him the honour of an official anointing ceremony in return for direct military action against the Longobards.

The Lombard Legacy

The Longobards may have disappeared into the history books and museums, but their presence lives on in the northern Italian plains across which they spurred their horses. The pattern of countless farms and small villages retains the character of their ancient tribal settlements, the *casali*, in which the big arcaded barns around a courtyard are incorporated into a dwelling house in such a way as to create an easily defensible stronghold. Their Germanic language became an integral part of modern Italian; many words connected with war (*guerra*), like *scudo* (shield), *elmo* (helmet) and *spada* (sword), are Longobard, as well as equestrian terms such as *staffa* (stirrup) and *briglia* (bridle). Even such everyday words as *casalinga* (housewife) and *guinzaglio* (dog-lead) betray a Longobard origin, and so, too, do the hundreds of place-names ending in -ago, -ara or -engo – Asiago, Martellago, Novara, Lendinara, Marengo, Offanengo. To a hot-blooded Neapolitan or Sicilian, the sober, hardworking character of the northern Italians is the ultimate legacy of this ancient German descent.

LEFT: an old postcard of Verona's Roman amphitheatre.
RIGHT: Charlemagne, first Holy Roman Emperor.

Under Pepin's successor, Charlemagne, who was crowned as the first Holy Roman Emperor by Pope Leo III on Christmas Day 800, the last Longobard king of northern Italy, Desiderius, was deposed. Pavia, for a time the provincial capital of the new imperial domain before being overtaken by Milan and Verona, became a leading centre for training civil servants and lawyers as well as the earliest of Italy's university towns. While successive emperors, especially Otto III (983–1002), did their best to establish a bulwark of secular power in the north against the Longobard legacy, popes showed themselves more than prepared to assert the Church's rights and privileges.

Charlemagne had been ready to countenance the breathtaking piece of forgery known as the Donation of Constantine, whereby a so-called territorial grant from the Emperor Constantine to Pope Silvester guaranteed sovereignty over an area which became an independent papal state and remained one until 1870. In more positive ways, the Church contributed forcefully to stability and continuity throughout Italy during the most unstable periods of early medieval history.

In the north, landscape and society both underwent serious changes as a result of the introduction of monasticism by the Benedictine order during the 7th and 8th centuries. By the year 1200 the Lombard plain, the foothills of the northern Apennines and the Emilian region were dotted with monasteries and convents large and small, incorporating extensive farm buildings and dedicated to forest clearances and irrigation schemes, as well as the daily round of church services.

When Venice Was But Wattle

The rise of Venice from a huddle of huts to one of the medieval world's most powerful cities took place in a mere few hundred years. In the 5th century, as Goths and Huns threatened, refugees from the northern cities of Grado and Aquileia sought safety among the islands of the nearby lagoon. They organised themselves into a primitive democratic community, living in wattle cabins with boats moored at the door and trading in salt, waterfowl or fish. In time, the islanders elected a *Dux*, the Latin word for leader, which local dialect rendered as *Doge*. The settlement assumed the title of the old imperial province of Venetia, named after the Celtic Veneti tribe.

First wave of Romanesque

The inspiration for many to join the monastic orders was initially offered not so much by Italians as by wandering monks from Ireland, who travelled south across France and Germany along pilgrim routes to Rome. One such was St Columbanus, whose abbey of Bobbio near Piacenza, founded in 612, became one of the most widely respected centres of learning in Europe during the early Middle Ages.

Irish monks also helped to found the monastery at Nonantola, east of Modena, whose distinctive architecture and sculpture were influential in creating the first wave of the Romanesque style, which dominated church architecture from Scotland to Spain during the 12th century.

It was the bishops of the various cities, however, who did most to earn respect for the Church among the ordinary men and women of northern Italy in the troubled centuries following the Roman imperial collapse. Towns such as Parma, Reggio and Cremona all relied on their respective bishops as the ultimate representatives of authority, whether spiritual or secular, and such figures were expected, when necessary, to put on armour, carry weapons and ride horses into battle. Many were canonised after their deaths and proved redoubtable protectors of their cities through miraculous intervention at times of crisis.

When the Hungarians threatened Modena in the early 10th century, for example, prayers were directed to St Geminianus, who had been the town's first bishop 600 years earlier. He had driven away marauding Huns by blanketing the city with a dense fog, and now his timely intercession brought about the same result with the Hungarians. The fact that the Emilian plain on which Modena stands has always been notorious for its thick fogs may also have helped. ❑

Left: the Doge, like the Pope, was elected for life.
Right: a 17th-century view of Venice's Rialto Bridge.

CITY STATES AND DYNASTIES

Street fights, power battles, clan allegiance, courage and cunning shaped the communities as they grew into powerful, independent city states

As the towns of northern Italy grew more prosperous during the 11th and 12th centuries, so they became increasingly unwilling to accept the authority of emperors, popes or bishops. Instead, the most powerful citizens began to reach out towards gaining control over the surrounding countryside, the *contado* as it was called, reducing the local barons to submission, revising outworn tax systems and introducing ambitious schemes for improving agriculture. Within the cities themselves, the old warrior aristocracy gave way to a bourgeois nobility, unembarrassed for the time being by its associations with trade and always able to boost its numbers by granting titles and honours to families whose fortunes had risen through shrewd business dealings.

For this very reason, thought the German Bishop Otto of Freising, the towns of northern Italy "greatly exceed the other cities of the world in wealth and power". The prosperity of these *comuni* – Milan, Bologna, Cremona and others – was based largely on trade in textiles and dyestuffs, securing a deep sense of collective loyalty among their inhabitants. Even today an Italian's first allegiance is to his home town, to his *campanile*, the bell tower which punctuates the skyline on the plains of Lombardy and Emilia. In everything from politics to football *campanilismo* is a vital influence, just as it was 900 years ago.

Birth of the Lombard League

The rising power of the communes met its match in 1152, when the German prince Frederick Barbarossa was named Holy Roman Emperor. Determined to assert what he believed was his God-given authority, he demanded control of everything from tax-gathering to the appointment of magistrates. The infuriated communes, led by Milan, united as the Lombard League and began a 20-year struggle against imperial dominance, which only ended when Frederick conceded full sovereign rights to each city in return for its recognition of him as overall ruler. The Lombard League soon became a symbol of Italian unity, and the story of the conflict was eventually to inspire the leaders of the Risorgimento the 19th-century struggle for nationhood *(see page 46)*. In 1848 Giuseppe Verdi chose the League's signal victory at Legnano as the theme of the patriotic opera *Aida*.

LEFT: German prince Frederick Barbarossa being crowned Holy Roman Emperor.

RIGHT: Malatesta, 15th-century ruler of Rimini.

The growth of elites and aristocracies among the citizens of the communes led at length to major power struggles between individual families jostling for leadership and, ultimately, for outright domination of the town and its surrounding *contado*. The strife between Montagues and Capulets forming the background to Shakespeare's *Romeo and Juliet* has its foundation in the history of 14th-century Verona, where members of the Montecchi and Capuleti families, aided by their households and hangers-on, fought running battles in the city streets. Here and elsewhere the richer clans had started to build themselves fortified palaces which could be used both as storehouses for merchandise and as symbols of pride and defiance in the face of their rivals.

Street battle for power

Mantua's story during the 13th and 14th centuries provides a typical example. From about 1260 onwards the commune became increasingly dominated by the Buonaccorsi family. In 1272 Pinamonte Buonaccorsi, combining an immense fortune with personal courage and political skills, became the city's effective ruler from his grimly imposing crenellated *palazzo* in Piazza Sordello.

For more than 50 years the Buonaccorsi held sway in Mantua until, in 1328, Luigi Gonzaga, head of a peasant clan from the village of Polirone, who had made a series of shrewd land deals with local monasteries and bought up city property, carried out a spectacular *coup d'état*. In a ferocious street battle on a moonlit August night, Pinamonte's cousin, Rinaldo Buonaccorsi was severely wounded but managed to escape to his palace, where he died on the threshold after slipping in his own blood and hitting his head against one of the great gates which he had earlier ordered his servants to close behind him.

The rise of the Gonzagas to more or less royal status – Holy Roman Emperor Sigismund in 1433 allowed them to display the imperial eagle on their coat of arms – is typical of what was happening elsewhere in an Italy increasingly dominated by powerful clans seeking ever more blatant affirmations of their aristocratic significance. Certain northern Italian cities, on the other hand, saw an implicit menace in such overwhelming predominance among members of a single family.

The republic of Venice made the most deliberate effort of all to limit the power of individual

Genoa, La Superba

Genoa was so successful as a commune that it soon became a fully independent state. It drew its wealth from a rapidly expanding trade and maritime empire, knocking out the rival republics of Pisa and Amalfi before shifting its attention to Venice, its main competitor in the East during the 12th–13th-century crusades. Genoa maintained trading centres in the Greek Islands, the Black Sea, Tunisia and Egypt, and acquired such riches that the city became known as "La Superba". Money was almost the only unifying force in a commune notorious for political unrest among its merchant aristocracy. The Genoese retain a reputation in Italy for being cynical, mercenary and mean.

citizens by creating a political mentality which focused on the state rather than on the fulfilment of personal ambition. Since the early Middle Ages its ruler had been an elected Doge, chosen from among a limited number of senators, themselves members of the so-called Grand Council whose composition was restricted to families whose names were inscribed in *The Golden Book of the Republic*. A system of committees, the Ten, the Thirty and so on, acted as checks and balances on one another's power, and an impressive range of sumptuary laws, controlling everything from the height and style of buildings to the colour and sleeve-length of official robes, reminded everyone that the state and the rule of law came before everything else.

NO FUN BEING A DOGE

Of Venice's first 25 Doges, three were murdered, one was executed, three were judicially blinded, four deposed, one exiled, four abdicated, one killed by pirates and one made a saint.

Venice's success was based both on this deep sense of corporate identity and on the skill with which its merchants learned to seize on whatever commercial advantages came their way from other states, both in Italy and in the rest of Europe. The Fourth Crusade in 1204 had brought the Republic spectacular gains in the Eastern Mediterranean through its shrewd exploitation of the crusaders' greed and internal dissensions, which led to the sack of Constantinople. The long feud between Genoa and the other great northern Italian maritime power, Venice, finally came to an end in the Chioggia War (1378–81). Genoa was soundly defeated and, with naval supremacy assured, the Venetians then turned their attention towards the land. One by one the mainland towns of Padua, Verona, Bergamo and Treviso fell into Venetian hands, and by the middle of the 15th century the territory controlled by the Republic stretched almost to the gates of Milan. Venice itself, meanwhile, had become Europe's fastest-growing and most prosperous city, the centre of a trade network stretching as far as China, Russia and Africa, and commanding a Mediterranean empire that included the Ionian islands, Crete and Cyprus.

Even a natural disaster on the scale of the Black Death, sweeping across northern Italy during the 14th century, had no long-lasting effect on the mounting affluence in town and

LEFT: a sea battle in the War of Chioggia (1378–81) fought between the Genoese and the Venetians.
ABOVE: the Lion of St Mark, symbol of Venetian power.

country. Drainage and land clearance projects improved productivity on the Lombard plain, where the planting of rice was introduced, making *risotto* a characteristic regional dish. Mulberry trees, planted on the slopes of the Alpine foothills, fostered a thriving silk industry, and the pasturing of large cattle herds in the fields around Parma and Reggio encouraged the production of *grana*, the hard cheese known to us as Parmesan.

RISOTTO FROM SPAIN

The first rice in Italy was planted at Pisa in 1468 by the Spaniards, who had been introduced to the crop by the Arabs.

The growth of northern towns echoed this prosperity, nowhere more so than Milan, where

the Visconti family had gradually risen to power in the 14th century's closing decades. On 5 September 1395 the imperial legate ceremonially invested Gian Galeazzo Visconti as duke, and the new ruler immediately set out to challenge the might of neighbouring states such as Savoy, Ferrara and Venice. It looked, indeed, as if the whole of Italy were in danger, especially when Gian Galeazzo moved south into Tuscany to take possession of Pisa and Siena, and wrested control of Bologna from the Pope. When he died unexpectedly in 1402 the various potentates struck back swiftly at his successor Filippo Maria Visconti, who was filled with the same territorial ambitions but was not nearly as efficient a soldier as his father. In the ensuing, prolonged war, Filippo Maria saw his son-in-law change sides and join the enemy alliance formed by Florence, Venice and the Pope.

On Filippo Maria Visconti's death in 1447, Francesco Sforza took possession of Milan after a long siege and began embellishing his city with fine churches, hospitals and new fortifications. Resolved to turn Milan into a capital appropriate to a state that could rival Florence or Naples as a major player on the Italian political stage, he gathered around him artists, musicians, technocrats and humanist scholars in what soon became one of the most brilliant of all Renaissance courts. Francesco was the son of a *condottiere*, a soldier of fortune, one of that ruthless mercenary breed which hired out its services to Italian rulers in need of a competent military leader. The great Renaissance sculptors Donatello and Verrocchio left us memorable bronze statues of two of them, astride their warhorses, in Padua and Venice respectively.

Leonardo in Milan

Milan's cultural life attained its utmost splendour under Francesco's nephew, Ludovico il Moro ("the black"), who succeeded him in 1480. The inspired Tuscan architect Bramante arrived to stage elaborate masques and pageants for the court and to design the ducal mausoleum and Santa Maria delle Grazie. In the same convent church Leonardo da Vinci painted his *Last Supper*. Summoned from Florence, he became Ludovico's scientific and technological adviser.

The envy of rival states at length brought the Sforzas to their knees. In 1499 Milan fell to a combined force of Venetians and Swiss, joined by King Louis XII of France, which drove Ludovico into exile. Even if the French and Spanish governors of Milan continued to employ Sforza princes and their agents in governing Lombardy, the city became a pawn in the power games of alien monarchs. The rest of Italy might have taken warning from the fact that in the first 30 years of the 16th century the Milanese changed rulers 11 times. ❑

LEFT: head of Filippo Maria Visconti (1392–1447) on a Milanese gold ducat coin.
RIGHT: Bianca Maria Sforza, wife of Francesco.

HEYDAY OF THE VENETIAN REPUBLIC

At its zenith, the Venetian Republic was a political heavyweight, queen of the Adriatic and an effective power player in world affairs

"Many a subject land looked at the winged lion's marble piles, where Venice sat in state, throned on her hundred isles," wrote Lord Byron as he reflected on the glory that was La Serenissima. He was writing of the Venetian heyday, between the 14th and 16th centuries, the age of empire, a golden age of conquest abroad and patriotic display at home. Citizens declared themselves "Venetians first, Christians afterwards", implying a greater duty to State and empire than to God. "Redeem us, O Christ," sang the choir in St Mark's, to which the response was distinctly unorthodox: "To the Most Serene and Excellent Doge, Health, Honour and Victory Perpetual." Paradoxically, the Republic's strength lay in its perceived weakness, in the belief that Venice was always alone in the world, forced to fend for itself and shun the shifting sands of political allegiances. In turn, rivals envied the Venetians' autonomous approach and the mercantile spirit of a great trading empire – not to mention their shrewd mastery of foreign affairs and good governance of the Republic at home.

OSTENTATION AND PURITANISM

La Serenissima's role as a Mediterranean power was perfectly captured by Venetian artists, for both patrons and posterity. The Republic was fed on a diet of pomp, with sumptuous receptions and lay and religious feasts; some of these are celebrated in the paintings of Bellini and Carpaccio. However, the Venetian taste for portraying pageantry went beyond the dictates of patrons. Moreover, despite a reputation for extravagance, the Republic harboured a puritanical streak. The prominence of black costumes in 16th-century Venice led a modern historian to liken the scene to "a Swiss Sunday". Yet in this authoritarian, regimented and censorious city, some nobles lived so lavishly that the State imposed laws governing dress codes and the gilding of gondolas.

▷ AWARDS FOR THE FAVOURED
On special occasions, the Doge would distribute medals, such as this 17th-century silver *osella*, to the Gran Consiglio, the council of nobles which had elected him.

△ SEALED LIPS
Secret denunciations could be posted in a *bocca di leone* ("lion's mouth" letter box). The boxes were placed in various locations across the city.

▷ WEDDED TO THE SEA
The Bucintoro, the Doge's barge, was lavishly decorated with gilded carvings and used for important state visits. On Ascension Day it carried the Doge to the Lido, where he would perform the ceremony of Venice's Marriage with the Sea, a famous city tradition captured on canvas by Canaletto (1657–1768).

△ SEAT OF THE SENATE
An 18th-century painting by by Gabriele Bella shows the room where the Doge would consult his 200 senators.

▽ ENDURING BEAUTY
Visitors to the Doge's Palace can still admire Tintoretto's decoration of the Sala del Senato, dating from 1574.

◁ **NAVAL POWER**
Venetian naval power was second to none. Here Holy Roman Emperor Frederick Barbarossa, who was in conflict with the Pope and the Lombard League, surrenders to Doge Ziani in 1176.

▽ **DOGE'S FINERY**
Doges wore distinctive hats, made of embroidered silk and adorned with precious stones, such as this *corno* worn by Doge Barbarigo (1485–1501).

OUTPOSTS OF EMPIRE

Military towers, citadels and lighthouses on the Croatian coast, Cyprus and Crete *(above)* attest to the reach of the Venetian empire. Such imperial power was born of patriotism, geography and trading supremacy. Venice bordered two worlds, the Byzantine and Muslim East and the Latin-Germanic West. As gateway to the East, the city traded incense, precious metals, slaves, silks and spices for northern staples, including salt and wheat. The purpose of Venetian imperialistic ambitions was to preserve trade routes and consolidate commercial opportunities. As a result, Venice became a melting pot for "Jews, Turks, Armenians, Persians, Moors, Greeks and Slavs... negotiating in this great emporium, which is always crowded with strangers" (John Evelyn).

The conquest of Croatia was achieved in the 10th century, and Venice soon developed trading posts in the Aegean, Black Sea and Syria. In 1204 The Sack of Constantinople gave Venice "one quarter and half a quarter" of the Roman Empire. Valour was expected in the name of glory: blind Doge Dandolo stormed Constantinople at the age of 90.

NOBLE COURTS TO NATIONHOOD

As the city states grew rich, they became prey to the big powers. Finally, the French Revolution showed them how they could become free

Always attractive to invaders from elsewhere in Europe, Italy in the 16th century lay at the mercy of the armies of France and Spain, both eager to gain control of its rich resources, human and material. Louis XII's invasion, successful to begin with, involved him eventually in the League of Cambrai, an alliance formed by Pope Julius II and designed to curb the overweening territorial ambitions and political self-confidence of the Venetian Republic. In 1509 Venice was severely defeated at the Battle of Agnadello, but it managed to hang on to most of its lands. As a result the Pope was lured away from the league, but he kept Spain as an ally. Louis now found himself facing a new confederation, the so-called Holy League of all the Italian states, whose battle-cry "Out with the barbarians!" both echoed an ancient hatred of French invaders and anticipated the spirit of the 19th-century Risorgimento.

Emperor Charles dominates Italy

Louis's successor, François I, attempted a further bid for mastery in northern Italy, but his disastrous defeat at Pavia in 1521 at the hands of Holy Roman Emperor Charles V (Charles I of Spain) was the prelude to a complete overturning of the established order throughout the Italian peninsula. In 1527 Rome was sacked and humiliated by imperial troops, and only in 1529 was peace concluded, effectively making Charles master of Italy. Though a member of the Sforza family was given the duchy of Milan, this was a mere gesture of dynastic politeness. The Genoese, shrewd as ever, saw which way the wind was blowing and committed their entire fleet, led by the great admiral Andrea Doria, to the Emperor's service.

Charles V, half Spanish and half Habsburg, was now the most powerful man in Europe – or, as he had good reason to believe, in the entire world. He boasted that the sun never set on his empire, which stretched halfway round the world. In Italy, however, he had to reckon with a resurgent Papacy, determined to recover international prestige and moral authority. In 1545 Pope Paul III, on behalf of his son Pier Luigi Farnese, persuaded Charles to create an independent duchy from the cities of Parma and Piacenza and their surrounding territories. Another small but important north Italian state was created in 1598 on the death of Alfonso d'Este, Duke of Ferrara. Pope Clement VIII claimed the duchy as a papal fiefdom, since there were no legitimate heirs. In compensation, Alfonso's bastard son Cesare was allowed to move the Ferrarese court to the city of Modena, where he became a sovereign duke.

The papal annexation of Ferrara ended one of the most enlightened of the smaller Renaissance states. The d'Este family were enthusiastic patrons of art, literature and music. In 1516 the poet Ludovico Ariosto had published

LEFT: Princess Maria Louisa di Parma (1751–1819), mother of King Charles V of Spain.
RIGHT: Venetians drinking chocolate.

the first of three versions of *Orlando Furioso* (1516, 1521 and 1532), his stupendous epic fantasy of love and chivalry, composed in Ferrara and very loosely based on d'Este history. This in turn inspired Torquato Tasso, another Ferrarese protégé, to write a more serious, loftier epic, *Gerusalemme Liberata*, a tale of the First Crusade. Both poems were among the most widely imitated and admired in 16th-century Europe.

Painters and musicians

In Mantua, meanwhile, the Gonzaga dukes had prospered through a series of marriages among illustrious families, not just in Italy but also within the Valois and Habsburg dynasties of France and Austria. Splendid buildings such as the Palazzo del Te, adorned with frescoes by Giulio Romano, and the stately domed church of Sant'Andrea, designed by Leon Battista Alberti, had proclaimed the exalted ambitions of the Gonzaga dynasty.

Like the d'Este, with whom there were marriage links, the family used its wealth to patronise painters and composers. Under Vincenzo I, who succeeded to the dukedom in 1587, a splendid picture collection was gathered together, including works by the young Peter Paul Rubens, who visited the court in person. Here, too, came musicians, led by Claudio Monteverdi whose opera *Orfeo* received its first performance at Mantua in 1607.

Opera, the fashionable new art form in early 17th-century Italy, found its keenest audiences in Venice. The state, for all its skilful diplomacy, had never fully recovered from its defeat at Agnadello and from the sacrifice to the Turks in 1570 of one of its prized imperial possessions, the island of Cyprus. Still more serious had been the loss of its Eastern spice markets to Portugal and Spain. The decline was at first barely perceptible, and until the close of the 17th century, when a costly war with Turkey and trade competition with France weakened it beyond recovery, Venice was still regarded with awe, envy and curiosity by travellers visiting its domains from other parts of Europe. The Republic's ancient system of government by committee was closely studied among political theorists, especially in England and Holland. Attempts within the state to make the administration more democratic were resisted by its aristocracy, though a mounting financial crisis meant that by 1700 several *nouveau riche* families had been able to buy their way into the prestigious *Golden Book*.

As the 17th century progressed, northern Italy fell an increasing prey to the great-power manoeuvres of Austria, France and Spain. While a duchy like Modena prospered owing to the shrewd operations of its d'Este rulers (one princess, Maria Beatrice, became Queen of England in 1685 as the wife of King James II), Mantua was less fortunate, losing practically all its assets though the diplomatic miscalculations of the last Gonzaga heirs. The most abiding success among the older ruling dynasties was that of the house of Savoy, based on its capital at Turin. The dukes played the game of alliances so skilfully that they raised their state to the dignity of a kingdom, known as Piedmont, or as Sardinia from the island they acquired through the Treaty of Utrecht.

TRAVEL BUGS

Travel during the days of the Grand Tour lacked the comforts of even the cheapest expedition today. To describe a hotel as "lousy" had a vivid meaning.

Sites for the Grand Tour

Even if ancestral feudalism prevailed in the countryside, the nobility in Venice's mainland possessions, in the territories of Parma and Modena, and above all in Lombardy, were beginning to take their rural estates more seriously as sources of investment. The early 18th century saw the start of improved roads and waterways and the building of handsome villas surrounded by parks and formal gardens.

The transfer of power in Lombardy from Spain to Austria in 1714 brought new life to Milan, and during the reigns of Maria Theresa and Joseph II the city entered fully into the spirit of the European Enlightenment, with a vigorous intellectual life encouraged by a benign Habsburg government. Milan became a favourite haunt of foreign visitors on the Grand Tour, while Venice entered on a new, if not surprising, final phase of its existence as an independent capital. The once powerful and dignified Serenissima became the favourite pleasure resort of those in search of non-stop entertainment and sexual adventure, whether in the legendary Carnival, the licensed gambling dens, the opera houses or even certain of the convents. No wonder a disgruntled political reformer among the Republic's senators referred to it as "a boxful of puppets".

Most of the Italian states were taken wholly by surprise when the French Revolution, from its outbreak in 1789, began sending sinister ripples across the Alps. The thriving bourgeoisie

LEFT: portrait of Barbara Gonzaga, daughter of Ludovico, by Mantegna (*c.*1431–1506).
ABOVE: an operatic recital in 17th-century Venice.

in cities of mainland Venice such as Brescia, Verona and Padua welcomed the new doctrines of political liberty and equality, and Genoa, by now thoroughly decadent, leaped at the chance of overturning the Doge and senators and devising a revolutionary government for itself. This gesture had been inspired largely by the French invasion of Lombardy in 1797, led by Napoleon Bonaparte, then a young general, whose ancestors were Tuscans settled in Corsica. When he seized outright power in France, Napoleon took it upon himself to reorganise Italian affairs, making his brother-in-law Eugène de Beauharnais viceroy of Milan and Venice.

THE SPOILS OF WAR

Many works of art in the Louvre in Paris are spoils of war taken by Napoleon. The French destroyed churches and dissolved monasteries, seizing their riches.

Napoleonic government in northern Italy was not an unmixed blessing. The French were often seen as arrogant and patronising, but the regime planted the seed of a united Italian state in which justice and taxation could be administered with universal fairness. Young men of bourgeois families could entertain ambitious career prospects, and children of both sexes gained access to a decent secular education. When Napoleon and his armies were beaten at Waterloo in 1815, and the old rulers returned to their various states under the watchful eye of Austria (to whose Habsburg dynasty most were related), these freedoms were not forgotten. In the years immediately following the Napoleonic wars, Milan, with an enlightened nobility and bourgeoisie, became the natural flashpoint for the earliest stirrings of what historians call "Il Risorgimento", the movement towards natural unity among the eight sovereign states of which Italy now consisted.

In 1821 a revolution was attempted by Milanese members of the secret society known as the Carbonari and, although the ringleaders were executed or exiled by the Austrians, their example was an inspiration to other fledgling "patriotic" movements. Ten years later it was Modena's turn to rebel, when the factory-owner Ciro Menotti tried to overthrow the harsh regime of the hated Duke Francesco IV and was executed by firing squad.

Like its neighbouring duchy of Parma, Modena was a satellite of the Austrian Empire, whose province of Venetia-Lombardy was run by combining well-intentioned efficiency with the ruthless surveillance of an extensive spy network. Only in 1848 did the first cracks start to appear in the reactionary Habsburg government apparatus. The two dukes of Parma and Modena were driven out by their subjects, Milan's citizens revolted against Austrian troops and, most heroic of all, Venice expelled its civil and military governors, resumed its ancient republican charter and kept imperial troops at bay in a siege lasting nearly a year.

Piedmont holds the key

Each of the revolutions had looked towards the strong, well-drilled army of the kingdom of Piedmont for an ultimate guarantee of success. With Charles Albert at its head, the Piedmont force which invaded Lombardy in 1848 seemed to bring dreams of unification close to reality. Charles Albert's decision-making unfortunately failed to catch his best ideals (he was known as *il re tentenna*, "King Ditherer"), and his defeat by the Austrians at Custoza was

LEFT: the French in Italy; illustration from Paris's *Le Petit Journal*, 13 May 1893.
RIGHT: combined French and Piedmontese forces routed the Austrians at the Battle of Solferino in 1859.

the result of fatal hesitations. A further debacle at Novara in 1849 drove him into exile.

His son Victor Emmanuel II set out to rally international support for a united Italy under Piedmontese rule, helped by his astute prime minister Camillo di Cavour. Though the 1848 revolutions had failed, "the Italian question" was now a European issue, and Austria could no longer sustain its image as the bringer of peace and order to northern Italy.

In 1858 Cavour's skilful negotiations with Napoleon III persuaded the latter to declare war on Austria, and the Austrian Emperor Franz Josef II saw his armies defeated at the battles of Solferino and Magenta. The combined French and Piedmonte campaign was assisted by the great freedom-fighter Giuseppe Garibaldi *(see box below).*

The treaty Austria was finally forced to make at Villafranca in 1859 surrendered the whole of Lombardy, including Milan, together with the ducal territories of Parma and Modena, to Piedmont, which became the Kingdom of Italy under Victor Emmanuel II. Only in 1866, when Austria was worsted in a war with Prussia, did the Veneto and Friuli join the kingdom, foreshadowing the complete unification for which so many had fought for half a century. ❑

CAVOUR AND GARIBALDI

Count Camillo di Cavour (1810–61) was one of Italy's greatest statesmen. Originally a successful and progressive agriculturalist and industrialist, he gradually came to believe in the need for Italian unity and independence, which he felt was best achieved through the leadership of Piedmont, the strongest Italian state. To raise support for the Italian cause he travelled to England and France, and he also contributed Piedmontese troops to the Crimean War, thus winning a place at the peace conference, where he brought the Italian question to the attention of Europe.

The key to Cavour's eventual success was his alliance with Giuseppe Garibaldi. Garibaldi had honed his fighting skills as a mercenary in South America, where he had been exiled for his part in a republican plot in Genoa in 1834. It was in South America that Garibaldi first formed his famous Red Shirts. He returned to Italy in order to fight in the revolutions of 1848; his bravery and determination quickly made him a popular hero and caught the attention of Cavour. After helping defeat the Austrians in northern Italy, Garibaldi went south to capture Sicily and Naples.

Cavour was appointed Italy's first prime minister in 1861, under the new king, Victor Emmanuel, but he died only four months later and never saw the complete unification of Italy, which was not achieved until 1870.

DUCE DUCE DUCE
TOLLIO
GARUTI
ALFREDO
ZULATO
EZIO
BOSI
DUILIO
SINIGAGLIA
ORLANDO
ANTONINI
MARIO

THE TUMULTUOUS 20TH CENTURY

Finally united, Italy was nearly torn apart again when Benito Mussolini took the country into a disastrous alliance with the Third Reich

Italy became a fully unified nation on 20 September 1870, when the army of King Victor Emmanuel II entered Rome, until then capital of the independent Papal States. Nothing could have prepared the many thousands of Italians who had actively engaged in the Risorgimento for the problems nationhood now brought in its wake. The alienation of ordinary people from an over-centralised government was made worse by an obsessive bureaucracy, a failure by the authorities to deal with various forms of corruption and a sense that the king and his ministers, eager to modernise the new state and place it on an equal footing with the great European powers, really did not understand the concerns of the people they ruled.

Northern Italy had the advantage over the southern provinces of possessing an improved road system, railway links between several of the principal towns and some light industry, mostly in Lombardy and the Veneto. After 1870 a deliberate attempt was made to create a state rail network, and cities such as Turin, Milan and Bologna soon became the focus of a steady drift of migrant workers from the old country estates. The bitter memory of a peasant life in which there was seldom enough to eat, and nothing belonged to the farmer beyond his clothes and household furniture, has burned deep into the national psyche, and most Italians would always rather live in a town. Hence the decidedly utilitarian look of much of the agricultural landscape in the Po Valley, a countryside inhabited for profit rather than pleasure.

Boulevards and parks planned

During the 19th century's closing decades the character of larger towns underwent important changes. Their ramparts were pulled down, citadels and barracks demolished at the same time, and tree-lined boulevards, parks and gardens laid out instead. Certain old princely residences were adapted for alternative uses: the Duke of Modena's palace became a military academy, and at Colorno near Parma the ducal summer retreat was turned into an asylum. On the outskirts of Genoa heavy industry sprang up to sustain Italy's shipbuilding drive, designed to modernise the merchant fleet and to produce ironclad battleships which, by 1890, made Italy's navy the world's third-largest.

LEFT: Fascist congress at Modena, 1934.
RIGHT: Mussolini's various pacts with Hitler cemented the bond between the Fascist states.

The gradual sophistication of the northern industrial base brought with it an inevitable tension between the growing urban labour force and its employers. Anarchism became popular among workers in the towns of Emilia and Romagna, and Italy's first big industrial strikes broke out in the textile factories of the Piedmontese town of Biella. An independent workers' party developed in Lombardy during the 1880s, dedicated to union activism and concentrating on attempts to mobilise peasant labourers. In 1884 demonstrations immediately broke out in the villages around Mantua, spreading quickly to other parts of Italy where unemployment and high prices had severely hit the farming community.

Poverty and prosperity

In the countryside, life seemed to slide from bad to worse, and malnutrition and disease threatened the poorest in parts of Emilia and the Veneto. The two largest cities, Milan and Turin, continued to grow and prosper. Venice, reconciled to its destiny as an art capital, began encouraging tourism as a serious investment, with new hotels and steamboat services up and down the Grand Canal.

Events like these forced social change on a country preparing to enter a period of prosperity, marking the fastest growth rate of any European country in the years immediately before the Great War. Under its prime minister, Giovanni Giolitti, the nation courted diplomatic approval among great powers, while setting itself up as their commercial competitor. Turin began to rival Milan as a centre for new industries, chief among them the Fiat automobile firm, founded by a group of young, speed-obsessed aristocrats led by Gianni Agnelli. He started producing cheap Fiat models on an assembly line, while the factory also built aero-

In the very centre of Milan during May 1898, there was an incident which summed up the post-Risorgimento failure. General Bava Beccaris, the city's army commandant, suspicious of activities involving a group of beggars gathered outside a Capuchin monastery, rallied troops and stormed the building. When hostile crowds took to the streets the general ordered his men to charge the demonstrators, and 50 people were killed. The response of King Umberto was to award Bava Beccaris a hero's welcome in Rome and a medal. This indication of the monarch's sympathies brought him a violent end two years later at the hands of the anarchist assassin Gaetano Bresci.

planes and engines for submarines. Other north Italian businesses achieved similar success in the early 1900s as international brand names, including Pirelli tyres and Olivetti typewriters.

The *belle époque* in Italy was an era when the flourishing bourgeoisie enjoyed lavish cinema epics made in increasingly busy film studios, operas like Puccini's *Tosca* or *Madama Butterfly*, outrageous art events organised by the young iconoclasts of the Futurist Movement and the poetry of that unblushing self-publicist Gabriele D'Annunzio *(see page 287)*. Further pleasures included motor racing and seaside holidays, the latter becoming an institution during July and August.

Italy remained neutral in World War I until May 1915, when popular demonstrations urged the government to join in the conflict on the side of Britain and France. The major theatre of war for the Italian army lay in the country's northeastern corner, where disputed territory in the Tyrol, Istria and around Trieste offered a suitable pretext for attacking the Austrians, still viewed with suspicion only half a century after their expulsion from the rest of Italy. Unfortunately, the handling of military operations by General Cadorna and his staff revealed the army's unreadiness, and after the disastrous Battle of Caporetto in 1917 the nation faced the possibility of upheaval from within through strikes, peace protests and the overall weakness of the government. Even when, with the help of allied contingents from Britain and the US, Italian troops avenged their earlier defeat by a second battle at Caporetto, the ensuing peace brought a sense of disillusionment and betrayal of expectations.

DISASTER STRIKES

The great disaster of World War I was the battle of Caporetto in 1917. Austria took almost 300,000 prisoners and there was a bout of strikes and protests.

LEFT: the early 1900s saw Italian companies from Martini to Marconi making headway in world markets.
ABOVE: Puccini's *Madama Butterfly* was a sensation.

Mussolini steps in

A footloose young journalist from Predappio named Benito Mussolini seized his opportunity to capitalise on the atmosphere of political tension. He secured valuable backing from landowners, industrialists and police chiefs for his new Movement, Fascism, using icons and symbols from Italy's Roman past to project its dynamic image. By 1925 he had more or less gained control of the government, and, although Italy was still a constitutional monarchy under Victor Emmanuel III, Mussolini became effectively its overall dictator.

As "Il Duce", a title based on the Latin word for leader which the Venetian and Genoese had accorded to their heads of government, Mussolini conducted a savage colonial war in Ethiopia and sent squadrons to Spain to fight for Franco's nationalists in the civil war. Northern Italy initially welcomed the new Fascist order, viewing it as a guarantee of stability, though certain areas remained sceptical.

Racial laws and resistance

Personal vanity as much as anything else drew Mussolini closer to Germany's Nazi regime.

Growing dependence on Germany for raw materials made "Il Duce" readier to accept Hitler's demands, which included a tougher attitude towards Italy's Jewish population. Since unification, several Jews had played an important role in public life, from which religious prejudice had earlier barred them in the various sovereign states. There was no strong tradition of anti-Semitism in Italy, however, and in places such as Venice, Genoa and Ferrara, Jews were seen as pillars of society. The racial laws passed in 1938 marked a further step towards the total submission to Germany's behests which led to Mussolini's declaration of war in 1940.

Italy was hopelessly unprepared for war, and an attempted invasion of Greece was only sustained with the help of heavy German reinforcements. British and American forces crushed the Italian armies in North Africa and began a series of devastating air attacks on major industrial centres. The mood in Italy was one of widespread disillusion with Fascist propaganda and of a deepening sense of shame at the country's involvement in a war it seemed to be losing. In 1943, as the Allies landed in the south, Mussolini tendered his resignation to the king. General Badoglio took charge of the government and offered Italy's surrender.

A new phase of the war began when the Germans invaded, seizing control of the north and installing Mussolini as leader of a puppet Fascist state ruled from Salò on Lake Garda. Mussolini installed his mistress, Claretta Petacci, here and became little more than a blustering figurehead, incapable of controlling the thuggish extremists who joined him. The Germans, meanwhile, rounded up Jews to be sent to concentration camps and punished those who maintained links with the various partisan groups mobilising in the north.

Ordinary Italians now fought with honour and courage against the Germans throughout the north. The annals of 1943–5 are full of moving episodes in which everyone from farmers' wives and schoolteachers to priests and children played a part. Greatest credit belongs to the partisans, whose role in weakening the German hold on Italy was played down or shamefully undermined by British and American politicians fearful of Communist influence.

Peace and recovery

In April 1945, a few days after Mussolini and Claretta were captured, shot and hung upside down in Milan's Piazzale Loreto, peace was declared and Italy's process of rapid recovery began. By the end of the 1950s Milan had become the nation's economic capital, associated with a sequence of rapidly changing governments involving the right-wing Christian Democrats and excluding the Communists for whom most northerners tended to vote.

The end of the Cold War in the early 1990s led to new political alignments in the north, with media tycoon Silvio Berlusconi forming a Conservative grouping, Forza Italia, alongside the neo-Fascist Alleanza Nazionale. Berlusconi's centre right government took office in 2001, with Forza Italia governing in coalition with the National Alliance and the Northern League. Since then there has been a great deal of instability, including the resignation of Foreign Minister Renato Ruggiero in January 2002, after Cabinet disputes regarding Italy's position on Europe. In July 2002 Claudio Scajola, the Interior Minister and one of the Prime Minister's closest aides, also resigned from government. This came after a row over labour law reform and left-wing terrorism. The terrorists claimed descent from the infamous far-left Red Brigade, which caused instability in the 1970s and 1980s in a bloody campaign of kidnapping and murder.

TERRIBLE REPRISALS

The worst German reprisal was in the winter of 1944 when the entire population of almost 2,000 living in and around the village of Marzabotto near Bologna was massacred by firing squads.

The second Berlusconi government has the dubious distinction of being the longest to last in Italy's republican history. However, after losses in regional elections and internal problems in his coalition he was forced to tender the resignation of his government in April 2005. But, just three days later on 23 April, he formed a new government with few changes.

LEFT: Axis allies – Mussolini and Hitler.

ABOVE: a guard of honour greets Hitler's arrival for talks with Mussolini at Italy's Brenner Pass in 1940.

Berlusconi's main opposition rival, Romano Prodi, has had a long political career, starting in 1978 and including presidency of the European Commission from 1999 to 2004. If the results of the regional elections in April 2005 were repeated on a national basis in the general election due in 2006, the centre-left coalition led by Romano Prodi would win as decisively as the Casa della Libertà did in 2001.

The current unrest brings to mind the immortal line of a character in Lampedusa's great novel of aristocratic decline in 19th-century Sicily, *Il Gattopardo (The Leopard)*: "If we want things to stay as they are, things will have to change." Time will tell. ❑

ARISTON

BAGNINO
SPIAGGIA LIBERA ATTREZZATA
- VENERE AZZURRA -
AREA con POSTAZIONE a RICHIESTA

THE CONTEMPORARY SCENE

Consumerism and conviviality, conformity, chaos and clannishness are the keynotes of northern society

The light-hearted "*terrazza* law" is often cited as an explanation for the cheery resilience of Italian life. According to café society logic, because the sun shines and people can dine *alfresco*, all troubles will eventually evaporate. Although the southern mindset readily indulges in *carpe diem*, the northern approach is more rooted in reality: seize the day and sun oneself, but also sacrifice inner life and leisure to making and spending money or shoring up one's image. Life beyond the sunny café terrace tends to remain a shadowy web of petty provincialism, stifling convention and rampant consumerism, underpinned by a clannish network of interest groups and the extended family.

Civic-minded northerners usually admire the perceived order and incorruptibility of public life north of the Alps. Compared with Italy, these are countries in which dealing with the authorities, setting up a company, lying in a hospital bed, paying bills or posting letters all seem fairly simple procedures. South of the Alps, however, the state is either feared or flouted.

Paradise postponed

The former Italian-based American writer Gore Vidal commented that while the genius of America was to separate the state from religion, the genius of Italy was to separate the state from the people. As Matt Frei, a BBC foreign correspondent, once remarked, if the country could only re-invent the relationship between the individual and the state, "it would shorten queues in banks, deliver letters on time, open museums, improve the traffic and the health system. If it could do that, Italy, with its culture, weather, beauty, humanity, humour, industry, inventiveness, unselfconscious eccentricity and delicious food, would surely be the closest thing to paradise on earth."

In the meantime, contemporary society is a paradoxical mixture of creativity, conformity and chaos. "In Italy there are neither angels nor devils, only average sinners," was the witticism of Giulio Andreotti, seven times premier. With its culture of patronage and corruption, the Italian democratic system defies most rules of a democracy. In response, the average tax-dodging northerner dedicates considerable energy and inventiveness to foiling the system, a complex bureaucracy whose wheels are oiled by *galoppini*, unofficial facilitators skilled in speeding up procedures by fair means and foul. In a recent abuse of benefits, thousands of supposedly blind pensioners were found to hold driving licences, while star footballers were receiving disability pensions.

PRECEDING PAGES: *il mare* or *la montagna* – Italians will opt for one or the other for their summer retreat. **LEFT AND RIGHT:** the August exodus to the sea, and carnival time in Venice – in such a convivial society the instinct is to join not escape the crowds.

Such irregularities seep into every area of life. A landing at Milan's Malpensa airport may be marred by thoughts of the billions of illicit *lire* mixed into the fresh cement. Even the taste of a *cappuccino* in Verona is soured by the *tangente,* the bribe that was necessary to produce the processing plant. Subversion of regulations is an ancient pastime, with cunning *(furbizia)* praised over probity. Indeed, after Trieste was ceded to Italy from the old Austro-Hungarian empire in 1918, taxes were promptly doubled on the assumption that people never paid more than 50 per cent of their dues. If guile fails, Catholic society still offers the path of confession, contrition and absolution.

In the recent past, the north has been content to leave politics to southerners and to concentrate on making money. However, northerners have been politically radicalised by the protest movements of the 1990s and by the increasing appeal of federalism as a solution to their grievances. In the late 1990s, the region positioned itself as the new Italy, turning its back on a baroque political structure steeped in *clientelismo* (nepotism). Yet the region remains deeply old-fashioned, despite its faddism. It is a paradox that, although priding themselves on their free-spirited nature, the people live in a conservative, over-regulated society. As Matt Frei says: "From the formal greeting to the social ritual of the *passeggiata*, the life of the

URBAN MYTHS: ONE

Italians are resolutely urban, drawn to the cosy ideal of living in a small or medium-sized town. The classic northern town is self-contained, self-sufficient and inward-looking. It may well be on a hill-top with modern culture grafted onto a medieval settlement. Such traditional towns regularly top European surveys for superb quality of life. For the northerners, provincial life represents security, modernity, comfort and conviviality while the countryside tends to represent the past, with its primitive conditions and poverty.

Large towns such as Modena, Padua and Verona can be seen as smaller versions of the successful provincial town at which Italians in the north excel. Not that smaller towns have a monopoly on beauty and quality of life. For all its inconvenience, Venice is praised as a deeply liveable city, while Bologna is regularly voted the place with the best quality of life in Italy. Even unsung cities such as Milan have their passionate fans, praising secret courtyards and hidden gardens. In the wintry elegance of 18th-century Turin, present-day citizens can cast their eyes along the dark streets and see glittering temples of consumerism basking in the luminosity of the Alps.

Turin and Detroit may both be noted for their car industries, but the Italians are certain that their city has a better quality of life.

average Italian is defined by a set of rules as complex as those of a secret monastic sect."

Northerners are not by nature law-abiding, perceiving the long arm of the law as yet another infringement on personal liberty. Paying taxes, parking in designated places and queuing are seen as similar unnecessary constraints. In a country where civic awareness is undeveloped, there is an assumption of lawlessness in most dealings with the state. Whether it is struggling against the telephone company or the tax office, battles with the authorities absorb a great deal of energy. Yet the law is only one of the arms which the individual uses in his essentially lawless struggle. In state schools, rebellion for the sake of rebelling is par for the course, as are strikes against educational reforms.

In truth, citizens are torn between tradition and rebellion, conformity and individuality. Despite a sense of chaos, social life is neatly ordered, underpinned by excessive planning. A young couple may decide to marry in exactly three years' time, or move into a house of their own in five years' time; a healthy, middle-aged couple may plan where to be buried in the family vault. Commenting on the cloying social packaging of northern life, Tim Parks, the Verona-based novelist, says: "*Cappuccino* until 10, then *espresso; aperitivo* after 12; your pasta, your meat, your *dolce* in bright packaging; light white wine, strong red wine, *prosecco*; baptism, first communion, marriage, funeral."

LEFT: catching up on today's news in Parma.
ABOVE: to market in Alto Adige. Despite northern Italy's dominant industrial base, it still clings to a strong rural tradition.

Unshakeable conservatism

At heart is "the extraordinary power of convention, the thorough-going, unshakeable conservatism of a people whose favourite delusion is that they are not bound by delusion". The writer Jonathan Keates would concur with the Italian correspondent John Hooper, who sees the rituals underlying the specious modishness of life: "A lot of what is Italian that is presented to the outside world is hyper-modern or hyper-vogueish, be it Ferrari cars, Versace ties, dried tomatoes or balsamic vinegar. Yet Italy remains profoundly old-fashioned and hidebound, not only by bureaucratic inefficiency but also by practices intended to limit competition and protect this or that interest group."

This archipelago of interest groups is at the heart of society. Even family companies are often organised in such a way as to minimise taxes and employers' contributions. Bizarrely, according to tax returns, employees seem to earn more than their employers while professional people and specialised craftsmen can claim subsistence levels despite running several homes or boats.

Italians have always taken refuge in tribalism, a complex system of extended loyalties whose survival validates virtually any course of action. "Me and my clan, my family, my shop, we'll manage – and all the rest can go to hell" is the crudest version of this philosophy, as expressed by Hans Magnus Enzenberger, an observer of Italian society.

URBAN MYTHS: TWO

Small towns continue to flourish in northern Italy because the people like to feel the embracing comfort of a life contained. At the simplest level, citizens create a cosy little world of "their" baker, dressmaker, ironing-lady or picture-framer, conveying the social status of a patron rather than of a mere consumer. Personal recommendation here is everything: *Il mio falegname di fiducia* (my trusted carpenter), often a moonlighting civil servant, could not work for anyone of indiscriminating taste. In its attachment to provincialism and small-town values, Italian society combines cosiness and pride in equal measure, making urban life stultifyingly narrow yet also deeply pleasurable.

Family ties

It is a cliché that Italy is not a country but a mosaic made up of 10 million families. As the cornerstone of a conservative society, *la famiglia* is a sophisticated network of patronage and power. Marriage is still seen as a contract for life, not necessarily severed by infidelity. Belonging to a northern family is still a cradle-to-the-grave commitment, with children treated as miniature adults, sons cosseted and daughters trained to be competent but generally more docile. (For a woman, faking subservience is a small price to pay for power in the family.)

Miraculously, the family seems impregnable, despite the rise in social mobility and divorce, the constraints of small apartments, the caprices of domineering parents, the lowest birthrate in Europe, and the virtual absence of state child support. Even so, the population is the first in the world to possess more pensioners than teenagers and children. By 2050 the ratio will rise to three to one if this resolutely consumerist society continues to eschew *bambini* in favour of beautiful houses and holidays in Bali. The Pope's concern is so great that he has instructed the Italians to "rediscover the culture of life and love ... and their mission as parents".

In the meantime, however, nearly 60 percent of pampered Italians under 34 still live at home. *Mammismo*, an unhealthy attachment to one's mother, tends to afflict sons, who are termed *mammoni*, mummies' boys. For all offspring, parents are looking for a state of *lo starbene*: a steady job, preferably in the family business or as a civil servant *(statale)*. Parents tend to buy or build their children houses so money can be spent on consumer durables rather than rent.

The cloying but comforting rituals of family life are revealed in the saying "*Natale con i tuoi, Pasqua con chi vuoi*" (Spend Christmas with your family, but Easter with whoever you wish). Yet, given the overweening importance of the family, friends (and lovers) come a distant second, with soulmates spurned in favour of a network of useful acquaintances for whom the game of gifts and favours is second nature. Jonathan Keates is scathing about the superficiality of social chit-chat and of society's shared fear of solitude: "The tyranny of family life proscribes individualism, annihilates outline and perspective. Without secrets, without worlds apart, without moments of determined solitariness, the grain and colour of personality are rubbed away." Even the Italian concept of *individualismo* is more "me-firstism" than genuine originality.

Fortunately, there are compensations for the complacency and money-making ethos of northern life. Convention and consumerism may be part of the social warp and weft but conviviality is the real religion. On a good day, the forfeiture of liberty seems a small price to pay for the inbred gregariousness of Italians.

Luigi Barzini condemned his fellow-countrymen for their "eternal search for shallow pleasures and distractions," but the sociologist Luciano Gallino presents the case for the other side: "However ridiculous it may seem, Italian food and sociability are important elements in a civilisation." Conviviality is inextricably bound up with eating well, which is one of the highest aims of Italian existence.

On average, compared with Britain, a similar country in terms of wealth, Italy possesses three times the number of retail outlets, and twice the number of cafés. Tellingly, "foodie" or "privacy" are not familiar terms in the local lexicon. An appreciation of good food is the prerogative of all, while privacy is the preserve of none. The emphasis is on the everyday values of sociability, simplicity and pleasure. *Allegria* is a blend of bubbly *joie de vivre* with copious sunshine, good company and collective high spirits. *Allegria* is infectious, as are sybaritic living and a communal way of life. Its much rarer counterpart is a fleeting melancholy induced by solitude, abysmal autumn weather and seasonal tax rises.

Jonathan Keates muses on the certainties of middle-class life in quiet-living, consumerist Middle Italy: "The shops will always bulge with acquisitive lures and promises, the appalling television channels will be there to offer the bromide and novocaine of endless game shows, and the news magazines will order their graver thoughts on matters a little more global than the thousand different ways of preparing a risotto or the chances for Juve and Samp in the league championships." On a sunny day, even this cynical appraisal of a soulless *dolce vita* has considerable appeal. ❑

The Slow Food Movement

As gourmets delight in pointing out, Italy is the only country in the world where the marketing strategy of McDonalds has been hampered by the birth of the Slow Food Movement.

LEFT: appreciation of good food is a prerogative of all.
ABOVE: children are cosseted and *la famiglia* remains sacred, yet Italy has the lowest birthrate in Europe.

REGIONALISM RULES

"We have made Italy, now we must make the Italians," declared Massimo d'Azeglio (1798–1866), prime minister of Piedmont, after the creation of the Kingdom of Italy

Before 1945, says the cookery writer Claudia Roden, "You could divide Italy according to cooking fats: there was butter in the north, pork fat in the centre and olive oil in the south. The Italy of polenta and rice was the north, and the Italy of pizza and dry pasta was in the south." Now, she thinks, the borders have been blurred, and pizza and pasta have triumphed. However, regional flavours survive in rich sauces and robust attitudes; national uniformity is only notional, even in politics, language and culture. As Massimo d'Azeglio, a shrewd architect of national unity, declared: "To make Italy out of Italians, one must not be in a hurry."

Identity crisis

If regionalism is a religion in northern Italy, then Italian-ness is a mere cult. In 1815 Metternich, the Habsburg prime minister, famously dismissed Italy as a "geographical expression". The country is a collection of peoples, with the disparate regions remaining diverse. National sentiment is restricted to sport, be it the resurgence of Ferrari or the mixed fortunes of the national football team.

Local loyalties cast a long historical shadow over the contemporary scene: distinctive regional identity was a factor in keeping Italy disunited. This was compounded by the fragmented nature of the city states, duchies, republics and Papal States, each with its own allegiances and cultural traditions. Until 1861 the regions were separate, independent, even rival states, who submitted to different rulers and were protected by sovereign armies. The people's common refrain was: *"Franza o Spagna, purché si manga."* (France or Spain, it matters little as long as we get fed.)

Turin, sandwiched between the great powers of France and Austria-Hungary, was frequently overrun and has retained a foreign flavour. Indeed, Count Cavour saw Turin as the nodal point between "German and Latin races", with the Piedmontese alone possessing the better qualities of Latins and Germans. In Piedmont, the pervasive French influence is reflected in the region's penchant for fussy French cuisine, at odds with plainer Italian country fare. The Austro-Hungarian influence in Lombardy, Friuli-Venezia Giulia and the Veneto helped to instil a tradition of sound administration and fair taxation. In the case of Venice, Austrian pragmatism overlays an exotic eastern heritage, the Republic's role as the hub of a trading empire with Africa and the Levant.

Whether living in famous cities or in one-horse towns, citizens generally carry their home town around for life, like a standard. Just as exile from home is the greatest fear, so "local boy made good" is the classic communal myth. Deeply ingrained regionalism also dictates fierce rivalry, just as civic pride implies competition. Such warped local patriotism is

LEFT: Alto Adige has a distinctly Austrian flavour.
RIGHT: Bolzano is the bilingual capital of Alto Adige, with both Italian and German being spoken.

predicated on the belief that Italy would be paradise without *"gli altri"*, fellow Italians from rival regions and cities.

Borderlands

For a country that superficially seems so clear and culturally distinct, Italy abounds in borderlands. The country's frontiers were only definitively fixed in 1954, when Italy's dispute with what was then Yugoslavia was settled. Yet even within northern regions that are undeniably Italian there are alien pockets, places on the edge little stirred by a national consciousness. One such anomaly is Trieste; as a splinter in the Habsburg Empire, Trieste gave *Mitteleuropa* its only access to the Mediterranean. In 1963 Friuli-Venezia Giulia was also accorded special status because of its Slovene-speaking population in the Trieste hinterland.

In the north it is hard to find Italy pure and undiluted. The region has its share of mini-states, including Campione d'Italia, a slice of Italy in Swiss territory. The world's oldest republic, San Marino, has a seat in the UN but lives on pageantry and postage stamps. Seborga, an enterprising principality behind the Italian Riviera, unilaterally declared its independence in 1995 but has yet to be officially recognised.

The Italian Constitution granted a measure of autonomy to French-speaking Valle d'Aosta and Italian-German-speaking Trentino-Alto Adige. Known as Südtirol in German, Alto Adige is the most complex case, a region spiritually Austrian but legally Italian. In 1919 the dismantling of the Austro-Hungarian Empire resulted in the Tyrol being divided, with South Tyrol awarded to Italy and eventually swallowed up by the new region of Trentino-Alto Adige in 1948. The Italian state's gerrymandering ensured an Italian-speaking majority but, until recently, left the German-speaking population dissatisfied. Culturally, Bolzano (Bozen), the German and Italian-speaking capital of Alto Adige, still feels like an Austrian city, with its mountain chalets, brass bands, neat window boxes, and its banks built with a most un-Italian disregard for security.

Northern Italy abounds in linguistic differences past and present. Piedmont shares more than a frontier with France: French was the court language until the mid 19th-century, and

OLD MIGRANTS AND NEW IMMIGRANTS

Since 1945 more than 6 million southerners have migrated to the northern industrial heartlands, but in more recent years the influx of non-European Union immigrants has resulted in new ethnic communities, who currently comprise 2 percent of the population, with a burgeoning underclass of illegal immigrants. In major northern cities such as Milan and Genoa, the social strain of immigration has been increasingly felt, particularly with the arrival of boatloads of North and West Africans, Albanians and citizens from the former Yugoslavia. (Non-European Union immigrants now comprise a quarter of the prison population.) Their presence has played into the hands of the instinctive racist tendencies shared by many northern Italians, and swelled the ranks of the secessionist movements. In critical northern eyes, today's immigrant could be an Eastern European prostitute in Milan, an Albanian cleaner in Turin, or a North African trader in Genoa.

While acceptance and integration look remote, the humanity of Italians ensures that many illegal immigrants are treated with tolerance, at least on a personal level. Moreover, Italians are gradually adjusting to the phenomenon of African-Italians speaking the language fairly fluently. Even so, mixed marriages or friendships across the racial divide still tend to be taboo.

the local dialects reflect French and old Tuscan influences. Count Cavour was as much Swiss and French as Piedmontese, since his mother was from Switzerland and his grandmother from Savoy. As prime minister, Cavour still spoke better French than Italian, never travelled south of Florence, and was more familiar with the culture and history north of the Alps.

LINGUA FRANCA

French was the language of the court in Piedmont until the mid-19th century, when only a tiny minority of the country spoke standard Italian. King Victor Emmanuel never mastered it.

Today citizens still delight in pointing out almost "incomprehensible" dialects, from the guttural *bergamasco* in Bergamo to the Provençal French of Valle d'Aosta or the Frenchified dialects of the Alpine Piedmontese hinterland.

Regional dialects and languages

Although the advent of television led to greater linguistic homogeneity, regional dialects and even languages survive. In the 1990s the state approved the teaching of minority languages at elementary schools in certain regions, and permitted the street names Italianised by Mussolini to revert to their original forms. (In the area around Trieste, place names were already written in Italian and Slovene, with Italian and German used in Alto Adige.) The promotion of minority languages was both a genuine admission of cultural diversity and a sop to regionalist separatist sentiments. As a result, Ladin, the Latin-based language spoken by a minority in Trentino-Alto Adige, was given special status. Languages granted similar recognition included German (in Alto Adige), Slovene (around Trieste), Friulano (in the northeast), Provençal French (in Valle d'Aosta and Turin) and Occitano (in Turin and Cosenza). As well as asserting their differences in dialects, cuisine and folklore, the regions have become hotbeds of political debate. Northerners express their political and economic differences in their attachment to parties with radical aspirations, from the left-wing efficiency of Emilia to the secessionist movements that flourish in Lombardy and the Veneto. These leagues combine protest against political corruption with a more ancient rebellion against the capital. The state is perceived as siphoning off northern taxes and diluting

LEFT: a souvenir vendor, one of the new generation of African-Italians, on the Riviera.
ABOVE: "regionalism first, nationalism second".

northern identity. To staunch federalists, even Italian unification was a historical error.

Lombardy, the Veneto and Piedmont spearhead the federalist movement. Although the Lombards have been the dominant force since the creation of the first modern league in 1982, the equally prosperous citizens of the Veneto are challenging their leadership. The Movimento Nordest (Northeast Movement), based on the Catalan model, aims to make northern Italy autonomous.

ARRIVISTE CELTS

"The Lombards were upstarts and newcomers descended from the Celts, and only arrived on the Italian peninsula in the 9th century." – The Venetian League.

Protection of profits

On one level, the federalist movement is fuelled by fierce regional pride and by resentment against poorer regions and the "thieving" state. Supporters of the leagues complain of their taxes being squandered in the south by the state machine. Certainly, autonomy would free the regions from the dead hand of bureaucracy, but for self-righteous northerners the primary aim is the protection of home-grown profits. Yet such grievances are underpinned by a sense of history as a living inspiration, from glorious ceremonials to a commemoration of valiant causes. South of Milan the nondescript town of Pontida regularly re-enacts the 1176 Battle of Legnano, a victory of the Lombard League over imperial forces. The pageant represents a rejection of the modern state and an indictment of Italian unity. The glue of national solidarity runs very thinly.

The questioning of the nation state is not restricted to Italy, but it has assumed a distinctly local character. Even if the leagues fail to find a leading role in the national democracy, they have succeeded in rousing regional passions. With Italy desperate to flaunt its European credentials, passions run extremely high on both sides of the political divide, with supporters of unity equally vehement.

Although his influence may be on the wane, Umberto Bossi, leader of the Northern League (part of a coalition with Forza Italia and the National Alliance), is the rabble-rousing mouthpiece of working-class anger, with a rallying cry of "*C'è l'ho duro!*" (I've got a hard-on). Yet guile is also part of his armoury: when speaking to a hardline audience in Bergamo, Signor Bossi is a separatist; speaking to the Venetian League, he is a regionalist; when in Rome, he is a federalist, and when in Sicily, he becomes pro-autonomy. In 1996 his Northern League created the surreal and self-styled country of Padania, complete with passports and currency.

In 2001 the Northern League rejoined forces with Berlusconi's coalition, in spite of previous disagreements. The League is currently the most loyal party to Berlusconi's government, except of course Berlusconi's own. Latterly it has muted its demands for independence, focusing instead on devolution while remaining within the framework of Italy. In the European Parliament its MEPs work within the grouping Independence and Democracy.

Despite all disclaimers, northerners like being Italian, provided that it is graced with a local dimension in politics, food and wine. Thanks to regional prosperity and an instinct for compromise and consensus, the north remains one of Italy's success stories. Northern confidence is not dented by its cultural and social diversity, or the controversies surrounding separatism. In the words of the Italian playwright Ennio Flaiano, "Things are tragic but not serious." ❑

LEFT: the Northern League's rabble-rousing leader, Umberto Bossi, campaigns for devolution.

Football Fever

Football, like opera, is a national obsession and a source of patriotic pride. The pre-match atmosphere in Milan's San Siro stadium is a festival of explosions, pounding drums and choreographed clapping, with stands decked in banners, dapper fans embracing fur-clad companions, and families devouring mounds of *porchetta*-filled *panini*, fresh ham rolls; only *caffè borghetti*, strong, sweet coffee, fuels the competition. Even so, the rivalry between the two Milanese sides explodes in a post-match finale in which the winning fans parade a coffin draped in the losers' colours.

The game thrives on classic regional and city rivalries: the major northern teams include Juventus, AC Milan, Inter Milan, Sampdoria (one of two Genoa teams) and Parma. Milan proclaims itself the capital of European soccer while Juventus, one of the world's richest clubs, prides itself on tactics, stamina and strength. Milan and Rome have two teams apiece, and Berlusconi's AC Milan is a rival to Fiat and Agnelli's Juventus at Turin.

The major Italian clubs are envious of the lucrative sponsorship and merchandising deals that can be struck by foreign rivals. Instead of rushing to the souvenir stands for replica shirts, more than 2,000 Juventus fans show their loyalty by taking skiing holidays on the Valle d'Aosta slopes where the team retreats for winter training. Refined Italian fashion sense precludes the donning of football strips as leisurewear: the major sides must be content with merchandising exquisite packages of wine, olive oil and *panettone* Christmas cake in club colours.

Nonetheless, Italian imports have enriched foreign football, despite their reputation as precious individualists rather than team players. In turn, Inter Milan and AC Milan have sides studded with foreign players. According to Gianluca Vialli, former Juventus star and manager of Chelsea: "In Italy, foreign footballers are idols, we treat them like kings." However, Berlusconi has complained that there is no spirit to his all-star Milanese side and called for more home-grown players.The current decline in standards has also been attributed to the lack of investment in youth training, accentuated by a marked preference for buying ready-made foreign players. Even Vicenza, a first-division club with a reputation for nurturing young players, recently abandoned its youth programme.

Known as the Azzurri, the Blues, the national side has had mixed fortunes. Just as Mussolini launched the 1934 World Cup as a celebration of the Fascist state, so Italia 90 was staged as a showcase for state-of-the-art stadia and "*la nuova ricca Italia*", the newly wealthy, corruption-free country. In the end, the 1990 World Cup was better remembered as a quagmire of kickbacks and political mismanagement. Italy, three times world champions, followed this with defeat in the 1994 World Cup final and a disappointing performance in 1998. In that year Italian football was struck by doping scandals which cast a shadow over Serie A, the world's premier football league, sullying the reputations of such lofty sides as Parma, Bologna and Juventus. Critics aired their suspicions that the sudden development of muscle mass in star players owed much to steroid abuse.

RIGHT: a packed-out Juventus crowd at the Stadio delle Alpi, Turin.

In the 2000 European Championships, Italy contested the final with France but missed the coveted title. In the World Cup in 2002, South Korea beat them in the quarter-final, causing many Italian tears to be shed. Though with players such as Alessandro del Piero, Francesco Totti and Paolo Maldini – Italy's most capped player – the Azzurri seemed poised for greater fame and fortune, they also failed in the 2004 European Championship. They nonetheless remain one of the world's most respected footballing nations. ❑

47
co taxi
VE 8553

PRINCES OF INDUSTRY

"The dynamism of Italian enterprise contrasts strongly with the inertia of the institutions." – Charles Richards in "The New Italians"

There is nothing incestuous about Benetton, says Luciano Benetton of his family business worth several billion pounds to his children: "We stick together and decisions are made quickly." As a "typical" family firm, albeit one on a grand scale, Benetton reflects the region's traditional strengths: the firm is heir to an ancient crafts and textiles tradition, and is imbued with a belief in design skills and functional beauty. Although industrial giants such as Benetton and Fiat are not wholly representative of the region's success, they share a family ethos and an almost Protestant work ethic. Linked to a belief in the redemptive powers of paternalism, this is sober-suited capitalism with a social conscience.

Northern Italy is the powerhouse of the Italian economy, driven by an entrepeneurial spirit and a paternalist past. Compared with its competitors, the north cannot compete on price, economies of scale or research and development. High labour costs also mean an undue concentration on the luxury end of the market. Instead, the region plays to its strengths, foremost of which is an exceptional concentration of successful family-run companies. With a dense web of small and medium-sized companies, the north is the model for Italian capitalism, producing a range of specialist goods. Flexibility, follow-up, a reliable network of suppliers and a commitment to quality and detail also characterise the northern model. (A thriving black economy also accounts for about a quarter of Italy's GDP.)

Commercial continuity

Even though northern Italy only industrialised itself in the 1950s, commerce and merchant capitalism flourished as far back as the middle ages. In a medieval version of the post-war "economic miracle", cities such as Milan, Genoa, Cremona, Pavia and Piacenza led the way, trading in textiles and crafts. In many cases a tradition of making similar things for centuries has given the region the edge in confident styling. Unlike the French and British service economies, the Italians are still fully engaged in making things, from white goods to red Ferraris, spectacles to sportswear, pullovers to Parmesan cheese. Wool and silk are transformed into fabrics and fine clothes, felt into hats, leather into shoes; metal turns into arms, helicopters, cars and carriages; wheat becomes pasta; fruits of the forest and cured meats are sold as specialised foodstuffs.

In modern times, Turin and Milan have driven the economic engine of northern industrialisation, with Olivetti, Montedison and Pirelli coming to prominence in the 1920s. The economic boom of the 1950s transformed Italy from an impoverished country into one of the wealthiest in the world. The AGIP petroleum company also redrew the industrial map of post-war Italy; Enrico Mattei exploited the discovery of

LEFT: the late Gianni Agnelli, patriarch of the Fiat dynasty. **RIGHT:** Italian stallions – a clutch of Ferraris at the company's factory in Modena.

The Fiat Family

The late Gianni Agnelli, patriarch of the Fiat dynasty, famously said that, in order to run a successful Italian company, "You need an uneven number of directors; and two is too many." Such autocratic attitudes have helped make Fiat the force that it is.

As Italy's largest industrial group, Fiat is worth over £35 billion and is the world's fifth-largest car producer, second only to Volkswagen among European manufacturers. In passing, Fiat has swallowed up Alfa Romeo, Ferrari, Lancia and Piaggio

motorbikes. The company also controls banks and insurance companies, and has concerns in the construction, aerospace and defence industries, not to mention fashion, food, publishing, the media and sport, including Juventus, Italy's most prestigious football club.

As a family affair, Fiat ensures that it is not just another car company but part of the Italian social fabric. With a management noted for its shrewdness and political connections, Fiat has never been afraid to face down governments. The Agnelli family exerted discreet pressure on Mussolini to prevent Ford from entering the domestic market in the 1920s. Fiat has since been helped by the fact that Italy is one of the most protected markets in Europe (high tariffs on imported cars remained in place until 1961). Susanna Agnelli's spell as Italian foreign minister in the 1990s coincided with lucrative new South American contracts for the firm. As for the press, Fiat owns *La Stampa*, the influential Turin daily, and the company's influence across the media guarantees acts of editorial self-censorship in the company's favour.

The Agnelli, from Piedmontese landowning stock, founded Fabbrica Italiana Automobili Torino (Fiat) in 1899, and in the process made modern Turin. In 1912 Giovanni Agnelli travelled to the United States to study Henry Ford's methods and production lines. The Agnelli formula was to fuse American-style production techniques, management and devotion to profit with old-fashioned northern Italian philanthropism and stylishness.

Fiat produced the first car in Turin in 1899, and in 1923 built brutalist Lingotto factory, praised by Le Corbusier as "one of industry's most exciting spectacles". Here the Topolino model moved up the production line from floor to floor until emerging on the rooftop test track. The company later abandoned Lingotto to move to the Mirafiori complex in the city suburbs. However, the revamped Lingotto plant remains a testament to the industrial giant, a hotel and conference centre complete with the surreal rooftop track.

Fiat rode the economic boom of the 1950s, providing most ordinary families with their first small car. The company prospered during the 1950s and by the 1970s had 15,000 workers in Turin, rising to 150,000 by 1980. Fiat was swept up in the corruption scandals of the early 1990s, with Romiti and other top executives arrested for paying bribes to win a contract on the Milan metro. At the height of the scandals, "VIP" came to mean *visti in prigione*, or spotted in prison.

By the 1990s, turnover was between 5 and 7 percent of Italian GDP, with over 2 million workers dependent on Fiat-related companies. However, aggressive marketing from foreign competitors has pushed Fiat's share of the domestic market below 50 percent. The company's strategy has been to diversify but to remain a family firm and resist mergers. Ironically, the fate of the Agnellis' company stake may depend on what Fiat's new, non-family chairman, Paolo Fresco, does for the share price. Currently the outlook is not good. Latest predictions are that the future is in fewer but better cars. ❑

LEFT: Alfa Romeo, once a competitor, is now part of the £35 billion Fiat empire.

methane gas in the Po Valley to build an enormous empire embracing petrochemicals, roads, engineering, textiles and nuclear power. Turin was transformed from being the capital of the Kingdom of Savoy to the car capital, a new industrial giant within a united Italy.

Fiat, to an outsider, is Turin. Yet according to sociologist Luciano Gallino, "They could close Fiat tomorrow and Turin would survive." The city is no longer simply Fiat, but an engineering, electronic and computing centre, as well as a showcase for contemporary architects and designers. The Piedmontese are practical people with a gift for mechanics and engineering, as well as some of the best technical institutes in Italy. But Turin is not a typical motor-manufacturing city. With superior coffee and a negligible crime rate, Turin and its hinterland are devoted to the good life: Piedmont produces vermouths, including the famous brands of Martini and Cinzano, owned by the Agnelli dynasty, as well as magnificent wines. As for fashion, Alessandria is the city of Borsalino hats, famed as the world's finest, while the Biella Valley is the loom of the Italian textile and clothing industry *(see page 83)*. Even the unemployed are largely involved in the thriving *economia sommersa*, the black economy.

CAR CITY

"Visitors think Turin is industrial, a car-manufacturing city like Detroit; but Turin is not Detroit." – local resident Giuseppe Galimi.

Milan's banking infrastructure and role as the hub of the media and service industries has made it Italy's de facto capital in commercial affairs. The city's role as fashion and design capital, and its ability to reinvent itself, has brought it prestige and people. Milan has always been a magnet for hard-working migrants from the south, such as the late Gianni Versace, and it also draws commuters from the Lombardy hinterland, notably Brescia, which acts as a New Jersey to Milan's Manhattan. Lombardy, the Milanese hinterland, is the richest and most populous region in Italy, producing a quarter of GNP and a third of all Italian exports. With an average income double that of the south, Lombardy has few rivals. Only the Veneto, Italy's fastest-growing economy, could conceivably outstrip it, given the success of small and medium-sized companies in sectors as diverse as fashion and furniture. Benetton is merely the Veneto's shop window for related family firms providing services and a pool of skilled labour.

ABOVE: Genoese architect Renzo Piano's bold transformation of the former Fiat factory in Lingotto into a cultural centre.

Family fortunes

Northern Italians are at ease with the concept of a firm as a family empire, whatever its size. Fiat may be a car company, but the major shareholder is the Agnelli family, and control passes dynastically. As for the fashion and textile industry, family groups are the norm, from Benetton to Missoni, Ferragamo to Ermenegildo Zegna.

Being an orphan or a self-made man is no impediment to founding a family firm: Milanese Leonardo del Vecchio was both, and has made Luxottica, a world leader in designer spectacles, a company to pass to his offspring.

The north has an illustrious pedigree of paternalist benefactors, mostly from sober Piedmontese stock. The classic case was Camillo Olivetti, who founded the typewriter firm that became a computer and telecommunications giant. In building workers' model villages in Ivrea, near Turin, he was motivated by a sense of community and social duty. This corner of Piedmont has a tradition of industrial patronage dating back to the 1840s.

Ermenegildo Zegna, the textile tycoon, founded Centro Zegna in Trivero, a socially enlightened project complete with hospital, school, shops and sports centre. He also created and substantially funded road-building and reafforestation projects, blasting tunnels through rocks to create a superb nature reserve. The same spirit of enlightened paternalism has always been part of the Fiat philosophy, with social housing in the industrial flatlands around Turin constructed to accommodate the influx of southern migrants in the 1950s.

Fame and shame

The princes of Italian industry include the pantheon of golden names, from Agnelli to Armani, Benetton to Ferragamo. Then there are the tarnished stars such as Silvio Berlusconi; the lost souls, such as Carlo de Benedetti; and the tragic victims of the corruption scandals, such as Raul Gardini. The Agnellis, founders of Fiat, the country's most successful company, dominate the industrial establishment's *salotto buono,* or high society *(see page 72)*.

Silvio Berlusconi still clings to his media empire, despite being found guilty of financial corruption. During his brief spell as premier in 1994, he exploited his brand name, running the country as a corporation, and promoting the association between football and politics; he even called his cabinet the Azzurri, a term normally reserved for the national squad. As prime minister he controls all six national TV channels (directly or indirectly), as well as TG4 and the national newspaper, *Il Giornale*.

Carlo de Benedetti, formerly head of Olivetti, was jailed during the corruption scandals of the 1990s. When running the computer giant, de Benedetti admitted to paying bribes, which he presented as an unavoidable evil of the murky system, with its absence of a free market. "We Italians dislike genuine competition amongst ourselves." Raul Gardini, former head of the Ferruzzi agro-industrial empire and the country's paymaster of bribes, committed suicide in 1993 rather than face the consequences.

United colours

By contrast, Luciano Benetton's star is in the ascendant. To outsiders he may simply be the prince of pullovers, but in the region of Veneto this taciturn entrepreneur is a major employer, a political force and a family figure writ large. Although the Benetton group is the world's largest buyer of wool, it is still run like the family knitwear firm it was in the 1950s.

At the age of 20, Luciano Benetton sold his accordion to finance the knitting machine his sister needed to launch the family business.

However, despite 5,000 shops in 120 countries, the high-profile clothing company is only the tip of the iceberg. It produces around 110 million garments per year and generates a total turnover of around €2 billion. The family conglomerate embraces banking, motor racing, sportswear and food, forming the 16th biggest group in Italy. Set amongst orchards and vineyards near Treviso, the headquarters are modelled around a corporate village and the family's Palladian villa. The cosy family atmosphere is maintained at mealtimes: the Benetton clan dines together, while the canteen serves workers with fresh produce from the family's kitchen gardens.

Benetton's talent was to reshape the traditional small-scale structure of the Italian textiles industry into an organisation capable of competing on world markets. Yet it is the provocative marketing campaigns that have made Benetton's name. Oliviero Toscani was the creative supremo and showman responsible for combining slick marketing with a social crusade. Luciano Benetton approved a billboard photo of a Catholic priest in full dress kissing a nun on the lips. "It was a joke to show that the habit doesn't make the priest," said Benetton. It was banned in Italy after Vatican protests, but won the Eurobest Award in Britain. (Toscani has been replaced by 27-year-old British photographer James Mollison. The crusade continues, but the cutting edge has gone.)

According to Toscani, "Companies are the new churches; it is only through them that problems can be solved." Certainly, the fervour attached to company life is matched only by the region's economic success. In 1987 Italy won a coveted place on the table of the G7, largely thanks to the performance of the northern economy. By the late-1980s export boom, "made in Italy" had become an international hallmark of style and quality.

Although the recession and corruption scandals of the 1990s rocked confidence in Italy's business empire, the region's strengths enabled the world's fifth-largest economy to bounce back. The current challenge is to combat "spaghettiphobia"; this is the fear that many foreign companies have of investing their money in Italy. The appeal of quality consumer goods made with Italian style and attention to detail should outweigh any scruples about corruption and bureaucracy. ❑

LEFT: Luciano Benetton surveys his flock.
ABOVE: a perennial design classic, Piaggio's Vespa motorscooter was introduced in 1946.

POP

RZIO

A SENSE OF STYLE

For the cognoscenti, Italy is a design showcase, excelling at ineffable chic and the art of understatement

A character in Tim Parks's *Mimi's Ghost* accuses the Italians of considering beauty "more as a consumer product than as something of spiritual value, a question of owning a particular shirt and tie, a particular style in furnishing". Certainly, the practised materialism of the contemporary northerner implies having an eye for the right Ferrari, floor tiles or Fendi fur coat rather than relishing the intricacies of restoring Leonardo's *Last Supper*.

Milan may be the design showcase, but most northern cities are citadels of good taste, with smart shops and shiny people committed to sophisticated consumerism. A northern city is also a stage set designed for preening and posturing, a place *fare bella figura*, to cut a fine figure.

Appearance is all

Although Milan remains the focus for fashion and creative innovation, a sense of style is in the Italian genes. Insolent chic and the flaunting of wealth are allied to a deep aesthetic sense, insouciant grace, and a gift for understanding the spirit of a treasured place or object. People have an innate pride in making things beautiful, *fatta ad arte*, although not necessarily built to last. Linked to a sense of beauty is the belief that visual awareness is a birthright for all.

In this baroque society, appearances are everything, with every age and caste possessing its uniform, usually a model of good taste. The Carabinieri, along with all Italian police forces, take pride in their decorative dress code: Armani naturally was commissioned to design their lightweight summer costume. The criminal fraternity are equally slavish followers of fashion: the successful *mafioso* tends to team an Armani suit with a Moschino waistcoat and Pollini shoes; even in prison, privileged *mafiosi* insist on wearing Fila and Tacchini sportswear. The uniform Italian look has been successfully marketed abroad: the England football team, for example, is just one of many squads that feel more stylish playing in Umbro, part of the Ferragamo empire.

To pass the appraising gaze of a Milanese requires a crash course in cultural one-upmanship. A certain nonchalance, cool conservatism, understated chic and the correct brand of sunglasses send the right messages. Not that style is simply a question of conspicuous consumption: a pullover slung jauntily around one's shoulders can say more than a designer label. If in doubt, the look of de luxe anonymity is the safe sartorial badge of modern Italy. To convey social status, it helps to have an entourage and to avoid public transport.

While the northerners are rarely philistine in fashion, conformity triumphs over originality. Although city slickers pride themselves on their individuality, dressing appropriately for the season and occasion is considered more important than dressing to please oneself or one's mood.

PRECEDING PAGES: a boutique in trendy Genoa.
LEFT: Carla Bruni on the catwalk.
RIGHT: Milanese chic for sale.

To be accidentally overdressed for, say, a visit to a park or pizzeria can be a cardinal sin; equally, a mere "stroll" can be taken to mean parading in all one's finery. As for beach etiquette, dress codes are often enforced on the Ligurian Riviera. A few years ago the Mayor of Diano Marina, an inconsequential Ligurian resort, caused a sensation by banning ugly women from his beaches.

The fashion map

Despite the internationalism of the fashion world, northern design houses pride themselves on their deep regional roots. Milan is the undisputed fashion capital, while Lombardy and Emilia Romagna have the greatest concentration of *alta moda* (haute couture) houses *(see page 219)*. Missoni, the colourful knitwear label, is based in Lombardy, while Emilia dominates the leather industry, from shoes to bags, belts and accessories. Patrick Cox, the Italian-based shoe designer, praises local manufacturers for excelling at choice, availability, delivery and sheer quality. The region also has La Perla, the sexy lingerie company, and Mandarin Duck, the chic luggage firm; few professional women would be without their supple Duck handbags. North of Turin, Piedmont's Biella Valley is the centre of the textile industry, and home to the exclusive Ermenegildo Zegna fabric and menswear firm. Benetton, based in the Veneto, is one of Europe's most profitable production lines *(see page 74)*.

Milan's reputation for fashion has not developed by chance but by design. An innovative industrial culture, sound mass-production techniques and a role as a melting pot set the city on a successful course. The prestigious Prada and Gucci labels are part of the Italian fashion renaissance, a reminder that the battle between Gucci kitten heels and Prada mules is as crucial to the economy as the fortunes of Fiat. The contribution of fashion to Italy's balance of payments is second only to that of tourism.

The 1980s, the archetypal designer decade, witnessed the triumph of Italian taste, a strong trend that continues despite the corruption scandals of the 1990s. These implicated a roll-call of top designers, with luminaries such as Armani, Ferre, Krizia and Versace admitting to paying bribes to the tax authorities.

The north has always been a magnet for the most talented designers, with stars such as Versace coming from the poor south to the heady heights of Milan. Most of the top Milanese-based designers are deeply traditional, serving a resolutely bourgeois clientele. Innovation might be elsewhere, but the northerners know how to treat fashion as opera while delivering collections of sleek sophistication.

Unlike the London fashion scene, Milanese designers are not besotted with youth or creativity; and unlike the Parisians, the Milanese are prepared to put profit before prestige, wearability before exclusivity. The essence of the Italian look is timeless classicism, no cultural fusion but a clear statement of identity. Since

POLITICALLY CORRECT DRESSERS

Off-duty, a young right-winger favours a Barbour jacket and Timberland boots while his left-wing counterpart chooses a checked shirt, jeans, a long pullover and a Loden coat. Gianfranco Fini, leader of the Fascist party, reassures putative followers with his conservatively cut grey suits and rimless glasses. On the other hand, Fausto Bertinotti, leader of the diehard Marxist Rifondazione Party, has given Communism a safely capitalist image with his preference for Burberry trench coats and English tweed. The dyed-in-the-(designer)-wool revolutionary is often called the best-dressed man in Parliament, the propounder of champagne Communism.

functional simplicity is increasingly dominating the catwalks, the Milanese designers look set to be a main influence in the next decade.

A basic philosophy

In a country that worships visual display, competitiveness and creativity are inevitable. Style is also an emblem of high seriousness, with great attention accorded the simple purchase of a picture or a place mat. Design is no mere styling but a philosophy involving creative alchemy and a crafts-based aesthetic, brainstorming and problem-solving skills, allied to a talent for interpreting mass culture. Fortunately, the world remains in thrall to Italian taste, inviting native talent to style American furniture, Japanese cameras, German limousines and French family cars. In styling, foreign status symbols are often products of *la linea italiana*, Italian style.

FELLOW TRAVELLERS

City buses are the preserve of the poor: nuns, students, tourists and the self-consciously left-wing.

Umberto Eco, best-selling novelist and questing culture-surfer, sees design in elevated Italian terms: "Design does not mean that I am commissioned by a more or less interesting industrial firm to bestow a form upon a more or less stupid product." Instead, it means to have carte blanche to reinvent the world through a single object. These are always seductive consumerist objects made with grace, style and the design flair imprinted in the Italian genes.

In 1946, the Italian architect Ernesto Nathan Rogers stated that design should be all-embracing, "from the spoon to the city". Italian designers have dutifully filled our world with vintage Vespa scooters and Olivetti typewriters; black Anglepoise lamps and sexy red Alfa Romeos; sleek Alessi kettles and Artemide lighting; Achille Castiglioni cutlery and rustic terracotta tiles. Among the everyday objects cast in sinuous sculptural forms are sleek chrome kitchen appliances and twirly pasta quills. In turn, Giandomenico Belotti's Spaghetti Chair was literally inspired by squiggly pasta. As a result of such diversity, the inimitable character of *la linea italiana* has a continuing impact on international taste.

The north is known for its smooth, streamlined objects, from washing machines to motorbikes. Creatively, however, designs can be functional or futuristic, elitist or democratic. Northern design has depended on the creative

LEFT: Giorgio Armani is one of the most successful fashion designers in the world.

ABOVE: Murano glass perfume flasks – or works of art?

cross-fertilisation between crafts, art and architecture. Giò Ponti, the 20th century's greatest modernist, believed that Italy had been created half by God and half by architects. He detested the superfluous and favoured practical, perfect forms such as his Superleggera, the consummate chair, a sculpted lightweight piece. Indeed, Italian chairs, desks and lamps have often been designed by major architects, which explains the rationality and rigour of the finished products.

The irrepressible spirit of Italian design taps into avant-garde movements in politics and the arts. Above all, design is still treated as

an artistic impulse, with practitioners often possessing a background in art or architecture. Gaetano Pesce's flamboyant foam chairs are gorgeous iconic objects that wittily evoke both traditions: *Sunset in New York* (1980) is a sofa with skyscrapers reflected on glass flooring. Italian products are a synthesis of both form and function.

Northern design remains a noisy, chaotic, unbureaucratic world, with "radical" studios and colourful personalities. Foremost among the design studios are the Milanese Alchymia (1976) and Memphis (1981). Founded by Ettore Sottsass, Memphis changed the domestic landscape, rejecting cosy domesticity and derivative designs, along with the notion that "form follows function": these objects were stars in their own right.

Design capital

Due to Fiat's troubles, Turin may no longer be the industrial capital, but it is fast becoming the industrial design capital of Italy. Car design originated in Turin, and Pininfarina's name is associated with everything from Ferrari to the Austin A40 and the StreetKa. Another legendary designer, Giorgetto Giugiaro, is not only associated with Maserati but also the Fiat Uno and the Volkswagen Golf. Just as he has created some of the world's best-known cars, his striking Atrium of glass, brushed steel and wood has caused a sensation in the city.

The famous Genovese architect, Renzo Piano, has done much to revitalise the Antico Porto at Genoa, and continues to weave his inventive magic at Lingotto – the former Fiat factory, which is now a multi-purpose complex – while Gae Aulenti is creating the Olympic Village and Arata Isozaki is rebuilding Turin's city stadium and redesigning the area to include a new Palasport. Massive investment and development projects are under way, including a new railway system and metro, part of which is scheduled for completion in time for the Winter Olympics in 2006. The decline in heavy industry has prompted the city to turn its attention to diversification and cutting-edge design blended with an extraordinarily rich culture. Turin's future looks bright, futuristic and ever more competitive.

Technical versatility

Italy has a talent for transforming the mundane and everyday into the beautiful. At best, northern style marries form and function, accessibility and aesthetics. Yet the design spectrum has room for divergent views, particularly regarding the importance of practicality. Anna Piaggi, fashion guru, daring stylist and an editor of Italian *Vogue*, declares: "Originality is of little use without practicality."

At the other end of the scale, Alessi kettles are design icons rather than kitchen implements. "I prefer it if they work," concedes Alberto Alessi, "but I don't think people buy an Alessi kettle to boil water." Indeed not: a fashion statement is its own *raison d'être*. ❑

LEFT: fine footwear – Italian leather shoes.

Textile Valley

Armani, Valentino and Versace represent only the most glamorous tip of the Italian fashion industry. Paris, Milan and London may be great fashion centres, noted for style and marketing, but Piedmont's unprepossessing valleys remain Europe's main textile manufacturing centre. Most European designers source their fabrics in northern Italy, from Chanel and Hugo Boss to Paul Smith, to Marks and Spencer whose spokesperson explains: "It is simply a matter of going to where the best skills are. One of our manufacturers goes back five generations; and there is a lot of investment in fabrics and new technology."

Even American designers such as Ralph Lauren and Calvin Klein recognise the superior quality and creativity of the Italian manufacturers and prefer to have their top range of clothes sewn in Italy. As for the French, although most of the *prêt-à-porter* collection is sourced in Italy, patriotic designers such as Hermès are loath to admit that they use the northern Italian Loro Piana mill.

The Biella Valley, nestling in the alpine foothills of Piedmont, is home to more than 200 textile mills which produce luxury cashmere, mohair and worsted fabrics, as well as innovative man-made textiles. The valley was once the poor cousin of France's Lyon, Britain's Bradford or Italy's Como but is now the country's foremost textile centre. Biella is without equal as a wool-spinning centre, spinning the thread ever thinner, softer and finer. The mills process superb merino wool from Australia, raw silk from China, and untreated cashmere from Inner Mongolia. (It takes the entire working life of a single goat to make one luxury cashmere sweater.)

Although Biella has been a textile centre for several centuries, it more than doubled its share of the international market between 1980 and 2000. According to the fashion editor Gianni Bertasso: "The Italians unashamedly stole ideas from the British and the French, but their real merit was to invest money in innovation in the 1970s, when the rest of the global market assumed that the textile industry had reached its peak."

With well-paid skilled workers, the Biella Valley is at the forefront of research and development. Microtene 10,000, produced in Trivero, is an impermeable polyester so light that 9,000 metres weigh under 0.4g. Not that tradition is ever forgotten. Ludovico Barbera, a local designer, says: "Working with cloth is like making a good wine: the longer it is left to mature, the better the product."

Biella has a tradition of industrial patronage dating back to the 1840s, when Ermenegildo Zegna, an enlightened benefactor, built schools, hospitals and a nature reserve. This menswear giant from the village of Trivero in the Biella Valley produces the cloth used in more than 30 per cent of the world's luxury menswear market and supplies such labels as Gucci, Romeo Gigli, Valentino and Jil Sander. As Anna Zegna, marketing manager of the sober Piedmontese Zegna family firm, points out: "The valley's production system stretches from the raw fibre to the finished product." The company's austere 19th-century mill produces 21st-century fabrics with a mixture of laser technology and old-fashioned techniques. Teasels, which still grow wild in southern Italy, are used to raise a napped surface on fine woollen cloth

RIGHT: Piedmont produces some of the finest fabrics in the world.

At the other end of the scale is Zegna's High Performance suit, described as the nearest fashion will get to a Ferrari. Made of thread finer than a human hair, the garment keeps the wearer warm in winter and pleasantly cool in summer, and ensures that an executive can step off a plane in a perfect, crease-free suit. ❑

ART AND ARCHITECTURE

Some of Europe's finest Romanesque and Renaissance art can be found in the towns and villages of northern Italy

Comparatively little survives to remind us that northern Italy was one of the most affluent and sophisticated areas of the Roman empire. A few of the largest structures have endured, however, as symbols of imperial grandeur. The arena at Verona, for example, one of the largest ever to have been built, is still in use, though gladiatorial contests and wild-beast fights have been replaced by colourful performances of operas by Verdi and Puccini.

Equally impressive is the triumphal arch of Emperor Augustus at Aosta, in the Piedmontese Alps, erected in 24 BC to commemorate the defeat of a local Celtic tribe. A bastardised version of the Roman architectural grand manner is to be found at Ravenna, where the mausoleum of Theodoric the Goth overawes us with ponderous masonry and a domed roof.

Unrivalled early Christian art

Ravenna is more famous for its outstanding examples of late Roman and Byzantine mosaic art. The 5th-century tomb of Empress Galla Placidia is adorned with panels showing Christ as a shepherd amid apostles and evangelists, all against a rich blue ground. At Aquileia the vast basilica's mosaic floor is full of Biblical imagery. This traditional Roman art form was renewed under the Byzantine emperors, and in other Ravenna churches, such as Sant' Apollinare in Classe, as well as in the cathedral baptistry, the sheer sumptuousness and scale of the mosaic design are unrivalled in early Christian art. As the church established itself as a significant force in medieval Italian society, so a wave of cathedral building began in the larger cities, intended to create both a spiritual focus for the townsfolk and a symbol of civic pride for the commune. Parma led the way in 1058, followed by Modena in 1099 and Ferrara 40 years later. The first two cathedrals are noted for their outstanding sculptural detail, by some of the earliest named artists in Europe. In the baptistry at Parma, Benedetto Antelami designed a striking sequence of scriptural panels and representations of the calendar months with their zodiacal signs and respective labours. At Modena, Wiligelmo was keener on extravagant fantasy carvings, though over the north door he placed the earliest known image of King Arthur, Guinevere and the Knights of the Round Table.

LEFT: the Byzantine Basilica San Vitale, Ravenna. **RIGHT:** staircase, Palazzo Contarini del Bovolo, Venice.

Romanesque art of the 11th and 12th centuries flourished most notably at Verona, where the church of San Zeno Maggiorc was decorated on its main doors with vigorous bronze reliefs showing Biblical episodes, and in Venice, where the basilica of San Marco most obviously reflected a synthesis between native styles and those of Venice's trading partner, and rival, Byzantium.

The basilica contains exquisite mosaic work, especially in the Capella di Sant' Isidoro, but perhaps the most hauntingly beautiful examples of this in the Venetian lagoon are to be found in the cathedral on the island of Torcello.

The high Middle Ages of the 13th and 14th centuries brought the Gothic style to northern Italy, and its features, such as pointed arches and ballflower moulding, are to be found in Bologna's great church of San Petronio, begun in 1390, in the design of heavily gilded panel paintings intended to hang above altars and shrines. Giotto, the leading Tuscan painter of the 14th century, paid a visit to Padua, and his frescoes for the Scrovegni chapel (1303–05) were a seminal influence on Italian art.

The ultimate medieval flourish was provided by Milan Cathedral, for which the Visconti family in 1386 presented an entire marble quarry. So powerful was the impact of its embellished pinnacles and arched buttresses that 16th-century architects working on its completion made no attempt to overwhelm the general Gothic effect with more than a few details of Renaissance classicism.

Unquestionably the most brilliant fusion of Gothic and Renaissance occurs in the Certosa di Pavia, one of Italy's loveliest buildings but among the least visited by foreign travellers. Begun in 1396, it is still the church of a Carthusian monastery, but contains enough to remind us that it was also a princely mausoleum for the Visconti and Sforza families. An almost incredible lavishness in its stone carving, iron work, stained glass and marquetry contrasts tellingly with the simple life led by the monks in their cells.

The Renaissance painters

While the Certosa was being built, during the 15th century, the earliest major painters of northern Italy were developing their individual styles. Andrea Mantegna (1431–1506) turned a typically Renaissance passion for the classical past into a uniquely personal, romantic distillation of Greek and Roman themes. His brother-in-law Giovanni Bellini (1435–1516)

became one of the most admired and influential artists of his time, noted above all for the radiance and delicacy of his altarpieces, featuring the Virgin and Child attended by groups of saints. Bellini worked mainly in the various towns belonging to the Venetian Republic, and Mantegna's major achievement, the frescoed Camera degli Sposi, is in Mantua, where he built himself a house.

Ferrara meanwhile was evolving its own important school of painters under the patronage of the d'Este dukes. Cosimo Tura, appointed court painter in 1458, led the way with his highly idiosyncratic style, using grotesque landscape backgrounds and angular, dramatically posed figures. His pupil Francesco Cossa (1438–81) left the exuberantly allegorical frescoes of the months of the years adorning Ferrara's Palazzo Schifanoia.

Country Style

Andrea Palladio (1508–80) was one of the most influential architects of the Veneto, where the farming estates of the aristocracy mattered as much as their palaces on the Grand Canal *(see Palladian Style, page 121)*.

The accumulated wealth of Venice made it a focus for aspiring young painters from the surrounding provinces, several of whom became Giovanni Bellini's pupils. Lyrical and profound, Giorgio da Castelfranco, known as Giorgione, born around 1478, was a classic example of youthful genius stifled by premature death, at 32. From the Alpine region of Cadore, Titian (Tiziano Vecellio) was one of the longest-lived of all Renaissance painters, an incomparable colourist whose style had made several fascinating experimental shifts by the time he died in 1576 aged 91.

The rising generation of Venetian artists who learned from Titian included two painters with markedly differing styles. Paolo Caliari (1528–88), called Veronese from his home town of Verona, expressed the sheer visual excitement of his era in grandly conceived canvases and fresco cycles, while Jacopo Robusti, called Tintoretto (1518–94), made dramatic experiments with light and composition during a highly prolific career.

Further west, in the region of Emilia, a lively and original tradition of painting had developed, beginning with the significant figure of Antonio Allegri, known as Correggio, from the town near Reggio Emilia where he was born in 1489.

Left: the ornate cupola of St Mark's, Venice.
Above: frescoes at Villa Barbaro in Maser by Paolo Veronese.

Baroque

During the latter half of the 16th century the wealthy city of Bologna became the art capital of Italy; its sensuous, poetic idiom nurtured by Annibale Carracci (born 1560) and his cousin Ludovico. The early Baroque artists who followed in their wake, notably Domenichino and Guido Reni, found fame not only in Italy but also throughout northern Europe, and collectors such as King Charles I of England and the Swedish Queen Christina paid high prices for their work. Perhaps the most successful of all the Emilian Baroque painters came from the little town of Cento near Modena. Giovanni Francesco Barbieri (1591–1666) was known as

Guercino, "little squint-eyes", a nickname which soon brought him fame as a painter of rapturous saints and erotically charged biblical scenes. The fanciful and excessive aspects of the Baroque style which typefied architecture and decorative arts in South Germany, Sicily and Spain left northern Italy relatively untouched. The rulers of the various states were generally too preoccupied with diplomacy to spend much time on adorning their palaces, though the charming little summer residence of the dukes of Modena at Sassuolo, created during the mid-17th century and recently restored, is an exception.

Court Painters

In the 18th century there was a great diaspora of Italian painters who became travelling artists among the courts of Europe, carrying their skills as far afield as Lisbon and St Petersburg.

Eighteenth-century townscapes

Towns and cities, meanwhile, were left largely unaltered, apart from Turin, which was carefully re-planned by Duke Charles Emmanuel II (died 1675) and his successors. When the duchy of Savoy became a kingdom in 1720, the newly enriched Victor Amadeus II built a splendid basilica at Superga in appreciation for his victories in the Spanish War of Succession. Its designer was Filippo Juvarra, who also created the grandiose royal summer palace of Stupinigi, a sort of Torinese Versailles. Beginning with such panache, the 18th century saw an exciting renewal of painting, especially in the towns of the Veneto, which had not forgotten their Renaissance heritage. The art of the portrait was revived in the city of Bergamo by the slightly eccentric and always memorable Vittorio Ghislandi, known as Fra Galgario (1655–1743), while in Venice itself Sebastiano Ricci (1659–1734), made a deliberate study of the grand manner of Veronese and Titian, paving the way for other travelling artists among the courts of Europe.

The most triumphant reassertion of Venetian art as a mixture of brio, fantasy and vivid colouring, with notes of worldliness and humanity enlivening even the most solemn spiritual moments, came from the brush of Giambattista Tiepolo (1696–1770). He started out as the creator of impressionistic altarpieces for Venice's churches, and had soon mastered the art of fresco painting, devising such daring effects on ceilings and walls (Vicenza's Villa Valmarana, Udine's episcopal palace) that he began to receive major commissions from elsewhere in Europe; it was during a visit to Madrid that he died. Tiepolo's artist contemporaries were much patronized by British travellers on the Grand Tour, none more so than Antonio Canal, "Canaletto" (1697–1768), whose views of Venice furnished classic images of the city in its closing decades as an independent capital. Canaletto had started his career as apprentice to his father, who was a theatrical scene painter.

Trend-setting Milan

Milan, under Napoleonic rule 1800–15, led the way as a centre of new fashions and fresh ideas, and it was here that Italy's greatest 19th-century painter, Francesco Hayez (1791–1882), chose to work after an apprenticeship in Venice. Hayez aspired to fame as the creator of exalted historical themes based on meticulous studies of costume and decor, but his true gift lay in portrait painting, and his images of his contemporaries, Milanese aristocrats, poets, musicians or fellow artists, are some of the most intense from the turbulent Risorgimento age.

Venice went on inspiring painters, however, and the last and best among many who sought to revive Canaletto's tradition of the *veduta* or cityscape was Ippolito Caffi (1806–66), destined to die in a naval battle against the Austrians. Venetian art schools had been heavily influenced, meanwhile, by the lonely genius of Antonio Canova (1757–1822), the great sculptor of his age. Though he spent much of his working life in Rome, Canova was determined to return to his birthplace at Possagno, near Asolo, north of Venice, where he built himself an austerely lovely *tempietto* (little temple) as a mausoleum.

Sculpture in northern Italy found another remarkable practitioner at the close of the 19th century. Medardo Rosso, working in Paris as well as Milan and Turin, devised forms which both evoked realistic situations from urban life and sought to reproduce, through bronze, clay or wax, the fluidity of living movement.

His world, that of the newly industrialised northern cities, was what in 1908 inspired the Futurists, led by the poet Marinetti and artists such as Umberto Boccioni and Giacomo Balla, to begin their deliberately eccentric revolution against the classic traditions of Italian art. Their strident gospel of modernism, obsessed with speed, power and aggression, contributed to a national state of mind which, only a decade later, would accept the ideology of Mussolini and his Fascist cohorts. ❑

LEFT: the Aquilino chapel, San Lorenzo, Milan.
ABOVE: a sculpture by Futurist Umberto Boccioni.
RIGHT: de Chirico's *Turin Melancholy* (1915).

Venetian Artists

The most impressive and influential painters of northern Italy found patronage from the wealthy Republic

The Venetian school embodies a poetic, painterly sensibility at odds with the rational, monumental and sculptural Florentine style. The lagoon artists were painters of colour, light, texture and space, reflecting the ambiguity of their shimmering, watery world. Paradoxically, the inclusiveness of the Venetian vision and the varied sources of patronage meant that Venetian art was less formulaic than other schools, with the greatest painters free to form their own inimitable personal styles.

With his sweet sensibility and expressiveness, Bellini freed Venetian painting from Byzantine stiffness. Carpaccio captured the texture of everyday Venetian life, with his pink-hued palaces, curious chimneys and canal-side crowds. Tintoretto brought religious fervour, while Titian, the complete Renaissance man, elevated Venetian art to universal grandeur with his ineffable technique and monumentality. Tiepolo, the Rococo "poet of light" who brought the great era to a dramatic close, delighted in a palette of pastel tones, matched by ethereal scenes of Olympian grandeur.

Giovanni Bellini (*circa* 1430–1516) is often considered the founder of the Venetian school and one of the best-loved Venetian painters. He worked in Padua, Ferrara and Verona but has left many masterpieces in his home city. A number are known as *sacre conversazioni* ("holy conversations") because of the rapt stillness of mood. These are not all limpid, idealised Madonnas: in his poignant *Pietà* in the Accademia, the suffering Virgin cradles her son in her arms, her careworn face a testament to Bellini's expressive powers; the city of Vicenza looms in the background, showing the painter's love of landscape and his skill at opening out a canvas. The church of the Frari is home to another Bellini masterpiece: the *Madonna and Saints* is a subtle and luminous triptych of the Virgin flanked by saints and cherubic angels, one trilling on a flute, the other strumming a mandolin. The musical motif recurs in Bellini's work, reinforcing the notion of music as a symbol of order and harmony. The charming church of San Zaccaria displays a superb Bellini altarpiece noted for its beguiling interplay of colour and light in a rich blend of reds, golds and blues. This soft and lyrical work embodies the inner harmony implicit in the finest works of Quattrocento and High Renaissance art. Although overshadowed by Bellini, Vittorio Carpaccio (*circa* 1465–1523/6) was the most Venetian of artists, with his vivid pictorial cycles and miniaturist precision.

Titian (*circa* 1487–1576) was the supreme artist. The church of the Frari contains two of his masterpieces, notably *The Assumption* (1516–18), a work whose revolutionary nature caused it to be rejected by the Friars; they relented, and the work made Titian's international reputation. Unlike his rivals, Titian could make his illusionistic altarpiece command attention from afar. Vibrant colours helped, with the counterpoint of a golden sky set against the glowing red of the Virgin's robes. Titian aligned the work exactly with the opening of the rood screen so that one's eye is drawn through the Gothic choir towards this magnificent altarpiece. In the same church, the Pesaro altarpiece depicts a theatrically illuminated yet off-centre Madonna in the presence of Saint Peter and of Titian's patrons, the Pesaro family. For the first time the portrait of a patron and his family was made part of a devotional painting, thus breaking the strict division between the sacred and secular worlds.

Tintoretto (1518–94) restricted his world to Venice. Despite being made official painter to the Doge in 1574, Tintoretto lived a precarious existence, often painting for the costs of the materials alone; he died penniless. However, his humble background gave him sympathy for the lives of the poor, a theme which, combined with religious fervour, distinguishes him from many contemporaries. The confraternity of the Scuola Grande di San Rocco represents Tintoretto's crowning glory. Magnificent Mannerist paintings adorn every surface; the works are larger than life, full of chiaroscuro effects and floating, plunging figures striking dramatic poses. Tintoretto's parish church was Madonna dell'Orto, the most assured Gothic church in Venice. This is very much a shrine to the artist, who is buried there. The church contains a clutch of early works, with the *Presentation of the Virgin* showing Tintoretto's familiar theatricality and grandiosity.

Tiepolo (1696–1770) was the last great Venetian painter, graced with a sublime style and virtuosity reminiscent of the Old Masters. Tiepolo's credo was that "the mind of the painter should always aspire to the sublime, the heroic and perfection". According to art critic Adriano Mariuz, in practice this meant "a sophisticated clientele who could appreciate the wit and sensuality of Tiepolo's interpretations of mythology". However, the greatest of Rococo painters also produced a riot of picturesque detail and enough charm to seduce the most casual observer. In Ca' Rezzonico, Tiepolo proves himself a master of scenic illusion, creating mirages of light and air and orchestrating figures in large composition

Apart from the *trompe l'oeil* paintings in Ca' Rezzonico, Tiepolo's work can be admired in numerous Venetian churches. La Pietà, the waterfront church, is a feast for the senses, and Tiepolo's celebrated frescoes are best seen during a concert of Baroque music. ❑

LEFT: detail from the Bellini altarpiece (1505) in San Zaccaria, Venice.
ABOVE: the Rococo grandeur of Giambattista Tiepolo (1696–1770).

THE MUSICAL TRADITION

Italy has given the world opera, the musical scale, the piano, the accordion and fabulous Stradivarius violins

Without the Italian sensibility, the world of music would be deaf to the seductive strains of Vivaldi and the nobility and intensity of Verdi. Italy is rightly known as the home of music, with Milan's image inextricably bound up with La Scala. When opera houses burn down, as they still tend to do, people cry in public and the country grieves.

Fortunately, northern Italy still has more major opera houses than it deserves; opera is on home ground and rejoices in its natural mode of expression. One of the charms of such an instinctive approach is the superb staging, the art of the grand gesture, untempered by northern European reserve. Productions can be sweeping, sensual and lush, appealing to the heart, not the head. Yet, at its purest, the performers' skill at stirring elemental passions is matched by the cool perfectionism of the staging. In inimitable Italian style, the irreverence of opera-goers only serves to intensify the experience.

Vibrant heritage

However, northern Italy's contribution to Western music goes beyond plush Rococo interiors and impassioned outpourings of Verdi. Musical history has been shaped by a clutch of northern cities, from Milan and Venice to Mantua, Parma, Verona and Cremona, each with a separate, flourishing tradition.

As for composers, Monteverdi, Verdi, Vivaldi and Donizetti are northern names to conjure with. Dedicated opera-lovers are rewarded with Verdi's dramatic power and Donizetti's light touch and gift for melody. Musical form and development have a distinctive northern stamp; Donizetti dedicated himself to the art of *bel canto*, the traditional emphasis on fine tone and ornamentation. The language of music remains resolutely Italian.

Northern Italian music also embraces memorable madrigals, solemn melodies and the purest Gregorian chant. The first violin sonatas of note were written by a Lombard, Biagio Marini of Brescia, in 1629: works of Baroque passion, energy and drama. Today the lush strings of the Venetian composer Albinoni perfectly chime with the public's taste for haunting

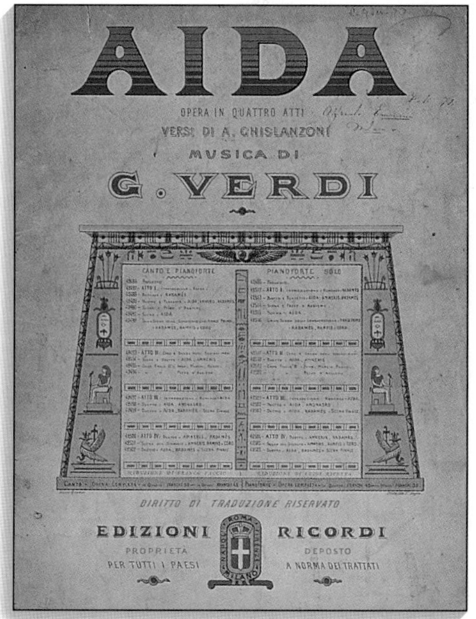

Baroque music. As for musical instruments, Cremona has been the capital of violin-making since the 16th century *(see page 95)*. Indeed, it is not too fanciful to see the curves of violins echoed in the spiral cornices of city palaces. Nor is it a coincidence that northern Italy is at the forefront of the trend towards a return to playing on authentic period instruments.

Venetian musicianship

"Venice was once the cradle of classical music, the birthplace of opera, the crucible of the concerto and the nerve-centre of a neo-classical revival." As critic Norman Lebrecht suggests, the city built the world's first opera house,

LEFT: the genius of late Baroque music, Antonio Vivaldi (1678–1741).

RIGHT: Verdi is one of Italy's best-loved composers.

created the first publicly funded system of music education and inspired composers as great as Bach, Handel, Wagner and Britten. Although it took a Tuscan monk, Guido d'Arezzo, to devise the musical scale, a Venetian printer, Ottavino Petrucci, invented a method of printing music with moveable type. Other Venetian keynotes are struck by Albinoni (1671–1750), whose works are characterised by charm and urbanity, and by Antonio Vivaldi (1678–1741), who acted as a model for such composers as J.S. Bach. The popularity of *The Four Seasons* can blind one to Vivaldi's genius as a leading exponent of late Baroque music.

Operatic origins

Opera was Italy's crowning musical achievement, a rousing art form which may have emerged in 14th-century Florence but was perfected by Claudio Monteverdi (1567–1643) in Mantua and Venice. On becoming master of music at St Mark's in 1613, the Lombard composer spent two decades composing sacred services and sumptuous polyphonic music. The opening of San Cassiano in 1637, the first public opera house, provided Monteverdi with the impetus to restage his earlier works. He took the madrigal beyond its traditional form, forging the development of the dramatic madrigal

The northern lakes have inspired some of the grandest Italian opera. In 1813, Rossini composed *Tancredi* in Cernobbio, on the shores of Lake Como, an example followed in 1831 by Bellini, with the composition of *Norma*. Although Bellini was born in Sicily, he moved north, and his ravishing melodies helped make him the dominant composer in Milan. Equally entranced by Lake Como's subtle light, Verdi chose Cadenabbia to compose *La Traviata* in 1853. Further north, in the mountainous reaches of Alto Adige, Dobbiaco, near Bolzano, provided the peace sought by Gustav Mahler (1860–1911). The composer's quaint cottage has become an appealing restaurant.

that paved the way for Baroque opera. Until then opera had been confined to noble wedding celebrations and princely courts. In one sense, Monteverdi and Venice represent the true birth of opera; henceforth, opera was no longer a ducal distraction, the plaything of a courtly society, but a dynamic new art form favoured by a demotic public.

The emergence of opera was helped by the fashion for declamation, with strong emotions expressed as sighs and sobs rather than description. In Monteverdi's opera *Orfeo* the title role

ABOVE: Venice's La Fenice, before the fire of 1996.
RIGHT: an 1819 view of La Scala, Milan.

was taken by a *castrato*, a male soprano or contralto with an unbroken voice. *Castrati* were in great demand in the 17th and 18th centuries, because of their flexible and voluptuous voices.

Given that Rossini and Puccini were born just outside northern Italy, Monteverdi, Donizetti and Verdi represent the region's greatest operatic talents. Gaetano Donizetti (1797–1848) was born in Bergamo into a poor family, and trained in Bologna before becoming enamoured of Rossini and the Neapolitan style. His reputation, based on his light touch and feeling for melody and sentiment, was sealed by *Lucrezia Borgia* (1833), first performed at La Scala, and *Lucia di Lammermoor* (1835), his tragic masterpiece.

SEX APPEAL

Farinelli (1705–82) was the most famous *castrato*. His singing and stage presence caused women to faint from excitement.

Giuseppe Verdi (1813–1901) was born in humble circumstances in Busseto, a village near Parma, and trained as a local church organist. Although he was denied entry to the prestigious Milan Conservatory, Verdi moved to Milan, where his first and last operas were premiered, and enjoyed a stormy relationship with La Scala.

CREMONA: HOME OF STRADIVARIUS VIOLINS

Cremona is an exceptionally musical town. It is famous for the composition of medieval sacred music, and it was here that the composer Claudio Monteverdi) was born in 1567 (*see Lombardy, page 229*).

Cremona is also the home of the world's greatest cellos and violins: Antonio Stradivari (1643–1737) created instruments of incomparable workmanship, carved out of maple and spruce, with segments of pear, poplar and willow wood, which today rank among the highest-priced instruments in the world. The Stradivarius is still a byword for sublime sound and beauty of tone, an instrument so sensitive that it is considered to have a soul.

The city still basks in its musical reputation, with an internationally acclaimed school of violin-making and the Monteverdi Festival, staged in the city's neoclassical Teatro Concordia-Ponchielli, to which musical pilgrims come from all over the world.

Given their tangible sense of life, the Stradivarius violins on display in the Cremona civic museum are regularly taken out of their cases and played. Maxim Vengerov, regarded by many as the finest contemporary violin virtuoso, plays a Stradivarius (dating from 1723), which enables him to achieve an alchemy between maestro and instrument.

Nabucco and subsequent operas were applauded as patriotic works and political gestures: the response of an oppressed people symbolised the Italians' suffering under Austrian domination. During the Risorgimento, walls were daubed with the acronym V(ittorio) E (manuele) R(e) D'I(talia), a reference to the first king of Italy, eventually crowned in 1861. However, Verdi's gifts marked him out as a genius rather than a mere patriot; he possessed intense dramatic power and a dark forcefulness, as well as a delight in humanity, subtle characterisation, and an ability to express contrasting emotions. By the time Verdi died in Milan, in the antiquated and atmospheric Grand Hotel, he was regarded as Italy's best-loved composer, deserving of his enduring cult following.

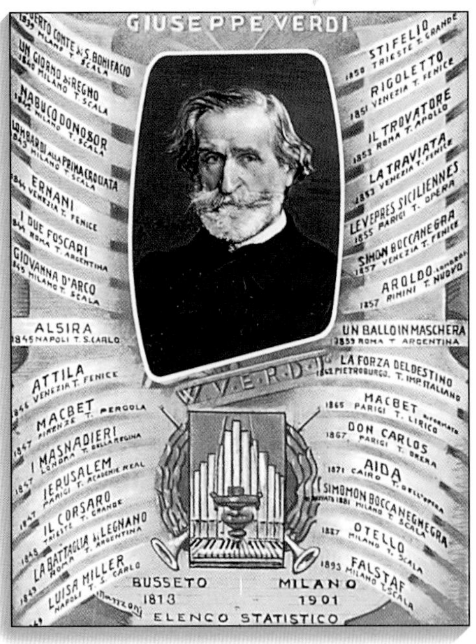

Temples to tradition

"An opera house is like a sponge that absorbs the best of man's creativity," claims the film director Franco Zeffirelli, with classic Italian grandiloquence. Beyond the gilt and stucco interiors, the glittering opera houses *(teatri lirici)* are mostly neoclassical theatres rebuilt after numerous fires. Historically, the rivalry of noble courts gave birth to countless private opera houses, which gradually opened their doors to the public, the first in Venice in 1637. It is no coincidence that the greatest concentration of historic opera houses is found in Lombardy and Emilia, places linked to the great courts at Cremona, Parma and Mantua. The fashion spread, and by the 18th century there were 20 *teatri lirici* in Venice alone.

Today opera houses range from the proficient and praiseworthy to the lacklustre. Milan's La Scala *(see below)* is the premier opera house, even though all Italy's opera houses are prestigious symbols of regional pride. While there are major opera houses in Naples, Florence and Rome, La Fenice (the Phoenix) in Venice enjoys greater prestige, despite its tragic history. Venice's "Phoenix" has lived to rue its name after fires in 1836 and 1996. Diva Joan Sutherland mourned the loss of "the most beautiful opera house in the world"; singing in La Fenice, she said, felt like singing inside a diamond. La Fenice burnt down a month before Woody Allen was due to play there. On hearing the news, the director's wry comment was: "It

La Scala

La Scala opera house in Milan, a symphony of red, cream and gold designed by Giuseppe Piermarini, opened in 1778 with a performance of an opera by Antonio Salieri, Mozart's great rival. All the great Italian composers have written for La Scala, in particular Rossini, Donizetti, Bellini, Puccini and Verdi. The opera house underwent a period of glory with performances of Verdi's patriotic works, and it experienced its early 20th-century heyday under Toscanini's direction.

Arturo Toscanini (1867–1957) was born in Parma but emigrated to the United States because of his opposition to Fascism. As musical director of La Scala, in the 1920s, he had been hugely influential in shaping the repertoire and maintaining the prestige of the opera house. At the turn of the century he had also been responsible for bringing Wagner into the operatic repertoire. As a lover of Italian opera, the magnetic but autocratic Toscanini, with a gift for interpreting composers' intentions, won the admiration of Verdi and Puccini. In 1926 he conducted the premiere of *Turandot*, Puccini's last opera, to great acclaim. Despite Mussolini's attempts to promote Rome Opera over La Scala, the Milanese never lost their musical supremacy. After La Scala was damaged by bombing in 1943, Toscanini personally contributed to its rebuilding.

must be a music lover; they heard I was coming." The red-and-gold Rococo confection is being rebuilt as before, but until its completion chic opera-goers are going to the new Teatro degli *Arcimboldi*. On the next rung down in terms of size, though not necessarily scope, are Parma, Genoa, Bergamo, Modena, Bologna and Turin. Parma's Teatro Farnese is a ravishing early 17th-century theatre modelled on Palladio's Teatro Olimpico in Vicenza. The all-wooden theatre was built by the Farnese as an act of one-upmanship, to out-do the Milanese; it could seat 3,000 and was the largest theatre of its day. Parma's plush Teatro Regio was built at the behest of Empress Marie-Louise in 1828, and is considered the best place to hear a performance of anything by Verdi.

GLITTERING GLORY

"Singing in La Fenice is like singing inside a diamond."
– Dame Joan Sutherland

Bologna's Teatro Comunale, which opened in 1763, also has Verdi associations, having staged the premiere of *Don Carlos* in 1867. Given the demands of the Bolognese aristocracy, the auditorium was designed to double as a ballroom, with the raising of the floor to the same level as the stage. Brescia's Teatro Grande, dating from the early 18th century, has also staged landmark performances of works by Verdi, Puccini and Rossini.

Mantua's musical tradition is as honourable as the enlightened Gonzaga court that fostered it: Monteverdi's *Orfeo* was first staged in 1607 in the Gonzagas' ducal apartments. Later, the city's Teatro Scientifico was finished in time to provide a stage for three of Mozart's newly composed symphonies in 1770.

As for Verona, the city's Teatro Filarmonico so impressed Mozart that he became musical director of the orchestra in 1771. Otherwise the city is best known for its operas in the open-air Arena *(see next page)*.

LEFT: a postcard celebrating Giuseppe Verdi (1813–1901) and his opera premieres.
ABOVE: the legendary diva, Maria Callas.

Curtains for opera?

In recent years, opera houses have been buffeted by strikes, budgetary cuts and even arson attacks. In response to excessive bureaucracy and a funding crisis, the Italian government in 1997 announced the privatisation of all opera houses, starting with La Scala. As a result the opera houses became *enti*, state-run enterprises managed as self-financing institutions, although paradoxically still eligible for up to 40 percent

Opera in the Open Air

Italian opera and classical music are not restricted to Milan's La Scala. Northern Italy as a whole has some of the best music festivals in Europe, from the Rossini Festival performed in Pesaro to the Verona Opera Festival held in the Roman Arena, a glorious summer junket for Europe's opera-going elite. (The romantic Puccini Festival at the composer's lakeside home is held in Tuscany's Torre del Lago.)

Renowned international singers rise to the challenge of open-air opera: at times the unaccompanied voices struggle to make an impact, given the background babble – not to mention distant car horns and police sirens – that typifies any such Italian event. In the end, the sense of occasion, the spectacle and the elemental passions ensure that the occasion is a triumph. "Every time I step onto the stage and glance towards the stalls and tiers, my heart is squeezed in a vice-like grip. It's the immense embrace of a thousand lighted candles, of a thousand people that await my voice." Such was Pavarotti's emotional response to the impact of performing Verdi's *Requiem* in Verona.

The Arena di Verona Festival was devised in 1913 as a way of celebrating the centenary of Verdi's birth, and has continued ever since, save for interruptions during wartime. Travel companies often offer weekend breaks with tickets to the festival included. The festival's historic setting, in the ancient Roman Arena, and the latter's superb acoustics have drawn singers as great as Callas, Caballé and Domingo.

If filled to capacity, the Arena holds an audience of more than 16,000 people, as many as the combined capacity of La Scala, Covent Garden, Bayreuth and the Metropolitan Opera. Verona's favourite opera is Verdi's *Aida*, which makes the best use of the vast stage space. The spectacle of the triumphal march is something to behold, with over 400 spear-carriers, captives, soldiers, slaves, trumpeters, dancers and singers.

Any opera in Verona is a charming exercise in Italian class distinctions: the bars in the Arena serve only champagne and cola, with nothing in between. The *gradinata*, the cheap seats in the unnumbered stands, are populated by serious opera-loving locals who unwrap pungent picnics of salami and olives. As dusk falls in the steep tiers of the Arena, a brief hush descends and the audience lights candles in order to read the libretto. Just as the Arena is engulfed by tiny flickering flames, the privileged patrons commanding the best *poltrona* and *poltronissima* seats in front of the stage take their places, often accompanied by cat-calls from less fortunate members of the audience.

state funding. La Scala has traditionally been one of the most heavily subsidised opera houses in Europe. Compared with Covent Garden, La Scala stages fewer performances but receives double the subsidy. The cost of one Milanese production can equal an entire season's budget at a rival opera house. Italy's premier opera house has ostensibly been privatised, but with a sweetener of $57 million from the state; cultural supremos were fearful that their flagship would otherwise fall off its pedestal.

La Scala's justification for such largesse is that, at its best, it still stages lavish productions on an unparalleled scale. However, bol-

stered by sponsorship from banks and car companies, La Scala's future looks increasingly secure. The new Milanese foundation is looking forward to making further lucrative merchandising deals, raiding its prestigious musical museum to produce miniature busts of Verdi for the Japanese market.

Musical chairs

Although Italy has produced some fine young mezzos and sopranos, it has taken to importing tenors from the United States and other big voices from Eastern Europe. Italy suffers from a shortage of singers with big voices, who can sing loudly over heavy 19th-century orchestration.

This is particularly true of the Verdi masterpieces, such as *Il Trovatore*, which makes casting problematic. According to critic Rupert Christiansen, the score requires "a strong yet exquisitely pure soprano of the type that the Italians label *spinto*; a rich and forceful *mezzo*; a tenor who can light fires; and a baritone who can be both villain and charmer". The charge is that most singers lack the stamina, physique and training to produce the amplitude, richness and fullness of sound required of a live performance. Given the dearth of suitable home-grown talent, critics claim that the tradition of Italian dramatic sopranos and baritones is defunct.

BLIND DATE

Andrea Bocelli is a great classical tenor whose blindness prevented him from following a conventional career. He was spotted singing in a piano bar by the rock star Zucchero, introduced to Pavarotti, and a musical marriage was born.

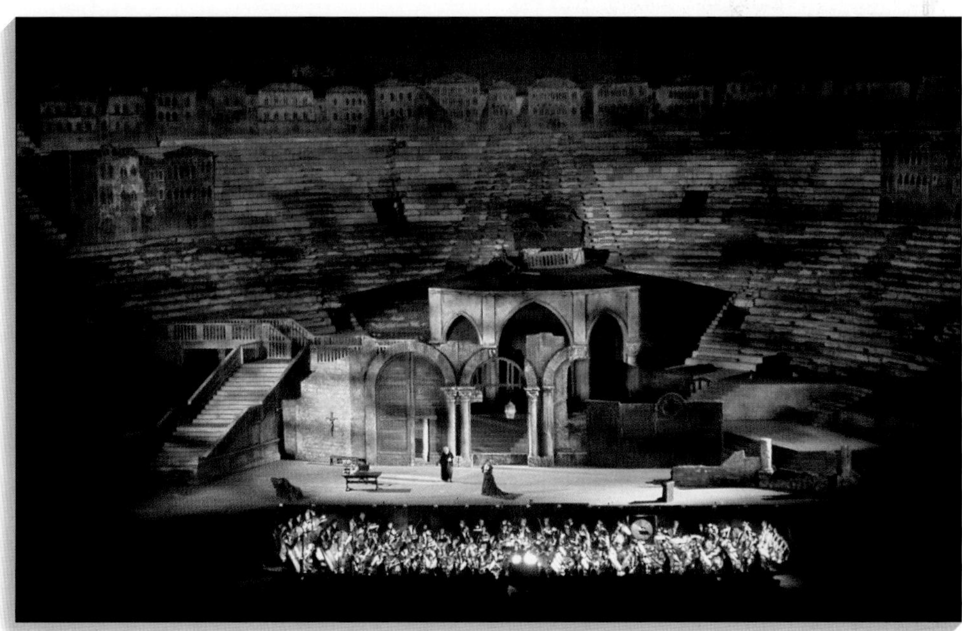

Certainly, the gradual demise of the ensemble system means that it is no longer realistic to cast the great Verdi operas with Italian-speaking singers of the first rank. Apart from Pavarotti, one notable exception is Giuseppe Giacomini from Padua, a singer sought after because of the Verdian timbre of his voice. Although Italian divas have graced the stages of the great *teatri lirici*, only Cecilia Bartoli stands out in the present-day. Even so, she is acclaimed for her Mozart roles rather than her interpretations of home-grown classics.

Yet any vocal disappointments are compensated for by the quality of conducting, an Italian forte since Toscanini. His first public performance was Verdi's *Aida*, which he conducted from memory after he had been asked to step in at short notice.

Among today's *maestri*, Riccardo Muti is considered the world's most charismatic conductor of Verdi. Until his resignation in April 2005 *(see page 209)*, he conducted at Milan's La Scala and he runs the Ravenna Music Festival, close to his home. Muti's predecessor, Claudio Abbado, directs productions around the world, as well as in Ferrara. Conductors Daniele Gatti, Riccardo Chailly and Giuseppe Sinopoli have also found fame abroad, notably at Amsterdam's Concertgebouw, London's Covent Garden and the Dresden Opera House. But to the outside world, Italy is forever linked with tenors, from Caruso and Gigli to Pavarotti and the lyrical romantic Andrea Bocelli. ❑

LEFT: Alto Adige has its own distinct musical heritage.
ABOVE: Verona's Roman arena provides a dramatic stage for many Italian operas.

SALUMERIA
CARNI SUINE I. Q.ta - tel. 27801
KING
CAMP
SPECIALITA' SICILIANA
Bottarga
DI TONNO
E DI MUGGINE
POMIDORO
GARANTITI
ESSICATI AL SOLE
MOSTARDA
Sperlari

CAMPARI

G.ALBERTIN
OLIO D'OLIVA E DI SEMI
Bottarga
DI TONNO
E DI MUGGINE

CAMPARI

RUSTIC AND CLASSIC CUISINE

"The cooking of Italy is really the cooking of its regions, regions that until 1861 were separate, independent and usually hostile states." – Marcella Hazan

Culinarily speaking, Italy is more of a salad bowl than a melting pot. Northern tastebuds are tickled by distinctive regional styles and dishes as diverse as the people themselves. Slav buffets, Balkan flavours and Hungarian goulash await visitors to Trieste. In Venice, filling Austrian pastries vie with oriental spices. In Turin, culinary schizophrenia shows itself in peasant-style dishes covered with sophisticated French sauces. Emilia is the kingdom of pasta, while the Veneto and Piedmont favour risotto, leaving Lombardy torn between rice and polenta. With its sauerkraut and dumplings, the Alpine Trentino-Alto Adige embodies the culinary clash between Italian and Austrian traditions. By contrast, seafaring Liguria relishes a summery, vegetable-based cuisine but makes less use of fish than one would expect of a coastal region.

Minestrone of tastes

"We have made Italy, now we must make the Italians," declared Massimo d'Azeglio, the Piedmontese statesman. But forging a common cuisine out of pasta and polenta has proved elusive. A national cuisine was first codified by Pellegrino Artusi in his influential *La Scienza in Cucina* (1891), still the most authoritative Italian cookery book. Artusi's aim was to "develop a common cuisine so that Italians could understand one another at table". However, the book promotes certain strands of refined northern cuisine at the expense of regionalism and rustic fare, elevating a pseudo-French concept of refinement over Italian regional authenticity. As British food critic Jonathan Meades points out: "There is only so much refinement Italian cooking can take before it becomes denatured." Not that culinary refinement is without an ancient lineage. The tradition of noble courts from late medieval and Renaissance times has enriched Italian regional cuisine.

PRECEDING PAGES: culinary adventures await you.
LEFT: the ancient art of Parmesan-making.
RIGHT: cutting the cheese.

Apart from pasta and pizza, little in Italy is national except such styles as *alla parmigiana*, cooking with cheese, bequeathed by Parma to the rest of the country. Yet the issue is not so much the struggle between national and regional styles, nor even between sublime cuisine and wholesome peasant fare. Instead, most

forward-thinking chefs are concerned with reinterpreting regional tradition: adapting the best of the past to contemporary trends and more health-conscious tastes.

Geography on a plate

At the European level the Italians make pleas for protectionism, and their olive oil, *panettone* cake, Parma ham and Parmesan cheese are just a few of the products that have privileged status. Most Italians are against the globalisation of packaged food, but few realise that certain protected products are less local than they seem. Bresaola, dried salted beef, may be the pride of the Alpine Valtellina area in Lombardy, but most of the beef is Argentinian; only the curing process is local. Even so, most northern Italians tend to eat more local food than their counterparts abroad. A typical meal might include pasta from Bologna; salad from Cremona; pizza yeast from Pavia; eggs from Vicenza; veal and milk from Lombardy; basil from Imperia in Liguria; flour from the Po Valley; Parmesan from Parma; sugar and peaches from Ferrara.

The best regional cuisine is both robust and refined: Emilia Romagna is the flagship of Italian gastronomy. Bologna, the capital, typifies the commitment and conviviality the world has come to associate with the finest Italian cooking. Pellegrino Artusi instructed his readers to "make a deep bow to Bolognese cooking, it deserves it". Bologna, a gastronomic paradise since the Middle Ages, remains Italy's undisputed culinary capital. The city is even known as "Bologna *la grassa*" – Bologna the fat. But "Bologna the rich" would be more appropriate given the city's feel for the good life, *il culto del benessere*. In this hearty, elaborate cuisine, the emphasis is on velvety sauces, pasta, meat, charcuterie and cheese. Foodies are enamoured of this opulent style, rich in pork fat, butter and oil, and equally high in cholesterol levels. *Fritto misto* is a case in point, delicious but dangerous: an array of breaded or deep-fried morsels, from sweetbreads to slivers of ham, chicken to courgettes, and brains to bananas, all bound in a béchamel sauce.

Not for the Squeamish

Northern cuisine is not for the squeamish. All parts of a pig go into the pot: ears, liver, bladder and guts. In Bergamo pitiful songbirds' beaks peer out of beds of *polenta*. Flavoured lard is enjoyed in Valle d'Aosta, as is sausage from castrated sheep in Valle Camonica in Lombardy. Horse is eaten in Emilia and Vicenza, while stewed donkey is devoured in Mantua, as is *torta di sangue*, a baked blood delicacy. (For this, the chicken's throat is slit, and the blood spills into a bowl of beaten egg yolks and sugar.) Also in gory Lombardy, *tinca* is a local fish either boiled alive or forced to swallow a tablespoon of white wine vinegar to cleanse its insides before cooking.

As for meat, Parma ham *(prosciutto di parma)* remains the Italian *antipasto* (first course) of choice, but the north abounds in distinctive cured meats. *Salama da sugo* from Ferrara is a succulent sausage made from minced pork, liver and tongue. Legend has it that the dish was created by Lucrezia Borgia to revive battle-weary troops; indeed, it is still served to soldiers home on leave. Neighbouring Modena produces ravioli stuffed with minced meats or *bollito misto*, mixed boiled meats, including beef, veal, tongue and pig's trotters. A *mortadella* from Bologna can have the circumference of a dinner plate and be studded with black peppercorns, with green pistachios protruding through the pale pink flesh. *Brodo*, a velvety meat broth, is matched by *stracotto*, a slowly simmered stew flavoured with cinnamon and nutmeg.

Ferrara is known for certain Jewish dishes such as smoked goose and marzipan desserts. Other regional sweets in Emilia Romagna include fritters, chestnut cakes, *tortelli* stuffed with chocolate, and myriad cholesterol-laden concoctions made with candied peel or brandy-soaked biscuits.

Venice and the Veneto

Like the winds across the lagoon, Venetian cuisine blows hot and cold. Much is filling, cold-weather, comfort food: thick soup and creamy risotto suitable for sustaining marooned travellers as the mists close in. Yet the cuisine can also be sophisticated and light, from fish risotto, sprinkled with shrimps, to carpaccio, wafer-thin raw beef dressed with olive oil, often served with rocket and Parmesan. For seafood-lovers, the cuisine can be memorable, with soft-shelled crabs from Murano, plump red mullet, pasta heaped with lobster or black and pungent with cuttlefish ink *(seppie alla veneziana).* Trademark dishes include cuttlefish risotto and *baccalà* – dried salt cod, prepared with milk and herbs or Parmesan cheese and parsley.

SLOW BUT SURE

The role of Italy's esteemed Slow Food Movement is "to be a bastion against the sadness of the hamburger and the pretensions of haute cuisine".

As the hub of a cosmopolitan trading empire, Venice was bristling with foreign communities, each with its own culinary tradition. As a bazaar city, Venice raided the recipe books of the Arabs, Armenians, Greeks, Jews and Turks. Trading posts in the Levant gave the city access to *spezie* (spices), the secret of subtle cookery. Pimento, tumeric, ginger, cinnamon, cumin, cloves, nutmeg, saffron and vanilla show the oriental influences; pine nuts, raisins, almonds and pistachios play their part. Rice was introduced from Spain by the Arabs and remains the most versatile aspect of local cuisine. *Risi e bisi* (rice and peas) is a thick soup flavoured with ham, celery and onion. A Middle Eastern-inspired dish is *sarde in saär*, tart sardines marinated in the standard Venetian sauce, *saor*. Reflecting later conquests, the exoticism of Middle Eastern cuisine is tempered by French cuisine and stodgy Austrian fare.

If Venice, "the marketplace of the eastern and western lands", spells cosmopolitan cuisine, the Veneto remains more provincial, more rooted in the land. Treviso is the main supplier of radicchio (red endive) which, raw, grilled or fried, finds its way into risotto, pasta and salads.

As well as being a rice-growing region, the Veneto is Italy's chief area for poultry production, from chicken and goose to guinea fowl and duck. Offal, spicy black pudding, horsemeat and kid *(capretto)* are also local delicacies, matched by wholemeal spaghetti *(bigoli)*, subtle cheeses and honey. Pastries, cakes and desserts, flavoured with cinnamon and nutmeg, remain a Venetian forte. The Venetians introduced cane sugar to Europe and have retained their sweet tooth, as has the Veneto at large. The chic resort of Cortina d'Ampezzo tempts après-skiers with deep-fried fritters, while Vicenza responds with *fugazza vicentina*,

LEFT: making fresh pasta verde.
ABOVE: rustic Milanese bread.

a popular Easter cake, and Verona brings Christmas cheer with *Pandoro di Verona*, a light, fluffy, mass-produced sponge cake.

The northeast

Austro-Hungarian and Balkan influences prevail in the least Italian of regions. In this rustic yet austere corner of the Balkans, Yugoslav-style raw beef is eaten with creamy Slav cheese, while a snack may consist of Hungarian pastries, stuffed with fruit and spices. Even so, the prominence of seafood, soups and risotto remains a legacy of Venetian rule, while the goulash, sausages, and strudel denote Austrian influence.

Trentino-Alto Adige is another distinctive border region, a mountainous area offering Alpine food with an Italian twist. Wholesome peasant-style dishes prevail, from hearty pork and beef smoked sausages to polenta dishes and pulse-filled soups. Culinary keynotes are minestrone with beans and potatoes, alpine trout poached in white wine, and ravioli filled with chicken and roasted and smoked meats. Trentino risotto can be made with wine, or with *finferli* mushrooms, second only to Tuscan *funghi porcini* (ceps) in quality. Variations include apple risotto or *risotto alle castagne o alle noci*, a rice dish with chestnuts or walnuts.

PASTA AND REAL BOLOGNESE SAUCE

Local lore has it that tortellini were inspired by Venus's belly button: when a Bolognese innkeeper espied the goddess in bed, he rushed to the kitchen to create his masterpiece. As if in homage to the goddess, the local tortellini association still claims that each sheet of pasta must be "as round as the moon and as soft as a caress". Each large Emilian town possesses a secret recipe for tortellini stuffed with minced meats, blended with herbs, broth and Parmesan. One shop even boasts tortellini "*buoni da ingannare i mariti*", good enough to fool husbands.

Tagliatelle, another local pasta, was supposedly invented in 1487 to honour Lucrezia Borgia's golden hair, but a hair-splitting recent regulation determined that each strand should be precisely eight millimetres wide, one-12,276th part of the height of Bologna's main leaning tower. Since then, anything else is simply not tagliatelle. Equally well known is *cannelloni ripieni di tortellini*, a filling pasta dish stuffed with ham, mozzarella, cream and butter. *Cappelletti* are stuffed with brains and minced turkey breast. To go with the pasta is *ragù*, the authentic Bolognese sauce that bears little relation to bastardised versions served in restaurants abroad; the real thing contains 20 ingredients, from chicken liver, carrots and celery to ham, minced beef, mushrooms, nutmeg, parsley and red wine.

Austrian influence prevails in Alto Adige, and even in Trentino itself. Typical dishes include smoked meats, sauerkraut cooked in lard, roast venison with polenta, red cabbage goulash and other filling stews. Dumplings are preferred to pasta, and bread dumplings are confusingly known as *canederli* in Italian but *knodel* in German. The best-known dish is *strangolapreti* – gnocchi made with potatoes, bread or spinach and coated with butter or cheese. Desserts are Austrian-inspired pastries such as strawberry cake *(erdbeertorte)* or strudel stuffed with apples, nuts and raisins.

Lombardy

"Here, the foods of the rich, based on meat and dairy products, meet the staples of the poor – maize and pasta – overladen by the fast food of the modern world," states the renowned cookery writer Claudia Roden. This is creamy cuisine designed for the palate of the northern industrialist, with saffron-tinted *risotto alla milanese* the signature dish. As in the Veneto, rice has been the natural choice of the urban upper classes since its introduction by Spanish rulers in 1535. This lavish Lombard cuisine favours combinations of rich, complex foods to display their sophistication. As such, it is a carnivore's delight, with beef, veal, pork and poultry dishes predominating. Yet it is also a poor polenta region: whether fried, baked or grilled, the white or yellow maize meal once formed the peasants' staple diet. Served in place of pasta or bread, filling white polenta accompanies fish, while yellow polenta is usually served with the rest.

The region produces some of the best meat in the country, from veal and beef to pork and poultry: hence such stalwarts as *costoletta alla milanese*, veal fillet fried in breadcrumbs, and *osso buco*, shin of veal in white wine served with risotto.

Less well-known outside Italy are *casseula*, a stew of mixed cuts of pork with vegetables, introduced from Spain by the Gonzagas, and *bollito*, boiled meats and offal cooked in a pot and served thinly sliced. The Lombards are also fond of sausages and cured meats *(salami)*, such as mortadella, and bresaola, beef fillet, salted, dried, then smoked.

LEFT: market day in Venice.
ABOVE: Italian cakes are works of art.

Good cheese

Gorgonzola, the greenish-blue veined cheese, originated in the foothills of the Alps near Milan. This cows'-milk cheese has a piquant flavour and is ideally served runny or as a sauce for pasta, polenta or risotto. Grana Padano, originally made by the Cistercian monks of Chiaravalle in 1100, is similar to Parmesan. Moist chunks are eaten with fruit.

Taleggio, a strong cheese with a texture like Camembert, is used in risotto and terrines. Bel Paese, the mild processed cheese, exists in its rusticincarnation, while creamy mascarpone is used in sauces.

Piedmont

The keynotes of Piedmontese cuisine are elegant French flourishes and filling country cuisine. The opulence of Piedmontese cuisine reflects the influence of France and the royal house of Savoy. Smooth truffle-scented risotto, rich cheeses and red meat represent the antithesis of *cucina nuova*. A classic dish is *vitel tonn*: sliced roast veal and tuna fish served cold in a mayonnaise, and garnished with capers and gherkins.

Fontina, the best cows'-milk cheese, comes from the Alpine region of Valle d'Aosta. Fondues *(fonduta)* are made from this chewy semi-soft cheese, which can be mild or piquant. *Gnocchi alla bava* are potato dumplings coated in Fontina cheese and white wine. This mountainous region is also noted for its salami, terrines and cured meats. By contrast, the woods around Alba are truffle-hunting country, providing such delicacies as *tagliolini* pasta coated in *salsa di tartufi bianchi*, white truffle sauce. The countryside was the inspiration for *bagna cauda*, a garlic and anchovy dip which accompanies raw peppers, artichokes, celery and potatoes. More substantial are meat dishes such as a *fritto misto* of brains, liver and sweetbreads fried in egg and breadcrumbs. Equally typical are *brusato al Barolo*, braised beef marinated in Barolo wine, or *bollito*, boiled meats.

Desserts include russet-skinned pears stewed in Barolo wine, baked peaches stuffed with amaretti macaroons from Saronno, or *zabaione*, a dessert made with Marsala and egg yolks. Turin is proud of its *gianduiotti*, hazelnut chocolates, a reminder of its 18th-century role as a founder of the European chocolate industry.

Healthy Liguria

Liguria is the most Mediterranean region, and it has the most vegetarian-friendly cuisine and the healthiest diet. There is little meat and dairy produce, but an array of vegetables sandwiched into the narrow strip between the sea and the hills. The mild climate is ideal for tomatoes and artichokes, peaches, apricots and lemons. Liguria's signature dish is pesto sauce, made from basil, olives, pine nuts or walnuts, Parmesan or sheep's cheese and garlic, ground and pounded into an aromatic pulp. It is usually served with *trenette verdi*, ribbon-shaped pasta or *trofie*, light gnocchi. Liguria also produces the only olive oil to rival the finest Tuscan varieties: a delicate, sweetly scented, greeny-golden concoction. Trademark dishes are *pansoti*, ravioli-like pasta stuffed with ricotta and herbs, and minestrone *alla genovese*.

For a coastal region, the fish is unexceptional, with favoured dishes including fish soup *(scippin)*, stews *(buridda)* with anchovies and mixed fish, fried onions and pine nuts, and *stoccafisso in umido*, salt cod cooked with tomatoes, potatoes, pine nuts, garlic and sultanas.

Slow Food Movement

The Slow Food Movement was born in Bra in Piedmont in 1986, dedicated to countering fast- or junk-food culture. Its manifesto declared, "Let us rediscover the flavours and savours of regional cooking and banish the degrading effects of fast food." The Movement now has more than 80,000 members spread across five continents. On alternate years it organises a huge food fair in October at the Lingotto in Turin, the Salone del Gusto. The latest venture of the Movement is by far its most ambitious – the University of Gastronomic Science. This is the world's first institution to elevate food and drink to a full-blown academic discipline with three-year degree courses and, for a master's qualification, a further two.

Signature dishes

Italian cooking may be less coherent, less classic than French cuisine, yet the rich diversity of Italy's regional cuisine is greater than the sum of its parts. Even similar pasta dishes are distinguished by local preparations. Every region has its signature dishes, from *risotto alla milanese* (Milanese saffron risotto) to *fegato alla veneziana* (Venetian calf's liver) and *ragù alla bolognese* (Bolognese sauce). Above all, local dishes are a reflection of regional pride. As the old dictum runs: "*Dimmi come mangi e ti diro chi sei* (Tell me what you eat and I'll tell you who you are)." ❑

LEFT: some like it hot – chilli peppers.

Parmesan Cheese

Italy's most prestigious cheese has been praised since Etruscan and Roman times, with a Latin paean to Parmesan in Martial's verse. Correctly known as Parmigiano Reggiano, these hulking cartwheels of cheese originated in Emilia Romagna and were lauded in Petrarch's poetry and Boccaccio's Decameron. Parmesan's fame soon spread: Queen Elizabeth I shipped it to England in great quantities, and an elderly Molière even attributed the revival of his flagging dramatic powers to the chese. Today the cheese's praises are sung by a consortium which jealously protects its reputation. Despite the popularity of Parmesan on the world market, the majority of cheese is destined for Italy.

Parma and Reggio Emilia form the epicentre of the production zone, with a thousand small cheesemakers in the surrounding region. The straw-coloured cheese has been documented since the 13th century, and the production methods have remained unchanged ever since. Parmesan belongs to the Grana family of cheeses, including Gran Padano from Lombardy. However, Parmesan-makers insist that their "artisanal" cheeses are superior to industrially produced brands. Parmesan's cachet lies in its trusty artisanal methods and natural ageing process, as well as in the absence of preservatives or anti-fermenting agents. It takes 1.4 million tonnes of milk to yield 85,000 tonnes of Parmesan. The strictness of the specifications ensures the superb quality promised by the Parmigiano-Reggiano seal. Such superiority is reflected in the cost of this king of Italian cheeses.

Parmesan is made from a mixture of morning and evening milk from cows who graze on grass in spring and summer pastures. The cream is removed from the evening milk and turned into butter, with the resultant semi-skimmed milk mixed with full-fat morning milk. The concoction is then heated in huge copper cauldrons, shaped like inverted bells, with goat's kid rennet used as the curdling agent. After separation, the whey is fed to the local pigs while the curds are broken down, drained and pressed into round moulds. When firm, the cheese is floated in brine to absorb salt before being stamped with its name, date and provenance; Parmigiano Reggiano should be branded on the outer crust. The drums of cheese, weighing over 30 kilos (66 pounds) each, are then stacked on wooden slats in cellars that hold up to 200,000 cheeses at one time, and matured for between 18 months and three years. During the ageing process, the cheeses are constantly checked, turned and aired: more mature cheeses are drier and have a chalky look whereas younger cheeses are more moist. The golden Parmesan is stored in bank vaults, both to preserve its freshness and to protect it: in Emilia Romagna, cheese is as valuable as money.

Parmesan can be grated or eaten as a wedge, with the cheese "opened", rather than cut, using an almond-shaped knife. Since the 16th century, chunks of the best Parmesan have traditionally been served with grapes and pears. However, it can also accompany an aperitif or a dessert of figs, apples, peaches or nuts. The popularity of Parmesan on pasta is due to its distinctive, lingering aroma and the fact that it melts without leaving a stringy residue. The best Parmesan crumbles in the mouth, while the edible crust can also be used in soups.

RIGHT: wedges of Parmigiano Reggiano.

Parmesan enjoys a reputation as the most versatile and restorative of cheeses. Little wonder that Italian doctors have long promoted Parmesan's curative powers, particularly for those under six or over sixty. In order to hedge their bets, and perhaps to placate the powerful cheese lobby, doctors also prescribe Parmesan as an aid to digestion for greedy patients of all ages. ❑

CAFÉ SOCIETY

Cafés – and coffee – are serious business in northern Italy, and the fine fin-de-siècle furnishings still make them atmospheric places to visit

The informal Italian *gelato* law stipulates that the further south one travels, the better the ice cream. Fortunately, the converse is that the further north one travels, the better the cafés. Turin, Trieste, Venice, Milan and Padua offer grandly historic cafés of great warmth and elegance. The northern climate favours formal, stylish retreats, intimate indoor cafés built against the vagaries of the weather. Yet the northern café culture owes much to Mitteleuropa, and the dowager ambience of the most monumental Italian cafés has much in common with cosmopolitan cafés in Vienna or Budapest, Paris or Prague.

Nobility and Art Nouveau

Caffè Cova is a Milanese institution on Via Montenapoleone. Founded in 1817, it was patronised by the 19th-century nobility. Students of Italian history can savour the genteel atmosphere where Mazzini and Garibaldi reputedly redrew the political map of Italy. Far grander is the Art Nouveau Giardino d'Inverno, in the Principe di Savoia, one of Milan's smartest hotels. Camparino, in Galleria Vittorio Emanuele, is also an Art Nouveau shrine, and a classic place for commuters to take *aperitivi* before they face the evening rush hour. Alternatively, Bar Giamaica, in the Brera district, is the place for erstwhile hippies who have mellowed into corporate suits. Although this 1960s bohemian rendezvous has been commandeered by models, designers and sundry creatives, it retains a raffish air.

Even the smaller provincial centres can conceal coffee houses of national repute. Trieste has a long and honourable tradition of coffee houses; the celebrated Caffè San Marco is a languorous study in elevated café style: frescoed Art Nouveau, gloomy mahogany fittings, polished brass and red velour drapes.

Venetian classics

Under the arcades of the Piazza San Marco is a cluster of distinguished coffee houses. Caffè Florian, considered the prince of coffee houses, was founded in 1720 and is the oldest surviving café in Italy. Although heavily restored, it is a tribute to 18th-century splendour. As an erstwhile literary haunt, Florian's welcomed Byron, Dickens, Goethe, Mann, Proust and George Sand. It has long numbered musicans amongst, its patrons although Richard Wagner kept away for fear of running into Giuseppe Verdi. Writers and artists still meet in Caffè Florian, though more for show than to listen to the melancholy airs of the cello and violin *virtuosi.*

On the basis that Harry's Bar is the best bar in the best city, the famed Bellini cocktail is cheap at any price. This is a legendary Venetian bar, resolutely unglitzy apart from a clientele of visiting celebrities and celebrity-watchers. The lure of classic cocktails and a good gossip have drawn prominent personalities, from Churchill and Chaplin to Bogart and Bacall,

ABOVE: the perfect cappuccino.
RIGHT: entertainment at Venice's Caffè Florian.

Fellini and Mastroianni, Sinatra and Madonna. Hemingway found inspiration in its "Montgomery", a Martini made with 15 measures of gin to one of vermouth, the same ratio of troops to enemy employed by the military strategist.

Savoy fare

Café culture reaches new heights in Turin's turn-of-the-century cafés, temples dedicated to pleasure and politics. Caffè Torino, once the favourite of the royal court, is still a high society haunt, noted for its elegance, cocktails and superb service. Caffè Specchi is one of a select band to line the bourgeois boulevards, a place to pass drowsy hours sitting and sipping cocktails or coffee. Caffè Mulassano, with faded gilt and panelled interior, is a rival turn-of-the-century temple to coffee, hot chocolate and cake-eating. By contrast, the glamorous bar in the Turin Palace strikes an exotic note, with a tented ceiling conjuring up an Oriental harem.

The intimate Al Bicerin is an early Ottocento café, originally a Sunday treat for prim dowagers attending Mass in the church opposite. The *bicerin*, the house speciality, is a heady mixture of hot chocolate, coffee and cream. Yet Al Bicerin is also a landmark in Piedmontese history, the preferred café of Count Camillo di Cavour, the architect of Italian unification. Caffè-Pasticceria Baratti, set in a *fin-de-siècle* arcade, is a steamy spot for lovers of the *cioccolata calda*, a melting hot chocolate concoction. Caffè San Carlo, once frequented by Risorgimento patriots and intellectuals, claims to make the best coffee in Italy, rivalled only by Florian's in Venice.

Stefano Cavallero, its owner, sees the café as the lynchpin of Italy's social life, whether "neighbourhood cafés, football cafés, business cafés, bohemian cafés or intellectual cafés. Cafés are the first places where young people meet and the last places where old men say goodbye. Cafés keep Italians together." ❑

COFFEE THE WAY THE ITALIANS LIKE IT

The perfect *espresso* should have an aroma so intense that it bites. It should also have a *crema*, a head, whose consistency is determined by the fats and volatile oils in the coffee beans. To produce a good rounded taste, the beans should be a judicious blend of burnt arabica and robusta. *Caffè ristretto* is a double-strength *espresso* more akin to an electric shock than a cup of coffee. *Caffè latte*, an *espresso* mixed with steamed milk, can be drunk for breakfast, as can *cappuccino*, but never after a meal. *Caffè macchiato* is a single shot of *espresso* with a dash of foaming milk, while *caffè corretto* is fortified with a slug of spirits, whether *grappa*, cognac or whisky.

WINE ON THE MAP: TRAILS AND TASTINGS

Tracking down the greatest northern Italian wines is a delightful duty and a rewarding way of getting to know different regional landscapes

The region boasts many of Italy's best-known wines, from quaffable Valpolicella, fizzy Lambrusco and crisp Soave to Piedmont's powerful Barolo and Barbaresco, wines worthy of pilgrimages. The Veneto is a significant wine-producing region, encompassing the area from Venice to Lake Garda, and plays host to VinItaly in Verona, the country's largest wine fair. Amongst the biggest regional names are sparkling Prosecco and the red, cherry-like Bardolino, as well as fruity Valpolicella from around Lake Garda and dry Soave, produced east of Verona.

Although Lombardy cannot compete with the Veneto, its Franciacorta red, white and sparkling wines, produced around Lake Iseo, have been lauded since Roman times, and praised by Pliny himself. The Collio district of Friuli produces crisp, fine white wines, from Riesling Italico to Pinot Grigio, while Liguria is noted for red Dolcetto, and Emilia Romagna produces Italy's best sparkling red Lambrusco.

THE KING OF WINES

However, Piedmont has a monopoly on the greatest wines. Barolo and Barbaresco are produced on the western shore of Lake Maggiore and benefit from a sub-alpine climate and southern exposure. These wines are justly famous, and have brought a quiet prosperity to the villages around Alba and Asti. They are made from the noble violet and raspberry scented Nebbiolo grape, the finest red grape in northern Italy, and matured in oak or chestnut casks. If Barolo is the king of wines, Barbaresco is the queen, lighter and more elegant. At the humbler end of the Piedmontese scale, the bubbly appeal of Asti Spumante still enlivens a party.

△ **BAROLO VINEYARDS**
At its best, Barolo, grown in southern Piedmont, is a powerful, individualistic long-lived red wine that lives up to its reputation.

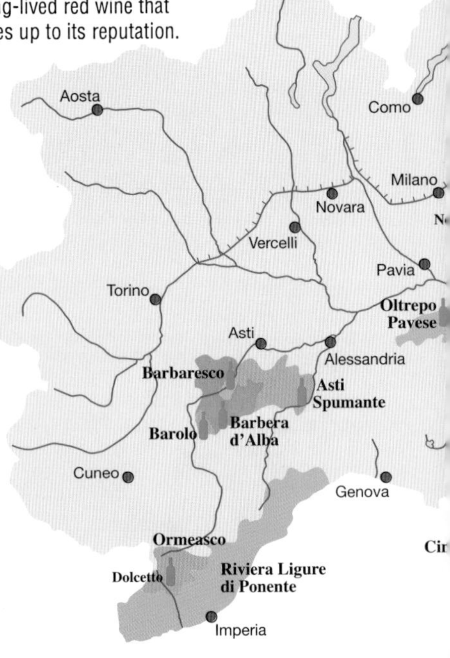

◁ **BUBBLY**
Prosecco, which can be dry or sweet, works best as a dry sparkling aperitif.

▷ **TYROLEAN TASTES**
Eppan, in the Alto Adige, sells wine with labels in both Italian and German.

◁ **MEDIEVAL MERRIMENT**
Harvesting the grapes – an annual scene, here depicted in Torre dell'Aquila, the charmingly frescoed tower in the Castello del Buonconsiglio, Trento.

△ **LIGURIAN NECTAR**
The hill-sides around Corniglia and the Cinque Terre villages produce noted white wines.

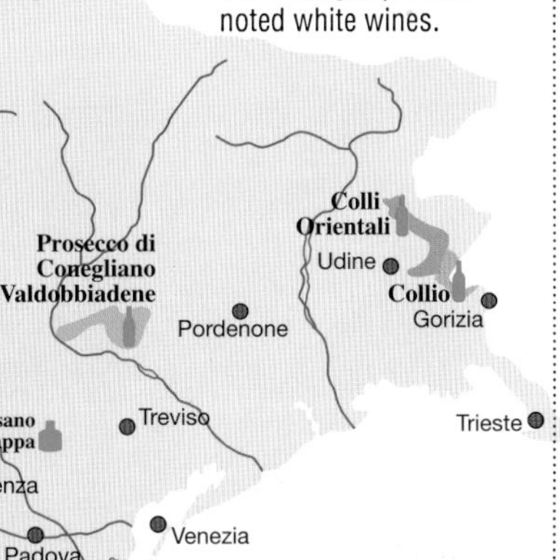

▽ **SCENIC SLOPES**
Neat, vine-clad hillsides and prosperous estates represent harmonious northern wine country.

◁ **HARVEST TOAST**
Rossesse di Dolceacqua, Napoleon's favourite wine, can be sampled in Liguria.

▷ **KING OF WINES**
Barolo, described as "earthy, truffly, smoky and mysterious."

WINE TOURS AND GRAPPA TASTINGS

Northern Italy is well supplied with *enoteche*, centres of excellence for wine-tasting, sales and promotion. The finest examples, such as Dozza and Barolo, are frequently located in such impressive settings as historic castles and make a convenient starting point for a leisurely trail around the most celebrated wine estates of the region.

In Emilia Romagna, Dozza boasts the impressive medieval Sforza fortress of La Rocca, where, following a visit to the castle, you can sample Emilian wines such as Barbera and Lambrusco in the medieval cellars.

In the Veneto, the Strada del Prosecco is a celebration of Italy's most popular sparkling wine, with an accessible wine-tasting route centred on Conegliano and Valdobbiadene.

In Lombardy, the Franciacorta area by Lake Iseo lends itself to wine-tastings and vineyard visits.

The regions of Trentino and the Veneto are the foremost producers of the famous firewater known as *grappa*, which is distilled from grapes.

VILLAS AND GARDENS

Lord Byron called Italy "the garden of the world", and the north, with its array of gorgeous Palladian villas and geometric gardens, does not disappoint

Bewitched by operatic gardens in the northern Italian lakes, Henry James described himself as "fairly wallowing in a *libretto*". Edith Wharton, who wrote the Edwardian travellers' bible to Italian gardens, praised such landscapes for their "breadth and simplicity", a composition of "marble, water and perennial verdure". From the Renaissance onwards, villas were embellished by sculptors, painters, cabinet-makers, plasterers and landscape gardeners. Whether models of Renaissance restraint, Classical Palladian design or Baroque theatricality, they possessed vistas framed by greenery, topiary and sculpture. Today the north still embraces some of the country's most enchanting villas and gardens.

The patrician ideal

From an architectural point of view, the Veneto possesses the greatest heritage, the blueprint for the patrician villa. Largely designed by Palladio *(see page 121)*, these UNESCO-listed villas spread in an arc embracing Rovigo, Vicenza, Treviso and Venice. To the west, on the Ligurian Riviera, villas and gardens grace the outskirts of Genoa and hug the coast close to Portofino. Further north, lakeside Lombardy is noted for its patrician residences, from Baroque Isola Bella to exuberant Villa Carlotta on Lake Como, where landscaped gardens hug the hill in a shower of hibiscus, bougainvillea and citrus trees. Isola Bella was a barren rock before being landscaped by the Borromean princes in the 17th century. Their lasting testament is a series of lofty terraces encrusted with statuary and fountains, complemented by grottoes studded with shells, fossils and coloured coral.

While the patrician ideal was a country villa surrounded by formal gardens and a working farm estate, a number of northern gardens are showpieces in their own right. The botanical gardens in Padua, dating from 1533, are the oldest university gardens in Italy devoted to medicinal plants and scientific research. Also in the Veneto, the Giusti gardens in Verona are equally distinctive, embellished with grottoes and terraces, and used as an open-air theatre in Renaissance times. The Giardino Reale in Monza near Milan is an inspired Italianate version of English Romanticism: royal parkland studded with alpine glades, lakes and lawns.

Renaissance summer solace

During the Renaissance the villa was reinvented as a gracious retreat and framed by geometric landscaped gardens *all'italiana*. With airy loggias and panoramic belvederes, the Tuscan Renaissance villa broke the mould of enclosed medieval gardens. Steeply terraced gardens enjoyed vistas of parterres, stairways and pergolas, lemon groves, laurels and lilies, with olive groves and vineyards beyond. The Venetian nobility and merchant class soon followed suit, commissioning villas beside the

PRECEDING PAGES: Villa Hanbury botanical garden.
LEFT: the romantic gardens of Villa Carlotta, Como.
RIGHT: lilies at Villa Hanbury, Ventimiglia.

Brenta Canal and in the foothills of the Alps. Moving to the country also enabled polite society to escape the summer heat of the Venetian Lagoon and Po Valley.

A villa society

The early 16th century coincided with a fashion for country living and witnessed the emergences of villa society. The relationship between the rural economy and the ruling classes meant that the Venetians could invest any income earned from maritime trade and make profits from their new lands. In so doing, they could believe in the ennoblement of agriculture whilst also achieving their less noble goal: the glorification of the dynasty. The merchant class was as industrious on *terra firma* as it was in the lagoon city. The land was drained and farmed. In summer, the villa became a society haunt for noble Venetian patrons, first as a focus for humanist gatherings and finally as a setting for festivities.

From the 1520s a stream of city-dwellers built country retreats, villas adorned with waterside gardens. Villas were often designed so that they would be reflected in the Brenta River or Canal, and formal pools were integral to the overall composition of the grounds.

An architectural garden was traced with paths and greenery, and landscaped *all'italiana* to suit the tastes of the times. Mathematical order prevailed, with clipped cypresses, laurels and myrtles, topiary, scented herbs and sculpture. Dwarf fruit trees were popular, with lemons, quinces and pomegranates generally grown.

In Renaissance times the villas became the hubs of prosperous agricultural estates, and a harmonious part of the landscape. The leading architects of the day were summoned to design the villas, from Michele Sanmicheli and Jacopo Sansovino to Palladio. By the same token, the greatest artists, from Veronese to Tiepolo, were invited to decorate the interiors.

Palladian trail

Palladio treated his creations as Roman stages encased in theatres of greenery. He favoured superb natural settings, airy porticoes, and loggias crowned by triangular pediments. The blend of architectural coherence and compositional elegance pleases the eye as simplicity personified. However, the Classical design and decorative detail mask the virtuosity of the design, cast as it is in mathematical ratios.

Villa Rotonda, technically known as Villa Capra, is a Palladian masterpiece famed for its photogenic setting, shallow dome and four identical façades. Set in the hills outside Vicenza, this summer retreat was designed as an architectural set-piece, a stage for admiring the undulating view flowing from the majestic columns and staircase. Villa Foscari, known as La Malcontenta, vies with La Rotonda as Palladio's most admired creation. The villa, raised on an elevated pedestal to protect it from floods, displays a temple-like façade reflected in the Brenta river.

Villa Emo Capodilista, east of Vicenza, is another Palladian gem, and, like Villa Saraceno to the south, accepts paying guests. Villa Barbaro in Maser, in the foothills of the Dolomites, is one of the Veneto's grandest villas, designed by Palladio and frescoed by Veronese.

The northern lakes, particularly Como and Maggiore, are home to some of the region's most splendid villas and gardens. Lake Como has long had the most exclusive lakeside villas, many of which are owned by celebrities. Villa Carlotta was the work of Princess Carlotta of The Netherlands, who landscaped the formal gardens and park in the 1860s. The dazzling azaleas and rhododendrons provide a colourful contrast to the villa's cool Neoclassical interior. By contrast, the Baroque splendours of Isola Bella on Lake Maggiore often blind visitors to the charms of the neighbouring Isola Madre and its luxuriant botanical gardens.

Dignity and harmonious proportions have served as a model for later villas in the Veneto. Villa Arvedi, set in Cuzzano, near Verona, dates from 1650 and has a complex Classical garden, with allegorical statues, geometrical hedges, a grotto, amaze and an orangery. By contrast, Villa Pisani in Stra is an 18th-century affair, decorated by Tiepolo. The garden owes much to French classicism, with the villa and the outbuildings set some distance apart, and a maze, rustic portals, and a belvedere with a spiral staircase leading to a raised loggia.

LEFT: Villa Cordelina, Montecchio Maggiore.
ABOVE: the terraces of Villa Serbeloni, Bellagio.

Geometry and perspective

Italianate gardens conjure up a picture of graceful geometry. Attention is paid to the proportions between the height of a wall and the width of a path, or to the alternation of sunny parterres and shady woodland. The grandest gardens may indulge in sweeps of landscape, with waterworks and pergolas in the foreground, possibly culminating in the *pièce de résistance*, a *scaletta d'acqua:* a water staircase with a grotto, fountains and classical statuary. Though less dependent on artifice and dramatic effects than Roman and Tuscan models, the Renaissance gardens in the Veneto play the same games with geometry and perspective. Given that Renaissance man saw himself at the centre of the universe, the wish to impose his will on the countryside was ever-present.

Villa Cicogna Mozzoni, in the hills north of Varese, was a hunting lodge until it was remodelled in 1559 as a classic Lombard Renaissance villa. The *trompe-l'oeil* Mannerist frescoes and loggia painted with plants and peacocks complement the framed vistas of parterres and forested slopes. The Renaissance garden is a tiered affair, inspired by Medici gardens in Florence and Papal gardens in Rome; a double staircase framed by cypresses and dotted with statuary connects the villa and grounds. The effect is seamless, a procession of loggias, box hedges, classical pools, fountains and a grotto.

French influence

The formality of French Classical gardens was difficult to transplant to the more rugged Italian terrain but succeeded in parts of the flatter Veneto, even if on a far smaller scale than the Classical châteaux garden around Paris. By comparison, Isola Bella is a deeply Italian Baroque extravaganza in the lake district, a fanciful terraced pleasure garden bursting with vegetation from all over the world.

Villa Trissino Marzotto, near Vicenza, has medieval gardens remodelled in Rococo style in the 18th century. In the grounds, striking features include the wrought-iron gates and curtain of cypresses leading up to the belvedere; wooded areas give way to sweeping lawns and terraced gardens with statuary and arches.

Anglo-Saxon attitudes

As fashions changed, some Classical gardens were transformed into *giardini inglesi*, English Romantic parkland and woods. The Italian tendency to remodel nature to man's own design gave way to the English approach, whereby man saw himself as aiding nature in creating a naturalistic effect.

Villa Pallavicino, set in Stresa, on Lake Maggiore, is a 19th-century villa whose gardens combine Romantic and Classical elements. Enlarged by the Duca di Villambrosa, who had a passion for tree-planting, the park abounds in horse chestnuts, copper and purple beech, maple and magnolia, majestic sequoia and oak. The parkland is complemented by Italianate gardens dotted with secret arbours, rose bowers, statues and fountains, as well as greenhouses filled with exotic and ornamental plants.

The lush gardens at Sigurtà, on Lake Garda, are an Italianate approximation of English parkland. It is full of flowering plants and majestic trees interspersed with terraces, lakes and a ruined castle. In the Edwardian heyday of genteel tourism, the northern lakes delighted visitors with seemingly careless vistas of azaleas, rhododendrons and camellias. At the same time the Italian Riviera, the Riviera dei Fiori, lived up to its floral name, with a profusion of camellias, magnolias and palms along the seafront.

A privileged minority still strives to recreate the classic villa garden of the aristocracy, an ornamental affair of statuary, topiary, fountains and stone paths. But to most Italians a garden means crops, vines, olives and an orchard, or at least an untidy vegetable patch.

Chic city-dwellers may have recently taken to spending a fortune on minuscule, status-symbol balcony gardens, but even those with more space tend to focus on creating a lovely terrace and ignoring the rest. Even here, tomatoes, a lemon tree or basil plants often take pride of place over pots of geraniums; in Italian minds, there is no contest between the rival claims of food and flowers. ❑

LEFT: Verona's Giusti gardens.

Palladian Style

Palladio's treatise *The Four Books of Architecture* was hugely influential in popularising Classical architecture. If the term "Palladian" has entered the language, it is a compliment both to the Italian's superb buildings and to his legacy as a scholar. The Renaissance genius Andrea di Pietro della Gondola was dubbed Palladio by Count Tressino, his patron and mentor, one of the enlightened Venetian landowners who had the foresight to commission Palladio's villas.

Palladio was born in Padua in the Veneto in 1508, and worked as a mason on Mannerist monuments in Vicenza, but he only fully formulated his Classical philosophy after visiting Rome in the 1540s. As the leading architect of his day, he pioneered a radical classicism that was too bold for Venetian tastes. Consequently he received few public commissions, and none for city palaces, which made him dependent on the patronage of the religious orders and the largesse of the Venetian landed gentry.

Authentic Palladian villas are found in the Po Valley between Venice and Vicenza, with some of the most celebrated situated along a stretch of the Brenta Canal. The architect also designed a bridge at Bassano del Grappa, in the foothills of the Alps, before dedicating the end of his career to transforming the Venetian skyline with his bold buildings. Be it church, bridge or villa, Palladianism is noted for its Classical restraint, a chaste and restrained style at odds with theatrical Baroque. Yet the villas, in particular, often pose architectural puzzles, from a square house built around a dome to a circular house constructed with square walls.

Palladio's designs for villas were a marriage between ancient Rome and the modern world, with the elevated tastes of the leisured classes allied to a sober and humane classicism stripped of excess. In the Roman hills, Palladio was impressed by the Tivoli villas, from the curved staff wings to the elevated monumental façades and stylised projecting pediments. He then proceeded to reinterpret the greatest Roman architecture for the Venetian bourgeoisie. Inspired by the Pantheon in Rome, certain villas are designed on the lines of a votive temple. An unwavering sense of proportion and perspective is reflected in the façades, the pedimented porticoes and the bold, airy interiors. The subtle, spare designs are enhanced by broad domes, graceful columns and Corinthian capitals.

Taken as a whole, Palladio's work on Venetian churches and the villas of the Veneto make him one of the outstanding architects of all time. Tempered by Palladianism, even Venetian Baroque was a relatively sober form. The rest of northern Italy witnessed a return to Palladian values in the 18th century, with dignified villas built for the nobility, and grandiose city palaces designed for wealthy *arrivistes*.

Palladian villas in the Veneto influenced architectural styles all over the Western world, especially in the United States, England and Ireland.

RIGHT: Villa Foscari, Veneto, designed by Andrea Palladio and built c.1560.

The use of the Graeco-Roman temple front as a portico was probably the most imitated feature. Villa Rotonda provided the model for London's Chiswick House and countless English stately homes, as well as inspiring imitators in Ireland and America. London's National Gallery, the Capitol in Washington DC and the Metropolitan Museum in New York are testaments to the pervasiveness of Palladianism. Thomas Jefferson, the American President and author of the Declaration of Independence, transplanted Palladian style to Virginia, where he cultivated a transatlantic Italian renaissance. Nonetheless, in terms of Classical design and decorative detail, the villas in the Veneto represent the purest form of Palladianism. ❑

WALKING AND WILDLIFE

Green tourism is a growth area in northern Italy, with spring and autumn the best seasons for hill-walking

Walkers drawn to the penitential aspect of mountain-climbing can satisfy their bodies and souls in the uncharted wildernesses of northern Italy. They will encounter jagged mountain peaks looming menacingly, stony mule tracks, torrential rain, and scrambles up strata of unyielding rock. Unattainable summits spur the walker to greater endeavours in the metaphysical sense. Yet, in a flash, vistas open up to reveal a clear blue sky over snow-capped peaks, serene woodland or a sighting of a chamois or an ibex. The descent may take in panoramic views from natural balconies, thundering waterfalls and copses of oak and chestnut. Beyond awaits a more ordered landscape, with alpine meadows punctuated perhaps by olive groves and vineyards. Material rewards take the form of filling polenta, venison and red wine in a cosy alpine refuge.

Mountains to coastal paths

Le Corbusier, the great French architect, described the Dolomites as the most beautiful natural sculpture in the world. British and German pioneers of alpine tourism "discovered" them in the 19th century, since when their landscape of peaks and perpetual glaciers has become a popular destination for foreign hikers. Yet so have the Ligurian coastal paths climbing through vineyards and terraced olive groves; the mists and marshland of the Po Delta; the coppiced woodland of the Emilian Apennines; and the balmy micro-climates of the great northern lakes.

Apart from gentle hill-walking and strenuous hiking, the north offers the full range of associated sports, from mountaineering and orienteering to rock and glacier-climbing. Winter adds alpine and cross-country skiing to the menu, as well as dog-sledding and long-distance excursions on snow shoes.

A number of walking itineraries are rich in military sites. Trentino, for instance, offers the Path of Peace, a World War I line of fortifications and communication trenches carved out the mountains separating Italy and Austria *(see page 126)*. Further south, in the Apennines, on the border between Emilia Romagna and Tuscany, walkers can explore the war sites along the Gothic Line. During World War II the Germans built substantial fortifications in these rugged valleys.

LEFT: the Stelvio Pass.
RIGHT: hiking amid the hills and mountains of Trentino.

Taking the high road

The Alps are criss-crossed with long-distance paths linking chestnut groves with rugged alpine panoramas. The *strade bianche* are the dusty white roads of rural Italy, while the *alte vie* are high long-distance paths, with the most spectacular being the *alte vie delle Dolomiti*, the high Dolomite trails. The most arduous routes are the so-called "*vie ferrate*", iron ladders, named after the spaghetti lines of iron cables that are implanted into the steeper rock gradients. Real ladders are used to scale sheer cliff walls in a sport that is still considered walking rather than mountain-climbing and is popular with the Italians and Germans in the Trentino Dolomites. Ice picks and a head for heights are a prerequisite for such alpine trails.

The north provides a taste of the region's best parks and nature reserves. Gran Paradiso, Italy's foremost national park, is a magnificent wilderness, with its waterfalls, meadows, glaciers and rare alpine flora. On a par with its northern neighbour is the sprawling Parco dello Stelvio, Italy's largest national park, which straddles Lombardy, Trentino and the Alto Adige. The profusion of lakes has led to the area being dubbed "the Finland of Italy". Most major parks have visitor centres where one can usually hire a bicycle, find detailed walking itineraries or book a local guide. National parks are patrolled, and keepers impose on-the-spot fines for such infractions as disturbing animals or picking flowers, mushrooms or berries.

Piedmont and the Gran Paradiso

The ruggedness of the terrain makes the region more suitable for long-distance walking, mountaineering and skiing than for gentle strolls. While the cultivated land is among the most profitable in the country, particularly the prized vineyards, almost half the region is mountainous. The alpine landscape was modelled by glaciers during the last Ice Age. Today the Dolomites abound in spruce, Scots pine, mountain pine, silver fir, larch, ash, silver birch and rowan. The wilder areas allow sightings of the golden eagle, chamois and marmots. Long-distance walks link the area around Cuneo to the Valle di Susa and Gran Paradiso. However, committed hikers tend to head straight for the Gran Paradiso. Swathes of woodland and precipitous peaks provide a background for fast-flowing streams, botanical gardens and carpets of alpine flora. The sure-footed ibex is the sym-

THE ITALIAN ALPINE CLUB

The CAI, the Italian Alpine Club, with recognised centres and schools in the main resorts, provides qualified mountain guides and instructors in every imaginable sport. The *rifugi*, invaluable mountain refuges providing hearty meals and even simple rooms, also tend to be run by the CAI. Turin and in Trento have museums showing its members' achievements, including their participation in Antarctic expeditions.

Upmarket independent tour operators offer hiking holidays, with accommodation varying from converted palaces, castles and convents to the simplest farms and *agriturismo (see page 126).*

bol of the park and, along with the chamois, is best seen in May or June on the lower valley slopes, or in late summer on the higher slopes. Since the last lynx was killed here in 1914, visitors must be content with sightings of chamois, marmots and mountain hares, or golden eagles, black woodpeckers and snow finches. The Val di Cogne area provides easy access to the park and is not far from the alpine garden in Valnontey, with its dramatic views of glaciers. Paths are well-marked, including *alta via 4*, a long-distance trail that traverses the park.

BEAR FACTS

The Adamello Brenta national park is the preserve of roebuck, chamois and foxes as well as being the last northern Italian refuge of the rapidly disappearing brown bear.

Oasi Zegna, set in the alpine foothills near Biella and Trivero, was founded in the 1930s by Ermenegildo Zegna, a far-sighted industrialist. Although the product of paternalism, the park has served its purpose as a pastoral retreat for the company's textile workers. The nature reserve, which embraces alpine pastureland and fir woods, is dotted with wildlife trails. The wolf may have died out in the area, but badgers, marmots and stoats survive, as do chamois and roe deer, eagles, owls and chaffinches – a reasonable tally for a region devoted to hunting.

Trentino

The region proclaims itself a walkers' paradise. Mountains crown the landscape; over half the region is covered by woods and alpine pastures, with high-altitude hiking popular in all seasons. In terms of guides, facilities, organisation and the sheer variety of outdoor pursuits, Trentino is unparalleled in Italy. Hikers are rewarded with tumbling streams, dramatic mountain gorges, and crags looming overhead. Brenta, an archetypal Dolomite group, intimidates with its towering pinnacles of limestone and rock surfaces that have an orange sheen when they catch the light. Equally appealing in the summer months are Trentino's 300 lakes. Particularly delightful are the walks around the lesser lakes, with Lake Tenno, Lake Cavedine and Lake Molveno encircled by footpaths. In summer, Lake Tovel can be tinged red by red algae.

Trentino offers numerous archeological and geological trails as well as organised excursions in search of alpine flora, usually beginning in the local botanical gardens. Fans of military

LEFT: monarch of the South Tyrol.
ABOVE: marmots of the Oasi Zegna nature reserve.
RIGHT: the endangered brown bear.

history can follow the Path of Peace *(see page 123)*. The path, which covers the Adamello, Ortles, Cevedale and Marmolada glaciers, would take a month to complete so is best restricted to certain stages.

The largest alpine park

The impressive Parco dello Stelvio, known as Stilfs in German, is the largest national park in the Alps, encompassing 40 lakes and the alpine massif of Ortles-Cevedale. As an indication of the ruggedness of the terrain, a tenth of the area is covered by glaciers. The Passo di Stelvio, Europe's second highest mountain pass, connects with Bolzano and the Alto Adige and is a hiking centre in summer, doubling as a ski resort in winter.

There are visitors' centres in Cogolo and the Val di Rabbi, in addition to access from Bormio. Marked trails and numerous alpine refuges permit observation of chamois, marmots, ibex and golden eagles.

Valle di Peio, part of the park, is a noted trekking centre, with summer routes equally suited to winter excursions on snow shoes. Walkers travelling in small groups may be rewarded by occasional sightings of deer, ibex, marmots or eagles.

RURAL TOURISM

Agriturismo originally referred to spartan rooms in working farms. Now the term can be used to describe any rural accommodation, from simple renovated cottages to restored medieval farms or luxurious converted convents. *Agriturismo* flourishes in much of the north, including Liguria, Emilia Romagna and Trentino– Alto Adige.

The larger or more luxurious rural enterprises may organise hiking or horse-riding excursions. Well-organised regional tourist offices provide lists and accurate descriptions of the *agriturismo* facilities. Successful rural ventures make profits from selling specialist honeys, truffle pâtés, bottled artichokes, olives and jams. A *degustazione*, or tasting of the estate wines and farm produce, is the best part of rural life.

Agritur is a rural initiative popular in the Trentino region. Although it tends not to provide accommodation, it is usually a specialised farm with a simple restaurant. Legally, it can only sell its own products, such as honey, cheese, yoghurt and salami. In Trentino, *Agritur* also offers the opportunity to meet bee-keepers and cattle-farmers at work. Standards of *Agritur* establishments vary enormously: the inn could be a simple place in which to hang up one's walking boots for a while, or represent a gastronomic experience serious enough to draw committed skiers from the slopes.

The chic winter ski resort of Madonna di Campiglio lies at the head of Val Rendenna, a typical pastoral valley. From Cles, near Tuenno, a wooded path leads to Mostizzolo, which opens out into the mountain pass of Campo Carlo Magno. From there, there is a descent to Madonna di Campiglio, a place for well-deserved après-ski posing in one of the trendy local inns. In summer this is also an ideal base for exploring the Brenta and Adamello ranges as well as for following the "five lakes" itinerary.

NEOLITHIC ART

Europe's finest rock carvings can be found at Val Camonica north of Boario Terme. Created by Neolithic hunters and farmers these sheer rock faces were used as a canvas for scenes of everyday life as well for drawings to appease the gods.

For serious hikers, the cable car from Madonna di Campiglio connects with Groste, where a beguiling path leads to Rifugio del Tucket, a mountain refuge. From here, there is access to one of the most popular *vie ferrate*, the "iron paths" along the stunning Sentiero Orsi in the Brenta group. Progress along these paths is aided by a mountain guide provided with ladders or by rungs fixed to the rock.

Mountaineers and climbers are well served by this craggy region. Mountaineering across glaciers of varying difficulty is available in the Valle di Fasse, Valle di Fiemme or Lagorai. Experienced rock-climbers can attempt the vertical ascents around Lake Garda and the Colodri near Arco. The mild lakeside micro-climate makes climbing possible in winter. Sheer cliffs also await expert and novice climbers near Cavalese, in the Valle di Fiemme, as well as in the Val di Sole, Predazzo and Moena.

Alto-Adige

Better known as the South Tyrol, this is Germanic borderlands with a Tyrolean feel, a landscape dotted with hamlets and onion-domed churches. Beyond the quaint villages await dramatic glaciers and scenes of intrepid paragliders floating amidst the snow-capped peaks. Gentler trails wind through domesticated rolling farmland, a patchwork of well-tended fields, orchards and vineyards. These hikes trace the charming meadows around Bad Ratsches and Compatsch, with an opportunity for stops in rustic inns and Germanic spas. Tougher challenges are posed by the Schnals (Senales) glacier or the Seiser Alm range in the Dolomites. The Sciliar national park, accessible from Bolzano, has steep rock faces and peaks.

The Lakes

Compared with the serious hiking on offer in the Dolomites, this region favours a gentle pace. Tucked into the foothills of the Alps, the silvery-blue lakes offer alpine walks in pearly mists or more Mediterranean strolls closer to the shore. Framed by majestic mountains, the lakes abound in balmy micro-climates favourable to citrus fruits and palm trees. Lake Maggiore is well served by paths and cycle tracks, on both the Lombard and Piedmontese banks. From Laveno, a 5km (3-mile) climb leads to the rocky sanctuary of Santa Caterina del Sasso. Around unspoilt Lake Iseo, Provaglio represents the start of a nature itinerary that takes in the peatbogs at the foot of Monte Provaglio and the reed-beds which provide refuge for water fowl. Monte Isola, the traffic-free fishermen's island in the centre of the lake, is best explored by bicycle.

LEFT: the Parco dello Stelvio is the largest national park in the Alps.
RIGHT: winter hiking in Madonna di Campiglio.

From the centre of Como a gentle stroll leads

to Villa Olmo, a gracious villa on the lake. A cable car also connects the town of Como with Brunate, the starting point for scenic hiking in the hills. With its confluence of dramatic peaks and a serene lake shore, the quaint resort of Bellagio is a good base. An invigorating afternoon's stroll can be made from the lakeside Villa Melzi to Monte San Primo by way of streams and mills. At Tremezzo one can join the lakeside route known as Tremezzina, linking several villas and gardens.

Lake Garda, despite being the most developed lake, offers good walking routes, whether from the Brescia, Verona or Trento shores. From the lakeside resort of Malcesine, a cable car connects with a number of mountain paths and convenient *rifugi* for lunch. The adventurous can choose to make the return journey by mountain bike. The castle resort of Sirmione is an ideal base for exploring the Grottoes of Catullus, while the picturesque villages of Tremosine and Tignale, perched on rocky crags, open onto a series of inviting footpaths.

On the Veneto shore, an appealing walk leads from the wine-producing village of Bardolino to Garda itself. Closer to Desenzano is a Mediterranean landscape of vineyards and olive groves. The lush atmosphere is even more pronounced around Gardone Riviera, a resort blessed with a steamy micro-climate producing palms, banana trees and tropical plants.

Lombardy's great art cities, including Bergamo, Mantua and Cremona, offer unusual walks in their vicinities. West of Mantua lies the Mincio reserve, a network of canals and reed beds which is the preserve of marsh turtles, river crab and otters. In Cremona a riverside route leading from Via del Sale traces the floodbeds and wends past poplars and birches to Porto Polesine. North of Boario Terme lies Val Camonica, Europe's finest park of rock carvings, an "open-air museum" created by Neolithic hunters and farmers. Reached via Capo di Ponte, these sheer rock faces bear scenes of everyday life as well as magical, propitiatory drawings to appease the gods.

The Veneto and Emilia Romagna

This is varied terrain, from the watery Po Plain, a bird-watching paradise, to the Emilian Apennines, rugged hill-walking country. While the Veneto can offer both mountains and hills, the marshland and waterscapes are arguably more distinctive. However, given the relative flatness of most of the terrain, the Veneto is perfect cycling country. The regional tourist office provides clear guides outlining the best cycling itineraries, whether linked to Palladian villas, lakeside retreats and the coastal route, or giving more energetic rides through the verdant Euganean hills or the vineyard-clad slopes of Soave. The river Sile, which connects Castelfranco Veneto and Treviso with Venice, includes inviting stretches of marshland. Although sections of the nature reserve can be explored on foot, more enterprising visitors will take to canoes or *burchi*, typical flat-bottomed boats built to traverse the reed-beds. The rural route to Treviso passes mills, dams, brickworks, villas and large country estates.

The Po Delta lies in a maze of waterways between Ferrara and Ravenna. This precious nature reserve, shared between the Veneto and Emilia Romagna, and just beyond the bustling Adriatic beach resorts, is a timeless landscape characterised by shallow lagoons and dunes, mudflats, low dykes and salt pans. For those who value solitude there are opportunities to walk or cycle along the high banks of the *valli*, the fishing lagoons curled into the delta branches of the meandering river Po. The only signs of life are wealthy weekenders using the *casoni*, the shuttered fishing huts, as a base for catching eels, sea bass and flounder. The eels for which this region is famous are caught in reed-walled traps as they try to answer the call of the Sargasso Sea. The misty marshland is the preserve of herons, egrets and mallards, as well as Camargue-style white ponies.

The Emilian Apennines, within easy access of Bologna, provide rugged hill-walking country. Covering the mountains on the Tuscan border, the terrain spans sharp ridges, coppiced woodland and mysterious leafy hollows dotted with dilapidated sanctuaries. Less arduous walks traverse valleys littered with long-abandoned hamlets. In the hills are traces of the loamy platforms used by the *carbonari* who worked the soot-encrusted charcoal-burners. Walkers seeking historical trails would do well to trace the war sites along the Gothic Line *(see page 123)*.

Liguria

The rocky Ligurian coast, riddled with coves and creeks, makes for beguiling walking country, complete with spellbinding sea views. The lush landscape, sandwiched between the Alps and the Apennines, provides a backdrop of juniper, myrtle and lentisks and the scent of thyme, rosemary and lavender. The rocky hinterland provides sightings of marmots, white hares and lizards, as well as walks to mountain sanctuaries.

The Impero Valley, close to Imperia, has walks through olive groves, chestnut and oak woods. Monte di Portofino is a protected area which embraces the chic resort of Portofino. Walks through the wooded countryside afford spectacular views over the idyllic gulf and a jagged coastline rich in Mediterranean flora.

One of the loveliest walks is to the renowned abbey of San Fruttuoso.

The Cinque Terre coastal villages have the most rewarding walking trail in the region. Idle ramblers can choose to follow a short stretch of the so-called "lovers' path" that hugs the dramatic coast. Serious hikers will tackle longer stretches of the rocky coastline, travelling between the five quaint fishing villages. The arduousness of the steep slopes and sheer drops into the sea is compensated for by the sight of terraced vineyards and olive groves clinging to the hillsides. After such exhilarating sights, the relaxing boat trip to Portovenere proves a welcoming temptation for sore, tired feet. ❑

LEFT: apricot trees in blossom.
RIGHT: cherry trees abound in the fertile country of Emilia Romagna.

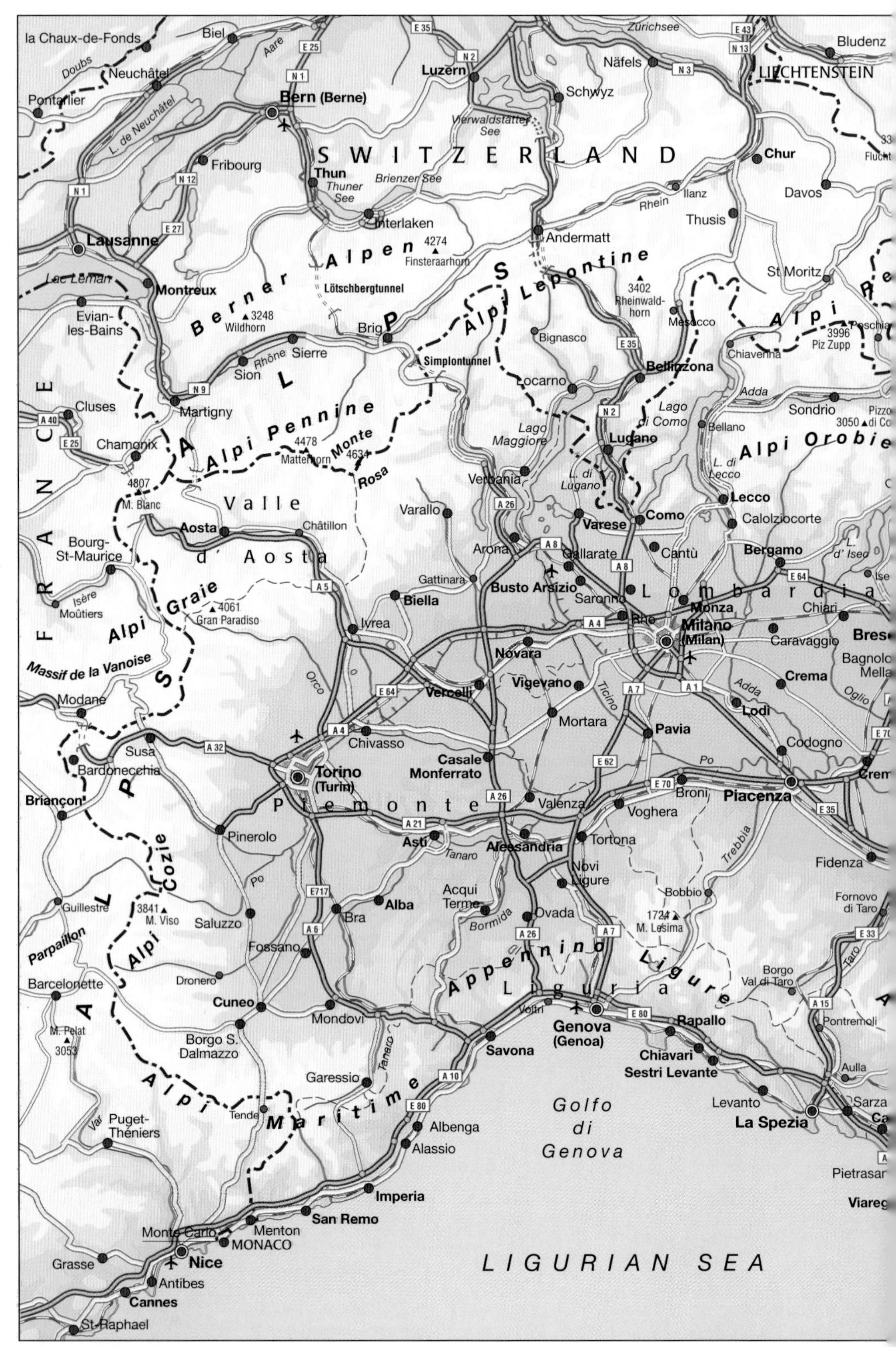
SWITZERLAND
FRANCE
LIECHTENSTEIN
MONACO
Bern (Berne)
Luzern
Näfels
Schwyz
Bludenz
Chur
Davos
Ilanz
Thusis
St Moritz
Fribourg
Thun
Thuner See
Brienzer See
Interlaken
Lausanne
Lac Léman
Montreux
Evian-les-Bains
Andermatt
Berner Alpen
4274 Finsteraarhorn
Lötschbergtunnel
3248 Wildhorn
Brig
Sierre
Sion
Rhône
Martigny
Simplontunnel
Alpi Lepontine
3402 Rheinwald-horn
Mesocco
Bignasco
Locarno
Bellinzona
Chiavenna
3996 Piz Zupp
Lago di Como
Lago Maggiore
Lugano
L. di Lugano
Bellano
Sondrio
Alpi Orobie
L. di Lecco
Lecco
Calolziocorte
Como
Varese
Cantù
Bergamo
L. d' Iseo
Cluses
Chamonix
Alpi Pennine
4478 Matterhorn
Monte Rosa 4634
4807 M. Blanc
Valle d' Aosta
Aosta
Châtillon
Varallo
Verbania
Arona
Gallarate
Busto Arsizio
Saronno
Lombardia
Monza
Rho
Milano (Milan)
Chiari
Caravaggio
Crema
Lodi
Bourg-St-Maurice
Isère
Moûtiers
Alpi Graie
4061 Gran Paradiso
Massif de la Vanoise
Gattinara
Biella
Ivrea
Novara
Vigevano
Mortara
Pavia
Ticino
Adda
Oglio
Codogno
Modane
Bardonecchia
Susa
Briançon
Chivasso
Torino (Turin)
Casale Monferrato
Vercelli
Orco
Piemonte
Valenza
Voghera
Broni
Piacenza
Po
Pinerolo
Asti
Alessandria
Tanaro
Tortona
Novi Ligure
Trebbia
Fidenza
Alpi Cozie
3841 M. Viso
Guillestre
Saluzzo
Alba
Bra
Acqui Terme
Bormida
Ovada
Bobbio
1724 M. Lesima
Fornovo di Taro
Parpaillon
Fossano
Dronero
Appennino Ligure
Liguria
Barcelonette
Cuneo
Mondovì
Borgo Val di Taro
Taro
Voltri
Genova (Genoa)
Rapallo
Pontremoli
M. Pelat 3053
Borgo S. Dalmazzo
Savona
Chiavari
Sestri Levante
Aulla
Alpi Maritime
Garessio
Tende
Puget-Théniers
Var
Albenga
Alassio
Golfo di Genova
Levanto
La Spezia
Sarza
Pietrasanta
Viareggio
Imperia
San Remo
Menton
Monte Carlo
Nice
Grasse
Antibes
Cannes
St-Raphael
LIGURIAN SEA
la Chaux-de-Fonds
Biel
Doubs
Neuchâtel
Pontarlier
L. de Neuchâtel
Aare
Zürichsee
Vierwaldstätter See
Rhein
E 35
E 25
N 1
N 2
N 3
E 43
N 13
N 12
E 27
N 9
A 40
E 25
E 35
N 2
A 26
A 8
A 4
A 5
E 64
A 7
A 1
A 32
E 62
E 70
A 21
E 717
A 6
A 26
A 7
E 80
A 10
E 80
A 15
E 33

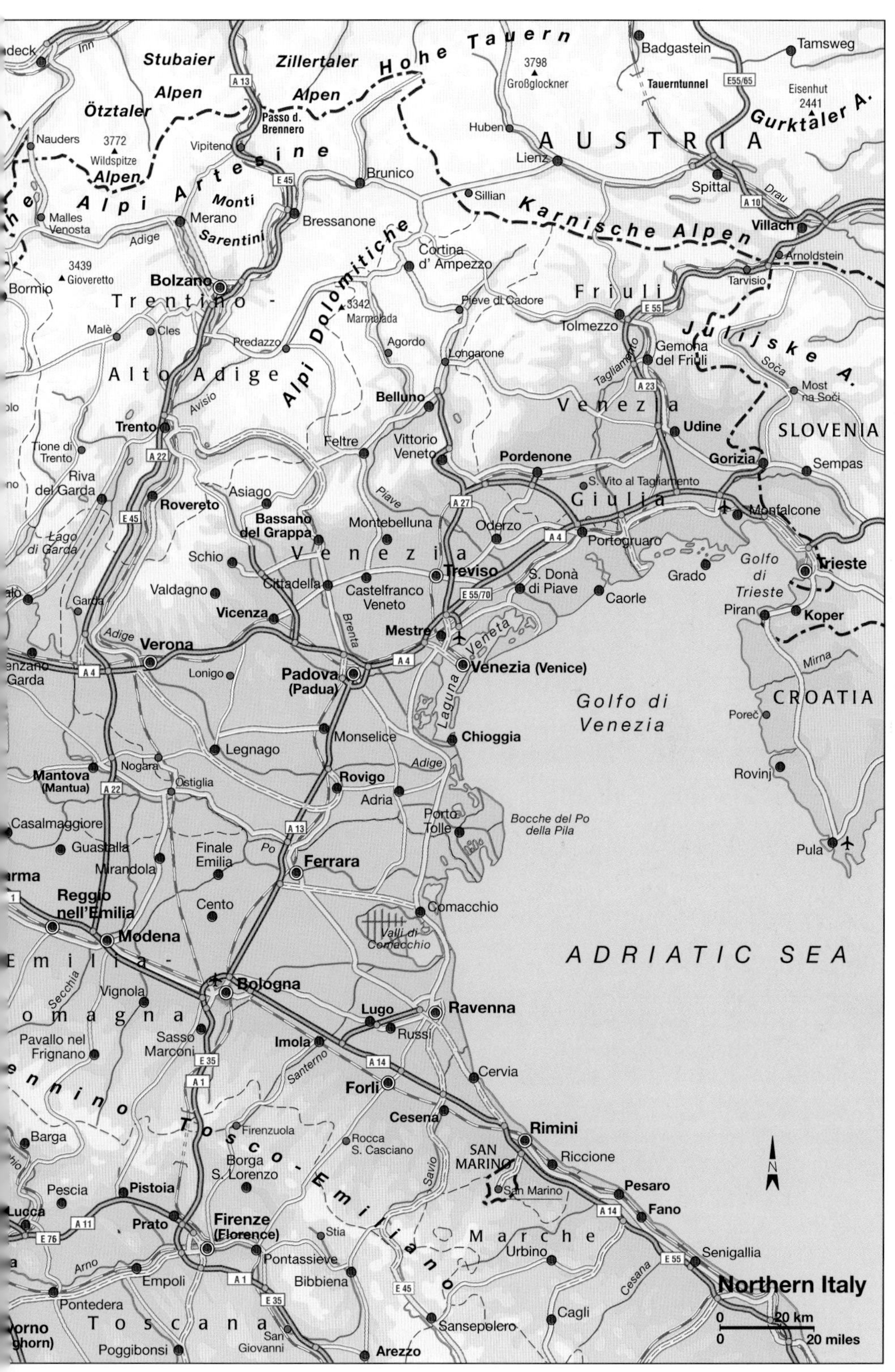
Stubaier Alpen
Zillertaler Alpen
Hohe Tauern
Ötztaler Alpen
Nauders
3772 Wildspitze
Passo d. Brennero
Vipiteno
Alpi Artesine
Monti Sarentini
Malles Venosta
Merano
Adige
Bressanone
Brunico
Sillian
Karnische Alpen
Alpi Dolomitiche
Cortina d' Ampezzo
3439 Gioveretto
Bormio
Bolzano
Trentino -
Alto Adige
3342 Marmolada
Pieve di Cadore
Malè
Cles
Predazzo
Agordo
Longarone
Belluno
Avisio
Trento
Tione di Trento
Riva del Garda
Feltre
Vittorio Veneto
Asiago
Rovereto
Bassano del Grappa
Montebelluna
Lago di Garda
Schio
Veneto
Cittadella
Castelfranco Veneto
Treviso
Valdagno
Vicenza
Garda
Verona
Mestre
Brenta
Lonigo
Padova (Padua)
Venezia (Venice)
Laguna Veneta
Monselice
Chioggia
Legnago
Nogara
Ostiglia
Mantova (Mantua)
Rovigo
Adria
Adige
Porto Tolle
Bocche del Po della Pila
Casalmaggiore
Guastalla
Mirandola
Finale Emilia
Po
Ferrara
Reggio nell'Emilia
Cento
Comacchio
Valli di Comacchio
Modena
Emilia-Romagna
Secchia
Vignola
Bologna
Lugo
Ravenna
Russi
Imola
Pavallo nel Frignano
Sasso Marconi
Santerno
Forlì
Cervia
Appennino Tosco-Emiliano
Cesena
Rimini
Riccione
Barga
Firenzuola
Rocca S. Casciano
Borgo S. Lorenzo
SAN MARINO
San Marino
Savio
Pescia
Pistoia
Pesaro
Lucca
Prato
Fano
Firenze (Florence)
Stia
Marche
Urbino
Pontassieve
Senigallia
Arno
Empoli
Bibbiena
Cesana
Pontedera
Toscana
Cagli
Livorno (Leghorn)
Poggibonsi
San Giovanni
Sansepolcro
Arezzo
Badgastein
Tamsweg
3798 Großglockner
Tauerntunnel
Eisenhut 2441
Gurktaler A.
Huben
AUSTRIA
Lienz
Spittal
Drau
Villach
Arnoldstein
Tarvisio
Friuli-Venezia Giulia
Tolmezzo
Julijske A.
Gemona del Friuli
Tagliamento
Soča
Most na Soči
Udine
SLOVENIA
Pordenone
Gorizia
Sempas
S. Vito al Tagliamento
Monfalcone
Piave
Oderzo
Portogruaro
S. Donà di Piave
Caorle
Grado
Golfo di Trieste
Trieste
Piran
Koper
Mirna
CROATIA
Poreč
Rovinj
Pula
Golfo di Venezia
ADRIATIC SEA
A 13
E 45
A 22
A 4
A 27
E 55/70
E 55/65
A 10
E 55
A 23
A 1
E 35
A 14
A 11
E 76
N
Northern Italy
0 20 km
0 20 miles

PIZZA
PASTA - SPAGHETTI
GELATI - ARTIGIANALI
DI NOSTRA PRODUZIONE
Bar Galleria

PLACES

A detailed guide to the entire region, with principal sites clearly cross-referenced by number to the maps

Despite its surface gloss and bourgeois air, northern Italy is far from being either a cohesive entity or yet another pocket of modern cosmopolitan Europe. The region's charm resides instead in its local character and customs. Sophisticated Milan may embody most visitors' preconceptions of the entrepreneurial north, but Trieste and Bolzano offer the unmistakable whiff of *Mitteleuropa* with their alpine scenery, chalets and cowbells, sauerkraut and strudel.

Since most northern regions retain their local character, this book presents places within their official demarcations. The only exceptions are the Lakes, which span several official regions but are more naturally treated a whole, and Emilia Romagna, which, given its diversity, is accorded an additional chapter dedicated to the Adriatic Coast.

As a general rule the rural north is best explored by car while, conversely, the historic cities reveal their secrets more readily to pedestrians. However, each region abounds in convenient touring bases and unusual thematic itineraries. In the Veneto, travellers can follow the Palladian villa trail or simply succumb to the romance of Romeo and Juliet in Verona. Just west, in Trentino-Alto Adige, the spectacular Great Dolomites Road links the two regions, crossing dramatic mountain scenery en route to prestigious ski resorts and scenic Tyrolean castle trails. Friuli-Venezia Giulia represents the exotic gateway to the Balkans and the Austro-Hungarian legacy evoked by Trieste. The genteel Lakes district encapsulates the best of the north, with its beguiling resorts and palatial villas. Even prosaic Lombardy has historic Bergamo and musical Cremona, not to mention Milan, the country's business, fashion and design capital.

As for the Ligurian Riviera, visitors can choose between chic Portofino and the gentrified fishing village of Camogli, while the Adriatic coast dismisses such pretensions with its brashly appealing resorts. The coherent time capsules of Bologna and Ferrara make ideal springboards for exploring the art cities of Emilia Romagna while, further north, cool Piedmont responds with the vivid contrast between Turin, Italy's suave car capital, and the mountain wildernesses and rolling vineyards of the hinterland. Asti is synonymous with sparkling Spumante, while neighbouring Barolo and Bardolino represent the region's finest red wines. Indeed, any geographical tour of northern Italy would also be a gastronomic feast, embracing wine and truffles from Piedmont, *polenta* dishes from Trentino, Milanese risotto, Venetian seafood, *tortellini* from Bologna and succulent Parma ham and Parmesan cheese from Parma. Although visitors are advised to march on their stomachs, the north is a feast for all senses. ❑

PRECEDING PAGES: summer in the Dolomites; the monastery of San Giorgio, Venice, at dusk; façade of the Duomo, Milan.
LEFT: Galleria Vittorio Emanuele, Milan.

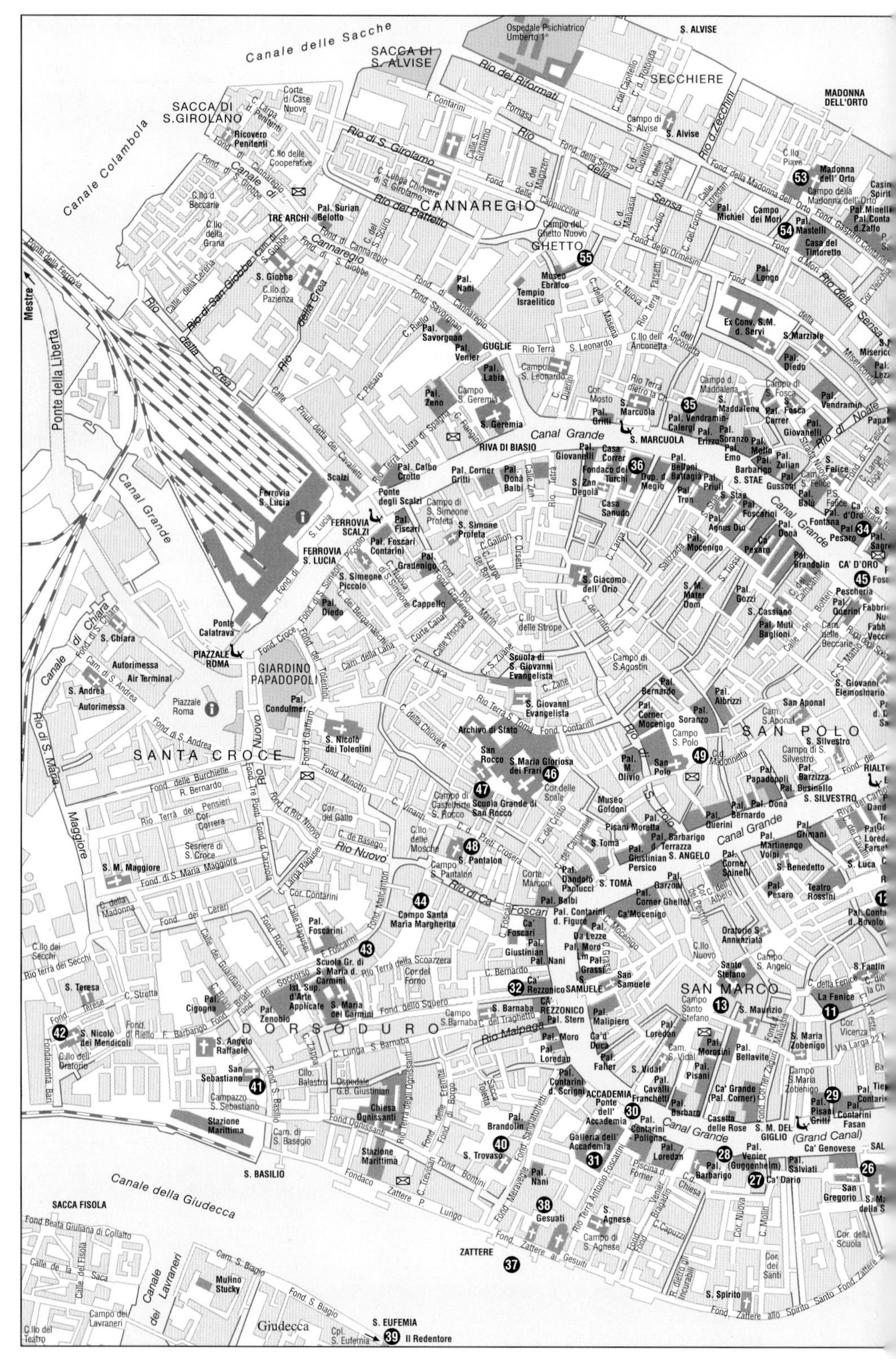

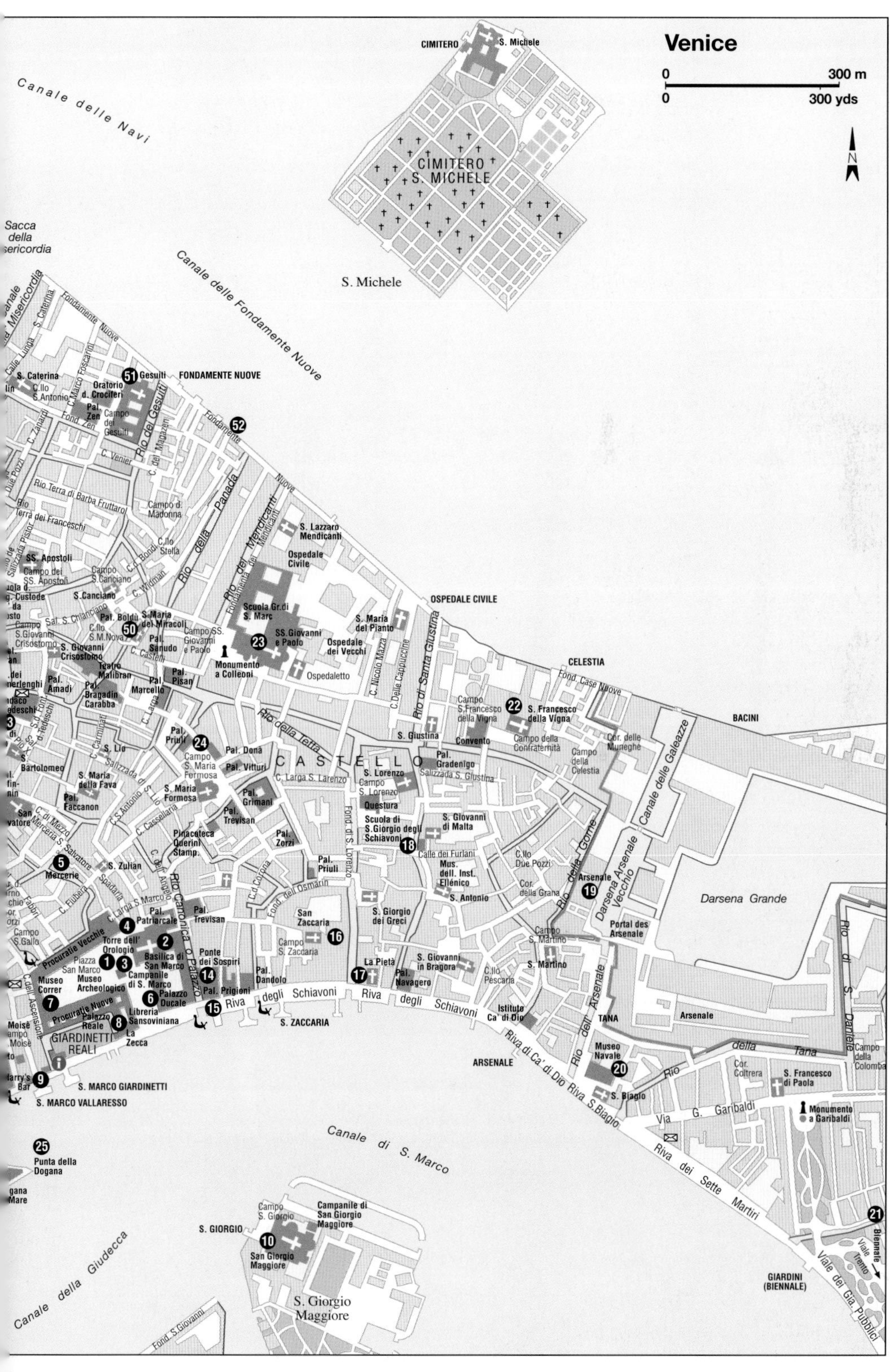
Venice
0 300 m
0 300 yds
N
Canale delle Navi
CIMITERO
S. Michele
CIMITERO S. MICHELE
Canale delle Fondamente Nuove
FONDAMENTE NUOVE
Gesuiti
OSPEDALE CIVILE
CELESTIA
BACINI
CASTELLO
Darsena Grande
Arsenale
TANA
ARSENALE
Riva degli Schiavoni
S. ZACCARIA
S. MARCO GIARDINETTI
S. MARCO VALLARESSO
Canale di S. Marco
Punta della Dogana
S. GIORGIO
San Giorgio Maggiore
S. Giorgio Maggiore
Canale della Giudecca
Via G. Garibaldi
Riva dei Sette Martiri
GIARDINI (BIENNALE)
Biennale
Viale dei Gia. Pubblici
Basilica di San Marco
Palazzo Ducale
Ponte dei Sospiri
Museo Correr
Mercerie
Scuola Gr. di S. Marc
SS. Giovanni e Paolo
Monumento a Colleoni
Teatro Malibran
Ospedale Civile
S. Francesco della Vigna
Museo Navale
Monumento a Garibaldi

VENICE

"A commercial people who lived solely for gain – how could they create a city of fantasy, lovely as a dream or a fairy tale?" – Mary McCarthy

Map on pages 140–141

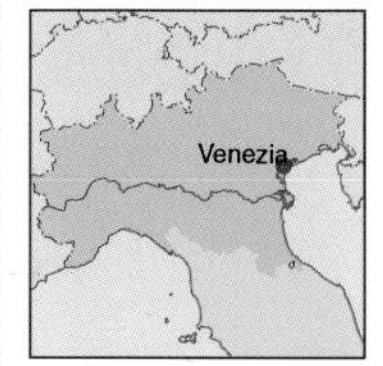

Venice is the city we have all been to, if only in our imaginations. Yet its essence remains as elusive as the slippery lagoon-dwellers themselves. Venice is a state of mind, a canvas for projecting one's poetic fantasies: there is monumental Venice and mournful Venice, domestic Venice and eclectic Venice, seductive Venice and secret Venice. In a city awash with ghosts, melancholy and nostalgia await around most dark canal corners, from Hemingway's bar to Wagner's bed, or the Jewish ghetto to the cemetery islands.

Monumental Venice dazzles with its Baroque stage sets, Palladian churches and Gothic palaces; eclectic Venice beguiles with Byzantine mosaics and carnival capers; seductive Venice can go serenading in the grandest cafés or catch one unawares in a wisteria-clad garden. Henry James gives us domestic Venice: "a narrow canal in the heart of the city, a patch of green water and a surface of pink wall, a great shabby façade of Gothic windows and balconies".

Yet even this fails to do justice to this watery chimera of a city, with its mercurial climate, shimmering light and mood of impermanence. The physical uniqueness of Venice can only be felt, not described.

LEFT: fishing nets in the lagoon.
BELOW: a gondolier.

A living museum

In a city that provokes possessive passion, tourism is almost as ancient as Venice itself. "His gondolier, being in league with various lacemakers and glassblowers, did his best to persuade his fare to pause." Even in Thomas Mann's Venice, the fleecing of tourists was part of the Venetian experience.

Although traditionally cosmopolitan and tolerant, Venetians will admit to an impatience with mass tourism; nor do they wish to live in a museum but in a living city. To them, Venice is not a frozen expression of beauty but an everyday affair of neighbourhood cafés and fish markets, gondolas and garbage barges. A Venetian élite may still meet to strains of Vivaldi at the fireside of a freshly gilded salon. Yet most Venetians prefer a prosaic stroll and a meal out: understandable when a stroll encompasses more magic and drama than are available on the formal stage. Proust best captures the poetic and prosaic nature of a place in which "the simplest social coming and going assumes at the same time the form and charm of a visit to a museum and a trip to the sea".

San Marco

Venice is traditionally divided into six *sestieri* (districts), a practice followed here, with the addition of the Grand Canal, which winds its way through the heart of the city. An astonishing 50 percent of visitors fail to stray further than St Mark's Square. Yet, unlike

The Lion of St Mark.

many official city squares, **Piazza San Marco** ❶ belongs to the citizens as well as to visitors; Venetians drink at the grand cafés, even if they often save money by standing up, and some may attend Mass at the Basilica or even dance at the open-air Carnival. However, for most of the day, St Mark's belongs to the pigeons, crowds and souvenir-sellers; only in early evening does it revert to a semblance of solitude. Piazza San Marco has acted as the heart of the Republic ever since the earliest settlement shifted from Torcello to central Venice. Yet Venetian notions of glory caused it to be remodelled in Renaissance times, with such success that it was later famously dubbed "the finest drawing room in Europe" by Napoleon. Like many visitors to Venice, he then proceeded to repaint it in his own image, even rearranging the furniture and literally moving the walls. However, given the city's talent for fusing influences into a beguiling Venetian whole, the square has retained its essential character.

In spite of high prices, visitors to Venice should not spurn San Marco's opulent cafés. With their string quartets and pretentious airs, they are part of the performance art that is Venice. Each café has its charms: **Caffè Quadri** basks in the morning sun and an 18th-century ambience, while **Caffè Florian**, its more celebrated rival, lies in the shade until noon; **Caffè Lavena** serves the best coffee without the beau-monde atmosphere. Even out of season, these historic haunts captivate, as one sips cocktails or Prosecco amid elegant stucco-work, red damask walls, Murano chandeliers and gilded mirrors.

Basilica di San Marco (St Mark's Basilica) ❷ (open Mon–Sat 9.30am–5pm, Sun 2–4pm; daily from 7am for worshippers; due to strict security measures all bags now need to be left in the Ateneo San Basso on Piazzetta dei Leoncini – a free left-luggage service) is the centrepiece of the square. The

BELOW: Basilica di San Marco.

SAVING VENICE

Floods have become a way of life in Venice, and the city faces a soggy future. As global warming continues and sea levels rise, Venice has been subjected to increasing flooding. Its position at the head of the lagoon also makes the city vulnerable to storm surges. Until recently the most posited solution to the problem was the installation of flood gates which would span the three entrances to the lagoon and be closed whenever high waters threatened.

But the scheme faltered on environmental grounds. In 1999 the government decided that it risked undermining the lagoon's fragile ecosystem: by being shut off from the sea too often the lagoon would be turned into a quagmire. Instead, experts favoured raising the ground level of the city and cleaning waters polluted by industrial waste and maritime traffic. However, supporters of the Hose dam project have not given up. As the head of a European Union research body declared: "Do you prevent the lagoon from turning into a lake or do you save Venice and its historic heritage? Personally, I would save Venice."

However, the Mayor of Venice believes that subconsciously the international community does not wish to save Venice: "From Byron to Mann to Woody Allen, they have all hankered after Atlantis."

façade of the Basilica is currently being restored. San Marco, modelled on Byzantine churches in Constantinople, transposes the essence of an eastern basilica to the West. Indeed, to critic Mary McCarthy it was "an oriental pavilion, half pleasure house, half war tent, belonging to some great satrap". Charles Dickens was spellbound: "Opium couldn't build such a place... dim with the smoke of incense; costly in treasure of precious stones and metals; glittering through iron bars; holy with the bodies of deceased saints." The Basilica was consecrated in 832, intended as a mausoleum for St Mark's relics and as the Doge's ceremonial chapel. In 976 the church burnt down after a riot but was rebuilt between 1063 and 1094, probably supervised by a Greek architect. Since Venice still recognised the cultural supremacy of Byzantium, the Basilica echoed eastern models. At the same time, Doge Selvo (1071–84) asked merchants to return with rare marbles and semi-precious stones to adorn the Basilica.

The Greek-cross plan is inscribed in a square, and crowned by a cluster of five cupolas, one over each arm of the cross and its centre. These are linked to one another by loggias and arcades. The bewildering contrast is between the oriental domes and rounded Byzantine arches and the Gothic ornamentation of the central roofline. Most of the garish mosaics on the façade are 17th-century copies, with the only intact 13th-century one depicting the arrival of St Mark's relics in the Basilica (set above the doorway on the far left). The exterior brickwork of the central apse is reminiscent of Santa Fosca in Torcello. The Baptistry doors are framed by the **Pilasters of Acre**, two ancient Syrian pillars plundered from Acre in the Holy Land after a victory over the Genoese in 1258. These 6th-century sculpted marble columns stand beside a porphyry stump known as the *pietra del bando*, where the laws of the Republic were proclaimed. In the cor-

Map on pages 140–141

Carved detail, St Mark's central door.

BELOW: view from the Campanile.

During the summer, visitors to the Basilica are channelled along set routes – to linger long is virtually impossible. Although it is open for worshippers from 7am, tourists are not allowed access until after 9.45am. The best option is to arrive early or late.

ner are the **Tetrarchs** or Moors, a 4th-century Egyptian work representing Diocletian and his fellow rulers who governed the Roman Empire.

After the conquest of Constantinople in 1204, Venice celebrated with a display of looted treasures. The **horses** were Byzantine booty and once stood atop a triumphal arch in Rome before gracing the hippodrome in Constantinople and adorning the façade of San Marco; because they symbolised the Venetian Republic's independence, Napoleon had them harnessed to a chariot in Paris for 18 years. Now returned, the originals are displayed in the **Biblioteca Nazionale Marciana** (open daily 9am–7pm), with copies on the façade.

Other plundered treasures include the **Madonna Nicopeia**, a sacred 10th-century icon adorning the Altar of the Virgin. Officially, St Mark's remains are encased in a sarcophagus under the altar, but sceptics believe that they were destroyed in the fire of 976. Behind the altar, often swamped by crowds, is the **Pala d'Oro**, a superb Byzantine altarpiece studded with gems. The **Treasury** incorporates a 9th-century corner tower from the first Doge's Palace and displays Byzantine gold, silver and glassware.

The interior is studded with **mosaics**, one of the chief glories of San Marco and amongst the most superb Byzantine examples in Italy. They date from 1071, and were first created by craftsmen from Constantinople; while the majority are from the 11th century to the 14th, more continued to be added until the 18th century. The result is an illustrated Bible using 4,000 square metres (43,000 sq. ft) of mosaic. Even the windows of this extravaganza were walled up to make more space for mosaics. As a rule of thumb, the lower walls depict saints, with the middle section featuring the Apostles, and the domes dedicated to Christ Pantocrator, the Ruler of All. The Basilica pavement is an oriental carpet

BELOW: the distinctive stonework of the Palazzo Ducale.

interweaving floral, animal and geometric motifs. The mosaics of marble, porphyry and glass depict allegorical and naturalistic scenes.

A striking feature of the square is the **Campanile** ❸ (open daily July–Aug 9am–9pm, Apr–June and Sept–Oct 9am–7pm, Nov and Mar 9am–4pm), a replica of the original tower that collapsed in 1902. From the top – accessible by lift – there is a superb view across the city and lagoon to the Dolomites, even if the canals themselves are not visible. In the past, foreigners were only permitted to climb the tower at high tide to prevent them from espying secret navigational channels.

The piazza's other tower is the Renaissance **Torre dell'Orologio** ❹ (1496), still under lengthy restorations, which boasts a gilt-and-blue-enamel clockface featuring the signs of the zodiac and the phases of the moon.

Behind the Clocktower, keen shoppers can plunge into the **Mercerie** ❺, the shadowy maze of alleys running between the Rialto and San Marco. Named after the haberdashers' shops that once lined the route, this engaging bazaar specialises in marbled paper, Murano glass and carnival masks. The church-filled squares radiating from the Mercerie include Campo San Salvatore whose cloisters are now home to the Telecom Italia Future Centre, (www.futurecentre.telecomitalia.it), charting the advances in information technology.

Map on pages 140–141

The clockface on the Torre dell'Orologio.

The Doge's Palace

The **Palazzo Ducale (Doge's Palace)** ❻ (open daily Apr–Oct 9am–7pm, Nov–Mar 9am–5pm) was the seat of the Venetian government from the 9th century until the fall of the Republic in 1797. Yet while rival mainland cities were building grim fortresses, the Venetians indulged in a light and airy structure, confident of the natural protection afforded by the lagoon. Apart from

BELOW: the Palazzo Ducale is a magnificent showcase of Venetian art and craftmanship.

The secret itinerary (itinerari segreti) *offered at the Doge's Palace explores the "shadow palace", with its secret passageways, state inquisitors' room, torture chamber, prisons and Piombi – "heads" from where Casanova made his escape in 1755 (open Apr–Oct daily at 10am and 11.30am in English; at other times in Italian or French).*

being the Doge's official residence it acted as the nerve centre of the Republic, containing offices and armouries, council chambers and chancellery, courtrooms and dungeons. The Palace was a symbol of political stability and independence as well as a testament to Venetian supremacy and a glorious showcase of Venetian art, sculpture and craftsmanship. Yet there was also a shadow palace, a secretive machine with state inquisitors, spies and torturers in residence.

Architecturally the palace is a Venetian hybrid, a harmonious fusion of Moorish, Gothic and Renaissance. Although often considered the symbol of Gothic Venice, the palace's distinctive façades, recently restored, were inspired by the Veneto-Byzantine succession of porticoes and loggias. However, the Gothic inversion of spaces and solids reached perfection in the floriated style of the southern corner, with a mass of masonry seemingly floating on air. The palace has two of the finest Gothic façades in existence, visions of rosy Verona marble supported by delicate Istrian stone arcades.

The recently revamped **interior** is magnificent, but visitors are usually channelled along specific routes. Many of the carved capitals on the portico were replaced by 19th-century copies, but the restored originals can now be seen in the **Museo dell'Opera** beside the entrance hall, set in the former prisons. The rooms reveal the inner workings of the Serene Republic, from the voting procedures to the courts of law. The Scala d'Oro, designed by Sansovino in 1555, was a ceremonial staircase intended to overawe ambassadors.

Museo Correr ❼ (open daily 9am–7pm), the museum of Venetian civilisation, is housed in the Procuratie Nuove, with the entrance in the Napoleonic Wing. The Neoclassical rooms make a fitting setting for Canova's sculptures. The first section is a romp through Venetian history, from Doges' caps to the fall of the Republic. Those without a taste for coins and battle memorabilia can proceed to the charming gallery, which focuses on 13th–16th century Venetian art. Near by, the Biblioteca Nazionale Marciana, also known as **Libreria Sansoviniana** ❽ (open daily 9am–7pm; for a full tour tel: 041-5208788), is a cool classical building set in an extended loggia. Designed by Sansovino in 1537, this long, low building houses the precious collection of manuscripts bequeathed by Petrarch in the 14th century. The superb salon of the original library is covered with paintings by Veronese and Tintoretto. Just west, on Calle Vallaresso, is **Harry's Bar** ❾, the world-famous watering hole where the Bellini cocktail was invented.

By boat, the island of **San Giorgio Maggiore** ❿ lies just a few minutes away. Seen from afar, the majestic Benedictine monastery appears suspended in the inner lagoon. Today the monks remain the sole island residents, enhancing the mood of spiritual seclusion. **San Giorgio** (open daily 9.30am–12.30pm, 2.30–6.30pm) is the finest monastic church in the lagoon. Here Palladio showed his mastery of the classical idiom, using the basic geometric volumes of cube, pyramid and sphere. Based on Alberti's precepts, this is a Christian church founded on classical principles and mathematical proportions. The façade is composed of two overlapping temple fronts, with a central portico. For fabulous views, a lift whisks visitors to the top of the **belltower**, modelled on St Mark's.

BELOW: Bocca di Leone, Palazzo Ducale.

From the ashes

A few minutes from San Marco is **La Fenice** ⓫, the legendary opera house. Destroyed by fire in 1996, "the Phoenix" finally rose from the ashes in December 2003, and Verdi's *La Traviata* officially reopened the tiny theatre in 2004 – a symbolic opera since it received its world premiere in the same place in 1853.

Palazzo Contarini del Bovolo ⓬ (open daily 10am–6pm), concealed in a maze of alleys off Campo Manin, is a late Gothic palace celebrated for its 15th-century arcaded staircase. *Bovolo*, meaning snail shell in Venetian dialect, describes the delightful spiral staircase which is linked to loggias of brick and smooth white stone. Near by is **Campo Santo Stefano** ⓭, a long, theatrical space lined with palaces and cafés. The Augustinian monastic church of **Santo Stefano** has a Gothic main portal and an entrancing ship's-keel ceiling; a canal flows under the church, which gondolas can pass along if the tide is low.

Map on pages 140–141

The famous Ponte dei Sospiri (the Bridge of Sighs).

Castello

If St Mark's Square is the drawing room of Europe, in Napoleon's celebrated phrase, then **Riva degli Schiavoni** is its sumptuous bedroom. The waterfront is awash with cultural links, reminders of famous past residents, from Wagner and Tchaikovsky to Dickens. But sailors, shipwrights and merchants also came here, from Dalmatia, Eastern Europe, Greece and Egypt, attracted by the prospect of work at the Arsenale shipyards and quaysides. The cosmopolitan legacy lingers on in sizeable Greek and Slav communities as well as a small Armenian quarter. The sights are scattered, with much space occupied by the Arsenale, whose looming walls and towers are visible from afar.

Ponte dei Sospiri ⓮, the most famous bridge in Venice, crosses the canal to

BELOW: San Giorgio Maggiore.

Part of the city's impeccable front.

the "new" prisons. Built between 1595 and 1600, the Bridge of Sighs provided a link between the Doge's Palace and the courtrooms and cells, allowing interrogators to slip back and forth. This covered stone bridge acquired its legendary name from the lamentation of prisoners as they confronted their inquisitors.

The bridge marks the beginning of **Riva degli Schiavoni** ⓯, the best-known stretch of Venetian waterfront. Now crowded with tourists and souvenir-sellers, this quayside once thronged with slave-dealers and merchants. (Its name refers to either slaves or Slavs, who were often synonymous in Venetian minds.) The quayside was widened and paved in 1782 and has been a popular Venetian promenade ever since. Over the bridge stands a horseback monument to **Vittorio Emanuele** (Victor Emmanuel), the first king of a united Italy.

San Zaccaria ⓰ (open 10am–noon, 4–6pm, closed Sun), set on the Campo of the same name, is a Renaissance masterpiece graced by Coducci's curvilinear façade and a Gothic belltower. The church was founded in the 9th century and acted as a Venetian pantheon, with eight early Doges buried in the crypt. The original Byzantine basilica forms the crypt below San Tarasio chapel, an atmospheric spot usually lying under water. The chapel itself is decorated with Gothic frescoes and several lovely 15th-century altarpieces. In the north aisle of the main Gothic church is a glowing altarpiece by Bellini.

A stroll along bustling Riva degli Schiavoni leads past waterfront cafés to the newly restored **La Pietà** ⓱ (open 9.30am–noon, 4–6pm), Vivaldi's (1678–1741) musical base in Venice. The church was superbly remodelled by Massari in the 18th century and transformed into the city's leading concert hall. The cool oval interior was designed with acoustics in mind, aided by curving lines, low vaulted ceilings and the filigree-like choir galleries. The church is a feast for the senses, with Tiepolo's celebrated frescoes best seen during a concert of Baroque music.

BELOW: gondolas on the Canale Grande.

Tucked into Calle dei Furlani, **San Giorgio degli Schiavoni** ⓲ (open Tues–Sat 9.30am–12.30pm, 3.30–6.30pm, Sun 9.30am–12.30pm) is the loveliest confraternity seat in Venice. Dating back to the Middle Ages, these *scuole* were charitable lay associations close to the heart of Venetian life. This one was intended to protect the interests of Slavs from Dalmatia (Schiavonia), the first Venetian colony. On its completion in 1501 the confraternity commissioned Carpaccio to create a painting cycle in honour of the Dalmatian patron saints. The *scuola* boasts the only Venetian pictorial cycle to have survived in its original site. This cycle is characterised by dramatic storytelling. In particular, the St George paintings are bold chivalric scenes, depicting a veritable knight in shining armour and a dying dragon in a place of desolation, with the ground littered with skulls, vipers and vultures.

Further east along Riva degli Schiavoni is the vast expanse of the **Arsenale** ⓳. As the *vaporetto* no longer runs through this closed military zone, the best way to see the Arsenale is to get off at the *vaporetto* stop Arsenale, on the Riva degli Schiavoni, and stroll down to the wooden bridge that stands opposite the entrance to the heart of the naval complex. From the middle of the bridge you get a good view. Founded in 1104, the Arsenale was the symbol of Venetian maritime might. This secretive military and naval complex became the largest medieval shipyard in Europe and a powerhouse of industrial planning. It was also an armaments site. The oldest part is the **Darsena Vecchio**, sandwiched between St Mark's Basin and the lagoon. The complex remained in continuous use until 1917, when the dockyards were dismantled lest they fall into enemy hands. Since then the Italian navy has been ensconced, with the dockyards used as a storage and repair site.

On the waterfront stands the **Museo Navale** ⓴ (open Mon–Sat 8.45am–1.30pm, closed Sun). Apart from naval maps, nautical instruments and weaponry, the intriguing collection displays models of Egyptian and Phoenician craft and Greek triremes. The Venetian focus is naturally on gondolas and galleys, but includes a replica of the last Bucintoro, the legendary state barge. Near by, the **Giardini Pubblici** are the permanent location of the **Biennale** ㉑, a glamorous summer forum for contemporary art. The Biennale has been held in these Napoleonic gardens in odd-numbered years from June–Sept since 1895. Described as Disneyland for adults, the event is garish, sprawling and pretentious but also chic and challenging. The gardens are home to about 40 permanent pavilions representing as many different countries.

San Francesco della Vigna ㉒ (open daily 8am–noon, 3.30–7pm) is set in an isolated, somewhat shabby area. Goethe even required a compass to reach this remote spot. However, this Franciscan church represents an architectural milestone: both Sansovino's first creation in Venice and the first flowering of the High Renaissance in Venice. The façade and crowning pediment were designed by Palladio, and the tall belltower is a familiar city landmark.

SS Giovanni e Paolo ㉓, known as **San Zanipolo**, (open Mon–Sat 7.30am–

Map on pages 140–141

The waterfront is the location of Venice's finest hotels, like the Danieli. Even Proust was enchanted by his room here: "When I went to Venice I found that my dream had become – incredibly but quite simply – my address." The hotel's terrace is still a superb place to toast the end of a war or the beginning of a romance.

BELOW: Riva degli Schiavoni.

"Like some great lady on the threshold of her salon… with her domes and scrolls, her scalloped buttresses and statues forming a pompous crown, and her wide steps disposed on the ground like the train of a robe."

– HENRY JAMES
(Description of La Salute)

12.30pm, 3–6.30pm, Sun 3–7pm) is set on the square of the same name. Guarding the great Gothic church is the finest equestrian statue in northern Italy. This restless horse and rider commemorate Bartolomeo Colleoni (1400–76), a celebrated *condottiere*. The church is dedicated to Saints John and Paul, and its sheer scale invites comparisons with the Frari, its fellow giant. San Zanipolo, too, is an austere church, founded in the late 13th century but only consecrated in 1430. Its Gothic pinnacles can be seen from both banks of the Grand Canal, with the roofline displaying statues of the Dominican saints. The church is the Pantheon of Venice, honouring illustrious leaders from admirals and noblemen to the odd artist. Above all, this was the last resting place of the Doges, with magnificent monuments to 25 of them, including the sculpted Renaissance tomb of Doge Giovanni Mocenigo.

Campo Santa Maria Formosa ㉔ is a lovely asymmetrical space dotted with flower, fruit and junk stalls. Set in the heart of Castello, it is the archetypal Venetian square. The *campo* rests on its laurels, sure of each Venetian element: the shadowy alleys running into a sunlit space; a striking Renaissance church; palaces from three different periods; a covered well-head surrounded by pigeons; everyday cafés filled with stallholders; even a gondola station *(stazio)*. The Renaissance parish church of **Santa Maria Formosa** (open Mon–Sat 10am–5pm, Sun 1–5pm) is an endearing sight, with its bulging apse and Baroque belltower.

Grand Canal (Canale Grande)

The Grand Canal was considered the register of the Venetian nobility, with the palaces symbolising patricians' status and success. Once a waterway for merchant vessels, the canal now welcomes simpler craft, from gondolas to garbage barges. The palaces remain as a testament to the city's imperial past, but the sea is a great leveller, with low tide revealing the slimy underpinnings of the noblest *palazzo*. The palaces represent a subtle fusion of styles: a Gothic design may be graced with round Renaissance arches and pilasters, while a sweep of oriental tracery echoes the Byzantine tradition.

BELOW: the magnificent interior of the palace of Ca' Rezzonico.

Known affectionately as the *Canalazzo*, the Grand Canal makes an appealing evening diversion. After most tourists have returned to the mainland is the ideal time for a leisurely look. Pick up a No. 1 *vaporetto* and slip into one of the coveted seats on the prow. The palaces present a seductive face: the illuminated windows, revealing gleaming Murano glass chandeliers, red silk-clad walls and the odd summer party spilling onto the balconies are an invitation to dream.

Day or night, **Punta della Dogana** ㉕ is the start of a popular Venetian walk around the point. **Dogana di Mare**, the sea customs post, occupies the triangular tip where ships and cargoes were inspected before being allowed to drop anchor in front of the Doge's Palace. Still used as a customs house, this is the only Republican civic building to have maintained its original function. Guarding the entrance to the Grand Canal is the Baroque basilica of **La Salute** ㉖ (open daily 9am–5.30pm). Officially dedicated to the Madonna, the church was begun in 1631 as a thanksgiving for delivery from the plague. Longhena, the architect, wished it to be "strange, worthy and beautiful", and succeeded magnificently. La Salute marks the end of Venetian Mannerism and heralds an era of bold Baroque statements. Devised before Rome's Bernini and Borromini masterpieces, it became one of the few Italian churches to challenge the supremacy of Roman Baroque. The clinical interior boasts a spectacular central plan, with its revolutionary octagonal space surmounted by a huge dome.

Another waterside landmark is the gently listing **Ca' Dario** ㉗, one of the most delightful palaces on the canal. Henry James adored the façade for its intricate pattern of roundels and plaques of precious marble and porphyry. Known as a *cielo-terra*, a self-contained structure, it is only accessible by water or through a door in the walled garden. However, five centuries of scandals, suicides and suspicious deaths have left Venetians wary of this unfortunate palace which lies empty. Next door, **Palazzo Venier** ㉘ is a white, truncated structure also known as "*Nonfinito*" (unfinished). Legend has it that the owners of Ca' Grande opposite forbade further building as it would block their view.

The building now houses the **Peggy Guggenheim Collection** (open 10am–6pm, later in summer, closed Tues), named after the American modern-art collector Peggy Guggenheim (1898–1979). On show is work by such names as Chagall, Dalí, Klee, Braque, Giacometti, Kandinsky, Bacon and Sutherland. Most major movements are represented, from Picasso's Cubist period to Severini's Futurism, from Mondrian's Abstract works to Surrealist masterpieces by de Chirico, Delvaux and Magritte. The gardens are filled with sculptures, including works by Henry Moore and Marino Marini, whose *Angel of the Citadel* sports a provocative erection – often concealed by the closed watergates.

Virtually opposite is the **Palazzo Pisani Gritti** ㉙, a legendary Venetian hotel,

Map on pages 140–141

To ponder on the ghosts of Venice, choose from the sophisticated stage sets at the glitziest hotels: the Gritti Palace, overlooking the Grand Canal, was one of Hemingway's haunts; or the Art Deco Hôtel des Bains, where Visconti shot Death in Venice.

BELOW: the famous Grand Canal (Canale Grande).

An example of Venetian Gothic – Villa Barbaro, where Henry James stayed.

also known as the Gritti Palace. The Gritti terrace offers a grandstand view of the Grand Canal, lying diagonally opposite the church of La Salute. This is one of the most sumptuous hotels in Venice, linked to writers as diverse as Hemingway and Graham Greene.

The **Accademia** ㉚ is a popular meeting-place. The distinctive wooden bridge, built in 1932 and restored in the 1980s, replaced a cast-iron bridge dating from the time of the Austrian occupation. Beside it is the Accademia boat stop, with the world's greatest collection of Venetian paintings in the **Galleria dell'Accademia** ㉛ (open Mon 8.30am–2pm, Tues–Sun 8.30am–7pm), the city's most popular gallery. The collection is housed in La Carità, a complex of church, convent, cloisters and charitable confraternity. Since the gallery is lit by natural light, it is best to choose a bright day. Early rooms display Byzantine and Gothic works noted for their symmetry and static decorative style on a gold background. The masterpieces include Renaissance and Mannerist works by Carpaccio, Bellini, Giorgione, Titian, Tintoretto and Veronese, and 17th- and 18th-century works by Tiepolo, Guardi and Canaletto.

Ca' Rezzonico ㉜ recently restored to its former glory, lies on the left bank, by the boat stop of the same name. Designed according to Longhena's plans, this ponderous Baroque palace was where the poet Robert Browning (1812–89) died. This is probably Venice's most famous *palazzo* and one of the few open to the public on the Grand Canal. Inside, the **Museum of 18th-Century Life** (open 10am–6pm, closed Tues) is an opulent showcase for Tiepolo's *trompe l'oeil* ceilings and Guardi's 18th-century genre paintings. The interior is magnificent: boldly restored, daringly frescoed and richly embellished with glittering chandeliers and period pieces.

BELOW: the quayside near the Ponte di Rialto is home to numerous cafés and restaurants.

Ponte di Rialto (33), which traditionally divides the city into two, was the only bridge across the Grand Canal until 1854. The single-span bridge, created in 1588–91 by Antonio da Ponte, is lined with shops selling shoes, silk scarves and jewellery. The quaysides where iron, coal and barrels of wine used to be unloaded are now overrun by restaurants and souvenir stalls.

Beyond is the **Ca' d'Oro** (34), home to the Franchetti Gallery, among the city's top galleries (open Mon 8.15am–2pm, Tues–Sun 8.15am–7.15pm), one of the loveliest Gothic palaces, set beside the landing stage of the same name. The Veneto-Byzantine influence is clear in the design, from the oriental pinnacles to the ethereal tracery. On the sumptuous façade the friezes of foliage and mythological beasts were originally picked out in gold, giving it its popular name "the golden house". Inside, the artistic highlights include a delightful *Annunciation* by Carpaccio, Titian's *Venus*, and Andrea Mantegna's poignant *St Sebastian*.

Palazzo Vendramin-Calergi (35), on the same bank of the canal, was inhabited by aristocrats, Doges and even Wagner (who died here), before becoming the city casino. Although built before 1500 by Coducci, the palace was inspired by classical principles and built in a three-part design. The casino has coffered ceilings, chandeliers and marble fireplaces, and jasper columns looted from Ephesus in Turkey. Opposite is the **Fondaco dei Turchi** (36), a former trading base for Turkish merchants, whose **Museum of Natural History** (open Sat–Sun 10am–4pm) has been refurbished, but only the dinosaur section and aquarium are open, together with an ecological presentation of the lagoon. It was built in 1227 for the Pesaro family, but in 1621 was leased to the Ottomans, who created bedrooms, shops and servants' quarters. In keeping with Muslim custom, doors and windows were sealed off, and the building contained a mosque and Turkish baths.

Map on pages 140–141

The church of San Simeone Piccolo has now been upstaged by a fourth bridge over the Grand Canal, the only one to be illuminated at night. Connecting the station with the road terminal, this new, elegant bridge was designed by the Spanish architect Calatrava.

BELOW: the Ca' d'Oro.

Carnival masks – the perfect souvenir of the theatricality of Venice.

Dorsoduro

Dorsoduro is the most charming quarter for idle wandering, with wisteria-clad walls, secret gardens and distinctive domestic architecture. Its name simply means "hard back", since the district occupies the largest area of firm land in Venice. This is the chicest *sestiere*, with the grandest section defined by the Punta della Dogana, the Gesuati and the Accademia.

The **Zattere** ㊲ stretches all the way round Dorsoduro's southern shore, with its quaysides flanked by cafés and churches, boathouses and warehouses. This promenade was created in 1516 and named after the cargoes of wood that were unloaded here (*zattere* are floating rafts). Its southern spur makes the most beguiling Venetian promenade, bracing in winter and refreshing in summer.

Further along the Zattere stands the grandiose church of the **Gesuati** ㊳ (open Mon–Sat 10am–5pm, Sun 1–5pm), a supreme example of 18th-century Venetian architecture. The façade, with its lofty Corinthian columns and Palladian motifs, was designed by Massari, an early Rococo architect. The theatrical interior boasts illusionistic Tiepolo frescoes (1739), visible in their original setting.

The **Zattere boarding stage** lies on this stretch of quays, with ferries to San Marco and the Giudecca. Set on the island of Giudecca, **Il Redentore** ㊴ (open Mon–Sat 10am–5pm, Sun 1–5pm) is a Venetian landmark. The Church of the Redeemer was built in thanksgiving for the end of the 1576 plague. Architectural purists feel that this Palladian masterpiece, inspired by the Pantheon in Rome, surpasses San Giorgio. Certainly, the façade is more subtle, resting on a rusticated pediment, with a sweeping flight of steps. From here, the eye is led to the lantern surmounted by the figure of Christ the Redeemer.

BELOW: the Palladian splendour of the church of Il Redentore, on the island of Giudecca.

From the Zattere it is a short stroll to **San Trovaso** ㊵ (open Mon–Sat 3–6pm), set on the canal of the same name. The medieval church was remodelled at the end of the 16th century in Palladian style. Opposite is the Cantinone Giá Schiavi, an atmospheric old wine bar. The **Squero di San Trovaso**, a picturesque gondola repair yard, is best viewed from further down the canal.

Following the Zattere westwards leads to **San Sebastiano** ㊶ (open Mon–Sat 10am–5pm), an early 16th-century church which is a classical canvas for Veronese's opulent masterpieces, painted between 1555 and 1565. The church is praised as a perfect marriage of the arts, with architecture, painting and sculpture in complete accord. Veronese's *trompe l'oeil* interior is an architectural flight of fancy created by frescoed loggias, columns and statues.

San Nicolò dei Mendicoli ㊷ (open Mon–Sat 10am–noon, 4–6pm) is the most remote waterside church in Dorsoduro. It is one of the oldest in Venice, founded in the 7th century but remodelled between the 12th and 14th centuries. The interior is one of the best-loved, with a single nave ending in a Romanesque apse and embellished with Renaissance panelling and gilded statues.

I Carmini ㊸ (open Mon–Sat 9am–4pm, Sun 9am–1pm) is the headquarters of the Carmelite Scuola Grande. Longhena's uninspired façade conceals a frescoed 18th-century interior. The Carmelites prospered during the Counter-Reformation and could

Map on pages 140–141

afford to summon the services of the greatest Rococo painter. Tiepolo repaid their confidence with a series of sensuous masterpieces. Classical concerts are given here periodically. Just beyond lies the lively **Campo Santa Maria Margherita** ㊹. One side of the square is bordered by palaces with overhanging roofs, a style rare in Venice both because of the fear of fire and through a desire to let light into dark alleys.

San Polo and Santa Croce

Centred on the bustling Rialto market, these adjoining districts *(sestieri)* are curved into the left bank of the Grand Canal. The hub of the left bank is the Rialto, "the marketplace of the morning and evening lands". Goethe's poetic description is fleshed out by writer Jan Morris, who loved the Rialto's "smell of mud, incense, fish, age, filth and velvet". The labyrinthine Rialto also contains several of the grandest churches and paintings in Venice. It is also the ideal place to indulge in a Venetian bar crawl, a *giro di ombre (see panel below).*

The Rialto is often described as "Venice's kitchen, office and back parlour". For Venetians it is not restricted to the graceful bridge but embraces the district curved around the middle bend of the Grand Canal. Its name (derived from *rivo alto*, high bank) refers to the first settlement of central Venice, which became the capital from 814. It was the powerhouse of the Venetian Empire, a crossroads between East and West, home to a mix of races. In this exotic marketplace, cargoes of spices and silks from the Levant were sold along with Slav slaves. Here northern Italian grain dealers and Flemish wool merchants rubbed shoulders with Jewish money lenders, Arab spice traders and German metal traders, as well as with Florentine and Lombard cloth merchants.

At the Pescheria (fish market).

Bàcari: Traditional Bars

Venice abounds in historic cafés and glitzy hotel bars, but beyond Harry's Bar and Florian's a humbler, cosier world awaits. Venetian wine bars, known as *bàcari*, are the places to indulge in a bitter *amaro*, the classic Italian *aperitivo* or a Venetian *spritz*, made with white wine, campari and soda water. Nor is a beer out of the question, whether a *birin*, a tiny glass, or the slightly bigger *birèta*. A *giro di ombra*, as they say in dialect, is a serious "wine crawl", with each tasting accompanied by a Venetian version of tapas such as *crostini* covered with cheese, *baccalà* (dried salted cod); home-cured salami; and *sarde in saor*, sardines in a marinade of onions and pine nuts. Typical *bàcari* are clustered in the Rialto market district. If early, try the rumbustious Do Morì (Mon–Sat 8am–8pm) on Calle de Do Morì. In a little corner of the Pescheria (fish market), Da Elio (Campo delle Beccarie, Tues–Sun 7am–7pm) serves *cichetti* and *ombre* – Venetian snacks and wine by the glass. The rustic Antico Dolo (Ruga Vecchia di San Giovanni San Polo 778, open 10am–3pm, 6.30–10pm, closed Sun) has specialities including tripe and other forms of offal. End a Rialto bar crawl in Bancogiro (Campo San Giacometto, closed Sun pm and Mon), a bar that brings the *bacaro* concept up to date without betraying its rustic roots.

BELOW: Al Bancogiro, a popular *bacaro* in the Rialto district.

The celebrated cookery writer Elizabeth David was entranced by "the light of a Venetian dawn so limpid and so still that it makes every separate vegetable and fruit and fish luminous with a life of its own".

Threading the labyrinthine alleys of the Rialto is an intoxicating experience. It remains a hive of commercial activity, with everything on sale between here and the Mercerie. The markets extend along the bank to the **Pescheria** ㊺, the fish market, set in an arcaded Neo-Gothic hall by the quayside. Brightly painted boats from the lagoon supply the main markets with fish and fresh vegetables. The adjoining **Campo delle Beccarie**, once a public abattoir, contains market overspill and a lively bar. The **Erberia** is the canalside fruit and vegetable market. Foodies find sensuous pleasure in the profusion of succulent salads, asparagus, baby artichokes, bunches of red peppers and peachy *borlotti* beans.

The greatest Gothic church on the left bank is the **Frari** ㊻, officially known as **Santa Maria Gloriosa dei Frari** (open Mon–Sat 9am–6pm, Sun 1–6pm). This Franciscan complex was founded in the 13th century but rebuilt over the next 200 years. The adjoining monastic cloisters house the state archives and a thousand years of Venetian history. In keeping with Franciscan strictures, the bare brick is unadorned: poverty was the guiding principle of the mendicant orders. The barn-like interior is a stark framework for the artwork, a pantheon of Venetian glories. The choir chapels are lined with tombs of the Doges. The nave is dominated by a Gothic choir screen and lovely choir stalls, the only such ensemble to survive in Venice. The high altar is the focal point, a space illuminated by Titian's *Assumption*. The revolutionary nature of the painting led to its initial rejection by the friars; they relented, and the work made Titian's reputation. Henry James adored Bellini's altarpiece, a radiant *Madonna and Child*: "It is as solemn as it is gorgeous as it is simple as it is deep."

Scuola Grande di San Rocco ㊼ (open daily 9am–5.30pm), dwarfed by the Frari, is Tintoretto's crowning glory. His Mannerist paintings adorn every surface, the works full of chiaroscuro effects and figures striking dramatic poses. The painter's bold Biblical scenes, executed between 1564 and 1587, provoke strong responses. Henry James found the air "thick with genius" yet palpably human: "It is not immortality that we breathe at San Rocco but conscious, reluctant mortality." In the evening, this splendid stage acts as a backdrop for Baroque recitals.

BELOW: the Erberia fruit and vegetable market.

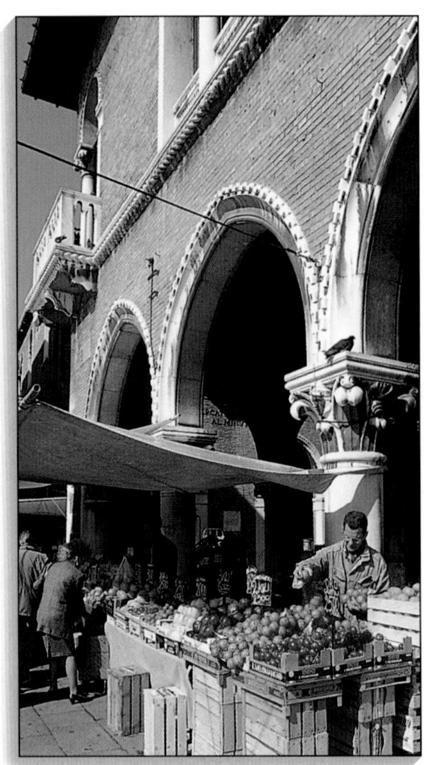

Campo San Pantalon ㊽, a canalside square lined with crumbling palaces, is home to the astonishing church of **San Pantalon**. It follows common Venetian practice by which interiors are often finer than exteriors. The unfinished façade gives no indication of the splendours within. The Baroque ceiling paintings by Fumiani (1650–1710) depict the martyrdom and glory of St Pantalon in a tour de force of perspective which projects the nave high into the sky. The ascent into heaven is peopled by boldly foreshortened figures clambering, floating or flying. On completion of the ceiling, the artist supposedly stood back to admire his work before slipping off the scaffolding to his death.

For a burst of everyday life, head towards **Campo San Polo** ㊾. After San Marco it is the largest square, once dedicated to bull-baiting, tournaments and processions. Today it makes do with carnival balls, film screenings, impromptu football matches, student gatherings and romantic assignations, appropriate for a square linked to the exploits of Giovanni Casanova.

Cannaregio

Cannaregio is the most northerly district, designed for those who have tired of monumental San Marco. The name comes from *canne*, meaning reeds, indicating Cannaregio's marshy origins. As the district closest to the railway station and the mainland, Cannaregio is the most densely populated. Yet it is also an ancient quarter, site of the world's first Jewish ghetto and the last bastion of working-class Venetians. Walks in the melancholic backwaters at the edge of the city trace a landscape of peeling façades and humble workshops, broad canals and wind-buffeted quays.

Santa Maria dei Miracoli 50 (open Mon–Sat 10am–5pm, Sun 1–5pm) now restored, rises sheer from the water, like a marble siren awaiting the call of the sea or the embrace of a foolish sailor. No wonder the church is a favourite with Venetian brides. Perfect proportions and seductive charm make this a Renaissance miracle in miniature. Its dazzling display of pastel marble presents a vision of pale pinks and silvery greys, of pilasters adorned with interlaced flowers, mythical beasts and cavorting mermaids. Visitors are dazzled by the cumulative effect of this church, with its inlaid marble, bas-reliefs and statues.

The Gesuiti 51 (open daily 10am–noon, 4–6pm) is often confused with the Gesuati, the other major Jesuit foundation, in Dorsoduro district. The Jesuits were never popular in Venice, a city which put patriotism before the Papacy and declared: "Venetians first and Christians second." After their banishment was revoked, the Jesuits returned to Venice and in 1715 started to rebuild on the site of a medieval church. The Gesuiti is still run by the Order and is the seat of the American Jesuit University. Set into a line of severe houses, the Baroque, angel-bedecked façade reveals an exuberant interior, graced by Titian's *Martyrdom of St Lawrence* and Tintoretto's *Assumption.*

Fondamente Nuove 52, the windswept "new quays" bordering the northern lagoon, were actually created in the 1580s. Before that, this now desolate stretch was a desirable residential district, with summer palaces and gardens lapped by the lagoon waters. Fondamente Nuove is the main boarding stage for the islands, with services to San Marco in the other direction. Although the quays seem inhospitable, especially in winter, the stirring lagoon views, encompassing the cemetery island of San Michele, count for much. These quaysides are the best departure point for visits to the outlying islands of **Torcello, Murano and Burano.** Torcello, the most remote, was the first settlement, and contains magnificent Byzantine mosaics in the basilica. Burano is a lively, painted fishing village, while Murano has been the centre of the Venetian glass industry since medieval times.

Madonna dell'Orto 53 (open Mon–Sat 10am–5pm, Sun 1–5pm), set on a square of herringbone design, is a shrine to Tintoretto *(see page 91)*. Tintoretto apart, the church is a treasury of Venetian painting from the 15th century to the 17th. The quirky campanile is topped by an onion-shaped cupola, the first belltower to greet visitors as they speed across the lagoon from the airport. Often bathed in a warm light, the church is a masterpiece of Venetian Gothic. The austere, brick-faced interior also makes a good starting point

Map on pages 140–141

CHORUS, the association of Venetian churches, issues a special pass allowing access to 13 of the city's most important churches (tel: 041-2750462; www.chorus-ve.org). For other churches there is a rival pass from Associazione Sant' Apollonia (tel: 041-2702464).

BELOW: your gondola awaits…

Map on pages 140–141

for exploring Tintoretto's genius; he lived near by, and this, his parish church, is decorated with works created *in situ*. His humble background gave him sympathy for the lives of the poor, a theme which, combined with religious fervour, distinguishes him from many of his contemporaries. A memorial bust of the artist watches over his grave in a side chapel.

Before crossing the bridge over Fondamenta Madonna dell'Orto to **Campo dei Mori** ➎➍, stand on the quayside and glance across at the Gothic **Palazzo Mastelli** opposite. To the right of the filigree balcony is a relief of a laden camel, lending the palace an eastern flavour. The owners were Levantine merchants whose origins are alluded to in the worn reliefs of turbaned Moors on the Campo dei Mori façade. On Rio della Sensa, beyond the *campo,* is **Tintoretto's house**, marked by a plaque and a bas-relief of the painter. This relatively humble abode was where the artist lived from 1574 until his death in 1594.

A bronze relief in the Ghetto Nuovo recalls the deportation and death of 200 Venetian Jews in World War II.

These faintly mournful waterways are flanked by Flemish-looking houses and neglected palaces, a contrast to the tall tenements of the **Ghetto** ➎➎ *(see box opposite)* further west. In the 1890s the de Goncourt brothers were moved to describe these melancholy, slightly menacing canals as "a district in decay, like an antique sculpture eaten away by rain and sun".

Despite its name, **Campo del Ghetto Nuovo** is the heart of the world's oldest ghetto, a fortified island created in 1516. Three of Venice's five remaining synagogues are set around the square, as is the **Museo Ebraico**, a museum of Jewish history (open Sun–Fri 10am–6pm; multilingual tours of the synagogues every hour Sun–Thur 10.30am–3.30pm). Beyond the square and bridge lies the **Ghetto Vecchio**, created in 1541, with two more synagogues. Visitors may follow in Woody Allen's steps by lingering by the Jewish bakery or kosher restaurant. ❑

BELOW: an artisan opens up shop. **RIGHT:** a canalside walkway in Cannaregio.

The Jewish Ghetto

Jews were first mentioned in Venetian records in the 10th century, as passengers banned from travelling on Venetian ships. As an ambitious trading city, Venice feared competition from Levantine merchants. Persecution soon drove waves of refugees to Venice, but Venetian policy was ambivalent, wavering between toleration and persecution.

While Jewish doctors, traders and textile merchants were tolerated, pawnbrokers and moneylenders were resented. Although hefty levies on moneylending meant that Venice profited, Jews were treated as second-class citizens, forbidden to settle in Venice. As Shylock says in Shakespeare's *The Merchant of Venice*: "I will buy with you, sell with you, talk with you, walk with you… but I will not eat with you, drink with you, nor pray with you."

From the 14th century onwards there were attempts to restrict Jews to the mainland, resulting in the decree of 1423 forbidding them to own property. Jews were forced to wear distinguishing badges, yellow skullcaps or red hats. When Mestre was destroyed in 1509, the Jews sought refuge in Venice until rampant prejudice led to the creation of the ghetto. In 1516 the expanding Jewish community was given its own closed living quarters, the ghetto, both as a reward for contributing funds for the defence of the city and as a means of future control. Since this new home was within sight of the former foundry or *ghetto*, the term came to mean a closed Jewish quarter.

The ghetto was damp and dark, and the living space was cramped because the local community multiplied in spite of persecution. In time the houses grew as high as the foundations permitted, an exception to normal Venetian building practice. The population density was three times greater than that the most crowded Christian suburbs. After the Ghetto Nuovo (1516), two newer settlements, the Ghetto Vecchio (1541) and Ghetto Nuovissimo (1633), provided temporary relief from overcrowding.

The decline of Venice ultimately affected the Jews; in 1655 there were almost 5,000 people in the ghetto, with numbers falling to 1,500 a century later. The Jewish tax burden often led to bankruptcy or emigration. This long farewell ended in 1797 with the Napoleonic invasion; at last the ghetto gates were flung open: even Jews were entitled to liberty, equality and fraternity. This brief dream was soon dispelled by the restoration of Austrian rule. But times had indeed changed, and Jews were among the most passionate upholders of the revolutionary aims of 1848. Jews only became full citizens in 1866, when Venice became part of the Kingdom of Italy.

Today the local Jewish community numbers 600, with few choosing to live in the former ghetto. Nonetheless, the ghetto remains at the heart of Jewish life, with fine synagogues and a cultural centre; a nursery and an old people's home; even workshops selling liturgical objects and a kosher bakery offering unleavened bread. The Jews may live elsewhere but they break bread here. Tours of the ghetto are available: book through the tourist office or at www.jewishvenice.org. ❑

RIGHT: buildings as tall as those found in the ghetto are unusual elsewhere in Venice.

LIFE AS A MASQUERADE

Carnival in Venice is supreme self-indulgence, a giddy round of masked balls and private parties suggesting mystery and promising romance

Carnival in Venice is a 10-day pre-Lenten extravaganza, culminating in the burning of the effigy of Carnival in Piazza San Marco on Shrove Tuesday. As an expression of a topsy-turvy world, carnival is a time for rebellion without the risk of ridicule. The essence of the "feast of fools" lies in the unfolding Venetian vistas: masked processions heading towards Piazza San Marco past shimmering palaces, with surreal masqueraders tumbling out of every alley. As the revellers flock to Florian's café in Piazza San Marco, the air is sickly-sweet with the scent of fritters and the sound of lush Baroque music. Carnival capers include costumed balls, firework displays and historical parades, all staged by the carnival societies.

SPIRIT OF RESISTANCE

Carnival is often dismissed as commercialised and chaotic, but Venetian traditionalists view it differently. The leader of a venerable carnival company sees the event as saving his city: "Life in Venice is inconvenient and costly. With the carnival, we give a positive picture and show the pleasure of living here. Carnival is a form of resistance. By resisting the temptation to leave, we are saving the spirit of the city for future generations."

▽ THE GREAT LEVELLER
A mask makes everyone equal. Masqueraders are addressed as *"sior maschera"* (masked gentleman) regardless of age, rank or even gender. One way of preserving some individuality is face-painting.

△ SELECT CARDS
A select group of Venetians still appears as *tarocchi*, fortune-telling tarot cards. These famous cards supposedly reached Europe from the East, through Venice. The star of the pack is the Queen of Swords, her costume rich in silver cabalistic signs.

▽ WINDOW DRESSING
Masks originally allowed the nobility to mingle incognito with the common people in *casini* (private clubs), but ar[e] now an excuse for all-purpo[se] revelry. This shop window displays fantasy masks, which are creative rather tha[n] authentic, and appeal to individual tastes.

△ **THE NOBLE LOOK**
Costumes can be historical, traditional or simply surreal. The classic Venetian disguise of the 17th and 18th centuries was known as the *maschera nobile*, the patrician mask. The carnival companies wear noble Renaissance and Rococo costumes *(left)* as a matter of course.

▽ **VOLTO FACE**
The patrician *maschera nobile* and witty *commedia dell'arte* masks are among a number of authentic disguises. While this cumbersome ruff is pure fantasy, the white mask looks to the past for inspiration: it is a modern variant on the slightly sinister *volto*, the traditional Venetian mask.

MASTERS OF DISGUISE

Mask-makers had their own guild in medieval times, when a *mascheraio* (mask-maker) helped a secretive society run smoothly. Modern masqueraders must choose between masks in leather *(cuoio)*, china *(ceramica)* or papier mâché *(cartapesta)*. Papier mâché and leather masks are the most authentic.

Antique masks are rare, since neither material readily stands the test of time or the Venetian climate. Authentic mask-makers both reinterpret traditional designs and create new ones. In the case of papier-mâché masks, the pattern is made from a fired-clay design, which generates a plaster-of-Paris mould. Layers of papier-mâché paste are used to line the mould and thus create the mask. When dry, the paste gives the mask a shiny surface akin to porcelain. Polish and a white base coat are applied before the eye holes are cut and decorative detail is added. This painting process can be simple or highly artistic. Of the alternatives to papier mâché, leather masks are hard to fashion; ceramic designs, ideal as hand-held masks or as wall decorations, are often adorned with fine fabrics. Places to browse include Laboratorio Artigiano Maschere (Barbaria delle Tole, Castello 6657, tel: 041-5223110) and Ca' del Sol (Fondamenta dell'Osmarin, Castello, tel: 041-5285549). Near by is Mondonovo – one of Venice's most creative mask-makers (Rio Terra Canal, off Campo Santa Margherita, tel: 041-5287344).

THE VENETO

Sandwiched between the seemingly dreary plain, the dramatic Dolomites and the exotic lakeside, the Veneto is very far from uniform

Maps:
Area 168
City 170

At first sight the terra firma towns pale into insignificance before Venice, the shimmering capital. As a centre of European art and architecture, Venice colours the local culture: graceful Venetian-style loggias adorn modest hilltop towns; the soft, sensuous Venetian atmosphere shines through the paintings of Giorgione and Titian. In the Veneto's civilised cities and landscaped countryside, trade with the famed Republic has left a legacy of impressive merchant palaces and Palladian villas. The presence of paintings and sculpted images of the Lion of St Mark also testifies to the Venetian influence. However, certain terra firma towns have resisted the cultural imperialism of Venice; Verona, Vicenza and Padua have had sharply separate identities since Roman times, and even the smaller centres possess clear personalities.

The Veneto is a fertile plain bounded by the Adriatic coast and the Po to the south, and by Lake Garda to the west. Around Vicenza and Padua the plains and gently rolling hills are prime villa country, revealing world-famous Palladian villas. In economic terms, the Veneto is Lombardy's keenest competitor, and often outdoes its dominant neighbour, with a concentration of efficient companies in sectors as diverse as furniture and high-tech, clothes and wine. Only Venice *(see pages 143–60)* is an exception to the economic boom: with business costs 10 percent higher than on the mainland, the city simply relies on tourism.

PRECEDING PAGES: the rolling, wooded hills of Bassano.
LEFT: café society in the Piazza Bra.
BELOW: Romeo's beloved Juliet, immortalised in bronze.

Romantic Verona

As the largest city after Venice, **Verona** ❶ is a place of great provincial charm. It also exudes the sophistication that comes of being a significant centre, long before the Venetian Empire presumed to swallow it up. Verona has a rich Roman and Etruscan past but was dominated by feudal families until the Venetian Republic took control (1402–1797). From 1797 to 1859 it was ruled by Austria, and it was only 20 km (12 miles) from the frontier of the old Austro-Hungarian Empire until the end of World War I.

Verona was the birthplace of Catullus, the Latin lyric poet, and of Veronese, the great Venetian painter. As the setting for Shakespeare's *Romeo and Juliet*, the city is still a magnet for lovers. Contemporary Verona is a prosperous city at ease with itself, an aesthetically pleasing swathe of pale pink stone curling along the banks of the River Adige, its streets paved with precious marble and lined with discreet restaurants and chic designer shops.

Piazza Bra Ⓐ stands at the centre of civic life, presenting an elegant, languid space lined with cheerful cafés. The square is completely dominated by the **Arena** Ⓑ (open Sept–June Tues–Sun 9am–6pm, July–Aug Tues–Sun 8am–3.30pm, Mon 1.45–7.30pm; last

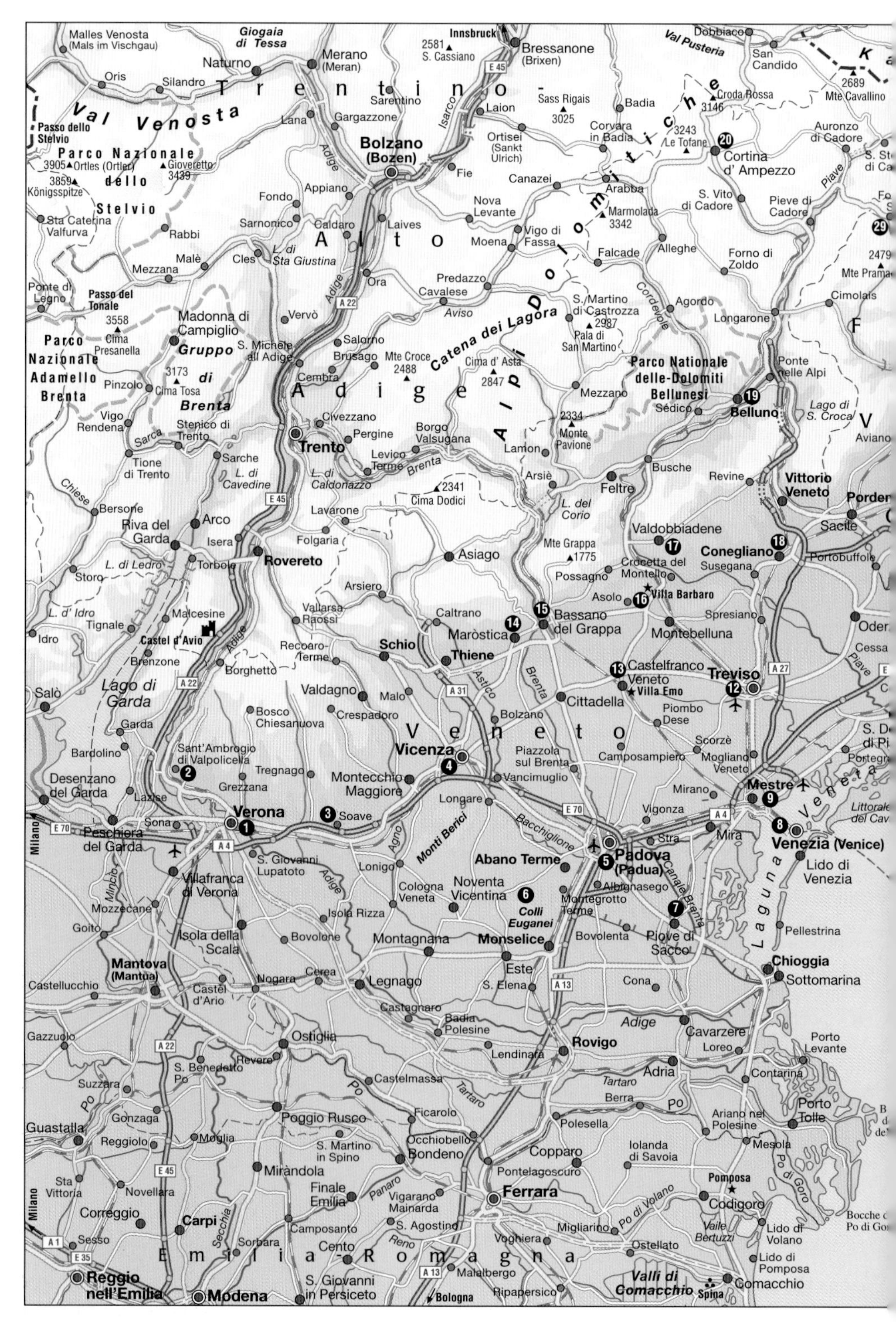

entry 45 minutes before closure; admission charge; tel: 045-8003204), the greatest of the city's Roman monuments. The elliptical amphitheatre, dating from the 1st century AD, is the third-largest in existence. Built of pale pink Veronese limestone, it provides the backdrop for Italy's most theatrical open-air operatic festival. **Piazza delle Erbe** Ⓒ is a sociable, domestic square, revealing the cosy heart of the city. Occupying the site of the Roman forum, it is dotted with cheerful market stalls and flanked by impressive palaces. The adjoining **Piazza dei Signori** Ⓓ, the main public square during the Renaissance, has an impressive array of civic buildings. From the top of the 12th-century **Torre dei Lamberti** (open Mon 1.30–7.30pm, Tues–Sun 9.30am–7.30pm) there are spectacular views over the city.

Casa di Giulietta Ⓔ (open Mon 1.30–7.30pm, Tues–Sun 8am–7pm; admission charge; last entry 45 minutes before closure) at Via Cappello 23, just off Piazza delle Erbe, complete with the requisite marble balcony and romantic courtyard, is the supposed home of Juliet, Shakespeare's tragic heroine – a fictional shrine, even if the Montagues and Capulets did actually exist. **Sant' Anastasia** Ⓕ (open Mon–Sat 9am–6pm, Sun 1–6pm), the city's largest Gothic church, with a fresco by Pisanello, is set just north in the medieval quarter. Around the bend in the river awaits the red-and-white striped **Duomo** Ⓖ (open Mon–Sat 10am –5.30pm, Sun 1.30–5.30pm), which is mainly Romanesque in the lower sections and Gothic towards the top. Near by stands Ponte Pietra, a Roman bridge detonated by the retreating Nazis in 1945 but rebuilt using the original materials. Further along the river looms **Castelvecchio** Ⓗ, Corso Castelvecchio 2, a 14th-century fortress that controls the main city bridge. An innovative and imaginative civic art gallery (open Mon 1.30–7.30pm, Tues–Sun 8.30am–7.30pm; tel: 045-594734) is carved into the castle walls. The collection is rich in medieval, Renaissance and Mannerist works, from Pisanello to Bellini and Tintoretto.

San Zeno Maggiore Ⓘ (open Mon–Sat 8.30am–6pm, Sun 1–6pm) lies to the west; an impressive church dedicated to Verona's patron saint, it is popular for weddings.

The ruling Scaligeri dynasty who ruled Verona from 1277 to 1387 were patrons of learning and benefactors to painters and poets, including Dante Alighieri (above).

Founded in the 5th century, it is essentially Romanesque; the lofty interior is adorned with an altarpiece by Mantegna. The Romanesque and Gothic cloisters are part of the former Benedictine abbey.

The **Tomba di Giulietta and Museo degli Affreschi** Ⓙ (open Tues–Sun 9am–7pm; tel: 045-8000361), set by the river, south of the Arena in Via Shakespeare, is a slightly spurious Juliet shrine. The so-called tomb lies in a crypt below the cloisters of **San Francesco al Corso**, a former monastery which is now a museum devoted to Shakespeare and 16th-century Verona. Just north, also beside the river, stands **San Fermo Maggiore** Ⓚ, a complex of two superimposed Benedictine churches dating from the 8th and 11th centuries. Highlights are the frescoed interior and the wonderful ship's-keel ceiling. From here, a short stroll across the bridge leads north to the Renaissance **Giardino Giusti** Ⓛ (open daily 9am–dusk), grand formal gardens with shady arbours and waterfalls.

Further north still at Regaste Redentore 2 is the **Teatro Romano** Ⓜ (open Mon 1.30–7.30pm, Tues–Sun 8.30am–7.30pm; admission charge), occupying a pleasing position on the hill. Like the Arena, the Roman theatre is used for the summer festival of dance and opera. Steps beside it lead up to **Castel San Pietro** Ⓝ, a characterless fortress constructed by the Austrians on the site of a ruined Visconti castle. Just beyond the theatre is the Romanesque church of **Santo Stefano** Ⓞ, the city cathedral until late medieval times. On the far side of Ponte Garibaldi, around the bend in the river, is the Renaissance church of **San Giorgio in Braida** Ⓟ, studded with precious paintings by Veronese and Tintoretto. The riverside piazza beside the church presents a fittingly romantic farewell to Verona.

It is no coincidence that Verona plays host to VinItaly, the country's major wine fair: the city is the hub of a thriving wine-producing region. **Sant'Ambrogio di**

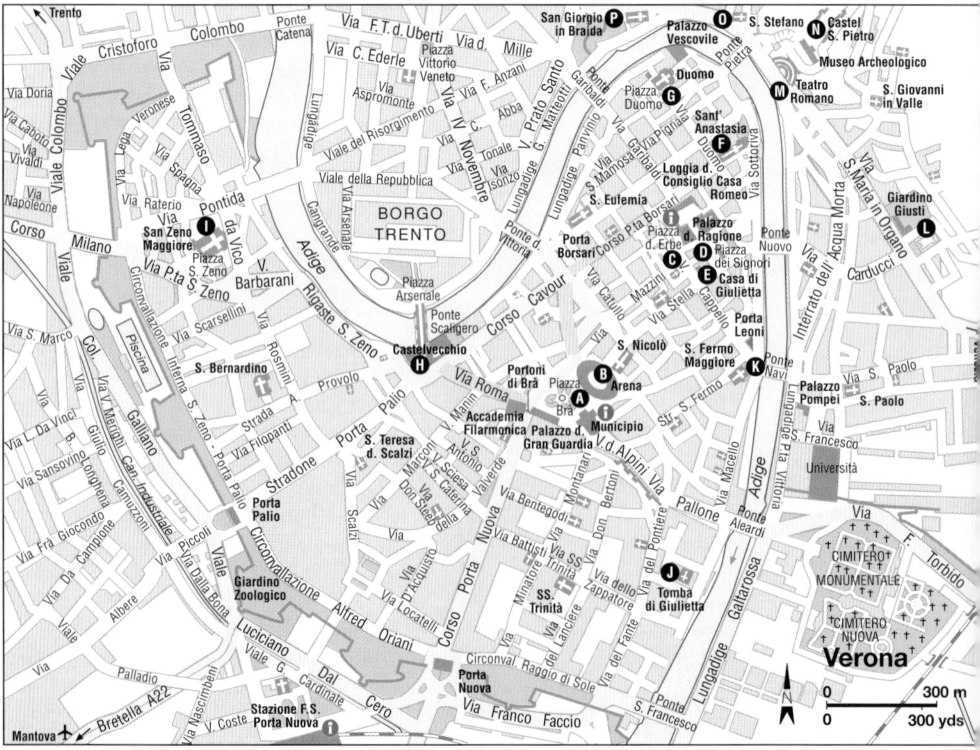

Valpolicella ❷, just west of Verona, is noted for the eponymous fruity red wine. **Soave** ❸, which lies in the Verona hinterland, is best known for its dry white wine. The fortified town is enclosed by Gothic defensive walls, hemmed in by towers and crowned by a castle known as **Rocca Scaligeri** (open Tues–Sun 9am–noon, 3–6.30pm; tel: 045-7860036), named after its 14th-century founders.

Map on pages 168–169

The Palladian trail

Vicenza ❹, which lies equidistant between Venice and Verona, is set against a backdrop of mountains. Palladio (1508–80), the leading 16th-century architect, was responsible for at least a dozen of its city palaces, not to mention countless villas in the surrounding countryside. The impressive array of Palladian buildings belies the fact that the city was heavily bombed during World War II. Contemporary Vicenza is sleek and glossy, content with its cool, classical image; the city centre, partly bounded by medieval walls, feels a world away from the city's current source of wealth, a "silicon valley" electronics industry.

Vicenza's 1st-century AD Roman Cripto-portico remains, as does a stretch of Roman road on Corso Fogazzaro, with crafts work-shops clustered in the adjoining porticoes.

The historic heart is best explored on one of the free guided tours provided by the tourist office (Piazza Matteotti 12; tel: 0444-320854; www.vicenza.org), a pleasant stroll which takes in the city bridges, from Ponte Foro, with its remaining Roman arches, to Ponte Pusterla, with a quaint mill race. The Roman theatre which inspired Palladio was dismantled in his lifetime, the marble recycled in city palaces. Palladio's main works include Palazzo Chierati, the Teatro Olimpico and, on a hill just outside town, the famous Villa Rotonda.

On Piazza dei Signori, the city centre, stands his imposing **Basilica** (open Tues–Sun summer 10am–7pm, winter 9am–5pm), his first public project – a classical remodelling of a Gothic courthouse. A daily market takes place in

BELOW: built in 1580, the Teatro Olimpico is claimed to be the world's oldest surviving indoor theatre.

Padua's golden age between the 12th and 14th centuries left an impressive cultural legacy, including many works by great artists, such as the Guattamelata *by Donatello.*

BELOW: the magisterial elegance of the villa La Rotonda.

the shadow of the basilica, with canny shoppers more interested in cheese and salami than in the copper-clad roof and double order of loggias. Here also is Palladio's stately **Loggia del Capitaniato** (1571), now the town hall, was the residence of the Venetian military commander. Just south is the **Basilica Palladiana Cattedrale** (open Tues–Sun 9am–5pm), a gloomy Gothic affair incorporating elements from earlier basilicas, with a door designed by Palladio.

Teatro Olimpico (open Tues–Sun 9am–4.45pm, July–Aug until 7pm; admission charge), Palladio's theatrical last work, was begun in the year of his death and finished by his gifted successor, Scamozzi. Intended as a stage set for classical tragedies, it lays claim to being the world's oldest surviving indoor theatre. This masterpiece of wood, brick, stucco-work and statuary represents a coherent piece of classical reconstruction. The Card Musei is a good value cumulative ticket allowing entry to the Teatro Olimpico, Museo Civico and Museo Naturalistico-Archeologico.

At the end of Corso Palladio, on the site of the former docks, stands **Palazzo Chiericati** (open Tues–Sun 9am–4.45pm, July–Aug until 7pm; admission charge), dating from 1551 and housing the civic museum and art gallery. The highlights of the collection are Venetian paintings by Tintoretto and Veronese and Flemish works by Memling and Van Dyck. **Palazzo Barbarano da Porto** (open Tues–Sun 10am–6pm; admission charge), set on Contra Porti just off Corso Palladio, is exceptional in being the sole building in Vicenza entirely designed and supervised by Palladio. Its chief features are an impressive loggia, a grand entrance, and sumptuous decoration by Veneto artists. In 1999 it opened as a centre for Palladian studies, the Museo Palladiano, and aims to be the world's main display case for his work. There are also excellent temporary exhibitions.

Map on pages 168–169

La Rotonda (open mid-Mar–early Nov; grounds Tues–Thur 10am–noon, 3–6pm; interior Wed 10am–noon, 3–6pm; admission charge; tel: 044-321793) nestles in the hills south of Vicenza. This exquisite villa, graced by solemn flights of steps and a ravishing dome, is an ostentatious monument to the owner's vanity.

At Contrà di Santa Corona 25, the **Galleria di Palazzo Leoni Montanari** (open Fri–Sun 10am–6pm, but variable; admission charge; tel: 800-578875) has a superb collection of Venetian paintings, including works by Canaletto and Pietro Longhi. On the top floor there is also a collection of 120 Russian icons.

TIP

Padova Arte, a combined ticket, provides access to all major city monuments and museums.

Centre of learning

Padua ❺ (Padova in Italian) ranks with Florence and Bologna as one of the main Italian centres of learning. The 12th–14th centuries represent a vigorous period in the city's history, typified by the building of basilicas and the expansion of the university. Although Venice held sway after 1405, Padua experienced a Renaissance flowering with Mantegna and Donatello, and benefited from grand Venetian schemes, including new public buildings and ramparts. The locals are proud of their city as the last resting place of St Anthony of Padua, honoured with a seven-domed basilica that closely resembles a mosque.

Most visitors instinctively head to the **Cappella degli Scrovegni** (open daily 9am–7pm; book in advance; tel: 049-2010020, lines open Mon–Fri 9am–7pm, Sat 9am–1pm; admission charge includes Eremitani Museum), which contains the most complete cycle of frescoes ever attributed to Giotto (1267–1327), who created it at the height of his powers (1303–5). After extensive renovation, the frescoes were reopened to the public in March 2002. Dedicated to the Virgin, the Life of Christ and the Last Judgement, the cycle displays great narrative force and naturalism, with vivid, humanised figures.

Below: Giotto's *Adoration of the Magi*, Scrovegni Chapel, Padua.

The neighbouring **Eremitani Musei Civici** (open Tues–Sun 9am–7pm; Nov–Jan, 9am–6pm), housed in the cloisters of a reclusive Augustinian order, is a cluster of collections, including archaeological, Roman and Venetian sections. Among artistic highlights are Renaissance bronzes, a Giotto Crucifixion, and paintings by Bellini, Titian, Tintoretto and Tiepolo. Near by, facing the remains of the Roman amphitheatre, stands the **Eremitani** church (open summer Mon–Sat 8.15am–12.15pm, 4–6pm, Sun 9.30am–12.15pm, 4–6pm; winter Mon–Sat closes 5.30pm, Sun closes 5pm). In the Ovetari chapel are fragments of frescoes by Mantegna (produced 1454–7), survivors of an Allied bombing raid in 1943, one of the worst artistic tragedies of the war.

From the Eremitani it is a short stroll to Piazza Cavour, the town's heart, and a historic coffee house. **Caffè Pedrocchi**, facing the university, is designed like a classical temple, and lined with Empire mirrors and velvet banquettes. The café has been a salon for students, academics and intellectuals since 1831. It was in these Egyptian Revival surroundings that Stendhal debated political utopias, and political plots were hatched during the Risorgimento. Today the café also functions as an **arts complex and exhibition centre** (open Tues–Sun 9.30am–12.30pm, 3.30–6pm; admission charge).

From the 16th century, when gracious summer retreats were first built along the waterway connecting Venice with Padua, the summer ritual involved transporting the family goods and furniture from Venice along the Brenta Canal.

Palazzo del Bò, the seat of the university, lies a stone's throw from Caffè Pedrocchi, on Via VIII Febbraio. The building is named "the ox" after an old inn sign that once hung near by. Founded in 1221, the university is second only to Bologna in seniority and can name Galileo among its professors; he taught physics here from 1592 to 1610. Among sights visited on the guided tour is the anatomy theatre, founded in 1594 as part of the university's school of medicine.

Further south, just within the city walls, lies the lush **Orto Botanico** (open daily 9am–1pm, 3–6pm; admission charge), the oldest university botanical gardens in Europe, founded in 1545. Around the corner from the university, separating the bustling **Piazza delle Erbe** and Piazza della Frutta, looms the monumental **Palazzo della Ragione** (open Tues–Sun 9am–7pm, Nov–Jan until 6pm; admission charge). These arcaded medieval halls housed the city council and law courts in the early 13th century.

The **Basilica di Sant'Antonio** (open daily 7.30am–7.30pm), is a splendid place of pilgrimage erected in honour of St Anthony. It is a poor man's St Mark's, echoing the Venetian model but incorporating Lombard and Tuscan styles. The assimilation of Eastern and Western traditions can be felt in the fusion between Byzantine domes and minarets and the Romanesque-Gothic structure. Inside are works by Donatello and Titian.

Elsewhere in the city, Paduan churches are often memorable. On Piazza Duomo stands the plain, 16th-century cathedral, flanked by the more impressive Romanesque baptistry. The restored **Battistero del Duomo** (open daily 10am–6pm) is adorned with 14th-century frescoes. By contrast, **Santa Sofia** (open daily 9am–noon, 4–6.30pm), the city's oldest church, is a remodelled 6th-century brick basilica graced by a lovely Veneto-Byzantine apse.

BELOW: canal bridge, Treviso.

Rovigo, south of Padua, marks the Veneto gateway to the Po Delta. Rovigo itself is an uninspiring town that borders a flat, wild and wet landscape, notorious for muggy summers, freezing winters and a sense of desolation. Known as the *bonifica*, this eerie land is not to everyone's taste, but beach-lovers can find consolation in the cluster of bustling coastal resorts in the Veneto *(see The Adriatic, page 341)*.

The Po Delta

The **Po Delta** straddles two administrative regions, the Veneto and Emilia Romagna. The former has been slow to grasp the conservation=tourism equation, but, prompted by government and environmentalists, is now tackling the pollution of the Po, which causes a yellowish haze to pervade the air.

Much of the Venetian plain is flat and featureless, so the rolling **Colli Euganei** (Euganean Hills) ❻ make a refreshing change from cultural pursuits. Southwest of Padua, this region is noted for its spas and mud treatments, whose healing properties have been recognised since Roman times. The sweetest spa is **Arquà Petrarca**, a medieval village where Petrarch spent his last years (1369–74).

The slow journey along the **Canale Brenta** ❼ provides a placid showcase for the Veneto's rural treasures. From March to October a *burchiello*, a long Venetian boat, leaves Venice on Tuesday, Thursday and

Saturday (tel: 049-3774712 or contact Padua Tourist Information (APT), Galleria Pedrocchi, tel: 049-8767927) and crawls along the canal to Padua, passing about 70 Renaissance villas as well as the Villa Pisani at Strà, infamous as the setting of Mussolini's first meeting with Hitler, in 1934. (The alternative road route connects Padua and Strà.)

The trip takes in visits to the 18th-century **Villa Pisani**, also known as Villa Nazionale (open Tues–Sun, Apr–Sept 9am–7pm, Oct–Mar 9am–4pm; admission charge; tel: 049-502074), which rivals a palace in ambition and scale, and the distinctive **La Malcontenta** (open Apr–mid-Nov Tues and Sat 9am–noon or by appointment; tel: 041-5203966; admission charge), also known as Villa Foscari. This showy villa (1558–60) has a vaulted *piano nobile* modelled on the interiors of the ancient Roman baths.

While **Venice** ❽ *(see pages 143–60)* is universally acclaimed, industrialised **Mestre** ❾ on the mainland is best known as the badly polluting hinterland. Further east, **Caorle** ❿ was a traditional fishing port until transformed into a bustling Adriatic resort. With its Romanesque belltower and pedestrianised historic centre, Caorle also makes a pleasant place for browsing. Just inland, **Portogruaro** ⓫ is a Venetian-style town with Roman remains and an archaeological museum, Museu Nazionale Concordiese (open daily 9am–7pm; tel: 0421-72674), a testament to the once thriving Roman city of Concordia.

Proud and prosperous

Treviso ⓬, situated between Portogruaro and Venice, is a prosperous provincial town and a beacon of economic excellence. Treviso's origins are Roman, but the city flourished during the Middle Ages, when it minted its own coinage.

Map on pages 168–169

Treviso is proud of its cuisine, based on traditional local produce. Radicchio is used in salads, soups and risottos, and local asparagus, famed for its fragrance and succulent flavour, is usually served with hard-boiled eggs and oil.

BELOW: cruising past Villa Pisani on the Brenta Canal.

The Good Ski Guide *describes Cortina's spider's-web runs as "flattened and widened in typical Italian style, so that the beautiful people do not become too tired to enjoy the extensive après-ski afterwards".*

After annexation by Venice in 1389 it assumed strategic importance as the guardian of the Republic's northwestern frontier. The city walls date from the period of Venetian domination. A single bombing raid in 1944 destroyed almost half the city, but much has been restored. **Calmaggiore**, the grandest commercial street, is lined with frescoed Gothic façades and porticoes. It connects the **Duomo San Pietro** (Cathedral; open Mon–Sat 7.30am–noon, 3.30–7pm, Sun 7.30am–1pm, 3.30–8pm) with Palazzo dei Trecento, the town hall; both were casualties of the 1944 bombardment. The Duomo is notable for its Romanesque crypt and a frescoed chapel containing Titian's *Annunciation* (1570). Set in the lee of the 16th-century town walls, the Dominican church of **San Nicolò** outshines the Cathedral; amid impressive Sienese frescoes are works by Tommaso da Modena (*c.*1325–76). **Buranelli** is the most pleasing quarter, with ancient palaces overhanging the water and a low stone bridge. The **Museo di Santa Caterina** (Via Santa Caterina; open Tues–Sun 9am–12.30pm, 2.30–6pm; tel: 0422-544864) is the new seat of the Musei Civici (Municipal Museums) in Treviso. This former monastery stands next to the church of the same name and the adjoining cloister has archaeological finds on the ground floors and a modern art gallery on the upper floors.

Between Treviso and Casale is the watery region of **Il Sile**, dotted with old mills, farmhouses and villas. The walled town of **Castelfranco-Veneto** ⓭, which once defended Treviso's western borders, lies between Treviso and Bassano del Grappa. Attractions include porticoed palaces and a Palladian cathedral with an altarpiece by Giorgione (1478–1511). The town makes a good springboard for a Palladian villa tour, with the magnificent **Villa Emo Capodilista** (open Apr–Oct Mon–Sat 3–6pm, Sun 10am–12.30pm and 2.30–7pm, Oct–Mar weekends only 2–6pm; tel: 0423-476414/476334; admission charge) within easy reach, at Fanzolo di Vedelago.

Maròstica ⓮ is a delightful medieval town, tucked inside 14th-century walls. It is celebrated for its delicious cherries and its bizarre chess festival: in the second weekend in September in alternate (even) years, the porticoed main square is transformed into a giant chessboard with costumed citizens acting as chess pieces. This is supposedly a re-enactment of a 15th-century game which resulted in the feudal lord giving his daughter away in marriage to the victor.

BELOW: Bassano del Grappa.

Favourite firewater

Bassano del Grappa ⓯ sits astride the River Brenta in the lee of Monte Grappa. This lovely castellated town, with arcaded squares and quaint alleyways lined with frescoed houses, is noted for its ceramics, white asparagus and the famous firewater known as grappa. The Veneto is a leading producer of the spirit, made from the lees left over from wine production. Despite war damage, much of the medieval fabric has remained, notably the **Ponte Coperto**, the covered bridge designed by Palladio. Piazza Garibaldi, the town's heart, is dominated by a 13th-century tower and overlooked by the Gothic San Francesco church. In the adjoining monastery, the **Museo Civico** (open Tues–Sat 9am–6.30pm, Sun 3.30–6.30pm; admission charge) shows works by Longhi and Tiepolo. **Monte**

Grappa, 32 km (20 miles) north, is reached via a scenic route through forests and pastures culminating in vistas stretching towards Venice and Trieste. Just east is **Asolo** ⓰, a picturesque walled town set amid the lumpy foothills of the Dolomites and dominated by the high-walled Rocca, the hilltop fortress. Its winding alleys are flanked by frescoed Renaissance palaces and Gothic arcades. The town has long been beloved of writers, from Henry James and Robert Browning – who dedicated a book of verse to Asolo – to the travel writer Freya Stark, who lived in a local villa. From the fortress and similar vantage points there are views of snow-capped Monte Grappa, the lower slopes covered by cypresses and vineyards, olive groves and pomegranate orchards.

Map on pages 168–169

The road from Conegliano to Valdobbiadene is known as the "Prosecco trail".

Villas and vineyards

The Veneto abounds in 16th–18th-century villas designed as rural retreats. Around the smaller towns and villages are idyllic rural estates, not the hubs of working farms but showy suburban villas. In Maser, close to Asolo, stands **Villa Barbaro** (open Mar–Oct Tues, Sat–Sun 3–6pm; Nov–Feb Sat–Sun 2.30–5pm; admission charge). The interior is a *trompe l'oeil* frescoed affair by Veronese. Just outside Vicenza is **Villa Valmarana ai Nani** (open Tues–Sun 2.30–5.30pm; tel: 0444-543976), a grandiose 18th-century villa noted for its Tiepolo frescoes. Visitors can stay at the restored Palladian **Villa Saraceno** (open Apr–Oct Wed only 2–4pm; tel: 0444-891371) at Agugliaro, part of the Landmark Trust.

Valdobbiadene ⓱ with its vineyard-studded hills, produces some of the Veneto's best wines, from sparkling white Prosecco to light Chardonnay and Verduzzo, full-bodied red Cabernet Sauvignon and Refosco. Near by, in Crocetta del Montello, the 17th-century Palladian **Villa Sandi** is attributed to Andrea Pagnossin, an architect from Treviso.

BELOW: the terraced hillsides of the Veneto.

Conegliano ⓲ enjoys an appealing setting amid orchards, vineyards and gentle hills. The name is synonymous with Prosecco, a sparkling white wine. The town is the birthplace of Cima da Conegliano (1460–1518), a colourist influenced by Bellini. His beguiling *Madonna and Saints* adorns the high altar of the 14th-century cathedral. The adjoining Scuola dei Battuti is a frescoed palace decorated in Venetian and Lombard style.

Belluno ⓳ stands on a rocky spur at the meeting of the Piave and Ardo rivers, encircled by lofty peaks, with the Dolomites to the north and the Belluno pre-Alps to the south. The **Piazza del Duomo** contains a 16th-century cathedral and baptistry with a Baroque belltower, as well as the Palazzo dei Rettori, with a porticoed façade, a loggia and mullioned windows. The **Piazza delle Erbe** is lined with Renaissance palaces. Belluno's cuisine betrays Alpine and Venetian influences, with mountain gnocchi and game flavoured with spicy Venetian sauces.

Cortina d'Ampezzo ⓴, capital of the Dolomites, vies with Zermatt and Kitzbühel as Europe's loveliest Alpine resort. Ringed by spectacular peaks and spires, with pink towers and cliffs soaring out of forests and snowfields, Cortina offers 140 km (88 miles) of pistes, extended to over 1,120 km (700 miles) on the linked Dolomiti Superski area. ❑

LLOYD TRIESTINO

FRIULI-VENEZIA GIULIA

This is where the Venetian and Austrian empires met between lagoons and limestone mountains. Its attractions number churches, castles and the delightful backwater port of Trieste

Map on pages 168–169

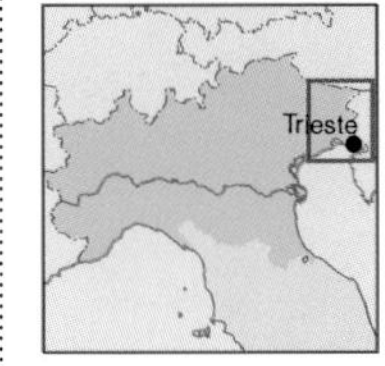

The name of Friuli-Venezia Giulia implicitly suggests a botched job, and the region is all too frequently portrayed as a briefly favoured child of the Austrian Empire, which made Trieste its principal port and Grado a health resort, a half-breed Slavic region in cahoots with Yugoslav communists, or a Fascist enclave that produced the only concentration camp in Italy in World War II. But as you travel around its extremities – and even venture into neighbouring Austria and Slovenia – it is quite clear that all of this is not only still homogeneously Roman territory, but also, more recently and more lastingly, is still in the thrall of the Venetian Lion of St Mark, a figure that appears on gateways and public buildings everywhere.

That is not to say it doesn't have its interesting corners, regional dialect differences and special charms. It also has its special problems: the region suffered badly in an earthquake in 1976, when several towns were severely damaged, particularly in the northeast. Other fatal earthquakes occurred in 1222 and 1516.

PRECEDING PAGE: the Villa Manin, Passariano.
LEFT: Piazza dell' Unità, Trieste.
BELOW: Trieste's waterfront.

The central plain

The last Doge of Venice had his country residence at the palatial **Villa Manin** (open Tues–Sun 9am–12.30pm, 3–6pm; winter 9am–noon, 2–5pm) in **Passariano ㉑**, some 25 km (15 miles) east of the manufacturing town of **Pordenone ㉒**. Built to resemble St Peter's in Rome, its spacious rooms house exhibitions, and there is a large formal garden.

The villa lies in the heart of the flatlands which stretch around the River Tagliamento. As well as fish and game, the area is famous for its smoked meats; the "Strada dei Castelli e del Prosciutto", a route of castles and meats, runs near the river, reaching a high spot at the town of **San Daniele del Friuli ㉓**, set on a hillock. This is a good stopover, where a plate of sweet-cured Daniele ham (prosciutto) with some bread and a carafe of wine can be wholly sustaining. Here, too, is the small church Sant'Antonio Abate, with what are considered to be the best Renaissance frescos (now restored) in Friuli-Venezia Giulia.

Udine ㉔, 48 km (30 miles) east of Pordenone, is one of the great finds in Friuli-Venezia Giulia. Animated and full of *osterie* where the local white wines are drunk in generous balloon glasses, its architectural mix blends into an exciting, historical whole – a true satellite of the great Venetian Republic. Visitors will immediately fall upon the lovely Renaissance Piazza della Libertà where the arcaded, pink-and-white-striped **Loggia del Lionello** is a pristine relic of a glorious past. It is named after its benefactor, a goldsmith named Nicolò Lionello. The building opposite, the Loggia di San Giovanni, is by Bernadino da Morcote, and the

The Lion of St Mark above a doorway at Gorizia Castle.

columns with the Lion of St Mark and the statue of justice are from 1614. Beneath an arch in the corner of the square, a cobbled hill, flanked by a Venetian Gothic portico built in 1487 under the Venetian governor, Tommasso Lippomano, leads to the **castle** he inhabited. Destroyed first in the 1511 earthquake, and damaged in that of 1976, it is now a museum and art gallery, Galleria d'Arte Antica (open Tues–Sat 9.30am–12.30pm, 3–6pm, Sun 9.30am–12.30pm). Beside this great civic building is the church of **Sant'Odorico**, a Romanesque relic with a certain grace. Within walking distance of the Piazza della Libertà is the **Archbishop's Palace** (open Wed–Sun 10am–noon, 3.30–6.30pm), where Giambattista Tiepolo created a triumphant ceiling with *The Fall of the Rebellious Angels*.

The new **Galleria d'Arte Moderna di Udine** (GAMUD; open Tues–Sat 9.30am–12.30pm, 3–6pm, Sun 9.30am–12.30pm; tel: 0432-295891) showcases both Italian and foreign 20th-century art.

Earthquake towns

East of Udine the land rises in the Cast Mountains and the borderlands of Slovenia. **Gorizia** ㉕ is dominated by the medieval castle, and an onion-domed church gives it a distinctly Slav flavour. Among the town's treasures at **Cividale del Friuli** ㉖ is the **Tempietto Longobardo** (open Apr–Sept Mon–Sat 9.30am–12.30pm, 3–6.30pm, Sun 9.30am–1pm, 3–7.30pm; Oct–Mar Mon–Sat 9.30am–12.30pm, 3–5pm, Sun 9.30am–12.30pm, 2.30–6pm; admission charge), a remarkable 8th-century Lombardic relic with fine 14th-century frescoes.

The country road from Cividale to **Gemona del Friuli** ㉗ in the Carnia Mountains is a rural ride among vineyards. The earthquake that struck in 1976 wreaked its worst at Gemona, where 1,000 died. **Venzone** ㉘, 18 km (11 miles) further

BELOW: Cividale del Friuli, Gorizia.

north, also suffered severely in the earthquake, particularly the church, now rebuilt.

Above Venzone, the high roads of the Carnia Mountains go west to Cortina, north to Austria and east to Slovenia. **Forni di Sopra** ㉙ on the western route is a clutch of villages and a base for mountain hiking and riding, as is **Arta Terme** ㉚ on the northern road, where walkers enjoy the flower-filled meadows. The last main town before the Slovenian and Austrian borders in the east is **Tarvisio** ㉛, a mountain resort with an Austrian flavour.

Map on pages 168–169

The coast

The Venetian lagoon continues round into Friuli-Venezia Giulia, flat and full of marshes, bird sanctuaries and fishermen's thatched *casoni*. Much of the lagoon is not accessible, but the two principal resorts, Lignano and Grado, are well-established holiday spots. **Lignano Sabbiadoro** ㉜ has 8 km (5 miles) of beach, eight marinas and an aquatic park. The spa resort of **Grado** ㉝ is where people come to eat seafood and have fun. A relaxing break amid the canals of the Isola d'Oro is a *vinotherapia* treatment at the Hotel Savoy di Grado (www.hotelsavoy-grado.it; tel: 0431-897111), Via Carducci 33. Developed in France, vinotherapy, or "wine therapy", detoxifies the skin with baths of red vine leaves and grape juice.

Just inland from Grado is the jewel of Friuli-Venezia Giulia, **Aquileia** ㉞. A Roman port abandoned to the marshy wastes after attacks by the Huns in the 5th century, it is little more than a village now. Its major attraction is the **basilica** (open daily, summer 9am–7pm, winter 8.30am–12.30pm, 2.30–5.30pm; free), which has a stunning Roman mosaic floor. Stretching the entire length of the nave, it was laid down in 314, but the current building was consecrated in 1031 under Patriarch Poppo, who had the mosaics covered; they did not see daylight

BELOW: fishing boats moored at Grado's harbour.

Mosaic in the 13th-century apse of Duomo San Giusto, Trieste.

again until 1909. Major restoration has taken place, and the mosaics were polished stone by stone. They depict Biblical tale and mythological scenes.

East of Aquileia there is little access to the coast until **Monfalcone** ㉟ and the last strip of Italy that squeezes between the Carso hills and the Gulf of Trieste. Halfway down is **Miramare** ㊱ (open summer daily 9am–7pm, ticket office closes 6.30pm; admission charge), the castle of the Archduke Ferdinand Josef Maximilian of Habsburg-Lorraine, who became Emperor of Mexico and there met his fate. With his wife Charlotte, daughter of Leopold I of Belgium, he built his dream palace on a promontory between 1856 and 1860. It is the best relic of the Austro-Hungarian Empire in Italy and plays a part in that story, which in summer is re-enacted in a *luce e suoni* (*son et lumière*; for information, tel: 040-224143). The Italianate gardens go down to the sea, which is a conservation area (park/gardens open Apr–Sept 8am–7pm, Mar and Oct until 6pm, Nov–Feb until 5pm; admission charge).

The **Grotta Gigante e Museo Speleologico**, (Giant Cave and Spelaeological Museum; for information and guided tours tel: (040) 823859; entrance fee) is only 15 km (9 miles) from Trieste on the Carso of Trieste, and is arguably the biggest tourist cave in the world.

Trieste ㊲ is both an intriguing modern port town and a delightful backwater. Its modern prosperity dates from 1719, when it was made a free port and an important outlet for the Austro-Hungarian Empire, and Empress Maria Theresa oversaw its rebuilding. It was the headquarters of the Italian high command in World War I, and after a turbulent World War II it did not come under Italian administration until 1954. The great traveller Richard Burton, the German poet Rainer Maria Rilke and the Viennese psychoanalyst Sigmund Freud were among

BELOW: the waterfront, Trieste.

its famous visitors. James Joyce taught and drank around the town, and it is easy to see a similarity between Trieste and Dublin. This is a special place, full of different dialects. As Joyce's biographer, Richard Ellmann, wrote: "The residents of Trieste, who had congregated there from Greece, Austria, Hungary and Italy, all spoke the dialect with special pronunciations. The puns and international jokes that resulted delighted Joyce."

Trieste's generous waterfront is centred on the 19th-century **Piazza dell'Unità d'Italia** (Italy's largest sea-facing piazza), surrounded by the serried portals of the town hall (1877), Palazzo del Governo, Lloyd Triestino building, Hotel Duche d'Aosta and the Baroque Palazzo Piterri (1790). A further showpiece is the canal and former harbour that runs up to the Neoclassical church, designed by Pietro Nobile in 1849.

First stop after these must be the castle and cathedral of **San Giusto** (open daily Apr–Sept 9am–7pm, Oct–Dec 9am–5pm), a simple Romanesque basilica once joined to another, giving it no fewer than four naves, with a lovely mosaic floor. Many religions worship in the town, including Serbian Orthodox at the neo-Byzantine San Spiridione, Greek Orthodox at San Nicolò and Jews at the 1912 Tempio Israelito, one of the largest synagogues in Europe. There is no shortage of museums, and pleasant surprises include the **Civico Museo Revoltella** (open Mon, Wed–Sat 9am–2pm, 4–7pm, Sun 10am–7pm; July and Aug until 10.30pm; admission charge) where there are some excellent genre paintings, such as Lionelli Balestieri's *Beethoven*, acquired at the 1901 Venice Biennale.

The last resort is **Muggia** 38, a developed fishing village where the Lion of St Mark still roars above archways. Beyond is the border, and Slovenia, where the concrete sea wall is replaced by grass. ❑

Trieste has some wonderfully atmospheric cafés, such as the Liberty-style Caffè San Marco, where you can breakfast on *cornetto* or *briosce*, feast on Viennese pastries for tea, or while away the early evening with an *aperitivo*.

BELOW: the understated elegance of San Giusto cathedral.

TRENTINO-ALTO ADIGE

As a region with a dual identity, Trentino-Alto Adige keeps one foot in Italy and the rest of the body in the South Tyrol, with its spirit adrift somewhere in the mountains

Map on page 190

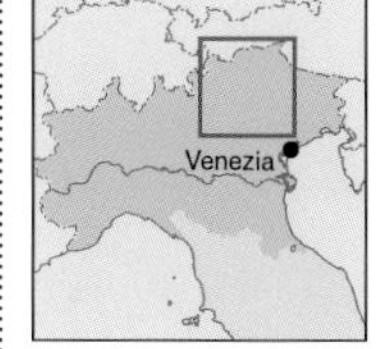

Trentino-Alto Adige and cultural ambiguity go together like snow and mountains. Its mind and passport may be in Italy, but its history is Austrian, its heart is in the South Tyrol, and its stomach is in *Mitteleuropa*. Austro-Hungarian culinary influences are clear, from dumplings and apple strudel to the typical winter dish of *polenta e crauti*, with sauerkraut. In 1946 the area was granted a greater degree of autonomy by the sanctioning of a special statute for the creation of the Trentino-Alto Adige region, and it now enjoys one of the highest standards of living in Italy.

The region's linguistic identity is torn between Italian and German. Compared with the Tyrolean Alto Adige, where many speak German as a first language, Trentino generally feels Italian in language and culture, although a Ladin-speaking minority lives in the valleys. Ladin is a Romance language, once spoken over much of Central Europe but now restricted to the South Tyrol, parts of Switzerland and Friuli. Trentino's other linguistic minority is the German-speaking group in the Valle dei Mocheni, an attractive rural area inhabited by people of German origin, descendants of those who came to work in the mines in the 16th century. In Alto Adige (South Tyrol) most signs appear in both Italian and German.

PRECEDING PAGES: Runkelstein, Bolsano (Bozen). **LEFT:** harvesting among the hills. **BELOW:** it is hard to miss the region's German cultural heritage.

Alpine culture

Since Roman times, the Brenner Pass and the Adige Valley have been the easiest Alpine crossing points. The Adige Valley was also the main route from Innsbruck and western Austria, via the Brenner Pass, to the cities of Venice and the Po Valley. Both Trentino and Alto Adige lie in the heart of the Alps and share traditions of conservatism, hospitality, environmental concern, quiet prosperity and a passion for mountains.

Scenery ranges from the domesticated to the wild, from sunny lakeside vineyards to the stark peaks and spires of the Brenta range. Much of the region is wooded or mountainous, yet the valley floors are carpeted with apple orchards. The Valle di Non, between Lombardy and the South Tyrol, is traditionally the wealthiest valley, as is shown by the verdant pastures and spring blossom. The lakes, with slopes covered in olives or vines, enjoy the most temperate climate in Trentino. The local parks are home to roe deer, chamois, mouflons, marmots, eagles, black grouse and the bearded vulture. The brown bear is the emblem of the Adamello Brenta park, but there are probably fewer than 10 left. Strict environmental laws ensure that nature is protected: lake water is constantly monitored, and even mushroom-picking is regulated.

As over half the terrain is covered in woods and mountains, the appeal of the great outdoors is obvious. Sports enthusiasts indulge in hang-gliding in the

A sign you are in mushroom country.

Dolomites, as well as hiking, mountaineering and rock-climbing. For those who don't want to brave the rocky ascents, hiking is a good option. There are ski resorts to suit every taste, with snowboarding, dog-sledging or scenic excursions on snowshoes as alternatives. In summer, lakes offer sailing and windsurfing, while the River Noce in the Val di Sole is the place for rafting and kayaking. Some organised cruises ply the lakes, but private motor boats are banned; even on Lake Garda, they must hug the Brescia shore on the Lombardy side.

Capital of Trentino

Trento ❶, the capital of the autonomous province of Trentino, lies at the foot of Monte Bondone. This prosperous yet provincial city exudes a curious air of Alpine homeliness and quiet sophistication. Trento was part of the Holy Roman Empire from the 10th century; it owes its fame to the Council of Trent, summoned in 1545 to face the crisis in Catholicism, notably the threat posed by the popularity of Lutheranism and Calvinism. The Pope and Emperor Charles V quibbled about

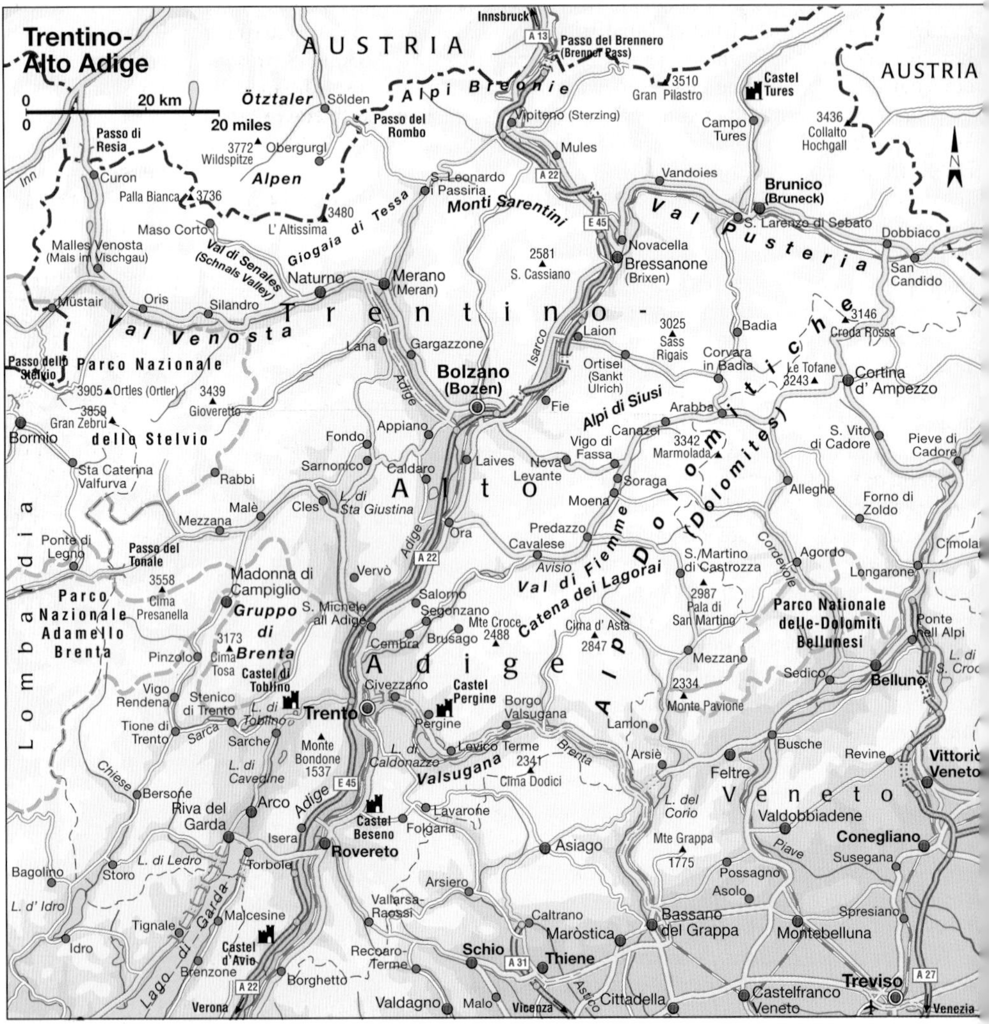

Map on page 190

the location, but Trento, set at the intersection between the Italian and Teutonic worlds, seemed an ideal choice: an Italian-speaking town within the German-speaking empire, situated on the easiest Alpine crossing.

The partly pedestrianised town centre is lined with impressive mansions. Via Manzi, Via Belenzani and the area around the Duomo, in particular, have richly frescoed Renaissance palaces. The Cantone is one of several quaint city corners which open onto attractive loggias and balconies. The profusion of pastry shops and homely *weinstube* (inns) paint a convincing picture of *Mitteleuropa*, but Trento nails its Italian colours to the mast: in the Piazza Dante gardens stands a monument to the great Florentine poet Dante Alighieri (1265–1321), erected in 1896 as an act of national pride, in defiance of the Austrian rulers.

Trento was ever a model of Roman Catholicism, as is revealed by the local dish, strangolapreti *("priest stranglers"), distinctive gnocchi which evoke the popular indignation against the avarice of some clerics.*

Piazza Duomo, the bustling heart of the town, is home to summery café terraces and boisterous Tyrolean bands. The Baroque fountain of Neptune with his trident recalls the city's Roman name, Tridentum. During the June *Mangiarbene* food festival, the square is strewn with tables laden with salami, meat stew, polenta, *canederli* (dumplings) and apple strudel. The Romanesque **Duomo** is surprisingly harmonious, considering it was built over an extended period and incorporates the remains of a 6th-century basilica. Highlights are the Romanesque apse, the gaudy Baroque altar and a rose window representing a wheel of fortune. Behind looms the crenellated **Castelletto**, the first fortified seat of the prince-bishops. Adjoining the cathedral is the fiercely battlemented, recently restored **Palazzo Pretorio** (open Wed–Mon 9.30am–12.30pm, 2.30–6pm; admission charge) which houses the Diocesan museum.

The **Castello del Buonconsiglio** (open high season, daily 10am–6pm, otherwise 9.30am–5pm; admission charge) is an underrated castle. The seat of the prince-bishops of Trento until the secularisation of the bishopric in 1802, the bastion contains an exquisitely frescoed Gothic tower, late-medieval and Renaissance wings and sumptuous Baroque apartments. The castle served as an Austrian military court during World War I, and played a symbolic role in the myth-making of Italian irredentism. In the "martyrs' pit", below the medieval town walls, the Austrians executed three patriots for treason in 1916.

Castelvecchio (1239–1486), the oldest part of the castle, is centred on an arcaded courtyard. A loggia in Venetian Renaissance style leads to the Bishops' Room, frescoed with images of princely clerics. The **Magno Palazzo** (1528–36) is a Renaissance affair, with frescoed walls and elegant loggias acting as a counterpoint to the medieval town walls and towers. The showpiece is the Gothic **Torre dell'Aquila**, containing a cycle of the months (1390–1419). The frescoes contrast peasants' labours with the noble high life.

The Sass Underground Archaeological Area, **Tridentum** (open Tues–Sun, June–Aug 10am–noon, 2.30–7pm, Sept–May 9am–noon, 2.30–6pm; tel: 0461-230171), is a large, recently excavated section of the Roman town, discovered in the basement of the Teatro Sociale and Piazza Cesare Battisti. Part of a paved street, a segment of a city wall, a house with mosaics and courtyards are all on view from a newly built visitor centre.

BELOW: the Piazza Duomo, at the heart of Trento.

The arcaded courtyard at Castello del Buonconsiglio.

Just outside the town lie the slopes of **Monte Bondone** ❷, accessible by cable car from Trento. Once the preserve of charcoal-burners, the kilns are now as abandoned as the ruined watchtowers. Set beside a mountain refuge at Viotre is the **Giardino Botanico** (Botanical Garden; open June–Sept daily 9am–noon, 2.30–5.30pm; admission charge). Among over 2,000 species of flora in these botanical gardens are foxgloves and edelweiss, gentians and lilies.

Castel Toblino ❸ (open Mar–Oct, closed Tues; tel: 0461-864036), west of Trento, is one of the most romantic castles in the region, a lakeside fortress that has been sensitively converted into a restaurant. Toblino is set on a small island, which becomes a peninsula when the water is low in the enchanting Lago di Toblino. The 12th-century castle, built over Roman remains, was remodelled in Renaissance times, and porticoes and loggias grace the inner courtyard. The turreted **Maso Toresella**, set on the lake shores, is the loveliest-looking wine estate in Trentino.

Lakes and fortresses

Between Castel Toblino and the massive Lake Garda lies **Lago di Cavedine** ❹, created by an enormous post-glacial landslide. Now used to generate hydroelectric power as well as pleasure, the peaceful lake is subject to strict environmental controls. Further south, **Riva del Garda** ❺ is an engaging resort on Lake Garda, the largest inland lake in Italy. The town, set on the fjord-like tip of the lake, is dominated by a rocky escarpment. On the lake stands the truncated **Rocca di Riva**, a moated medieval fortress linked to the town by a drawbridge. The museum within (open Tues–Sun, mid-Mar–mid-June and mid-Sept–early Nov 9.30am–12.45pm, 2.15–5.30pm, mid-June–mid-Sept 9.30am–6pm; July–

BELOW: the Old Town, Riva del Garda.

TRENTINO CASTLES

As a border region, Trentino has always been a bulwark against outside enemies. The strongholds encompassed feudal tower houses, lofty medieval bastions clinging to the rocks, and Venetian Renaissance courts. The mountain ridges are also dotted with Austro-Hungarian forts, often turned into military outposts during World War I. Recently the region has restored its finest castles, with some converted into hotels, restaurants, conference centres or the seats of wine estates. In summer they become the cultural focus for folklore and fireworks, exhibitions and classical concerts. During Trentino's Vinum Bonum – a summer wine and music festival – wine-tastings take place in lovely settings, including such historic haunts as Castel Toblino, Castel Pergine and the Castello di Rovereto *(see page 194)*.

The Adige Valley has long been an important trading route and eased the path of invading armies. Thus the Adige has the greatest concentration of castles, but the region as a whole bristles with bastions. In the prosperous Valle di Non there are patrician castles, tower houses and fortified manors, but many are privately owned and not open to the public. The design of the castles reflects changing tastes, with Gothic frescoes giving way to Renaissance loggias or lavish Baroque stucco-work.

Aug daily; admission charge) has finds dating back to the Bronze Age. There is also an art gallery with works from the 16th–20th centuries and many temporary exhibitions. The castle belonged to a succession of feudal lords and prince-bishops before serving as an Austrian barracks. From here it is a short stroll to the picturesque maze of the old town.

Only the northern tip of the shore of **Lago di Garda** ❻ is in Trentino, with the rest shared by the Veneto and Lombardy. Garda is subject to the *ora*, a bracing breeze that blows over the lake every afternoon, helping make neighbouring **Torbole** the best place for windsurfing. Just north of Riva stands **Castello di Arco** (open daily, variable times; admission charge; tel: 0464-583511), a castle perched on a jagged peak. The ruined watchtower and imposing bastions survey the Valle di Sarca, once the route to the Po Valley. In September this is the venue for the World Climbing Championships. When water levels are low, **Lago di Ledro** ❼, lying just west of Garda, reveals the soggy stumps of a prehistoric village off the southwestern shore. Items from here dating from 4,000 BC are on display in the museum at Rocca di Riva *(see above)*.

East of the two lakes is an impressive castle, visible from the main north–south motorway. Scenically set on grassy slopes framed by jagged peaks, **Castel d'Avio** ❽ (open Feb–Dec Tues–Sun 10am–1pm, 2–5pm) is a striking feudal bastion. The strategic location, overlooking Val Lagarina, enabled it to protect trading routes between the Mediterranean and northern Europe. Also known as Sabbionara d'Avio, the castle is reached by a steep path from the car park. The overwhelming impression is of terraces, towers and three sets of solid walls. The interior contains a baronial court extended by the Venetians, with Gothic frescoes depicting the battlefields of love and war.

A breeze on Lake Garda.

BELOW: the Varone gardens, Riva del Garda.

The vineyards of Trentino.

Second city

Rovereto ❾, Trentino's second city, reveals an engaging medieval and Renaissance heart, despite unprepossessing modern quarters. The city was shelled by the Italians in World War I, and the scars remain. In the Miravalle quarter the Maria Dolens bell rings daily at sunset in memory of the fallen in all wars. A long-distance **Path of Peace** also traces the line of the battlefields, leading to the Adamello and Marmolada glaciers.

In the town centre, the River Leno is lined with silk-workers' tall houses. Silk-making was introduced in the 16th century and helped make Rovereto the region's chief industrial centre 200 years later. World War I caused great damage, but the historic centre still has a faded charm, with frescoed façades, loggias and portals adorned with family crests. The winding **Via della Terra** is the backbone of the picturesque medieval quarter, linking the church of San Marco with the Gothic civic tower and the **Castello** (open Tues–Sun 10am–6pm; tel: 0464-438100; admission charge), which came into being as a moated military fortress guarding the Adige Valley crossing. The crenellated bastion was remodelled by the Venetians but still follows the rugged contours of the rock. The castle has served as a poorhouse, a Napoleonic garrison and an Austrian barracks before becoming a war museum and a school of hotel management.

MART, the **Museum of Modern and Contemporary Art of Rovereto and Trento** (Corso Bettini 43; open Tues–Sun 10am–6pm, Fri until 9pm; tel: 0464-438887), reopened in a brand new site in 2002, designed by contemporary Swiss architect Mario Botta. This large, airy museum is dedicated to the art of the 20th and 21st centuries.

BELOW: the "Bell of Peace" at Rovereto.

Until the 18th century much of the surrounding countryside was given over to mulberry orchards and the silkworm breeding that supplied the local industry. Today, the slopes are covered in vineyards. In the Lavini di Marco area south of the town, a bizarre **Dinosaur Trail** can be picked out, but is best followed on a guided tour; 200 million years ago dinosaurs left their tracks in sandy causeways, which became fossilised in limestone.

Wines and spas

Isera ❿, an otherwise undistinguished area, is home to vineyards producing the dry, full-bodied ruby-red Marzemino wine. Production, extending between the mountains of Baldo and Bondone, is centred on the slopes of the Lagarina Valley overlooking Rovereto. De Tarczal (tel: 0464-409134) is one of the finest producers of the noble varietal wine which was favoured by the imperial court. During the **Vinum Bonum** summer wine and music festival, concerts and tastings take place in numerous settings, from the de Tarczal villa to rustic cellars and historic castles, throughout Trentino. The **Casa del Vino** (tel: 0461-822820) is a wine centre that promotes prestigious local brands, harvest festivals and wine and food fairs. North of Rovereto, near the village of Besenello, looms **Castel Beseno** ⓫ (open Tues–Sun, Apr–June and Oct 9am–noon, 2–5.30pm, July–Sept 9am–6pm; admission charge), the largest castle in Trentino, incorporating massive bastions and gun emplacements.

Valsugana, about 20 km (12 miles) from Trento, covers Lake Caldonazzo and a cluster of spa towns centred on Levico Terme. The hills are dotted with ruined Austro-Hungarian forts. The long-distance **Path of Peace** runs along the 1914–18 front line, connecting the Tonale Pass, Rovereto and Marmolada. The valley makes a relaxing centre for Alpine and cross-country skiing, trekking, riding, water cures or sheer indulgence.

Lavarone ⓬ is a small resort set on the hillside above a tiny lake. The crest of the hill is dotted with Austrian forts, trenches and war cemeteries, while the lakeside path is named after Sigmund Freud, who spent a few summers there. Separated from the lake by a mountain ridge is **Lago di Caldonazzo** ⓭, which offers swimming, sailing, windsurfing, canoeing, water-skiing and fishing. The water is extremely pure, and it is the only lake where water-skiing is permitted.

At 1,500 metres (4,900 ft) above sea level, in the oldest part of the town, **Levico Terme** ⓮ claims to be the highest spa resort in Europe. The waters descend from a great height through galleries dug in the Middle Ages to facilitate the extraction of minerals. The 19th-century spa has a dignified air and is dotted with Art Nouveau villas, mostly hotels set in spacious grounds. The water has a high iron and arsenic content. Patients seeking distractions from diseases can shop for local handicrafts, from copper and brassware to hand-carved wooden toys and furniture. At **Panarotta 2002**, a ski resort north of Levico, the use of snow cannons for artificial snow ensures skiing until April.

Just north is the **Valle dei Mòcheni**, a curious cultural enclave inhabited by descendants of 16th-century German miners, who uphold many of their forebears' traditions as well as their language. Attractive wooden farmhouses are visible in such villages as Palù del Fersina, as are stretches of abandoned

Substantial local dishes worth sampling in the Valsugana region include polenta with mushrooms or game, salmon trout, sausages and cured meats.

BELOW: Tyrolean gentlemen of the Alto Adige enjoy a game of cards.

mines. Towering over Lake Caldonazzo is **Castel Pergine** ⓯ (tel: 0461-531158), an impressive Gothic castle, remodelled in the Renaissance. It is now a renowned (but reputedly haunted) hotel and restaurant (the latter is closed on Monday).

Cembra ⓰, a wine-producing town between Trento and Cavalese, has the steepest terraces in Trentino. It is also the gateway to the rugged **Valle di Cembra**, noted for its Alpine climate, steep gorges and flower-bedecked hamlets. Part of the valley has been scarred by porphyry quarrying, which provides paving stones and building slabs for cities all over Europe. The **Sentiero Rosa** is a relaxing 7-km (4-mile) trail linking villages on the northwestern side of the valley; en route are views of vineyards, porphyry quarries and Alpine terraces. In **Segonzano**, just east of Cembra, there is the strange spectacle of curious natural pyramids, carved over thousands of years by the wind and the rain.

In Pinzolo, close to the Madonna di Campiglio resort, the church of San Vigilio displays macabre frescoes of a Dance of Death (1539).

Madonna di Campiglio ⓱, the most stylish ski resort in Trentino, is second only to Cortina d'Ampezzo as a haunt of the sleekly pampered winter sports set. The annual skiing trip is seen as a northern Italian right rather than a privilege. There is après-ski aplenty. The winding main street is the scene of a nightly parade, a *passeggiata* encompassing window-shopping for skiwear and shades followed by *vin brûlé* (mulled wine) in cosy rustic inns. Madonna di Campiglio is at the head of Valle Rendena, nestling between the Adamello and Brenta groups, part of a cluster of slopes which, with the linked resorts of Marilleva and Folgarida, provide 120 km (75 miles) of mainly tree-lined pistes. Although Madonna itself does not connect with the vast Dolomiti Superski area, the not too distant resorts of Cavalese, Canazei and Moena do.

Set in west Trentino, the **Parco Nazionale Adamello-Brenta** ⓲ is the last

BELOW: the Alpine meadows of Seiser Alm.

refuge of the brown bear, but red deer, roe deer, foxes and marmots are more in evidence. (The elusive brown bear is best seen in the Spormaggiore or San Romedio sanctuaries in the upper Valle di Non.) For most visitors, the austere landscape is the greatest draw, embracing majestic glaciers, such as Mandron, and Alpine lakes, streams, waterfalls, deep fir woods and dolomitic rocks. The visitor centre is on Lake Tovel, but Lake Molveno further south is also appealing.

Cavalese ⓳ is the chief resort for the **Valle di Fiemme**, a valley carpeted with spring flowers and the name given collectively to the 11 small villages and towns. The grandest building is the sumptuously frescoed Palazzo della Magnifica Comunità, seat of the medieval council.

San Martino di Castrozza ⓴ basks in archetypal Dolomites landscape, lying at the foot of the pinnacle-crowned mountains. Rising to almost 3,200 metres (10,500 ft), the Pale di San Martino is the main mountain group in the southern Dolomites. Chair-lifts and a cable car give access to stunning views over glaciers and craggy peaks soaring over meadows and woodland. Violin-maker Stradivari used to collect spruce for his instruments here, giving it the name "Forest of Violins". San Martino is also the springboard for visits to the **Lagorai** mountains, a popular place for horse-riding and hiking. In summer the Suone delle Dolomite Festival combines a passion for mountains and music in open-air concerts conducted in Alpine meadows.

Map on page 190

The Valle di Fassa was the fiefdom of the prince-bishop of Bressanone (Brixen) until 1802. As such, it had to pay tithes of 68 sheep and pigs.

Valle di Fassa

Canazei ㉑ is the main resort for the Ladin-speaking Valle di Fassa. The Ladin Campitello carnival is both a cheerful interlude and an affirmation of local culture. The resort has expanded to absorb surrounding hamlets, but the valley's tradition of hospitality survives, as do the typical Alpine chalets with painted façades in the upper part of the town. Spectacular views of the Dolomites lie in wait at Belvedere and Sass Pordoi, reached by cable car.

From Canazei skiers can set out on the famous Sella Ronda, a great touring experience in stunning scenery. The circular ski route leads around the mighty Sella limestone massif, with villages dotted around it, offering 26 km (16 miles) of downhill trails in a single day. The route is linked by a variety of uphill transport including many new high-speed cable cars, gondolas and chair-lifts (and fortunately few drag lifts nowadays), all covered by the Dolomiti Superski ski pass. Canazei is also the best base for challenging climbs of the **Marmolada** range, the highest Dolomite peaks, and skiing on the Marmolada glacier.

The **Valle di Fassa**, which takes in the western slopes of the Marmolada range, includes the towns of Moena, Soraga and Campitello. **Moena** is noted for its Gothic church, welcoming inns and wood-carving. **Soraga** remains a rural community, as does **Campitello**, which marks the start of strolls along mule-tracks lined with votive crosses and is also a skiing village. The most magical landscape awaits beyond Predazzo, in the Lagorai and the jagged Catinaccio, where sunsets and refracted rays create a soft effect known as *enrosadira*, bathing the Dolomite crags in a rosy glow.

BELOW: the valleys and rocky crags of Valle di Fassa.

In the culinary clash between Italian and Germanic traditions, filling goulash and sauerkraut cooked in lard are the order of the day. The excellent wines also have a distinct Germanic flavour, from fruity Müller-Thurgau to delicate Sylvaner, crisp Gewürztraminer and dry Riesling Renato.

BELOW: until 1915, the Alto Adige region was part of Austria, and its people 97 percent German-speaking – a proud legacy for many of their descendants.

Alto Adige (Südtirol)

Known as the South Tyrol in English, this landlocked province dissociates itself from the rest of Italy, at least in cultural terms. The Tyrolean nature of the architecture in the Alto Adige is matched by the blond people, who are more lugubrious than Latin. The Tyrolean influence is present, too, in the soft Alpine meadows, the geranium-bedecked chalets and strudel-scented bakeries.

Bolzano (Bozen) ㉒ is the German-speaking capital of the Alto Adige (Südtirol). It lies on the Brenner transalpine route, linking the Latin south with the Germanic north. The gabled mountain chalets, brass bands and neat window boxes all seem distinctly un-Italian. The Tyrolean mood is a reflection of the cultural and artistic influences that prevailed from the 16th century until 1919. Bolzano still feels like an Austrian city, and the triumphal arch, built by Mussolini, raises thorny issues of race, identity and language. The finest houses lie in the area from **Piazza Werther** to Via dei Portici, an arcaded street lined with 17th-century mansions, and home to a colourful market, spilling out from Piazza Grano. The pink sandstone **Duomo** is roofed with multi-coloured tiles, restored after World War II damage. Dating from the 6th century, the cathedral incorporates Romanesque and Gothic elements. Two medieval churches, Chiesa dei Dominicani and Chiesa dei Francescani, decorated with School of Giotto frescoes, are also noteworthy; both have attractive cloisters.

The **Museo Archeologico dell'Alto Adige** (open Tues–Sun 10am–6pm, Thur until 8pm; admission charge) is set on Via Museo, a street of pastry shops. This is the final resting place of the mummified Ötzi the Iceman (estimated to have died 5,300 years ago), a Bronze Age man found in the meltwaters of a glacier in 1991. Austrian nationalists lost the battle to keep him on home soil, and he was reluctantly

returned from Innsbruck to Italy. Since 1998 he has been on display in a capsule of solid ice, protected behind bullet-proof glass. He is dressed in a leather loincloth, fur leggings, cape and cap, and waterproof grass boots. Despite mysterious burn marks and a small hole in his skull, the cause of death is unknown, but exposure is considered likely. It is possible to view the mummy through a small window.

Bolzano's summer climate is stifling, but cable cars swiftly transport citizens to the Alpine meadows. For motorists, the majestic **Dolomite Road** stretches from Bolzano to Cortina d'Ampezzo, following the central depression of the massif. This masterpiece of engineering was built in 1895 and served a military purpose during the 1914–18 campaigns.

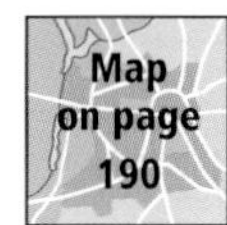
Map on page 190

Water therapy

Merano (Meran) ㉓, set at the head of the Val Venosta Valley, is a sedate spa town, popular with genteel visitors from all over Europe who enjoy the *belle époque* tearooms, gentle strolls and grim water cures. On Corso Libertà is the Kurhaus, the former pump-rooms, now converted into a concert hall. The Duomo di San Nicolò is a Gothic cathedral with a crenellated gable. The **Castello Principesco** (tel: 0473-230102), with its gabled façade, is the ancestral home of the Counts of Tyrol and the palatial residence of the Habsburg Archduke Sigismund.

The spa town of Merano also delights in a notorious "grape cure", which involves a copious diet of grapes for the duration of the regime.

A stroll through the medieval centre of town can take in Via Portici (Laubengasse), an arcaded promenade lined with painted houses. Merano's flower-decked promenades have boutiques and cafés as well as terraces and waterfalls. One of the most appealing strolls is **Passeggiata Lungo Passiro**, a "winter walk" linking the north bank of the river with the so-called Roman bridge. The "summer walk" meanders through a park planted with palms and pine trees. From the town, a cable car sweeps winter sports enthusiasts up to **Merano 2000**, a ski resort best suited to beginners, set on a conifer-clad plateau.

Parco Nazionale dello Stelvio (Stilfs) ㉔ is the largest park in the Alps, extending into Trentino and Lombardy. The best access to this land of snow-clad peaks and perpetual glaciers is via the visitor centres at Cogolo di Peio and the **Valle di Rabbi**. Park rangers accompany visitors on trips through larch and spruce forests with the sharp scent of resin in the air. Valle di Rabbi provides a good base for exploring the park. It is here that chamois decend to their summer pastures from the glaciated peaks. The landscape is dotted with farm buildings consisting of a cowshed on the ground floor and a barn or hay-loft above.

Malles Venosta (Mals im Vischgau) ㉕, the largest town in the west of Val Venosta, is a popular resort. The frescoed Carolingian San Benedetto church has a graceful Romanesque belltower, while the spires of the Gothic San Michele echo the jagged mountain peaks. The surrounding **Val di Senales (Schnals Valley)** ㉖ is a scenic ski centre. Just north of Malles, close to Burgusio (Burgeis) is the Benedictine **Abbazia di Monte Maria** (guided tours of crypt, 10am, 11am, 3pm, 4pm; closed Sat pm and Sun; admission charge; tel: 0473-831306), an impressive but remodelled abbey, its fine crypt decorated with 12th-century frescoes. At Slud-

BELOW: cooling off in Pragerwildsee.

erno (Schluderns), 4 km (2½ miles) southeast of Malles, medieval **Castel Coira (Churburg)** (open Tues–Sun 10am–noon, 2–4.30pm; admission charge) houses weaponry and armour.

Vipiteno (Sterzing) ㉗ is unquestionably a Tyrolean town, linking Bressanone with the Brenner Pass. As the centre of a previously prosperous mining district, Vipiteno was the possession of the Fuggers, the legendary banking dynasty, who redesigned the centre in Renaissance style. Via Città Nuova is flanked by grand palaces, including the late-Gothic town hall, the Palazzo Comunale. The arcaded main street is lined by Renaissance Tyrolean houses, with oriel windows and wrought-iron signs. The **Museo Multscher** (open Mon 2–5pm, Tues–Fri 10am–noon, 2–5pm, Sat 10am–noon; admission charge) on Via della Commenda, displays Renaissance sculptures. The mineral-encrusted valleys outside town include **Val di Racines**, noted for its waterfalls.

Seiser Alm is oddly named, as "alm" means alp but confusingly refers to a wide plateau here.

Bressanone (Brixen) ㉘, south of Brunico and Vipiteno, is also typically Tyrolean. The medieval heart is centred on the cathedral and the **Palazzo Vescovile**, which retains a pleasing galleried courtyard. The grand interior contains the **Diocesan Museum** (open Mar–Oct Tues–Sun 10am–5pm, Dec–Jan daily 2–5pm, cribs only; admission charge), with Romanesque sculptures and wood carvings, Renaissance altarpieces and a collection of cribs *(presepi)*. The remodelled Romanesque **Duomo** displays a Neoclassical west front but retains its Romanesque cloisters, adorned with Renaissance frescoes.

To the southwest of the town is **Castello di Velturno** (tel: 0472-855525), the summer palace of the rulers of Bressanone. Just north of the town stands the **Abbazia di Novacella** (tel: 0472-836189), a fortified monastery with fine frescoed cloisters, a Bavarian Baroque church and a Rococo library (guided tours, Mon–Sat 10am, 11am, 12pm, 3pm and 4pm; admission charge).

BELOW: cycling the Pordoi Pass.

Ortisei (St Ulrich) ㉙ is an attractive resort serving the Valle di Gardena and Alpe di Susi area, both delightful areas for Alpine hiking and skiing, linked to the huge Dolomiti Superski area of 1,220 km (758 miles). The valley is a centre of Ladin culture, and the library traces the origins of the language. South of town is the **Alpe di Siusi (Seiser Alm)**, the largest Alpine pasture in Europe, with quaint farmhouses and onion-domed churches.

From Ortisei, a cable car connects with Seiser Alm, a truncated peak encircled by the spiky spires of **Sassolungo (Langkofel)**. This mountain is dotted with old chalets and carpeted with Alpine orchids in spring. Sassolungo itself enjoys a view of the Sella, a seemingly castellated mass topped by towers. The **Passo di Sella**, linking Canazei and Valle di Fassa with Ortisei and Valle di Gardena, provides one of the most panoramic views in the whole region, and continues up to Passo Pordoi with its stunning views. A new lift system now connects Ortisei directly to the Sella Ronda circuit *(see page 197)*.

East of Vipiteno is **Brunico (Bruneck)** ㉚, a quaint town surveyed by a Gothic castle. Brunico's narrow alleys lead to a medieval gate and the church of Saint Ursula. To reach the popular winter-sports area, take the Riscone cable car to Plan de Corones. ❑

Italy with a German soul

The region is composed of two autonomous provinces – Trentino, which is some 98 percent Italian-speaking, while Alto Adige, often more commonly referred to as Südtirol, is very German in character. Most ethnic Germans felt wronged at the hands of the Italian Fascists after World War I. Indeed, German-speaking irredentists have never accepted the Italian annexation of the South Tyrol, which was part of the deal the Italians struck with the Allies in return for joining the war against Austria-Hungary in 1915. By claiming all the territory up to the Brenner Pass, the Italians put the desire for clearly defensible borders above the demands of linguistic and ethnic distinctions. The South Tyrol was duly split.

In the 1920s Mussolini transformed the population, bringing in Italians from the Veneto and the south as well as erasing German place-names and suppressing German culture and language. In 1939 Mussolini held a plebiscite to offer German-speakers the option of moving to post-*Anschluss* Germany. Over 200,000 chose Nazi Germany over Fascist Italy, proof that Il Duce's Italianisation policy had failed. In 1946 an international agreement stipulated that Austria renounced any territorial claim on condition that the rights of the German-speaking minority were respected.

In 1948 the Italian state engineered the creation of a new province to ensure an Italian-speaking majority in the enlarged entity. The provinces of Trento and Bolzano were duly merged to form Trentino-Alto Adige, with its own regional parliament and administration based in Trento. However, aggrieved German extremists perpetrated terrorist attacks from the late 1950s onwards, making a new political accommodation a priority.

With the aid of the United Nations, a *pacchetto*, or package of concessions, was finally agreed between Italy and Austria, and adopted in 1969. The measures allowed for greater local autonomy, with Bolzano able to protect the rights of all language groups.

Today German-speakers outnumber Italian-speakers by two to one in Alto Adige, with the latter mainly settled in the towns and the former in the country. Since 1996 there has been a political drive to "Germanise" place-names across the region, which has provoked an Italian backlash. Italian-speakers claim that their racial forebears had inhabited the region since Roman times. Equally aggrieved was the minority population of 20,000 speakers of Ladin, a language close to Latin, who claim to have been settled in the region for 2,000 years. Ladin-speakers are noted for their entrepreneurial flair.

In recent years South Tyroleans have been granted increased autonomy by Rome, and showered with mammoth subsidies. This has served to dim the secessionist ambitions of the materialistic *Südtiroler* (South Tyroleans). As the best-protected minority in Europe, they have simply no reason to envy their poorer Austrian neighbours living in the North Tyrol. ❑

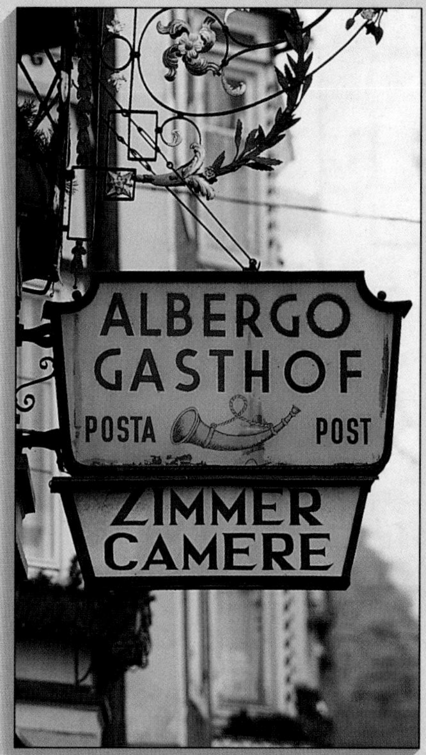

RIGHT: a sure sign of Trentino-Alto Adige's bilingual heritage.

MILAN

The fashion industry has put the city on the international map as a sophisticated place. But it's a one-dimensional image: the reality is much more complex

As the country's fashion capital, Milan is not slow to flaunt its credentials: even the airports are emblazoned with the Armani logo in sky-high lettering. In the chic Montenapoleone shopping district, Bar San Babila sells designer sandwiches named after Moschino, Versace and other dead fashion legends. At its sartorial best, Milan is a well-tailored, cosmopolitan city that puts on a show with panache, and Milan's Fashion Weeks are top-drawer events for every cosmopolitan "fashionista". At a Dolce & Gabbana party, foreign stars gather by fountains overflowing with rose petals and pick from silver platters piled with pomegranates. Yet this picture of the city is only a snapshot. Behind the scenes lies the cool practicality of a prosaic capital: serious, sober and locked into its quintessential northernness.

PRECEDING PAGES: the umbrellas of Milan; the Duomo in a downpour.
LEFT: the Duomo's Gothic spires.
BELOW: homegrown fashion: Prada Milan.

Undisputed capital

Once an inconsequential city on the Lombard plain, Milan rose to fame as the Roman stronghold of Mediolanum. After developing as an early Christian centre, it consolidated its power as an independent medieval commune. The Visconti (1277–1447) were enlightened despots whose empire-building caused them to be regarded as the city state's natural rulers. Under Gian Galeazzo Visconti (1385–1402) the mercantile city prospered and the northern empire expanded. The pragmatic Sforza dynasty then turned Milan into a vibrant Renaissance centre until Spanish rule (1535–1713) spelt cultural stagnation. During the Enlightenment, Austrian rule replaced Spanish decadence with economic progress and helped engender the industrious spirit that characterises the city today.

Italian unification led to the integration of the northern industrial cities into a cohesive national economy and gave a further boost to Milan. Since 1900 the city has led industrial design, a position consolidated by the impact of Bauhaus rationalism in the 1920s and the advent of mass production in architecture in the 1930s. After enduring Fascism and Allied bombing, Milan was confirmed in its pre-eminence by the economic miracle of the 1950s when the burgeoning design industry came into its own. Today Milan still dominates the fashion and industrial design calendar, from international trade fairs to the spring/summer, autumn/winter couture and ready-to-wear collections.

Milan remains Italy's undisputed business capital, a sophisticated metropolis dedicated to moneymaking and the pleasure principle. As the engine of economic growth it is also a symbol of the country's north-south divide: Rome may be the country's capital, but Milan is the powerhouse. This ponderously handsome city

Milan
0 400 m
0 400 yds
N
Piazzale Cimitero Monumentale
Via E. Tazzoli
San Antonio di Pádova
Stazione Porta Garibaldi F. S.
Garibaldi F.S.
Stazione Centrale (Central Station)
Gioia
Grattacielo Pirelli (Pirelli Tower)
Piazza S. Freud
Viale L. Sturzo
Piazza L. Einaudi
Via G. B. Pirelli
Via Donato Bramante
Via Ceresio
Via Carlo Farini
Via M. Quadrio
V. P. Maroncelli
Via N. Bonnet
Corso Como
Via C. De Cristoforis
Via F. Viganò
Via Melchiorre Gioia
Via A. Vespucci
Via d. Liberazione
Via Vinc. Viviani
Via Fabio Filzi
Via A. Cappellini
Piazza S. Gioachino
Via Marco Polo
Piazzale Princ. Clotilde
Via G. Galilei
Via V. Pisani
Via F. Casati
Via P. Lomazzo
Via G. B. Bertini
Via Paolo Sarpi
Piazzale A. Baiamonti
Viale Pasubio
Viale Monte Grappa
Viale F. Crispi
Bastiani di Porta Nuova
Via G. Bruno
Via A. Rosmini
Via G. B. Niccolini
Via Donato Bramante
Via G. Giusti
Via Luigi Canonica
Viale Montello
Via di Porta Volta
Via A. Volta
Via Varese
Consiglio
Santa Maria Incoronata
Via Milazzo
Via Marsala
Via Solferino
Via Castelfidardo
Fatebenefratelli
Ospedale F.B.F.
Corso di Porta Nuova
Via A. Appiani
Viale Monte Santo
Piazza della Repubblica
Repubblica
Via Manzoni
Piscina Cozzi
V. Vittorio Veneto
Bastioni di Porta Venezia
Leonardo's Horse
Via F. Melzi d'Eril
Via V. Alfieri
Piazza E. L. Morselli
Via D. Cirillo
Via L. Cagnola
Via C. M. Maggi
Largo la Foppa
Moscova
Via Garibaldi
Via Tenaglia
Via San Marco
Via G. Parini
Via F. Turati
Intend. d. Finanza
Viale Elvezia
Via A. Bertani
PARCO
Piazza Sempione
Arco della Pace
Arena (Stádion Civico)
Via Legnano
Corso Garibaldi
Chiesa Anglicano
Via Statuto
Via Moscova
San Angelo
Zoo
GIARDINI
Porta Sempione
Viale Malta
Via Palermo
Largo C. Treves
Via Montebello
Turati
Via D. Manin
Acquario (Aquarium)
Via d. Chiostri
San Simpliciano
San Marco
Via Cernaia
Chiesa Protestante
Palazzo Dugnani
PUBBLICI
Torre del Parco
SEMPIONE
Napoleone III
Via L. Albertini Rivoli
Palazzo Crivelli
Questura
Piazza Cavour
Via Palestro
Via Pontaccio
Via Fatebenefratelli
Via dell'Annunciata
Archi di Porta Nuova
Palazzo C. Svizzero
Villa Reale Galleria d'Arte Moderna
Viale Gadio
Viale E. Zola
Via Molière
Viale E. Alemagna
Palazzo dell'Arte
Lanza
Via Tivoli
Via Fiori Chiari
Via Fiori Oscuri
Pinacoteca di Brera
Palazzo Cusani
Via Borgonuovo
Palazzo Borromeo d'Adda
Teatro Manzoni
Palazzo dei Giornali
Piazza
Pinacoteca
Museo d'Arte Antica
Museo del Collezionista d'Arte
Foro Buonaparte
Via Mercato
Santa Maria del Carmine
ORTO BOTANICO
Via F. Gabba
Via Marina
Palazzo del Senato
San Pietro Celestino
Castello Sforzesco (Sforza Castle)
Roccetta
Via Sella
Via del Carmine
Via Brera
Monte di Pietá
Via Monte di Pietà
Montenapoleone
Palazzo Bagatti-Valsecchi
Via Senato
Via Venezia
Via A. Saffi
Viale Gadio
Via P. Paleocapa
San Giuseppe
Via dell'Orso
Museo Poldi-Pezzoli
Palazzo Melzi di Cusano
Via della Spiga
Palazzo Serbelloni
Ferrovie Stazione Nord Milano
Castello
Via Cusani
Via Broletto
Teatro alla Scala
Via G. Morone
Palazzo Belgioioso
Via Monte Napoleone
Museo di Milano
Via Bagutta
Via S. Andrea
Cadorna
Largo Cairoli
Cairoli
San Tomaso
Via A. Boito
Via Verdi
Casa d. Manzoni
Via Alessandro Manzoni
Corso Damiano
Via G. Boccaccio
Via Vincenzo Monti
G. Leopardi
Foro Buonaparte
Palazzo Clerici
Via Clerici
Museo Teatrale
Piazza d. Scala
Via M. A. Catena
Corso G. Matteotti
Basilica di San Babila
Santa Maria delle Grazie
San Nicolao
Via Dante
Teatro Dal Verme
Palazzo Marino (Municipio)
San Fedele
Via Bigli
Piazza S. Babila
Palazzo Bolagnos
Cenacolo Vinciano
Palazzo Litta
Palazzo Carmagnola
Via S. Margherita
Galleria Vittorio Emanuele
Palazzo Spinola
San Babila
Corso Magenta
Via Meravigli
Cordusio
Pal. d. Ragione
Via Agnello
Corso Vitt. Emanuele II
Via Borgog
Palazzo Durini
Palazzo delle Stelline
Via Togni
Museo Archeologico
S. Monastero Maggiore
Palazzo d. Borsa
Via G. Negri
Piazza Cordusio
Duomo
Via S. Radegonda
San Vito
Via Durini
Via Visconti di Modrone
Via A. De
Via S. Agnese
Via Nirone
Via Brisa
Piazza degli Affari
Via Bocchetto
Via Orefici
Piazza del Duomo
Palazzo d. Capitano di Giustizia
Corso Europa
Via V. Cerva
Via G. Carducci
Piazza S. Ambrogio
Via Valeria
Palazzo Borromeo
Piazza Borromeo
Pinacoteca Ambrosiana
Palazzo Reale
Piazza Fontana
Largo Augusto
Via C. Battisti
Sant' Ambrogio
Università Cattolica
Palazzo Stanga
Via S. Orsola
Piazza Mentana
San Satiro
Arengario
San Gottardo
Ufficio Comunal
Piazza San Stefano
Santo Stefano Maggiore
Corso di Porta Vittoria
Museo Nazionale della Scienza e della Tecnologia
Via Cappuccio
Via Santa Marta
Via Torino
Via Unione
Via G. Mazzini
Via Rastrelli
Via Larga
Via d. Signora
Via Sforza
Via Guastalla
Via Freguglia
Sant' Agostino
Circo Romano
Via Circo
Via Nerino
San Giorgio
Missori
Teatro Lirico
Piazza Velasca
Via Sant Antonio
Ca Grande (Università Statale)
Palazzo Sormani
Palazzo di Giustizia
Via E. de Amicis
Via Olona
Via Carroccio
Via Lesmi
Via Lanzone
Palazzo Stampa
Palazzo Trivulzio
Via Zebedia
Via P. d. Cannobio
Palazzo Greppi
Via Festa d. Perdono
Santissimi Barnaba e Paolo
GIARDINO
Via San Barnaba
San Bernardino a Monarche
Via C. Correnti
Via Stampa
Via S. Vito
Via Amedei
Corso Italia
Palazzo Annoni
Torre Velasca
Via Pantano
Via Francesco
GUASTALLA
Via F. Daverio
Via Ausonio
Via Aribergo
Via San Vincenzo
Piazza Resistenza Partigiana
Porta Ticinese
Piazza d. Vetra
Piazza S. Quasimodo
Via dei Cornaggia
(Ex. Osp. Maggiore)
Via Ces. da Sesto
S. Calocero
San Calocero
Colonne di San Lorenzo
Sant' Eufemia
Via S. Senatore
Piazza S. Nazaro
Corso di Porta Romana
Policlinico
Via M. Fanti
San Vincenzo in Prato
Anfiteatro Romano
San Lorenzo Maggiore
Via d. Chiusa
Via Crocefisso
Regina Elena
Viale Papiniano
Corso Genova
Via M. d'Oggiono
Via Conca del Naviglio
PARCO DELLE BASILICHE
Via Molino delle Armi
San Paolo Converso
Via Santa Sofia
Santa Maria d. Visitazione
Viale S. Calimero
Via Romana
Santi Innocenti
Via della Commenda
Via A. Lamarmora
Viale Coni Zugna
Porta Genova
Via G. Alessi
Via G. Ferrari
Via Arena
Via Vetere
Corso di S. Gottardo
Via C. D. Fante
Via G. Mercalli
San Calimero
Crocetta
Teatro Carcano
Corso C. Colombo
Viale G. d'Annunzio
San Eustorgio
Via Santa Croce
Via San Luca
Santa Maria dei Miracoli
Piazza Card. A. Ferrari
Istituto Ortopedico G. Pini
Via Quadronno
Via Orti
Viale Gorizia
Darsena
Piazza S. Eustorgio
Via M. Burigozzo
San Celso
Via S. Martino
Fr. d'Assisi
Corso Punta Vigentina
San Pietro dei Pellegrini
Genova F.S.
Via Vigevano
Porta Ticinese
Via Sambuco
Via C. Crivelli
Via Cassolo
Santa Maria delle Grazie al Naviglio
Strada Alzaia Naviglio Grande
Viale Gorizia
Piazzale XXIV Maggio
Viale G. Galeazzo
Piazzale Porta Lodovica
Viale Beatrice d'Este
Via Bianca di Savoia
Viale A. Filippetti
Pavia
Viale Col di Lana

Palermo would sacrifice wealth for prestige and power. Fortunately, Milan has substantially recovered from *Tangentopoli*, the "Bribesville" corruption scandals of the early 1990s. According to Roberto Peretta, an expert in Milanese affairs, *"Tutto come prima ma non proprio"* (All is as it was – but not exactly).

The civic centre

Piazza del Duomo ❶ has been the historical heart of the city since the Middle Ages, when the archbishop, the city's political ruler, maintained a palace beside the cathedral. Despite its sense of solidity, the square only attained its present form after Italian unification, when medieval buildings were demolished to emphasise grandeur. The square is dominated by the Duomo, the city's landmark cathedral, but is lined by severe palaces, notably the two monumental blocks built under Fascism. However, any architectural severity is softened by the presence of busy commuters, buskers and bag-sellers. The piazza is always bustling, particularly when open-air concerts enliven summer evenings.

The façade is currently under more than 7,000 sq. metres (75,000 sq. ft) of scaffolding while two years of restoration work is conducted. The work is concentrated on the upper part of the façade and its 12 spires.

The Duomo ❷ (open daily 7am–7pm) remains Italy's most famous unfinished masterpiece, which patrons continue to endow with statuary and stones. The work was begun under Gian Galeazzo Visconti in 1386 but continued until Napoleonic times, seamlessly blending Gothic, Baroque, Neoclassical and neo-Gothic styles. The building is considered Europe's biggest Gothic cathedral, but its authenticity is slightly compromised by the Baroque main doors and the main façade, which were added during the Counter-Reformation. Nonetheless, it is the clearest model of Gothic architecture in Italy, with numerous French-style flying buttresses and soaring pinnacles contrasting with the excessive width preferred by the native Lombard builders. It has a staggering 135 spires and 3,400 statues. The finest view is from the Piazzetta Reale, which reveals the full sweep of Gothic-Flamboyant glory, with arched buttresses and gables embellished with delicate spires and gargoyles. On the highest pinnacle stands the sacred *Madonnina*, the city protector, resplendent in glittering gold. From the roof of the Duomo, accessible by a steep climb or lift (9am–5.50pm daily; admission charge), there is a memorable view of the *Madonnina* soaring over the Gothic spires 109 metres (358 ft) above the ground.

BELOW: the Duomo is a temple of astonishing craftsmanship, as seen in this intricate cast-bronze door.

The English novelist D.H. Lawrence called the Duomo "an imitation hedgehog of a cathedral", because of its pointy intricate exterior. But inside, the church is simple, majestic and vast. Five great aisles stretch from the entrance to the altar. Enormous stone pillars dominate the nave, which is big enough to accommodate some 40,000 worshippers. In the apse, three large and intricate stained-glass windows attributed to Nicolas de Bonaventura shed a soft half-light over the area behind the altar. The central window features the shield of Visconti, Milan's ruling family during the 13th and 14th centuries.

In a small square to the right of the Duomo is the **Palazzo Reale** ❸. In the Middle Ages it was home to the city's rulers – the Visconti, Sforza and Torriani. In the 18th century the palace was rebuilt and decorated with gold leaf and stucco, and both Napoleon and Victor Emmanuel of Savoy lived here. It suffered in the

Among the Galleria's best cafés and restaurants are the Art Nouveau Camparino at no. 78, a classic spot for an *aperitivo* – especially a campari, as Davide Campari, inventor of the drink, was born here on the first floor. Other perfect people-watching spots include Biffi and, next door, the new Gucci café which, although not cheap, serves good, sophisticated snacks.

BELOW: inside the Galleria Vittorio Emanuele.

with gold leaf and stucco, and both Napoleon and Victor Emmanuel of Savoy lived here. It suffered in the 1943 bombardments, and the damage is still visible in the lovely, partly demolished Sala delle Cartialdi. Temporary exhibitions are staged in the Palazzo Reale (for information tel: 02-88451). The **Museo della Reggia** (tel: 02-875672) within the Palazzo has been under restoration since the 1980s. Work is expected to be completed in 2006, with 14 rooms on the first floor showcasing architecture and design. One wing on the ground floor houses the **Museo del Duomo** (open Tues–Sun 9.30am–12.30pm, 3–6pm; admission charge). Here the story of the cathedral's construction is told chronologically, and highlights include Jacopo Tintoretto's *Infant Christ Among the Doctors*.

The long-awaited new **Museum of the 20th Century**, also known as **Museo del Presente**, will combine the **Civico Museo d'Arte Contemporanea** (currently under restoration) on the second floor with the very stylish modern **Arengario** building on the corner of the Piazza del Duomo and Via Marconi. Predicted to open towards the end of 2006 and early 2007, this should be among Europe's top contemporary art galleries.

Galleria Vittorio Emanuele ❹, the magnificent arcaded gallery leading off the square, is known as *il salotto di Milano*, Milan's drawing room. Since its creation in 1864 the gallery, surmounted by a magnificent iron-and-glass cupola and lined by cafés and bookshops, has served as a meeting-place for Milanese of all ages and backgrounds. The gallery, originally created to honour the Austro-Hungarian emperor, was dedicated to Victor Emmanuel, the Italian king. The designer, Giuseppe Mengoni, intended the passage to link the cathedral with La Scala and the prestigious Via Manzoni.

The gallery opens onto the austere Piazza della Scala, home to **Teatro alla**

Scala ❺, Italy's premier opera house, which has now been opulently restored. The Neoclassical façade was built by Giuseppe Piermarini in 1776, but the main auditorium was faithfully reconstructed after bomb damage. Opera is a national passion, and is celebrated by the Milanese with typical Italian fervour. In this melodious city, the perfect pitch of the singers is matched by the sumptuousness of La Scala's red plush, and by the choice of neighbouring bars that play on a musical theme. Caffè Verdi, around the corner, is decorated with posters of the Three Tenors, Callas and Nureyev, while the neighbouring Grand Hotel et de Milan contains the famous suite where Verdi died.

La Scala's season traditionally opens on 7 December, the day of St Ambrose, the city's patron saint. This is the high point of the social calendar, signalling a season running until July, with opera interspersed with orchestral concerts.

The **Museo Teatrale alla Scala** (open daily 9am–12.30pm, 1.30–5.30pm; admission charge) is now housed again at La Scala after its temporary move to Corso Magento. It was closed for three years for renovation and reopened in December 2004 in a new layout designed by Pier Luigi Pizzi. The museum traces the fascinating history of opera and theatre in the city, with memorabilia, busts, posters and other objects connected to great musicians and composers such as Verdi, Toscanini and Puccini on show as well as temporary exhibitions. The visit includes a look into the theatre itself from one of the boxes – as long as there are no rehearsals under way. It displays a rich collection of musical instruments, operatic costumes and masks, as well as busts of the great operatic composers and conductors. Milanese audiences are hard taskmasters, with applause led by the official clapping societies. If the opera falls short of perfection, the *loggionisti*, those sitting in the gods, rain down abuse on fallen divas.

Riccardo Muti fell on his baton and resigned from La Scala in April 2005, ending his 19-year reign at Milan's glittering opera house after a bitter battle for power. The hot-tempered conductor declared that he had no choice but to leave after workers and musicians went on strike, forcing La Scala to cancel several performances.

BELOW: La Scala.

Museo Poldi-Pezzoli, a testament to 19th-century patrician tastes.

Casa del Manzoni ❻ (or Museo Manzoniano; open Tues–Sat 9am–noon, 2–4pm; admission charge), on Via Morone, is a shrine to Alessandro Manzoni, one of the country's best-known novelists – he was the author of *The Betrothed (I Promissi Sposi)*, generally acclaimed as Italy's only major 19th-century novel. The house where he lived from 1822 until his death in 1873 is now a small museum.

On Via Manzoni is the **Museo Poldi-Pezzoli** ❼ (open Tues–Sun 10am–6pm; admission charge; free audio-guide equipment), founded by a nobleman who bequeathed his home to the city on his death in 1879. The interior is a testament to 19th-century patrician tastes, with sundials and ceramics. Highlights include Renaissance paintings by Botticelli, Bellini, and Piero della Francesca.

From Via Manzoni, Via Santa Margherita leads to **Palazzo Clerici** ❽ (ring the bell). Set on Via Clerici, this impressive 18th-century palace is noted for a famous ceiling fresco by Tiepolo. Further south, just off the Piazza del Duomo, is the tiny **Piazza Mercanti**, the sole surviving corner of medieval Milan. Surrounding the square are former guildhalls and civic buildings, now banks and offices. The finest is the **Palazzo della Ragione** ❾, also known as the Broletto Nuovo. This medieval gem served as the council chambers and law courts.

Il Quadrilatero

BELOW: the Galleria Vittorio Emanuele has been a favourite Milanese meeting-place since 1864.

From Piazza Mercanti it is a short stroll or metro ride to the chic fashion district, centred on Via Monte Napoleone. The fashion showrooms are located between the elegant Brera district and Piazza San Babila in the *quadrilatero,* a quadrangle dubbed the "golden triangle" or *"triangolo della moda"*. **Via Monte Napoleone** ❿, known to cognoscenti as Monte Napo, offers Italy's greatest concentration of design and jewellery houses. Milan's fashion industry thrives on a ready supply of home-grown talent and a contemporary feel, essentially a creative twist on classic lines. These deep design roots lie in medieval craftsmanship, traditional skills which are prized in textiles, jewellery and leather goods, as well as in haute couture *(see Alta Moda, page 219)*. Yet so confident are the Milanese of their impeccable refinement that they can even do gross bad taste with aplomb, as Versace, Moschino and Dolce & Gabbana have demonstrated on occasion.

Map on page 206

The "vie" Monte Napoleone, Sant'Andrea, della Spiga and Borgospesso are home to all the great designer shops. A stroll down Via Monte Napoleone takes in Emilio Pucci – one of the longest-established fashion houses – Versace glitz, Gucci glamour, sumptuous cashmere from Loro Piana, Alberta Ferretti and their younger brand "Philosophy" in the adjoining shop, and much more. At the intersection of Monte Napoleone and Sant'Andrea, seek refuge from haughty sales staff in the Antico Caffè Cova. Founded in 1817, this is an obligatory stop on the fashion circuit. This chic, chandelier-hung *pasticceria* was favoured by Mazzini, Garibaldi and 19th-century nobility but today welcomes the *Milanese bene*, well-off citizens eager to exchange shopping tips over a coffee.

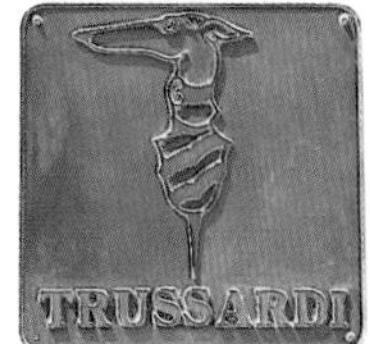

Famous names abound in this chic area.

On Via Gesù is the quirky Renaissance museum of **Palazzo Bagatti-Valsecchi** ⓫ (open Tues–Sun 1–5.45pm; admission charge), an eclectic collection in a nobleman's residence. Created by the Bagetti-Valsecchi brothers as an elegy for the Renaissance era, it is also a tribute to Victorian eclecticism. Authentic 16th-century furniture, ceramics and weaponry are mixed with reproductions of Renaissance art, but the result is more than a pleasing pastiche.

Piazza San Babila is a popular meeting-place for Milanese youth. Nearby is **Basilica di San Babila** ⓬, a 5th-century church sensitively remodelled in 1905 in an attempt to restore its 12th-century splendour. Nearby is the exhibition centre, **Fiera Milano City**, which hosts some 80 trade fairs annually including the fabled fashion designer collections. In the adjoining streets, sleek addicts of designer wear scour Via Sant'Andrea in search of Trussardi, Moschino, Fendi and Giorgio Armani. Pietro Veri is home to Ermenegildo Zegna menswear, and Corso Venezia to diffuse fashion lines. On ultra-chic Via della Spiga you will find Dolce & Gabbana, Moschino, Roberto Cavalli and Agnona – the womenswear arm of Ermenegildo Zegna. It is overlooked by the Carlton Hotel Baglioni's terrace "shisha bar" *(see page 366)* – a little corner of Morocco or Dubai in this glamorous part of town.

BELOW: Villa Reale.

Via Palestro leads through a chic residential district to **Villa Reale** ⓭, set in romantic grounds dotted with follies. The Neoclassical villa, built for a Milanese count in 1790, accommodated Napoleon and Josephine as well as Napoleon III. Today it houses the **Galleria d'Arte Moderna** (currently closed for renovation but guided tours are held Tues–Sun 9–11am), a collection of modern Italian paintings, with works by Cézanne, Sisley and Bonnard on the second floor. The former carriage house here is now the **Padiglione d'Arte Contemporanea** (open Tues–Sun, variable hours according to exhibitions). On the other side of Via Palestro are the **Giardini Pubblici** ⓮, the city's finest park, with pony trails and pavilions. Created in

For weary shoppers, the glamorous bar of the Four Seasons Hotel, set in a delightful former monastery on Via Gesù, provides a cosseted escape from rampant consumerism.

BELOW: the Pinacoteca di Brera houses one of Italy's finest art collections, with works by Mantegna, Raphael and Piero della Francesca.

the 1780s, the grounds incorporated the monastic kitchen gardens that bordered Corso Venezia, an area which in the 18th century was at the heart of Milanese intellectual life, and still abounds in grand palaces that were once literary salons. At Corso Venezia 55 is the **Museo di Storia Naturale** (open Tues–Fri 9am–6pm, Sat–Sun 9am–6.30pm; tel: 02-88463280), Italy's most important natural history museum. On the same side of the gardens is **Planetario Hoepli**, Italy's largest planetarium. The star shows beneath the dome are a delight.

The Brera quarter

This chic district adjoins the "golden triangle" and the castle quarter. The Brera was once a bohemian rendezvous for artists and rebels, but 1960s flower power has long since given way to early-21st-century materialism. This is *Milano bene*, an elegant district where well-to-do Milanese browse in designer boutiques and art galleries before flitting to fashionable cafés. Fortunately, relics of the old Brera remain, not least in the discreet palaces graced by secret courtyards and old portals, and by a handful of quaint cafés and theatres.

A stroll from La Scala along Via Verdi leads to the Brera quarter, which is also served by Lanza metro station. The best of it lies in the small pedestrianised area between Via Pontaccio and Via Brera, lined by 18th- and 19th-century palaces. Bar Giamaica on Via Brera, 32, is the place for erstwhile hippies who have mellowed into corporate executives. This 1960s haunt is a little down at heel nowadays but still popular. It also hosts occasional art exhibitions. **Via Fiori Chiari** ⓯ is the heart of a bustling little area packed with bars, restaurants and designer boutiques. This characteristic street is an obligatory stop on the evening summer *passeggiata*. On the third Saturday of the month an atmospheric antiques market spills over onto Via Fiori Chiari.

Pinacoteca di Brera ⓰ (open Tues–Sun 8.30am–7.15pm, but variable; admission charge; tel: 02-722631), founded by the Habsburgs in the late 18th century, represents one of the country's greatest art collections, especially for medieval and Renaissance Italian art. The museum, on Via Brera, was dramatically enlarged in Napoleonic times, as Napoleon sought to create a collection worthy of a new capital, albeit one subject to Paris. Since his fall did not result in the return of the plundered artworks, the Brera remains a treasure trove of northern European art. The somewhat austere palace has been modernised, and a pleasant café and bookshop created. The collection is particularly strong on Venetian and Lombard works from the 15th to the 18th century, with Renaissance artists particularly favoured. Italian masterpieces include works by Raphael, Piero della Francesca, Caravaggio and Mantegna, including his masterpiece, the dramatically foreshortened *Dead Christ* (Room 6), as well as modern works by Boccioni, Carrà and Morandi. The Venetians are represented by Veronese, Tintoretto, Titian and Carpaccio, with Bellini's *Madonna and Child* one of the finest works. Amongst foreign old masters, paintings by Rubens, Rembrandt and Van Dyck can be singled out. Look also for the 19th-century work by Francesco Hayez in Room 37; *The Kiss* is his most famous and passionate work.

Map on page 206

Via Pontaccio and Corso Garibaldi lead to **San Simpliciano** ⓱ (open daily 7am–noon, 3–7pm), on Piazza San Simpliciano, one of the city's most ancient churches, dating from the 5th century. Behind it are fine 15th-century cloisters. It is a short stroll back to Via Tivoli, which leads to the castle quarter.

The castle quarter

The castle quarter adjoins the banking district and is signalled by Foro Bonaparte, a grandiose semicircle created by the French Napoleonic forces. Dominating the district is **Castello Sforzesco** ⓲ (open Tues–Sun 9.30am–5.30pm; admission charge), the imposing castle founded by Galeazzo II Visconti (*c.* 1350) and rebuilt by Francesco Sforza in 1450. It was largely dismantled by the Napoleonic forces, who downgraded it to a barracks. The shell was rebuilt in 1893 to incorporate mock medieval and Renaissance flourishes such as the Filarete tower that dominates the façade. Renaissance interiors include Leonardo da Vinci's Sala delle Asse, a room decorated with a pattern of intertwined foliage. The castle museums house a display of Lombard sculpture, ceramics, furniture, tapestries, arms and a recently extended collection of musical instruments. The picture gallery (closed noon–2pm) features works by Bellini, Titian, Correggio, Tintoretto, Canaletto and Van Dyck. The highlight is Michelangelo's last work, *Pietà Rondanini* (Room 15), still unfinished when he died aged 89, now especially evocative after having been cleaned.

The castle is surrounded by so-called English gardens, which connect with the sprawling **Parco Sempione** ⓳, created in 1893 on the old parade grounds and terminating in a Neoclassical arch, l'Arco della Pace, to hail Napolean's entry into Milan. On the edge of the park is the **Acquario** ⓴ (open Tues–Sun

Madonna in Prayer, *attributed to Pietro Solari, in the picture gallery of the Castello Sforzesco.*

BELOW: the "English gardens" of Castello Sforzesco.

Fresco of St Ambrose in the Basilica di Sant'Ambrogio.

9am–5.30pm; free). The aquarium is housed in an appealing Art Nouveau building and displays the main marine habitats as well as a specialist library.

The **Museo del Collezionista d'Arte** (Via Sella 4, on the corner of Piazza Castello; open Mon–Fri 10am–6pm, Sat 10am–2pm; admission charge) is a fascinating private museum that reveals the difference between fake and real antiques. Visitors are encouraged to handle objects and to discover how to verify the originality of pieces. There is also a special section dedicated to understanding art by Leonardo da Vinci.

Porta Romana and the university quarter

This is a mixed, residential neighbourhood with student cafés and historic sights. It comes alive in early December for a medieval fair, *Oh Bej, Oh Bej*, set in Piazza Sant'Ambrogio, when stalls sell speciality sweets, pork snacks, children's toys and artisanal furniture. **Ca' Grande (Università Statale)** ㉑, set on Via Festa del Perdono, is the most imposing university building. The "big house", as it is known in Milanese dialect, is an attractive 15th-century brick building that housed the city's main hospital for five centuries. Now home to the humanities faculty, it is at the heart of Milanese student life. Closer to Sant'Ambrogio is the Università Cattolica, the Catholic rival to the state university. On Piazza Velasca, just around the corner, looms **Torre Velasca**, a bizarre tower built in 1958 to echo the city's predilection for massive medieval towers.

Beyond, on Piazza Sant'Ambrogio, is the **Basilica di Sant'Ambrogio** ㉒ (open daily 8am–noon, 2.30–6pm), a prototype for a Romanesque Lombard church, with its harmonious proportions and geometrical cross-vaulting. For many Milanese this solemn church is closer to their hearts than the lofty Duomo. A mood of subdued spirituality prevails in a place dedicated to the city's patron saint. Work began in 386, but the church was only completed in the 12th century. The legacy of St Ambrose lives on in the liturgy of the Milanese church as well as in Ambrosian chant. Traces of the early Christian Church remain: portions of walls and columns; marble and mosaic decorations; a jewel-encrusted medieval high altar; and a ciborium supported by columns of red porphyry. The **Museo della Basilica** (open daily 10am–noon, 3–5pm; admission charge) holds many treasures, incuding illuminated manuscripts and St Ambrose's robe.

Museo della Scienza e della Tecnologia Leonardo da Vinci (open Tues–Fri 9.30am–5pm, Sat–Sun 9.30am–6.30pm; admission charge) on Via San Vittore 21, is one of the most important science and technology museums in the world, with more than 15,000 exhibits. A complete gallery is dedicated to the Italian genius of the Renaissance period, Leonardo da Vinci. From here it is only a short walk to Leonardo's masterpiece.

BELOW: the Corso Venezia was once the centre of Milanese intellectual life; it still bears witness to the occasional debate.

Leonardo's *Last Supper*

The **Cenacolo Vinciano** ㉓ (open Tues–Sun 8.15am–7pm, last entry 6.45pm, variable; viewing limited to 15 minutes, by appointment only; admission charge; information and reservations, tel: 02-89421146, reservations only, tel: 02-4987588), housing Leonardo da Vinci's *Last Supper* (painted between 1495 and

1497), lights up the former refectory of Santa Maria delle Grazie. Since its restoration in 1999 the popularity of the painting means that it is best to book your visit as soon as you arrive in Milan. It has become difficult to get places to see the fresco, partly as a result of the popularity of *The Da Vinci Code*. Places are limited to 25 people every 15 minutes. The telephone booking number is available Mon–Fri 9am–6pm and Sat 9am–2pm. It is often engaged, but operators do speak English. The operator will give you a code number and the time of the visit. If you don't manage to book, there is a very small chance of getting returns on the day at the *Last Supper* booking office.

In deciding not to paint on wet plaster, Leonardo rejected received wisdom: dry plaster would allow him more time to retouch the work. However, excessive humidity combined with the faulty mixture used for binding the paint caused the fresco to deteriorate even during the artist's lifetime. The masterpiece was finally unveiled in 1999 after a 22-year restoration, with later accretions being stripped off to reveal the artist's original intentions. As a result, the restorers have revealed wonderfully vivid details such as flowers and bread, with the familiar murky brown sludge giving way to a startling luminosity.

The controversial restoration has divided critics, but Signora Brambilla, the chief restorer for two decades, is clear about her guiding principles: "I'm an artisan, not an artist, still less a scientist; aesthetic sensitivity is the most important thing for restoring any work of art." Although the public tends to approve of the brilliancy of the colours, the results of the restoration have dissatisfied many art critics, who feel that posterity has been given a pale ghost, a virtual Leonardo.

Facing the refectory is the lovely Renaissance church of **Santa Maria delle Grazie** (open Tues–Sat 7am–noon, 3–7pm, Sun and hols 7.30am–12.15pm,

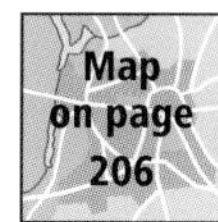
Map on page 206

When the prior accused Leonardo da Vinci of dawdling over the fresco, the master tartly replied that he was having difficulty imagining the face of anyone as evil as Judas, but that the prior's portrait could be used if the Church were really in such a hurry.

BELOW: flawed genius; da Vinci's masterpiece, *The Last Supper.*

RENAISSANCE MAN

Leonardo da Vinci lived in Milan and France as well as in his native Florence. In Milan he was supported between 1482 and 1515 by the Sforza, his powerful patrons, and he has left numerous masterpieces in his adoptive city. Yet despite the sublime beauty of his work and a supreme mastery of painting technique, Leonardo was chiefly interested in solving intellectual and philosophical problems of composition. As the quintessential Renaissance man he was ready to apply his mind to a wide range of fields, from the arts to applied sciences, from poetic portraiture to war machines, from anatomy to botany.

In addition to his paintings, Leonardo bequeathed the city new techniques in irrigation, canal-building and hydraulic engineering. As well as being a philosopher, a visionary, an architect, a medical draughtsman, a musician and a cartographer, he was the first artist to be universally acknowledged not as a skilled artisan but as an inspired genius whose mind encompassed the sum of human knowledge. However, whether this brilliance is visible in the restored *Last Supper* is open to debate, nor has Leonardo's flawed experimental technique confirmed optimists' expectations of a "reborn masterpiece".

The canal quarter has some excellent markets. Every Saturday the Darsena and Naviglio Grande are taken over by the Fiera di Senigallia, with stallholders displaying bric-a-brac along the canal banks. The Mercatone del Naviglio Grande is a slightly grander affair held on the last Sunday of the month.

3.30–9pm), with cloisters attributed to Bramante. Also on Corso Magenta is the **Palazzo delle Stelline** ㉔, an impressive cluster of palaces converted into a major exhibition centre and congress complex. On the same sedate boulevard is the palace from which the whole *Tangentopoli* political corruption scandal exploded in the 1990s. Milan has yet to live it down.

The canal quarter

Strictly speaking, this is the Ticinese and the Navigli, two overlapping districts southwest of the city centre, with shared characteristics. The Ticinese is the most atmospheric of Milan's *quartieri popolari*, the old working-class districts, and is named after the River Ticino, a tributory of the Po. The sprawling Ticinese runs into the youthful and faintly bohemian Navigli quarter, equivalent to the Parisian left bank. The Navigli were the navigable canals that used to flow across the city; now largely covered over, they survive in this quirky district (Porta Genova metro station). They have been reopened to pleasure boats, bringing new life to an area already populated by painters, artisans and students.

The **Pinacoteca Ambrosiana** ㉕ (open Tues–Sun 10am–5.30pm; admission charge), set on Piazza Pio XI, is a gallery founded by Cardinal Federico Borromeo in 1609. His more serious aim, represented by the illustrious library in the same building, was to defend Catholic orthodoxy against the challenge of Protestantism, and for this purpose, he created a research institute complete with a superb collection of illuminated manuscripts and ancient Bibles. The manuscripts in particular were intended to establish the only "true" version of the Bible, a response both to Luther's radical German translation and to the freer interpretation of sacred texts favoured by Protestantism.

BELOW: two wheels better than four.

The collection contains Cardinal Borromeo's favourite work, Caravaggio's *Basket of Fruit*, and also reflects the founder's preference for Flemish and Venetian art. However, later bequests have broadened the Pinacoteca's appeal by including medieval Lombard sculpture, German old masters and Tuscan Renaissance masterpieces. Foremost amongst the Venetian treasures is Titian's *Adoration of the Magi* and Rococo works by Tiepolo. Renaissance paintings include a luminous Botticelli Madonna, Raphael's cartoon for *The School of Athens*, and enigmatic masterpieces by Bramantino which delight in games of perspective. The collection also has *Portrait of a Musician*, a masterpiece attributed to Leonardo da Vinci. Certainly, it fulfils Leonardo's dictum, "There are only two subjects worthy of the painter: man and the concept of his mind."

On the ground floor is the **Biblioteca Ambrosiana** (open Mon–Fri 9.30am–5pm; closed two weeks in Apr and mid-Jul–end Aug; admission charge), one of Europe's oldest public libraries, founded by Cardinal Borromeo in 1607. The library houses a collection of illuminated manuscripts, Hebrew parchments, oriental and European Bibles, letters and antiquarian books. In addition to drawings by old masters, the collection contains a 5th-century copy of the *Iliad* as well as the *Codex Atlanticus*, complete with over a thousand pages of scientific and technical drawings by Leonardo da Vinci. Other treasures include Petrarch's annotated copy of Virgil's poems, and Piero della Francesca's treatise on painting.

Via Torino leads to the **Basilica di San Satiro** ㉖, a landmark church created with exquisite artifice. Founded in the 9th century, San Satiro was completely remodelled in Renaissance style in 1478. Bramante's skilful use of a classical idiom disguises the lack of space and, by integrating gilded stucco and *trompe l'oeil* effects, creates the impression of a chancel. While the 9th-century baptistry was incorporated into the remodelled church as the Cappella della Pietà, and graced with a Renaissance exterior, the Romanesque brick belltower is a testament to the earlier church.

San Lorenzo Maggiore ㉗, on Corso di Porta Ticinese, is often cited as the first centrally planned building in the Western world. It is Milan's tallest and most spacious church after the Duomo. Founded in the 4th century, this is a powerful evocation of an early Christian basilica. The 16th-century reconstruction remained faithful to the early Christian plan. The vast dome creates an awe-inspiring interior, with chapels radiating in a sunburst pattern. The most affecting section is the Sant'Aquilino chapel, the 4th-century mausoleum decorated with original mosaics. The **Colonne di San Lorenzo** are a group of Roman columns forming a portico. Opinion is divided as to whether the Roman remains formed part of a temple or of public baths.

Near by are the Portoni di Porta Ticinese, the medieval walls which were restructured in the 19th century. Corso di Porta Ticinese connects with Piazza XXIV Maggio, running south to the canal quarter. The Corso is lined with specialist shops, often devoted to crafts or cuisine. **Sant'Eustorgio** ㉘ lies on Piazza XXIV Maggio, at the end of the Corso. The church dates back to the 5th century but was rebuilt from the 11th century onwards. The Dominican foundation

Map on page 206

In the northwest, near Malpensa airport, is the very stylish Fiera Milano Rho Exhibition Centre. Crafted of glass and steel under the expert eye of Italian architect Massimiliano Fuksas, the buildings alone are a showcase, and give this area of Milan a welcome makeover.

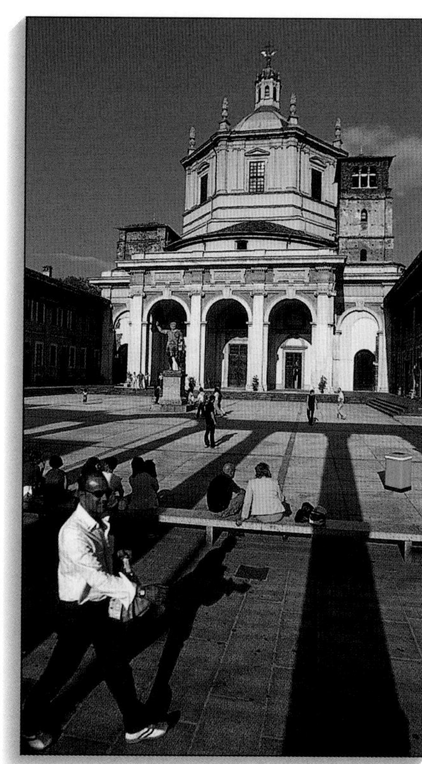

BELOW: San Lorenzo Maggiore.

Map on page 206

conceals a chapel in Tuscan Renaissance style. Also on the square stands **Porta Ticinese** 29, a Neoclassical arch built on the former Spanish walls.

Just beyond is the **Darsena** 30, or canal basin, representing the hub of the Navigli. **Alzaia Naviglio Grande** 31, which hugs the northern bank of the main canal, changes its mood according to the time of day; a sleepy afternoon spent browsing in antique and craft shops gives way to an exuberant summer scene. Vicolo Lavandai, just off the Darsena end of the canal, is one of the most attractive corners, with rustic cottages and a quaint wash-house.

The designer of the Pirelli Tower, Giò Ponti, proves the versatility of Italian industrial designers; apart from conceiving a Milanese landmark, he created the espresso machine, founded the magazine Domus *and established the Milan Triennale.*

The station quarter

As a slice of monumental Milan, the station quarter offers some of the city's grandest hotels, as well as a section of seedier Milan. Travellers leaving from the airport bus terminal or taking the train to other cities will have no choice but to pass through the district. The area has a certain appeal for fans of innovative modern architecture. The **Stazione Centrale** 32 is overwhelming in its conception and sheer size. With its marble terraces and mosaic floors, this Fascistic, triumphalist affair, designed by Ulisse Stacchini in 1912, is still the most splendid station in Europe. It is undergoing a major facelift that will be completed early in 2008. The historic entrance will be left intact, but the whole area will be transformed with new ticket offices, lifts and conveyor belts for passengers. A new shopping area will be created to host at least 100 shops as well as restaurants and a gym. Facing the station, **Excelsior Gallia**, one of the city's most traditional luxurious hotels, offers a taste of the high life in its sedate bar and restaurant, and on the adjoining Piazza d'Aosta soars the **Grattacielo Pirelli** 33, Milan's brutalist Pirelli Tower, designed by Giò Ponti in 1956.

BELOW: Milan's cavernous station.

The neighbouring **Piazza della Repubblica** 34 is a soulless square that is, paradoxically, home to several of the city's finest hotels and hotel bars. Giardino d'Inverno, set in the smart Hotel Principe di Savoia, has an Art Nouveau design, known as *lo stile liberty*, complemented by a classical fountain and statues in Carrara marble. It's a perfect escape from the hordes.

Leonardo's Horse (open daily 9.30am–6.30pm; free), Piazzale dello Sport 6, San Siro (to the north-west of the city, metro Lotto), is the largest equestrian monument in the world. Leonardo da Vinci worked on it from 1482 to 1499, completing the plaster original ready for casting in bronze. It had been commissioned by Milanese ruler Ludovico il Moro to commemorate his father, Francesco Sforza, but the great sculpture was destroyed by the French invaders who ousted il Moro. The present-day version was created by "Leonardo da Vinci's Horse Incorporation", founded by American pilot Charles Dent, whose aim was to bring the work, Leonardo's great dream, to reality. It was made by American sculptor Nina Akamu on the basis of Leonardo's many drawings, cast by the Tallix Art Foundry using 12 tonnes of bronze, transported to Milan, assembled and then inaugurated in 1999, exactly 500 years after Leonardo's original was destroyed. It is poignant that neither Leonardo, Ludovico il Moro nor Charles Dent lived to see the work become reality. ❑

Alta Moda

Commercially, the Milan-based fashion industry is far more successful than its Parisian counterpart, with the Italian *alta moda* (haute couture) collections considered more wearable. Milan's reputation for style is enhanced by the presence of well-known couturiers who contribute to the city's prestigious design courses, from Romeo Gigli to Luciano Soprani.

The fashion world fields designers with the aspirations of Renaissance princelings: the kitsch eroticism of Versace clashes with Armani's fluid lines, Romeo Gigli's romantic fantasies and Dolce & Gabbana's sense of fun. Certain designers cleave to tradition with quiet confidence. Cerutti continues to produce status-symbol suits for the rich and powerful, while Missoni, the grandparents of designer knitwear, have spent more than 50 years perfecting their blend of bright colours and eccentric hippy attitudes. If Armani reigns supreme as the king of classicism, Milan-based designers such as Dolce & Gabbana and Versace remain in the vanguard of youth culture, and have continued support from the world's highest-profile celebrities for their chic, kitsch and glamorous clothes. In the late 1990s, however, such sartorial pre-eminence was challenged by Prada, Gucci and Moschino. These reinvigorated logos were seen as provocative and playful yet glamorous.

Armani, the master of minimalism, specialises in sophisticated styling and softly tailored suits. His trademark deconstructed suits are object lessons in rigour and refinement, the quintessence of Italian classicism. Versace, the first superstar designer, was his sartorial polar opposite: vulgar, glamorous and sexually explicit. Armani's rivalry with Versace's "Rock and royalty" label was a running theme until the death of the "emperor of excess" in 1997. Despite the loss of the creative design genius, the firm thrives under his sister, Donatella. Dolce & Gabbana, whose credo is to "blur the lines of femininity and masculinity", are equally enslaved by sexual chutzpah. As for Moschino, although the founder died in 1994 the house still produces glitzy sunglasses and scarves as well as wittily self-referential T-shirts.

The 1990s witnessed the battle for the high ground between Gucci and Prada, former luggage firms that became the most coveted labels of the decade. Gucci, as famous for its feuds as for its frocks, no longer belongs to the Florentine family founders. Guccio Gucci is one of the few remaining dynastic members since the murder of Maurizio Gucci in 1995, a contract killing ordered by his former wife. Gucci designs are marked by a contemporary androgyny.

By contrast with the cool chic of Gucci girl, Prada woman depends on a creative alchemy in which off-the-wall ideas become functional clothes. As founder Miuccia Prada admits: "I am not exactly a designer but I know how to pull design elements together."

Certainly the quilted bag made from nylon, inspired by military bivouacs, has become a design classic. However, given the Italian beauty aesthetic, it isn't surprising that *stropicciato*, the grunge look, never caught on. ❑

RIGHT: Valentino's designs are among the most elegant in Italian fashion.

WHY "MADE IN ITALY" MEANS SO MUCH

Furniture, clothes, cars, typewriters, even kitchen appliances – the influence of Italian design has permeated the way we live and work today

Italian designers bask in their reputation for refinement, innate good taste and an eye for colour and line. "Quite simply, we are the best," boasts architect and cultural commentator Luigi Caccia. "We have more imagination, more culture, and are better mediators between the past and the future. That is why our design is more attractive and more in tune with the times than in other countries." Italian design is nothing if not inclusive. The traditional distinction between architect and industrial designer is blurred, with practitioners dabbling in fields as diverse as factory-building and furniture design, office lighting and graphics. In the words of Ettore Sottsass, one of the most influential designers, "Design should be a discussion of life, society, politics, food and the design itself."

MODERNISM TO POP ART

Since the 20th century Milan has led industrial design, reaching its apogee in the 1970s and 1980s. The Italians produced seminal designs for cars and lamps in the 1930s, matched by radios and motorbikes in the 1940s. Milan also pioneered innovative design in the 1950s, with the mass production of household appliances from cookers and washing machines to kitchen utensils. Italian modernism supplanted the post-war European taste for the safe, hand-crafted homeliness of Scandinavian design. Stylish kettles and coffee percolators became cult objects in the 1960s, followed by quirky Pop Art furniture and the fashion-designer chic of subsequent decades, from cool Armani to pared-down Prada. The inimitable character of *la linea italiana*, Italian style, still sets the standard for international design values.

▷ WASHED OUT
Zanussi's rigorous designs, streamlined look and user-friendly features have long made it a European market leader in the field of washing machines, refrigerators and other "white goods".

△ FERRARI FORMULA
The Ferrari Spider is one in a long line of fabulous cars from the most admired Italian manufacturer. Enzo Ferrari (1898–1988), the firm's founder, was also a noted racing-car designer.

▽ WINDOW-SHOPPING
A highly structured Prada suit adorns Milan's fashion district. Prada is the fashion company that best captures the Zeitgeist of the 1990s. Its designs made it the most copied (faked) label on the city streets.

△ **PLASTIC FANTASTIC**
A postmodern bookcase in laminated plastic, a bold design for the Memphis studio by Sottsass (1981). Memphis was the design event of the 1980s, a playful and much-imitated school inspired by Bob Dylan's song *Memphis Blues*.

◁ **TALKING POINT**
Italian design often takes ideas to their extreme, as in these eye-catching New Tone sculptural sofas by Atrium. This is subversive, unconventional, avant-garde living.

DESIGN CLASSIC
ıe Piaggio Vespa ("wasp"), st produced in 1946, came the symbol of eedom for the post- ar generation. The spa Lifestyle bag *bove)*, part of a trend r brand recognition d product versification, is an stere minimalist fering from the aggio stable.

CLASSIC CAR STYLE

Ever since the 1930s, Italian car design has been characterised by stylistic restraint, versatility and timeless elegance. At one end of the scale, the Italians still produce some of the greatest status symbols in the world. In the 1950s the beautiful Alfa Romeo convertibles spelt playboy raffishness; Ferrari's Spider, the ultimate in glamour, was produced from 1966 to 1992 – the only sports car to boast a longer production run than Germany's Porsche 911.

Yet the Italians have also had great success with Fiat's bland but eminently practical models. Topolino ("the little mouse") was launched to great acclaim in 1939, and continued into the 1950s. Giovanni Agnelli studied American mass-production techniques, and from the 1950s the family dynasty had a captive market, with customers eager for the inexpensive Fiat 500.

The car industry is based in the north, with Fiat in Turin, Alfa Romeo in Milan and Ferrari in Modena. The huge Fiat Lingotto plant was set up near Turin in the 1920s, and today the city's fortunes are still inextricably linked to Fiat.

The Italians also design for foreign manufacturers, including Mercedes and Rolls-Royce.

LOMBARDY

"Beneath is spread like a green sea
The waveless plain of Lombardy, Bounded by the vaporous air
Islanded by cities fair" – Percy Bysshe Shelley

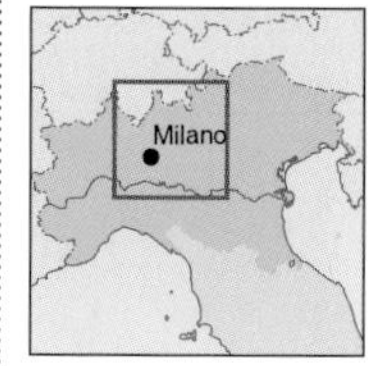

Lombardy, the Milanese hinterland, is the richest and most populous region in Italy, producing a quarter of its GNP and a third of all Italian exports. With an average income double that of the south, it has had a reputation for entrepreneurial flair since the Middle Ages, when the Como silk industry and the Milanese banks made the region a byword for reliability. Lombardy's prosperity was founded by its powerful independent cities, the antithesis of feudalism. The success story continues today: Brescia is synonymous with light industry and middle-class commuter-belt land, while Varese and its surrounding area compete with helicopters, silks, confectionery and specialised foodstuffs.

Although economically progressive, Lombardy is socially more conservative, a product of its chequered past and deep local roots. The resourceful Lombards are descended from waves of Teutonic tribes, with Pavia becoming the capital under the Goths. During the Middle Ages the cities rose to prominence as independent communes, but were later run by paternalistic aristocracies. Bergamo, Brescia, Como, Pavia, Mantua and Cremona were powers in their own right. Under the Gonzagas, Mantua had a Renaissance court illustrious enough to engage Mantegna (d. 1506) as court painter. The region also prospered under the Visconti and Sforza dynasties, with the arms and textile industries favoured. Arms manufacturing is still based in Brescia, and textiles are produced throughout the region. Venetian rule, lasting until the 18th century, brought stability and a sophisticated architectural veneer.

PRECEDING PAGES: poplars near Mantua.
LEFT: Alpine cattle in Lombard mountain pastures.
BELOW: Renaissance fountain, Brescia.

Separatist sentiments

Lombardy regained a sense of leadership during the Risorgimento, the movement for Italian unity. In 1860, when Garibaldi set sail for Sicily, half of his volunteers were from Lombardy. This region also led the way in industrialisation after World War II. Since then, however, feelings of resentment have set in, compounded by the Lombards' strong sense of identity. The desire to keep control of their regional riches has led to a rise in separatist sentiments. The Lombard resurgence of civic pride, in particular, followed the corruption scandals of the early 1990s.

Lombardy embraces diverse territory, from the Alps to the plains, from watery rice paddies around Mantua to the lush Mediterranean climate of Lake Garda, rich in olive groves and oleanders. However, to most Italian minds it is synonymous with the misty, oppressive climate of the Po Valley which afflicts the area around **Milan** ❶ among other places. The city *(see pages 205–18)* is the starting point for rural excursions. South of the city lies the Bassa Milanese, a curious region dotted with historic abbeys, border castles, extensive parks and large farms. The abbeys are the

To nostalgic separatists the 12th century represents the flowering of Lombardy, with its rich civic culture, burgeoning guilds and Gothic churches.

legacy of Benedictine monks who settled the marshy area during the Middle Ages. By contrast, the ruined fortresses reflect Milan's determination to defend its borders against threats from its rival, Pavia.

A stone's throw from Milan

Monza ❷, just 10 km (6 miles) from Milan, makes a pleasant trip, particularly for fans heading for the Italian Grand Prix in September. The Neoclassical Villa Reale adjoins the spacious **Parco di Monza**, (open daily 7am–7pm, until 8.30pm in summer), one of the largest enclosed parks in Europe. Once part of the Habsburg and Savoy hunting estates, this was created in its present form in 1805 by Eugène de Beauharnais, Napoleon's viceroy. The spacious grounds (800 hectares/2,000 acres) are ample enough to conceal a golf course and a cluster of working farms, plus the Autodromo di Monza, the Formula One racing track.

Abbiategrasso ❸, once an important port, is now a mere market town on the banks of the Naviglio Grande, which connects Milan with its rural hinterland.

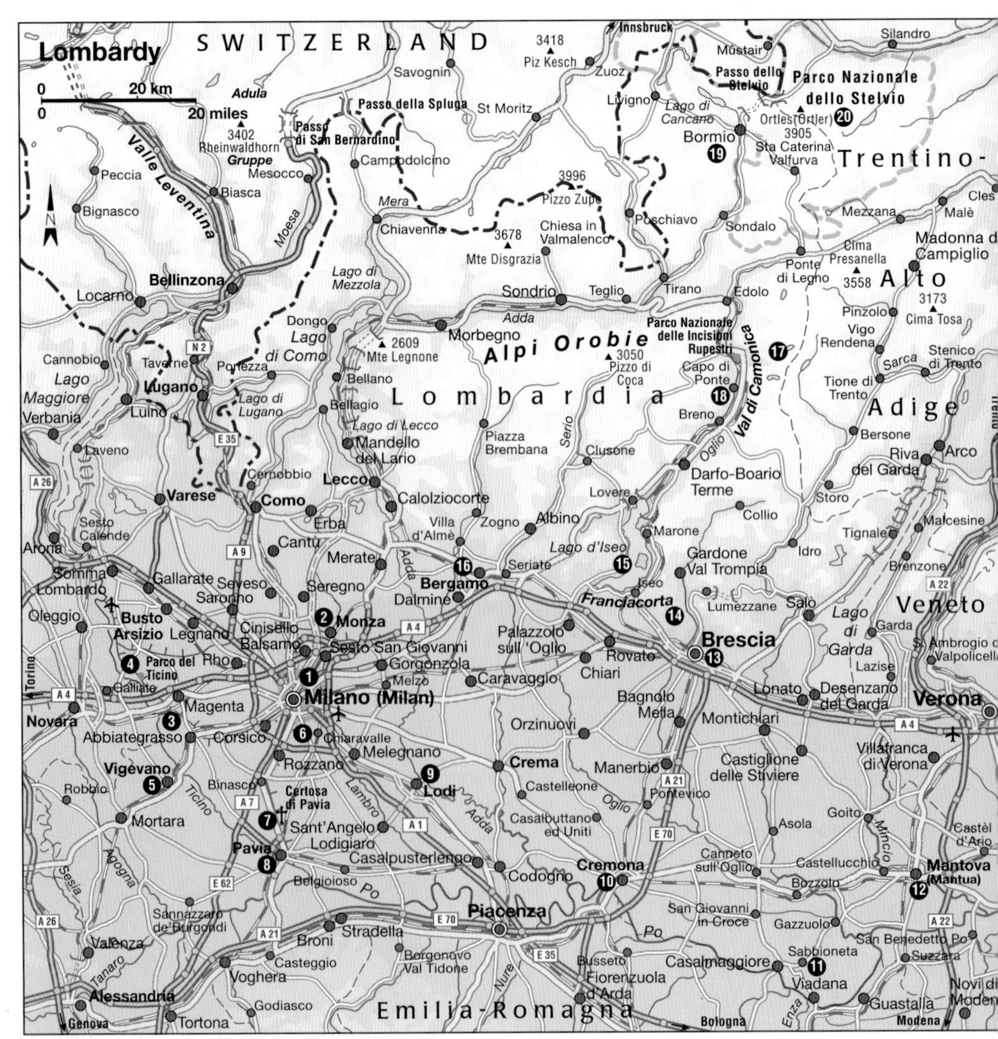

Map on page 226

The Castello, a Gothic fortress, was partly destroyed by Spanish troops in the 17th century but retains a ruined tower and mullioned windows. Outside town is **Abbazia di Morimondo** (open Fri–Wed 8.30am–noon, 2.30–5.30pm), one of the earliest examples of Gothic in Italy, created by Burgundian Benedictines, who were the first to drain and cultivate the once insalubrious marshes. The brickwork church, which dates from 1182, contains notable frescos and 16th-century choir stalls. Adjoining Abbiategrasso is the **Parco del Ticino ❹**, which stretches from Turbigo to Pavia, following the River Ticino, as it meanders through woods, water meadows and rolling hills. The park offers a variety of activities, from hiking, cycling and riding to canoeing and rafting.

Façade detail, Certosa di Pavia.

Vigevano ❺, just south of Abbiategrasso, has the huge Castello Sforzesco (open Apr–Sept Tues–Sun 8.30am–7pm, Oct–Mar Sun & hols 8.30am–8pm; free), occupied by two of Milan's major ruling dynasties, the Visconti and the Sforza. The 15th-century castle and the Piazza Ducale, a monumental Renaissance square, provide the setting for the historical Palio, a colourful competition which is staged in late spring and autumn. The surrounding countryside is noted for its rustic specialities, from salami risottos to omelettes made with wild herbs. It is also known for stylish shoe manufacturers.

Chiaravalle ❻ (open Tues–Sun 9am–noon, 2.30–6pm), set in a hamlet of the same name just south of Milan, is one of the loveliest abbeys in Italy. This Gothic masterpiece, founded by St Bernard in 1135, was Italy's most important Cistercian abbey. It conforms to rigid Cistercian principles but reflects the Lombard preference for brick. Decorated with 16th-century frescoes, the church is flanked by Gothic cloisters and a distinctive belltower.

Further south, 10 km (6 miles) from Pavia, stands the remarkable **Certosa di Pavia ❼** (open May–Sept Tues–Sun 9–11.30am, 2.30–6pm, Oct–Mar until 4.30pm, Apr until 5.30pm; free). The Carthusian monastery was founded in 1396 on the edge of an extensive park surrounding the Visconti castle in Pavia. Although created as a pantheon for the illustrious Visconti dynasty, the Charterhouse is better known as a decorative masterpiece in Lombard Renaissance style. However, since the Certosa took two centuries to build, the resulting complex also embraces Gothic and Baroque elements. The stunning Lombard façade (1473–9) is studded with marble sculptures and lacy windows. The late-Gothic interior is dotted with ornate vaulted chapels displaying Lombard sculptures, paintings and frescoes, including Renaissance funerary monuments to the d'Este dynasty. The cloisters form an atmospheric backdrop, with the Chiostro Piccolo, the small cloisters, distinguished by their decorative terracotta friezes.

BELOW: the garden cloisters of Certosa di Pavia.

By contrast, the Chiostro Grande houses the relatively luxurious monastic cells, which are still in use. In 1784 the monastery passed into Cistercian hands before being entrusted to the barefoot Carmelites. Now state property, the Certosa is still run by the Cistercians, who maintain a vow of silence. However, guided tours are led by a monk released from the vow.

Just south is the historic city of **Pavia ❽**, set on the banks of the River Tessin. Although founded in Roman times, Pavia rose to prominence as the capital

Locals recommend a sampling of the region's hearty peasant soups (minestre). *The best-known is* zuppa pavese, *a broth with an egg floating on the surface. The soup was supposedly given to François I of France to fortify him on the eve of the Battle of Pavia in 1525.*

of the Goths from the 6th to the 11th century and witnessed the coronation of Charlemagne as King of the Lombards in 774. The city later prospered as a medieval trading centre, possessing links with Amalfi and Venice. It was also resplendent during the Renaissance, when its court became the focal point for festivities throughout Lombardy. Pavia has preserved a number of Romanesque and Renaissance buildings, but the city's mood owes more to Austrian domination, from the citizens' self-composure to the stucco-faced buildings.

Castello Visconteo (open spring and autumn, Tues–Fri 9am–1.30pm, Sat–Sun 10am–7pm; winter and summer, Tues–Sat 9am–1.30pm, Sun 9am–1pm), in the north of the city, was built by Gian Galeazzo Visconti in 1360. Although designed as a pleasure palace rather than as a castle, it is flanked by two corner turrets, the remains of mock-defensive fortifications. Inside, the Museo Civico displays Roman and Egyptian exhibits, plus statuary, mosaics and frescoes salvaged from demolished Romanesque and Renaissance churches. The Pinacoteca in the east wing focuses on Lombard painting from the Middle Ages to the Renaissance.

San Michele Maggiore, on Via Paolo Diacono, is a Romanesque church built in mellow sandstone over a 7th-century Lombard basilica. The solemn, austere interior, reminiscent of Sant'Ambrogio in Milan, was where Federico Barbarossa was crowned Holy Roman Emperor in 1155. The neighbouring **Strada Nuova**, the elegant main street, is built over a Roman road that linked the north and south of the city. Lined with smart cafés and boutiques, Strada Nuova crosses the river over a grand, covered bridge that was reconstructed after bomb damage in World War II. The street's dignified air is underlined by the presence of an ancient university, famed for its faculties of law and medicine. Famous alumni include Christopher Columbus and physicist Alessandro Volta, who

BELOW: the Ponte Coperto, Pavia.

invented the electric battery in 1799. Founded by the Visconti in 1361, the university owes more to Renaissance designs, despite later remodelling in Neoclassical style. A series of inner courtyards leads to the historic anatomical theatre and the **Museo per la Storia** (open Mon 3–5.30pm, Fri 9.30am–noon; tel: 0382-5041), the science-based university museum.

Lodi ❾ has always been overshadowed by Milan, Mantua and Pavia, but the signing of the Peace of Lodi in 1454 signalled a period of peace and prosperity and marked the end of a struggle between Francesco Sforza and the Venetians for control over the Duchy of Milan. Although a minor town, Lodi has some impressive architecture. L'Incoronata, in particular, is a richly decorated church with a Renaissance portico and a gilded, stuccoed interior.

City of Monteverdi

Cremona ❿, languishing on the plains of the Po, relishes its reputation as the cradle of fiddle-making and the birthplace of the father of opera, Claudio Monteverdi. The violins came into being in 1566, when Andrea Amati developed the modern violin industry. Since then their spirit and form have been likened to an essay in Baroque architecture: the subtle, curvaceous forms of the instruments, cut from the finest woods in Lombardy or the Dolomites, are reflected in the cornices and pediments of the city palaces. The great Stradivarius was part of a long musical tradition that continues to shape city culture; Cremona has more violin masters and workshops *(botteghe liutarie)* than any other European city.

Cremona was a pawn of the Visconti and Sforza dynasties before falling into Venetian, Spanish and Austrian hands. However, its greatest square belongs firmly to the medieval period. **Piazza del Comune** is a beguiling square with

Portrait of Claudio Monteverdi by Domenico Feti.

BELOW: one of the many violin workshops in Cremona, home of Stradivarius.

TIP

Cremona makes for interesting shopping. Musicians can browse in the hundred violin workshops, while foodies can track down Cremona's wonderful nougat *(torrone)*, cheese and salami shops.

a cluster of imposing monuments. A sombre Lombard Romanesque cathedral, the **Duomo** is decorated with loggias and faced with polychrome marble; inside are Flemish tapestries and a 16th-century Lombard fresco cycle. The adjoining **Torazzo** (open Tues–Sun 10am–1pm; mid-Apr–Oct also 2.30–5.30pm; admission charge), the lofty crenellated belltower – the tallest in Italy, standing 113 metres (370 ft) high – is the symbol of the city, linked to the cathedral by a Renaissance loggia, and the octagonal Romanesque baptistry has a portico supported by a pair of weathered lions. Opposite the cathedral stands the **Loggia dei Militi**, the headquarters of the captains of the citizens' militia, built in 13th-century Lombard style. Completing the square is the **Palazzo del Comune** (open Tues–Sat 9am–6pm, Sun 10am–6pm; admission charge), the grandiose town hall, which dates from the 13th century. On display inside are some of the greatest violins ever made, of which the undoubted star is the Cremonese 1715, a Stradivarius complete with its original mysterious varnish.

The **Museo Stradivariano** (open Tues–Sat 9am–6pm, Sun 10am–6pm; admission charge) is set among the Baroque palaces on Via Palestro. The collection contains casts and models which attempt to explain Stradivari's genius. Nearby, on Via Dati, is the Museo Civico (times as above), a grand palace housing an archeological section and an art gallery presenting an overview of art from Cremona and the rest of Lombardy from Renaissance times onwards.

Glorious ghost town

Sabbioneta ⓫, set between Cremona and Mantua, is a rational expression of the Renaissance ideal, an orderly urban space provided with winter and summer palaces, a theatre, a hospital and a humanist library, schools and a synagogue, a

BELOW: Cremona's Romanesque cathedral.

printing office and a mint. In 1444 it was an undistinguished village, but by the end of the century it had been transformed into a glittering Renaissance court. As one of the first consciously designed Renaissance cities it drew on humanist architectural treatises and the precepts of Vitruvius. The city is also a tribute to the fertile mind of Vespasian Gonzaga, an extravagant and impetuous prince of a patron. (In a moment of rashness, he accidentally killed his son by kicking him in the genitals.) At his best, Gonzaga sought to create a humanist utopia bounded by star-shaped Renaissance walls. Sabbioneta fell into decline with Gonzaga's death in 1591 and became something of a glorious ghost town.

Piazza Ducale, the main square, has a pink-and-white-marble parish church and an elegant ducal palace, with a tower and loggia. The interior abounds in frescoed chambers and gilded ceilings. Behind it is the church of the **Incoronata**, the austere façade contrasting with the ornate interior. Designed as Vespasian Gonzaga's tomb, the octagonal church delights in chiaroscuro effects.

At the end of the Piazza Castello stands **Palazzo del Giardino**, a noble pleasure palace. The frescoed interior sports designs inspired by classical mythology. The other highlight is the **Teatro All'Antica**, a theatre modelled on Palladio's original Teatro Olimpico in Vicenza. The monuments in this rural backwater can only be seen on a guided tour (tel: 0375-52039) through ProLoco or the newer Ufficio Turistico del Comune (Piazza D'Arani 1; tel: 0375-221044).

The Po Valley

Cremona and Mantua are set in the Po Valley, an area with great resonance for northern Italians. The Pianura Padana, the interminable northern plain, is broken only by screens of scrubby poplars and mulberry trees. Summers are stifling

Map on page 226

Reading matter on a city news-stand.

BELOW: rice, the main crop of Lombardy.

and winters freezing, hence the popularity of the beach scene. Urban sophisticates may baulk at the brackish fishing lakes, silted-up river mouths, the canyons of poplars, lone belltowers, watery bleakness and unpeopled pall of it all. Close to Mantua is a rice-growing area, reminiscent of the rice paddies near Vigevano and Pavia. Lombardy, which has always employed advanced agricultural methods, introduced rice cultivation during the Renaissance, providing work for the peasants while satisfying the palates of the urban rich.

TIP

Mantua's marshy location, bordered by lakes on three sides, produces a muggy climate, but this makes for atmospheric boat trips on Lago Superiore, the western lake. The Parco del Minclo, close to the city, is a wetlands zone with opportunities for birdwatching, boating and cycling.

Melancholy Mantua

Mantua (Mantova) ⓬ is a stern, inward-looking, ponderously noble city. Surrounded by swampy lakes, this melancholy, masculine place was once a busy port. As an isolated city state, protected by its waters, it was ruled by the extravagant Gonzaga dukes, and survived as a showy but canny buffer state between Milan and Venice. From 1328 until 1630 the Gonzagas led one of the liveliest and richest princely courts, attracting artists of the calibre of Pisanello, Italy's Gothic master, and Mantegna, the leading Renaissance artist in northern Italy. The last great Gonzaga, Vincenzo I, was the patron of Rubens and of Monteverdi, who composed *Orfeo* for the court of Mantua.

Foreigners tend to associate Mantua with Mantegna's magnificent cycle of frescoes. In Italian eyes, however, modern Mantua is known for its staunchly separatist politics. It has a strong sense of identity and became a member of the Lombard League in 1167. As a sign of the recent revival of regionalism, in 1992 it became the first city to be ruled by a Northern League mayor, and is known as a power base for separatists. In 1996 the Movement announced its aim of creating an independent northern Italy under the name "Padania" *(see page 68)*. Its capital would be Mantua and elections organised by the party for a "northern parliament" – although with no international recognition.

BELOW: the sun sets over Mantua.

Mantua is blessed with a trio of impressive squares: the bustling marketplace of **Piazza dell'Erbe**; the medieval civic centre of **Piazza del Broletto**; and the cobbled Piazza Sordello, containing the seat of the ruling dynasty and the site of the Duomo, whose curious 18th-century façade gives way to a Renaissance interior, frescoed by Giulio Romano (*c*.1492–1546). Just east of the Broletto, set on Via Accademia, is the **Teatro Scientifico**, an 18th-century gem of a theatre. **Piazza dell'Erbe** is dwarfed by the domed Renaissance **Basilica di Sant'Andrea** designed by Alberti, the great architect and theorist, and based on Vitruvius' idea of a Roman temple. Mantegna, who died in Mantua in 1506, is buried inside the city's greatest church. From here one can wander through austere red-brick arches and admire the dignified façades of a seductive city which is rarely soft and mellow.

Palazzo Ducale (open Tues–Sun 8.45am–7.15pm, last entrance 6.30pm; admission charge), the playground of the Gonzaga dukes, monopolises the northeastern section of town. The Renaissance palace incorporates a basilica, political prisons and offices as well as Castello San Giorgio, the Gothic fortress that served as family apartments. The 500 rooms, frescoed by such artists as Pisanello and Mantegna, provide a snapshot of courtly

Map on page 226

life. Apart from the intimacy of Isabella d'Este's private chambers, the "dwarfs' apartments" demonstrate that dwarfs were fashionable accessories in royal courts. Elsewhere, Arthurian legends or coffered ceilings bring to life the lavish world of the Gonzaga court.

The centrepiece of the palace is the **Camera degli Sposi** (15 Mar–31 Oct, hours as for Palazzo; June–Sept, also Sat 9–11pm) decorated with Mantegna's beautifully restored frescoes of Ludovico II, his family, court and retinue. Painted between 1465 and 1474, these are frank portraits depicting hunting scenes, with pure-bred horses and sturdy mastiffs. The circular ceiling painting features a sumptuous garland with cherubs blessed with gossamer wings. The *trompe l'oeil* ceiling is also an early attempt (1474) at perspective painting.

At the far end of town stands the **Palazzo Te** (open Tues–Sun 9am–6.30pm, Mon 1–6.30pm; admission charge), an elegant country palace doubling as palatial horse stables and a boudoir for Gonzaga mistresses. The villa, constructed in harmonious classical style, has a frescoed interior (1525–35) which is largely the work of Giulio Romano, a gifted pupil of Raphael.

A meeting of like minds in Brescia.

Military minded

As a solid Lombard workhorse, **Brescia** ⓭ is not immediately appealing. However, a recent re-evaluation of its artistic heritage, prompted by the superb restoration of the Santa Giulia complex, has tempted the city to take tourism more seriously. As Brixia, Brescia was a Gaulish and later a Roman city which still retains vestiges of its glorious past. Medieval Brescia was a member of the powerful Lombard League, but by 1421 the Brescians, tired of regional rivalries and internal strife, had invited the Venetians to rule the city. Venetian

BELOW: the Palazzo Ducale in Mantua, home of the Gonzaga dukes.

Ruins of the Roman Temple, Brescia.

domination signalled a period of prosperity and rebuilding, characterised by the remodelling of the cityscape. Neighbouring iron-ore deposits also provided the basis for a firearms-manufacturing industry so profitable that the Venetians imposed severe emigration restrictions on producers.

The sinister and soulless **Piazza Vittoriale** usually referred to as Piazza della Vittoria is a ponderous tribute to Fascism, a symbolic hole where the heart of the city should be. The square only comes alive during the Mille Miglia, Italy's celebrated vintage-car rally each May. Fortunately the adjoining **Piazza della Loggia** is vibrant and harmonious, dominated by a clocktower and **Palazzo del Comune**, the Renaissance town hall. A note of grace is added by the square's Renaissance loggias, including one on **Monte di Pieta**, now the tourist office, with its façade studded with recycled Roman inscriptions.

Behind the clocktower looms the dome of the **Duomo Nuovo** (open Mon–Sat 7.30am–noon, 4–7.30pm, Sun 8am–1pm, 4–7.30pm), the curious 17th-century "new" cathedral, set on **Piazza Paolo VI**. On the east of the square squats the Romanesque **Duomo Vecchio** (open Apr–Oct Tues–Sun 9am–noon, 3–7pm; Nov–Mar Sat–Sun 10am–noon, 3–5pm), whose original dates to the 6th century. Known as the Rotonda, this softly lit basilica has a cylindrical dome supported by eight pillars. The impressive crypt incorporates medieval and Roman columns as well as mosaics from the Roman baths on the site of which it was built.

Santa Giulia Museo della Città (open Tues–Sun, summer l0am–6pm, Fri until 10pm; winter 9.30am–5.30pm; admission charge), set on Via dei Musei at the foot of the castle, is an innovative museum complex that showcases Brescia's past in relevant monuments from the Bronze Age to the present day. It incorporates an 8th-century nunnery, the Renaissance church and cloisters of Santa Giulia, the

BELOW: the Piazza Vecchia, Bergamo.

Romanesque oratory of Santa Maria in Solario, and the Lombard Basilica of San Salvatore. This church alone is a major monument, with its Byzantine influences and Lombard nave flanked by Roman columns. The Longobard and Carolingian section displays frescoes, jewellery and 8th-century terracottas. The Venetian section, rich in statuary and frescoes, depicts the city from the late Gothic and Renaissance periods, while the Roman section is notable for mosaics, bronzes and sarcophagi unearthed during excavations in San Salvatore.

The route from Santa Giulia to Via Piamarta passes the ruins of the city's remaining Roman gate. The Cydneo (Cydnean) hill that looms up behind Via dei Musei was the core of Roman Brixia. Via dei Musci, formerly the Decamanus Maximus, leads to the ruins of the forum in **Piazza del Foro.** Above stand the Corinthian colonnades and pediment of the Capitoleum, the Capitoline temple built by Vespasian in AD 73 and probably dedicated to Jupiter, Juno and Minerva. Next to the temple is the insignificant-looking **Teatro Romano,** which once held 15,000 spectators. The medieval Castello, set atop the Cydneo hill, possesses a Gothic tower built over Roman remains. The most interesting castle museum is the remodelled **Luigi Marzoli** (open June–Sept Tues–Sun l0am–5pm; Oct–May 9.30am–1pm, 2.30–5pm; admission charge), a tribute to Brescia's military might with an extensive collection of firearms.

Pasticceria *in Bergamo.*

Great escapes and Donizetti

Franciacorta ⓮, sandwiched between Brescia and Lake Iseo, is an appealing wine-growing region. **Lago d'Iseo ⓯** itself *(see Lakes, page 276)* is one of the least visited yet more engaging lakes.

The combination of cobbled streets, cypress-clad hills and mountain air makes **Bergamo ⓰** a refreshing diversion. Memories of the stifling Lombard plains are banished by Bergamo's delightful skyline and softly hued stonework. Although a significant settlement in Roman times, the city owes more to the late-medieval and Renaissance periods. Medieval Bergamo experienced independence before falling under the sway of the Venetians from 1428 to 1797. Today Bergamo is essentially two cities: the well-preserved *città alta,* or historic upper city, and the spacious but uninspiring *città bassa,* or lower city. The city on the plain possesses one extraordinary art gallery, but otherwise the sights are concentrated in the fortified *città alta,* easily reached by cable car. Bergamo is bound by a circle of defensive walls, built by the Venetians in 1560. At its heart is the **Rocca**, a fortress built to protect the Venetian Empire against the Milanese state; the restored *torrione* (tower) is open Sat–Sun noon–2.30pm). A leisurely stroll along the 5 km (3 miles) of **city walls** makes a fitting prelude or post-script to a summer visit.

With winding streets and mountainous climate, the upper city is particularly appealing under a snowfall. At the heart of the town lies **Piazza Vecchia**, a harmonious Gothic ensemble. Flanking the porticoed square are a lofty civic tower (which can be climbed, but the lift is indefinitely broken) and the Palazzo della Ragione, the much-remodelled medieval council chambers, complemented by a graceful fountain,

BELOW: the richly sculpted stonework of Cappella Colleoni.

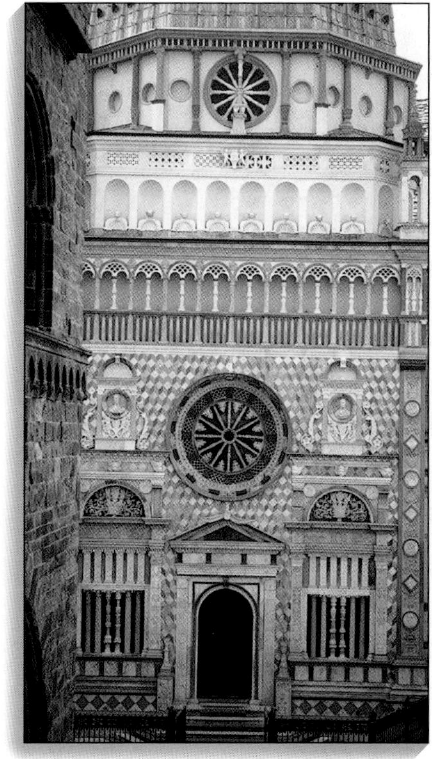

This town prides itself on gastronomy, and there are several good restaurants, delicatessens and bakeries showcasing the delicacies. The local passion for game-birds is also reflected in the sweet speciality of polenta e osei, *where confectionery baby birds peep out of confectionery polenta pies.*

and the Palladian-style Palazzo Nuovo, housing the city library. The adjacent Piazza del Duomo is home to the Gothic cathedral and the memorable **Santa Maria Maggiore**, an austere Romanesque basilica. Attached to the south wall is the **Cappella Colleoni** (open daily 9am–12.30pm, 2–6.30pm, Nov–Feb until 4.30pm; free), built in the 1470s as a funerary monument for legendary *condottiere* Bartolomeo Colleoni. The chapel is one of Lombardy's earliest set-pieces of Renaissance architecture.

In the lower town, the **Accademia Carrara** (open Tues–Sun 10am–1pm, 2.30–5.30pm; admission charge) displays one of the grandest arrays of Lombard and Venetian art, with paintings by such masters as Tintoretto, Bellini, Veronese, Tiepolo and Mantegna. Opposite the Carrara, the **Galleria d'Arte Moderna e Contemporanea** (open Apr–Sept 10am–1pm, 3–6.45pm, Oct–Mar 9.30am–1pm, 2.30–5.45pm; free) hosts excellent by contemporary artists.

On the pedestrianised Sentierone is the **Teatro Donizetti**, dedicated to Bergamo's celebrated son (1797–1848). Opera-lovers are rewarded with Gaetano Donizetti's light touch, gift for melody and art of *bel canto*. Just behind the Citadella is the **Museo Donizettiano** (Donizetti Birthplace Museum; open June–Sept Tues–Sun 9.30am–1pm and 2–5.30pm, Oct–Mar mornings only). Within are several of the Bergamo-based composer's artefacts such as his piano, furniture and portraits. The town's most famous son died here in 1848.

Cookery writer Claudia Roden is one of many to single out the local cuisine: "Bergamo, once part of the Serenissima, is more Venetian; Mantua has refined aristocratic traditions and is more like Emilia, to the south. But they do have things in common: they use enormous quantities of butter, lard and cream and all their cuisines are based on risotto, polenta and *minestre*."

BELOW: a statue in the early Renaissance chapel of Cappella Colleoni, Bergamo.

Prehistoric carvings

Val di Camonica ⑰, also known as Valcamonica, has the greatest concentration of prehistoric rock-carvings in the world. Situated just north of the spa town of Boario Terme, this rural valley has been inhabited since the Neolithic era. The carvings span a period of thousands of years, from Neolithic times (pre-2200 BC) until the Roman era. For generations the Camuni tribes of hunters and farmers made their mark by recording their symbols of everyday life. There are approximately 200,000 carvings on this glacier-seared sandstone, of which about 30,000 represent figures. The images vary in degrees of sophistication, from Stone Age scratchings to Bronze Age narratives.

Capo di Ponte ⑱ (tel: 0364-42140) marks the main entrance to the UNESCO-recognised **Parco Nazionale delle Incisioni Rupestri** (open Tues–Sun 8.30am–7.30pm, mid-Oct–Feb until 4.30pm; admission charge), the largest open-air display of rock-carvings in Europe.

The Parco Nazionale delle Incisioni Rupestri claims to possess the oldest representation of a rose, the rosa camuna, *an image duplicated throughout the valley and now adopted as Lombardy's official regional symbol.*

Springboard for the Dolomites

As a popular winter and summer resort, **Bormio ⑲** provides a convenient base for exploring the glacier-encrusted Dolomite mountains. It is also a gateway to the Stelvio National Park *(see Walking, page 126)*, the largest park in the Alps. **Parco Nazionale dello Stelvio ⑳** straddles Lombardy, Trentino and the Swiss border, encompassing alpine meadows, lakes and dramatic peaks. Although hunting is illegal on the Lombardy side, the wildlife over the Trentino border have been slow to sneak over. Access to the park is from numerous sites in Lombardy as well as from Trentino *(see page 199)*. These exhilarating snow-capped mountains could hardly make a more dramatic contrast with the muggy Lombard plains. ❑

BELOW: Capo di Ponte.

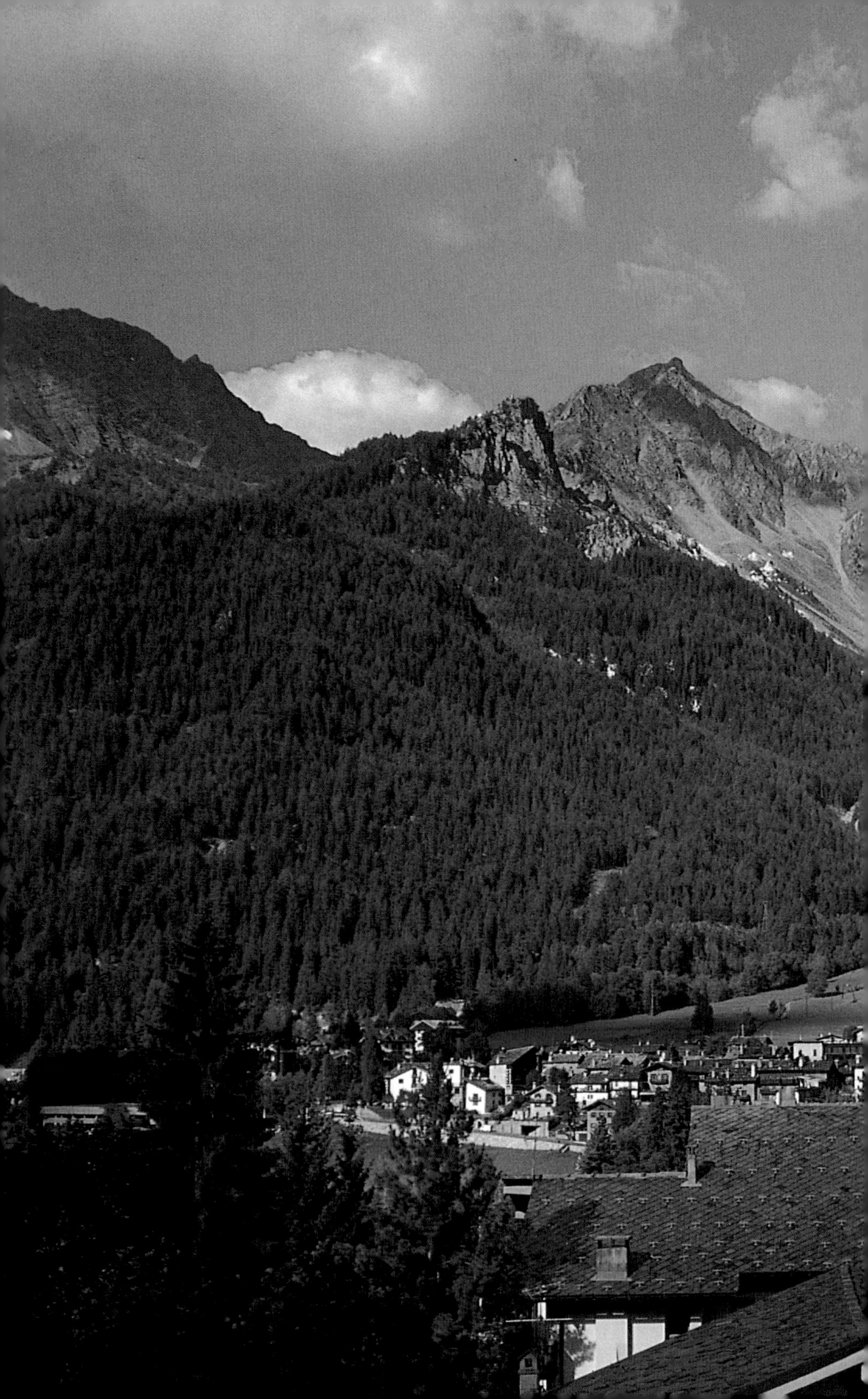

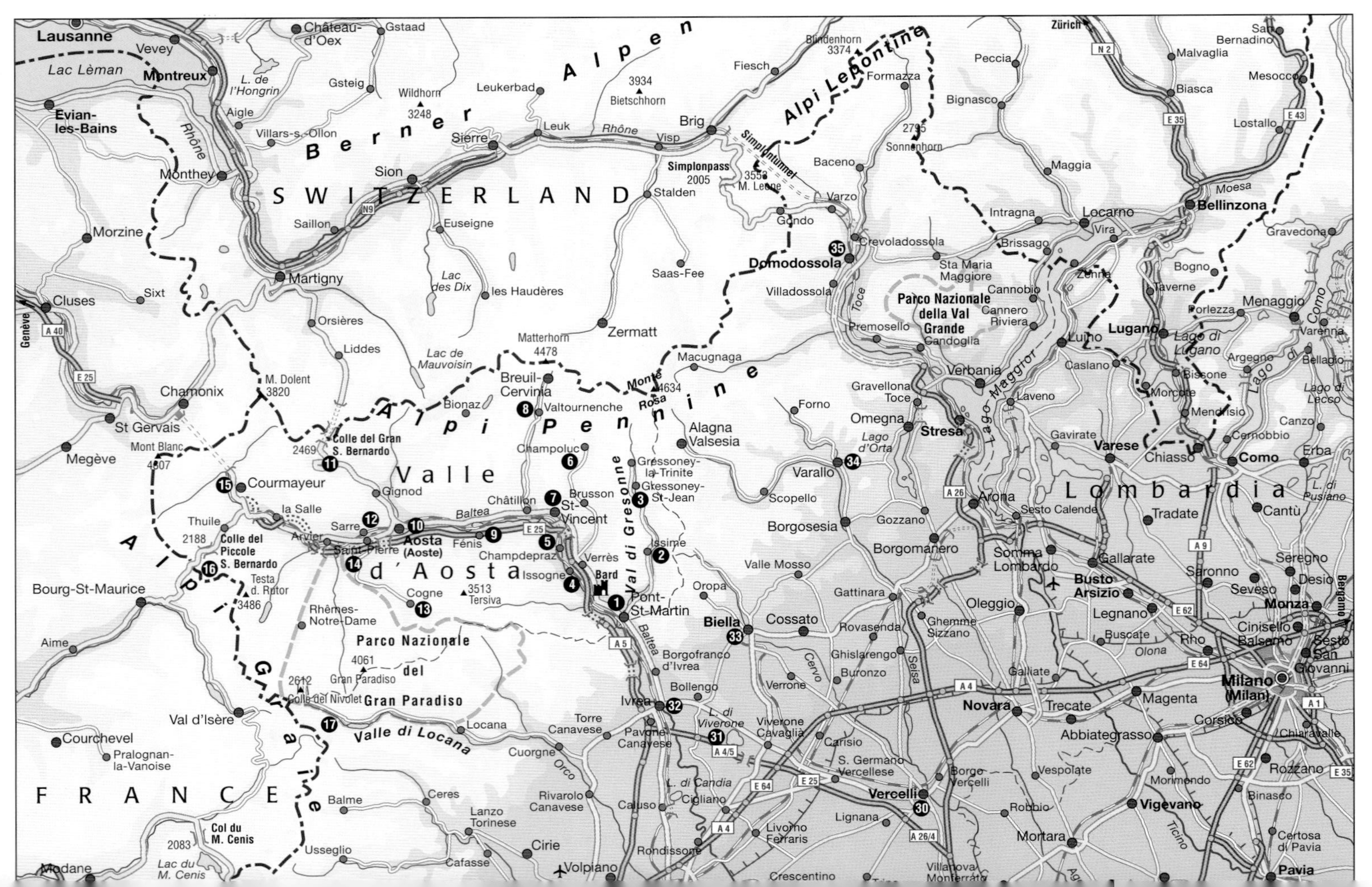

Lausanne
Lac Lèman
Evian-les-Bains
Vevey
Montreux
Morzine
Cluses
Genève
Sixt
Monthey
Rhône
Aigle
Villars-s.-Ollon
L. de l'Hongrin
Château-d'Oex
Gstaad
Gsteig
Wildhorn 3248
Berner Alpen
SWITZERLAND
Saillon
Martigny
Sion
Sierre
Leukerbad
Leuk
Rhône
Visp
Brig
3934 Bietschhorn
Fiesch
Blindenhorn 3374
Alpi Lepontine
Simplontunnel
Simplonpass 2005
3553 M. Leone
Gondo
Stalden
Saas-Fee
Euseigne
Lac des Dix
les Haudères
Zermatt
Matterhorn 4478
Lac de Mauvoisin
Orsières
Liddes
M. Dolent 3820
Chamonix
St Gervais
Mont Blanc 4807
Megève
Breuil-Cervinia
Bionaz
Valtournenche
Monte Rosa 4634
Macugnaga
Alpi Pennine
Alagna Valsesia
Gressoney-la-Trinite
Gressoney-St-Jean
Issime
Val di Gresonne
Pont-St-Martin
Bard
Verrès
Issogne
Brusson
St-Vincent
Champoluc
Châtillon
Champdepraz
Baltea
Fénis
3513 Tersiva
Aosta (Aoste)
Valle d'Aosta
Cogne
Gignod
Sarre
Saint-Pierre
Arvier
la Salle
Courmayeur
Colle del Gran S. Bernardo 2469
Thuile
2188
Colle del Piccolo S. Bernardo
Testa d. Rutor 3486
Bourg-St-Maurice
Aime
Rhêmes-Notre-Dame
Parco Nazionale del Gran Paradiso
4061 Gran Paradiso
2612 Colle del Nivolet
Valle di Locana
Locana
Alpi Graie
Val d'Isère
Courchevel
Pralognan-la-Vanoise
FRANCE
Col du M. Cenis 2083
Lac du M. Cenis
Modane
Balme
Ceres
Usseglio
Lanzo Torinese
Cafasse
Ciriè
Volpiano
Rivarolo Canavese
Cuorgnè
Orco
Torre Canavese
Pavone Canavese
Ivrea
Bollengo
Borgofranco d'Ivrea
Biella
Oropa
Cossato
Valle Mosso
Borgosesia
Scopello
Varallo
Forno
Lago d'Orta
Omegna
Gravellona Toce
Stresa
Verbania
Premosello
Candoglia
Parco Nazionale della Val Grande
Villadossola
Domodossola
Crevoladossola
Varzo
Baceno
2795 Sonnenhorn
Formazza
Bignasco
Peccia
Maggia
Intragna
Locarno
Vira
Brissago
Sta Maria Maggiore
Cannobio
Cannero Riviera
Zenna
Luino
Lago Maggiore
Laveno
Caslano
Lugano
Lago di Lugano
Bissone
Morcote
Mendrisio
Chiasso
Varese
Gavirate
Arona
Sesto Calende
Gozzano
Borgomanero
Gattinara
Rovasenda
Ghemme
Sizzano
Somma Lombardo
Busto Arsizio
Gallarate
Lombardia
Tradate
Como
Cernobbio
Erba
Canzo
L. di Pusiano
Cantù
Lago di Lecco
Lago di Como
Bellagio
Varenna
Argegno
Menaggio
Porlezza
Taverne
Bogno
Bellinzona
Moesa
Gravedona
Zürich
Malvaglia
Biasca
Bernadino
Mesocco
Lostallo
Seregno
Saronno
Seveso
Desio
Bergamo
Monza
Cinisello Balsamo
Sesto San Giovanni
Legnano
Rho
Buscate
Olona
Milano (Milan)
Magenta
Corsico
Chiaravalle
Rozzano
Binasco
Certosa di Pavia
Pavia
Morimondo
Vigevano
Ticino
Abbiategrasso
Trecate
Novara
Oleggio
Galliate
Vespolate
Robbio
Mortara
Borgo Vercelli
Vercelli
Villanova Monferrato
Crescentino
Lignana
Livorno Ferraris
S. Germano Vercellese
Carisio
Cigliano
L. di Candia
Caluso
Rondissone
Viverone
Cavaglià
L. di Viverone
Verrone
Ghislarengo
Buronzo
Cervo
Seisa

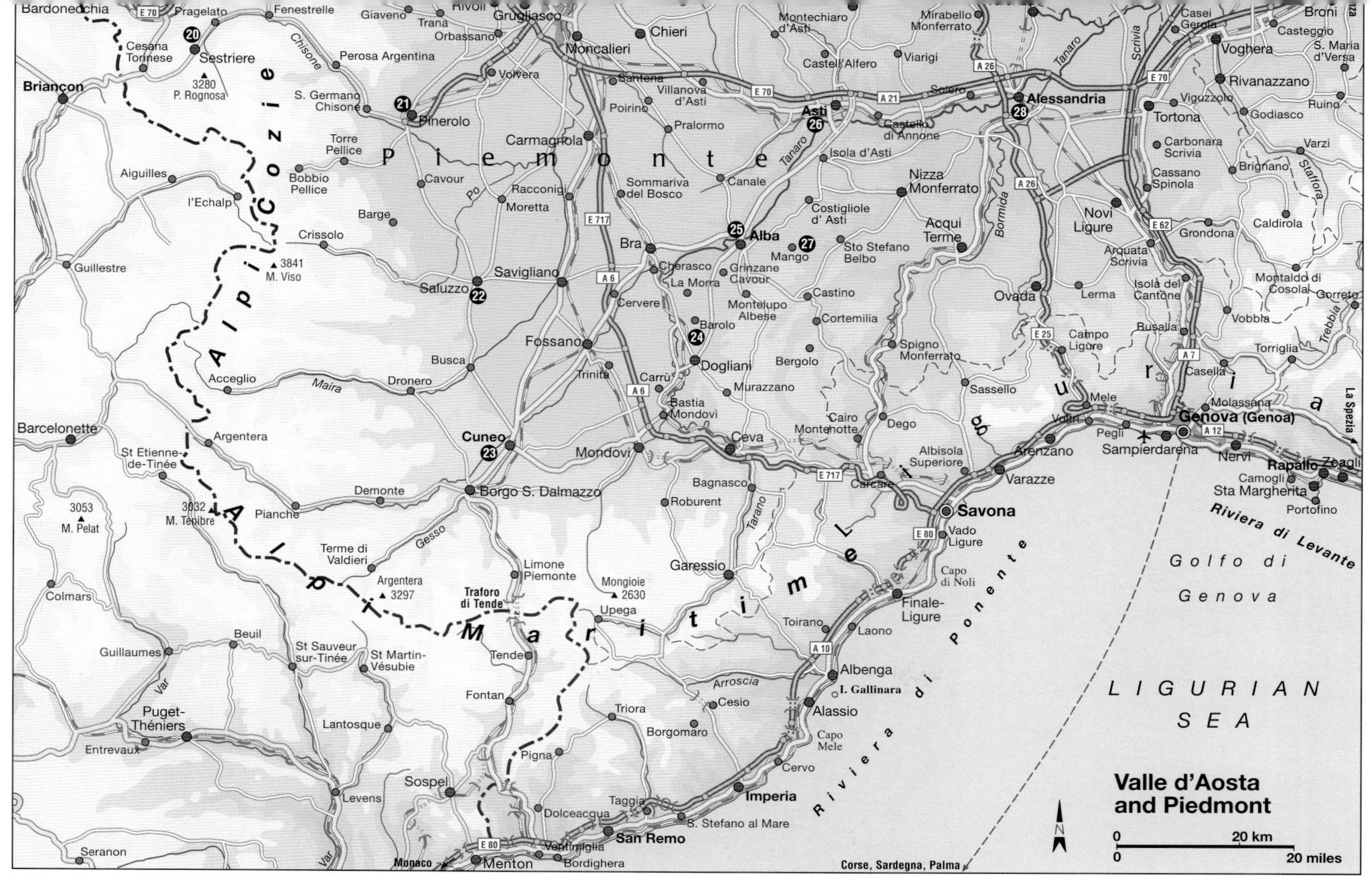
Valle d'Aosta and Piedmont
0 20 km
0 20 miles
LIGURIAN SEA
Golfo di Genova
Riviera di Levante
Riviera di Ponente
Piemonte
Liguria
Alpi Cozie
Alpi Marittime
La Spezia
Corse, Sardegna, Palma
Genova (Genoa)
Savona
Alessandria
Asti
Alba
Cuneo
Imperia
San Remo
Menton
Monaco
Briançon
Barcelonette
Pinerolo
Saluzzo
Savigliano
Fossano
Mondovì
Ceva
Dogliani
Bra
Carmagnola
Moncalieri
Chieri
Grugliasco
Sestriere
Pragelato
Cesana Torinese
Bardonecchia
Fenestrelle
Perosa Argentina
Giaveno
Trana
Orbassano
Volvera
Torre Pellice
Bobbio Pellice
Barge
Crissolo
Cavour
Racconigi
Moretta
Sommariva del Bosco
Cherasco
La Morra
Barolo
Grinzane Cavour
Canale
Mango
Costigliole d' Asti
Isola d'Asti
Nizza Monferrato
Acqui Terme
Ovada
Novi Ligure
Tortona
Voghera
Rivanazzano
Casteggio
Broni
Varzi
Busca
Dronero
Demonte
Borgo S. Dalmazzo
Limone Piemonte
Traforo di Tende
Tende
Fontan
Sospel
Garessio
Bagnasco
Albenga
Alassio
Finale-Ligure
Varazze
Arenzano
Sampierdarena
Nervi
Camogli
Sta Margherita
Rapallo
Zoagli
Portofino
3841 M. Viso
3297 Argentera
3280 P. Rognosa
3032 M. Ténibre
3053 M. Pelat
2630 Mongioie
Tanaro
Bormida
Scrivia
Po
Maira
Gesso
Var
A 6
A 7
A 10
A 12
A 21
A 26
E 25
E 62
E 70
E 80
E 717

VALLE D'AOSTA

The "Valley of Castles", centred on the Roman town of Aosta and surrounded by the highest peaks in Europe, is a great region for driving, hiking and taking cable-car rides

Map on pages 240–241

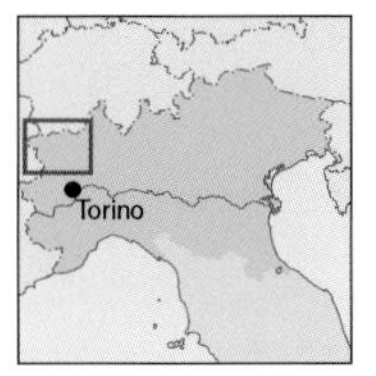

The Valle d'Aosta is the high road in and out of Italy. Bordering France on the western side is Mont Blanc (Monte Bianco; 4,807 metres/15,780 ft), and bordering Switzerland in the north are the Matterhorn (Monte Cervino, 4,478 metres/14,692 ft) and Monte Rosa (4,634 metres/15,203 ft), the three highest mountains in Europe. On the south side is the highest mountain entirely within Italy, Gran Paradiso (4,061 metres/13,323 ft), which gives its name to the spectacular surrounding National Park. The region takes its name not from the river that created the valley – the thundering Dora Baltea, which feeds the River Po – but from its main town, Aosta, named after Emperor Augustus who set up one of his chain of mini-Romes in the centre of the valley.

Accessible only along the river's course, the "Valley of Castles" is clearly of strategic importance, and its mountain passes, *fenêtres*, have been used by the great armies of European history, from Hannibal to Napoleon. The most important of these glacially eroded saddles are the Great St Bernard Pass, north of Aosta, leading to Switzerland, and Little St Bernard, south of Mont Blanc, leading to France. The 5.6 km (3½ mile) road tunnel through Great St Bernard was opened in 1964, the 12 km (7½ mile) Mont Blanc Tunnel the following year.

PRECEDING PAGES: Valle d'Aosta; where the towns meet the mountains.
LEFT: meadow in bloom, Val d'Ayas.
BELOW: a mountain man of Valle d'Aosta.

This is the supreme Alpine region of Italy, home to marmots, ibex, ermines and eagles, laid out with orchards, vineyards and meadows, bright with flowers and singing with trout-filled torrents. Wildlife is conserved in one national and one regional park, and in nine nature reserves. Glaciers glisten and snow is visible all year, though rainfall here is the lowest in Italy. Dairy farming is important; local "red-dappled" and "black-dappled" cattle move up and down the pastureland clunking their bells. Minerals have been exploited since the 15th century, and there is still some iron and steel production.

Mountain men

Woodcarvers, herdsmen and adroit mountaineers, the people are conservative and pious – St Anselm, an Archbishop of Canterbury, was born in Aosta in 1033. The French language, imposed by the Savoy Duke Emanuel Filiberto in 1561, is in evidence, and a Franco-Provençal culture dominates, with a minority Walser, German-Swiss, tradition in the upper valleys in the northeast.

In 1943 there was a move towards annexation with France after 20 years of Fascism under which local languages had been suppressed, workers were mandatorily imported from poorer areas, and an "Italianisation" of the region had been attempted. In 1944 several well-respected local nationalists were murdered by the Fascists. Three years after the end of the war the region was granted a degree of autonomy.

The lower valley

Pont-St-Martin ❶, overlooked by 12th-century Castello du Pont, was the main iron and steel town in the Valle d'Aosta until the end of the 19th century. The well-preserved bridge with a single arch, dating from the 1st century BC, crosses the River Lys, the first of half a dozen tributaries on the northern side of the valley, and the 34-km (21-mile) road traces it up the **Val di Gresonne** to the foot of Monte Rosa. The 16th-century church of St James the Elder at **Issime ❷** has a splendid external fresco of the Last Judgement by the d'Enrico brothers.

Further up, the 100-sq. km (39-sq. mile) Lys glacier is fed by a number of spectacular waterfalls. **Gressoney-St-Jean ❸** was founded by shepherds from the Swiss Valais, and *titsch*, an ancient German Walser dialect, is still spoken here. Near by is **Savoy Castle** (open Apr–Sept Fri–Wed 9am–7pm; Oct–Mar 10am–5pm, Sun until 6pm) and its botanical gardens (May–Oct), summer residence of Queen Margherita, widow of King Umberto I, who had it built in 1894. Simple, Nordic-looking, Walser buildings are scattered through the upper valley, which draws to a halt at **Gressoney-la-Trinité**, a major winter resort, also popular in summer with walkers and hikers.

Beyond Pont-St-Martin the main road passes the sturdy, cold fortress at **Bard**, to which Cavour was confined in 1831 for his liberal ideas. One of the most interesting castles is 10 km (6 miles) further on at **Issogne ❹** (open daily 9am–7pm, July–Aug until 8pm; winter 10am–5pm, closed Wed, Sun 10am–6pm; tours every 30 minutes; admission charge). More château than fortress, the three-storey building overlooking a courtyard with a pomegranate fountain (**Il Melograno**) was begun in 1480 by the local noble Challant family. Restored in the last century, it contains period furniture and objects, and delightful frescoes on the lunettes of the

BELOW AND RIGHT: friendly locals.

entrance portico which show street life and artisan workshops at the end of the 15th century. The next village on the same side of the river is **Champdepraz** ❺, the entry point to the **Mont Avic Regional Park**, a curious landscape of lakes and peat bogs which supports a rich flora and 1,000 species of butterfly.

Opposite Issogne is **Verrès**, with a 14th-century castle; from here a road winds up the **Val d'Ayas**, which follows the River Evançon 27 km (17 miles) to **Champoluc** ❻, another resort beneath Monte Rosa, passing the 50-metre (165-ft) **Isollaz** waterfall, a 10th-century castle at **Graines**, wooden houses at **Brusson** and a sparkling blue reservoir by the **Colle de Joux**.

Back in the valley, the main road climbs around **Montjovet** and then opens onto the broad valley around **St Vincent** ❼, a spa town and leisure centre, to **Châtillon** where a third valley, the **Valtournenche**, runs north. The town after which the valley is named lies 18 km (11 miles) away, and the great sliver of the Matterhorn beckons at each twist and turn.

In the small town square at **Valtournenche** ❽, tablets have been struck on the walls to commemorate the guides and climbers who have risked their lives in the mountains. **Breuil-Cervinia**, one of Italy's most popular ski resorts, is at the end of the road 9 km (6 miles) further on.

Of all the Challant family's castles, the finest is beyond Châtillon at **Fénis** ❾ (open daily Mar–Sept 9am–6.30pm, July–Aug until 7.30pm; tours every 30 minutes; tel: 0165-764263; admission charge). Every inch a proper castle, with towers, keeps, crenellations and a double curtain wall, it was built by Aimone de Challant in 1340. There are good frescoes in the courtyard, attributed to the school of Giacomo Jaquerio (1375–1453), and the building is used as the Museum of Valle d'Aosta Furnishings.

Map on pages 240–241

In chilly Valle d'Aosta, the locals have a penchant for fortified caffè valdostano nella grolla, *laced with wine, grappa and sugar. The* grolla, *or carved wooden drinking vessel, is supposedly descended from the grail, the chivalric cup of yore.*

BELOW: the castle at Issogne has some fine frescoes.

Strong stomachs are called for in Aosta. Larda *is a rasher of pure fat, a speciality which may be served with a plate of cold meats.* Polenta Valdostino *is another dish designed for the famished. This steaming bowl of solid polenta is topped with a doorstep of melted cheese.*

Aosta, the Roman hub

Beyond Fénis the valley opens generously to encompass **Aosta ⑩**, the region's capital (population 39,000). Built in 25 BC as a military camp, Augusta Praetoria was dissected by the roads to the passes of Little St Bernard and Great St Bernard. The best way to understand Aosta is as a traveller would have done in the time of Augustus, arriving at the lower end of the town over the Roman bridge, and crossing the River Buthier to the Roman **Arch of Augustus**, now squatting on a traffic island. From here the Roman road is a pedestrian precinct, Via Sant'Anselmo, where clogs, cuckoo clocks and mountain hooch are sold.

To the right is an intriguing series of ancient church buildings outside the city walls around the **Collegiata di Sant'Orso**. It has a highly original 15th-century façade, opposite a free-standing Romanesque belltower (1131). High under the church roof, between the middle nave and the loft, are some fine 15th-century frescoes. The handsome 16th-century wooden choir stalls were carved by Jeninus Braye. The crypt dates from the 12th century, as does the Romanesque cloister (open daily Mar–Sept 9am–7pm, July–Aug until 8pm; Oct–Feb 10am–12.30pm, 1.30–5pm; free), which has richly carved and animated capitals.

Via Sant'Anselmo leads to **Porta Praetoria**, a massively impressive stone entrance into the city. The two arched walls are 4.5 metres (14 ft 9 in) and 3.45 metres (11 ft 4 in) thick. Most of the Roman city walls, a perfect rectangle 572 by 724 metres (1,875 by 2,375 ft), remain intact. Inside the Porta Praetoria to the right are the remains of the Roman theatre and amphitheatre, where you can watch the ongoing restoration by taking the lift to a panoramic height of 23 metres (76 ft) (open in season 10am–5pm; guided tours lasting one hour depart every 30 minutes; admission charge; tel: 335-6747994).

BELOW: Aosta's Arch of Augustus.

The shopping lane then opens up into the main square, Plaza Emilio Chanoux, named after one of the leading Aosta nationalists murdered by the Nazis. This is a fine square for a coffee and a look at life. The tourist office and town hall are situated here, the latter built in 1839 after French troops had destroyed the Franciscan convent on the site. A lane in the right corner leads to the **Cathedral**, which has an intriguing façade with a polychromatic tableau above the main portal. Some of the finest treasures of Christian art in the valley are housed in the ambulatory in the **Museo del Tesoro** (open Apr–Sept daily 10am–noon, 3–6.30pm; Oct–Mar closed Mon; ask permission from the custodian; admission charge; tel: 0165-40413). The nearby **Archaelogical Museum** (open daily 9am–7pm; free) has plans of the Roman city and finds from the valley.

The upper valley

The Buthier torrent heads towards the Great St Bernard Pass to the north of the city. It soon divides, the right fork going east up the **Valpelline** valley, where there are old wood-balconied houses. During the French Revolution the Bishop of Paris holed up here in **Bionaz**. The valley ends at a vast dam which flooded the upper reaches in 1965. To the left, the road heads to **Colle del Gran San Bernardo** ⓫, where a hospice was founded in 1050 by St Bernard of Montjoux, patron saint of mountaineers; later, dogs named after him were trained to find people lost in snowstorms. The present building dates from 1825.

On the main road above Aosta is the castle of **Sarre** ⓬ (open daily summer 9am–6.30pm, winter 10am–noon, 1.30–4.30pm; admission charge; tel: 0165-257 539), Victor Emmanuel II's hunting lodge, decorated with horns from a thousand mountain goats. The king had set up a royal hunting reserve in 1856 on the

Map on pages 240–241

Bernard of Montjoux, born in 996, was a canon in Aosta Cathedral with responsibilities over the mountain passes. He did much to minister to the peoples of these remote areas, and built rest houses at the top of the passes (Great and Little St Bernard). In 1932 Pope Pius XI made him patron saint of mountaineers.

BELOW: Fénis Castle.

Map on pages 240–241

facing slopes of Gran Paradiso. In 1929 Victor Emmanuel III donated 21 sq. km (5,200 acres) of the park to the state; this became the **Parco Nazionale del Gran Paradiso**, Italy's first national park, which stretches over the mountain into Piedmont. On the Aosta side it lies between the **Valle Rhêmes** and the **Valle de Cogne**, the best entry point to the park. The drive up the **Cogne Valley** beside the river is delightful. **Cogne** ⓭ is a modest town and a good springboard for the hills. Just above it, at **Valnontey**, 1,700 metres (5,580 ft) up, is the **Paradisia Alpine Botanical Gardens** (open 2nd weekend June–2nd weekend Sept daily 10am–6.30pm; admission charge; period of maximum bloom: end June–mid-July), which has more than 1,000 flower species found in mountain regions all over the world.

Mountain flora.

The flora and fauna of the mountains is otherwise laid out in the **Natural History Museum** at the fairy-tale castle at **Saint Pierre** ⓮ (open daily 9am–7pm) just beyond Sarre.

The valley closes in as it heads towards Mont Blanc, and tempting glimpses of this majestic white lady come around each bend. The last major town is **Courmayeur** ⓯, where, along pedestrianised Via Roma, elegant shops brim with designer goods and mouth-watering delicacies. The **Museo Alpino Duca degli Abruzzi** (open Tues–Sun 9am–7pm) has a collection of snow-wear and memorabilia from mountain climbs and Antarctic expeditions. From here there are excursions to make, by ski in winter, on foot in summer.

The reopened Mont Blanc Tunnel lies ahead; or you can scale the mountain on the world's longest cable-car trip across the Aiguille du Midi to Chamonix in France. To the south, the S26 winds past the Pré Saint-Didier gorge to **La Thuile** and the **Colle del Piccole San Bernardo** ⓰, where a stone circle is called Hannibal's Circle after the invader and his band of elephants. ❑

BELOW LEFT: town scene, Courmayeur. **BELOW RIGHT:** Alpine views.

Skiing

Stunning scenery, excellent food and extensive snow-making facilities make Italy's resorts a popular choice. Snow lasts roughly from Christmas to Easter, pistes come in all shapes and sizes, and sports include snowboarding, snowmobiling, snowshoeing, snow-rafting, ski-joring, dog-sledging, sleigh rides, parapenting, ice-climbing, and polo played on frozen lakes. Après-ski is fully catered for, and restaurants can always be looked forward to; Italians know lunch is just as important as skiing.

Skiing in Italy began at the turn of the century in the Susa Valley, Piedmont, when Adolfo Kin in Sauze d'Oulx and the Smith brothers in Bardonecchia imported wooden skis to help them get about in the snow. Today these two towns are part of the **Milky Way** (Via Lattea), 400 km (250 miles) of piste that make up one of Europe's great ski circuits, taking in Montgenèvre in France. The circuit's centre is **Sestriere** in Piedmont, the Alps' first purpose-built resort, created by Gianni Agnelli in the 1930s, where the Alpine Skiing World Championships were held in 1997. Turin has been chosen to host the 2006 Olympic Winter Games. Most of the events will be held at Sestriere, Sansicario and Sauze d'Oulx.

Further north is **Courmayeur**, beneath Mont Blanc at the head of the Valle d'Aosta. This lovely old town has a good social life and abundant restaurants, particularly appreciated by visitors from Milan. Linked to Chamonix by the famous Vallée Blanche in France, it lies on the sunny side of the slope, which does not usually diminish its snowfall. **La Thuile**, an old mining town near by, is a good choice for escaping crowds.

Cervinia, more commonly known as Breuil-Cervinia (the Matterhorn), in the Valle d'Aosta is the most reliable resort for snow. Built up by Mussolini, it is rather lacking in soul, but is one of the largest resorts in the Alps. The village of **Valtournenche** just down the valley has genuine Italian atmosphere. Cervinia is linked with Zermatt in Switzerland, and ski passes are valid in both resorts. More ethnic, and quieter, are the Walser settlements in nearby **Monterosa** area: **Alagna**, off-piste paradise **Champoluc** and **Gressoney-la-Trinité**.

One of the most typically Italian resorts is **Bormio**, a Roman spa town with a pedestrianised centre of chic shops and low-key nightlife. Snow stays late, and the town is linked to the more lively **Santa Catarina** and in reach of St Moritz in Switzerland. **Livigno** in the Spol Valley is linked to St Moritz and Davos in Switzerland, and is one of the cheapest resorts. Both Lombardy resorts are around five hours from Bergamo or Milan.

The Dolomites in northeastern Italy offer the most glorious scenery and mile upon mile of intermediate terrain. Skiers in Verona head for chic **Madonna di Campiglio**, while skiers in Bergamo go to **Passo Tonale** and **Pontedilegno**; both are inexpensive, with easy slopes for beginners. The top Dolomite resort is **Cortina d'Ampezzo**, two hours from Venice. This is the smartest place to ski in the country. It is not overpriced, and anyone can watch the rich climb aboard helicopters in search of new snow thrills.

Where skiers go walkers can go, too, and ski-lifts and cable cars operate in many places throughout the summer. ❑

RIGHT: we have lift-off.

Caffè
Ristorante

ino
FFE
TORINO

TURIN

With a royal palace, some 40 museums, smart shops, elegant cafés and a replica of the famous Holy Shroud, there's plenty to see and do in Piedmont's capital

Map on page 254

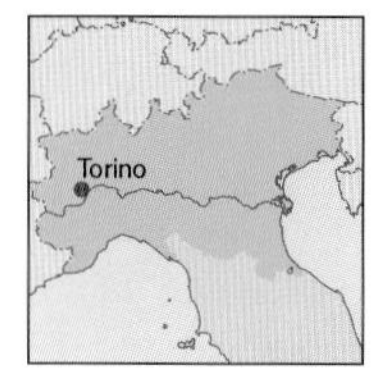

Italy's fourth-largest city (the metropolitan area totals about 1.5 million inhabitants) is a harmonious and noble collection of 18th- and 19th-century streets built where three rivers join the Po. From 1574 this was the seat of the House of Savoy, a duchy that once not only included Piedmont and the Valle d'Aosta but also extended into Switzerland and took in all the Savoie in France as well as the island of Sardinia. It was here that the Turin-born aristocrat Count Camillo di Cavour colluded with Victor Emmanuel of Savoy against the empires of France and Austria to bring about an independent and unified Italy (though Nice and Savoie were lost in the process) and, in 1861, provide Italy with its first capital. In every piazza and at every junction huge, moustached Emmanuels and Umbertos rise on plinths and warhorses, leaving no doubt about the satisfaction the House of Savoy felt in providing blue blood for an Italian monarchy.

For all their heroism, the aristocracy were wimps in the wet, insisting that colonnades line the main streets so they would never be bothered by rain. The result is that the heart of the city has a grand Baroque and Neoclassical air, with seamless arcades shading chandelier-hung, marbled cafés and smart shops suggesting nothing of the industrial city of Fiat and factory workers, of the late Antonio Gramsci (former leader of the Communist Party), of Red Brigade targets, of the hard-working city that Turin really is. It was also the host city for the 2006 Winter Olympics.

A flair for innovation and design has always been part of the Torinese character. The car, cinema, television, telephone and fashion industries have all flourished here, and continue to do so. As Turin moves ever forward, brand-new state-of-the-art railway and metro systems are under construction, with 15 km (9 miles) of lines being laid underground, out of sight and reclaiming and beautifying the industrial wasteland. The city has become a symbol of contemporary architecture and art whose hills, parks and gardens make it one of the greenest in Europe. Whether it is as the city of the House of Savoy, of cutting-edge design, of the much-debated Holy Shroud or of the home of Juventus football, Turin continues to reinvent itself.

Orientation

At first this seems like a one-street town. From the gates of the royal palace there is a clear view straight down the Via Roma and its handsome, colonnaded piazzas to the grand glass-and-iron railway station 1.2 km (¾ mile) away. Two lesser streets lead off from the castle in front of the royal palace: the colonnaded Via Po heads down to the attractive Piazza Vittorio Veneto and the River Po; in the opposite direction the pedestrianised Via Garibaldi makes for the older part of town.

PRECEDING PAGES: Caffè Torino.
LEFT: the dome of the chapel of San Lorenzo.
BELOW: the distinctive Mole Antonelliana.

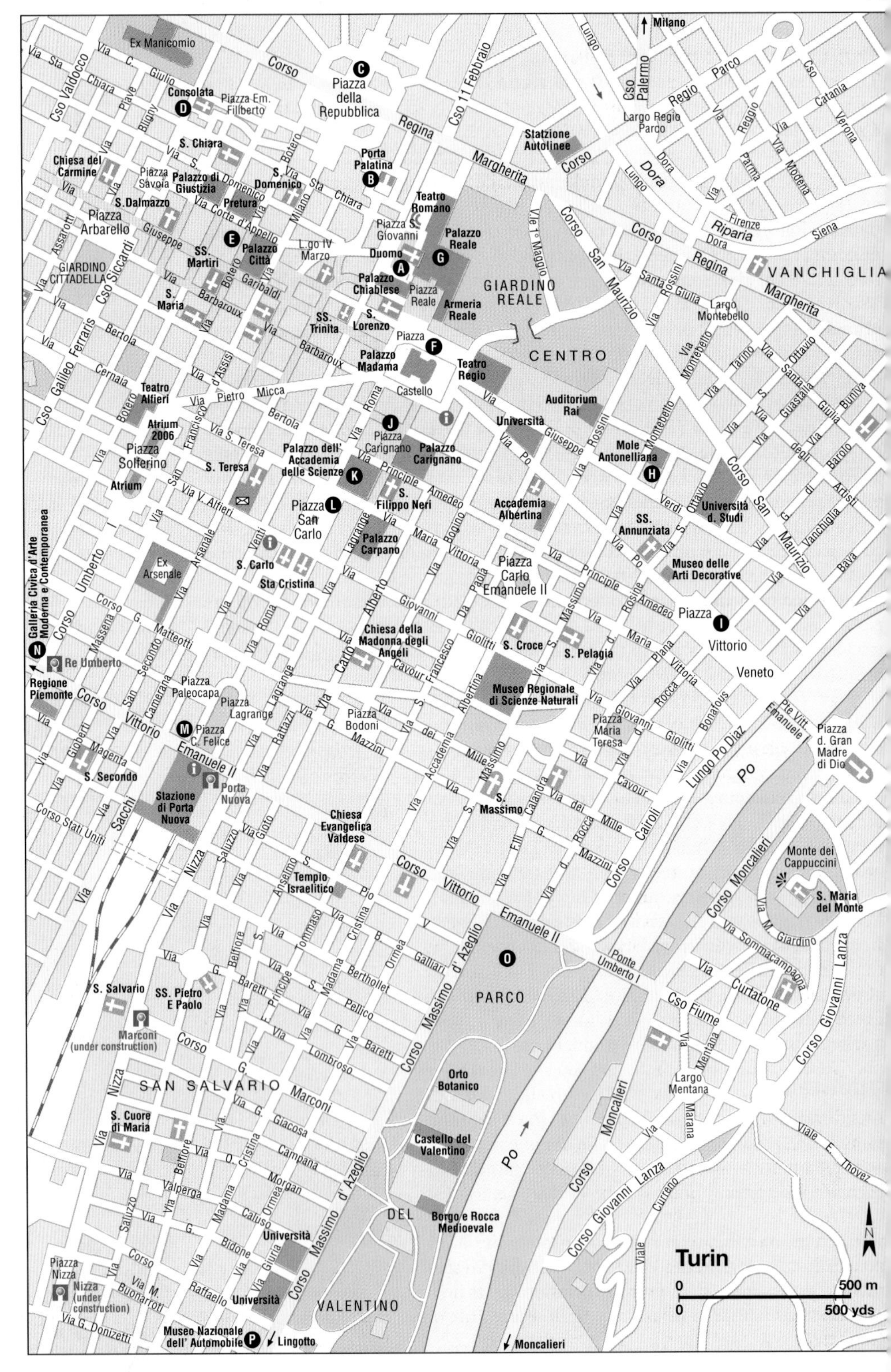
Turin
CENTRO
SAN SALVARIO
VANCHIGLIA
PARCO DEL VALENTINO
Piazza della Repubblica
Porta Palatina
Duomo
Palazzo Reale
Giardino Reale
Armeria Reale
Palazzo Madama
Teatro Regio
Mole Antonelliana
Palazzo Carignano
Piazza San Carlo
Piazza Carlo Emanuele II
Piazza Vittorio Veneto
Museo Regionale di Scienze Naturali
Stazione di Porta Nuova
Orto Botanico
Castello del Valentino
Borgo e Rocca Medioevale
Museo Nazionale dell' Automobile
Galleria Civica d'Arte Moderna e Contemporanea
Monte dei Cappuccini
S. Maria del Monte
Po
Milano
Lingotto
Moncalieri
0
500 m
0
500 yds

The cathedral and old town

There was a bishopric in Turin from around the 5th century, but the present cathedral was not completed until 1498. The **Duomo di San Giovanni Battista** **A** (open Mon–Sat 7am–12.30pm, 3–7pm, Sun 8am–12.30pm, 3–7pm) is a small but elegant Renaissance edifice designed by a Tuscan architect, Meo del Caprino. Beside it is a 60-metre (200-ft) brick campanile built 30 years earlier, topped by an 18th-century bell house by Filippo Juvara. At the back of the cathedral is an outstanding Baroque octagonal cupola built by Guarino Guarini in 1694, illuminating the black **Cappella della Sindone**, the chapel of the Holy Shroud *(see page 259)*, entered from inside the church or through the royal palace behind. In 1997 the cupola was seriously damaged by fire, and the chapel has remained closed. However, the Sindone was left miraculously unscathed. Both Guarini and Juvarra contributed enormously to the city's architecture, evolving a distinctive local Baroque style.

On the western corner with Piazza Castello at Via Palazzo di Città is the **Church of San Lorenzo** (open Mon–Fri 7.30am–noon, 4–7.30pm, Sat 7.30am–noon, 3–7.30pm, Sun 9am–1pm, 3–7.15pm, 8.30–10pm). For many, this is Turin's most beautiful church, although its plain exterior belies the beauty within – a fantasy of Baroque stucco, marble, gilding and sculptures. The highlight of the octagonal interior is the superb, lofty dome by Guarino Guarini, opulently decorated with elegant plays of shape and volume. The church also has on view a full-size replica of the Turin Shroud.

From the cathedral steps the remains of the Roman city are evident on the right in some fragments of the wall, theatre and **Porta Palatina** **B**, the main gate to the Po Valley. Walk through it to reach the **Piazza della Repubblica** **C**, the site of a market every morning and all day Saturday. There is also a flea market, the Balôn, on Saturday, which becomes the Gran Balôn antiques market on the second Sunday of the month. This is Europe's largest open-air market.

Beyond the market, by one of the Roman city's five corner towers, is the Piazza Consolata and Guarini's round church, **Santuario della Consolata** **D**, the Torinesi's favourite church (open daily 6.30am–12.30pm, 3–7.30pm). Around this ancient square are an old herbalist's shop and Al Bicerin, a tiny café famously frequented by the composer Puccini and still serving its renowned hot drink, the *bicerin*, made of coffee, chocolate and cream. Opened in 1763, it was much loved by Cavour, important politicians, nobles and intellectuals of the Risorgimento, and is still as atmospheric today, dripping with marble and mirrors. Nietzsche was a frequent visitor, and Alexandre Dumas mentioned Bicerin "among the good and pleasant things of the city" during his stay in Turin in 1852.

There are a number of old shops and manor houses in this former heart of the city. Jean-Jacques Rousseau lived at 11 Via dei Cappelli (now a wine shop) and was converted to Catholicism at a neighbouring hospice in 1728. The **Palazzo Città** **E** is the former grass market, just off the old Roman Via Dora Grossa, now Via Garibaldi, a pedestrianised throughfare full of character – Europe's longest pedestrianised street.

Map on page 254

On the Porta Palatina, gateway to the Po Valley.

BELOW: outside the Bicerin.

In Turin, café life is in the blood. The citizens have a passion for pastries and desserts, many of which were first created for the royal court of Savoy. For more information on Turin's cafés, see page 110.

Royal Turin

Via Garibaldi arrives at the centre of the town at **Piazza Castello** Ⓕ, where the only medieval monument in the city is found; it is known as the **Palazzo Madama** (open Tues–Sun 10am–8pm, Sat until 11pm; free; tours of the restored parts of the palazzo; tours during the week need to be booked, tel: 011-442 9912; www.comune.torino.it/palazzomadama) since two royal widows, Maria Cristina of France and Giovanna Battista of Savoy, made it their home. The Senate of the Kingdom of Savoy met in its Salone degli Svizzeri between 1846 and 1861, and for the next three years it housed the Senate of the Kingdom of Italy. The Swiss connection is confirmed by the statue of the Standard Bearer of the Swiss Army by Vincenzo Vela on the south side of the building, presented to the city in 1857 by the municipality of Milan. The Castello now contains the **Museo Civico di Arte Antica** (open Tues–Fri, Sun 10am–6pm, Sat until 8pm).

The royal buildings which lie to the north of the castle will not have gone unnoticed. Their near wing contains, on the ground floor, the **Biblioteca Reale** (open Mon and Wed 8.15am–6.45pm, Tues, Thur–Sat 8.15am–1.45pm; free). On the first floor is the **Armeria Reale** (open Wed and Fri 8.30am–noon, Tues–Thur and Sat–Sun 1.30–7.30pm; admission charge; tel: 011-543889). This is one of the world's richest collections of arms and armour, with oriental, Risorgimento and Napoleonic weapons, including 57 complete suits of armour and Emanuele Filiberto's 16th-century sword. The collection also features firearms and stilettos – types of Italian dagger. Outside, next to the Armeria, is a statue of Christopher Columbus, erected in honour of a soldier from the Americas who came to fight in World War I. It's supposed to bring good luck to rub the statue's little finger, which now gleams with the constant attention and, to date, has been replaced four times.

BELOW: Via Garibaldi runs through the heart of the Quadrilatero Romano.

Beyond, through the Piazza Reale, is the **Palazzo Reale** Ⓖ (Tues–Sun 8.30am–7.30pm, ticket office closes at 6pm; guided tours; admission charge). It is essential to visit the Royal Palace, which was built in 1660 by the architect Amedeo di Castellamonte and was used by the Savoy dukes, kings of Sardinia and of Italy, until 1865. Dripping gold and velvet, chinoiserie and chandeliers, the first-floor apartments around a plain courtyard are furnished with pomp and pretension. The palace grounds (Giardini Reali; open daily May & Oct 9am–5pm, June–Sept 8.30am–6.30pm) are modest but pleasant for a stroll. On the far side of the Castello, beside the restored **Teatro Regio**, now a façade of glass and metal as the old 18th-century theatre was burnt down in 1936, the Via Po leads down to the river, passing, on the left, Via Montebello, where the extraordinary **Mole Antonelliana** Ⓗ points its 167-metre (548-ft) spire at the sky as an emblem of the city. Named after its architect, Alessandro Antonelli (1798–1888), it was a synagogue and is now a fascinating cinema museum. The **Museo Nazionale del Cinema** (open Tues–Sun 10am–8pm, Sat 10am–11pm; admission charge) is on five levels. From the top of the panoramic lift there are superb views across the city. The Italian film industry was born in Turin, and from 1906 to 1916 the city was the world's film-production capital. This thrilling exhibition covers 3,200 sq. metres (34,000 sq. ft) at the heart of which is the Aula del Tempio (Temple Room), with comfortable loungers from where you can enjoy clips from films of today and yesterday on giant screens. Ten themed chapels are arranged around this main hall, dedicated to "cult films" – the themes are horror, sci-fi, love, death, animation, the absurd, truth, falsehood, experimental cinema and Turin as the city of film. Sequences from 200 films are screened and, in the Macchina del Cinema section, the secrets of editing, sound effects, casting and much more are fascinatingly revealed. Classic clips from the shower scene in *Psycho*, the obligatory car chase in *The Italian Job*, props like the egg from *Alien*, the head from *Jaws* and costumes ranging from Marilyn Monroe's bodice and Charlie Chaplin's bowler hat to Fellini's scarf, coat and hat are all exhibited.

The shops in Via Po's arcades include the aristocratic **Caffè Fiorio**, an ice-cream specialist, where Cavour drank and dreamed in its plush red 19th-century décor. Also along the Via Po is the **Museo delle Arti Decorative – Fondazione Pietro Accorsi** (Museum of Decorative Arts; Via Po 55; tel: 011-8129116; open Tues–Sun 10am–8pm, Thur until 11pm; tours in English and touch-tours for the visually impaired; admission charge). Housed in the noble 18th-century house of the famous Piedmontese antiques dealer, the late Pietro Accorsi, this museum opened in 1999. Thousands of rare objets d'art, furniture, porcelain, silver, paintings and tapestries make up this precious collection. Many of the treasures are from the 18th century and are displayed within 27 rooms. This dynamic Foundation also stages frequent temporary exhibitions, history-of-art classes and concerts. The street ends in the wide **Piazza Vittorio Veneto** Ⓘ, an elegant square looking across the Ponte Vittorio Emanuele to the 19th-century Gran Madre de Dio.

The Torino Card, obtainable from Turismo c/o the Atrium, Porta Nuova station or from the airport, is valid for 48 or 72 hours and gives free access to 30 museums in Turin and Piedmont.

BELOW: inside the Cinema Museum.

Map on page 254

The Risorgimento relived

On the south side of the Castello, near the grand Caffè Mulassano, the Via Accademia delle Scienze leads down to **Piazza Carignano** Ⓙ, Turin's political centre in the 19th century when it seethed with optimism and grand plans for an emergent independent state. On one side of the square are **Del Cambio**, where Cavour dined, which is still a prestigious restaurant serving traditional local dishes, and the Teatro Carrignano; on the other side is **Palazzo Carignano**, designed by Guarini, from 1861 to 1865 the seat of Italy's first parliament. It now houses the **Museo Nazionale del Risorgimento** (open Tues–Sun 9am–7pm; admission charge), and though 30 rooms may be more than one wishes to see concerning the Movement, the experience should not be missed.

Elegant façade, Piazza San Carlo.

Guarini designed the **Palazzo dell'Accademia delle Scienze** Ⓚ on the south side of the square for the Jesuits; it now houses the **Museo Egizio** (open Tues–Sun 8.30am–7.30pm; admission charge includes ticket for the Galleria Sabauda). Impressive treasures include the black granite statue of Rameses II and the two giant sphinxes at the entrance, which were part of the Drovetti Collection – the original nucleus of the Egyptian Museum. Also impressive is the Tomb of Kha and Merit, dating from around 1430 BC. Discovered in 1906 during the excavation campaign carried out by the Italian archaeological mission in Deir el Medina, it houses sarcophagi and statues, as well as furniture, garments, grooming items, vases of unguents and preserved food. The underground section has a large part of the original Roman walls found during renovation exposed (2.5 metres/8 ft thick and 7 metres/23 ft high). On the top floor is the **Galleria Sabauda** (same opening times). This is one of Italy's richest treasure troves of Italian paintings from the 14th–18th centuries. The whole collection will move to the Manica Nuova of the Palazzo Reale in 2007.

BELOW: exhibits from the significant collection of Turin's Egypt Museum.

Opposite the museum is **San Filippo Neri**, the city's largest church and a product of both Guarini and Juvara. On the far side of the Palazzo Carignano is **Piazza Carlo Alberto**, dominated by Marocchetti's equestrian statue of Carlo Alberto, Victor Emmanuel's father, who was also born in the palace. On the corner of Via Carlo Alberto is a plaque commemorating "Federico" Nietzsche's stay in the city in 1888.

Walk back up to Via Roma and **Piazza San Carlo** Ⓛ, the heart of this elegant thoroughfare, designed by Castellamonte, where a pianist might be playing at the Caffè Torino. Another equestrian statue by Marocchetti, that of Emanuele Filiberto (1831–8), is in the centre of this grand space of former noble homes and exclusive establishments, including, at No. 183, the still-active Circolo de Whist founded by the card-carrying Count Camillo di Cavour.

Via Roma and the railway station

Beyond the piazza, Via Roma becomes a street again where statues of two figures, refreshingly naked and unhorsed, represent Turin's two major rivers, the Po and the Dora. Ahead lies the final elegant square, **Piazza Carlo Felice** Ⓜ, with bandstand and ponds, sitting in front of the **Porta Nuova railway station** and the slightly seedier end of the town. The Corso Vittorio Emanuele runs in front of it, leading on the right hand to the **Galleria Civica d'Arte Moderna e Contemporanea** Ⓝ (open Tues–Sun 9am–7pm; admission charge). Known by its initials as the GAM, the museum has art from the 18th century to the present day.

The road to the left leads to **Parco del Valentino** Ⓞ, down by the Po. This is a popular park, with cafés and restaurants. At night it buzzes with clubs and bars. Within the park is a "medieval" village and fortress, **Borgo e Rocca Medioevale** (Viale Virgilio, Parco del Valentino; Borgo: daily 9am–7pm, free; Rocca: Tues–Sun 9am–7pm, admission charge). This is a faithful reconstruction of a 15th-century Piedmontese village and fortress created for the General Italian Exhibition of 1884. Tangles of alleyways and a drawbridge are all part of the "medieval" experience.

Two boats, the *Valentino* and *Valentina*, ply up and down the River Po and can be boarded at Murazzi at the end of Piazza Vittorio Veneto or from Borgo Medioevale (early June–late Sept Tues–Sun; Oct–May Sun and hols; information, tel: 011-5764733; reservations, tel: 011-744892).

Further afield

A number of sites outside the centre of Turin are accessible by public transport, taxi or car; check opening times locally before going. South of the Parco del Valentino, at Corso Unità d'Italia 40, is the **Museo Nazionale dell'Automobile** Ⓟ (open Tues–Sat 10am–6.30pm; admission charge), one of the most important motoring museums in Europe, as one might expect from the home of Fabbrica Italiana di Automobili Torino – Fiat. It has over 150 models (including the earliest Fiat, the *Itala* that won the world's longest automobile race in 1907), posters, paraphernalia and a bookshop.

Along the length of the "Spina" (or central backbone, running from south to north, which will cross the underground line), there are many projects underway including new arts centres, and, close to the Lingotto, the cultural and trade centre, the "Olympic District" for 2006.

BELOW: the Turin Shroud – the face of Christ?

THE TURIN SHROUD

The most venerated cloth in Christendom, the Sacra Sindone, is a length of linen, 4.34 metres (14ft 3in) long and 1.09 metres (3ft 3in) wide, wrapped around a corpse, from head to toe, leaving a faint image of both the back and the front of a naked body, a long-haired, bearded figure which has its hands clasped over its groin. Many believers maintain that this is the cloth wrapped around the body of Christ by Joseph of Arimathea after he was taken down from the Cross. Carbon dating and chemical analysis have proved inconclusive.

The shroud was brought to Turin from Chambéry in 1578 when the Savoys moved their capital, and has "miraculously" escaped theft and fire several times, most recently in 1997. The shroud is kept in a silver chest in a special chapel of black marble in Turin Cathedral and seldom goes on display, but a copy, a third smaller than the original size, is on view in the north side of the Duomo.

Its last public appearance was in 2000, and the next is scheduled for 2025. The mystery is far from solved, and the Institute of Sindonology in Turin is dedicated to continual study of the cloth. However, it remains an object of great reverence for believers and the merely curious alike.

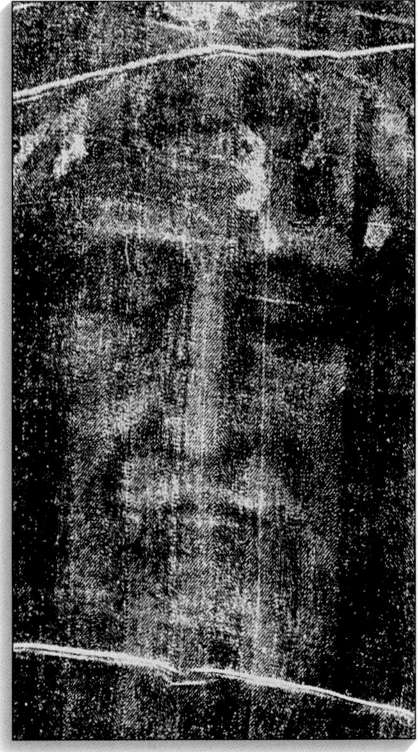

South of the city centre

South of the city centre was the heart of the car industry that put the "T" into Fiat, Fabbrica Italiana Automobili Torino, in 1899, and made Turin *the* city of cars. The areas of Lingotto, Italia 61, Mirafiori and Millefonti, once the power-house of the industry, are now being transformed in a multi-million-euro "suburbs project", and many new sporting facilities are being created here in honour of the Turin Winter Olympic Games in 2006.

Near by, between the Corso Unità d'Italia and Via Ventimiglia, is the area known as **Italia 61**, built in 1961 to celebrate the centenary of the Unification of Italy. The **Palazzo delle Mostre** (Via Ventimiglia) is now the **Palavela**, reworked by Gae Aulenti, and is the new 9,000-seat venue for ice figure-skating.

South of here is the concrete **Palazzo del Lavoro** (Via Ventimiglia 201), designed by Pier Luigi Nervi in the late 1950s. Large enough to contain St Peter's in Rome, this vast structure stages trade fairs and exhibitions.

Just west of Italia 61 is **Lingotto**, the cultural and trade centre which has risen on the site of the historical Fiat factory and has become the Olympic District and epicentre of the 2006 Games. Building began in 1917 on what was to become Europe's blueprint for the efficient mass production of motor cars. By 1939, the huge Mirafiori Fiat factory to the south had overtaken it, but production continued at Lingotto until 1982. Transformation came under the skilful eye of architect Renzo Piano, starting in 1986 when it became a multi-purpose exhibition centre, and today it's the setting for international events such as the biannual Salone del Gusto. The auditorium has superb acoustics, the shopping mall is vast, sprinkled with cafes and restaurants, and the two hotels, the Meridien and Art+Tech, Turin's first five-star hotel, are among the city's best.

BELOW: Lingotto, the epicentre of the 2006 WInter Olympics.

Map on page 254

Also here is the **Pinacoteca Giovanni e Marella Agnelli** (open Tues–Sun 9am–7pm; admission charge). Known as "Lo Scrigno" (jewel case), designed by Renzo Piano and opened in 2002, this futuristic building is made of wood, with a glass roof to give natural light to the collection of Agnelli treasures.

"Lo Scrigno" stands at the same height as "La Bolla" (bubble), also designed by Renzo Piano, which is an avant-garde conference hall crafted in steel and glass and in the shape of, not surprisingly, a bubble.

Superga is a hill opposite **Piazza Vittorio Veneto** on the other side of the Po. Filippo Juvarra took 40 metres (130 ft) off its top to create a flat space for his masterpiece, a Baroque basilica, **Basilica di Superga** (Strada della Basilica di Superga 73; open daily 9am–noon, 3–6pm, Nov–Mar until 5pm; Savoy tombs: Apr–Oct Mon–Fri 9.30am–1.30pm, 2.30–6.30pm, Sat 9.30am–7.30pm, Sun 1–7pm; Oct–Mar openings variable, usually weekdays by appointment only, Sat–Sun 9.30am–1.30pm, 2.30–6.30pm; tel: 011-8997456/8980083; admission charge), built to fulfil a vow made by Vittorio Amedeo II before the Battle of Turin in 1706, in which besieging French and Spanish forces were routed, and subsequently the resting place of the Savoy kings. A plaque also commemorates a tragedy which particularly touched the people of Turin: the death of the entire Turin soccer team, who were returning from Lisbon in May 1949 when their plane crashed behind the basilica.

The **Castello di Moncalieri** (Piazza Baden Baden 4; guided visits Thur, Sat–Sun every 45 minutes 9.30am–6.30pm; tel: 011-6402883) dates from the 15th century. On show are King Victor Emmanuel II's grand apartments.

Near by is the **Monte dei Cappuccini**, on which stand the church of **Santa Maria del Monte** (open daily 8.40am–noon, 3–7.30pm) and the **Museo Nazionale della Montagna Duca degli Abruzzi** (closed for restoration until the end of 2005 but temporary exhibitions usually open 9am–7pm).

Three royal residences are also within reach. To the north is the **Reggia di Venaria Reale** (open Tues, Thur, Sat, Sun, 9.30am–12.30pm, 2.30–5.30pm; or by arrangement, tel: 011-4593675), a vast echoing Baroque summer residence of the Savoys. To the west of the city is another summer palace, **Castello di Rivoli**, by Juvarra, which has a permanent modern art collection by European and American artists (open Tues–Thur 10am–5pm, Fri–Sun 10am–9pm). Since 1984 it has been the site for Turin's **Museum of Contemporary Art**, contrasting the old with the very, very new. It may seem at first a little jarring to see works by Gilbert and George and Jeff Koons in such a setting, with Maurizio Cattelan's stuffed horse suspended from a stuccoed ceiling, but contrasts are both dramatic and fantastic. There is a good museum café and next to the Manica Langa is the minimalist, cuboid Combal.Zero Restaurant. But the most impressive is **Palazzina di Caccia di Stupinigi**, a grand hunting lodge and grounds to the south of the city (open Tues–Sun, Apr–Oct 10am–6pm, Nov–Mar 9.30am–5pm; ticket office closes 1 hour earlier; admission charge). Built by Juvarra for Vittorio Amedeo II, the lodge was a favourite of Napoleon when "visiting" Italy. ❑

BELOW: the Basilica di Superga.

PIEDMONT

Risotto, truffles and some of Italy's finest wines are rich rewards for the traveller among the mountains and plains of Piedmont

Map on pages 240–241

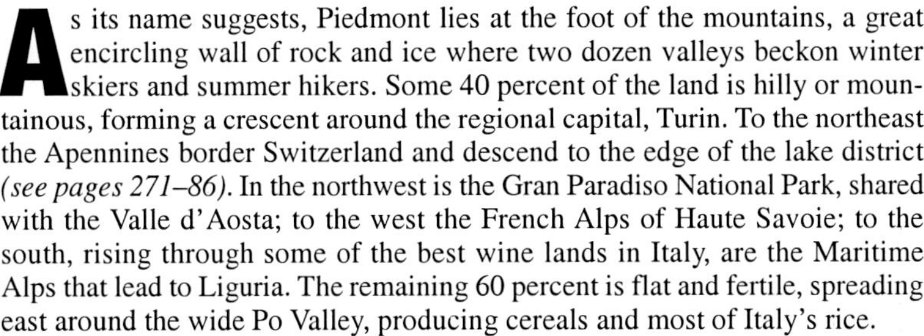

As its name suggests, Piedmont lies at the foot of the mountains, a great encircling wall of rock and ice where two dozen valleys beckon winter skiers and summer hikers. Some 40 percent of the land is hilly or mountainous, forming a crescent around the regional capital, Turin. To the northeast the Apennines border Switzerland and descend to the edge of the lake district *(see pages 271–86)*. In the northwest is the Gran Paradiso National Park, shared with the Valle d'Aosta; to the west the French Alps of Haute Savoie; to the south, rising through some of the best wine lands in Italy, are the Maritime Alps that lead to Liguria. The remaining 60 percent is flat and fertile, spreading east around the wide Po Valley, producing cereals and most of Italy's rice.

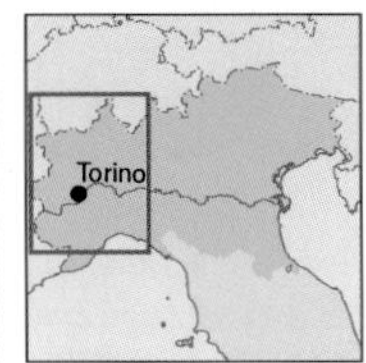

Mountains in the west

The southern slopes of the Gran Paradiso National Park, less accessible than those of the north, are wilder and less populous. Main access to the park is up the **Valle di Locana** 17 to the Orco Valley, where the road climbs to the 2,612-metre (8,570-ft) peak of Colle del Nivolet and a pass over the mountains which leads to the Val Savarenche in Aosta.

The main road west of Turin goes through the Susa Valley to France. After some 32 km (20 miles) it passes **Sacra de San Michele** 18 (open Tues–Sat 9.30am–12.30pm, 3–6pm, Sun 9.30am–noon, 3–6pm, mid-Oct–mid-Mar until 5pm; Sat evenings in Aug visits to the floodlit Monastero Nuovo, churches, monks' workshop and Torre della Bell'Alda; admission charge). Visible from miles around, this vast, imposing monastery clings to the peak of Monte Pirchiriano, 962 metres (3,156 ft) high. Begun in the late 10th century for the Benedictine monks on the Via Francigena – the pilgrimage route to Rome – it became an important study centre and was enlarged many times until the Benedictine Order was forced out in 1622. Now in the hands of the Rosminian fathers, the abbey is Gothic in appearance and, after major work in the 1990s, it has been restored to its former glory.

Susa 19 is an attractive small mountain town and a good centre for the exploration of the surrounding Alps. Shops brim with pastries, gifts and multicoloured alcoholic delights. Remains of Roman Segusio include an **amphitheatre** (open daily 7.30am–8pm), an aqueduct and the 3rd-century Porta Savoia, which owes its present wide arch to an enlargement in 1750. The *Arco di Augusto* (8 BC) was put up by Cottius, a local Gallic chieftain who threw in his lot with the Romans. There is a small museum in the castle at the top of the town.

From Susa the old road goes over the **Col du Mont Cenis** pass into France, but the motorway and

LEFT: cycling through the streets of Barolo.
BELOW: some of Italy's finest wine comes from this region.

Barolo vineyards. Piedmont has 20 denominated wines.

main road head for the **Fréjus** tunnel, now reopened after a bad fire in June 2004. Susa is as much a summer as a winter resort: the main winter resort is **Sestriere** ⓴, to the south in the Valle del Chisone *(see Skiing, page 249)*, reached through **Pinerolo** ㉑, an attractive town with an old centre and a fine 15th-century cathedral. There are a number of forts in the area, notably the extraordinary complex at **Finistrelle**.

Two other attractive mountain valleys are the upper **Po Valley**, which begins beneath Monteviso (3,841 metres/12,602 ft), where Italy's longest river starts its journey to the Adriatic Sea, and **Valle Varaita**. Both are approached through **Saluzzo** ㉒, which makes a pleasant stopover. **Cuneo** ㉓, 32 km (20 miles) south of Saluzzo, leads to the southern valleys, including the Stura and Vermengagna, verdant places with abundant flora.

Alba, Asti and the wine lands

Southeast of Turin, the flat landscape begins to roll into a sea of hills topped by castles and hamlets, most of which have only a few hundred inhabitants. First come the Roere and then the Langhe hills, running into the chalk Monferrato district in the east and rising to 900 metres (2,950 ft) as they approach the High Langhe and Liguria to the south. These are the wine lands of Barbaresco and Barolo, often called the Burgundy of Italy, not least because of the wines' high prices. The government has set up nine Enoteche Regionale, regional wine-tasting centres, in castles and other historic buildings, and these are backed up by wine shops and high-quality restaurants. This is a gourmet corner of the country, and tables are filled with white truffles, mushrooms and hazelnuts; it is also marketed as "the hills of salami, cheese and bread". Many of the villages have cel-

BELOW: the 14th-century façade of Asti's cathedral.

lars and places to taste wine as well as small rural and wine-related museums.

Barolo ㉔ is the king of the wines, and it comes from a village of the same name set in a triangle of vineyard between Alba, Dogliani and Cherasco. A modest village which can seem almost deserted, it has a castle with a museum of wine and the former residence of the Falletti family, Castello dei Marchesi Falletti di Barolo (open Feb–Dec, Mon–Wed, Fri–Sun 10am–12.30pm, 3–6.30pm; tel: 0173-56277; admission charge). The last Falletti marquesa is credited with vinifying the wine to make it last longer, thus creating the famous Barolo brew. Wines from the whole region are available in the Enoteca in the bowels of the castle; as well as the noble Barolo, they include the less expensive Nebbiolo.

Perched on the hill is the historical **Grinzane**, dominated by its beautiful medieval castle, **Castello di Grinzane Cavour** (Via Cavour 5; open Feb–Aug and Dec Wed–Mon 9.30am–12.30pm, 2.30–6.30pm; Sept–Nov daily; tel: 0173-262159). The famous Piedmontese statesman Count Camillo di Cavour used this as his country mansion in the 19th century. The **Ethnographic Museum** here displays some of Cavour's personal belongings and represents an authentic picture of life from the 17th to 19th centuries. There's also a small collection of Roman finds in the area, and some informative panels on the white truffle. This is the site of the white-truffles auction held every end of October or beginning of November when vast sums of money are exchanged for the "white gold". It is open by invitation only. Open to everyone, however, is the excellent restaurant serving typical Piedmontese cuisine and the Enoteca Regionale Piemontese Cavour, one of the finest regional wine cellars with an extensive collection of Piedmontese wines and grappa.

The Enoteca at **Barbaresco**, just east of Alba, is in the middle of the village, in the deconsecrated 19th-century church of San Donato.

Map on pages 240–241

Second to wine comes rice.

BELOW: stonework on Asti's magnificent Gothic cathedral.

Map on pages 240–241

Alba ㉕ is a quiet, genial country town with a good market on Saturday. At the heart of town is the Piazza Risorgimento, once the site of the Roman forum, now dominated by the red-brick **Cattedrale di San Lorenzo** (under restoration; normally open daily 7am–noon, 3–6.30pm). The symbols of the four evangelists, Matthew, Mark, Luke and John, are depicted on the exterior wall, which gives a clue to Alba's name. *Angelo* (angel) for Matthew, *Leone* (lion) for Mark, *Bue* (ox) for Luke and *Aquila* (eagle) for John. This has been the site of a church since the 7th century, but the overall impression nowadays is more Lombard Gothic.

Asti ㉖ is a livelier town which is at its most boisterous during the *palio*, a bareback horse race that thunders around the Campo de Palio on the third Sunday in September, when a wine festival also takes place. There is a Sunday antiques market in the square. Only a few remain of the great towers that once dominated the 13th-century town, and the highlight of the town is the airy, 14th-century **Cattedrale di Santa Maria Assunta** (open daily 8.30am–noon, 3.30–5.30pm), one of the finest Gothic works in Piedmont. It has an attractive portico of brick and tufa, in front of which outdoor concerts take place in summer. The **Cantine dei Marchesi Incisa della Rocchette** (open Sat, Sun, Mon 10am–noon, 3–5pm; tel: 0141-644647) has cellars and wine tastings. The Enoteca for Moscato d'Asti and Asti Spumante is the castle at **Mango** ㉗, some 30 km (20 miles) due south of Asti.

Flat lands of the Po Valley

From Asti the Po Valley travels some 40 km (25 miles) to **Alessandria** ㉘, once heavily fortified and now a busy modern town. Towns are broad and generous in these flat lands of maize and rice fields, among them **Casale Monferrato** ㉙, a

BELOW: Muscat grapes are the oldest variety in the region.

WINE

Italy's greatest red wines – Barolo and Barbaresco – come from around Alba. Rich, ruby-red, aged for two years in oak or chestnut and made from the Nebbiolo grape, these are the Burgundies of Italian wine. But there are other wines, too, ranging from young whites and slightly sparkling reds to the more characteristic reds, such as the Nebbiolo d'Alba. In all, there are 20 denominated wines in Piedmont, including Asti Spumanti.

Most wines with the word Alba in their title suggest full reds that age well, whether they are made from the Barabera, Dolcetta or Nebbiolo grape. Other Dolcettas are drunk young. Lighter and younger are the Roero wines, which have the local Arneis grape added; a Roero Arneis is a light white which can be drunk as an aperitif. Asti Spumante is a sparkling dessert wine. Made from grape-must, it goes well with Panettone Christmas cake. Moscato d'Asti is a slightly fizzy wine that is drunk young. Both are made from Muscat grapes, the oldest variety in Piedmont, which are also used in distilling a fine grappa.

There are Enoteche Regionali (government-backed wineries) where you can taste and buy at Acqui Terme, Barbaresco, Barolo, Anale, Canelli, Crianze Cavour, Mango, Roppolo and Vignale Monferrato.

fortified town beside the Po where there is a particularly fine synagogue and **Museo d'Arte e Storia Antigua Ebraica** (open Sun, 10am–noon, 3–5pm; or apply to the director's office, 44 Vicolo Olpes, tel: 1042-71807). Vineyards in the Monferrato produce superb Barbera and Gnignolino.

Map on pages 240–241

Vercelli ㉚ is the rice capital of the area and is a pleasant town, although mosquitoes are active in the heat. Its most notable building is the **Basilica of St Andrew**, completed in 1227 and one of the first Cistercian Gothic buildings in Italy. The **Lago di Viverone** ㉛, 32 km (20 miles) west on the S228, is a good place to drop in for a swim.

Ivrea ㉜, 16 km (10 miles) further on, lies on the Dorea Balteia emptying out of the Valle d'Aosta. The home of Olivetti, it has a lively shopping street leading up to a vast, rotting castle. The textile town of **Biella** ㉝ is a 30-km (18-mile) country drive north. **Biella Valley**, otherwise known as the Textile or Cashmere Valley, is now Europe's main textile-manufacturing centre and home to more than 200 mills which produce luxury cashmere, worsted fabrics and mohair. It is possible to visit the factory outlet or *spaccio* of Loro Piana and many others such as Colombo in Romagnano Sesia, just off the A26 autostrada *(see page 83)*. Eight km (5 miles) above Biella is **Oropa**, where an intriguing collection of churches has created a place of Marian pilgrimage.

The northern mountains

Biella lies in the lower hills that rise north to the Swiss border. Val Sesia and Valle Anzasca lead up to Monte Rosa, the former passing through the quaint village of **Varallo** ㉞, where cobbled streets and manor houses show signs of a prosperous past. Varallo is also famous for its **Sacro Monte** (open at all times; free), which can be reached by cable car or on foot. A *sacro monte* is a collection of chapels on a hillside, usually representing the Stations of the Cross. Of the nine *sacri monti* in this region of northern Italy, Varallo is the oldest and most important and was created a UNESCO World Heritage Site in 2003. The Franciscan friar Bernardino Caimi sought a suitable location in the late 15th century for recreating a miniature "Holy Land" in the west after returning from Jerusalem. Now there are 43 chapels, each depicting scenes with lifelike statues and frescoes, many of which are by the 16th-century artistic genius, Gaudenzio Ferrari. The early statues are made of wood, the later of terracotta. The fountain in the piazza outside takes the place of Chapel 44; made from a single piece of rock, crowned by the statue of Christ Risen and with its five spouts of pure spring water, it symbolises the five wounds of Christ.

Domodossola ㉟ is the main centre for the Val d'Ossola, Piedmont's most northerly valley, tucked up among the Swiss Alps. This once small medieval town is now sprawling, but it is the starting point for a railway that takes an hour-long scenic route east across the border to Locarno at the head of Lake Maggiore. It is also famous for its Saturday market. Domodossola also is the site of the northernmost Sago Monte – not only geographically but also for the influence of the nearby Swiss region. ❑

BELOW: local vineyard.

THE LAKES

"What can one say about Lake Maggiore, about the Borromean Isles, about Lake Como, unless it be that one pities those that are not madly in love with them" – Alexandre Dumas

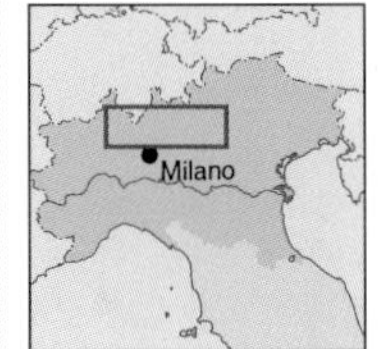

The lakes, set against snowcapped peaks or vine-clad slopes, evoke dreamy images of passing steamers, with the waterside cloaked in mysterious winter mists or summer heat hazes. Since their 19th-century heyday the lakes have drifted in and out of fashion, symbolising mournful sanatoria, inspiring poets or simply soothing the spirit. The lakes entranced Byron and Shelley, Stendhal and Ibsen, Freud and Nietszche, Goethe, Rilke and Thomas Mann. On Garda alone, each classic resort has its literary lion: Kafka is associated with Desenzano, James Joyce with Sirmione, D.H. Lawrence with Gargnano.

Lake Garda, the largest, seemingly as wide as a sea, was the first lake to be "discovered" by Grand Tourists, and it remains the most commercial, the most obviously Italian in character, with the greatest range of hotels and water sports. By contrast, Lake Lugano naturally exudes a Swiss atmosphere, while majestic Lake Maggiore is blessed with delightful islands, and Lake Iseo feels aloof, faintly sad and haunted. To connoisseurs, Lake Como, cradled by mountains, is perhaps the loveliest, both the most distinctive and the most refined.

Yet all the lakes have their share of sophisticated resorts, pastel-coloured fishing villages and sumptuous villas. On the major lakes, Baroque or classical villas are surrounded by verdant gardens, while gracious Art Nouveau hotels enjoy azalea-framed views. The vineyards and olive-clad hills are reminiscent of languid Mediterranean landscapes. The mild climate favours this lush vegetation, with citrus trees, rhododendrons and camellias set in the lee of majestic mountains. The shades encompass sludgy greens, browns and greys as well as Mediterranean pinks, reds, ochres and yellows. The lakes are best savoured from a waterfront terrace, from the shelter of camellia-scented gardens, or from the deck of a leisurely steamer. Hydrofoils are faster, but slower, open-decked steamers are more in keeping with the mood of the lakes.

PRECEDING PAGES: the lakeside town of Varenna.
LEFT: Bellagio, Lake Como.
BELOW: the lake at Villa Melzi, Bellagio.

Lago di Garda (Lake Garda)

Despite the presence of secluded villas in the shadow of the Alps, Garda is less status-seeking than Como and Maggiore. As the most southerly of the great lakes, it is blessed with the warmest climate and least "Swissified" atmosphere. The Dolomites to the north shelter Garda from the cold north winds, helping to create delightfully mild conditions. The distinctly Mediterranean micro-climate is emphasised by the profusion of olive groves and citrus plantations, palm trees and vineyards, lofty cypresses and vivid flowerings of magnolias, oleanders and bougainvilleas. The southern end of the lake is more tropical and languorous, broadening out over the Lombard plains; closer to the Dolomites the air can carry a hint of a chill and the scent of juniper. Water-skiing and motor boats are banned in the northerly, Trentino end of the lake, but there are fewer restrictions in the south, which makes it both busier and more at risk from pollution.

Riva del Garda ❶, one of the liveliest resorts on the lake, has an attractive town centre with a castle and compact medieval quarter. However, despite a pleasant beach, upmarket boutiques and turn-of-the-century hotels, the effect is tarnished by summer crowds and the undistinguished sprawl along the shore. Water-skiing and motor boats are banned in this stretch, as they are at neighbouring **Torbole** ❷. Yet Torbole remains a burgeoning water-sports centre, popular with young Austrians, Germans and Scandivians who are eager to race their windsurfers when the *ora*, the fierce local wind, whips up the right afternoon breeze. It is also on the World Cup circuit for windsurfing.

The Venetian authorities in Malcesine arrested Goethe (1749–1832) as a spy when they saw him sketching the castle. The event is now commemorated by a bust of the poet in an upper courtyard.

Malcesine ❸, set on the slopes of Monte Baldo to the south, is a family resort that combines the charms of a Mediterranean resort with the complexity of a medieval town. A crenellated castle soars over the red-tiled rooftops, the quaint café-lined port and a labyrinth of steep, cobbled streets overhung by balconies. The **Castello Scaligero** (open Apr–Oct daily 9am–9pm, Nov–Mar Sat–Sun 10am–4pm) houses the lake's natural history museum, the **Museo di Storia Naturale del Garda e del Monte Baldo**. From the Venetian **Palazzo dei Capitani** (open in summer, daily 9am–8pm), the 16th-century rulers controlled the port. From the town, a cable car leads up to Monte Baldo and superb views over the Dolomites.

Halfway down the shore stands the former bastion of **Torri del Benaco** ❹. This former Lombard stronghold lies on the Riviera degli Olivi, named after its olive groves. A crenellated feudal castle dominates the little port and overlooks the frescoed church of Santissima Trinità. Just around the headland and the

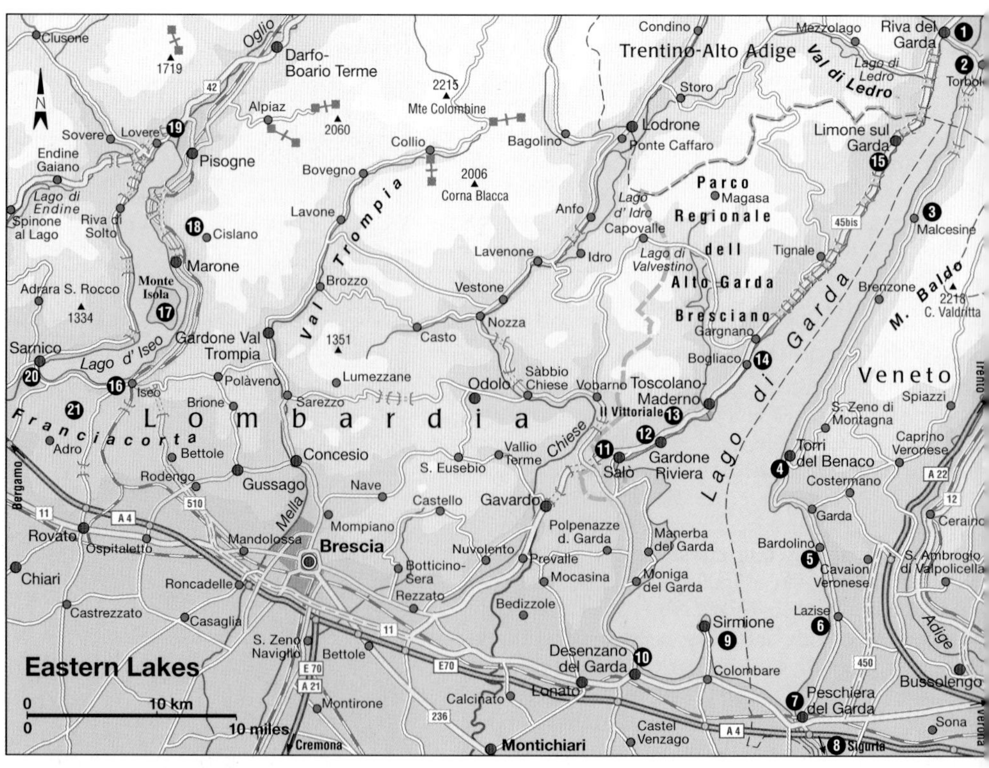

resort of Garda is **Bardolino** ❺, the high point of the wine-growing hills. The family resort itself has a cobbled, pedestrianised centre and is popular with Austrians and Germans. It possesses the curious Carolingian church of San Zeno and the Romanesque church of San Severo, as well as a ruined castle. However, wine-lovers will focus on tastings in the celebrated *cantine*, or Museo del Vino, or on visits to the vine-clad slopes. In the wide, southern section of the lake, lies **Lazise** ❻, ringed by medieval walls and dominated by a fine, privately owned castle. Close to the small port is the Romanesque church of San Nicolò, with School of Giotto frescoes. The 16th-century Dogana Veneta is a reminder that Lazise was a key customs post and Venetian military base.

Peschiera del Garda ❼, at the southeastern end of the lake, occupies a strategic site near the mouth of the River Mincio that drains the lake. **Gardaland** (open daily, late Apr–June 10am–6pm, late June–mid-Sept 9am–midnight, mid-Sept–Oct Sat–Sun 10am–6.30pm; admission charge; tel: 045-6449777), just northwest of town, is Italy's most popular theme park. From Peschiera it is a short drive (10 km/6 miles) to **Sigurta** ❽, near Valeggio, where the well-tended villa gardens (open Mar–Nov daily 9am–6pm, exit at 7pm; admission charge) are among the finest in the region. An exotic array of banana and palm trees gives way to lily ponds and an avenue of irises and valleys of roses; dramatically sited cypresses frame a colourful display of Chinese and Japanese plantings.

Scenic Sirmione

As the quaintest resort on the Lombardy bank, **Sirmione** ❾ sits snugly on a narrow peninsula jutting into the lake. The centrepiece of this scenic walled town is the moated fortress known as the **Rocca Scaligera** (open Apr–Oct Tues–Sun

Map on page 272

Bardolino, a favourite resort.

BELOW: relaxing at one of the lakes.

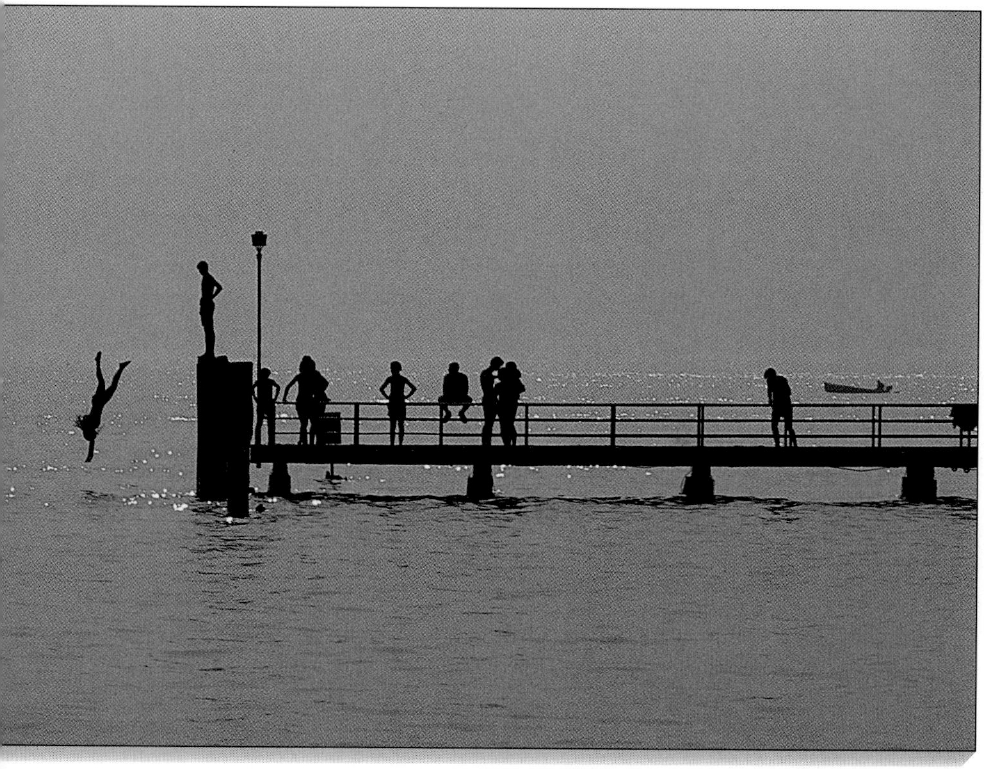

9am–7pm, Nov–Mar daily 8.30am–4.30pm), with the drawbridge on its landward side the only means of reaching Sirmione. Near by stands the porticoed church of **Santa Maria Maggiore**, carved out of a feudal tower. Although slightly claustrophobic and self-consciously cute, Sirmione's cobbled pedestrianised quarter is pleasant, with its boutiques, cafés and cake shops. Most of the hotels are strung along the uninspired strip that leads into Sirmione, but the lakeside promenades and archaeological trails are rewarding.

Long before Salò became identified with unsavoury politics, Lady Mary Wortley Montagu, a privileged visitor in 1750, praised the local setting as "an amphitheatre covered with woods of orange, lemon and pomegranate trees".

Via Catullo leads along the rocky promontory through olive groves to the church of San Pietro in Mavino, which dates from the 8th century. At the end of the peninsula lies the Roman archaeological site known as **Grotte di Catullo**, (open summer, Tues–Sat 8.30am–7pm, Sun 9am–6pm, until 4.30pm in winter) linked to the poet Catullus (87–54 BC), who died in Sirmione. The remains of ancient baths and vaulted disrobing chambers are reminders that the local thermal springs have been active since Roman times. Sirmione's spas now channel the sulphurous springs into a range of dubious water cures.

Desenzano del Garda ❿, often considered the gateway to the lake, is not the most relaxing resort. The traffic-choked centre gives way to a picturesque port before sprawling along the waterfront. Apart from the porticoed Piazza Malvezzi, the sites include the **Duomo**, which dates from the 16th century and displays a *Last Supper* attributed to Tiepolo. On Via Gramsci lie the remains of a 4th-century Roman villa, **Villa Romara** (open Tues–Sun 8.30am–7.30pm, mid-Oct–Feb until 5pm; admission charge). The 240-sq. metre (2,600-sq. ft) exquisite mosaic floor is the most extensive in northern Italy.

The wide stretch of water at the southern end of the lake, between Dezenzano and **Salò** ⓫, resembles an inland sea. The attractive resort is synonymous with

BELOW: Fascist leader Benito Mussolini – "Il Duce" – addressing his people in 1929.

PLAYGROUND AND PUPPET STATE

In 1943, Mussolini, who had fallen from grace and been imprisoned by the king and the Fascist Grand Council, was rescued from a mountain-top prison by the Nazis. "Il Duce" was swiftly installed as the ruler of a puppet republic operating from a sleepy resort on Lake Garda. The Republic of Salò represented Mussolini's last stand, a government with little power but all the trappings. Here he occasionally paraded for the benefit of German newsreels, discussed casualties over lunch with his neighbour, the German ambassador, and met his favourite mistress, Claretta Petacci, at 5 o'clock. In 1945 he was shot by partisans near Lake Como, with Claretta by his side; both were strung up by their heels with piano wire.

Gardone Riviera's pink-and-white Villa Fiordaliso was where Mussolini installed his mistress. Most features remain, down to the door handles embellished with swastikas. The villa is now an elegant hotel, and the Claretta Petacci suite is perfect for romantic encounters. Mussolini's wife, Rachele, was ensconced in Gargnano, 10 km (6 miles) away, in Villa Feltrinelli, which also became a hotel. Donna Rachele was more interested in her pet hens than in her sumptuous villa, which included 16 bedrooms, a billiard room and a private bunker.

one of the most shameful periods of Italian history, the Republic of Salò *(see opposite)* when it was a playground for the idling Italian aristocracy and war malingerers, with decadent German officers and Italian officials leading self-indulgent lifestyles while the Jewish round-ups were going on. Salò has a late-Gothic cathedral but its sites are less compelling than the weight of history.

Gardone Riviera ⓬ became a favoured halt in the days of the Grand Tour. Nestling among lush gardens, with its air of fusty grandeur, Gardone remains the most elegant and exclusive resort on Lake Garda. Steamers still dock by the cobbled quayside, while the lakeside promenade offers views over the whole southern section of the lake. Via Roma leads to the splendid botanical gardens of **Giardino Botanico Hruska** (open Mar–Oct daily 9am–7pm; tel: 0336-410877). Alpine plants and Mediterranean vegetation grow happily on this rocky spur, lying in the shadow of the Dolomite peaks. A delightful trail winds past artificial streams, exotic blooms, papyrus-filled pools and Buddhist shrines. The hotel **Villa Fiordaliso** (Corso Zanardelli 150, tel: 0365-20158), a very pretty, secluded lakeside villa, was where Mussolini dallied with Claretta Petacci *(see opposite)*. The chandelier-hung Grand Hotel also has a history: it was patronised by writers, from Vladimir Nabokov to Somerset Maugham, while Winston Churchill made it his base during painting holidays.

Above the resort is **Il Vittoriale** ⓭ (park and gardens open daily, Apr–Sept 8.30am–8pm, Oct–Mar 9am–5pm; guided tours of house Tues–Sun, Apr–Sept 9.30am–7pm, Oct–Mar 9am–1pm, 2–5pm; admission charge), an extraordinary shrine to Gabriele D'Annunzio, one of Italy's most flamboyant pre-war figures *(see page 287)*. The villa, framed by cypresses and oleanders, is set on gentle slopes overlooking the lake. The grounds are cluttered with bizarre monumental

Map on page 272

Vibrant bloom in the Hruska Botanical Gardens.

BELOW: magnificent scenery at Lake Como.

structures, from the brutalist open-air theatre to the lofty mausoleum containing D'Annunzio's body and the hangar on the hillside displaying the plane he used to fly over Vienna. The overall effect is of ugly monumentalism almost disfiguring the enchanting lakeside setting.

Bogliaco ⓮, just south of the better-known Gargnano, makes an inviting lunch stop. This erstwhile fishing village has a 15th-century parish church and the Villa Bettoni, encircled by Baroque gardens. Further north, named after the luxuriant lemon groves that represented the town's claim to fame before tourism took over, **Limone sul Garda** ⓯ completes the circuit back to Riva del Garda. Set amid the surviving lemon groves and cedars, Limone's ochre-coloured houses and cobbled streets are hung with bougainvillea.

Lago d'Iseo (Lake Iseo)

Lago d'Iseo measures 5 km (3 miles) at its broadest point, but most of the space is occupied by Monte Isola, the largest lake island in Europe. This resolutely untouristy lake depends on fishing and boat-making, and on the fabrication of nets of all descriptions. Its charms reside in the peaceful hamlets fringed by mountains and the cosy local inns. It is prone to fogs and fitful thunderstorms that descend without warning. **Iseo** ⓰, on the southern part of the lake, is a pleasant resort and a lively provincial town with a refreshingly unpretentious, friendly atmosphere. The bustling shops in the medieval quarter display a slice of provincial life, with huge Parmesans, salamis and mounds of fresh pasta eagerly devoured by local eyes. The liveliest part of the market occupies the recently-restored Jewish ghetto. Not far from Iseo is the large peat bog and nature site known as Torbiere, noted for its water-lilies and marsh reeds.

BELOW: a ferry on Lake Iseo.

Monte Isola (17), the island at the centre of the lake, resembles a mountain more than an island. The fishing villages are characterised by red-tiled roofs and cobbled streets. With its sudden mists, steep banks and timeless fishing traditions, the island can feel aloof and slightly menacing, a mood dispelled by an invigorating walk up through the chestnut groves. The summit of the island (600 metres/1,970 ft) is crowned by the frescoed church of Madonna della Ceriola.

On the eastern shore of the lake, **Cislano** (18), near the village of Marone, provides a curious natural spectacle of so-called erosion pyramids – bizarre rock formations similar to those found in the Dolomites. The UNESCO World Heritage Site, **Parco Nazionale delle Incisioni Rupestri** (National Rock Engravings Park) is open Tues–Sun 9am–1hr before sunset in summer, till 4.30pm in winter; entrance fee. **Lovere** (19), the major lakeside town in the north, is a pleasant resort with terraces tumbling down to the shore, but the narrow northern end of the lake is about 250 metres (820 ft) deep, which acts as a psychological deterrent to swimmers. The dramatic northern end is framed by high ridges and sheer cliffs that rise up from the shoreline.

Sarnico (20), at the southern end of the lake, served by the steamer which also chugs over to Iseo, marks the end of the circuit around the shore. This fishing village abounds in cluttered fortifications and breezy boatyards. Further inland lie the extensive vineyards of **Franciacorta** (21), a region that produces good champagne-method sparkling wine, and superior reds and whites. The hamlet of Erbusco is home to one of the finest gourmet restaurants in Italy. The 2-Michelin-star restaurant at **L'Albereta Hotel**, a 19th-century converted villa (Via Vittorio Emanuele 11; restaurant tel: 030-7760562, hotel tel: 030-7760550), is run by Gualtiero Marchesi, who is among the country's best-known gourmet chefs.

Map on page 272

You won't be disappointed by Erbusco's L'Albereta Hotel where Marchesi, an exponent of reinterpreted nouvelle cuisine, shows that superb seasonal produce and creative flair can go hand in hand with sensibly sized portions.

BELOW: a stroll by the water's edge, Lake Como.

Lago di Como (Lake Como)

Lake Como is most closely associated with the days of grand dukes and dowager empresses, of *fin-de-siècle* balls before the chill winds of democracy swept away the cobweb-encrusted aristocrats. The 19th century poet Shelley said that Lake Como "exceeds anything I ever beheld in beauty". Two centuries later the actor George Clooney has done a great deal to popularise Como with today's jet-set after the purchase of his multi-million euro villa. A restaurant called the Locanda on Comacina island in the middle of the lake is a treasure trove of photos of "A" list celebrities.

When Gianni Versace was murdered in 1998, his family chose to scatter his ashes in the grounds of his beloved Montrasio villa near Como.

With its pewter-coloured water and darkening mass of mountains, the deep, fjord-like Como has a less balmy climate than Garda, but it still has its sparkling days of serene blue waters, plus lakeside villages with steeply cobbled streets and cascades of geraniums, pastel villas and prettified hotel terraces.

The town of **Como** ㉒ is very touristy and traffic-choked nowadays but can be a good base for a lake-hopping holiday. It was a prosperous centre in the Middle Ages, and many of the city monuments owe much to the craftsmanship of the Maestri Comacini, the medieval master builders and sculptors who perfected the Lombard style. The silk and textile industries, which still flourish, also contributed to Como's prosperity and gracious living.

Just inland from the lake, the heart of the medieval quarter centres on the **Duomo** Ⓐ (open daily 7am–noon, 3–7pm). This splendid solemn cathedral represents the transition from Gothic to Renaissance. The highlights are the Gothic rose window and richly sculpted façade, with the central portal framed by Renaissance statues to Pliny the Elder and Younger. Adjoining the façade is the **Broletto** Ⓑ, the former town hall, an elegantly arcaded Gothic affair with triple-arched windows. A

BELOW: standing at ease; a wine press awaits the next season's harvest.

WINE LAKES

The fertility of the lake district emerged in the wake of the glaciation that formed the lake basins and retreated at the end of the Ice Age. One extremely fortuitous effect of the mild climate and myriad micro-climates is the number of fine vineyards in the region. The range of wines produced is greater than in most other Italian regions; types run from simple, sparkling Asti Spumante to the dry complexity of Bardolino.

Asti Spumante is produced in pressure tanks, using a special technique for processing the must of Muscat grapes. The full-bodied red wines of Barolo and Barbaresco come from the western shore of Lake Maggiore. Both are produced from Nebbiolo grapes, and aged in oak or chestnut casks – Barolo for at least three years, Barbaresco for two. Dry Soave, fruity Valpolicella and dry Bardolino come from around Lake Garda. There are also white wines from the plains of Lombardy, including Moscato and Riesling. These are complemented by red Valtellina wines from the mountains, or by the superior range of Franciacorta wines from Lake Iseo. As if this were not enough, the region is a noted producer of distilled Alpine drinks, made with forest fruits or herbs, not forgetting the powerful firewater known as grappa.

complete contrast to this is provided by the Fascist **Casa del Popolo** **C** (1936), a surprisingly harmonious piece of Fascist architecture.

The **Tempio Voltiano** **D** (open Apr–Sept Tues–Sun 10am–noon, 3–6pm; Oct–Mar 10am–noon, 2–4pm; admission charge), set in the public gardens, is named after Alessandro Volta (1745–1827), the physicist who invented the battery in 1799 and the units of electricity we know as volts. Volta was also credited with the discovery, made in the marshes around Lake Maggiore, that methane was an organic gas.

Porta Vittoria **E**, south of the Duomo, at the end of Via Giove, is a 12th-century gate 40 metres (130 ft) high, topped by five tiers of arches. Just south-west, on Via Vittorio Emanuele, on the site of a pagan temple, stands **San Fedele** **F**. The much-remodelled church dates from the 7th century, but it is essentially a masterpiece of Lombard Romanesque architecture built by the Maestri Comacini. The **Pinacoteca Civica** **G** (open Tues–Sat, 9.30–12.30pm, 2–5pm, Sun 10am–1pm; admission charge), in Palazzo Volpi on Via Diaz, contains the city art gallery, with paintings from the 14th to the 18th century. The **Musei Civici** **H** (open Tues–Sat 9am–noon, 2–5.30pm, Sun 9.15am–12.15pm), which flank **Piazza Medaglie d'Oro Comasche**, contain an archaeological collection plus a museum dedicated to the Risorgimento.

Just east is the **Museo della Seta** **I** (open Tues–Fri 9am–noon, 3–6pm, Sat by appointment only; admission charge), devoted to the town's traditional silk industry, which has flourished since the 16th century. Although silkworms are no longer bred on the lake, Chinese thread is woven and dyed here to the specifications of the top Milanese fashion houses. Italy produces 91 percent of Europe's silk, and Como produces 79 percent of this. Its annual production totals 3,200 tonnes of silk.

Maps: Area 281 Town 279

TIP

Fine silk can be bought at local factory outlets or at the Centro della Seta (on Via Volta and Via Bellinzona).

BELOW: the Gothic rose window at Como's cathedral.

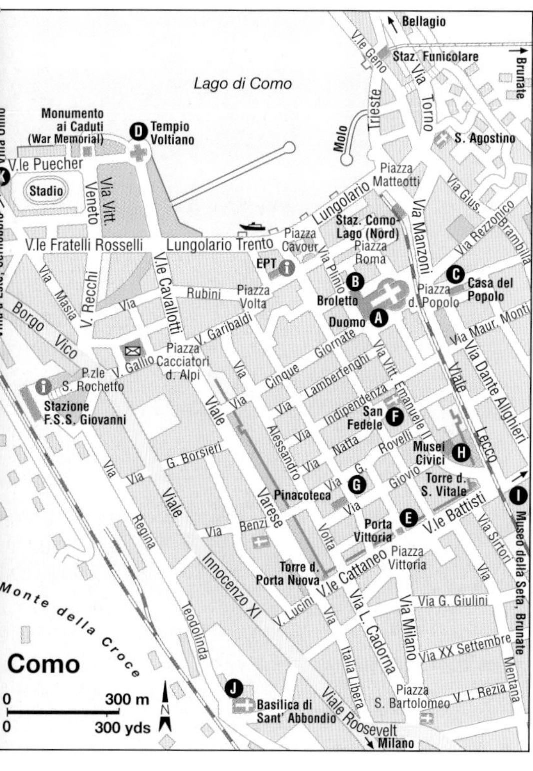

Sant'Abbondio

Languishing in the industrial suburbs is the **Basilica di Sant'Abbondio** Ⓙ, a frescoed Romanesque complex built by the Maestri Comacini and well restored in the 19th century. **Villa Olmo** Ⓚ (villa 9am–noon, 3–6pm; park summer 8am–11pm, winter 9am–7pm; frequent exhibitions in the villa – variable opening times; tel: 848-800687), 3 km (2 miles) north of Como, is an imposing Neoclassical affair, built in 1782 and set in formal gardens and wooded parkland. Since most visitors will succumb to lake-hopping, the waterside **Piazza Cavour** is the obvious place to go. Flanked by café terraces and ice-cream parlours, the touristy square lies a stone's throw from the main steamer and catamaran jetties. For peace and quiet, take the cable car from the waterfront by the main beach to Brunate, a village perched above the city, which marks the start of several appealing trails.

Elton John and Michael Schumacher are among the people who come as guests to the Villa d'Este today.

Neighbouring **Cernobbio** ㉓ was the resort favoured by the exiled Queen Caroline of England. In 1815, when Princess of Wales, she bought the Villa d'Este as a bolthole, but debt eventually forced her to sell it. The magnificent Renaissance estate is framed by cypresses and formal gardens, and dotted with Italianate grottoes and topiary. The **Villa d'Este** (open Mar–Nov; tel: 031-3481; www.villadeste.it) has been one of Europe's leading hotels since 1873.

Island retreat

Isola Comacina ㉔ is an attractive patch of greenery in the middle of Lake Como, best known as the setting for a spectacular folk festival and firework display on the weekend after the Feast of St John the Baptist (24 June). Facing the island is the gorgeous **Villa del Balbianello** (gardens open Apr–Oct Tues, Thur–Fri 10am–1pm, 2–6pm, Sat–Sun 10am–6pm; admission charge). The

BELOW: the Baroque splendour of Villa Carlotta.

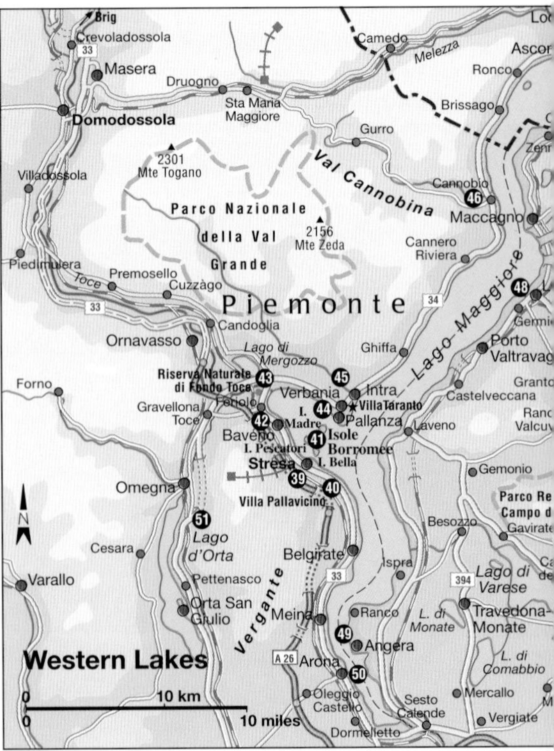

villa, now state property, is set on a rocky spur near Lenno and can only be reached by boat from Isola Comacina. In 1786 Cardinal Durini bought Balbianello as a retreat and transformed it into the most romantic villa on the lake. It was restored in the 1970s by explorer and supermarket heir Count Guido Monzini, who filled it with exotic artefacts. The gardens were used as the setting for the planet Naboo in the Star Wars film, *Attack of the Clones*.

A short lakeside stroll leads to the pale-pink **Villa Carlotta** ㉕ (open Apr–Sept daily 9am–6pm, Mar 9am–11.30am, 2–4.30pm; admission charge), a Baroque residence, with luxurious interiors and beautiful ceiling frescoes, which overlooks splendid formal terraced gardens. A wilder section of the grounds features a giant sequoia and a glade of lush ferns, with rhododendrons and a rockery. Elsewhere the tropical vegetation focuses on shrubs, succulents and trees from Australia and the Orient. The interior of the villa is somewhat disappointing, although the statuary includes Canova's erotic *Eros and Psyche*.

Menaggio ㉖, the next port of call, is a health resort with a young and sprightly atmosphere. There's a cluster of ochre and red houses by the harbour, plus an onion-domed church and a hillside studded with villas and gardens. **Colico** ㉗, further north on the eastern shore, nestling below the conical Monte Legnone, is the gateway to the nature reserve of **Piano di Spana**. **Varenna** ㉘ is a delightful steamer stop, with a beguiling old quarter stacked up on the lower slopes. The lush resort is surrounded by terraced gardens, cypresses and pine groves. The gardens of **Villa Monastero** (open Mar–Sept daily 9am–6pm, summer until 7pm; admission charge) are the finest on the eastern shore. This former Cistercian abbey was converted into a palatial residence in the 16th century and complemented by landscaped classical grounds.

Map on pages 280–281

Isola Comacina is well known for the Locanda dell'Isola Comacina (tel: 0344-55083), an inn with good rustic food.

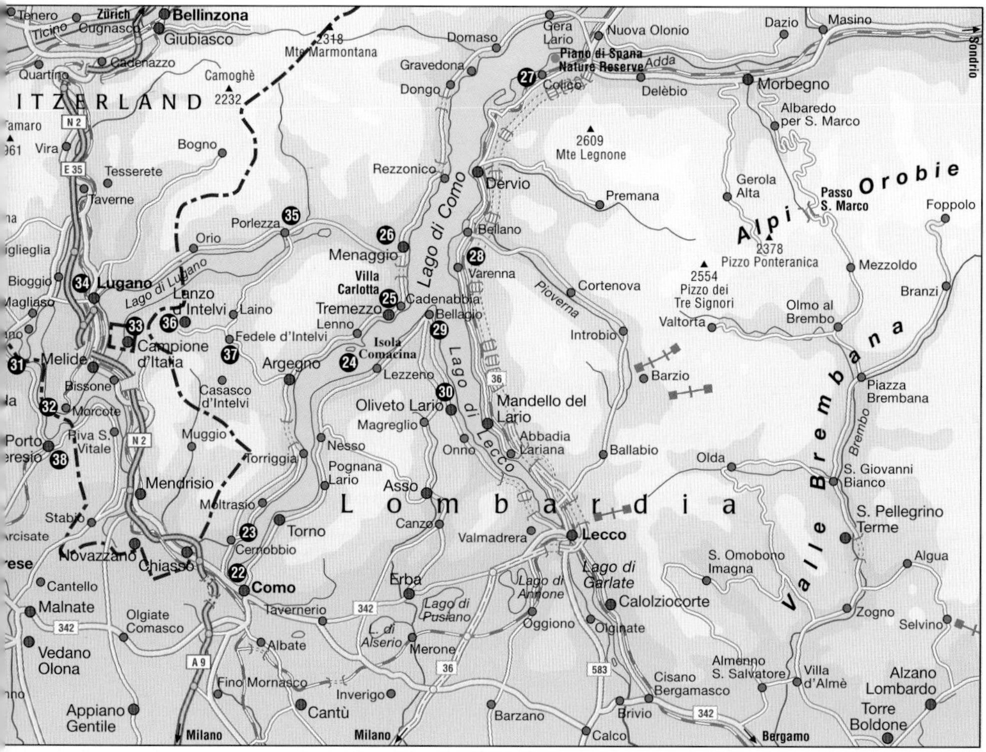

Poetry and promenades

Bellagio ㉙ rises up on a promontory that separates the southern arms of Lake Como. This gentrified resort commands a gorgeous position on the cusp of the lake. While neighbouring Menaggio has traditionally been popular with Germans, Bellagio has always appealed to the British and French. Stendhal (1783–1842) spent many summers here, attending the opera, fighting duels and falling for a woman "not conspicuously chaste", whom he pursued for 10 years.

Such is the spell of Bellagio and the Villa Serbelloni that in 1998 Las Vegas unveiled a replica of the resort in the guise of a casino and hotel complex.

From the bustling café-lined waterfront, Salita Mella leads up to the sheltered centre of Bellagio and the pleasing main shopping street at the top. The main square is graced by a Romanesque church with an intriguing baptismal font. From here it is an enjoyable stroll past pink and ochre houses and discreet villas to the Neoclassical **Villa Melzi** (open late Mar–Oct, daily 9am–6pm; admission charge).

On the crest of the hill stands a hotel that is part of the history of Bellagio. The **Grand Hotel Villa Serbelloni** (open end Mar–mid-Nov; tel: 031-950216) is the quintessential grand, lakeside hotel, once patronised by Russian princes and German counts. Now a palatial hotel and conference centre run by the Rockefeller Foundation, the Serbelloni still opens its gardens to non-residents.

South of Bellagio, on the Lecco arm of the lake, **Oliveto Lario** ㉚, set amid olive groves as the name suggests, presents a rural farewell to the lake.

Lago di Lugano (Lake Lugano)

Compared with Lake Maggiore and Lake Como, **Lugano** is wilder and more wooded yet distinctly less majestic. The waterfront is often inaccessible, with its shoreline too steep for a road, let alone a straggling hamlet. Two-thirds of the lake

BELOW: Baveno, Lake Maggiore.

comes within the Swiss canton of Ticino, which contains much of the best scenery. **Ponte Tresa** ❸❶ is a steamer-landing and curious border village with both a Swiss and an Italian side. **Morcote** ❸❷, known as "the pearl of the lake", is an appealing village en route to Campione d'Italia, and makes an inviting lunch stop.

Map on pages 280–281

Beyond is **Campione d'Italia** ❸❸, an Italian enclave in Switzerland, which is wedged halfway between Lugano and the border at Chiasso. Italian law may prevail, but the cars have Swiss number-plates, the postal service is Swiss, and the principality's budget is calculated in Swiss francs. Campione has a chequered past, but it looks cheerfully modern. For neighbouring Italians the glitzy casino is the main attraction, with wins spent in local designer boutiques. The greatest surviving historical monuments are the Oratorio di San Pietro (1326) and the Gothic and Baroque Madonna dei Ghirli, both the work of the Maestri Campionesi, who rivalled the Maestri Comacini from Como as the most skilled medieval master builders. These travelling Lombard craftsmen helped create some of Italy's greatest Romanesque cathedrals, including Cremona, Modena and Verona.

From Campione there are views across the lake to **Lugano** ❸❹, set in Ticino, and one of the leading Swiss cities. The Swiss took Lugano in 1512 and have held it ever since. Highlights of the old quarter include the Renaissance-frescoed church of Santa Maria degli Angeli and the Duomo, graced with a Lombard-Venetian façade. For most visitors, however, this smart resort is an opportunity to sample lakeside promenades and Swiss cuisine.

Porlezza ❸❺, at the northernmost end of the lake, is an appealing town where Italian flair prevails over Swiss sobriety. At Santa Margherita, further south, a cable car conects with the scenic Belvedere, known as "the balcony over Italy". Even more panoramic views unfurl from **Lanzo d'Intelvi** ❸❻, the ski resort above. The Alpine village, tucked into thick pine and larch woods, enjoys views over Lake Lugano and the Alps. The resort is part of the scenic Via d'Intelvi, a series of rural valleys centred on village churches decorated by the Maestri Comacini, the master builders. As a vital link between Lake Como and Lake Lugano, this route was heavily fortified in medieval times and also saw action during the Risorgimento battles of independence. **Fedele d'Intelvi** ❸❼, nestling among Alpine valleys and conifer forests, has the best Romanesque church in the region.

Concluding the lakeside circuit is **Ponte Ceresio** ❸❽, a port set on a sheltered bay south of Campione.

BELOW: lacemaking is one of the traditional crafts of the region.

Lago Maggiore (Lake Maggiore)

Although the northern part of the lake is centred on Swiss Locarno, **Stresa** ❸❾, with its faded *belle-époque* charm, was once one of the grandest 19th-century resorts. The elegant waterfront is still flanked by lovely Art Nouveau hotels and well served by steamers which spirit visitors away to the Borromean islands. The Grand Hôtel des Borromées, featured in Hemingway's *A Farewell to Arms*, is a relic of past glories. Just behind the waterfront, Piazza Cadorna is a pleasant café-lined square and shopping quarter. At Stresa Lido a cable car leads up to Monte Mottarone,

The Borromean dynasty originally intended Isola Bella as a pleasure palace, Isola dei Pescatori a rural retreat, and Isola Madre as an enchanted garden.

with views of glacier-crested peaks, the Monte Rosa ski slopes and the valleys around Domodossola, as well as a panorama of the Lombardy plain.

Just outside Stresa, off the Arona road, stands **Villa Pallavicino** ㊵ (park open Mar–Oct, daily 9am–6pm; admission charge), encircled by romantic "English" gardens. Gentle parkland and streams are complemented by more formal terraces, ornamental gardens and pergolas. The grounds are also home to a small zoo of llamas, antelopes, deer and kangaroos.

The **Isole Borromei** ㊶, which have belonged to the Borromean family since Renaissance times, present three enchantingly different faces: the Baroque fantasy of Isola Bella, the fishing village of Isola dei Pescatori (also known as Isola Superiore), and the verdant villa-park of Isola Madre. The Milanese Borromean family still owns the fishing rights to the entire lake. Steamers from Arona, Stresa, Verbania and Laveno criss-cross the lake, making frequent stops at the islands.

Isola Bella (palace open end Mar–Oct daily 9am–noon, 1.30–5.30pm; gardens open daily 9am–6.15pm; admission charge) is the centrepiece of these picturesque islands. This sumptuous palace and its lush pleasure gardens were a labour of love begun by the Cardinal of Milan, Count Carlo III Borromeo, in 1632, in honour of his consort, Isabella. The Baroque palace was largely completed by the couple's sons in the 1670s. The terraced gardens represent a Baroque masterpiece, graced with statuary, dramatic perspectives and grottoes.

The garden is a riot of colour in summer, full of exotic rarities, with butterflies flitting in and out of shady arbours, and is crowned by a shell-shaped amphitheatre, the setting for concerts and spectacles. A cobbled courtyard opens onto high-ceilinged rooms decorated with stucco-work and frescoes, often

BELOW: the gardens of Villa Palavicini. **RIGHT:** outside Locarno's Madonna del Sasso church.

Map on pages 280–281

emblazoned with a unicorn, the Borromean crest. The palace's lavish interior also displays a Tiepolo ceiling, Murano glass chandeliers, Flemish tapestries and Florentine marquetry. The highlights are the magnificent Empire-style ballroom, the cantilevered spiral staircase and the domed great hall.

Isola dei Pescatori once sheltered the lake's main fishing community. Today the village's secret passageways and tiny courtyards, accompanied by the sweet sound of birdsong, provide unexpected views of the lake or lead to the frescoed medieval parish church. **Verbano** (tel: 0323-30408) is a rustic inn overlooking the lake, and a sought-after destination for lunch. From the rocky beach beyond, there are views of Isola Bella framed by fishing nets and snoozing cats.

Isola Madre, set closer to Pallanza than to Stresa, is the largest and most languorous of the islands, with a 16th-century villa surrounded by lush gardens (opening times same as Isola Bella). The gardens, landscaped into five terraces, are the highlight of any visit, although the overall effect is curiously naturalistic. Planted with citrus trees, cedars and cypresses, mimosa and magnolia, the grounds are home to vivid parrots and bold white peacocks which strut through the azaleas and rhododendrons.

Baveno 42, set in the lee of a pink-granite mountain, is a more subdued version of Stresa. The resort, which once drew such honoured guests as Queen Victoria and Winston Churchill, remains a favourite with the British. In the historic centre, the church of Santi Gervasio e San Protaso is graced with a Romanesque façade and belltower; flanking it is an octagonal baptistry. From the waterfront there are views of lakeside villas and over to Isola dei Pescatori. At the end of the bay, between Baveno and Pallanza, lies the **Riserva Naturale di Fondo Toce** 43, a nature reserve and bird sanctuary.

BELOW: cruising Lake Iseo.

Map on pages 280–281

Pallanza ㊹, set on the headland, has a lovely waterside lined by magnolias and oleanders, with porticoed ochre and pink houses merging into a maze of alleys. The lakeside towns of Pallanza and **Verbania** ㊺ fade into one another, with the latter best known as the stop for **Villa Taranto** (open daily 8.30am– 7.30pm, last entrance 6.30pm; admission charge) and its impressive gardens, designed in the 1930s by a Scot, Neil McEacharn. Although theoretically botanical gardens, this is not a scientific collection but an exotic composition featuring fountains and waterfalls, Amazonian water-lilies and lotus blossoms.

The copper colossus of Carlo Borromeo at Arona.

Cannobio ㊻, a small resort near the Swiss border, is often neglected since it is set some way up the northwestern side of the lake. The centre of this erstwhile market town is wound around tight alleys, a pleasant harbour and the Renaissance church of Madonna della Pietà. From Cannobio a road leads west to Val Cannobina and the dramatic gorge of Santa Anna, with its tumbling waterfall and an adjoining church. Just south is the quiet resort of Cannero Riviera, set amid vineyards, olives and citrus groves.

Locarno ㊼, commanding a sheltered bay on the Swiss shore, is a crisp, well-ordered resort with a tree-lined lakeside promenade. Gamblers and browsers are drawn to the casino and shopping arcades. In the upper city stands Castello Visconti, a fort converted into an archaeological museum. A cable car climbs up to Madonna del Sasso.

Luino ㊽, lying on the Lombardy shore to the east, is a lively border town, with a famous market every Wednesday, and its historic centre remains appealing. Piazza Garibaldi contains a statue to the revolutionary freedom fighter, for it was here, in 1848, after his defeat at Custoza, that Garibaldi mustered an army to continue the struggle against the Austrians.

BELOW: a waterside café in Lake Como's port.

Further south is **Angera** ㊾, dominated by the **Rocca Borromeo** (open mid-Mar–late Oct daily 9am–5.30pm, Sun until 6pm) fortified castle, which has belonged to the Borromeos since 1450. **Arona** ㊿, facing Angera from the Piedmont shore, possessed a twin castle, which was demolished by Napoleon. The castle ruins surmount the town, but Arona is better known for its copper colossus of Carlo Borromeo, who asserted his authority during the plague of 1576.

Lago d'Orta 51, a mere 13 km (8 miles) long, lies in the province of Novara in Piedmont. Even Nietzsche fell in love with the beauty of this little lake. On the west bank, above Pella, Madonna del Sasso is a mountain sanctuary and forms the core of a pleasant group of hamlets. The lush promontory of Orta San Giulio, on the east bank, has island views, winding alleys and Baroque houses.

A path leads through woods, past 20 chapels dedicated to St Francis, to **Sacro Monte** (chapels open summer daily 9am–5.30pm). Next door to Sacro Monte stands the Gothic Palazzo dei Vescovi, housing a Benedictine monastery. But the lake's main attraction (reached from the east bank) is the **Isola San Giulio**, a tiny island with passing steamers, a pretty harbour, porticoes, pergolas and slate-roofed houses. The centrepiece is the Romanesque **Basilica of San Giulio** (open daily 9.30am–12.15pm, 2–6.45pm, winter until 5.30pm), built on the site of a hermitage. ❑

Superman and superkitsch

Il Vittoriale, on the shores of Lake Garda, is a shrine to Gabriele D'Annunzio (1863–1938), maverick, poet, megalomaniac, pantheist, aviator, aesthete and nationalist, who lived there from 1921 until his death. A bizarre amalgam of founding Fascist and soldier-poet, only half convinced by his own myth-making, D'Annunzio was enamoured of Nietzsche's concept of the Superman, which was misused by the Fascists to bolster their beliefs.

A right-wing nationalist who posed as the saviour of his country, he favoured Italy's entry into the war in 1915 and plunged into the fighting, carrying out several operations, such as flying over Trieste in 1915 and Vienna in 1918. Believing that Italy had been cheated by the 1919 Treaty of Versailles, he led an unauthorised invasion of the Dalmatian port of Fiume, which he ruled until 1921, on the basis that it had been promised to Italy before the war.

Such activities convinced Mussolini that the dangerous maverick should be pensioned off to Lake Garda. D'Annunzio accepted the house as a monument to his massive ego, and called it Il Vittoriale, probably in memory of Italy's victory over Austria in 1918. Wanting the house to be a grandiose national monument, he donated it to the state in 1923, in return for further funds and in recognition of his role as "the father of the fatherland".

The villa has two waiting rooms, a relatively cheerful one for favoured guests, and a gloomy temple for those D'Annunzio disliked. Throughout the house, walls and ceilings are studded with crests, arcane symbols, mottoes and secret messages. "I have what I have given" is carved over a doorway. The entrance to his study was intentionally low so visitors had to stoop, presumably to bow to the poet's genius. The solemn "leper's room" has a "cradle-coffin" bed where the poet mused on major deaths and commemorated war anniversaries, and the blue bathroom is a gilded cage for a fin-de-siècle aesthete. The funereal music room is a prelude to a cluttered map room and a monastic study, all three filled with exotic bric-a-brac, from Murano glass bottles to Islamic plates and Austrian machine guns.

The furniture, swathed in silks, chinoiserie, leopard skin and Italian flags, embraces Renaissance reproductions and fake Parthenon friezes. So that it should not prove a distraction, the bust of his lover, the actress Eleanora Duse, was covered with a cloth while the poet worked. Not that D'Annunzio was without a warped sense of humour: the dining room contains the poet's embalmed pet tortoise, which died of indigestion, placed on display as a warning against the dangers of overeating. In the extravagant gardens is the patrol boat D'Annunzio commanded during World War I. As an overview of D'Annunzio and his delusions of grandeur, Il Vittoriale leaves visitors amused and none the wiser. Curiously, it is treated with a mixture of reverence and impassivity by many Italians. ❑

RIGHT: maverick soldier-poet, Gabriele D'Annunzio (1863–1938).

SP 432A

GENOA

In marked contrast to some of the softer, safer Ligurian resorts, historic Genoa is a challenging, cosmopolitan port city which rewards exploration

Novelist Italo Calvino called Genoa one of his "invisible cities", a place of secret alleys and sunless courtyards, of banded façades in striped marble, of private squares and jewel-box interiors. Rubens called this, Europe's largest medieval town, "La Superba". The *caruggi*, the classic city alleys, are often buried under medieval tenements and linked by myriad passages. Sandwiched between the mountains and the sea, the capital of Liguria suffers from lack of space, but once one is inside the minute medieval courtyards or across the threshold of a narrow Renaissance palace, hidden spaces seem to multiply amidst the mirrored interiors. Critics tend to connect the city's lack of space with its sense of reserve. In a city without a central piazza the mood is one of wariness, underscored by a suspicion of outsiders common to all ports.

PRECEDING PAGES: the harbour at Vernazza.
LEFT: statue of Christopher Columbus, born in Genoa.
BELOW: the old town.

Maritime might

Founded in the 5th century, **Genoa** (**Genova**) swiftly became a trading city and rose to prominence as a maritime power. By the end of the 12th century it had defeated its arch rival, Pisa, and possessed ports and colonies from the Aegean to the Black Sea. However, mighty Venice posed a greater threat to Genoa's trading empire. During its 14th-century golden age Genoa was a factional city, albeit one controlled by shrewd oligarchs; bankers, merchants, nobles and rival brotherhoods possessed private armies and separate political agendas. Whereas Venetians were loyal to their Republic, the Genoese were faithful only to their faction and fortunes: the merchant bank was trusted more than the municipal government. The mercantile character of the city and the citizens' skill at moneylending have given the Genoese an undeserved reputation for meanness. As befits an erstwhile Republic that pioneered such modern devices as bills of credit, cheques and insurance, Genoese banking and business skills continue to be held in high regard.

The city has cultivated a patrician crust of enlightened patronage ever since Andrea Doria, admiral of the Genoese fleet and founder of the Doria dynasty, won independence from France in 1528. He negotiated a sound city constitution that remained in force until 1797, enshrining Genoese values and protecting the city's financial status. During the Risorgimento Genoa was a leading centre of republican ideas and counted as a native son Giuseppe Mazzini (1805–72), who put a united Italy on the political map.

With its reputation for obdurate independence and rugged individualism, Genoa was a centre of resistance against both Fascism and Nazism. Its industrial past, large working-class population and red-blooded refusal to submit have forged a political climate more attuned to left-wing administrations. Only in 1998 was the dominance of the left seriously challenged. However, as Italy's sixth-largest city and a member of the Milan–Turin industrial triangle, Genoa is not about to give up its traditional loyalties so readily.

The celebrated contemporary Genoese architect Renzo Piano calls Genoa "a secretive, inward-looking city, reflecting the prudent nature of the Genovese", whereas in 1846 Charles Dickens dismissed the city's "disheartening dirt, discomfort and decay".

As the largest port in Italy, Genoa has often been seen merely as a departure point or somewhere to pass through quickly en route to the resorts of the Italian Riviera. However, the Columbus celebrations in 1992, marking the 500th anniversary of the discovery of the Americas, gave the city a new dynamism and began the transformation of the harbour. The famous Genoese architect Renzo Piano built upon his work in the 1990s to give the Porto Antico a thorough facelift for the city's celebrations as European City of Culture in 2004. The city has embarked on a voyage of self-discovery and is embracing its new-found status with all the zeal of the discoverers and matchless Italian design. Once again it can claim Rubens's title, "La Superba".

The historic heart

As a port, Genoa cannot avoid dilapidation or the faint whiff of danger suspended in the salty air, especially at night. However, compensations lie in the hard-edged excitement generated by the waywardness of a real port. The intriguing *centro stórico* (historic centre) stretches from the old port to Piazza de Ferrari and Via Garibaldi. The Genoese middle classes recommend that this maze of alleys be ignored after nightfall, and follow this practice themselves. This attitude is born of natural caution tinged with racism, since the port is home to African immigrants as well as working-class Genoese. However, a modicum of street sense is enough to make an evening stroll pleasurable, especially since most of the city's best restaurants are tucked into the old town.

BELOW: Genoa's historic streets.

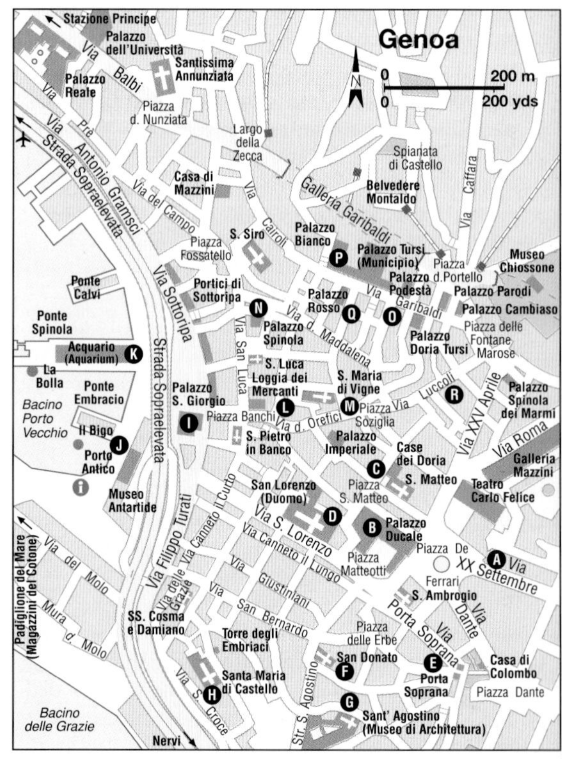

Map on page 292

The labyrinth of squares and palaces is testament to Genoa's medieval wealth and urban density: it was one of the largest cities in 14th-century Europe. Noble family homes were designed with several exits, covered passages linking different levels or houses; even a simple inn may have had a warren of rooms. A number of palaces are still inhabited by the original families. At night, beyond the Renaissance portals and façades of white marble and black slate, there are glimpses of simple family dinners taking place under grandly frescoed ceilings.

Via XX Settembre Ⓐ, a severe arcaded street, is a shop window on the elegant, classical quarter: the smartest shops, snootiest cafés and the old-world Bristol Palace Hotel. An air of safety and smugness pervades the street despite the discreet nightly presence of Russian prostitutes. Given the secrecy of the Genoese, it is only to be expected that, with the exception of **Zeffinino** (Via XX Settembre 20; tel: 010-591990), the best restaurants are invisible, tucked into the backstreets. The cool, slightly soulless air of monumental Genoa is sustained by the grand **Palazzo Ducale** Ⓑ, set on neighbouring Piazza de Ferrari. This hollow shell of a palace once symbolised the power of "La Superba", the ancient Republic. However, it feels a bit of a sham; with a Neoclassical façade looming over Piazza Matteotti and an over-restored interior remodelled after wartime bomb damage, it is reduced to staging art exhibitions and antiques fairs.

Just downhill, **Piazza San Matteo** Ⓒ offers the first glimmer of authentic medieval Genoa. The church of San Matteo dates back to the 12th century, but has a Gothic façade in the characteristic grey-and-white stripes that are Genoa's response to Pisan Romanesque. As well as the appealing cloisters (1308), the square is flanked by medieval palaces, decorated in Romanesque, Gothic and Renaissance styles.

Lion guarding San Lorenzo.

BELOW: Piazza de Ferrari.

Casa Colombo, where Christopher Columbus grew up.

Salita Arcivescovado leads to the cathedral, **San Lorenzo** Ⓓ (open daily 8am–11.45pm, 3–6.45pm). In the 9th century the threat of pirate incursions prompted city rulers to transfer the cathedral to the heart of the city. San Lorenzo was begun in 1200, but its eclectic design incorporates Romanesque, Gothic, Renaissance and Baroque elements.

From here, follow Canneto il Lungo, a narrow alley lined with crumbling palaces, to the medieval city's eastern limits. **Porta Soprana** Ⓔ, the twin-towered gateway, is the best-preserved section of the fortifications. The towers dominate **Casa Colombo de Cristoforo** (open Sat–Sun 9am–noon, 3–6pm), the reconstructed boyhood home of Christopher Columbus (1451–1506). The son of a local weaver, the city's celebrated navigator was destined for a career as a cloth merchant until fate intervened. Salita Prione leads through the atmospheric Piazza delle Erbe to the 12th-century church of **San Donato** Ⓕ with its octagonal belltower. Just south stands **Sant'Agostino (Museo di Architettura e Scultura Ligure)** Ⓖ (open Tues–Sat 9am–7pm, Sun 9am–12.30pm; admission charge), marooned in a bleak quarter which suffered heavy wartime bombardment. This deconsecrated Gothic monastery has been turned into a museum of Ligurian sculpture and frescoes, and works salvaged from Genoa's demolished city churches are displayed in the Gothic and Baroque cloisters.

Set in the original Roman *castrum*, closer to the port, **Santa Maria di Castello** Ⓗ can also claim to be at the heart of the medieval city. Built on ancient foundations, this early Christian church has a Romanesque façade. The building was modified by the Dominicans in Renaissance times, but the interior still contains Roman columns and Romanesque sculpture. Near by stands the **Torre degli Embriaci**, one of the few surviving medieval towers. Just beyond

BELOW: rooftop view of the city.

lie the bustling quayside and the porticoes of **Sottoripa**, with shops and stalls selling everything from fruit to fishing tackle. **Palazzo San Giorgio Ⓘ**, the port authority headquarters, commands a prominent position. Despite its harmoniously frescoed façade, this is a fusion of two palaces from different periods. From 1408 it was the seat of the Banco di San Giorgio, a banking syndicate and symbol of Genoa's financial might. It is also a reminder that while the city declined after the discovery of America, the wealth of the New World was channelled through its slick money markets. The Genoese were Europe's foremost bankers until they were supplanted by the Portuguese in the 17th century.

Map on page 292

TIP

If you are visiting one of the city's *pasticcerie*, try the *torta di mandorle*, a tasty almond cake made with preserved fruit.

The city port and surrounding area

Porto Antico Ⓙ, the old city port, formerly in a state of disuse and dilapidation, has now been transformed. The first major creation was Renzo Piano and Peter Chermayeff's visionary **Acquario Ⓚ** (Aquarium; open daily, Mar–June and Sept–Oct 9.30am–7.30pm, Thur until 10pm, Sat–Sun until 8.30pm; July–Aug 9am–11pm; Nov 9.30am–7.30pm, Thur until 10pm, Sat–Mon until 8.30pm; Dec–Feb 10am–7.30pm, Mon until 6pm, Thur until 10pm; last entrance normally 2 hours before closing; admission charge). The largest in Europe, it allows visitors to view marine life from surface and seabed levels; among the 600 different species and 6,000 creatures are grey sharks and dolphins. Also in the old port area is the **Antarctic National Museum** (Tues 10.30am–6.30pm, Wed–Sun 10am–6.30pm) which has a new exhibition area, Il Mondo dei Pinguini, dedicated to the recreation of sub-Antarctic conditions in which the museum's latest popular attraction of penguins live. To the west, an industrial zone fringes the modern **Porto Nuovo**. Next to the Aquarium, Renzo Piano's **La Bolla** (open Tues–Sun 9.30am–dusk) is a futuristic glass-and-steel bubble containing tropical plants and a collection of rare types of fern among which butterflies flit.

A stone's throw from the old port, bustling **Piazza Banchi** is in the heart of a friendly neighbourhood noted for its small market, varied shops and typical trattorias. This is an opportunity to try a fishy pasta dish or focaccia. The Renaissance **Loggia dei Mercanti Ⓛ**, set on the square, is where banking services were operated under the loggia, before it became the seat of Italy's first stock exchange in 1839. From here **Via San Luca**, one of the loveliest medieval streets, leads to Palazzo Spinola. Alternatively, Caffè Klainguti, a historic *pasticceria* on **Piazza Soziglia Ⓜ**, provides a welcome coffee break in dignified surroundings. Renzo Piano's **Il Grande Bigo** (open daily 10am–6pm, July–Aug 9am–11pm; times reduced in winter; admission charge) is an enormous crane, visible for miles, which whisks passengers 40 metres (130 ft) in a cylindrical lift for panoramic views over the city and waterfront.

The unique **Museo Nazionale dell'Antartide** (Antarctic Museum; open daily 10.30am–6.30pm) provides a fascinating insight into the little-known ecosystems of the South Pole.

In celebration of Genoa's status as European Capital of Culture in 2004, the **dockyards** (Darsena) have been entirely restored and renovated, creating a huge area of

BELOW: in the Acquario.

entertainment and culture dedicated to the sea and adventure. A museum complex, the largest in Europe, with over 20 exhibition areas, presents a voyage through time and the culture of the sea. The **Padiglione del Mare e della Navigazione** (Pavilion of the Sea and Navigation; open daily, Nov–end Feb 10.30am–5.30pm, Sat–Sun and hols until 6pm; Mar–May and Oct 10.30am–7pm, Sat–Sun and hols until 7.30pm; June–Sept 10.30am–7pm, Thur–Sun until 8pm; admission charge) on the third floor of the old cotton warehouse building is the new museum space for the Museo Navale at Pegli. The Pavilion features a permanent exhibition of merchant ships, from galleys to transatlantic steamers, and a new room dedicated to the trips of Christopher Columbus. There are helmets and armour from the 16th century, the 17th-century lodgings of a rich merchant, an old Genovese side street, a naval yard with all the machinery in full operation, and the deck of a brigantine schooner, moored to the dock – all in full scale. There are also several reproductions of famous ships and steamboats from various eras.

Also within the Magazzini del Cotone on the first floor is the **Città dei Bambini** (open Tues–Sun 10am–6pm; admission charge), a hands-on high-tech interactive space for three- to 16-year-olds.

Palazzo Spinola Ⓝ (open Tues–Sat 9am–7pm, Sun 2pm–7pm; admission charge), on Piazza Pellicceria, is tucked away in the former furriers' district but repays seeking out. The 16th-century palace, with frescoed ceilings and monumental staircases, has become a gallery displaying works by artists from Van Dyck to the Emilian Guido Reni.

Via Garibaldi Ⓞ is the noblest of streets, lined with sumptuous 16th-century palaces. In celebration of Genoa's status as a European City of Culture in 2004, it is now a "museum street" linking the main art collections, including the newly

BELOW: the revamped port area.

Map on page 292

restored Palazzo Doria Tursi with its splendid arcaded courtyard. **Palazzo Bianco** **P** (open Tues–Fri 9am–7pm, Sat–Sun 10am–7pm; admission charge) is a fine gallery displaying Flemish and Dutch paintings by Van der Goes, Van Dyck and Rubens as well as French and Spanish artists and a comprehensive collection of Genoese and Ligurian painting; the wealth of the city made it a magnet for foreign artists, especially the Flemish. Opposite, **Palazzo Rosso** **Q** (open Tues, Thurs and Fri 9am–1pm, Wed and Sat 9am–7pm, Sun 10am–6pm; admission charge), holds works from the Venetian and Genoese schools. The former is represented by Titian, Tintoretto and Veronese; the latter is typified by the work of Bernardo Strozzi.

If you are in search of dinner, take **Via Luccoli** **R** back to the old city. A classic pasta dish is *trennette al pesto,* with a sauce similar to French *pistou*, sweeter and more delicate than the Tuscan variety.

Outskirts of the city

Just east of Genoa is the picturesque fishing village of **Boccadasse**, which is popular with Genoese and tourists alike. Pastel-coloured houses are clustered around the little harbour, making this a very photogenic spot, where time appears to stand still.

To the southeast, the villa quarter of **Nervi** is famous for its sea promenade, the Passeggiata Anita Garibaldi, which winds above spectacular jagged rocks and through lush gardens perfumed with oranges. The grounds of the Serra, Gropallo and Grimaldi villas have been united into a romantic park, blending lush Mediterranean and exotic plants with the English garden style, including the spectacular rose garden in the grounds of Villa Grimaldi. ❑

BELOW: *The Cook,* by leading Genoese painter, Bernardo Strozzi.

I LOVE
LIDAYS!

THE LIGURIAN RIVIERA

The Ligurian coast offers a taste of the Mediterranean and the mountains, with hilltop castles, citrus groves, fishing villages transformed into chic resorts, and robust local cuisine

Map on pages 300–301

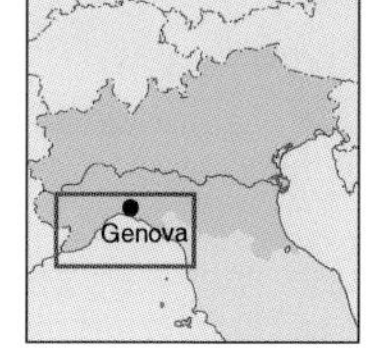

The vogue for sea-bathing on the Riviera did not become established until the 1930s. Until then a pampered foreign élite was more interested in winter cures and the therapeutic effects of the mild climate. The Italians had been swimming at San Remo since the 1850s, but the British, Germans and Russians regarded this as Italian perversity. The British, who were happy to swim at home, regarded the Mediterranean as suitable only for seaweed and anemone-hunting. However, for repressed northerners drawn to the winter resorts, the Riviera also represented a place to express smothered sensibilities.

Rugged individualists

The sea has determined Liguria's destiny as a trading region. As befits a former maritime state, Genoa *(see pages 291–97)* is cosmopolitan and raffish in equal measures. Its tough hinterland, Liguria, has always been a land of adventurous fishermen-sailors and shrewd merchant-wayfarers. In the 16th century its inhabitants, afraid of raids by marauding Turks and Venetians, built a series of coastal defences, which still survive. The Ligurians are an enterprising, pugnacious people, with the ingenuity to exploit the humblest of resources. Not that they lack subtlety; local excavations reveal their civilisation to be among the oldest and most sophisticated in Europe. Some complexity even pervades the language: French was the courtly language until the mid-19th century, and Ligurian dialects reflect French and Tuscan influences.

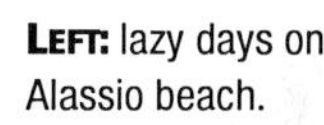

LEFT: lazy days on Alassio beach. **BELOW:** casting off.

Yet a symbiotic relationship with the sea is not synonymous with an affection for the coastal environment. Ecologists accuse Ligurians of indulging in disposable tourism, of turning sections of the coast into a concrete jungle. However, the steepness of the cliffs and the creation of protected zones have spared much of the area. Concrete jungles do exist, but so do ravishing and balmy lemon-scented surroundings.

The landscape embraces the dramatic wine-growing coast, the remote mountainous hinterland and the millionaires' playground, Portofino. The lush vegetation ranges from agaves and oleanders to citrus fruits, umbrella pines and tamarisks. A Mediterranean mantle of greenery survives in coastal pine groves and palm-fringed avenues. The jagged coastline harbours many architectural treasures, from bold Genoese-style churches to *belle-époque* villas. As for agriculture, the cultivation of flowers might have broken the economic dependence on olives but grapes, peaches, oranges and olives still grow in abundance.

Liguria, confident of its local cuisine, expects visitors to eat until they burst *(manja a crepa pansa)*. Yet Liguria also has the highest life expectancy of any region in Italy: a healthy, homely Mediterranean diet

Posing – but not for the camera.

helps foster such longevity, second only to that of the Japanese and Icelanders. Liguria has made a virtue of necessity, since the region has yielded little in the way of grain, meat, dairy products, or even fish. Instead, the cuisine focuses on freshly made pasta, gnocchi and stuffed vegetable dishes. Food is often dressed with vintage olive oil from Taggia and cooked with herbs such as thyme, oregano, basil and sage. Focaccia – *fugassa* in local dialect – is the fast food of the poor. Fish also makes an impact, from soup to seafood risotto. The terraced slopes provide ideal territory for vines and olives. "The... cuisine owes more to the country than the sea because it grew out of the hankerings of sailors who yearned for fresh green vegetables… and this is what their women made to please them," is cookery writer Claudia Roden's interpretation.

Riviera di Ponente

The **western coast** stretches from the French border to Genoa, taking in San Remo, Imperia, Albenga and Savona, as well as a host of attractive villages in the rugged hinterland. As the centre of Italy's cut-flower industry, this coast is often dubbed "Riviera dei Fiori". Certainly the terraced hills around Ventimiglia and San Remo are dedicated to the growing of roses, carnations and anemones. Even outside the greenhouses the hothouse climate ensures that this coast is well endowed with exotic gardens and palm-lined promenades. The Via Aurelia, successor to the ancient Roman road, offers the most engaging coastal scenery, only rivalled by views from the hillside villages in the wild hinterland.

Compared with polished Menton over the French border, **Ventimiglia ❶** appears scruffy and bedraggled, especially if one arrives by train. However, the approach by the coastal route is far more picturesque, with a carpet of

BELOW: La Mortola.

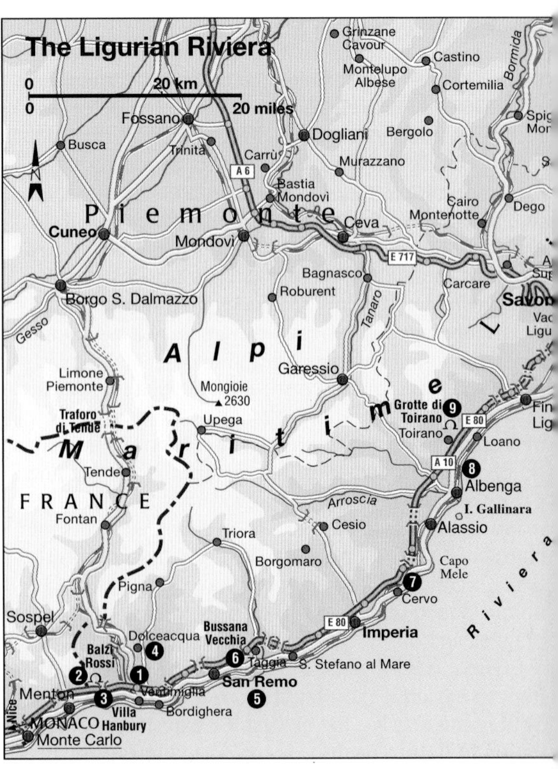

Map on pages 300–301

flowers covering the terraced slopes. The June Battle of Flowers festival pays homage to the town's best-known industry. After being swallowed up by Genoa in 1261, Ventimiglia became a border town surrounded by fortifications, vestiges of which survive. The medieval city, tucked into the left bank of the river Roia, is centred on the Romanesque cathedral and a cluster of dourly handsome civic buildings. The neighbouring church of **San Michele**, dating from the 8th to the 10th century, has an impressive crypt and Romanesque columns. The city has been inhabited since Roman times, but the Roman amphitheatre and other remains are engulfed by the modern lower city. However, for most people the city's greatest attraction is the **Friday market**, which invades the river bank, public gardens and part of Via Roma. The array of bags, shoes, clothes, fabrics, fruit and vegetables draws French residents from across the frontier and allows the canny Italians to have the last laugh on the chic French.

Prehistoric caves

Virtually on the French frontier, west of Ventimiglia, are the **Balzi Rossi** ❷ prehistoric caves (open Tues–Sun 9am–7pm; tel: 0181-38113; free). Set at the foot of red cliffs in **Grimaldi**, these caves contain fossils, human skeletons and Palaeolithic wall drawings. A study of these elaborate burials proves that the ancient Ligurians lived in one of Europe's most sophisticated societies. Apart from skeletons dating from 100,000 years ago, there are tools, weapons, fertility figures and a sketch of a breed of horse hitherto found only on the Russian Steppes. The museum (open daily 9am–7pm; admission charge) was established in 1898 by Sir Thomas Hanbury, an English botanist and merchant who is best known for his gardens.

Commanding a headland just east of the Balzi Rossi is his home, **Villa Hanbury** ❸ (gardens open Apr–mid-June daily 10am–5pm, mid-June–Sept daily 9am–6pm, Oct daily 10am–6pm, Nov–Mar Thur–Tues 10am–4pm; admission charge). Struck by the cape's beauty and climate, Sir Thomas transformed the grounds into a botanical paradise between 1867 and his death. His legacy was typical of his class and times: the British often succumbed to the creative urge to make a lasting mark. Hanbury created Japanese and Australian gardens as well as the newly restored perfume garden, full of scented pelargoniums, lavender and herbs. Today, exotic plants that Hanbury imported from Africa and Asia coexist with native Mediterranean vegetation. The exotic species include papyrus and eucalyptus, cacti and rubber trees.

On Hanbury's death his daughter-in-law Dorothy continued his work, but concentrated on landscaping rather than planting, creating paths, fountains, arbours and novel perspectives.

Further along the coast is the resort of **Bordighera**, linking Ventimiglia and San Remo. There is a contrast between the historic hillside town of Bordighera Alta, with defensive walls and maze of medieval alleys, and the elegant seaside resort, with its palm-lined avenues. In the Bordighera hinterland is the well-tended wine-producing village of **Dolceacqua** ❹, a picturesque place set amid vineyards and crowned by a ruined medieval castle. Other delights include a humpbacked stone bridge beloved by Claude Monet, quaint covered passageways, and a rose-coloured parish church with a Baroque belltower.

Sumptuous San Remo

Like Menton on the Côte d'Azur, **San Remo** ❺ made its name in the 1840s as an élitist winter resort. The mild climate, genteel atmosphere and beautiful surroundings attracted a foreign clientele, especially Russian and British aristocrats. Tourism received a further boost with the creation of sumptuous *belle-époque*

BELOW: the gentle waters of Dolceacqua.

hotels and the arrival of the railway in 1871. San Remo, sheltered by mountains, still enjoys the lush vegetation that once drew these visitors. Lying in the lee of the Ligurian Alps, the capital of the Riviera dei Fiori cultivates the flowers for which it is known. The mild climate also means that the palm groves are more reminiscent of Sicily or North Africa. The early morning flower market on Corso Garibaldi is a chance to appreciate the fragrant local blooms.

San Remo has two centres: La Pigna, the original medieval hilltop village, is outshone by the chic seaside resort. The palm-lined promenade of Corso Imperatrice is named after the Russian Czarina Maria Alexandrovna, a San Remo resident who filled the local gardens with palms in the 1870s. In the same street is another legacy of the Russian community: the eclectic **Chiesa Russa** (1913) (open Tues–Sun 9.30am–12.30pm, 3–6.30pm), an onion-domed fantasy of an Orthodox church. The 19th century saw the creation of sweeping avenues, a setting for healthy but gentle promenades. Corso Imperatrice and its extensions, Corso Matteotti and Corso Nino Bixio, form the city drawing room, with the Art Nouveau **Casino** (1906) at its heart. Tchaikovsky lived in this street, as did Edward Lear, the nonsense poet, and Alfred Nobel, the father of modern explosives and prestigious prizes. As the queen of the Riviera, San Remo may have glittered during the *belle époque* but is a slightly shabby dowager now.

La Pigna, the higher, historic heart of San Remo, was once the fiefdom of Ventimiglia's feudal barons. The bastion was designed to offer protection against Turkish marauders, who regularly sacked the coast for water supplies and slaves. The walled village later flourished, surrounded by vineyards and olive groves. In time, however, La Pigna became more isolated from the chic seafront settlement. Today's old quarter curls around the vestiges of the former castle, with a series of

Map on pages 300–301

The Russian Orthodox Church, San Remo.

BELOW: win a car – or lose your shirt – at San Remo's casino.

If you are feeling adventurous you can take the funicular railway from La Pigna to Monte Bignone, with its panoramic views and nature trails.

dark alleys and tunnels, sculpted portals and pastel-shuttered houses. At its heart stands **San Siro**, the Romanesque-Gothic cathedral (open daily 7–11.15am, 3–6pm), partly remodelled in Baroque style. From here one can stroll to the small fishing harbour to inspect the catches of crayfish, swordfish and whitebait.

Just inland from San Remo stands the curious ghost town of **Bussana Vecchia** ❻. Abandoned after an earthquake in 1887, the village was repopulated by a bohemian artists' colony in the 1960s, and Italian and foreign artists have turned the least damaged houses into arts and crafts shops to promote their wares.

Towards Genoa

Cervo ❼ is an engaging hilltop village set on a spur sloping down to the sea. Dominated by a castle, the well-preserved medieval centre clings vertiginously to the slopes. The upper part of the village is particularly pleasing, with its distinctive porticoes, medieval walls and white houses huddled against the hillside. Further east along the coast, **Alassio** was one of the most elegant resorts in the early part of the last century. Northern Europeans were drawn by the luxurious hotels, the sweeping sands, the flowering gardens and the hilltop villas. Today it is one of the Riviera's largest and most popular resorts, thanks largely to its fine soft sands which stretch for nearly 4 km (2½ miles).

Albenga ❽ was founded by the Romans and flourished between the 10th and 13th centuries, but when the sea moved further out the Romanesque city was marooned by the river. The medieval centre fans out from the piazzas of San Michele, IV Novembre and dei Leoni. This last, named after its three stone lions, is flanked by historic buildings, from the Comune Vecchio, the old town hall, to the cathedral of **San Michele**, graced with a Romanesque belltower cast in green-

BELOW: Alassio.

and-white marble. Inside are the remains of the original early Christian church, including the apse of the crypt and vestiges of a 4th-century floor. Beside the cathedral stands an octagonal baptistry with fine early Christian mosaics reminiscent of those at Ravenna. The **Museo Navale Romano** (open summer Tues–Sun 9.30am–12.30pm, 3.30–7.30pm; winter 10am–12.30pm, 2.30–6pm; admission charge; tel: 0182-51215) traces Albenga's maritime heritage and displays the cargo of a Roman ship that sank offshore around 100–90 BC.

Map on pages 300–301

Savona, lying between Albenga and Genoa, is a former Florentine port overshadowed by its industrial present: the busy port handles crude oil and Italian cars for export to Britain and the United States. As the oldest nucleus of the city, the port is dominated by a naval fortress and opens onto a cathedral, Renaissance palaces and an art gallery displaying works by Ligurian painters. The **Grotte di Toirano** ❾ (open daily 9.30am–12.30pm, 2–5pm, July–Aug until 5.30pm; guided tours: tel: 0182-98062) lie beneath the hill town of Toirano. This series of caves testifies to the importance of the Palaeolithic period in the region. Among the relics dating back to 80,000 BC are traces of human and bear footprints, the remains of other wild animals, and mud balls probably used as missiles; the chambers are festooned with dramatic stalagmites and stalactites.

Charles Dickens (1812–70) called the fishing village of Camogli "the saltiest, roughest, most piratical little place".

Pegli ❿, the faded haunt of the Genoese aristocracy, lies on the coast just before Genoa. Although now little more than a grand city suburb, it stands out for its collection of noble villas and gardens. The 16th-century **Villa Doria** used to contain the **Museo Navale** (now moved to the Padiglione del Mare in Genoa). The romantic **Villa Durazzo-Pallavicini** is set in glorious landscaped gardens (open Tues–Sun 9am–7pm, until 5pm in winter; admission charge). Inside the villa, the **Museo Civico di Archeologia Ligure** (open Tues–Fri 9am–7pm, Sat–Sun 10am–7pm) has interesting finds from local cave burials. Refined Pegli is now closer than it would like to be to the teeming port city of **Genoa** ⓫ *(see pages 291–7)*.

BELOW: topping up the tan.

Riviera di Levante

The **eastern coast** stretches from Genoa to La Spezia, taking in Camogli, Portofino and Rapallo as well as Chiavari, Sestri Levanti, the Cinque Terre villages and Lerici. For day trips to the coast, the Riviera di Levante, except for Portofino, is easily accessible by train from Genoa. Portofino, Portovenere and the Cinque Terre villages can also be reached on boat trips from Rapallo or Genoa.

Nervi ⓬, just east of Genoa, rose to prominence as a smart winter resort. Today this refined and hilly suburb is home to a trio of faded Genoese villas landscaped in English Romantic style, complete with lakes, avenues, rose gardens and a belvedere.

Camogli ⓭, the scenic gateway to the Portofino Peninsula, nestles at the foot of a pine-wooded slope. In the 18th century Camogli was known as "the port of a thousand white sails". Today the sailing fleet is gone, and this quaint fishing village symbolises the chicness of this stretch of coast.

For all its posturing, however, Camogli is more genuine than Portofino. The *porticciolo*, the tiny port at the foot of the promontory, is stacked with *case-torre*, the tall thin medieval houses that are typical of this coast; edged with dark-green shutters, they are painted in various shades, from ochre and rose to brick and burnt sienna. The village, riddled with steep stairways and vertiginous views, contains good seafood restaurants and stylish bars, and the medieval **Castel Dragone** houses an aquarium, the **Acquario Tirrenico** (open summer daily 10am–noon, 3–7pm; admission charge). The celebrated Sagra del Pesce festival takes place on the second Sunday in May, when the country's largest frying pan is used to cook sardines.

Portofino owes its salvation to a foreigner: in April 1945 German resident Baroness von Mumm pleaded with the Nazis to spare her beloved home from bombing; the commander complied over a fish lunch.

San Fruttuoso di Capodimonie ⓮, in the next bay, is a tiny fishing hamlet built around the abbey of the same name. Although San Fruttuoso can be reached by boat, the long trek from Camogli is as exhilarating as it is exhausting. A steep path traverses silvery olive groves, chestnut plantations and ruins in a patchwork of juniper, myrtle and wild asparagus. When not covered in mist, the cupola of the Benedictine abbey stands out against the Mediterranean landscape. The 11th-century complex embraces Romanesque cloisters and a crypt containing tombs of the Genoese Doria dynasty who, before their demise, added a defensive tower to protect the coast from marauders in the 16th century.

Portofino and Rapallo

Portofino ⓯, the most exclusive spot on the Riviera, can be reached by boat from neighbouring resorts; by foot, it is a two-hour trek from San Fruttuoso. Set on a picturesque promontory, this *faux* fishing village is adored by the stars, who arrive incognito to sample its atmosphere. After an intimate tryst in the world-famous Hotel Splendido (tel: 0185-267801), or a studiously simple supper in a rustic inn, preferably shared with a fisherman, it is back to the yacht and the next movie deal. Since its discovery by the British in the 19th century, Portofino has been the preserve of artists, film directors and the yachting set, and was the inspiration for Portmeirion in Wales.

BELOW: the abbey at San Fruttuoso.

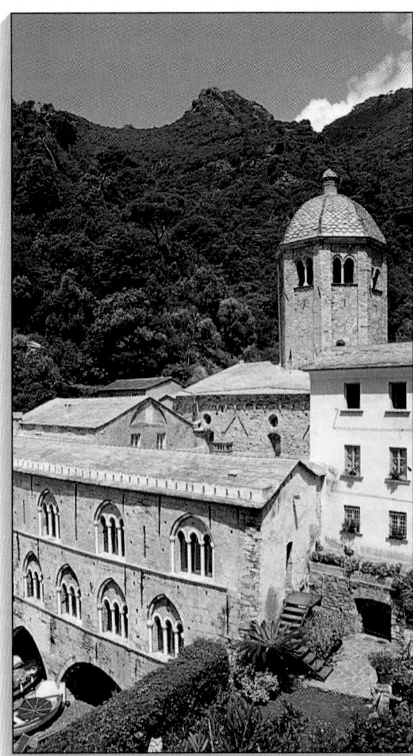

Portofino's illustrious past visitors include Edward VIII (the Duke of Windsor), Clark Gable and Frank Sinatra; the contemporary roll call features actors Harrison Ford, John Malkovich and Sophie Marceau, who have shot films here. Yet, even for the élite, seclusion only lasts from evening to first light: when the day trippers arrive, the spell is broken. During the day the medieval lanes studded with bijou boutiques are frequented by yachties in designer nautical wear. But it is easy to fall for the sailing boats at sunset, the portside *piazzetta* framed by picturesque *case-torre*, the lanes dotted with terraces and cute cats. The hillside beyond, surmounted by a castle, is studded with villas hidden by cypresses, chestnuts, palms and pines.

As a lush coastal nature reserve the **Promontory of Portofino** is satisfying walking country, with rock, bush and pine tumbling to the sea. From San Rocco di Camogli, a pleasant path leads to the cape of **Punta Chiappa**, past the Romanesque church of San Nicolò di Capodimonte. The luxuriant scrub provides a forest of heather, myrtle, broom, thyme and saxifrage, a perfect habitat for skylarks, barn owls and nightingales.

A panoramic route connects Portofino with the neighbouring resort of **Santa Margherita Ligure**.

Map on pages 300–301

Sandwiched between Portofino and Rapallo, Santa Margherita makes a lively touring base, more relaxed and less exclusive than Portofino. The attractions include a sandy beach, ruined castle and, perched on the headland, the lovely **Villa Durazzo** (tel: 0185-282449), surrounded by Italianate gardens (open daily 9am–7pm, 5pm in winter). The 16th-century Villa Durazzo is a charming mansion, richly decorated with statues and paintings, and housing the **Museo V.G. Rossi** (open 9.30am–6.30pm, until 4.30pm in winter), a reconstruction of writer Vittorio G. Rossi's study containing his books, paintings and possessions.

Rapallo ⓰, framed by attractive hills, is deservedly one of the most popular resorts on the Riviera, with a low-key yet lively atmosphere that satisfies old and young alike. The cultural and historical sights are quickly disposed of, leaving one time to appreciate the balmy atmosphere and gentle strolls along the seafront. If boredom sets in there are boat trips to other fishing villages on the coast, notably to the Cinque Terre. The genteel town is best explored in the early morning, when the food markets are enticing, or in the early evening when the shops and relaxed bars come into their own. Rapallo's chief sight is the seafront **Castello**, which once served as a prison. Although built in 1550 to defend the port against pirate raids, it was remodelled in the 17th century when the foundations were raised and the castle was endowed with a private chapel.

The **Museo del Merletto** (Lace Museum: open Tues–Wed, Fri–Sat 3–6.30pm, Thur, Sun 10am–noon; tel: 0185-63305) is a reminder of the way in which women traditionally occupied themselves while their fishermen husbands were at sea. The museum displays everything from chaste underwear to pillowcases for wedding trousseaus or a baby's baptismal best. From Rapallo a cable car leads up to **Montallegro**, a Marian sanctuary with panoramic views over the gulf.

Villa Durazzo at Santa Margherita Ligure.

BELOW: picturesque Portofino.

The Fortezza di Sarzello in Sarzana is characterised by deep moats and austere curtain walls.

Sestri Levante, further east, is attractively set on a peninsula, with a long promenade stretching the length of the bay. Another fishing village that has mutated into a resort, it has made a smoother transition than most. From here, the Cinque Terre villages are accessible by train, boat or on foot. The road from Sestri Levante to La Spezia becomes distinctly mountainous.

The famous five

At this stage the prospect of exploring the **Cinque Terre** ⓱ by foot is the more appealing. Five stunning villages surrounded by steep hills and vineyards, the Cinque Terre (Five Lands) present concentrated essence of Liguria. The classic route follows panoramic coastal footpaths to lofty sanctuaries, homely restaurants, Genoese-style striped churches and tiny ports. En route there are views of jagged coasts, pastel-coloured cottages, fishing nets drying in the sun and vineyards built using dry stone walls. The walk is Liguria in miniature, a pilgrimage for the spirit and the stomach. Via dell'Amore, a lovers' path wending along the coast linking Riomaggiore and Manarola, provides a typical flavour of the route. However, summer visitors in search of solitude may find these cliffside hamlets overrated; in August, stupendous views are little compensation for the crowds. A visit out of season reveals a wilder side, particularly on the rougher trails to the sanctuaries above the villages. Leave your car at Riomaggiore and take the short train journey to Monterosso, where the walk back begins.

Monterosso ⓲, the western gateway to this celebrated cluster of villages, is best reached by train. The village, which is slightly more commercialised than the others, overlooks a popular sandy beach. The main sights are the Convento dei Cappuccini, with a majestic view, and the parish church of San Giovanni Battista with its crenellated belltower. Many morning walks end in the Ristorante degli Amici, set just off the beach on Via Buranco 36 (tel: 0187-817544) and noted for grilled fish and seafood antipasti. From Monterosso one can also reach the other Cinque Terre villages by train, by boat or on foot. The **Sentiero Azzurro** follows the coast, linking the main villages in vertiginous views; the stretch to Vernazza is one of the more demanding sections, climbing through vineyards high above the sea and traversing narrow valleys on old footbridges before descending to Vernazza about two hours later. Alternatively, to lose the crowds, take the steep climb up to the remote 9th-century sanctuary of Madonna di Soviore.

BELOW: Riomaggiore, seen from the sea.

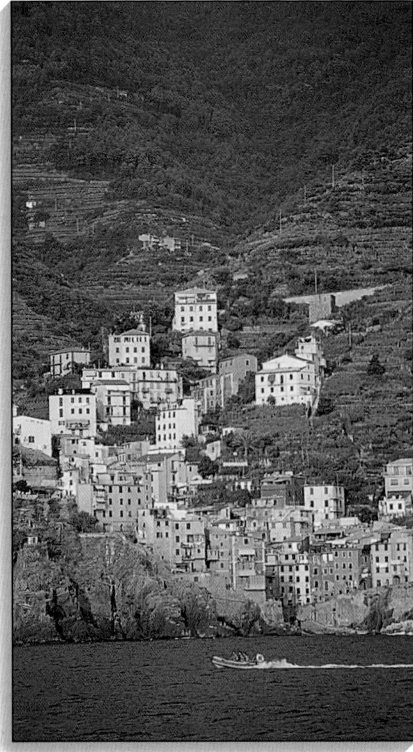

Vernazza ⓳, the most picturesque village, is also the most crowded, particularly on summer weekends. Wander through the winding backstreets, dotted with wine and craft shops, then have a clam soup or lobster lunch on a pretty terrace. The scene-stealer is the port itself, with tall painted houses clustered at the head of a sheltered cove. The port is overlooked by an atmospheric parish church in Genoese style. Vernazza's role as a trusted ally during the Genoese Republic means that the village has a more refined aspect than the others. The stretch from Vernazza to the unspoilt village of **Corniglia** ⓴ is slightly shorter than the previous one. As a farming and wine-growing community built atop a lofty promontory, Corniglia has always had a more inland character than the other Cinque Terre ports. The village is perched over the Cinque Terre's most beautiful and best beach. Lying on the northern side of the promontory, this beach, the Spiaggia di Guvano, is lapped by clear, warm waters and is one of Liguria's very few beaches where nudity is permitted. **Manarola** ㉑, roughly an hour from Corniglia on foot, is a colourful fishing village set amid geometrical patterns of terraced vineyards. After admiring the 14th-century church of San Lorenzo, follow the celebrated Via dell'Amore to **Riomaggiore** ㉒, a village carved into a narrow valley. The journey ends with a visit to the 14th-century church of San Giovanni Battista and a sight of the harbour, set against strata of the strange black rock that typifies the region. Walkers in a celebratory mood can toast the towering cliffs with dry Cinque Terre wine or Sciacchetrà sweet dessert fizz.

Map on pages 300–301

Shelley was working on his last great poem, The Triumph of Life, *when he was drowned on his way back to Lerici after visiting another English expatriate poet, James Leigh Hunt.*

Portovenere ㉓, easily reached by boat from Rapallo or Genoa, makes a delightful day out and is usually far less crowded than the Cinque Terre villages. The port sprawls along a promontory, with fish restaurants lining the harbour, sunbathers on the rocks, and fishing nets cast over the sea walls. In medieval times Portovenere was a fortified outpost of the Republic of Genoa, but the Genoese bastion was largely dismantled in 1453, and the present citadel is Baroque. In the upper part of the village beguiling backstreets lead to the Romanesque parish church of San Lorenzo, which has Gothic and Renaissance additions. From Piazza Spallanzani a gentle climb leads to **San Pietro**, a Gothic church in striped bands of black and white. From the terrace, a popular setting for open-air concerts, there are stunning views towards the Cinque Terre and Lerici. A staircase leads up to **Grotta Arpaia**, known as Byron's Grotto. This stretch of coast will forever be linked to the fateful musings of the English Romantic poets. Lord Byron, a strong swimmer then living in a villa in neighbouring La Spezia, loved the wildness of the waters around Portovenere. However, in 1822 his friend Shelley was drowned while attempting to sail from Livorno to Lerici, where he had a small house.

BELOW: if you love seafood, you'll love Portovenere.

From Portovenere there are boat trips to the **Isola Palmaria**, colonised by Benedictine monks in medieval times. Dominating the next bay is **La Spezia** with its sprawling naval shipyards, former arsenal and naval museum. The town and seaside promenades are overlooked by a medieval castle. **Lerici** ㉔, set on the other side of the so-called "gulf of poets", is illuminated by a picturesque castle that enchanted Byron, Keats and Shelley. This towering Pisan stronghold was enlarged by the Genoese, who remodelled it in Gothic style, adding a chapel. From Lerici a beguiling descent leads down to Fiascherino, a luminous bay.

Sarzana ㉕ once guarded the eastern frontier of the Republic of Genoa against Pisa. The hub of this fortified town is the Fortezza di Sarzello, a 15th-century Florentine citadel which was remodelled after the Tuscans had defeated the Genoese. Other attractions in the town include the Gothic cathedral and the Renaissance palaces flanking Piazza Matteotti. From here even landlubbers will probably be tempted to return to the Ligurian coast, with its soft interplay of sky and sea. ❑

CORTE

BOLOGNA

Bologna's galleries and museums are engrossing, but it is the red-brick city itself that is the central work of art. Follow this route to discover its network of porticoes and its friendly taverns

Map on page 314

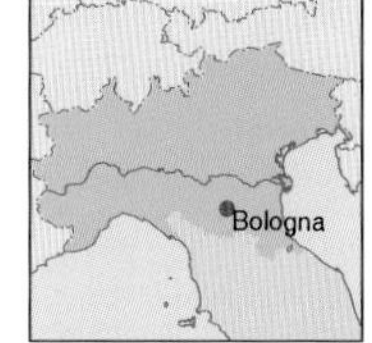

Bologna is one of the most civilised cities in Europe and was named European City of Culture in 2000, a monument to bourgeois bliss, personal pragmatism and public efficiency. As a stylish tribute to the beauty of urban life, Bologna unfurls a warm red-brick cityscape of arcaded streets and elegant palaces. It is also a paradigm of the good life, with its superb cuisine and cultured outlook, vibrant arts scene and youthful population, honest public administration and efficient public transport. The citizens are sociable, affable, open and cosmopolitan, proud of but not precious about their urban heritage.

Fat, learned and red

Bologna abounds in nicknames: *la Dotta*, "the Learned", referring to its role as an ancient university city; *la Rossa*, "the Red", in relation to its politics rather than its red-brick buildings; and, finally, *la Grassa*, "the Fat", an epithet linked to its reputation as a gourmandising city, the temple of Italian cuisine. Until recently it remained firmly in Italy's political red belt as a bastion of the Democratic Party of the Left (Democratici di Sinistra). Thanks to its passion for education, Bologna also remains a city committed to museums, with a new museum of Jewish culture, and a new library, the largest in Italy, opened for the Millennium. The **Museo Ebraico** (open Sun–Thur 10am–6pm, Fri 10am–4pm, closed Sat and Jewish festivals) in Palazzo Pannolini, Via Valdonica, has a section charting the history of Jews in Bologna and Emilia Romagna from the Middle Ages until today.

As for cuisine, stroll into delicatessens lining Via Caprarie to see mountains of *tortelloni*, salami and cheeses stacked beside spit-roasted chickens, rice croquettes and *marrons glacés*.

The city has been a centre of learning since the 7th century, when scholars from Ravenna settled near by. In 1088 the city's famous law school, the nucleus of one of the first universities in Europe, was founded. Bologna, bound by 14th-century walls and entered via 12 fine gates, developed as a coherent commercial city, with wealth created by merchants who developed the gold, clothing, silk and hemp industries. Like most major northern cities, medieval Bologna experienced power struggles between the church, the *comune* and the guilds, represented by the lawyers and bankers. In the 16th century it became part of the Papal States but continued to follow a communal, civic-minded path, with the common good placed before personal glory. In modern times Bologna's civic record has emphasised its hostility to Fascism and right-wing government. The region turned to Communism after leading the resistance against the Nazi occupation towards the end of World War II.

PRECEDING PAGES: Piazza Santo Stefano.
LEFT: last of the city's high towers.
BELOW: Via dell'Independenza.

Foreign correspondent Charles Richards refers to the teasing paradox of this fascinating city: "Bologna is radical chic, the showcase of Communism and women in furs; Third World causes and stolid bourgeoisie, big cars and a left-wing campus."

Today Bologna's political affiliations are clear in streets blessed with such names as Salvatore Allende and Martin Luther King. However, political ideology is tempered with pragmatism. As the former mayor, Walter Vitali, said: "Bologna is not the last bastion of Communism; we simply have a good, left-wing, social democrat administration." Bologna is a pioneering city: the first to introduce pedestrian precincts, to privatise certain social services, to permit gay couples to apply for communal housing, and to impose key environmental and health measures. With a population of only 600,000, its homogeneous urban design and lack of ugly suburbs, Bologna is *una città a misura dell'uomo*, a city built on a human scale, in which people live and work in the well-preserved historic heart (even if some workers live in the countryside and commute).

Andiamo in piazza

For a Bolognese, "*Andiamo in piazza*" ("Let's go to the square") can only mean a visit to **Piazza Maggiore** Ⓐ. The main square stands at the heart of this monocentric city, forming a majestic architectural ensemble, complete with open-air cafés, palaces and public buildings. One of the grandest is the **Palazzo del Podestà**, formerly the governor's palace, graced with a Renaissance façade, part of which houses the main tourist information centre (open Mon–Sat 9am–7pm, Sun 9am–2pm; tel: 051-246541). The palace is open during exhibitions only. Despite the elegant cafés, on most mornings the square is the preserve of old men in fusty clothes putting the world to rights; the afternoon sees the arrival of some of Bologna's 100,000 students, who cycle over for coffee and conversation.

Piazza del Nettuno Ⓑ, skirting the northern end of the main square, is centred on the muscular bronze statue of Neptune *(see pages 313 and 316)*. Facing

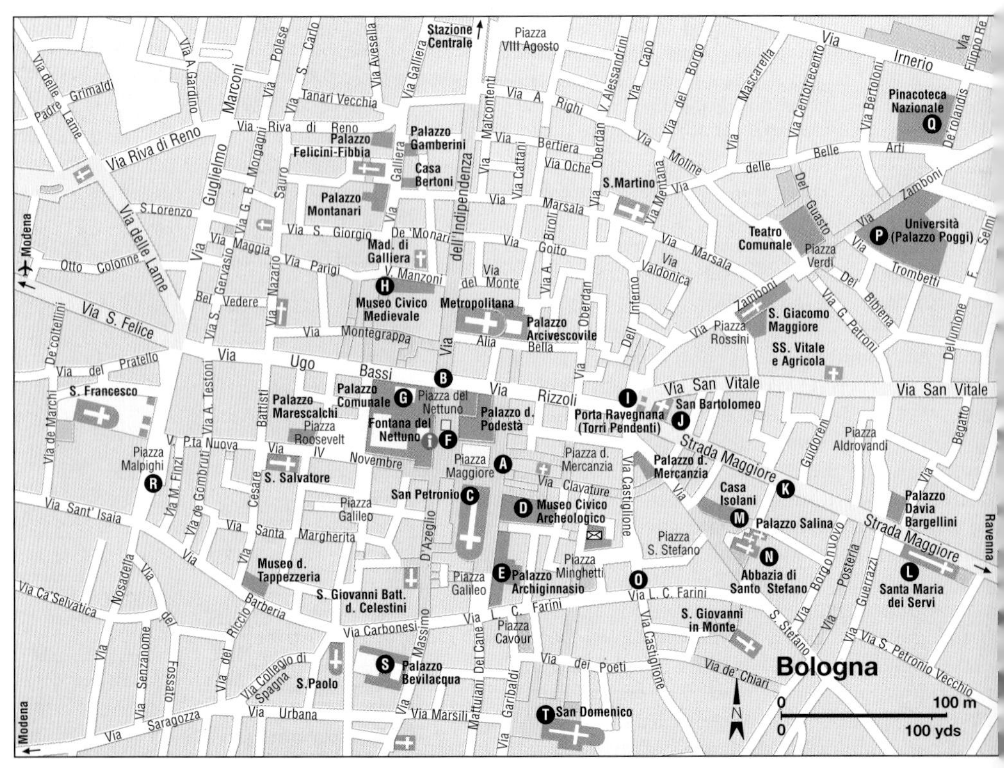

the Palazzo del Podestà is the looming bulk of **San Petronio** Ⓒ (open daily 7.15am–1pm, 2–6pm), the fifth-largest church in the world. Founded in 1390, it is dedicated to the city's patron saint, a 5th-century bishop beloved for the urban-planning projects he masterminded. The Gothic basilica testifies to the seemingly limitless wealth of the medieval city, although grandiose plans to make the basilica bigger than St Peter's came to nothing, and work on the unfinished façade was abandoned in 1650. The financial profligacy of the project was said to have helped turn Martin Luther against the Church. The basilica influenced Michelangelo, presenting an exotic expanse of pink marble in a sea of red brick. Particularly outstanding a re Jacopo della Quercia's bas-reliefs over the main portal, and the marble decoration on the lower part of the façade. Della Quercia was Sienese; the alien nature of marble in this red-brick city meant that marble sculptors were rarely from Bologna. Inside, the highlights are Giovanni da Modena's frescoed 15th-century Madonna, and the pulpit where St Bernard of Siena and Savonarola preached. The basilica provided a splendid setting for the coronation of the Holy Roman Emperor Charles V in 1530.

Behind San Petronio is the **Museo Civico Archeologico** Ⓓ (open Tues–Sat 9am–6.30pm, Sun 10am–6.30pm; admission charge). This well-designed archaeological museum paints a picture of Etruscan and Roman Emilia Romagna. Etruscan and Roman artefacts range from funerary urns and stelae to mosaics and a bust of the Emperor Nero. The collection is complemented by Egyptian artefacts as well as Celtic helmets and 6th-century bronze buckles.

Near by stands the **Palazzo Archiginnasio** Ⓔ (open Mon–Fri 8.30am–1.45pm, Sat 8.30am–12.45pm; free admission), now home to the municipal library but once the seat of the university. Set on Piazza Galvani, it occupies the site

Map on page 314

The writer and traveller Freya Stark remarked that San Petronio looked as if it had sunset built into its walls.

BELOW: Piazza Maggiore, Bologna's main square.

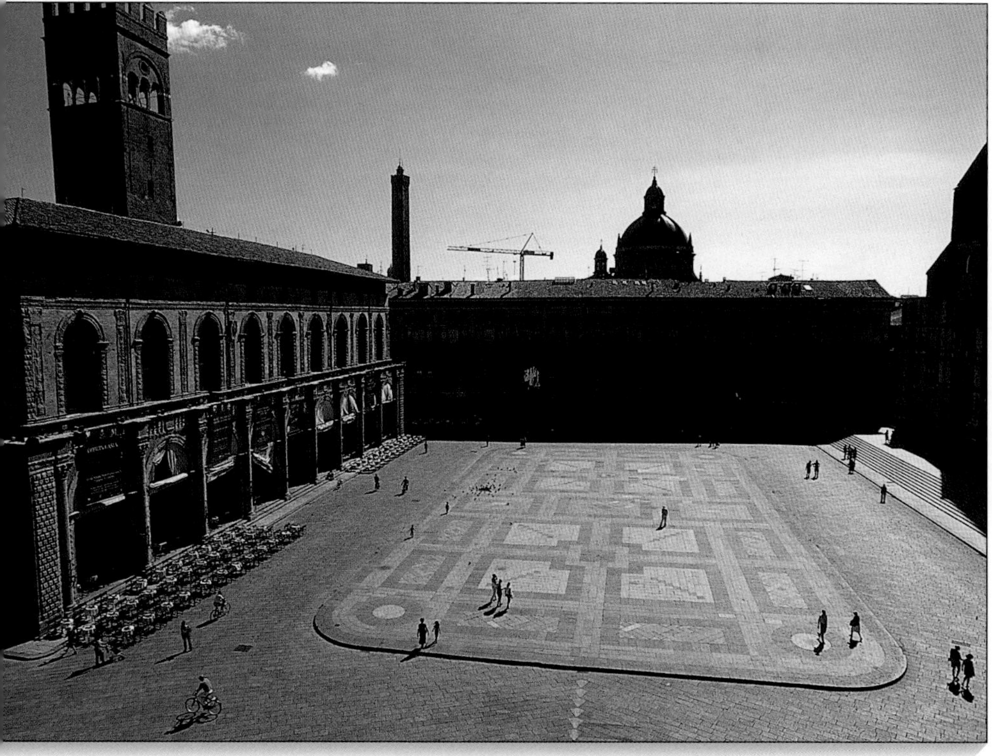

Neptune on top of his fountain.

intended for the left transept of San Petronio; funds were diverted to the palace instead. Built in 1563, it was intended as a home for all faculties, from philosophy and civil law to medicine and mathematics. Upstairs is the Teatro Anatomico, a compelling dissection theatre and a reminder that the world's first lessons in human anatomy were conducted in Bologna. This chamber, superbly restored after bomb damage in World War II, dates from the 17th century, but public medieval dissections were performed in similar surroundings. It is dominated by an operating table eerily supervised by statues of famous professors and skeletal figures, known as *gli spellati* or "the skinned ones".

To banish morbid thoughts it is enough to retrace one's steps to Piazza del Nettuno and the **Fontana di Nettuno** Ⓕ, the Fountain of Neptune (1563–66) by Giambologna, the Flemish artist who made his name in Florence. Neptune, unashamedly naked, trident in hand, commands four voluptuous sirens, each riding a dolphin. In the Baroque period the statue's erotic charge was considered so disturbing that bronze breeches were cast on the god and only removed in more liberated times.

On the west side of the square is the **Palazzo Comunale** Ⓖ, more correctly known as Palazzo d'Accursio, the town hall since the early 13th century. The panel outside the *palazzo* is covered in photographs of Bolognese intellectuals and partisans shot by the Nazis in 1944. The collection in the **Collezioni Comunali** (open Tues–Sun 10am–6.30pm, until 6pm on Sun; admission charge) includes paintings, sculpture and furniture. Pride of place is given to the **Museo Giorgio Morandi** (open Tues–Sun, 10am–6pm; admission charge), dedicated to the city's pre-eminent still-life painter. Morandi (1890–1964) had a predilection for painting bottles and bowls with great subtlety in sludgy colours. According

BELOW: the fountains near the town hall – the Palazzo d'Accursio.

to Umberto Eco, Bologna-based professor and best-selling author of *The Name of the Rose*, "Morandi can only be understood after one has trailed the arcaded streets of his city and understood how a seemingly uniform brick-red tint can define different houses and alleys."

The **Museo Civico Medievale e del Rinascimento** Ⓗ (open Tues–Sat 9am–6.30pm, Sun 10am–6.30pm; admission charge), on Via Manzoni 4, occupies a delightful palace. This charming and compact museum covers the period from the Middle Ages to the Renaissance. Highlights include collections of arms, ivory and glassware as well as Gothic sculptures and bronze statues.

Lofty views

The gate of **Porta Ravegnana** Ⓘ is dominated by the two relatively intact leaning towers **(Torri Pendenti)** that escaped demolition at the turn of the century. Such lofty towers characterised the medieval city skyline and testified to the power of the resident feudal families. To work up an appetite, visitors can climb 498 narrow steps 97 metres (320 ft) to the top of the **Torre degli Asinelli** (open daily 9am–6pm, winter until 5pm; admission charge), the taller tower, and be rewarded by a terracotta cityscape stretching into the villa-studded Apennine hills. The Asinelli is visible from most spots in the city; the Garisenda, its squatter companion, is half the size but leans three times as much. As a counterpoint to these historic towers in the city centre, there are contemporary Japanese-designed towers in the new business district.

San Bartolomeo Ⓙ, set beside the two towers, is a Baroque church with a lovely, highly decorated portico. In the north transept is a colourful Madonna by Guido Reni. **Strada Maggiore** Ⓚ runs east from the towers and follows

Map on page 314

Bologna-based professor and author Umberto Eco.

BELOW: Bologna is a city of piazzas and porticoes.

PORTICOES

Porticoes are a hallmark of Bologna – picturesque marble or brick affairs radiating from the city centre. These seemingly endless arcades stretch for 35 km (22 miles) and shelter shoppers and sightseers from inclement weather. The porticoes were a response to a housing crisis caused by the influx of students, migrants and merchants who flocked to Bologna in the 15th century. The first floors of houses were extended to form extra rooms suspended over the street. As well as providing space and shelter, these overhanging adjuncts were found to promote trade and social life, connect private and public areas, and even protect pedestrians from traffic. As a result the city has continued to build, rebuild or restore its porticoes until modern times.

The arcades from Porta Maggiore to Via Mazzini, the old Roman road, are the most impressive in the city, an early 17th-century affair forming a "sacred way" to the church of Santa Maria Lacrimosa. The early 18th century saw the completion of the world's longest porticoes, built to connect the city with a hilltop sanctuary. Composed of 666 arcades, the route winds up Colle della Guardia to Santuario della Madonna di San Luca, a distance of several miles.

the original line of the Roman Via Emilia, making a gentle introduction to the terracotta-hued shopping streets. **Santa Maria dei Servi** Ⓛ, set further down the street, is a 14th-century church with Gothic and Renaissance porticos, rich in works of art, with frescoes by Vitale da Bologna and a Madonna and Child panel painting by Cimabue. **Casa Isolani** Ⓜ, overlooking the same street, is an arts, commercial and residential complex carved out of traditional city palaces. Also known as Corte Isolani, it has Romanesque-Gothic porticoes supported by 12th-century beams. The complex, a warren of chic boutiques and cafés, connects with Via Santo Stefano, lined with churches and palaces.

Abbazia di Santo Stefano Ⓝ (open daily 9am–noon, 3.30–6.30pm, sometimes later; free) is the most bewildering of the city churches. Essentially a religious complex clustered around Santo Stefano, it's a harmonious ensemble formed from four churches, two chapels and two cloisters that date from the 5th century but are predominantly Romanesque. San Sepolcro (11th century) houses the elaborate tomb of St Petronius (Bologna's patron saint), built in imitation of the Holy Sepulchre in Jerusalem. **Via Castiglione** Ⓞ, running parallel to Via Santo Stefano, is another typical Bolognese street.

The oldest university?

Further north, the **Università (Palazzo Poggi)** Ⓟ (tel: 051-2099360) on Via Zamboni has been a seat of learning since the 16th century, when the campus transferred from the Archiginnasio. One of the first universities in Europe, dating from the 11th century, the law school was born out of a need to bring Roman law up to date, and resulted in Bologna becoming the pre-eminent European centre for civil law. At its height in the 13th century it numbered 10,000 students

BELOW: students take a break.

from all over Europe. Scholars included Petrarch, Copernicus, Dante Alighieri and Thomas Becket, subsequently martyred in Canterbury. The university has also specialised in the sciences, a reputation underlined by the pioneering radio experiments of local boy, Guglielmo Marconi (1874–1937). Bologna remains a centre of scholarship, and there are a number of international universities with campuses in the city.

The **Pinacoteca Nazionale** Ⓠ (open Tues–Sun 9am–7pm; admission charge), on Via delle Belle Arti, has one of the most appealing art collections in the country. The core collection embraces Emilian painters from the 14th century. As a reaction to the formalism of Tuscan Mannerism, the Bolognese School favoured simplicity and greater realism. These elements feature in the work of artists such as Annibale Carraci, Guercino and Guido Reni. A few works by Giotto and Raphael add a less regional perspective.

To the west of Piazza Maggiore, the delightful **Piazza Malpighi** Ⓡ is a colourful spot surrounded by a frescoed portico. On the same square is the romantic Gothic church of San Francesco. Further south, on Via d'Azeglio, **Palazzo Bevilacqua** Ⓢ is the boldest of Bologna's senatorial palaces. Built in Florentine rusticated style in 1474, this superb Renaissance building has a sandstone façade, wrought-iron balconies and a courtyard surrounded by a loggia.

The Basilica di San Domenico Ⓣ (open Tues–Sat 10am–12.30pm, 3–5pm, Sun 3–5pm; free) dominates Piazza San Domenico. Dating from 1228, it was remodelled in Baroque style but incorporates Romanesque walls. The interior displays the tomb of St Dominic, founder of the Dominican Order, decorated with sculptures by Nicola Pisano and Arnolfo di Cambio of the Pisan school as well as two by the young Michelangelo. ❑

Art critic Roberto Longhi praises Emilian painting as sincere, earthy and impulsive, "open to sin but also to redemption"; and local writer Renzo Renzi says: "It is openly human and therefore popular art in the best sense."

OSTERIE: TRADITIONAL TAVERNS

Bologna's *osterie* focus on genuine food and a cosy family atmosphere. They have their roots in proletarian wine shops, a cross between a tap room and a tavern. In 19th-century Bologna or Milan the typical tavern offered a daily diet of fried polenta and salt cod, steaming macaroni or left-over offal, washed down with rough wine. By the end of the century politics had prevailed over food: taverns were considered dens of iniquity. Under Fascism, these inns became notorious as focuses for subversion and seditious demonstrations. After the war they succumbed to fashion, with most surviving by emphasising their regional roots and traditional recipes.

Today, these family-run *osterie* attempt to promote Emilian hospitality and specialise in home-made food. In Bologna they often serve such standards as *bollito misto*, an abundance of mixed meats, from *cotechino* or *zampone* to tongue, shin, chicken on the bone, or stuffed *porchetta*. Recently, their cause has been championed by the influential *Slow Food (see page 105)*, a combined culinary campaign and international journal which aims to promote the pleasures of eating. An evening stroll along Bologna's Via del Pratello is an introduction to several inviting *osterie*.

BELOW: traditional Bolognese osteria.

EMILIA ROMAGNA

The medieval and the Renaissance mingle in the cities, museums and castles of Emilia Romagna, a discreetly sensuous land of plenty which also offers the best cuisine in the country

Map on pages 324–325

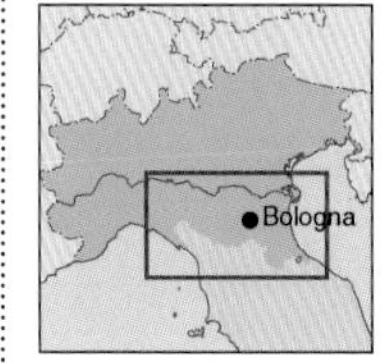

The broad river plain stretches languorously south from the sluggish River Po to the Apennines. There are cities, from Ferrara to Piacenza, which are treasure troves of galleries, churches and castles, and others, from Parma to Modena and Bologna, associated with gastronomy and good living. Historically the region has been dominated by ducal dynasties and tiny fiefdoms run by huge egos. The glory days of feudalism culminated in the claims of the d'Este, rulers of Ferrara, and the Farnese, who controlled Parma and Piacenza. Before 1860, Bologna and Ferrara were governed by Papal legates; the land to the northeast belonged to the Duke of Parma; and the Duke of Modena's possessions stretched across the mountains to Carrara and the Gulf of Genoa. Politically the region has been socialist since the 19th century, and it suffered in the struggle against Fascism and Nazism. In April 1945 the Allies launched an offensive from Ravenna, which led to the liberation of the region, supported by the partisans. However, Emilia's left-wing politics have more to do with the region's traditional anti-clericalism than with belief in a Communist utopia.

PRECEDING PAGES: the beautiful frescoed ceiling of Parma's Baptistry.
LEFT: Modena's Romanesque duomo.
BELOW: Palazzo Ducale Gardens, Parma.

The Emilian model

The post-war period witnessed the development of small and medium-sized companies, an economic success story which came to be known as "the Emilian model". Above all it is noted for the survival of city-specific industries, from tiles in Sassuolo to glassworks in Fidenza; Modena styles sleek Ferraris and Maseratis, while Parma produces ham and cheese. Emilia is the gastronomic heart of Italy, feeding the north with superb salami and sausages as well as cheeses. The region produces much of Italy's wheat and sugar beet as well as barley, tomatoes, rice, peaches and plums. It also produces almost a quarter of the country's beef and veal.

The dignified and unassuming city of **Piacenza** ❶ marks the border between Lombardy and Emilia Romagna, a frontier clearly carved by the yellowing River Po. Piacenza has the dubious distinction of being the coldest city in Italy, the price paid for its riverside setting on the Pianura Padana, the inhospitable Po Valley.

When Pope Paul III, a powerful member of the Farnese dynasty, wished to create a buffer zone between the Papal States to the south and Spanish domination in Lombardy to the north, he granted the new Duchy of Parma and Piacenza to his son, Pier Luigi Farnese, in 1545, with territory that originally fell within the jurisdiction of the Papal States. Piacenza became the first capital of the Duchy of Parma, graced with Renaissance walls, although the dynasty's greatest legacy was in Parma itself.

Emilia is prime pasta country and also produces the country's finest charcuterie, perfect food for a convivial, pampered people.

The historic centre is clustered around **Piazza dei Cavalli**, named after the *cavalli*, two early-Baroque bronze horses (1620–5) ridden by members of the Farnese dynasty. Flanking the square are the Gothic church of **San Francesco** and the **Palazzo del Comune** (1280), the Gothic town hall, noted for its mullioned windows and swallowtail crenellations. The Lombard-Romanesque **Duomo** (1122–1244) (open daily 7.30am–noon, 3–7pm) stands at the end of Via XX Settembre. The façade is cast in Verona marble and stone, enlivened by Romanesque capitals and sculptures. The impressive 14th-century belltower is surmounted by an iron cage installed in 1495 as a means of public punishment: offenders were suspended above the square and subjected to public ridicule.

Via Chiapponi leads to **Sant'Antonio**, which was founded in the 4th century and served as the cathedral until the 9th. As well as an exceptional 11th-century octagonal lantern and Gothic vestibule, the highlights include a rich interior with 9th-century frescoes. The **Museo Civico** (open Tues–Thur 9am–1pm, 3–5.30pm, Fri–Sat 9.30am–1pm, Sun 3–6pm; admission charge) on Piazza Citadella occupies the unfinished Palazzo Farnese. The museum holds a quirky collection of exhibits, from a Botticelli Madonna to a curious Etruscan bronze sheep's liver (the *Fegato di Piacenza*), used for divining the future.

Panoramas, pilgrims and the birthplace of Verdi

Castell'Arquato ❷ is a harmonious village with panoramic views, nestling in the hills of Piacenza. Piazza Alta, the hub of the village, is lined with appealing inns and flanked by the Romanesque church of Santa Maria and the fortified, Gothic **Palazzo Pretorio**, the town hall. Near by, the **Rocca Viscontea** is a 14th-century fortress bounded by ramparts and topped by pentagonal towers.

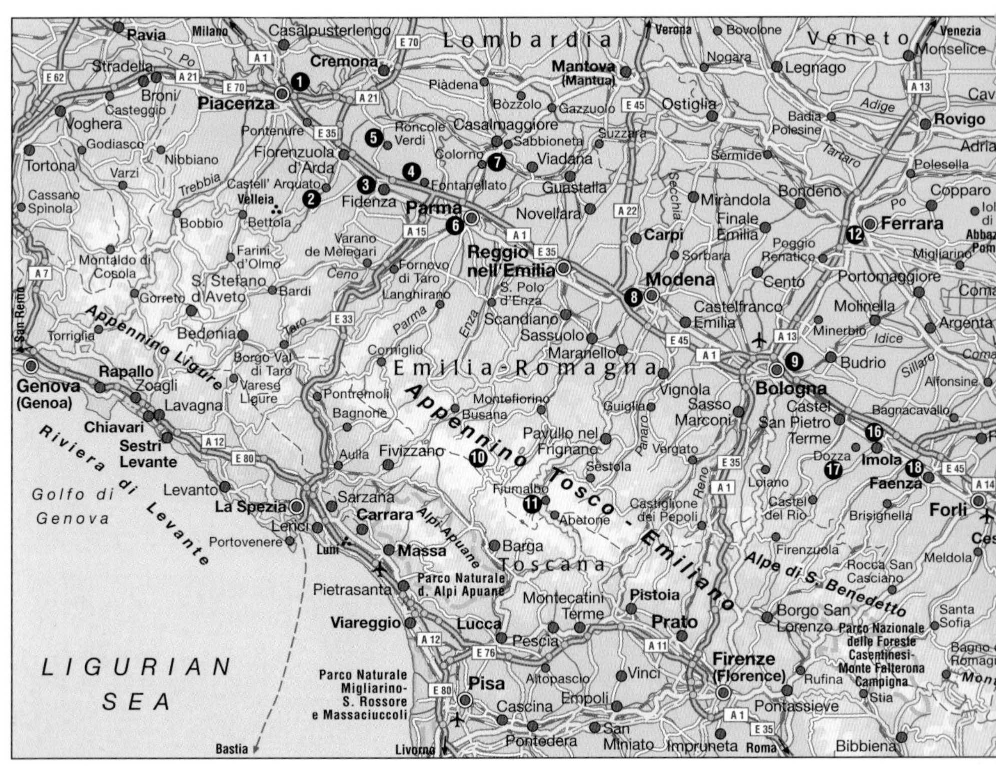

Map on pages 324–325

Fidenza ❸ is a historic halt on the Via Francigena, the main pilgrimage route to Rome. The cathedral of **San Donnino** is adorned by friezes depicting weary pilgrims, and is dedicated to a martyr who, after being decapitated by the Romans, managed to carry his severed head to the far side of the river.

The feudal castle of **Fontanellato ❹** (open Tues–Sun 9.30am–12.30pm, 3–7pm, winter until 5pm; admission charge), set 10 km (6 miles) west of Parma, seems to rise majestically from a glassy green moat. The castle belonged to the Sanvitale family from the mid-14th century until 1948, when the last count sold it to the town as a museum. The centrepiece is a mysterious chamber, adorned with frescoes by Parmigianino, mirrors and gilt, depicting the myth of Actaeon and the huntress Diana.

Roncole Verdi ❺ has an indisputable claim to fame as the birthplace of Italy's most famous composer. In Italy, Giuseppe Verdi (1813–1901) is revered as a genius who expressed the national spirit in his music. His birthplace has been turned into a museum, **Casa Natale di Giuseppe Verdi** (open Mar–Oct Tues–Sun 9.30am–12.30pm, 2.30–6.30pm; Nov–Feb Sat–Sun with reservation 9.30am–12.30pm, 2–4.30pm; admission charge; tel: 0524-97450). Just north of Busseto is **Villa Verdi** (open Apr–Oct Tues–Sun 9am–noon, 3–6.30pm; admission charge), bought by the composer with the proceeds from *Rigoletto* and filled with memorabilia. In Busseto itself the city castle accommodates the **Teatro Verdi**, dedicated to performing his works.

Detail on Fidenza's cathedral.

The city of cheese and ham

Parma ❻, sandwiched between Milan and Bologna, was fought over by France, the Papacy and the northern feudal dynasties; the Farnese dynasty made the

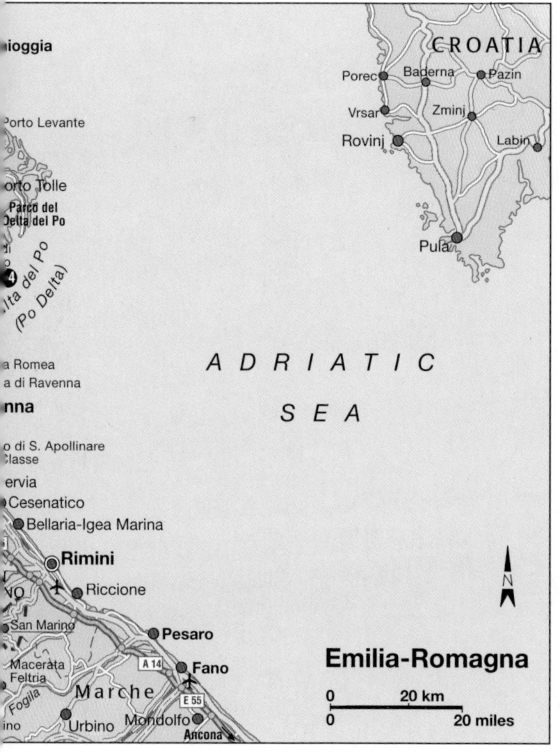

BELOW: Castell'Arquato.

greatest mark, ruling the city during its 16th- and 17th-century heyday. When the line died out in 1731 the Duchy of Parma passed into the hands of the Bourbons. The 1815 Congress of Vienna assigned it to Habsburg ex-Empress Marie Louise (1791–1847), Napoleon's estranged second wife, who is credited with transforming Parma into a bourgeois capital with an imperial air.

"I was, am and always will be a peasant from Roncole," wrote Giuseppe Verdi, Italy's best-known composer.

Modern-day Parmigiani have a reputation for bravery: Parma was the last Italian city to succumb to Fascism in 1922. Allied bombing raids destroyed a fifth of the city in 1944, but most of the medieval heart remains, matched by Renaissance frescoes and Neoclassical façades. Today Parma is a byword for fine living, with an urbane, prosperous population devoted to making and spending money. This chic, understated city abounds in civic pride and splendid architecture, yet tends to be neglected by foreigners in favour of Florence and Siena. The locals blame the climate: stiflingly hot in summer, snowy or foggy in winter, Parma is an acquired taste, as is the local accent.

Piazza del Duomo is a cobbled square bounded by the cathedral, belltower and baptistry as well as the bishop's palace, guarded by red-and-white marble lions. The **Duomo** (open daily 9am–12.30pm, 3–7pm), built between 1060 and 1073, displays a stepped façade in Lombard style as well as a Gothic belltower and a pink portal framed by lions. The Romanesque interior, damaged by an earthquake in 1117, was restored in 1130. Among the treasures within are a *Deposition* by Benedetto Antelami, one of the greatest medieval sculptors (this is his earliest known work, created in 1178 from a single piece of marble), and a Baroque pulpit. The dome, frescoed by Correggio in 1526, is awash with ethereal pyramids of frothy clouds and wispy saints. In this Assumption, Mary, borne by angels, is swept heavenwards in a swirling white cloak. Correggio

BELOW: *Parmigiano Reggiano* – king of cheeses.

(1489–1534 was largely self-taught. Noted for his sensuous style and *sfumato* technique, he also influenced Parmigianino, the fifth centenary of whose birth Parma celebrates in 2003. One of the most important painters in Italy in the first half of the 16th century, he was born Francesco Mazzola, and nicknamed Parmigianino after his place of birth. He was a disciple of Correggio and is famed for the grace of his figurative composition and original use of colour, making him the father of the European Mannerism Movement.

The adjacent **Baptistry** (open daily, closed 12.30–3pm) is an octagonal five-storey Romanesque affair cast in Verona's russet-pink marble. It was begun in 1196 by Benedetto Antelami, who also sculpted the three external portals and the stone reliefs depicting the labours of the months within. The building, finally finished in 1307 in transitional Romanesque-Gothic style, has been superbly restored. The galleried interior is adorned with one of the most awe-inspiring cycles of frescoes in northern Italy, anonymous Byzantine-influenced works.

San Giovanni Evangelista (open daily, closed noon–3pm) is a fine Renaissance abbey rising behind the cathedral apse. Beyond the Baroque façade and belltower is a Renaissance dome with splendidly sensuous Correggio frescoes. Near by are Renaissance cloisters, a refectory and a library used by the resident Benedictine community; close by is a Benedictine Dispensary (pharmacy open daily 8.30am–2pm; admission charge), complete with 16th-century apothecary's jars.

Piazza Garibaldi leads to the plush **Teatro Regio**, the premier opera house for the Verdian repertoire (tel: 0521-218678; www.teatroregioparma.org). Inaugurated in 1829, with Paganini as director of the orchestra, this much-loved building glitters in gold and white.

Map on pages 324–325

The galleried interior of the Baptistry.

BELOW: in the Po Valley, no part of the pig is wasted.

The **Palazzo della Pilotta**, an unfinished and bomb-damaged brick barn of a building, broods over the city centre. This maze of corridors and courtyards was a Farnese palace for almost 150 years until the line died out in 1731. It now houses several museums. The core of the collection of the **Museo Archeologico** (open daily 9am–7.30pm; admission charge) comes from finds in Velleia, a Roman settlement between Parma and Piacenza, but also includes Etruscan artefacts from the Po Valley. The **Galleria Nazionale** (open Tues–Sun 8.30am–1.45pm; admission charge includes Teatro Farnese) in the same palace houses an impressive art collection, with works by such great regional artists as Correggio and Parmigianino as well as by Fra Angelico, Leonardo da Vinci and Canaletto. Also within the palace is the **Teatro Farnese** (times as for Galleria Nazionale) a wood-and-stucco theatre modelled on Palladio's Teatro Olimpico in Vicenza. Commissioned in 1619, this was one of the grandest theatres in Europe and could seat 3,000 people. The interior is decorated with mythological figures and equestrian statues of the Farnese dynasty. Severely damaged during Allied bombing raids, it has been magnificently restored.

The Teatro Regio was also the setting for the first public performance by Toscanini, the celebrated conductor, who was born in Parma. He conducted Aida *entirely from memory.*

Just off neighbouring Via Meloni is the former convent of St Paul, containing the **Camera di San Paolo** (open daily 9am–1.45pm; admission charge). Also known as the Correggio Chamber, this room is a display case for Correggio's art, where High Renaissance tricks of perspective and chiaroscuro compete with *trompe-l'oeil* pillars and monochrome figures. It is adorned with allegorical frescoes of the four elements, fruit, foliage and mythological creatures.

Across the river from the Palazzo della Pilote is the **Palazzo Ducale** (open Mon–Sat 9.30am–noon; tel: 0521-230023; admission charge), a 16th-century Farnese palace, with landscaped grounds featuring a lake and an island. It

BELOW: hanging the ham.

PARMA HAM

Since Hannibal reputedly supped on Parma ham in 217 BC, the local meat industry has grown as fast as the pigs themselves. For around 2,000 years pigs in the Po Valley have provided the raw material for a thriving industry. Parma ham *(prosciutto di parma)*, the favourite Italian antipasto, comes from pigs bred for cured meats. The best Parma ham is sweet and succulent, marbled with pure white fat, while the mass-produced *prosciutto crudo* can be stringy, fatty or greasy. The pigs are a cross between an English and a Danish breed. Bred purely for their salami, and branded with the Ducal crown of Parma, these are the only pigs permitted in the production of Parma ham. They are fattened on chestnuts and whey, the milk left over from making Parmesan cheese. After being slightly salted, the raw hind thighs are hung in drying sheds to mature for about a year. Parma hams are even hand-massaged to improve the texture. With 6,000 pig breeders and 220 slaughterers, this is a profitable industry governed by vigorous controls regarding slicing and packaging monopolies. However, the Consorzio del Prosciutto di Parma, the local ham consortium, continues to fail in attempts to stop British supermarkets slicing, packaging and selling the ham for their own markets.

was remodelled in French style in the 18th century, with statues and a classical temple in the park (park and gardens open from dawn to dusk; free).

Given Parma's culinary prowess, visitors should sample the local ham and cheese, washed down with a flinty Sauvignon or a fizzy Lambrusco from north of Modena. Meat-lovers can try a speciality from Zibello: *culatello* salami, a choice slice of pig's bottom, which the poet D'Annunzio *(see page 287)* compared to the sweetness of his lover's breasts.

Castle country

Much of Parma province is flat, but the locals discern hidden beauty in this somewhat bleak terrain. However, now and again the crested profiles of fortified *castelli* cast shadows over the plains, for over a hundred ruined or intact castles are dotted throughout the province. While many were abandoned in Renaissance times, others were converted into palatial country mansions. Centred on Parma, a rambling castle route can take in Torrechiara, a masterpiece of military engineering, and Bardi, a bulwark built atop a rock of red jasper.

The most prestigious is undoubtedly **Colorno** ❼ (open by appointment; tel: 0521-312546), more like a French château or German *Schloss* than an Italianate castle. First designed as a medieval fortress, Colorno gained its present appearance after being remodelled by Ranuccio Farnese in 1660. In its heyday it was dubbed "the Versailles of Parma".

Colorno became a splendid stage set for festivities, with frescoed ceilings, 18th-century marble fireplaces and Neoclassical stucco-work. The restored interior is a blend of styles, but the Ducal apartments are impressive. In the grounds, Colorno's warm façades are reflected in the water, encircled by English-style

Map on pages 324–325

In Parma, no organ of any creature is ever dismissed as inedible. As the local expression has it: "Pork is like Verdi's music, every piece has its place."

BELOW: Piazza Garibaldi in Parma.

parkland. After 1860 the royal House of Savoy appropriated Colorno's best statuary and furniture to adorn palaces in Turin, Florence and Rome.

"The best Ferrari? It's the one we haven't made yet," says Enzo Ferrari, the founder of the famous car firm, who personifies the ambitious character of the Modenese and their passion for one-upmanship.

Modena: materialism and museums

Modena ❽, the historical rival to Bologna, is a place of comfort and prosperity set amid fertile countryside, synonymous with materialism, fast cars and big appetites. Enzo Ferrari founded his firm in 1939, and the company, now Fiat-owned, still produces cars in the industrial outskirts. Luciano Pavarotti has raised the profile of his home town in recent years by staging annual charity concerts. Modena is one of the country's richest cities, yoked to a consumer-oriented culture devoted to designer boutiques and shoe shops. In addition, it is the centre of the region's important livestock industry, has a healthy wine trade and is producer of Italy's best balsamic vinegar.

Yet commerce in Modena is allied to a finely honed aesthetic sense; shops are tucked into the graceful arcaded spider's web of streets. Looking good is a passion epitomised by the ritual *passeggiata* in the warren of historic alleys and along the airy boulevards to the south, built over the fortified ramparts demolished a century ago. It is hard to believe that medieval Modena resembled an inland Venice, lined with canals; the waterways have been filled in, but the curved streets and porticoes trace the swirl of the erstwhile canals.

This faded ochre city presents a harmonious face to the world with its elegant arcades and kaleidoscope of red roofs. The skyline is dominated by the **Torre Ghirlandina** (open Apr–Oct daily 9.30am–12.30pm, 3–7pm; admission charge), the leaning belltower close to the apse of the cathedral. The ravishing **Duomo** (open daily 7am–noon, 3.30–7pm) on Piazza Grande is one of the earliest Romanesque cathedrals in Italy. Founded by Countess Matilda of Tuscany, ruler of Modena, in 1099, and finished in the 14th century by the Campionese Masters, the pink Verona marble structure is a mirror of the medieval mind, with friezes of saints and monsters, pilgrims and knights, griffons and doves, dragons and deer, fruit and vines. The **Museo del Duomo** (open daily 9.30am–12.30pm, 3.30–6.30pm) contains impressive 12th-century metopes, low reliefs which once surmounted the flying buttresses.

BELOW: children playing outside Modena's Romanesque Duomo.

The cathedral is more than a match for the handsome **Palazzo Comunale** (Town Hall; open Mon–Sat 8am–7pm, Sun 3–7pm) on the far side of the cobbled square. Its austere interior is graced by a superb rood screen, a Romanesque masterpiece depicting scenes from the Passion, supported by Lombardy lions.

Modena's other museums are housed in an ex-arsenal northwest of the Duomo. **Galleria Estense** (open Tues–Sun 8.30am–7.30pm, except Wed, Thur and Sun pm; admission charge) on Piazzale Sant'Agostino houses a rewarding collection of Emilian and Venetian works. Emilia is represented by Parmigianino, Carracci and Guido Reni (14th–17th centuries), while the 15th- and 16th-century Venetian masters include Tintoretto, Veronese and the School of Canaletto. In the same palace is **Biblioteca Estense** (open Mon–Thur 9am–7.15pm, Fri–Sat 9am–1.45pm; admission charge), one of the richest libraries in Italy,

Map on pages 324–325

containing splendid medieval codices, a 1481 edition of Dante's *Divine Comedy* and the *Bible of Borso d'Este*, a 15th-century illuminated work with 1,200 miniatures.

The **Palazzo Ducale** (advance booking only; tel: 059-225671) is proof that the Modenese are as passionate about military life as they are about cars, clothes and food. This severe building was built for Francesco I d'Este in 1634, but since 1862 has been Italy's most prestigious military academy.

Theatrical flourish in Modena.

Hiking country and foggy Ferrara

Bologna ❾, the capital of Emilia Romagna, lies south of Modena and Ferrara, and has a chapter of its own *(see pages 313–19)*. The landscapes of **L'Appennino Tosco-Emiliano** (the Emilian Apennines) ❿, spanning the Emilian–Tuscan border, range from gentle green slopes to deep woods and Alpine crags. With traditional Apennine villages, lakes and mountain crests, it makes for ideal hiking country as well as hang-gliding, skiing and riding. From the Modena area, the Passo delle Radici follows the crest of the hills to Abetone, a noted ski and hiking resort on the Emilian–Tuscan border.

Fiumalbo ⓫, set in the shadow of Monte Cimone in the Modena section of the Apennines, is an inviting base for a rural holiday, in winter or summer. Despite the cluster of historic churches, the appeal of this traditional village resides in its steep, picturesque alleys, flanked by mountain streams. Fiumalbo's quaint setting and rustic Alpine houses provide an antidote to the more commercial charms of bigger neighbouring resorts such as Abetone.

Ferrara ⓬, dominated by the d'Este fortress, often erased by the winter mists, takes pride in its indefinability. Few agree on a definition of *ferraresità*,

BELOW: a farm near Vignola, in Bologna's rural hinterland.

There are over 100,000 bicycles in Ferrara, with special phone boxes created to enable riders to make calls without dismounting. Giorgio Bassani, who set the evocative The Garden of the Finzi-Continis *in Ferrara, used the bicycle as a constant, silent character in his stories of city life.*

the condition of being from Ferrara. To some it is summed up by the frescoed palaces, cobbled streets, fortifications, stone halls and echoing stairways; for others it is allegories and alchemical symbols, black magic and jaded appetites. (Ferrara, supposedly built on major ley lines, vies with Turin as Italy's capital of black magic.) Giorgio de Chirico, the metaphysical artist who immortalised Ferrara Castle, called his city the most mysterious and metaphysical of places.

The cradle of the Renaissance

The d'Este dynasty gained power in the late 13th century but enjoyed a cultural heyday in the Renaissance, when Ferrara became a splendid humanist court, served by Pisanello, Mantegna and Piero della Francesca. Ercole I (1407–1505) remodelled the city on open lines, with broad, palace-lined avenues complemented by a public park, an innovation for the period. Ferrara is often called the first planned Renaissance city, but that is an accolade it shares with tiny Pienza in Tuscany.

The sparkling court at Ferrara came to an end in 1598 when the seat moved to Modena, and the last d'Este duke was deposed by the French in 1796. Yet the legacy lives on in the cuisine: *cappellacci con la zucca*, Parmesan and pumpkin-stuffed ravioli, dates back to the days of the noble court. The Renaissance city also flickers into life in the May *palio*, a race on horseback carried out by the competing *contrade*, the eight historic city districts.

To avoid the perils of swooping cyclists, survey the cathedral from a café terrace on **Piazza del Duomo**. The **Duomo** (open Mon–Sat 7.30am–noon, 3–6.30pm, Sun 7.30am–12.15pm, 4–7.30pm; admission charge), a pink-and-white Romanesque-Gothic edifice, was founded in 1135 and dedicated to St George, the city's patron saint. The highlights are the lilting rhythms of the façade,

BELOW: the cobbled piazzas of Ferrara are often shrouded in winter mists.

the Romanesque sculptures over the main portal, and the Renaissance campanile.

The **Castello Estense** (open Tues–Sun 9.30am–5.30pm; admission charge), the d'Este dynastic seat until 1598, is surrounded by a milky-green moat. The bastion was begun in 1385 and built on a square plan with corner towers and battlements. A sober Gothic courtyard leads to a Renaissance staircase and frescoed rooms.

Map on pages 324–325

Via delle Volte, Ferrara's most characteristic medieval alley.

Palatial living

The Palazzo dei Diamanti (open daily 9am–7pm; admission charge), which commands Corso d'Ercole I d'Este, is named after its blistering marble façade, with a surface covered with more than 12,000 stones, sculpted in the shape of diamonds. Chiaroscuro effects and changes in colour occur as the light shifts throughout the day. The palace was begun in 1493 as a private d'Este home, and finished in 1565. Inside, a picture gallery focuses on the Ferrara and Bolognese schools (13th–18th centuries).

Palazzo Schifanoia (open Tues–Sun 9am–6pm; admission charge), set on Via Scandiana, celebrates the ostentation and carefree extravagance of 15th-century Ferrara. The d'Este designed the palace as a *delizia*, devoted to every whim. The name *Schifanoia* means "avoiding boredom". The Salone dei Mesi (Room of the Months) is frescoed with allegorical tales; the scenes of court life show the Renaissance relish in depicting the pleasures of the senses. The Renaissance **Casa Romei** (open Tues–Sun 8.30am–7.30pm; admission charge), on Via Savonarola, has been the seat of the university since 1963, and is a place where Lucrezia Borgia spent many days. Ferrara's university was founded by the d'Este in 1393 and drew such illustrious students as Paracelsus and Copernicus. **Palazzina Marfisa** (open Tues–Sun 9am–1pm, 3–6pm; admission charge), on Corso Giovecca, the former home of a d'Este noblewoman, houses a mixture of authentic and pastiche frescoes.

Few cities provide such a clear contrast between medieval and Renaissance urban planning. **Via delle Volte**, one of the most characteristic medieval alleys, is a vaulted affair curved into the urban fabric. By contrast, **Corso Ercole I d'Este**, which runs northwards from the castle, is a stern, straight Renaissance avenue. A walk along the city walls, of which there are some 10 km (6 miles), and tree-lined earthworks offers an invigorating overview of the 16th-century fortifications.

BELOW: Ferrara's 14th-century Castello Estense.

The ghetto

Ferrara once had one of the most flourishing Jewish communities in Italy. Unlike the Venetian rulers, the d'Este were noted for their religious tolerance and invited the Jews expelled from Spain in 1492 to settle here. But tolerance came to an abrupt end in 1627 when the Papal States imposed a ghetto, which survived until 1848.

You can take a Jewish trail which includes the ghetto, the synagogue and the Jewish cemetery in Via delle Vigne. On Via Mazzini there is a 700-year-old synagogue, one of the oldest surviving in Italy, and now home to the **Museo Ebraico** (open for guided tours Sun–Thur 10am, 11am and noon; admission charge).

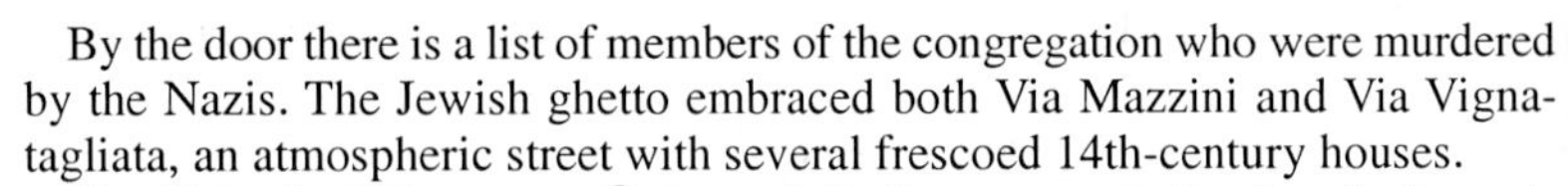

Map on pages 324–325

The fishing villages of Comacchio, Gorino, Goro and Mesola are the springboards for boat trips through the narrow canals to explore the mouth of the Po di Goro and the Valle di Gorino.

By the door there is a list of members of the congregation who were murdered by the Nazis. The Jewish ghetto embraced both Via Mazzini and Via Vignatagliata, an atmospheric street with several frescoed 14th-century houses.

The **Abbazia di Pomposa** ⓭ (open daily 9am–noon, 2–7pm) at Codigoro is an uninhabited Benedictine foundation in a dreamily remote location, strategically placed to allow the monks to control the Ravenna–Pavia route. The prosperous estate embraced medieval forests, salt pans and fishing lagoons. The complex, centred on an 8th-century Byzantine-Romanesque church, is graced by a slender belltower (1063). The monastery, rebuilt in the 14th century but abandoned 200 years later, has a fine refectory and chapter house decorated with School of Giotto frescoes. Near by stands the 11th-century **Palazzo della Ragione**, where the monks once meted out justice to the entire region.

The abbey is part of the mosaic of wetlands known as the **Delta del Po** (Po Delta) ⓮, a marshy wilderness extending north to Venice and south to Ravenna. **Comacchio** ⓯, a miniature Venice built over linked islands, lies deep in the Po Delta and frequently disappears into the mists. For centuries this distinctive fishing village, its fortunes founded on the local salt industry, was isolated from surrounding towns by treacherous marshland. It spans 13 tiny islands, criss-crossed by canals and connected by bridges, and is best explored by boat, easily booked at the quayside.

Comacchio's grandest sight is **Trepponti**, the monumental, triple hump-backed bridge spanning three canals. Beside the quay is the old fish market, a reminder that Comacchio is the Po's capital of eel-fishing. During the autumn, when the mature female eels attempt to rejoin the males in a mass exodus, the fishermen are waiting, as are the watergates that have been in place since Roman times.

BELOW: the Trepponti bridge in Comacchio.

Imola ⓰ is synonymous with racing. As the setting for the **San Marino Grand Prix** the Imola track is the focus of national hopes, particularly if the local Ferrari team is performing well. However, this medieval and Renaissance town also has subtler pleasures in store. South of Via Emilia, the medieval **Rocca** is the most impressive Imola castle. The 18th-century **Duomo** is dedicated to St Cassian, Imola's patron saint, an early victim of student rage: he was cruelly stabbed to death with the pens of his students.

Dozza ⓱, a medieval village set in vineyards near Imola, provides an opportunity to sample the best Emilian wines in a historic castle or local inn. Dozza is celebrated for its Enoteca, a regional wine-tasting centre, located in the restored cellars of Sforza fortress, known as the **Rocca** (open Tues–Sun 10am–noon, 3–6pm). The village is also known for the riotously painted contemporary façades which adorn its gates, doorways and walls.

Faenza, the origin of the word faience, spells ceramics in any language. For more than 500 years this town has produced the blue-and-yellow designs that have brought it international renown. The **Museo delle Ceramiche** (open Tues–Sat 9am–7pm, Sun 9.30am–1pm, 3–7pm; admission charge) on Viale Baccarini contains local majolica as well as Roman, medieval and contemporary designs from around the world. ❑

Pavarotti: Tenor of Tenors

The greatest tenor of his generation has homes in New York, Monte Carlo and Pesaro on the Adriatic coast, but his heart is in Modena, his home town, where he has a rambling estate. Luciano Pavarotti's humble origins are reflected in his name, which means "weaver of straw" in Modenese dialect. Music and football were his passions, as they are still.

As a child he recalls the suffering experienced during World War II by his family, who fled to the countryside to escape the bombing. He vividly remembers seeing in Modena the bodies of Italian partisans, murdered by the Nazis: "Every night masked men would come to your house to look for food, and to see if you harboured partisans. For every German killed, 10 Italians were hanged."

Pavarotti, renowned for his *bel canto* voice, regularly sang with José Carreras and Plácido Domingo as one of "The Three Tenors". Startlingly, he attributes his singing technique to his wet-nurse, who breastfed both him and the accomplished soprano Mirella Freni. As a five-year-old he was singing "*La donna è mobile*" for sweets, but his career was only launched with the winning of a Welsh choral competition.

Pavarotti attributes the length of his career to his late father, who continued to sing and record in his eighties, and his musical gift to the female members of his family: "I probably owe my way of singing to them – the lyricism, the softness, the affection." His agent describes his appeal differently: "When you leave a Pavarotti performance, he's given you something... he doesn't leave you unaffected; and in addition to his artistry, he's fearless."

One of the highlights of Pavarotti's career was singing in Verdi's *Requiem* at La Scala in 1967 in honour of the centenary of Toscanini's birth. The conductor Herbert von Karajan declared that Pavarotti's vocal chords had been touched by God. Yet Pavarotti, a blatant populist, is as happy singing Neapolitan love duets or crooning with international rock stars such as Sting and Tina Turner.

In 1998 Pavarotti staged his usual charity concert in Modena, to raise funds for the Bosnian city of Mostar: "My roots are in Modena, so that's why I wanted to create a big international event there."

A connection is often made between the bulkiness of "Big Lucy" and the food in his home region of Emilia Romagna, considered the best cuisine in Italy. Certainly he remains close to the earthy cuisine of Modena and adores feeding the visitors who flock to his charity concerts. Critics complain that his vocal powers are diminishing, but Pavarotti is sanguine about the future.

Pavarotti began a farewell tour in 2005, but was forced to cancel dates because of illness and back injury. In 2006 he was diagnosed with pancreatic cancer and required emergency surgery. His remaining appearances were cancelled because of ongoing treatment, and it is anticipated that his farewell tour will resume in 2007. ❑

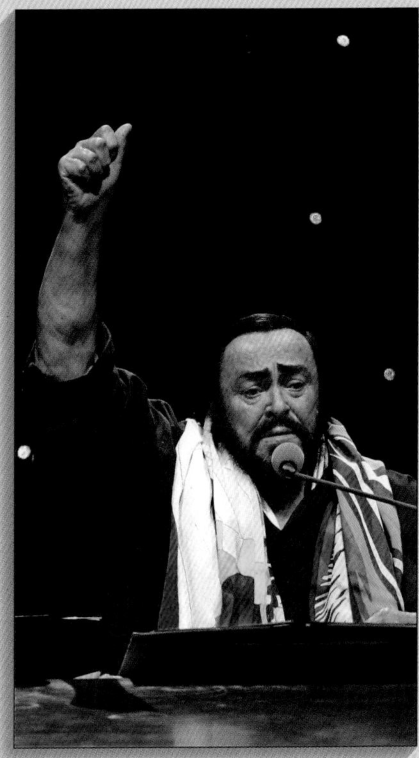

RIGHT: Modena-born Luciano Pavarotti, performing in Australia during his worldwide Farewell Tour.

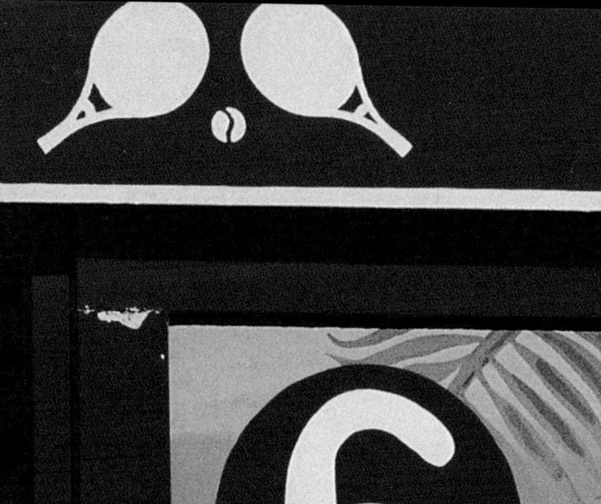
6

SQUALOSKA·195L

THE ADRIATIC

Beach culture meets Byzantine ruins in this curious and eclectic coastal region of smart resorts and secretive lagoons

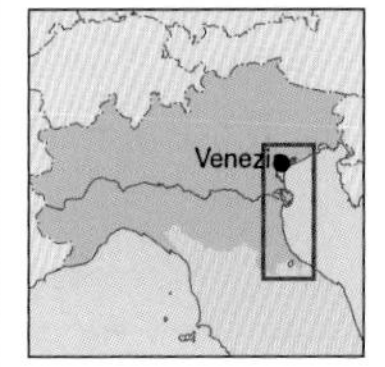

The Adriatic may be in Emilia Romagna, but the people are robust Romagnoli rather than smooth Emiliani, with a different history, culture and cuisine. They embody classic Italian attributes: Mediterranean values and an oriental past grafted onto a northern European culture. Culturally, a sense of ancient glory lingers on in Ravenna, the point of entry for the Eastern Roman Empire. Here and elsewhere linger echoes of Greek, Roman and Byzantine civilisations. Ravenna and Rimini, the main cities, are both of Roman foundation, if buried under layers of medieval brick. Romagna, too, had its great medieval and Renaissance dynasties: the Malatesta in Rimini once rivalled the d'Este in Ferrara. While Rimini was the first chic bathing establishment, the mass-tourism boom of the 1960s and 1970s put an end to any pretence that the coast was for the privileged few: the Adriatic was now one of Europe's most popular summer spots. Nowadays it is fashionable to dismiss the Adriatic resorts as depositories for tasteless Euro-trash, yet just as the local cuisine blends bourgeois and peasant styles, so the resorts appeal to aficionados of Byzantine art and to package holidaymakers, who are often one and the same.

PRECEDING PAGES: the Adriatic coast has a certain brash charm.
LEFT: Goro harbour.
BELOW: the beach at Rimini.

The Adriatic coast caters to all tastes, with sprawling, mass-market resorts in the south, and smaller, more exclusive ones sheltered by pine groves in the north. Yet if Rimini and Cattolica conform to the popular idea of a full-frontal beach holiday, the northerly Lido di Jesolo is proof that even the prim Venetians can provide downmarket fun, from trashy souvenir shops to family beach games and riotous clubs. More typical of the north coast are small, discreet bays fringed by pines and bounded by lagoons.

In the same way, the south is not without its sophisticated resorts: Riccione has a marble-clad pedestrian zone, packed with designer shops. This chapter covers the Adriatic coast from Chioggia to Rimini, although a few of the most northerly resorts are technically in the Veneto.

The Venetian coast

Eraclea Mare ❶, north of Venice, is set amid pine groves beside the Piave estuary. A peaceful family-oriented resort, it provides pale sandy beaches and the opportunity for riding trips deep into the estuary and lagoon area. Set just off the road to Jesolo, Venice and Padua, Eraclea could also be a base for more cultural tourism.

Lido di Jesolo ❷, marking the northern entrance to the Venetian lagoon, is the largest seaside resort in the Veneto. Dominated by package tourism, Jesolo satisfies the ice cream, pizza and parasol brigades. In addition the resort provides a good range of sports facilities, from riding to golf and tennis. Although

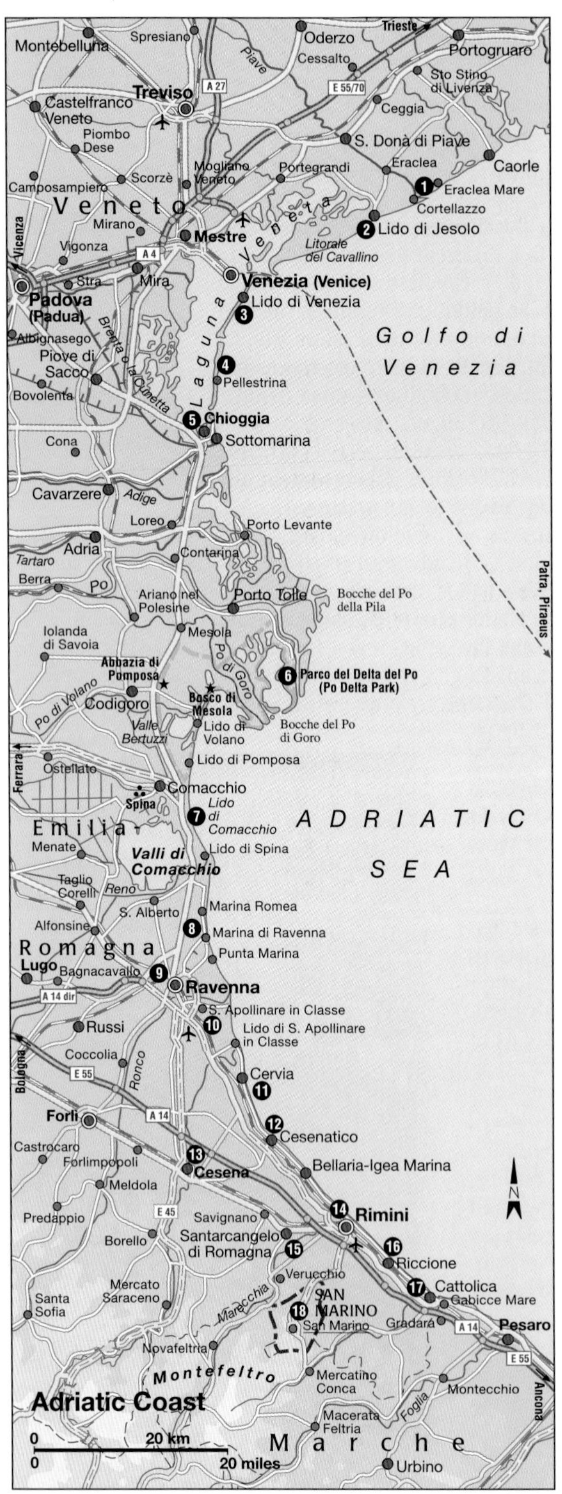

bland, it makes an acceptable base for visitors wishing to combine a beach holiday with cultural day trips to Venice. Among young Italians, Jesolo is synonymous with summer nightlife.

On sultry evenings the roads between Jesolo and Venice are full of young Venetians fleeing their claustrophobic culture for the vibrant coastal clubs.

Lido di Venezia ❸, better-known as Il Lido, is Venice's access to the beach. The long sandy shores are easily reached by boat from the historic heart of the city. The Lido has been a fashionable resort since the 1840s, when the cult for sea-bathing began. Today it makes an ideal base for family holidays; hotels generally have access to a private beach, and rooms are more spacious and less expensive than in Venice.

Pellestrina ❹, which protects Venice from the sea, is a narrow sliver of land stretching into the silvery-grey lagoon, forming a natural barrier enforced by the Murazzi, the giant sea walls, and thus saving Venice from periodic flooding. The island is a haunt of sunbathing Venetians and solitary walkers, with a quaint fishing village, gossipy bars and brightly coloured cottages. As part of the dyke which preserves Venice for the generations to come, Pellestrina plays an essential role in the Adriatic sea defences. (From Venice, the island is best reached from the Lido, with bus 11 to Alberoni connecting with the ferry for a five-minute boat ride to Pellestrina.)

Chioggia ❺, a bustling workaday fishing port, closes the Venetian lagoon to the south. The port is easily accessible from the lagoon city, or even by bicycle from the Lido. Chioggia covers two parallel islands and is often called a Venice in miniature, thanks to its historic heart criss-crossed by canals. The Roman port rose to prominence as the guardian of the river route to Padua, and as a self-governing medieval city it developed a lucrative salt-extraction industry. After this industry collapsed, Chioggia concentrated on fishing, a vocation it retains today. The port is noted for its boats: the *tartana*, an early type of trawler, and its colourful successor, the flat-bottomed *bragozzo*, suitable for fishing in the shallow lagoon waters. The trapezoid sail is decorated with heraldic, religious or family devices, from lions and compasses to madonnas and nicknames.

Visiting the bustling quaysides, painted fishing boats and the Granaio fish market, followed by an inevitably fishy lunch in restaurants considerably better and more reasonably priced than their grander Venetian counterparts, is the chief enjoyment. Chioggia's beaches lie 10 km (6 miles) down the coast at **Isolaverde** and **Sottomarina**.

The north coast: discreet lagoon resorts

From Chioggia to Ravenna the coast skirts the curious landscape of lagoons and marshland that characterises the Po Delta, the **Parco del Delta del Po** ❻. From the north the SS309, the main coastal road, follows Via Romea, the old Roman road, to the haunting Pomposa Abbey. En route, it passes the Mesola nature reserve, the **Gran Bosco della Mesola**, a thicket of holm oak, ash, elm and holly, with red deer roaming the forest glades. There were once deep forests covering the coastal strip between Ferrara and Ravenna, but these have dwindled dramatically. The forest, a d'Este hunting estate since 1490, remained in dynastic hands until 1758.

Just east are the **Bosco di Mesola** botanical gardens, full of indigenous marsh and woodland plants. Further inland is the crenellated **Castello di Mesola** (open Tues–Sat 9am–noon, 3–6pm; admission charge), one of the few d'Este castles secreted away in the Po marshes. Built in 1583, this pleasure palace was linked to sophisticated marshland drainage works, but the advantage of the locks and

TIP

Despite Chioggia's fine sands, you may prefer to swim further south, a fair distance from the polluted Venetian lagoon.

BELOW: risotto, a local speciality.

The Po Delta

The Po Delta is one of Italy's most important wetlands and a birdwatcher's paradise. This mosaic of marshes, dunes, mudflats and islands is called the Italian Camargue. Indeed, sturdy white Camargue ponies and bulls have been introduced successfully to the region. The Po, Italy's longest river, crosses Piacenza, Ferrara and Ravenna, splitting into streams and channels in the delta, with only one of its 14 mouths navigable. The delta extends 100 km (60 miles) from north to south and is dotted with nature reserves which are easily reached from the coast or inland area.

East of Ferrara the Po gradually disappears into a labyrinth of lagoons called *valli*, fishing lakes where eels begin their migration back to the Sargasso Sea. The Valli di Comacchio were formed in the medieval period when the area around the Po Delta subsided, creating a cluster of marshy valleys. Medieval monks introduced sophisticated drainage schemes before the d'Este Dukes of Ferrara appropriated the land and began their own reclamation schemes. Their initial success was reversed by both land subsidence and the engineering works of the Venetians, who diverted the course of the Po to prevent their own city from silting up.

With the advent of steam machinery in the early 19th century, mechanical drainage schemes led to a significant reduction in the marshland, thus shaping the present shallow salty landscape. In the 1950s, parts of the marshes were again drained to satisfy the demand for farming land, and a few roads were built. Farmers are constantly pushing for more marshland to be released, but ecologists are currently winning the battle to preserve the existing wetlands.

The area acts as a magnet for migratory birds since it is a key staging post on the route from Africa to Central Europe. Parts of the delta have been declared reserves, where birds can be seen in their natural habitats. The river-lagoon setting, with its expanse of mudflats and marshes, proves a welcoming environment for waterfowl, especially the native shelduck, with its distinctive black and brown markings. Among the bird-life are bean geese, greyish geese with yellow legs and bills, and greylag geese, distinguished by their pink legs. Reed warblers, bearded tits and purple herons are also common, as are gulls and terns, with coots and black terns congregating on the marshes in winter. More persistent birdwatchers may be rewarded with sightings of white egrets and curlew sandpipers, or great crested grebes building their nests on the banks. Apart from extensive oyster beds and the local eels, fishing focuses on sea bass, carp, grey mullet, flounder, tench and pike. The distinctive tree-toad is found wherever there is a profusion of cane, shrubs or trees.

Today the salty wetlands still preserve a number of *casoni*, fishing huts on stilts, some now the private retreats of Milanese industrialists. Visitors come here for the wildlife and the solitude: one can still walk or cycle along the banks of the fishing lakes without coming across another soul. ❑

LEFT: medieval monks were the first to realise the agricultural potential of the Po Delta marshes.

irrigation channels was nullified when the Venetians created a canal to stop their city silting up, thereby causing the Mesola area to silt up instead.

The villages on the sandy coast around Comacchio were formerly fishing settlements but in recent years resemble more closely simple resorts on the margins of life. Collectively known as the **Lidi di Comacchio** ❼, these resorts are strung out along the coast, stretching from Lido di Volano to the bigger and better-equipped resorts of Lido delle Nazione and Porto Garbaldi. All tend to present their public faces to the sea but turn their private faces to the lagoons that skirt the shore. The vineyards by the adjoining **Valli di Comacchio** fishing lakes were planted by Renata of France, who married into the d'Este dynasty in 1528. Her Burgundian wine is considered the only red wine suitable for accompanying local fish or eel dishes.

Lago delle Nazioni, the saltwater lake just inland from the Lido di Volano, provides extensive mullet and eel fishing. In summer the lake is also popular with sailors and water-skiers, and organised boat trips are run to explore the flora and fauna: the local marshes abound in swamp orchids and medicinal plants, with the reed-beds home to grebes, mallards and kingfishers. Bulls and Camargue Delta horses are bred on a neighbouring stud farm and seem to adapt perfectly to life on the marshes.

Map on page 340

One romantic who preferred lagoons to beaches was Giorgio Bassani, resident of Ferrara and author of the atmospheric "Garden of the Finzi-Conti". He regularly sought inspiration in the gentle water-scape of the delta.

Umbrellas and pines

Porto Garibaldi, just south of Comacchio, is the busiest, most established resort, a former fishing village dominated by water sports and lines of beach umbrellas. The name recalls Garibaldi's foiled guerrilla exploits and his flight in 1849 from Austrian pursuit, which led to the death of his pregnant wife.

Gently sloping beaches, interspersed with pine woods, stretch south from Porto Garibaldi to bustling Lido degli Estensi and exclusive **Lido di Spina**, with chic villas tucked into the pinewoods. Behind the dunes of Lido di Spina lie a lagoon and a nature reserve with considerable appeal to birdwatchers: in **Vene di Bellochio**, a population of coots, curlews, teals and marsh harriers appreciates the setting of sea lavender, dunes, reeds and rushes.

The Greco-Etruscan necropolis at **Spina**, just west of Comacchio, was discovered by chance during the drainage programmes of the 1950s. The finds, essentially funerary stelae and tomb furniture dating from 6 BC to the 3rd century AD, are now on display in Ferrara's archaeology museum. Those craving solitude may decide to shun the shore in favour of the lagoons. For those who look, there are still reed-cutters, skimming the surface in flat-bottomed boats, cantilevered fishing nets and *casoni*, the green-shuttered fishing huts on stilts.

Towards Ravenna the coastline is characterised by *pinete*, waving lines of umbrella pines as neat as beach umbrellas, framing greyish-green scudding seas. **Marina di Ravenna** ❽ is a well-established resort, with a wide beach, busy harbour, pine groves and sand dunes. The adjoining **Porto Cassini** is a good walking destination, with its 5 km (3 mile) dam that hugs the harbour. **Marina Romea**, just north, is one of the

BELOW: locally caught fish for sale at Comacchio.

TIP

Try the specialities of the coastal stretch: pasta-filled soups and grilled meats, including lamb and pork served with grilled courgettes or aubergines.

smartest resorts, with a pleasant harbour and paths winding through the pine groves. On sultry summer evenings, most strolls lead to *gelaterie* (ice-cream parlours) and cosy trattorias.

Byzantine time capsule

Ravenna ❾ was the last enclave of the Roman Empire in the West. At first sight, it seems like a provincial town that just happens to contain the world's greatest mosaics. Like Venice, Ravenna, which dates from 2 BC, was built on a series of islands in a lagoon. It was colonised by the Romans and, thanks to its strategic importance, proclaimed capital of the Western Roman Empire in 402. In the 5th and 6th centuries Roman and Byzantine cultures converged in Ravenna and bequeathed the city superb mosaics, transforming it into a luminous western Byzantium. Despite declining fortunes, and the silting up of the port, it remained prosperous during the Middle Ages and provided a refuge for Dante Alighieri, the great 14th-century Florentine poet. The city came under Venetian domination in the 15th century, and was controlled by the Venetians or the Papacy until 1859. Since the 1950s exploitation of offshore gas, the creation of a new port and chemical industries and the development of the coastal resorts, Ravenna has become a boom city once more.

Pieces of a mosaic

Ravenna's legacy is the sensuous melding of classical art and spirituality in a dazzling array of basilicas, baptistries and mausoleums. Dante described Ravenna's mosaics as the "sweet colour of oriental sapphires". As the mainspring of early Christian art, the mosaics acted as a poor man's Bible, illuminating the

BELOW: an early-Byzantine mosaic at Sant'Apollinare Nuovo shows Christ calling the fishermen Peter and Andrew to be his Apostles.

Scriptures by means of iconic images and stylised figures set against a gold background. They use such images as the drinking doves, symbolising the soul sipping from the fountain of eternal life. The early mosaicists were probably Greek artists from the court of Constantinople. These lustrous interiors were partly inspired by the memory of pagan temples, partly by the sense of awe provoked by the Gospels. As with all great art, the mosaics represent man's supreme striving for the absolute. Every Friday in summer the mosaics in the basilicas are open to the public until midnight, as are the mosaic shops.

The **Basilica di San Vitale** (open Apr–Sept daily 9am–7pm, Fri–Sat also 9–11.30pm, Oct–Mar until 4.30pm; combined ticket with next three sites), Ravenna's greatest monument, dates from the first half of the 6th century, the period of Byzantine conquest. The mosaics are sometimes seen as the summation of Roman culture, the last great flowering of art in the ancient world, but they can equally be seen as the first flowering of Christian art. The octagonal basilica is itself a masterpiece, a gabled, galleried brick building surmounted by a cupola, which has been dubbed the last building born of the Roman tradition and the first of the Romanesque. The highly decorated mosaics depict the court of Emperor Justinian I. They are characterised by a rich palette of blues and greens, from flowers and fields to sky and the glittering grandeur of the figures. The scriptural scenes illuminate Byzantine symbolism in a bold expanse of golden sky.

Beside the basilica stands the **Mausoleo di Galla Placidia** (open Apr–Sept, daily 9am–7pm, Oct–Mar, until 4.30pm), a mausoleum dedicated to Galla Placidia, the Christian half-sister of Honorius (the emperor who transferred the capital to Ravenna in 402), despite the fact that she is buried in Rome. This is

Map on page 340

The Basilica di San Vitale.

BELOW: a procession of virgins, Sant' Apollinare Nuovo.

generally agreed to be home to Italy's most beautiful 5th-century mosaics. Built between 425 and 450, it is bathed in green light which becomes aquamarine higher up the walls. The mystical atmosphere is intensified by the strikingly simple style of the mosaics, including the cobalt-blue sky sprinkled with gold stars. Despite the simple Christian iconography, the realism of the figures reflects the naturalistic Roman style as much as a nascent Christian one.

The vivid mosaics of Sant'Apollinare Nuovo inspired the Austrian artist Gustav Klimt (1862–1918), while the cobalt-blue sky and gold star mosaics in the Mausoleo di Galla Placidia are said to have inspired Cole Porter to write his classic song Night and Day.

Sant'Apollinare Nuovo (open daily, Apr–Sept 9am–7pm, Oct–Mar 9am–noon, 2–5pm), flanked by a cylindrical belltower, was built between 493 and 496. The mosaics in the palatine church depict a stately procession of martyrs and virgins and show the transition from naturalistic Hellenistic-Roman art to the more stylised tendencies of Byzantine artistry. Opposite stands the basilica of **San Giovanni Evangelista** (hours as above), with a sculpted marble portal. Dating from the 5th century but much altered, it was built by Galla Placidia. Legend has it that she had vowed to build the church in return for surviving a shipwreck on a voyage from Constantinople.

Further on, outside the centre, looms **Rocca di Brancaleone** (open 9am–7pm; admission charge), a Venetian fortress and one of the locations of the Ravenna Jazz Festival. Isolated in the greenery is the **Mausoleo di Teodorico** (open 8.30am–7pm) a curious Romanesque construction with Syrian and Nordic influences. It was built in 520 by Theodoric the Great, who designed it as his own mausoleum. Other superb buildings are the **Oratorio di Sant'Andrea**, covered in splendid mosaics, and the 5th-century **Battistero Neoniani**, with a frescoed cupola.

Despite being buried under the weight of its glittering mosaics, Ravenna struggles to retain its personality as a proud provincial town. The central **Piazza del Popolo** is lined with dignified 15th-century buildings built under Venetian rule. The **Duomo** was founded in the 5th century, but the lasting impression of it is of the bold Baroque façade.

BELOW: the Basilica di San Vitale dates from the first half of the 6th century.

Zona Dantesca, a slightly clinical quarter, honours Dante, who lived in Ravenna between 1317 and 1321. Exiled from Florence for political reasons, Dante completed *The Divine Comedy* in the city and is buried in the adjoining church of **San Francesco** (access to Dante's tomb: summer, 9am–7pm, winter, 9am–noon, 2–5pm). This 5th-century building was remodelled in chilly Neoclassical style and over-restored in the 1920s. In summer, classical concerts enliven the Franciscan cloisters, as do readings of Dante's works.

The city's cultural highlight, however, is the **Ravenna Festival**, a summer jamboree of symphony concerts, opera, ballet and organ recitals which attracts top conductors, from Claudio Abbado to Riccardo Muti. A number of these concerts are held outdoors or take advantage of settings in the Byzantine basilicas.

Sant'Apollinare in Classe ❿ (open Mon–Sat 8.30am–7.30pm, Sun 1–7.30pm; admission charge), set 5 km (3 miles) south, is a basilica of Byzantine mosaics dating from AD 533. The striking cylindrical belltower is one of the symbols of Ravenna. Visitors wishing to learn more about the art of mosaics could try one of the many courses on offer in the city; those more interested in buying can visit the shops selling hand-crafted modern mosaics or reproductions of the greatest Byzantine masters.

The southern coast: salt, sun and seafood

Although the Adriatic coast has been heavily commercialised, garden suburbs, tree-lined avenues, sandy beaches and trails through the pine groves are compensation for regrettable concrete strips. **Milano-Marittima** is a fashionable resort for young people, with packed beaches and popular cafés. By contrast, **Cervia ⓫**, just south, is a family-oriented resort, known for salt extraction since Etruscan times. As well as the salt flats and the surviving industry, the town still retains its 18th-century salt warehouses. Known as **Maggazzini del Sale**, these include a small museum in a salt tower dedicated to the "white gold" itself.

Southwest of Cervia is the **Riserva Naturale delle Saline di Cervia**, a complex of salt works encircled by a canal. The neighbouring **Terme di Cervia** health spa treats arthritis and other complaints with mud treatments.

Cesenatico ⓬ has long combined fishing and tourism, and the family-minded resort has proved particularly popular with German holidaymakers. The historic heart is centred on the harbour and canal, the **Darsena** and **Portocanale Leonardesco**. The canal was created in 1302 but redesigned by Leonardo da Vinci in 1502. Its right bank, lined with pastel-coloured merchants' houses, is a popular place for a stroll, while the left bank, dotted with fishermen's cottages, has some good seafood inns. **Piazza delle Conserve**, just off the canal, is also home to a bustling fish market and seafood restaurants, but more striking are the cone-shaped underground ice chambers where fish were stored in the days before refrigeration. The **Marineria** (Maritime Museum) (admission charge) displays a collection of Adriatic fishing boats with bold sails and hulls. The 7-km (4-mile) sandy beach provides well-organised activities, from cycling through the pine groves to boating, fishing and volleyball.

The only surviving building of Classe, Ravenna's ancient port, is the Basilica di Sant'Apollinare. Many mosaics have been uncovered during excavations at Classe, and it is expected that the project will yield more extraordinary finds, ranking it alongside the largest archaeological sites in Italy.

BELOW: the historic heart of Cesenatico.

Where life's a beach.

Cesenatico's well-deserved reputation as a gastronomic centre means that the best fish restaurants are generally full. Cuttlefish, squid, lobster, sea perch and mackerel are all on offer. The seafront is lined with seafood restaurants, while the inns in the Cesenatico hinterland tend to be the preserve of country cooking and grilled meats. Regional meals are generally accompanied by Sangiovese red, straw-coloured Trebbiano or crisp white Albana wines.

Cesena ⓭, a mere 12 km (7 miles) from Cesenatico, makes a pleasant excursion into the hinterland. The profusion of seasonal fruit is a reminder that the town is one of the main exporters of strawberries and peaches. Apart from a cathedral with Romanesque traces, Cesena is proud of its 14th-century castle **Rocca Malatestiana** (open Mar–Nov Tues–Sun 9.30am–12.30pm, 3–7pm) and magnificent **Malatesta Renaissance Library** (open Mon–Sat 9am–12.30pm, 3–6pm, Sun 10am–12.30pm). In lofty Madonna del Monte, the 15th-century sanctuary overlooking the town, Benedictine monks diligently restore manuscripts and antiquarian books.

Capital of the Riviera

As Europe's biggest beach resort, **Rimini** ⓮ has been dedicated to tourism since 1830, when the Italian Riviera began to be developed in response to the new fashion for sea-bathing. The vast beach is one of the safest in Europe, with motor craft banned within 500 metres (545 yards) of the shore. However, Rimini's role as unofficial capital of the Riviera has overshadowed its considerable artistic heritage. It was founded by the Romans in AD 268 and prospered as a Malatesta fiefdom from the 13th century onwards. There are distinctive Roman and Renaissance monuments, even if most visitors are only drawn to the seafront

BELOW: a Rimini beach lifeguard.

Map on page 340

and tree-lined promenades. Rimini forms two distinct entities, contrasting the quiet historic centre with the bustling coastal strip.

Borgo di San Giuliano, set at the landward end of Porto Canale, is a fishermen's quarter of quaint cottages and medieval alleyways. Here, too, is Ponte Tiberio, the best-preserved of the Roman bridges built in the first century AD, with a view of the park and the hills stretching into the distance. From here Corso d'Augusto leads to the historic centre and **Piazza Cavour**, which is flanked by old palaces, including the 14th-century Palazzo del Podestà, and an arcaded 18th-century fish market. With an attractive cluster of cafés and bars, Piazza Tre Martiri, built over the old Roman forum, is a favourite city meeting-place. Just west towers the **Arco d'Augusto**, a Roman arch erected in honour of Augustus in 27 BC.

South of Piazza Tre Martiri stands the **Tempio Malatestiano** (open Mon–Sat 8am–12.30pm, 3.30–7pm, Sun 9am–1pm, 3.30–7pm; free), the city's most celebrated monument. Sigismondo Malatesta (1417–68), the notorious ruler of Rimini, commissioned this Renaissance gem from Leon Battista Alberti, the great Florentine architect. The Gothic church of San Francesco was remodelled as the embodiment of Renaissance architectural values. The interior houses the Malatesta tomb as well as works of art by Piero della Francesca, Duccio and Giotto. Ostensibly designed as a chapel, the building became a monument to the debauched Malatesta himself. Given the man's evil reputation, combined with the bacchanalian scenes depicted within, Pope Pius II declared it "a temple of devil-worshippers" and had an effigy of Malatesta burned on the street.

The beaches, which stretch for almost 15 km (9 miles), are crowded but well-groomed and clean, with the sea regularly monitored for pollution. Facilities

BELOW: master film director, Federico Fellini.

FEDERICO FELLINI

Italian film directors are particularly influenced by their environments, and Federico Fellini (1920–93), who was born and raised in Rimini, was no exception. His Oscar-winning *Amarcord* (1974), one of the seminal films of the 1970s and perhaps his most popular and accessible work, turned Rimini into a virtual reality world. It was sweet revenge on the "inert, provincial, opaque, dull" Adriatic seaside resort he left in search of Roman chic. Through his central character in *Amarcord*, a young boy called Titta, Felllini explored his own youth and rites of passage.

He first gained popular and critical acclaim in Britain and the US in 1959 with *La Dolce Vita*, which starred Marcello Mastroianni, Italy's leading actor. He described his films as "a marriage of innocence and experience". The Adriatic was always a reference point for Fellini: in a sense it was his canvas, even if he recreated his boyhood city far away, in the Cinecittà studios in Rome. For more information contact the Fellini Association (Via Angherà, 22, tel: 0541-50085).

Inaugurated in 2003, the little Museo Fellini (Via Clementini 2; open Tues–Fri 4–7pm, Sat–Sun 10am–noon, 4–7pm; tel: 0541-50085) celebrates this late, but very great director.

include beach volleyball, paddle-boats, a windsurfing school and the Rovazzurra theme park. A seafront *passeggiata* around the marina and down Viale Vespucci is a nightly ritual for many visitors. Diners can sample clams or sea snails *(lumache di mare)*, two of the local specialities. Fans of Federico Fellini may call in on the **Grand Hotel** (1908), the Adriatic's most historic hostelry. Fellini used the place as a backdrop for various films, including *Amarcord* *(see previous page)*. This eclectic hotel is one of the few along the coast that can equal the grandest on the French Riviera.

TIP

In summer a shuttle bus connects all the Rimini nightclubs, while the Treno Azzurro ferries clubbers between Rimini and Cattolica.

Around Rimini

Santarcangelo di Romagna ⓯, west of Rimini, is a walled hilltop town with a historic castle, curious caves and a welcoming atmosphere. This erstwhile Roman settlement became a Malatesta fiefdom in the 13th century, only to be ceded to the Montefeltro clan in 1462, and to pass swiftly from Borgia and Venetian rule to the Papal States in 1505. The pretty medieval nucleus is a warren of alleys, steeply raked steps and picturesque window boxes framed against weather-beaten walls. The core of the town is the **Rocca**, the medieval fortress remodelled by Malatesta in 1447 and protected by medieval gates. Carved into the rock are ancient grottoes once used as refuges, wine cellars and possibly even tombs.

Once back on the coastal strip south of Rimini, sophisticated beach-lovers are drawn to the distinguished resort of **Riccione** ⓰. Built on a chessboard pattern, the resort combines pleasant garden suburbs and villas with beach life. Riccione, formerly a smart Edwardian resort, likes to reinvent itself. Traditionally at the forefront of fashion, it was the first Italian city to popularise the miniskirt and topless bathing, the first to welcome gay couples, the first to promote water parks. **Aquafàn** (open June–mid-Sept daily 10am–6.30pm; discos at night; admission charge; tel: 0541-603050) is the most famous of these.

Certainly Riccione has little interest in attracting mainstream package tourism, preferring to cultivate a faithful Italian clientele, many of whom are second-home owners from Bologna. The upmarket pedestrian zone of Viale Ceccarini cossets visitors with designer shops, background music, fresh flowers and invitations to stop for leisurely seafood suppers.

Cattolica ⓱ enjoys a sheltered climate, with the resort set in the lee of the hills. As the fastest-expanding resort in this area it prides itself on its pragmatic approach to tourism, specialising in inexpensive package holidays for young couples or families. Cattolica is also the Adriatic resort that attracts the highest number of non-Italian visitors, primarily Germans, Britons and Scandinavians.

Despite its somewhat bland image, the resort provides an acceptable base for exploring the art cities of southern Emilia Romagna. Its attractions include the lively summer nightlife, the pier of Punto Verde, and the medieval villages tucked into the hinterland. Cattolica is a border town, serving as a gateway to the Marche region and to the quaint principality of San Marino *(see facing page)*. ❑

BELOW: Rimini's Grand Hotel – one of the finest on the coast.

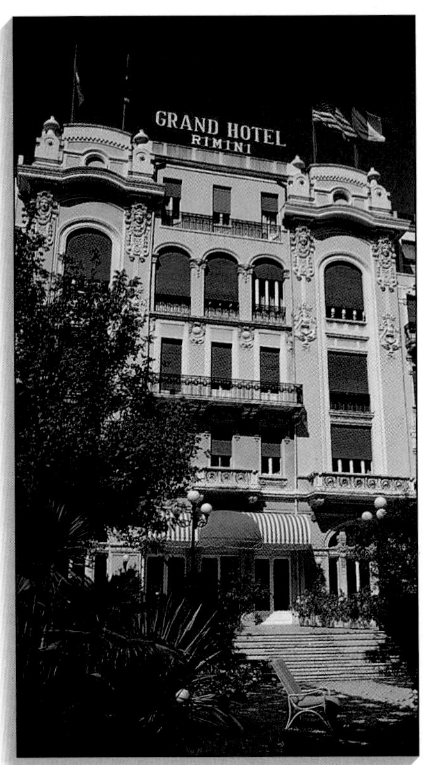

San Marino, Toytown State

On the motorway outside Europe's oldest and smallest republic a sign says: "Welcome to the Republic of San Marino, land of freedom." Founded by St Marinus, patron saint of freedom, **San Marino** ⓲ encompasses 61 sq. km (23½ sq. miles) of tax-free terrain. The 26,000 inhabitants of this independent city state survive on the proceeds of sales from perfumes, stamps, ceramics and duty-free wine.

According to legend, the Republic was founded by a Dalmatian stone-cutter who had fled persecution from Emperor Diocletian in AD 301, only to end up establishing a duty-free haven on the inhospitable slopes of Monte Titano. Thanks to San Marino's tax-free status the state coffers are suitably full, with stamp-collecting representing 10 percent of all revenues. The state prides itself on having given the world its first postal service, in 1607, but, as with all such mini-states, the stamps are grander than the territory.

Although paranoia is rife in this antiquated 700-year-old political system, tyranny is unlikely. The Republic is governed by two regents from opposing parties so that they can keep an eye on one another; these joint heads of state are only in office for six months, so they have no time to build up personal power bases. Moreover, any citizen is legally entitled to make an official complaint about a regent's conduct, and judicial proceedings may be instigated as a result. Citizens are fully involved in political life and have the most assiduous voting record in Europe.

On 3 September the Sammarinesi citizens celebrate the foundation of the Republic with a crossbow competition and a game of bingo. The Museo delle Armi Moderne in Contrada della Pieve has a plethora of crossbows.

San Marino fields a "national" football team, conducts its own foreign policy, and has a seat at the United Nations and a centuries-old tradition of neutrality. Peace was only recently concluded with Sweden; until then San Marino had officially been on a war footing after neglecting to sign the Peace of Westphalia in 1648. However, according to a Swedish diplomat, Scandinavian citizens in San Marino need not be concerned: "There are only six or eight of them left, mostly ladies married to locals. They're certainly not prisoners of war." San Marino insists that it has not been to war since 1462, when it did battle with the Malatesta dynasty in Rimini. But for such a pacific state San Marino is inordinately keen on arms. The Republic sells such arcane weaponry as muskets, halberds and arquebuses, although simple Korean bayonets are also on sale in the shops. You can get a trophy stamp in your passport for a modest fee.

The Sammarinesi equate personal profit with the prosperity of the state; even the Franciscan monks sell a sickly liqueur to the unsuspecting public. Most visitors to San Marino succumb to a sheet of stamps or sweet Moscato wine. The more adventurous can buy arquebuses and crossbows or Korean bayonets, if they can face the furore at international departures. ❑

RIGHT: the citadel of San Marino.
OVERLEAF: Portofino.

INSIGHT GUIDES

Travel Tips

First to Fly A3
in 2006
In this ever changing world,
Singapore Girl, you're a great way to fly.
SINGAPORE AIRLINES
A STAR ALLIANCE MEMBER
singaporeair.co
BANGKOK · TOKYO · AMSTERDAM · AUCKLAND · NEW DELHI · LOS ANGELES · OVER 55 MAJOR CIT

CONTENTS

Getting Acquainted

The Place 354
Geography.................. 354
Climate 354
Government 354
Economy.................... 354

Planning the Trip

Visas and Passports .. 354
Money Matters 354
What to Wear.............. 355
Tourist Offices 355
Getting There 355
Customs Regulations.. 355
Animal Quarantine...... 355
Public Holidays 356
The Orient Express 356
Car Trains 357
Package Tours............ 357

Practical Tips

Business Hours 357
Tipping 357
Media 357
Postal Services 358
Telephone 358
Area Codes 358
Calling Home 358
Local Tourist Offices.... 358
Consulates.................. 359
Medical Services 359
Security and Crime 359
Women Travellers 359
Personal Security........ 359

Getting Around

By Air 359
By Rail 359
By Coach.................... 360
Ferries and Hydrofoils 360
In Milan...................... 360
In Venice 360
The Lakes 361
Milan Metro map........ 361
Taxis 361
Private Transport........ 362
Driving Speeds 362

Where to Stay

Choosing a Hotel 362
Venice Hotels 362
Hotel Groups 364
Veneto........................ 365
Friuli-Venezia Giulia.... 365
Trentino-Alto Adige 365
Milan.......................... 366
Lombardy 367
Valle d'Aosta 368
Piedmont.................... 368
The Lakes 369
Liguria & Riviera 370
Emilia Romagna 371
San Marino 371
The Adriatic................ 371

Where to Eat

What to Eat 372
Restaurant Listings......372
Venice........................ 372
Veneto........................ 374
Friuli-Venezia Giulia.... 374
Trentino-Alto Adige 374
Milan.......................... 375
Lombardy 376
Valle d'Aosta 376
Piedmont.................... 376
The Lakes 377
Liguria & Riviera 378
Emilia Romagna 378
San Marino 379
The Adriatic................ 379

Culture

Music 379
Theatres 380

Nightlife

Late Spots.................. 381

Festivals

Special Events............ 381
Calendar 381

Outdoor Activities

National Parks 382
The Alps 382

Sport

Spectator Sports 383
Other Sports 383

Shopping

Shopping Areas 384
Clothing Size Chart 384

Language

Language Tips............ 384
Basic Communication 384
Pronunciation &
Grammar................ 386
Menu Decoder............ 386
At the Shops 388
On The Road 390
Health 391
Emergencies 391

Further Reading

General 391
Other Insight Guides .. 392

Getting Acquainted

The Place

Area: Italy: 301,308 sq. km/ 116,335 sq. miles
Population: 57.5 million
Language: Italian, with some French (Aosta), German (Trentino-Alto Adige) and mountain dialects near the borders; Venetian dialect
Religion: Roman Catholic
Time Zone: Central European Time (GMT plus 1 hour, EST plus 6hrs)
Currency: Euro
Weights and Measures: Metric
Electricity: 220 volts. Take an adaptor to operate British three-pin appliances and a transformer to use 100–120 volt appliances.
International Dialling Code: 39

Geography

The Alps form a natural boundary between Italy and neighbouring France, Switzerland and Austria. Below the Alps are the Italian Lakes. The Dolomites provide a second tier of mountains above Venetia and Trentino-Alto Adige. At a right-angle to the Alps, heading right down the country, are the Apennines, which form the Riviera's west coast. Between the two is the Po Valley, where most of Italy's cereals are grown. The Adriatic's coastal plains produce long, sandy beaches.

Climate

- In the Alps and Apennines, winters are long and cold, while summers are short and cool.
- In the Pianura Padana, around Milan, there are foggy winters and hot, humid summers.
- In the rest of the region, winters are mild, and hot, dry summers are tempered by sea-breezes.

Government

Italy's President is elected for a term of seven years by Parliament, which is composed of two houses: the Senate (with 315 members) and Chamber of Deputies (630 members). The president nominates the Prime Minister and, on the latter's advice, the Cabinet.

After a period of constitutional corruption in the early 1990s, Italy reduced its dependence on proportional representation and moved towards a "first-past-the-post" system, under which the country elected its first left-wing government, a loose centre-left coalition, in 1996. Silvio Berlusconi's Forza Italia came to power in 2001, in coalition with the National Alliance and the Northern League. The controversial Berlusconi resigned in 2005. The centre-left leader, Romano Prodi won a closely-fought election in 2006.

The regions have strong political affiliations, and special autonomous status has been granted to five of them. Northern Italy is influenced by federalist tendencies and a separatist party, the Northern League, attracts about 10 percent of the vote. They campaign for an independent northern Italy, which they call Padania.

Economy

Italian industry (motor and electrical goods manufacturing, chemicals, sulphur, mercury, iron and steel) is concentrated in the north, where the Alps provide a source of hydro-electric power. Italy is the world's largest producer of wine and olive oil and Europe's foremost producer of silk, mainly from Lombardy.

Milan is the economic capital of Italy and centre of the design industry, rivalling Paris as Europe's fashion capital. Italy's economic strength lies in the creativity and industry of its small and medium-sized companies, especially those in Lombardy, Piedmont, the Veneto and Emilia Romagna.

Planning the Trip

Visas and Passports

EU citizens do not need a visa or a passport to enter Italy: an identification card valid for foreign travel is sufficient, in the case of the UK where there are no ID cards a passport is mandatory. Visitors from the following countries need a passport but not a visa providing they do not stay for more than three months: Australia, Austria, Barbados, Canada, Iceland, Jamaica, Japan, Kenya, South Korea, Kuwait, Malaysia, Maldives, Malta, Mexico, Monaco, New Zealand, Niger, Norway, Paraguay, Poland (for a stay up to 30 days), Singapore, Switzerland, Trinidad and Tobago, United States, Uruguay, Venezuela (up to 60 days). Other nationalities should contact their nearest Italian consulate.

You are supposed to register with the police within three days of arriving in Italy. In fact, this procedure will be taken care of by your hotel, whatever the level of accommodation. If you are not staying in a hotel, contact the local police station.

Money Matters

The monetary unit is the euro. Travellers' cheques are recommended as they can be replaced if stolen or lost. However, commission will be charged for changing them. Most shopkeepers and restaurateurs will not change money, so it is best to change a limited amount at the airport when you arrive, especially if it is the weekend, when banks are closed. Try to avoid changing money in hotels, where the commission tends to be higher than in banks.

Animal Quarantine

Pets must be vaccinated against rabies, and you should obtain an officially stamped document stating that your animal is healthy. This should be done no more than a month before you arrive in Italy.

Banks generally open from 8 or 8.30am–1.30pm and for 1½ hours in the afternoon (usually 2.30–4pm). You will find current exchange rates are published in the press and posted in banks. Rates fluctuate considerably.

Credit cards and cash machines: In cities, many restaurants, hotels, shops and stores will take major credit cards (Visa, American Express, Diners Club, MasterCard and Carte Blanche) but most petrol stations require cash. Don't rely on using credit cards in country areas or in many smaller restaurants. Cash still speaks volumes in Italy.

What to Wear

The Italians are known for their sense of style, so expect a fashion parade if you are visiting such upmarket cities as Milan. A light jacket will be adequate for summer evenings. In winter the climate can be cold and wet across northern Italy. Note that you may be barred from entering churches if dressed in shorts or short skirts, or if your shoulders are uncovered.

Tourist Offices

Australia: Italian Government Travel Office (ENIT), Level 26, 44 Market Street, Sydney 2000, tel: 02-96262 1666, e-mail: enitour@ikng.com.au
Canada: Suite 907, South Tower, 17 Bloor Street East, Toronto, Ontario MN4 3R8, tel: 416-925 4882, e-mail: enitcanada@on.aibn.com
UK: Italian State Tourist Board (ENIT), 1 Princes Street, London W1R 8AY, tel: 020-7408 1254, fax: 020-7493 6695, e-mail: enitlond@globalnet.co.uk
US: Italian Government Travel Office (ENIT), Suite 1565, 630 Fifth Avenue, New York, NY 10111, tel: 212-245 4822, fax: 212-586 9249, e-mail: enitny@italiantourism.com
Suite 2240, 500 North Michigan Avenue, Chicago 1, Illinois 60611, tel: 312-644 0996, fax: 312-644 3019, e-mail: enitch@italiantourism.com
Suite 550, 12400 Wilshire Blvd, Los Angeles, CA 90025-12400, tel: 310-820 1898, fax: 310-820 6357, e-mail: enitla@italiantourism.com

Getting There

By Air

In addition to the national airline, Alitalia, most airlines run direct flights to Italy, including many charter flights with low-cost tickets.

Intercontinental: Italy has 29 main airports, but the main hubs are Roma Leonardo da Vinci (known as Fiumicino) and Milano Malpensa.

European and charter: There has been an explosion in the variety of low-price tickets from British firms such as easyJet and Ryanair. These airlines fly to numerous airports across northern Italy, including Brescia and Turin.

Marco Polo Airport, Venice is located at Tessera on the mainland 13 km (8 miles) north of Venice. To reach Venice there is a choice of public bus to Piazzale Roma (around 30 minutes); private land taxi (20–25 minutes); the Cooperativa San Marco water launch which crosses the lagoon to Piazza San Marco via the Lido (45 minutes); or a water-taxi, which costs six times as much as the public launch.

Treviso Airport, 30 km (19 miles) north of Venice, is an alternative for travellers to Venice or the Lakes. Charter flights are available from London Gatwick, no-frills airline Ryanair from Stansted and a coach service runs to Venice.

Verona Airport is one of the most convenient airports for reaching the Lakes or the Veneto region. Charter flights arrive from London, Frankfurt, Paris and several other cities, low-cost carriers from London (Stansted).

Milano Malpensa 2000 Airport, Milan's intercontinental airport, 45 km (28 miles) from the city centre, opened its second terminal in time to celebrate the Millennium. It is served by several major companies including Alitalia, British Airways, British Midland and Lufthansa. The Malpensa Express runs from 5.30am to 1.30am from the airport's Terminal One to Cadorna station in the centre of Milan; The journey takes around 50 minutes. An Air Pullman bus ferries passengers between the airport and the Air Pullman office outside the Stazione Centrale, Milan's main train station. You can buy a ticket a few minutes before departure from the Air Pullman office.

Customs Regulations

Used personal effects may be imported and exported without formality. The import of narcotics, weapons and pirated materials is forbidden. Since the atrocities of 11 September 2001, no sharp objects, including scissors and tweezers, are allowed in hand-luggage on planes.

Alcoholic drinks, tobacco and perfume can be imported in limited quantities, depending on your nationality.

Duty-free shopping for EU citizens within Europe ended on 1 July 1999. Goods on which duty has already been paid in another EU country may be freely imported, provided the amount falls within what might be reasonably described as "for personal use".

For US citizens, the duty-free allowance is: 200 cigarettes, 50 cigars or 3 lb tobacco; 1 US quart of alcoholic beverages and duty-free gifts worth up to $100.

The airports at Genoa, Milan, Turin and Venice all have duty-free shops.

Public Holidays

- **January** New Year's Day (1)
- **March/April** Good Friday, Easter Monday
- **April** Liberation Day – *Anniversario della Liberazione* (25)
- **May** Labour Day – *Festa del Lavoro* (1)
- **August** Assumption of the Blessed Virgin Mary – *Ferragosto* (15)
- **November** All Saints – *Ognissanti* (1)
- **December** Immaculate Conception of the Blessed Virgin Mary – *Immacolata Concezione* (8), Christmas Day (25), St Stephen's Day (26)

Saints' Days

In addition to these national holidays, almost all cities have a holiday to celebrate their own patron saint, for example:

- **St John the Baptist**, 24 June (Turin and Genoa)
- **St Ambrose**, 7 December (Milan)
- **St Mark**, 25 April (Venice)
- **St Petronius**, 4 October (Bologna)

Milano Linate, Milan's other airport, is around 8 km (5 miles) from the centre. This airport is now used mainly for flights within Italy, although low-cost carriers such as easyJet fly here. The ATM bus 73 travels regularly (5.30am–midnight) from the front of the airport (Piazzale del Aeroporto) to its terminus on Piazza S. Babila at the corner of Corso Europa. The STAM shuttle connects Linate with the Stazione Centrale and runs approximately every 30 minutes.

Bergamo Airport is convenient for exploring the Lakes, including Lake Iseo and Lake Como, as well as Milan, Mantua and the rest of Lombardy. Bergamo is served, amongst others, by Gandals, which flies from London's City Airport.

The tiny **Brescia Airport** is well situated as a base for visiting Lake Garda, Lake Iseo, Verona, the Dolomites and Trentino-Alto Adige. Brescia is served by charter flights, including Ryanair, which travels from London Stansted.

Turin Airport is small but handy for the Piedmontese hinterland and the wine country around Barolo and Bardolino. It is also well situated for the Gran Paradiso National Park and the Valle d'Aosta. Alitalia and Ryanair fly here.

Genoa Airport which is also served by Ryanair, is small but well placed for exploring Genoa and the Ligurian coast.

Bologna Airport, another small airport, is served by Alitalia and British Airways. The Aerobus (a shuttle bus) can whisk you into the city centre in around 20 minutes; the same journey by taxi will take around 15 minutes.

Additional airlines include:

Aer Lingus: tel: 0818-365000; www.aerlingus.com

BMI Baby: tel: 0870-264 2229; www.bmibaby.com

easyJet: tel: 0870-600 0000; www.easyjet.com

Flybe: tel: 0870-567 4564; www.flybe.com

Volare Airlines: tel: 01293-562266; www.volare-airlines.com

MyTravelLite: tel: 0870-156 4564; www.mytravellite.com

By Car

When calculating the cost of travelling to Italy by car, allow for motorway tolls as well as accommodation en route and petrol. Motorists driving through Switzerland will need to purchase a *vignette*, an annual road pass (around £17) which can be bought either at the border or at any national tourist office. If you want to travel by toll-free roads in Italy, they are listed in the Italian State Tourist Office's *Traveller's Handbook*.

The usual route from France to Italy is via the Mont Blanc Tunnel (between Chamonix and Courmayeur) or from Switzerland through the Gran San Bernardo Tunnel (between Bourg St Pierre and Aosta). Some of the many Alpine passes are seasonal, so check the viability of your route with the tourist board or a motoring organisation before setting off. Alternatively, motorists can head down the French autoroute to Nice and cross the border at Ventimiglia on the Riviera.

To take your car into Italy, you will need your current driving licence (with an Italian translation unless it is the standard EU licence), your vehicle registration document (which must be in the driver's name or supported by the owner's written permission for the driver to use the vehicle) and Green Card insurance. You must carry a warning triangle in case of breakdown.

By Coach

The cost of travelling to Italy from Great Britain by scheduled coach is not much cheaper than travelling by air. National Express Eurolines runs coaches from London Victoria, via Paris and Mont Blanc, to Aosta, Turin, Genoa, Milan, Venice, Bologna, Verona, Padua and Parma. To book from London, contact: National Express Eurolines, Victoria Coach Station, Buckingham Palace

The Orient Express

This is a wonderful way to reach Venice in style – certainly the most romantic. The service operates from March to November, with two trains a week departing London on Thursday and Sunday, and leaving Venice on Wednesday and Saturday. From London, the train stops in Paris, Düsseldorf, Cologne, Frankfurt, Zurich, Innsbruck and Verona. The whole journey takes 28 hours, 30 minutes.

If you wish – and if you can afford it – you can travel both ways on the Orient Express, but you must stay a minimum of five days in Venice. Sybarites can check into the luxurious Cipriani Hotel *(see Where to Stay)*, which is owned by the same group as the Orient Express.

Alternatively, buy a single either to or from Venice, and Alitalia will throw in a single ticket to allow you to complete your journey. For reservations, tel: 0870-544 8259.

Car Trains

The following rail services will transport cars to Italy:

- Paris–Milan
- Boulogne–Lille–Milan
- Schaerbeek (Brussels)–Milan
- Hertogenbosch (The Netherlands)–Domodossola–Genoa–Milan
- Hertogenbosch–Chiasso–Milan
- Düsseldorf–Cologne–Milan–Genoa
- Hamburg–Hanover–Verona
- Munich–Rimini
- Düsseldorf–Cologne–Bolzano
- Vienna–Venice
- Boulogne–Alessandria

Road, London SW1W 9TQ, tel: 020-7730 8235, www.eurolines.com.

By Rail

Rail travel is not a particularly cheap option unless you are visiting different places in Italy as part of the Inter-Rail or Eurail schemes. These provide a month's unlimited train travel in Europe for anyone under 26 at a very reasonable price.

The entire Italian rail sytem is operated by Trenitalia www.trenitalia.it. The Rail Pass, Family Card and Kilometric Card (which allows one or more people to travel a specified number of kilometres at a special rate) can be purchased at any major train station in Italy. The fastest trains operate on the networks between the major cities, while the regional trains are fairly slow. **Note:** Once you have purchased your ticket you must stamp it before entering the train in the special yellow machines that can be found all along the platform. Failure to do so will result in a fine.

For details of rail travel contact:
Australia: CIT, 123 Clarence Street, Sydney. Tel: 02-9299 4574.
UK: Rail-Europe. Tel: 0870-584 8848; Italian State Railway, Marco Polo House, 3–5 Landsdowne Road, Croydon, Surrey. Tel: 020-8686 0677.
US: CIT, 342 Madison Avenue, Suite 207, New York, NY 190173. Tel: 1-800 223 7987/212-697 1482.

When travelling from the UK via Paris, you must change in Paris (from the Eurostar terminal at the Gare du Nord to the Gare de Lyon).

ETR (Eurostar), EC (Eurocity) and TEE (Trans Europe Express) trains connect Italy with the main European cities. A supplement is charged and seat reservation is obligatory. For train information, call the same number from anywhere in Italy: 147-888088. Alternatively, check routes on the official railway website: www.fs-on-line.com.

Package Tours

From the UK, Ireland or the US, this is usually the easiest and most economical way to visit places such as Venice and the Lakes. It is an advantage to travel with a company that has good local representation. Brochures are generally available from your travel agent. The following are among the most reputable UK companies now specialising in travel to Venice and other parts of Italy.

Citalia
Marco Polo House,
3–5 Landsdowne Road, Croydon, Surrey, tel: 020-8686 0677, www.citalia.co.uk

Magic of Italy
Kings House, 12–42 Wood Street, Kingston-upon-Thames, Surrey KT1 1JF, tel: 0870-027 0500, fax: 020-8939 0411, www.magictravelgroup.co.uk

Inghams Travel
10–18 Putney Hill, London SW15 6AX, tel: 020-8780 4433, www.inghams.co.uk

Italian Expressions
104 Belsize Lane, London NW3 5BB, tel: 020-7435 2525, fax: 020-7431 4221, www.expressionsholidays.co.uk

Italiatour
9 Whyteleafe Business Village, Whyteleafe Hill, Whyteleafe, Surrey CR3 0AT, tel: 01883-621 9000, fax: 01883-625 222, www.italiatour.co.uk

Sunvil Holidays
Sunvil House, 7/8 Upper Square, Old Isleworth, Middlesex TW7 7BJ, tel: 020-8758 4722, fax: 020-8568 8330, www.sunvil.co.uk

Practical Tips

Business Hours

Shops are usually open for business 9am–12.30pm and 3.30 or 4pm–7.30 or 8pm. In areas serving tourists, hours are generally longer than these. Shops often close on Monday (or Monday morning only). Some close on Saturday. Almost everything closes on Sunday.

Tipping

It is customary to tip various people for their services, especially in restaurants and hotels, although Italians don't always adhere to this practice. Most restaurants continue to impose an outdated cover and bread charge *(pane e coperto)* of around 5 euros, although it has "officially" been eliminated in most cities. Often there is an additional 10 percent service charge added to the bill. If the menu says that service is included, a small additional tip is discretionary. If service is not included, it is usual to leave between 12 and 15 percent of the bill.

Media

The Italian press is concentrated in Milan and Rome. Most of Italy's 80 daily newspapers are in private hands. The biggest papers are *La Repubblica* and *Il Corriere della Sera*, which publish regional and northern editions. Most major cities publish weekly listings magazines which are worth getting, even for visitors with basic Italian.

The local tourist office will have information on current happenings.

Television stations include RAI (the national network with three channels), the Vatican network, plus seven national and more than 450 local commercial stations.

Postal Services

Post office hours are usually 8am–1.30pm, but many towns have a main office which is open throughout the day. Stamps may also be purchased from tobacconists *(tabacchi)*. The post office can provide such services as *raccomandata* (registered) and *espresso* (express).

You can receive mail addressed to *Posta Restante*, held at the *Fermo Posta* window of the main post office in every town, picking it up personally with identification.

You do not have to queue to post mail; use the red letter-boxes near tobacconists or stations.

Telephone

The most convenient way to use public telephones is to buy phone cards *(schede telefoniche)*, which are sold at *tabacchi* and newspaper kiosks in denominations of 2.50, 5 and 10 euros. As many telephone boxes are frequently out of order, better options include public telephones in bars, Telecom Italia offices and the larger post offices. Phone calls from hotels tend to be very expensive, usually an additional charge of some 25 percent. Less expensive rates apply to calls made after 9pm and at weekends. You can also make calls using a British BT chargecard or one of the cards issued by AT&T, Sprint, NCI and other North American long-distance telephone companies. This allows more flexibility by charging the calls to your home address.

Area Codes in Italy

To call Italy from abroad, dial 39 followed by 0 and the area code. For numbers outside your area and for all local calls, dialling must be preceded by 0 and then the area code (obtainable free from Information: dial 12). The area codes (including the initial 0) of main cities are: **Rome** (06), **Milan** (02), **Bologna** (051), **Genoa** (010), **Florence** (055), **Pisa** (050), **Venice** (041), **Turin** (011), **Como** (031), **Verona** (045).

Calling Home

To call abroad from Italy, dial 00, followed by:

Australia 61
Canada 1
Ireland 353
New Zealand 64
UK 44
US 1

Then dial the number, omitting the initial "0" if there is one.

- European directory enquiries: 4176
- European operator assistance: 15
- Intercontinental operator assistance: 170
- Telegrams and cables: 186

Local Tourist Offices

Every major town has an **Azienda di Promozione Turistica** (APT) or **Informazione e Accoglienza Turistica** (IAT). For addresses and phone numbers, check the directory or the Yellow Pages under "ENIT". Together with helpful information, main APT offices offer a free city map, a list of hotels, and museum hours and addresses. APT offices in the main areas are listed below.

Almost every town in Italy has a **Touring Club Italiano** (TCI) office, which provides free information about points of interest. Telephone numbers are listed in the local telephone book. The club also produces some of the best maps and food and wine guides in Italy.

Turin

Turismo Turino (**APT**) has two information offices: Piazza Castelli 161, tel: 011-535181/535901, fax: 011-530070.
Also Stazione di Porta Nuova (railway station), tel: 011-531327, fax: 011-5617095, www.turismotorino.org

The Riviera

Contact **APT Genova**, Via Acqua Verde Stazione, Piazza Principe, 16126 Genoa, tel: 010-576791, fax: 010-581408, www.apt.genova.it

Milan

IAT offices are located at:
Stazione Centrale, Galleria Partenze, tel: 02-72524360/370. Open Monday– Saturday 8am–7pm, Sunday 9am–12.30pm and 1.30–6pm.
Also **APT**, Via Marconi 1, Piazza del Duomo, tel: 02-72524360, fax: 02-72524350, www.milanoinfotourist.com
Open Monday–Friday 8.30am–8pm (until 7pm in winter), Saturday 9am–1pm and 2–7pm (until 6pm in winter), Sunday 9am–1pm and 2–5pm.

The Lakes

APT Lago di Garda/Trentino, Giardini di Porta Orientale 8, 38066 Riva del Garda, tel: 0464-554444, fax: 0464-520308, www.gardatrentino.it
APT Como, Piazza Cavour 17, 22100 Como, tel: 031-269712/ 3300111, fax: 031-240111, www.lakecomo.org
APT Lake Maggiore, Corso Zanitello 6/8, Verbania, tel: 0323-503249, fax: 0323-556669, www.lagomaggiore.it
APT Bergamo, Viale Vittorio Emanuele 20, 24121 Bergamo, tel: 035-213185, fax: 035-230184, www.apt.bergamo.it
Open Monday–Friday 9am–12.30pm and 2–5.30pm.

Venice and Veneto

APT offices in **Venice**:
San Marco, Giardini ex Redi, tel: 041-5226356, fax: 041-5225150, under the arcades of the piazza. Open Monday–Saturday 9am–12.30pm and 3–7pm.
Ferrovia Santa Lucia (train station), tel: 041-5298727, fax: 041-719078.
Open daily 8am–7pm.
The APT provincial headquarters is at Castello 4421, tel: 041-5298711, fax: 041-5230399. www.provincia.venezia.it/aptre
Open daily 8am–7pm.
APT Verona, Via degli Alpini 9 (close to Piazza Brà), 37100 Verona, tel: 045-8068680, fax: 045-8003638, www.tourism.verona.it

Consulates

There is the following limited local consular representation in northern Italy:

Milan

- British Consulate,Via San Paolo 7, tel: 02-723001.
- US Consulate, Via Principe Amedeo 2/10, tel: 02-290351.

Venice

- British Consulate, Dorsoduro 1051, tel: 041-5227207.

Other nationalities will need to contact their **embassies in Rome**:

- Australia: Via Alessandria 215, Rome, tel: 06-852721.
- Canada: Via G.B. de Rossi, Rome, tel: 06-445981.
- Ireland: Piazza Campitelli 3, Rome, tel: 06-6979121.
- New Zealand: Via Zara 28, Rome, tel: 06-4417171.

Medical Services

In cases of real need, such as medical aid or ambulances, call the Public Emergency Assistance number, **113**. This service operates on a 24-hour basis, and, in the principal cities, response will be in the main foreign languages. Dial 112 for the Carabinieri immediate-action service. Certain tourist cities offer medical interpreting services.

To receive free treatment in cases of illness, accident or even childbirth, EU citizens (and citizens of countries with other ties to Italy, such as Brazil, Monaco, and the former Yugoslavia) must obtain (in their country of residence before arriving in Italy) the E-111 form. This form is to state that the bearers are registered with their national health service and therefore have the right to the same assistance offered to Italian citizens. (Note: it won't provide repatriation, which you may require in the case of serious illness.) Citizens of non-EU countries must pay for medical assistance and medicine.

Health insurance is recommended for travelling in Italy. Keep receipts to claim for medical expenses.

Most hospitals have a 24-hour emergency department called *Pronto Soccorso*, but a stay in an Italian hospital can be a grim experience. For more minor complaints, go to a *farmacia*, identified by a sign displaying a red cross in a white circle. Pharmacists give advice and suggest over-the-counter drugs, including antibiotics. Normal opening hours are 9am–1pm and 4–7.30 or 8pm, but outside these hours the address of the nearest *farmacia* on duty is posted in the window.

Security and Crime

The main problems are pick-pocketing, bag-snatching and robbery. Get insurance coverage against these occurrences. If you are the victim of a crime (or suffer a loss) and wish to make claim you must make a report at the nearest police station and get documentation to support your claim. When you need a policeman, dial **113** (or 112 for the Carabinieri, a national police force which is technically a branch of the army).

If driving, lock your car and never leave luggage, cameras or other valuables inside, particularly in major cities.

Women Travellers

The difficulties encountered by women travelling alone in Italy are often overstated. Women often have to put up with much male attention, but it is rarely dangerous. Ignoring whistles and questions is the best way to get rid of unwanted attention.

Personal Security

- Don't linger in non-commercial areas after dark
- Don't carry all your cash with you; leave some in the hotel
- Use travellers' cheques rather than large quantities of cash
- Never leave your luggage unattended
- Keep valuables in the hotel safe (most hotels provide a storage service)
- Deposit your room key at the desk before going out.

Getting Around

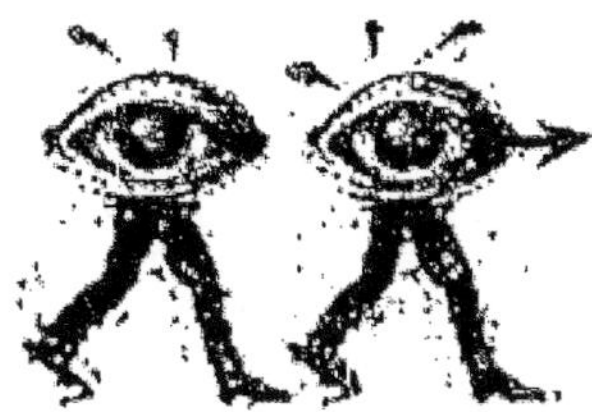

Public Transport

BY AIR

The major centres and towns of touristic interest are connected by flights provided mostly by Alitalia. Smaller airlines are ATI, Alisarda (to and from Sardinia) and Aligiulia. Flying in Italy is expensive compared with taking the train, but it can be useful for long distances. Discount flights are often available if you are prepared to arrive and return on certain days, but such fares must be booked in Italy. For detailed information, contact your nearest travel agent or Alitalia office.

Infants under two years accompanied by an adult have a 90 percent discount; children over two years and under 12 have a 50 percent discount, and young travellers of 12–21 years have a 25 percent discount.

BY RAIL

The cheapest, fastest and most convenient way to travel is by train. Train information is available from the *Uffici Informazioni* at most major stations, listed in the telephone directory under *Ferrovie dello Stato*. You can also telephone 147-888088 or visit the official railway website: www.fs-on-line.com.

Local trains are called *Locale*, *Diretto*, *Interregionale* and *Espresso*. When travelling considerable distances or along major lines, the faster *InterCity*, *EuroCity* and *Eurostar* services are the best bet – the supplemental charge being well worth the time saved and the extra comfort. The *Pendolino* is the fastest, most comfortable train, and requires a supplement and reservation. It is a good idea to buy tickets and make reservations for the *IC/EC/ES* and *Pendolino* in advance, and this can be done at any travel agency as well as at the station.

If you are planning to make more than several train journeys, consider buying the inexpensive official train timetable book from any station kiosk. If travelling a fair distance, it is worth reserving a seat as trains tend to be crowded.

Good fare reductions and special offers are available for groups and young travellers, and it is worth making enquiries about these when you arrive in Italy. Tickets are valid for two months. Passengers must stamp their tickets in the station before boarding. If for some reason that is not possible, you must find the conductor before he finds you.

BY COACH

Each province in Italy has its own inter-city bus company and each company has its own lines. It is worth taking buses, especially when you are going to the mountainous interior, where they are generally faster than the train. Some of the principal coach companies operating long-distance travel from the main cities are listed below.

Milan

Autostradale, Viaggi, Via Luca Belkami, tel: 02-801161. Services across Lombardy and the Lakes. The firm also runs guided tours, which can be booked through the tourist office. Eurolines is next door, tel: 02-72001304.

Trentino-Alto Adige

SAD, Via Conciapelli 60, Bolzano, tel: 0471-5582414. Services along the coast from Genoa to Varazze (Riviera di Ponente) or Recco (Riviera di Levante).
APT Tourist Office, Piazza Walther 8, tel: 0471-307000.

Genoa

AMT, Piazza della Vittoria 88, tel: 010-5997414. Services from Genoa to Alassio, Rapallo and Milan.

TRAVEL WITHIN MILAN

The bus and tram service (ATM) is fast and efficient. Tickets must be purchased in advance at tobacconists *(tabacchi)* or news-stands and are good for 75 minutes of travel.

The Metropolitana Milanese (MM) is the best subway in Italy. MM has three lines (1, 2 and 3) which serve almost all the city and the hinterland. Usually tourists get on line 3, which runs south from near Stazione Centrale to Piazza del Duomo.

Tickets are sold at machines in stations, in most *tabacchi* and at news-stands. Tickets allow 75 minutes of travel. A day ticket is valid on all forms of transport. Other good-value tickets are the 24-hour ticket, the 2-day ticket, or the book of 10 tickets.

TRAVEL/TRANSPORT WITHIN VENICE

The city is small enough to be covered on foot, and a good map is essential for exploring the maze of small streets and squares. Pick one up from the tourist office.

The main form of public transport is the *vaporetto* or water bus. The most scenic line is the

Ferries and Hydrofoils

There are a great many ferryboat and hydrofoil speedboat lines that offer connections between the mainland and Italy's many large and small islands. The services run by the State Railways, Tirrenia, Grandi Navi Veloci, Trans Tirrenco Express, Moby Lines and SNAV companies provide all the connections with Sicily and Sardinia. Many other lines connect the peninsula with the smaller islands. Here is some basic information regarding shipping lines:
Ferrovie dello Stato (State Railways): Civitavecchia–Golfo Aranci (Sardinia): departures many times a day for passengers with cars. Crossing takes nine hours.
Tirrenia Navigazione: This Genoa-based line operates sailings to Sardinia, Sicily and Tunis, as well as Naples–Palermo, Civitavecchia–Olbia or Cagliari (both direct and via Arbatax). The connections with Sardinia are daily for passengers and cars, with both day and night runs. Tirrenia also runs Genoa–Porto Torres, Genoa–Cagliari and Naples–Cagliari (all to Sardinia), with an average crossing time of 12–20 hours.
Trans Tirreno Express: Livorno–Olbia, particularly during the high season.
Grandi Navi Veloci: This line offers connections from Genoa to Corsica, Sicily, Sardinia and Spain (Barcelona) for passengers and cars.
Moby Lines: This line offers a ferry service from Genoa to Corsica and further to Sardinia (in summer only).
Toremar/Siremar/Caremar/SNAV: Toremar offers connections to the Tuscan islands (Elba, Giglio), while Siremar runs to the Aeolian islands, Caremar runs from Naples to the Naples Gulf islands (Capri, Ischia), and SNAV connects Naples and Palermo.
Aliscafi: This is a hydrofoil speedboat line which connects Naples and the islands Ischia, Capri and Procida.
Adriatic: This service carries passengers and cars from Venice, Trieste, Ancona, Pescara, Bari and Brindisi both to the Adriatic and foreign ports.
To obtain further information about fares and schedules, call in at any of the many travel agencies or the APT offices.

No. 1 Accelerato, which takes you slowly down the Grand Canal. Line 82 provides a faster service down the Grand Canal, making only six stops and going west as far as Tronchetto (the car park island) and east to San Zaccaria (and the Lido in summer). The circular line No. 52 provides an enjoyable ride around the periphery of Venice and takes in the island of Murano.

Passengers who have not bought a ticket before boarding will be surcharged; tourists have to pay more than residents, who get reduced rates. Twenty-four-hour or three-day passes are available. Children under 1 metre (3 ft) high travel free, but a suitcase costs as much as an adult passenger.

A private and more costly water-taxi service can be hired from most hotels in the city. If arriving at your hotel with luggage, you will need to tip someone to help carry it up to the building.

Water-Taxis and Gondolas

The alternatives to water buses are water-taxis and, of course, gondolas. The former take up to four people and, like regular taxis, display meters. You can find taxi "ranks" at main points in the city. To understand the complex system of charges for water transport, pick up a free copy of *A Guest in Venice* from any major hotel.

Current prices are around €73 for 50 minutes and €91 after 8pm. However, you can always try to strike a bargain, but do remember that a singing gondolier – whatever the age – costs extra. Gondolas booked as a group convoy may be cheaper – if you can face it! A recommended route is Bridge of Sighs, Santa Maria Formosa and Rialto Bridge, returning via the Grand Canal.

Very much cheaper, for those who want a quick taste, are the *traghetti* gondolas, which simply ferry people across the Grand Canal in six different places where no bridge is convenient (and cost 40 cents per crossing).

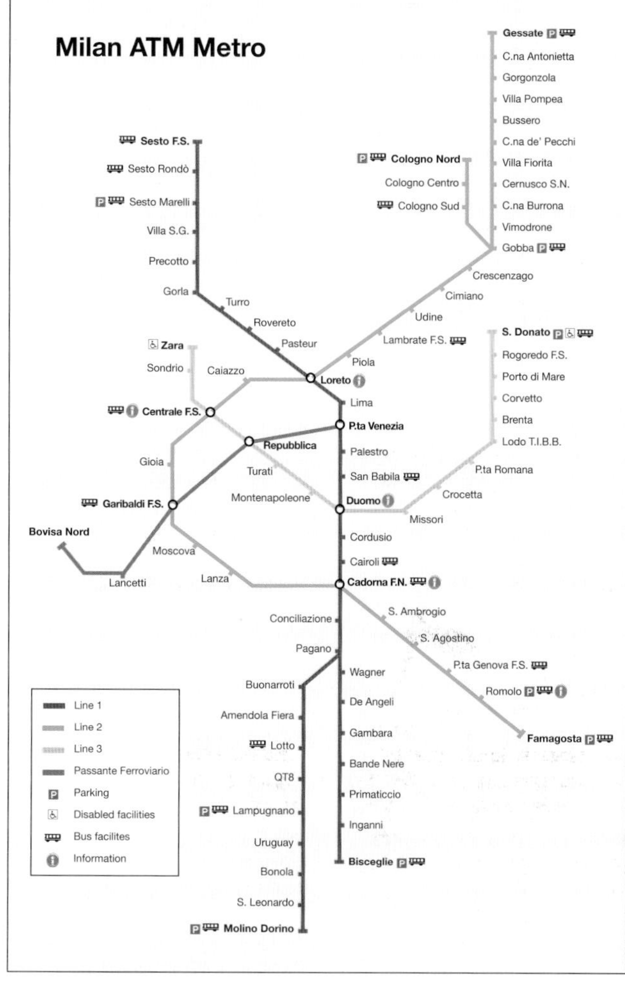

TRAVEL WITHIN THE LAKES

One of the most relaxing ways of viewing the lakes is from the deck of a steamer. All major towns on the lakes have ferry connections for passengers and a number of towns are linked by car ferry as well: Verbania–Laveno on Lake Maggiore; Menaggoio–Bellagio–Varenna on Lake Como; and Maderno–Torri del Benaco on Lake Garda.

The Maggiore and Lugano steamers cross the border between Italy and Switzerland, so the usual border procedures apply. The larger vessels have on-board restaurants. For a trip along the full length of Lake Garda, from Desenzano to Riva. allow around 4½ hours.

Cruises are regular features during summer, and disco ships are also common. Real, old-fashioned paddle steamers are still used.

TAXIS

Cabs are found at taxi ranks or paged by telephone rather than hailed in the street. When you call, the operator will tell you the call letters of the taxi and approximately how many minutes it will take to arrive.

Fares are clocked up on meters. There is a fixed starting charge and then a charge for every kilometre (and a standing charge for traffic jams). Taxi drivers are obliged to show, if asked, the current list of additional charges. Extra charges are added for night rides, around €2.60 (10pm–7am), luggage, journeys outside town and journeys on Sunday and public holidays. It is a general rule to leave a small tip, rounding off the fare to the nearest euro.

Private Transport

BY CAR

In Italy, you must drive on the right. The motorways *(autostrade)* are fast and uncrowded (except in summer), but Italians frequently drive faster than the speed limit. Nearly all *autostrade* charge tolls, and you pay as you exit.

It is compulsory to wear seat-belts at all times, and infants up to nine months must occupy a baby seat. Children between nine months and four years must sit on the back seat.

Pay attention to street signs advising no parking because police are strict on illegal parking and will remove vehicles found in no-parking areas. You'll need plenty of cash to reclaim your car. Try to park in a garage for the night: it will be a little expensive, but much safer.

Hitchhiking is forbidden on the *autostrade* and is not advised for women travelling alone, especially in the south.

When travelling into the **mountain areas** during the winter months, it is advisable to call 194 for road conditions. When there is ice and snow, chains will be required. It is also now obligatory to illuminate headlights at all times.

Car Rentals

Hiring a car is expensive in Italy, as is petrol. Major car-rental firms such as Avis, Hertz and Europcar are represented in most cities and at all airports, though local firms often offer better rates. Agencies are listed in the Yellow Pages under *Autonoleggio*. Collision-damage waiver and recovery in case of breakdown are usually included in the price of hiring a vehicle, but be sure to check exclusions carefully. Additional insurance cover is usually available at fixed rates. Also, make sure that the price you are quoted includes VAT (IVA), which is levied at 19 percent.

The renter must be over 21 and must be in possession of a valid driver's licence (an EU licence, an international driving licence or a national driving licence with Italian translation). A deposit equal to the cost of hiring the vehicle is usually required, or a credit-card imprint.

Driving Speeds

The following speed limits apply to cars in Italy:
Urban areas: 50 km/h (30 mph)
Roads outside urban areas: 90 km/h (55 mph)
Dual carriageways outside urban areas: 110 km/h (70 mph)
Motorways *(autostrade)*: 130 km/h (80 mph); for cars less than 1,100cc: 110 km/h (70 mph)

Calling a Taxi

You can call for a taxi by dialling one of the following numbers:
Bologna: 372727 or 534141
Milan: 6767, 5353, 8585, 8383 or 5251
Turin: 5737 or 5730
Venice: see *Water-Taxis and Gondolas*
• Check the *Tutto Città* (first page) or the Yellow Pages for other towns.

Where to Stay

Choosing a Hotel

Italy has a wonderful variety of accommodation in all categories, from grand villas to small family-run hotels, as well as the newly developing sector of *Agriturismo* – farm holidays. All the major international chains are represented in Italy, with Jolly and Hilton being two of the most common. However, there are also burgeoning groups of highly individualistic hotels that have banded together to present a common front. They tend to be independent hotels that are linked by their atmosphere, style and cost to others in different areas.

Be sure to call or write beforehand to verify facilities and make reservations. Smaller hotels are not always cheaper – some of the more exclusive small hotels match the grand hotels in style and expense – but even inexpensive hotels usually offer basic comforts and good service.

Hotel Listings

The following listings offer a selection of hotels at all levels. Your travel agent or the APT offices in Italy can give more complete information on these and other hotels.

VENICE

Note: Hotel rates in Venice are about 30 percent higher than those on the mainland, but the prices are usually worth it for the atmosphere.

Grand Hotels

Cipriani
Isola della Giudecca 10
Tel: 041-5207744
Fax: 041-5203930
www.hotelcipriani.it

A small oasis hidden on the tip of the island of Giudecca, the Cipriani feels far removed from the city centre. Among its comforts are lavish bedrooms furnished with Fortuny fabrics, a swimming pool (one of few private pools in Venice), gardens and tennis courts, a yacht harbour, piano bar and a launch service which whisks you, in a couple of minutes, to San Marco. **€€€€**

Danieli Hotel
Riva degli Schiavoni 4196
Castello
Tel: 041-5226480
Fax: 041-5200208
www.danieli@luxurycollection.com
Part of the Starwood Luxury Collection, the Danieli is rich in memories of eminent guests – George Sand, Alfred de Musset, Dickens, Balzac, Wagner, kings, princes, stars – and still attracts the rich and famous. The roof-garden restaurant has a splendid view over the lagoon. **€€€€**

Gritti Palace Hotel
Campo Santa Maria del Giglio 2467
San Marco
Tel: 041-794611
Fax: 041-5200942
www.luxurycollection.com/grittipalace
This legendary elegant Venetian hotel is renowned for its formal luxury, charming setting (right on the Grand Canal) and discreet, attentive service. Doge Andrea Gritti lived here, and the hotel still has the air of a private *palazzo*. Hemingway, Churchill, Herbert von Karajan and Greta Garbo all stayed here. **€€€€**

Hotel des Bains
Lungomare Marconi 17
Lido di Venezia
Tel: 041-5265921
Fax: 041-5260113
This grand old hotel in the Lido is remembered for its role in Thomas Mann's *Death in Venice*. It is located across the road from its private beach. Facilities similar to those at the Excelsior *(see below)*. **€€€€**

Londra Palace
Riva degli Schiavoni 4171
Tel: 041-5200533
Fax: 041-5225032
www.thecharminglife.com
www.hotellondra.it
This elegant, recently renovated hotel is a flagship of the Charming Hotels group *(see Hotel Groups below)*. One hundred windows overlook the lagoon. **€€€€**

Luna Baglioni
Calle Larga del'Ascension 1243
San Marco
Tel: 041-5289840
Fax: 041-5287160
www.baglionihotels.com
The oldest hotel in Venice, dating its origins back to a Knights Templar lodge in existence in 1118, for pilgrims travelling to the Crusades. It's been operating as an inn since the 16th century. Grand public rooms decorated in noble Venetian style, with frescoes from the school of Tiepolo, stucco-work and paintings. Recommended for its setting, close to St Mark's. Refined Canova restaurant. **€€€€**

Price Categories

Price categories are based on double occupancy without breakfast:
€ = under €150
€€ = €150–250
€€€ = €250–350
€€€€ = €350 and above

Monaco & Grand Canal
Calle Vallaresso 1332
San Marco
Tel: 041-5200211
Fax: 041-5200501
E-mail: mailbox@hotelmonaco.it
Beautifully located in the San Marco area, overlooking the Grand Canal, this is an impressive 18th-century *palazzo*. The warm and welcoming atmosphere, complemented by stylish décor have made the hotel very popular. The acclaimed terrace restaurant overlooks the Grand Canal, and Harry's Bar is just a stroll away in the same street. **€€€–€€€€**

Westin Excelsior Hotel
Lungomare Marconi 41
Lido di Venezia
Tel: 041-5260201
Fax: 041-5267276
www.westin.com
A member of the Westin group, this is a huge luxury beach hotel with a façade reminiscent of a Moorish castle. Attractions include numerous sports facilities and a free launch service to Venice. **€€€€**

Small Hotels and B&Bs

Accademia Villa Maravage
Fondamenta Bollani 1058
Dorsoduro
Tel: 041-5210188
Fax: 041-5239152
www.pensioneaccademia.it
Reservations should be made months in advance for this sought-after *pensione*. Close to the Accademia gallery, it is a 17th-century villa with delightful gardens front and back. **€€**

Agli Alboretti
Rio terà Foscarini 884
Accademia
Tel: 041-5230058
Fax: 041-5210158
www.cash.it/alboretti
Located next to the Galleria dell' Accademia, this family-run 2-star hotel is noted for its warm welcome and courteous service. Twenty-three air-conditioned rooms and a peaceful, private garden. **€–€€**

Bucintoro
Riva San Biagio 2135
Castello
Tel: 041-5223240
Fax: 041-5222424
Simply furnished, friendly *pensione* on the waterfront at the end of the Riva degli Schiavoni with splendid views over the Basin of San Marco and the island of San Giorgio Maggiore. **€€**

Flora
Calle dei Bergamaschi 2283/A
San Marco
Tel: 041-5205844
Fax: 041-5228217
www.hotelflora.it
Charming, friendly hotel within five minutes' walk of Piazza San Marco. The garden, with fountains and flower beds, is particularly appealing. Bedrooms vary enormously and can be quite basic; best are 45, 46 and 47. **€€**

La Calcina
Zattere ai Gesuati 780
Dorsoduro
Tel: 041-5206466
Fax: 041-5227045

www.lacalcina.com
This russet-coloured inn is situated along the charming quayside of the Zattere in the Dorsoduro district. John Ruskin, the aesthete and art critic, stayed here in 1876. Each bedroom is different, and there is a considerable price differential between them as not all have been modernised. Appealing views over the Giudecca Canal. **€€€**

La Fenice et des Artistes
Campiello della Fenice 1936
San Marco
Tel: 041-5232333
Fax: 041-5203721
www.fenicehotels.it
Within a stone's throw of the Fenice opera house, this low-key, yet sophisticated hotel is usually popular with actors, musicians and artists. **€€–€€€**

Locanda la Corte
Calle Bressana 6317
Castello
Tel: 041-2411300
Fax: 041-2415982
www.locandalacorte.it
This very pleasant little Gothic *palazzo* takes its name from the picturesque inner courtyard where breakfast is served. Rooms are decorated in Venetian style. **€–€€**

Metropole
Riva degli Schiavoni 4149
Castello
Tel: 041-5205044
Fax: 041-5223679
www.hotelmetropole.com
In front of St George's Island. Beautifully furnished with a lovely collection of antiques. This boutique hotel has been romantically renovated and offers excellent service. **€€€€**

Palazzo Duodo
Calle dei Fabbri, Ramo Duodo 1014
San Marco
Tel: 041-522 5832
Fax: 041-5239151
www.palazzoduodo.com
Very centrally located, this B&B set in a Venetian *palazzo* offers three suites – green, red and white. There is a lift and each suite has a private bathroom. Extremely good value. **€**

Ponte Chiodo
Ponte Chiodo 3749
Cannaregio
Tel: 041-241 3935
www.pontechiodo.it
Near to the Ca' d'Oro, this very centrally located B&B has six bedrooms. Shared bathroom in all but one of the bedrooms. **€**

Quattro Fontane
Via Quattro Fontane 16
Lido di Venezia

Hotel Groups

The following is a selection of the most noteworthy hotel groups.

Charming Hotels
This delightful group of luxurious, independent Italian hotels is characterised by its impeccable taste in atmospheric locations, use of authentic antiques and excellent traditional cuisine. There are Charming Hotels in Como, Milan and Venice, amongst other places. Call, toll free, outside Italy from Australia, Belgium, France, Spain, Switzerland, UK and US +800-24276464, in Italy call 840-707575, www.thecharminglife.com

Sina Hotels
This small hotel group, founded by an Italian aristocrat, runs a collection of stylish and luxurious hotels in six major Italian cities: Milan, Parma, Viareggio, Florence, Perugia and Rome. The hotels are all different yet have a certain elegance and formality in common. Call, toll free, Central Reservations 800-273226, www.sinahotels.com

Turin Hotels
This group began in Turin and manages traditional, classic hotels in the regions of Piedmont and Liguria. The hotels are characterised by high Piedmontese standards of service, classical or Neoclassical buildings and excellent cuisine. They are all 4-star and include the Turin Palace Hotel *(see page 369)* and the Excelsior Palace Hotel in Rapallo. Hotels can be booked through Turin Hotels International, Turin, tel: 011-5151911, fax: 011-5617191, www.thi.it.

Logis d'Italia
This group operates on the same principles as the better-known French group, Logis de France. The group's 90–100 hotels are found all over Italy and are listed in the *Logis d'Italia* guide, available from bookshops or the Italian tourist office. The group's principles are founded on value for money, hospitality and size (most are small, and many are family-run). Hotels can be booked through a central reservations system in Milan, tel: 02-48519285, fax: 02-48519265, or booked direct. A typical hotel in the group is Hotel Select in Rome.

Jolly Hotels
Formed in 1949, this is now the largest Italian hotel group; tel: 0800-7310470, www.jollyhotels.it

Starhotels
This Italian group specialises in hotels in the heart of cities such as the 4-star Savoia Excelsior in Trieste *(see page 365)*. For reservations from the UK, tel: 800-313132, from Italy tel: 800-860200, www.starhotels.it

Starwood Hotels and Resorts
Upmarket properties located throughout Italy and the world. For reservations from the UK, tel: 0800-353535, www.starwood.com

Leading Hotels of the World/Leading Small Hotels of the World: Consortium of upmarket properties. From the UK, tel: 00800-10101111 www.lhw.com

Abitare La Storia
This new hotel grouping operates under the banner of "Bringing History Alive" and "Hospitality in Historical Houses". It is an association of independently run hotels, each of which is housed in a historic *palazzo* or villa, often with lovely grounds. The keynotes are tradition and atmosphere, often matched by a choice of good regional cuisine. Tel: 05776 32256, E-mail: mailbox@abitarelastoria.it

Tel: 041-5260227
Fax: 041-5260726
www.quattrofontane.com
This small, gabled 4-star hotel lies in secluded gardens, making it one of the most charming hotels on the Lido. This is the place for visitors who are looking for comfort and pleasant surroundings without the formality of the larger luxury hotels. Courtyard for summer dining. Reserved beach. **€€€€**

San Cassiano
Calle della Rosa 2232
Santa Croce
Tel: 041-5241768
Fax: 041-721033
www.sancassiano.it
One of the few hotels actually on the Grand Canal, the San Cassiano is converted from a 14th-century *palazzo.* About half the rooms have canalside views looking across to the Ca' d'Oro. **€€€**

Santo Stefano
Campo Santo Stefano 2957
San Marco
Tel: 041-5200166
Fax: 041-5224460
www.hotelsantostefanovenezia.com
This small hotel, occupying a former palace watchtower, is a welcome addition to the Venetian scene. It is set on one of the city's most spacious and stylish squares, close to the Accademia. Small but tastefully furnished rooms lit by Murano glass chandeliers. Babysitting service. **€€–€€€**

Saturnia & International
Calle Larga XXII Marzo 2398
San Marco
Tel: 041-5208377
Fax: 041-5207131
www.hotelsaturnia.it
Very romantic 4-star hotel housed in an original 14th-century palace close to bustling Piazza San Marco. Both intimate and comfortable. **€€€–€€€€**

VENETO

Verona

Due Torri Baglioni
Piazza S. Anastasia 4
Tel: 045-595044
Fax: 045-8004130
www.duetorriverona@baglionihotels.com
This grand classical *palazzo* has been well converted into a luxurious hotel and has an excellent, if rather formal, restaurant with a fine wine list. **€€€€**

Gabbia D'Oro
Corso Porta Borsari 4/A
Tel: 045-8003060
Fax: 045-590293
www.hotelgabbiadoro@easynet.it
Highly acclaimed, elegant small hotel offering sheer 5-star luxury. Probably the best hotel in Verona. **€€€€**

Giulietta e Romeo
Via Tre Marchetti 3
Tel: 045-8003554
Fax: 045-8010862
www.giuliettaeromeo.com
Well-established 3-star hotel just a few steps from the Arena. Recently sympathetically refurbished. **€€–€€€**

Porta Palio
Via Galliano 21
Tel: 045-8102140
Fax: 045-8101771
www.comfortinn.com/hotel/it436
Modern and comfortable 3-star hotel located just behind the historic centre. **€€–€€€**

Victoria
Via Adua 8
Tel: 045-590566
Fax: 045-590155
www.hotelvictoria.it
Set in the heart of the old quarter of Verona, this historic *palazzo* has been creatively yet sensitively converted. The bedrooms are superbly inviting, while the reception rooms incorporate Roman and medieval remains, including some mosaics. **€€€–€€€€**

Vicenza

Campo Marzio
Viale Roma 21
Tel: 0444-545700
Fax: 0444-320495
www.hotelcampomarzio.com
A convenient hotel, though not particularly individual. It is near the park and within easy reach of the railway station. **€€–€€€**

Price Categories

Price categories are based on double occupancy without breakfast:
€ = under €150
€€ = €150–250
€€€ = €250–350
€€€€ = €350 and above

FRIULI-VENEZIA GIULIA

Trieste

Grand Hotel Duchi d'Aosta
Piazza Unità d'Italia 2
Tel: 040-7600011
Fax: 040-366092
www.magesta.com
This hotel has 55 rooms and is very charming, with big, well-furnished rooms, and efficient service, in a convenient, central position. Be sure to try the excellent restaurant (Harry's Grill). **€€€**

Jolly
Corso Cavour 7
Tel: 040-7600055
Fax: 040-362699
www.jollyhotels.it
Jolly-style hotel with the usual great service and comfort. **€€€**

Starhotel Savoia Excelsior Palace
Riva del Mandracchio 4
Tel: 040-77941
Fax: 040-638260
www.starhotels.it
Imposing façade on the seafront very close to the centre. **€€€**

Udine

Astoria Hotel Italia
Piazza XX Settembre 24
Tel: 0432-505091
Fax: 0432-509070
www.hotelastoria.udine.it
Set in the historic centre of this lovely old town, this is a delightful and peaceful spot. Attentive and professional service. **€–€€**

TRENTINO-ALTO ADIGE

Bolzano

Scala-Stiegl
Via Brennero 11
Tel: 0471-976222
Fax: 0471-981141

www.scalahot.com
This turn-of-the-last-century hotel is situated within walking distance of the old city centre. In spite of all its modern comforts, it has managed to maintain its historic ambience with a spacious garden, restaurant and swimming pool. In the same family for three generations. **€–€€**

Merano

Villa Tivoli
Via Verdi 72
Tel: 0473-446282
Fax: 0473-446849
www.villativoli.it
Set in its own gardens, this Liberty-style small hotel is an oasis of tranquillity and is highly acclaimed. Meals are served al fresco on a panoramic terrace. **€–€€**

Rovereto

Leon d'Oro
Via Tacchi 2
Tel: 0464-437333
Fax: 0464-423777
www.rovhotels.com
Acclaimed hotel (56 rooms) offering a warm, intimate atmosphere in peaceful surroundings in Trentino's lovely city – second only to Trento. **€–€€€**

Trento

Albergo Accademia
Vicolo Colico 4–6
Tel: 0461-233600
Fax: 0461-230174
www.accademiahotel.it
In a 14th-century historic building situated in the middle of the old town, on a tiny square near the Piazza Duomo. The charming hotel has been completely renovated. Big and spacious rooms are bright and comfortably furnished. The restaurant is famous for its good cuisine, especially fish. **€€**

Buonconsiglio
Via Romagnosi 16/18
Tel: 0461-272888
Fax: 0461-272889
A stylish, modern hotel suitable for business and leisure travellers. Well-equipped and close to the historic centre. **€**

Hotel America
Via Torre Verde 50
Tel: 0461-983010
Fax: 0461-230603
www.hotelamerica.it
Long-established hotel set in the historic heart of Trento, close to the Castello del Buonconsiglio. Good service. **€**

Villa Madruzzo
Località Cognola
Via Ponte Alto 26
(3 km from centre)
Tel: 0461-986220
Fax: 0461-986361
www.villamadruzzo.it
A grand hill top villa set in charming grounds. An elegant interior is matched by pleasing service and good traditional cuisine. **€–€€**

MILAN

Grand Hotels

Carlton Hotel Baglioni
Via Senato 5
Tel: 02-77077
Fax: 02-783300
www.baglionihotels.com
Overlooking the ultra-chic Via della Spiga, this luxurious hotel offers the ultimate in elegance and refinement. Rooms are furnished with exquisite silk brocades, antiques and marbled bathrooms. There are 92 sound-proofed rooms, some of which have sunroofs and nine opulent suites. Outside terrace with very fashionable tented "shisha bar" – hubbly-bubbly pipes and Middle Eastern nibbles. **€€€€**

Cavour
Via Fatebenefratelli 21
Tel: 02-620001
Fax: 02-6592263
www.hotelcavour.it
Located in the fashion and designer district, the Quadrilatero, this modern hotel offers every comfort. **€€–€€€**

Excelsior Gallia
Piazza Duca d'Aosta 9
Tel: 02-67851
Fax: 02-66713239
www.excelsiorgallia.it
Luxury-category, historic hotel located close to Stazione Centrale, near the air terminal and business centre. Part of Le Meridien hotels and resorts. Expensive, but the service is perfect. **€€€€**

Four Seasons
Via Gesù 8
Tel: 02-77088
Fax: 02-77085000
www.fourseasons.com
This is one of Milan's best hotels, both in terms of atmosphere and unadulterated luxury. Converted from a 15th-century monastery, with lovely rooms overlooking delightful cloisters. Favoured by film/music stars and fashion personalities. Magnificent Il Teatro gourmet restaurant (open evenings only) and the less rarified La Veranda restaurant. **€€€€**

Grand Hotel et de Milan
Via A Manzoni 29
Tel: 02-723141
Fax: 02-86460861
www.grandhoteletdemilan.it
Milan's most historic hotel, founded in 1863 and containing the celebrated suite where Verdi died. Set north of the Duomo, on one of the city's most prestigious streets close to La Scala. Popular Don Carlos restaurant. Sumptuous décor and antiques. **€€€€**

Hermitage
Via Messina 10
Tel: 02-318170
Fax: 02-33107399
www.monrifhotels.it
Elegant and characterful hotel of 119 rooms (eight suites also available). The garden and veranda are especially delightful. **€€€**

Jolly Hotel President
Largo Augusto 10
Tel: 02-77461
Fax: 02-783449
www.jollyhotels.it
Grand and comfortable. Excellent member of the Jolly chain. 234 rooms; seven suites; free transport to Linate Airport. **€€€–€€€€**

Principe di Savoia
Piazza della Repubblica 17
Tel: 02-62301
Fax: 02-6595838
www.luxurycollection.com
Located north of the cathedral, a classic luxury hotel, with superb service. The ultimate in elegance and luxury. 341 bedrooms, 63

suites; swimming pool and sauna, health/spa centre. **€€€€**

Villa San Carlo Borromeo
Piazza Borromeo 20, Senago (12 km/7 miles north of Milan)
Tel: 02-994741
Fax: 02-99474241
www.hotelvillasancarloborromeo.com
This 5-star luxury hotel, set in 6 hectares (14 acres) of parkland, is awash with antiques, Murano chandeliers, frescoes and beautiful works of art. There is a permanent museum of art and many visiting exhibitions. The rooms and suites take their names from artists, writers and composers and are all individually designed. Shuttle service on request from Linate (20 km) and Malpensa (30 km) airports. **€€€€**

The Westin Palace
Piazza della Repubblica 20
Tel: 02-63361
Fax: 02-654485
www.westin.com
In the heart of Milan, this elegant and sophisticated hotel offers impeccable service and amenities. **€€€€**

Price Categories

Price categories are based on double occupancy without breakfast:
€ = under €150
€€ = €150–250
€€€ = €250–350
€€€€ = €350 and above

Small Hotels and B&Bs

Antica Locanda dei Mercanti
Via San Tomaso 6
Tel: 02-8054080
Fax: 02-8054090
www.locanda.it
Small, charming hotel set in an 18th-century palace in a pedestrianised area, near La Scala. Each room is individually decorated, but common features include personal "libraries", wrought-iron bedsteads and marble bathrooms. **€€**

Antica Locanda Leonardo
Corso Magenta 78
Tel: 02-463317
Fax: 02-48019012
www.lelloc.com
Small, family-run hotel offering a warm welcome. Enviable location very close to the church of Santa Maria delle Grazie. **€–€€**

Antica Locanda Solferino
Via Castelfidardo 2
Tel: 02-6570129
Fax: 02-6571361
This former inn in the characterful, arty Brera district has just 11 rooms. Comfortable, well located and highly regarded. **€–€€**

Ariston
Largo Carrobbio 2
Tel: 02-72000556
Fax: 02-72000914
www.brerahotels.com/ariston
This is a so-called "ecological" hotel which manages to be both comfortable and environmentally correct. Rooms are well furnished and the atmosphere is friendly. One floor is given over to non-smokers. All guests have unlimited use of the hotel bicycles. **€–€€**

Caffelletto
Via Procaccini 7
Tel: 02-3311814/3311820
Fax: 02-3313009
www.caffelletto.it
Two apartments offering B&B are available in Corso Vercelli, in a good neighbourhood close to Leonardo's *Last Supper*. The ground-floor apartment is very spacious in the "faded elegance" style and represents extremely good value, although there is no air conditioning. **€**

Gran Duca di York
Via Moneta 1
Tel: 02-874863
Fax: 02-8690344
www.ducadiyork.com
Centrally located close to the Duomo, this is a very popular boutique hotel with just 33 rooms. It is housed in a former 18th-century *palazzo*, recently very stylishly renovated. This good-value hotel attracts a faithful following. **€€**

Spadari al Duomo
Via Spadari 11
Tel: 02-72002371
Fax: 02-861184
www.spadarihotel.com
Exclusive little jewel of a boutique hotel just around the corner from the Duomo and La Scala. The first "art hotel" in Italy, this was developed around a private collection of art by contemporary artists and designer furniture. The result is a collection of 40 lovely rooms, all individually designed. Very popular. Rooms 72 and 74 have jacuzzis. **€€–€€€**

The Gray
Via San Raffaele 6
Tel: 02-7208951
Fax: 02-866526
www.thegray@sinahotels.it
In the heart of Milan, very close to the Duomo, the Scala and Galleria Vittorio Emanuele, this designer boutique hotel has become one of the city's most fashionable. The 21 rooms are all individually styled. **€€€€**

LOMBARDY

Bergamo

Agnello d'oro
Via Gombito 22
Tel: 035-249883
Fax: 035-235612
Small inn in the upper city with 20 simple but comfortable rooms and a fine restaurant serving traditional Lombardic cuisine. **€**

Excelsior San Marco
Piazza della Repubblica 6
Tel: 035-366111
Fax: 035-366159
Impressive modern hotel with efficient service and good facilities. Roof garden. **€€**

Mantua

Il Leone
Piazza IV Martiri 2
Tel: 0375-86077
Fax: 0375-86770
The rather simple facade of the former house of the Gonzagas conceals this remarkable hotel with rooms with an inner courtyard and swimming pool. Cultivated lounge, big and comfortable rooms and an excellent restaurant. **€**

Rechigi
Via Calvi 30
Tel: 0376-320781
Fax: 0376-220291
www.rechigi.com

Central location. This hotel is both elegant and comfortable. Permanent collection of modern art in the hall. **€–€€**

San Lorenzo
Piazza Concordia 14
Tel: 0376-220500
Fax: 0376-327194
www.hotelsanlorenzo.it
Typical city hotel near the cathedral. The spacious rooms and beautiful salons are partly furnished with antique furniture. Good service. Pretty garden on the roof. **€€**

Pavia

Excelsior
Piazzale Stazione 25
Tel: 0382-28596
Fax: 0382-26030
Reliable city hotel opposite the station. Although the exterior is not especially pretty, the interior is well tended. **€**

Price Categories

Price categories are based on double occupancy without breakfast:
€ = under €150
€€ = €150–250
€€€ = €250–350
€€€€ = €350 and above

VALLE D'AOSTA

Aosta

Classhotel Aosta
Corso Ivrea 146
Tel: 0165-41845
Fax: 0165-236660
www.classhotel.com
Well located at the old gates of the city, this hotel is popular with both tourists and business clients. A good standard of comfort. **€–€€**

Europe
Piazza Narbonne 8
Tel: 0165-236363
Fax: 0165-40566
Set in the historic centre, this is a traditional hotel, noted for its peace and quiet as well as elegance. **€€**

Milleluci
Località Porossan Roppoz 15
Tel: 0165-235278
Fax: 0165-235284
www.hotelmilleluci.com
Pleasant, traditional inn with 31 rooms in a panoramic and peaceful position with views over the city. Swimming pool. **€–€€**

Courmayeur

Gran Baita
Strada Larzey
Tel: 0165-844040
Fax: 0165-844805
www.sogliahotels.com
Luxurious hotel offering high standards, conveniently located for the cable-car station, in a quiet position. Panoramic terrace with fabulous views of Mont Blanc, swimming pool and health spa. **€€–€€€**

Grand Hotel Royal e Golf
Via Roma 87
Tel: 0165-831611
Fax: 0165-842093
E-mail: info@hotelroyalgolf.com
In the pedestrianised area in the heart of town, this luxurious and comfortable hotel provides an oasis of calm away from the tempting shops. Well-appointed rooms look out towards Mont Blanc. There's also a health centre. **€€€–€€€€**

La Baita
Località Plan Checrouit
Tel: 0165-843570
Fax: 0165-846641
This rustic mountain hotel sits 1,800 metres (905 ft) high at the top of the cable car above Courmayeur. **€€**

Courmayeur-Entrèves

La Grange
Strada La Brenva
Entrèves (3 km from Courmayeur)
Tel: 0165-869733
Fax: 0165-869744
www.lagrange-it.com
This charming small hotel (23 rooms) is situated in the pretty mountain village of Entrèves, a hidden corner of the Aosta Valley at the bottom of Mont Blanc. **€**

Hotel La Brenva
Courmayeur-Entrèves
Tel: 0165-869780
Fax: 0165-869726
www.labrenva.com
This cosy inn with only 12 rooms has the atmosphere of a mountain chalet, with wood panelling and balconies facing Mont Blanc. It also has an exquisite restaurant, La Brenva. **€–€€**

PIEDMONT

Alba (Cuneo)

Savona
Via Roma 1
Tel: 0173-440440
Fax: 0173-363475
www.hotelsavona.com
Centrally situated on the main piazza, this very comfortable hotel is good value and also offers suites. A separate restaurant is a temple to the truffle – the "white gold" of Alba. **€–€€**

Canelli (Asti)

Agriturismo La Casa in Collina
Località Sant'Antonio 30 (2 km/1 mile west of Canelli and 29 km/18 miles from Asti)
Tel: 0141-822827
Fax: 0141-823543
E-mail: casaincollina@casaincollina.com
This lovely house sits on a hill, overlooking vineyards and enjoys stunning views of the snowy peaks of the Alps. There are six spacious rooms furnished with period pieces and antiques, and the views from the breakfast room are splendid. **€**

Chiaverano d'Ivrea (Turin)

Castello San Giuseppe
Tel: 0125-424370
Fax: 0125-641278
www.castellosangiuseppe.it
Comfortable country hotel with a gorgeous garden in part of the well-preserved old Castello San Giuseppe. Some rooms have jacuzzi baths. **€–€€**

Turin

Art Boston
Via Massena 70
Tel: 011-500359
Fax: 011-599358
www.hotelbostontorino.it
Very tasteful hotel, designed with a sense of exclusivity and originality. All the common areas are hung with works of contemporary art, and

there is an oriental theme in some of the newly decorated bedrooms. **€€–€€€**

Genio
Corso Vittorio Emanuele II 47
Tel: 011-6505771
Fax: 011-6508264
www.hotelgenio.it
Comfortable, family-run hotel, close to Porta Nuova station. The rooms have recently been refurbished very elegantly. **€€**

Grand Hotel Sitea
Via Carlo Alberto 35
Tel: 011-5170171
Fax: 011-548090
www.thi.it
Traditional hotel with elegant furnishings and marble bathrooms. Located in the heart of the city, but the ambience is both relaxing and luxurious. **€€–€€€**

Jolly Hotel Ambasciatori
Corso Vittorio Emanuele II 104
Tel: 011-5752
Fax: 011-544978
www.jollyhotels.com
Large, modern hotel, favoured by businesspeople. Good location and service. **€€**

Le Meridien Art+Tech
Via Nizza 230, Lingotto
Tel: 011-6642000
Fax: 011-6642001
www.lemeridien-lingotto.it
This 5-star hotel is a monument to cutting-edge design with such gurus of style as Philippe Starck, Antonio Citterio and Giò Ponti's handiwork much in evidence. The glass-roofed central hall also has three ultra-fast glass lifts. In the bedrooms, plasma-screen TVs and exhilarating power-showers are standard, as are allergy-free bed linen and carpets. From the jogging track on the roof there are glorious, panoramic views of the Alps. **€€€€**

Le Meridien Lingotto
Via Nizza 262, Lingotto
Tel: 011-6642000
Fax: 011-6642001
www.lemeridien-lingotto.it
Housed in part of the orginal Fiat factory, one of the most spectacular testaments to industrial architecture, this hotel has every luxury and comfort. As well as being ultra-stylish, the facilities and service are exemplary. **€€€–€€€€**

Starhotel Majestic
Corso Vittorio Emanuele II 54
Tel: 011-539153
Fax: 011-534963
www.starhotels.it
Good location in the centre of the city, opposite the Porta Nuova station. The hotel has recently been renovated and also offers "executive rooms" with internet access, fast modems and fax machines. **€€–€€€**

Turin Palace Hotel
Via Sacchi 8
Tel: 011-5625511
Fax: 011-5612187
www.thi.it
A traditional, classic and elegant hotel offering a good restaurant. Excellent service. **€€–€€€**

Victoria
Via Nino Costa 4
Tel: 011-5611909
Fax: 011-5611806
www.hotelvictoria-torino.com
Highly acclaimed, classic hotel in the middle of the city, but quietly situated. Remarkable in that each room has been designed in a different style and with a lot of imagination, including English country-house style with antique and oriental furniture. **€€**

Villa Sassi
Strada Traforo del Pino 47
Tel: 011-8980556
Fax: 011-8980095
www.villasassi.com
This hotel is housed in an 18th-century villa, in a great park in the foothills of Turin. Only 16 bedrooms, but excellent service and comfort. Very good restaurant, also open to non-residents. Exclusive. **€€–€€€**

THE LAKES

Bellagio (Lago di Como)

Grand Hotel Villa Serbelloni
Via Roma 1
Tel: 031-950216
Fax: 031-951529
www.villaserbelloni.it
This fabulous Neoclassical patrician villa has been converted into one of the finest hotels in northern Italy. The views, grounds, facilities, full health spa and service are all impeccable. **€€€€**

Como

Barchetta Excelsior
Piazza Cavour 1
Tel: 031-3221
Fax: 031-302622
www.hotelbarchetta.com
Very comfortable modern hotel in a central location. Request a room overlooking the lake. **€€€**

Villa d'Este
Via Regina 40
Cernobbio
Tel: 031-3481
Fax: 031-348844
www.villadeste.it
Overlooking Lake Como, this fabled hotel offers the highest standards of unashamed luxury with every possible amenity. Open March–November. **€€€€**

Isole Borromee (Lago Maggiore)

Hotel Verbano
Via Ugo Ara 2
Isola dei Pescatori
Tel: 0323-30408
Fax: 0323-33129
www.hotelverbano.it
The Isola dei Pescatori is one of the smallest and most romantic among the Islands in the midst of Lake Maggiore. The Verbano has 12, slightly old-fashioned but charming rooms with wonderful views over the lake. **€–€€**

Sirmione (Lago di Garda)

Grand Hotel Terme
Viale Marconi 7
Tel: 030-916261
Fax: 030-916192
www.termedisirmione.com
Elegant, well-modernised hotel overlooking the lake, in attractive grounds. Good facilities include a pool, sauna and fitness centre. **€€€–€€€€**

Desirée
Via San Pietro 2
Tel: 030-9905244
Fax: 030-916241
www.hotel-desiree.it
Situated right in the heart of Sirmione, close to the spa and the ruins of Catullo, this a cheerful, welcoming small hotel with 34

rooms. Offering bright, comfortable accommodation and genuine, warm hospitality, the hotel enjoys an exceptionally quiet setting, in a largely traffic-free zone, surrounded by a garden of palm trees. Outdoor swimming pool. **€–€€**

Varenna (Lecco/Lago di Como)

Palazzo Arzaga
25080 Carzago di Calvagese della Riviera
Tel: 030-680600
Fax: 030-6806270
www.palazzoarzaga.com
Very luxurious, 5-star hotel set in a stunning location within easy reach of Lake Garda, Brescia and Verona. This 15th-century palace of pleasure and pampering also has its own spa and golf course. Member of Preferred Hotels & Resorts Worldwide. **€€€€**

LIGURIA & RIVIERA

Alassio

Diana Grand Hotel
Via Garibaldi 110
Tel: 0182-642701
Fax: 0182-640304
www.dianagh.it
Good service, a swimming pool and a terrace garden in high season. Half board mandatory in high season. Private beach. Closed January–February. **€€**

Bordighera

Grand Hotel del Mare
Via Portico della Punta 34
Tel: 0184-262201
Fax: 0184-262394
www.grandhoteldelmare.it
Exclusive hotel overlooking the sea, preferred by adults for its quietness, its comfort and its beautiful rooms. **€€€**

Camogli

Cenobio dei Dogi
Via Cuneo 34
Tel: 0185-7241
Fax: 0185-772796
www.cenobio.it
This hotel, in a wonderful spot overlooking the sea, is surrounded by a splendid park. It is well known for its salt-water swimming pool, its private beach and its nightclub during the summer. **€€–€€€**

Genoa

Bristol Palace
Via XX Settembre 35
Tel: 010-592541
Fax: 010-561756
www.hotelbristolpalace.com
Despite its modest entrance, a well-furnished hotel – particularly the dining room, which is decorated in the Louis XVI style. **€€€**

Jolly Hotel Plaza
Via M. Piaggio 11
Tel: 010-83161
Fax: 010-8391850
www.jollyhotels.it
Two period buildings linked by a modern nucleus, transformed into a centrally located, pleasant hotel. 133 rooms. **€€–€€€**

Locanda di Palazzo Cicala
Piazza San Lorenzo 16
Tel: 010-2518824
Fax: 010-2467414
www.thecharminghotels.com
This recently opened hotel is housed in a delightful 16th-century *palazzo* in the heart of the old city. Large, airy rooms with high arched ceilings combine a nostalgic atmosphere with modern convenience. **€€–€€€**

Portofino

Splendido
Viale Baratta 16
Tel: 0185-267801
Fax: 0185-267806
E-mail: reservations@splendido.net
One of Italy's finest hotels, very popular with the glitterati. This hotel is a peaceful oasis along a street lined with olive trees, affording a splendid view of the Portofino promontory. Open end March–mid-November. **€€€€**

Rapallo

Hotel Europa
Via Milite Ignoto 2
Tel: 0185-669521
Fax: 0185-669847
www.hoteleuropa-rapallo.com
Part of the Turin Hotels group, this Art Nouveau hotel was restored to its former glory in 1996. Fine restaurant, fitness centre. **€**

Excelsior Palace Hotel
Via San Michele di Pagana 8
Tel: 0185-230666
Fax: 0185-230214
www.excelsior@thi.it
Beautifully appointed hotel overlooking the Gulf of Tigullio and Portofino. Every amenity, including swimming pool, health spa and conference facilities. **€€€€**

San Remo

Paradiso
Via Roccasterone 12
Tel: 01845-71211
Fax: 01845-78176
www.paradisohotel.it
A member of the Logis d'Italia group, this very pleasant hotel is tucked away in a quiet, leafy spot with easy access to both sea and the historical centre. **€–€€**

Royal
Corso Imperatrice 80
Tel: 0184-5391
Fax: 0184-661445
www.royalhotelsanremo.com
Luxury hotel surrounded by terraced gardens filled with flowers and palm trees. Big, comfortable rooms overlooking the sea or hills. **€€€–€€€€**

Santa Margherita Ligure

Agriturismo Roberto Gnocchi
Via Romana 53, San Lorenzo della Costa (2.5km/1½ miles west of Santa Margherita Ligure)
Tel/fax: 0185-283431
A stay here is like being a guest in a country house. Lovely views of the sea from the terrace. Booking essential. Open May–15 October. **€€**

Imperiale Palace
Via Pagana 19
Tel: 0185-288991
Fax: 0185-284223
www.hotelimperiale.com
Luxury, big hotel in the classic tradition, surrounded by a tropical garden. Old-fashioned décor with antique furnishings.**€€€–€€€€**

Metropole
Via Pagana 2
Tel: 0185-286134
Fax: 0185-283495
This elegant, traditional hotel is run most professionally. Smart

restaurant which specialises in Ligurian dishes. Closed November. **€€€**

Sestri Levante

Grand Hotel dei Castelli
Via alla Penisola 26
Tel: 0185-487220/485780
Fax: 0185-44767
www.rainbownet.it/htl.castelli
Quiet and pleasant hotel in front of the church of San Niccolò, surrounded by a big park and overlooking the sea. An elevator descends to the hotel's private beach. 29 rooms. **€€–€€€**

Ventimiglia

La Riserva di Castel d'Appio
Castel d'Appio 71
Tel: 0184-229533
Fax: 0184-229712
www.lariserva.it
5 km outside Ventimiglia, this is a small place with a wonderful view of the Riviera dei Fiori and the Costa Azzurra. **€–€€**

Price Categories

Price categories are based on double occupancy without breakfast:
€ = under €150
€€ = €150–250
€€€ = €250–350
€€€€ = €350 and above

EMILIA ROMAGNA

Bologna

Grand Hotel Baglioni
Via Indipendenza 8
Tel: 051-225445
Fax: 051-234840
www.baglionihotels.com
In the historic heart of Bologna, this former 18th-century *palazzo* is yet another example of the Baglioni group of hotels' winning combination of style, elegance and comfort. **€€€–€€€€**

Jolly Hotel de la Gare
Piazza XX Settembre 2
Tel: 051-281611
Fax: 051-249764
www.jollyhotels.it
Near station and the Alitalia terminal. Large and comfortable; recently refurbished. **€€€**

Orologio
Via IV Novembre 10
Tel: 051-7457411
Fax: 051-7457422
www.cnc.it/bologna
This former *palazzo* has very stylish rooms and offers great comfort and excellent service. **€€€**

Royal Hotel Carlton
Via Montebello 8
Tel: 051-249361
Fax: 051-249724
www.montifhotels.it
This big central hotel is extremely comfortable but a little anonymous. Excellent service with recently renovated restaurant. **€€–€€€**

Ferrara

Duchessa Isabella
Via Palestro 70
Tel: 0532-202121
Fax: 0532-202638
In the heart of Ferrara, this elegant, frescoed 15th-century *palazzo* features inlaid ceilings, a collection of antique clocks, a lovely garden, and dishes based on Renaissance recipes for dinner. 27 rooms. **€€€**

Hotel Ripagrande
Via Ripagrande 21
Tel: 0532-765250
Fax: 0532-764377
www.ripagrandehotel.it
This Renaissance palace forms part of Abitare La Storia (Living History), a group of historic independent hotels *(see Hotel Groups, page 364)*. Fine public rooms, good cuisine and a central location. **€€**

Modena

Canalgrande
Corso Canalgrande 6
Tel: 0592-17160
Fax: 0592-21674
www.canalgrandehotel.it
This Neoclassical hotel is pleasingly situated and very comfortable. Large garden and alfresco dining in summer. **€€**

Parma

Starhotel du Parc
Viale Piacenza 12/C
Tel: 0521-292929
Fax: 0521-292828
www.starhotels.it
Early 20th-century building with 169 rooms very close to the centre. This very comfortable, highly acclaimed hotel is pleasingly decorated in the Liberty style. **€€–€€€**

Villa Ducale
Via del Popolo 35/A
Tel: 0521-272727
Fax: 0521-780756
www.popnet.it/villaducale
Charming villa set in appealing grounds. Recently restored, the 47 bedrooms are pleasantly furnished. Welcoming and attentive service. **€€**

SAN MARINO

Grand Hotel San Marino
Viale Antonio Onofri 31
Tel: 0549-992400
Fax: 0549-992951
www.grandhotel.sm
This modestly sized hotel of 63 rooms is probably San Marino's grandest and appeals both to tourists and business clients. **€–€€**

Titano
Contrada del Collegio 31
Tel: 0549-991006
Fax: 0549-991007
www.sanmarinosite.com/htitano
This comfortable hotel lies in the heart of the old town of San Marino and is one of the town's best (and the oldest). The Titano has a spacious terrace overlooking the Apennines and valley, and a recommendable restaurant. **€**

THE ADRIATIC

Ravenna

Bisanzio
Via Salara 30
Tel: 0544-217111
Fax: 0544-32539
www.bisanziohotel.com
Modern and comfortable hotel, with simple rooms, good service and a romantic garden. Close to the most important monuments. **€–€€**

Jolly
Piazza Mameli 1
Tel: 0544-35762
Fax: 0544-216055
www.jollyhotels.it

Price Categories

Price categories are based on double occupancy without breakfast:
€ = under €150
€€ = €150–250
€€€ = €250–350
€€€€ = €350 and above

Hotel with excellent standards and a recently renovated restaurant, La Matta. **€€**

Rimini

Duomo
Via G. Bruno 28
Tel: 0541-24215
Very fine hotel in the old town with comfortable and elegantly furnished rooms and a small garden. **€€**

Grand Hotel
Parco Federico Fellini 1
Tel: 0541-56000
Fax: 0541-56866
www.grandhotelrimini.com
Elegant early 20th-century hotel with beautiful garden. The rooms are tastefully furnished with antique furniture. Guests are the rich and the beautiful. Echoes of Fellini. **€€€–€€€€**

Santarcàngelo di Romagna (Rimini)

Hotel della Porta
Via Andrea Costa 85
Tel: 0541-622152
Fax: 0541-622168
www.italiaabc.it/az/dellaporta
This comfortable hotel is situated in a small village, only 15 km west of Rimini. The carefully restored building consists of two houses. Spacious rooms are very well looked after and equipped in the traditional style of Emilia Romagna. **€€**

Where to Eat

What to Eat

The gentle lifestyle of Italy is partly a product of its civilised eating habits: eating and drinking in tranquillity at least twice a day are the norm here.

Italian breakfast *(colazione)* is usually light and consists of *cappuccino* (espresso and steamed milk) and a *cornetto* (pastry/croissant), or simply *caffè* (black and strong espresso).

Except in the industrialised cities, *pranzo* (lunch) is the big meal of the day. It consists of *antipasto* (hors d'oeuvre), a *primo* (pasta, rice or soup) and a *secondo* (meat or fish with a vegetable – *contorno* – or salad). Cheese and/or fruit usually follows. Italians usually drink coffee *(espresso)* after lunch and/or a liqueur, such as *grappa, amaro* or *sambuca.*

Traditionally, dinner is similar to lunch, but lighter. However, in the cities people are tending to eat less at lunchtime and making dinner the major meal of the day.

Every region in Italy has its own typical dishes: Piedmont specialises in pheasant, hare, truffles and *zabaglione* (a hot dessert made with whipped egg yolks and Marsala wine); Lombardy is known for *risotto alla Milanese* (saffron and onions), minestrone, veal and *panettone* (a sweet Christmas bread with sultanas and candied fruits); Trentino-Alto Adige is the place for dumplings and thick soups to keep out the cold.
See also the chapter on Rustic and Classic Cuisine, page 103.

Where to Eat

Italy has thousands of restaurants, trattorias and *osterie*. If you do not want to have a complete meal, you can have a snack at the bar or at *tavole calde* and *rosticcerie* (grills).

If you go to a restaurant, don't order just a salad: the waiters may look down on you and treat you with disdain. If you think a complete meal is too big, forgo the *antipasto*, but take a *primo* and a *secondo* at least.

The restaurants listed below have been recommended by Italian food writers and/or the authors of this guide. It is difficult to generalise about prices, since much depends on the choice of wine and menu selection. Even noted chefs may offer a less expensive, but restricted, menu in conjunction with the main menu.

VENICE

Castello

Al Covo
Campiello della Pescaria 3968
Tel: 041-5223812
Enthusiastically run restaurant serving fish fresh from the lagoon, wild duck (seasonal) and wonderful home-made desserts. Great wine list. Lunch is less expensive than dinner. Highly recommended by food critics. Closed: Wednesday and Thursday. **€€€**

L'Aciugheta
Campo San Filoppo e Giacomo
Tel: 041-5224292
Excellent, good-value *bàcaro* but also has a proper menu featuring a variety of dishes from Adriatic fish to truffles and oysters. Popular with Venetians and also for its fine Friuli wines. Closed: Monday. **€–€€**

Dorsoduro

Ai Gondolieri
Fondamente de l'Ospedaleto 366
Tel: 041-5286396
Near the Guggenheim Museum, this popular restaurant specialises in meat and game. Also serves exceptional risottos. Booking essential. Closed: Tuesday. **€€€**

Cantinone Gia Schiavi
Fondamente Nani 992
Dorsoduro
Tel: 041-5230034
Located on Rio di San Trovaso, this canalside wine bar is extremely

popular with locals. Do as the Venetians do and enjoy *cichetti*, typical bar snacks, with a glass of wine. It is especially atmospheric at the Venetian cocktail hour, 7–8pm. Closed: at 9.30pm and Sunday dinner. **€–€€**

Taverna San Trovaso
Fondamenta Priuli 1016
Tel: 041-5203703
Cheap, cheerful trattoria and pizzeria for standard Italian cuisine. Great setting on the canal. Closed: Monday. **€€**

Giudecca

Do Mori
Fondamenta Sant'Eufemia
Giudecca 588
Tel: 041-5225452
Good, Venetian home cooking specialising in fish dishes. For an alternative to the high prices of Harry's Dolci and the legendary Cipriani, this establishment, formed, by a breakaway group from Harry's Bar, could be the better-value option. Closed: Sunday. **€€**

Harry's Dolci
Fondamenta San Biagio 773
Tel: 041-5224844
Similar food to Harry's Bar in San Marco, but cheaper. Specialities are the *dolci* (cakes), which are served all day. A terrace for summer overlooks the Giudecca. Closed: Tuesday and November–mid-March. **€€€**

Hotel Cipriani
Fondamente San Giovanni
Giudecca 10
Tel: 041-5207744
www.hotelcipriani.it
One of the finest city restaurants, set within the most luxurious city hotel. The elegant restaurant spills out onto a glorious summer terrace. Dishes include *carpaccio*, clams with asparagus, scampi and *calamari*, and veal with artichokes. Closed: early November–mid-March. **€€€€**

San Marco

Al Graspo de Ua
Calle de Bombaseri 5094
Tel: 041-5200150
Close to the Rialto Bridge. This well-established fish restaurant, under its wooden roof, is centuries old, and has a long tradition of excellent cooking. It is a delight for those seeking local colour. National cuisine. Closed: Monday in January. **€€€–€€€€**

Al Volto
Calle Cavalli
San Marco 4081
Tel: 041-5228945
This is Venice's oldest *enoteca* (wine bar), where you can choose between tastings from several thousand different wines. Try a variety of *ombre* (small glasses of wine) accompanied by *cichetti*, traditional Venetian snacks. Extremely popular. Open: 10am–2.30pm, 5–10.30pm. Closed: Sunday. **€**

Antico Martini
Campo San Fantin 1983
Tel: 041-5224121
Close to the site of the Fenice opera house. Elegant and intimate, serving Venetian and international cuisine. Closed: all day Tuesday and Wednesday lunch. Reserve. **€€€€**

Antico Pignolo
Calle dei Specchieri 451
San Marco
Tel: 041-5228123
Classical Venetian ambience in this highly regarded restaurant. Venetian and traditional specialities include fresh fish. Exceptional wine list and attentive, professional service in four spacious dining salons where well-spaced tables ensure your privacy. **€€€€**

Caffè Quadri
Procuratie Vecchie
Piazza San Marco 120
Tel: 041-5222105
www.quadrivenice.com
As well as the famous bar, this is the setting for a fine restaurant, the only proper one on the piazza, serving Venetian specialities as well as creative twists on classic Italian cuisine. Innovative and traditional Venetian dishes. Prices are predictably high but acceptable by Venetian standards. Closed: Monday out of season. **€€€€**

Canova
Luna Hotel Baglioni
Calle Larga dell'Ascensione 1243
Tel: 041-5289840
Exquisite dishes served in the gracious surroundings of the Canova restaurant of the Baglioni Hotel. An extensive menu includes Venetian specialities and international cuisine, all prepared with fresh seasonal ingredients. Excellent service and extensive wine menu. Booking essential **€€€€**

Harry's Bar
Calle Vallaresso 1323
Tel: 041-5285777
This bar/restaurant was a favourite haunt of Hemingway; it is now mainly patronised by very wealthy Venetians, expatriates and American tourists. Good home-made pastas at exorbitant prices. Open daily. **€€€€**

Le Bistrot de Venise
Calle dei Fabbri 4685
Tel: 041-5236651
Atmospheric bistro-cum-wine bar behind St Mark's. Seafood delicacies such as lobster and scampi and elaborate Venetian menus feature. **€€€**

San Polo

Antica Bessetta
Salizada de Ca' Zusto,
Tel: 041-721687
Rustic trattoria just north of San Giacomo dell'Orio specialising in Venetian home cooking. It is a good spot in which to sample seafood risotto, *risi e bisi*, or the catch of the day. Closed: Tuesday and Wednesday. **€€–€€€**

Antico Dolo
Ruga Vecchia San Giovanni
San Polo 778
Tel: 041-5226546
Close to Do Mori *(below)*, this rustic inn began life as the haunt of the boatmen who plied the Rialto, delivering fresh produce to the markets. Good snacks including *baccalà* (salt cod) and *bruschetta* are served in the bohemian and buzzing atmosphere. Restaurant

Price Guide

The price of a three-course meal for two with wine:
€ = under €25
€€ = €25–50
€€€ = €50–100
€€€€ = over €100

Price Guide

The price of a three-course meal for two with wine:
€ = under €25
€€ = €25–50
€€€ = €50–100
€€€€ = over €100

menu available in the evening – reservations necessary. Open: noon–10.30pm. Closed: Monday. **€–€€**

Do Mori
Calle de Do Mori
San Polo 429
Tel: 041-5225401
Popular and hugely atmospheric inn serving a good range of Venetian tapas. Choose tiny sandwiches, *tramezzini*, stuffed with crab, aubergines or shrimps accompanied by a glass of wine. Open: 8.30am–9.30pm Monday–Saturday. **€**

Osteria Da Fiore
Calle del Scaleter
San Polo 2202a
Tel: 041-721308
Acclaimed for its superb food, this is regarded as one of Italy's top restaurants. It has one Michelin star. The very stylish *osteria* is popular with locals, foreigners and celebrities, especially during the Venice Film Festival. Exquisitely subtle Venetian cuisine with seasonal specialities. Closed: Sunday and Monday. Booking essential. **€€€€**

Trattoria alla Madonna
Calle della Madonna 594
Tel: 041-5223824
This is a popular fish and seafood restaurant near the Rialto. It offers good value for Venice, and hence is always crowded – the service can be brusque. Closed: Wednesday. Reserve on weekdays. **€€–€€€**

Santa Croce

Antica Bessetta
Salizada de Ca' Zusto 1395
Tel: 041-721687
Near San Giacomo dell'Orio, off the beaten track. Authentic family-run trattoria, a temple to Venetian cooking. Highly recommended by food critics. Closed: January–February, Tuesday and Wednesday lunch except April–October. Reserve. **€€–€€€**

VENETO

Padua

Dotto di Campagna
Via Randaccio 4, Ponte di Brenta
Località Torre (4 km out of town)
Tel: 049-625469
Classic furniture, typical cuisine. Try *pasta e fagioli* (pasta and beans) and *baccalà* (dried salt cod). Closed: Sunday evening, Monday and August. Reserve. **€€**

Verona

12 Apostoli
Vicolo Corticella San Marco 3
Tel: 045-596999
Very atmospheric restaurant; excellent service and cuisine in an ancient building with frescoes by Casarini. Closed: Sunday evening, Monday, Christmas and mid-June to mid-July. **€€€**

Il Desco
Via Dietro S. Sebastiano 7
Tel: 045-595358
Located in a lovely old *palazzo*, this very elegant, highly acclaimed restaurant holds two Michelin stars. Elia Rizzo's superb cooking combines rare and expensive ingredients with the more traditional. Closed: Sunday, Monday and festivals. Booking essential. **€€€€**

Locanda di Castelvecchio
Corso Castelvecchio 21/A
Tel: 045-8030097
This elegant restaurant in a beautiful corner of the old town still has the ambience of an old *osteria*. Friendly service and exquisite Veronic cuisine. Closed: Tuesday and Wednesday lunch. **€€**

Vicenza

Cinzia e Valerio
Piazzetta Porta Padova 65/67
Tel: 0444-505213/512796
Set on the ancient city walls, an elegant restaurant with fish specialities. **€€–€€€**

FRIULI-VENEZIA GIULIA

Trieste

Al Bagatto
Via Venezia 2 (corner of Via Cadorna)
Tel: 040-301771
Flavoursome seafood and fish served in small but very gracious surroundings. Very popular, so booking advised. Closed: Sunday. **€€–€€€**

Antica Trattoria Suban
Via Comici 2
Tel: 040-54368
Friendly and simple, belonging to the same family since 1865. Good regional cuisine based on traditional recipes. Closed: Monday lunch and all day Tuesday. **€€€**

Antico Caffè San Marco
Via Battisti 18
Tel: 040-363538
The grandest *belle-époque* café in the city. Closed: Monday lunch and Tuesday all day. **€€**

Udine

Alla Vedova
Via Tavagnacco 9
Tel: 0432-470291
Very old Friulian restaurant, with outdoor tables in summer. Good traditional cooking. Closed: Sunday evening and Monday. Reserve. **€€**

Là Di Moret
Viale Tricesimo 276
Tel: 0432-545096
Traditional cooking based on classical and Friulian influences. Closed: Sunday and Monday lunch and two weeks July–August. **€€–€€€**

TRENTINO-ALTO ADIGE

Bolzano

Laurin
Via Laurin 4
Tel: 0471-311000
Liberty-style, very pleasant restaurant in the Park Hotel, Laurin. The Mediterranean-style cooking of chef Luca Verdolini and brigade is highly innovative. Very good wine list and an especially attractive bar. Closed: Sunday lunch. **€€–€€€**

Trento

Chiesa
Parco San Marco 64
Tel: 0461-238766
On the first floor of a 17th-century palace with a cloister. Very refined. Closed: Sunday. **€€€**

Le Tire-Bouchon
Via Milano 148
Tel: 046-1261456
In a former *cantina*, this acclaimed restaurant has recently been renovated in classic-modern style. Excellent food, sublime desserts, very attentive service and it stays open late, too. Closed: Sunday. **€€–€€€**

Lo Scrigno del Duomo
Piazza del Duomo 29
Tel: 0461-220030
Elegant atmosphere in 17th-century building. The ground floor is an *enoteca* (wine bar) offering a range of wines and snacks. The restaurant above is recommended for its excellent regional cuisine, inspired by the rich lands of Trentino, and holds a Michelin star. Booking essential. Closed: Monday. **€€€–€€€€**

Osteria a Le Due Spade
Via Don Rizzi 11 (corner Via Verdi)
Tel: 0461-234343
In the heart of the historic centre this 16th-century *osteria* is a temple to gastronomy specialising in the rich flavours of Trentino. It holds one Michelin star – so booking is essential. **€€€€**

Osteria Il Cappello
Piazza B, Lunelli 5
Tel: 0461-235850
Small, rustic, yet elegant restaurant. The owners manage it with a lot of enthusiasm. The menu is small but exquisite, the service excellent and the atmosphere friendly but quiet. The regional dishes and fish dishes are recommended. Closed: Sunday evening and Monday. **€€**

MILAN

Armani/Nobu
Via Pisoni 1
Tel: 02-62312645
Modern, minimalist ambience located in the Emporio Armani. Original and innovative cuisine. On the ground floor there is a sushi bar, while upstairs the restaurant offers fusion food combining the flavours of Japan with South America and the West.Closed: Sunday and Monday lunchtime, August and Christmas. **€€€–€€€€**

Bice
Via Borgospesso 12
Tel: 02-76002572
In a prime location between Via della Spiga and Via Montenapoleone, this restaurant is popular with *fashionistas* and specialises in both Milanese and Tuscan specialities. Booking essential. Closed: Monday, Tuesday lunch and August. **€€€–€€€€**

Boeucc
Piazza Belgioioso 2
Tel: 02-76020224
Sophisticated, design-conscious restaurant attracting the glamorous. Milanese cuisine the speciality. Booking essential. Closed: Saturday, Sunday lunch, August and Christmas/New Year. **€€€€**

Cracco-Peck
Via Victor Hugo
Tel: 02-876774
Carlo Cracco took just three years to earn two Michelin stars in 2004. Still one of Milan's top restaurants, the creative cuisine interprets traditional dishes with great flair. The décor is elegant and sophisticated, and service is impeccable. Booking essential. Closed: Sunday and Saturday lunch; 3 weeks in August; Christmas and New Year; lunchtime mid-June–August. **€€€€**

Il Barretto al Baglioni
Via Senato 5
Tel: 02-77077
The Carlton Hotel Baglioni's elegant restaurant is rather like a gentleman's club – both refined and stylish. Dishes vary from Milanese specialities to international cuisine and the high standard of cuisine is matched by the impeccable service. Booking essential. **€€€€**

Il Luogo di Aimo e Nadia
Via Montecuccoli 6
Tel: 02-416886
A temple to gastronomy, this is acclaimed as one of Italy's top restaurants and holds one Michelin star. Some Tuscan influence characterises the deceptively simple but superbly executed dishes. Closed: Saturday lunch, Sunday, August and Christmas. Booking essential. **€€€€**

La Dolce Vita
Via Bergamini 11
Tel: 02-583303843
Romantic and sophisticated spot with candles and coffered ceilings, whose kitchen stays open until midnight. Lombard specialities, nouvelle cuisine and gourmet menus (less pricey at lunchtime). Closed: Sunday. **€€€–€€€€**

La Scaletta
Piazzale Stazione, Porta Genova 3
Tel: 02-58100290
Modern ambience, with a library and international level cuisine. Good French/Italian cuisine, home-made pasta and bread. Very fashionable. Open evenings only. Closed: Sunday. Reserve. **€€€€**

Mauro
Via Colonnetta 5 (corner of Via Cesare Battisti)
Tel: 02-5461380
This quiet restaurant has the advantage of being open on Sundays – a rarity in Milan. Traditional fish dishes are the speciality, and Florentine prints on the wall reflect the owner's Tuscan roots and style of cuisine. Booking essential. Closed: Monday, Saturday lunch and August. **€€–€€€**

Sadler
Via Conchetta corner of Via Troilo 14
Tel: 02-58104451
Highly acclaimed creative cuisine (two Michelin stars) in a modern, elegant and prestigious setting. Excellent, professional service. Specialities include fish and white truffles (in season). Open for dinner only. Closed: Sunday and for a period in January and August. Reservations essential. **€€€€**

Sadler Wine & Food
Via Monte Bianco 2/A
Tel: 02-4814677
Elegant, but informal, this is a smaller version of Sadler on Via Conchetta with continuous opening

from midday until 11pm. Cuisine based on classical favourites. Closed: Sunday and for a period in January and August. **€€–€€€**

LOMBARDY

Bergamo

Agnello d'Oro
Via Gombito 22
Tel: 035-249883
Good regional food in an old hotel in the upper part of town. Closed: Sunday evening, all day Monday and January. Reserve. **€€€**

Da Vittorio
Viale Papa Giovanni XXIII 221 (Città Bassa)
Tel: 035-213266
One of Italy's top restaurants, this two-Michelin-star temple to gastronomy serves regional specialities with style and flair. Seasonal scampi carpaccio with onion purée or crispy suckling pig. Mouth-watering desserts. Booking essential. Closed: Wednesday and August. **€€€€**

Lio Pellegrini
Via San Tomaso 47
Tel: 035-247813
Highly acclaimed, atmospheric former sacristy, serving Tuscan specialities. There is every form of home-made pasta, including ravioli stuffed with ricotta and chives. Closed: all day Monday and Tuesday lunch. Reservations recommended. **€€€–€€€€**

Trattoria del Teatro
Piazza Mascheroni 3
Tel: 035-238862
With 19th-century furniture and simple but delicious food. Located in Città Alta, featuring specialities such as *baccalà* (salt cod) with polenta. Closed: Monday. **€**

Mantua

Il Cigno Trattoria dei Martini
Piazza Carlo d'Arco 1
Tel: 0376-327101
In a wonderful piazza, in an ancient building. The service is as excellent as the regional cooking taken from recipes passed down through the generations. Closed: Monday, Tuesday and August. Reserve. **€€€**

Price Guide

The price of a three-course meal for two with wine:
€ = under €25
€€ = €25–50
€€€ = €50–100
€€€€ = over €100

VALLE D'AOSTA

Aosta

Le Foyer
Corso Ivrea 146
Tel: 0165-32136
Set just outside Aosta, this restaurant offers excellent fish and Italian cheeses. Closed: Monday evening and all day Tuesday. **€€€**

Vecchia Aosta
Piazza Porte Pretoriane 4
Tel: 0165-361186
Set within part of the old city gateway, this restaurant serves French and regional specialities, ravioli, various stuffed pastas and venison with pomegranate. Closed: Wednesday except July and August. **€€€**

Breuil-Cervinia

Les Neiges d'Antan
Località Crêt de Perrères 10
Tel: 0166-948775
Situated on a mountain 4 km from Breuil-Cervinia, this restaurant with rooms serves typical Valdostana cuisine. Try the *fonduta*. Open: 6 December–1 May and July–15 September. Reserve. **€€€**

Gignod

Locanda La Clusaz
La Clusaz
Statale Gran San Bernardo
Tel: 0165-56075
Set 5 km north of Aosta at La Clusaz, this charming inn has 14 rooms as well as a frescoed medieval interior. Acclaimed restaurant whose specialities include grain soups, polenta and dishes made with chestnuts or bacon. Closed: 10 May–15 June and 3 November–3 December; lunchtime except Saturday, holidays and August. **€€€**

Saint-Pierre

Les Écureuils (Agriturismo)
Località Homené-Sainte Marguerite
Tel: 0165-903831
This small restaurant 8 km outside Aosta belongs to the farmhouse of the Gontier family. Nearly everything on the menu is a product from their own farm and of excellent quality. Some products, for example the home-produced superb goat's cheese, jam and preserved fruits of the forest, are sold as well. Closed: December–January. **€€**

Valgrisenche

Perret
Località Bonne 2
Tel: 0165-97107
Located 2 km outside Aosta, this cosy hotel restaurant, with its impressive fireside, serves simple, typical regional meals; the four-course menu changes daily. Closed: mid-May–June and mid-October–mid-December. Reserve. **€€**

PIEDMONT

Turin

AB+
Via della Basilica 13
Tel: 011-4390618
Creative Mediterranean cuisine in a magical atmosphere in the Quadrilatero, created by clever lighting and panels of contemporary art. Closed: Sunday. **€€€**

Al Bicerin
Piazza della Consolata 5
Tel: 011-4369325
Once the favourite haunt of Dumas and Cavour among many other famous regulars, this café's origins date back to 1763. It is the place to try another speciality of Turin, the heavenly *bicerin* – coffee with chocolate and cream. (This is a historic café, not a restaurant.) **€€–€€€**

Al Garamond
Via Pomba 14
Tel: 011-8122781
Both classic Piedmontese and Mediterranean dishes are on offer here in this centrally located yet quiet, esteemed restaurant. There is an excellent wine list and very

good service in a smart atmosphere, deemed by many to be one of Turin's top restaurants. Closed: August. **€€€**

Caffè Torino
Piazza San Carlo 204
Tel: 011-545118
Famous historic café with gilded mirrors, frescoed ceiling and twinkling chandeliers where little has changed since it opened in 1903. Expensive but great for a cocktail or maybe a vermouth – a Torinese invention **€€**

Combal.Zero
Piazza Mafalda di Savoia-Rivoli
Tel: 011-9565225
Located inside the Rivoli Castle, home of the Contemporary Arts Museum, this stylishly minimalist restaurant offers very creative cuisine. Specialities include fish with black truffles, foie gras and beef – especially *gelatina di manzo al Porto*. Excellent service and now the proud holders of a Michelin star. A unique and unforgettable experience by the chef Davide Scabin. Closed: Monday and Tuesday. Booking essential. **€€€–€€€€**

Del Cambio
Piazza Carignano 2
Tel: 011-546690
Opened in 1757, one of the most beautiful restaurants in Italy and the oldest in Turin. 19th-century furniture and atmosphere. Typical regional and national cuisine. Closed: Sunday and August. Reservations advised. **€€€€**

Tipinifini
Via Matteo Pescatore 9D
Tel: 011-19702053
New, very fashionable restaurant with a trendy atmosphere and good Mediterranean cuisine. Closed: Monday. **€€**

Trattoria Mongreno
Strada Comunale Mongreno 50
Tel: 011-8980417
A welcoming and intimate atmosphere, offering traditional Piedmontese menus as well as creative, at times quite daring recipes, to match flavours. Summer terrace. Closed: Monday noon. **€€€–€€€€**

Tre Galli
Via Sant'Agostino 25
Tel: 011-5216027
Typical wine bar with a great selection of wines and good food, with special attention to typical Piedmontese products. Closed: Sunday. **€–€€**

Tre Galline
Via Bellezia 37
Tel: 011-4366553
Typical old-fashioned *piola* (a meeting-place to drink wine and eat snacks), recently refurbished, serving regional cooking. Each evening brings a different Piedmont cheese speciality. Closed: all day Sunday and Monday lunch. Reserve. **€€€**

Vintage 1997
Piazza Solferino 16H
Tel: 011-535948
Elegant interior and good location but above all every dish on the menu is spectacular to behold as well as to eat. For the very hungry, there's the *menu del Vintage*, a 13-course feast that covers the full range of the Michelin-starred restaurant's cuisine. Closed: Saturday lunch and Sunday. **€€€–€€€€**

THE LAKES

Lago di Como

Al Porticcioli
84 Via Valsecchi 5–7
Tel: 0341-498103
Excellent restaurant specialising in fresh fish and seafood. Choose your crustacean fresh from the tank. Closed: Monday and Tuesday, and periods in January and August; normally open evenings only. Reservations advised. **€€€**

Antica Osteria Enoteca Casa di Lucia
Via Lucia 27, Lecco
Tel: 0341-494594
This old, established *osteria* in the old part of the town Acquate has a big restaurant with wooden tables and a fireplace. You will find dishes that are typical of the region on the menu, e.g. *ossobuco* with mushrooms. Closed: Saturday lunch and Sunday. **€€–€€€**

Lago di Como/Cernobbio

Gatto Nero
Via Monte Santo 69
Rovenna (4 km inland from Cernobbio)
Tel: 031-512042
Glorious location in the hills with beautiful views over the lake and terrace dining in summer. Very attentive service in atmospheric, rustic restaurant where the specialities are both fish and meat, plus a very good cheeseboard. Closed: Monday and Tuesday lunch. Reservations necessary. **€€€**

Harry's Bar
Piazza Risorgimento
Tel: 031-512647
Smart watering-hole (and restaurant) by the lake, especially popular for late night drinks. Closed: Tuesday. **€**

Lago di Como/Torno

Ristorante Belvedere
Piazza Casartelli, Torno
Lago di Como
Tel: 031-419100
Gloriously situated overlooking the lake, this friendly restaurant excels in good, unfussy cooking with *lavarello* (lake fish) and pasta specialities. Popular, yet not too touristy, but book ahead for a table alongside the lake on the lovely vine-covered terrace. Beautiful views at sunset. Open daily in summer. **€€–€€€**

Lago di Garda/Bardolino

Il Giardino delle Esperidi
Via Mameli 1
Tel: 045-6210477
Good food on a menu which changes every fortnight to reflect seasonal specialities. Pleasant rustic ambience. Closed: Tuesday and Wednesday lunch. **€€–€€€**

Lago di Garda/Torbole

Piccolo Mondo
Via Matteotti 7
Tel: 0464-505271
Acclaimed hotel restaurant in a quiet position with a beautiful garden. Excellent service where the speciality is the cuisine of Trentino. Closed: Tuesday and 3 weeks in February. **€€€**

Lago Maggiore/Verbania

Osteria dell'Angolo
Piazza Garibaldi 35
Pallanza (Verbania)
Tel: 0323-556362
Cosy restaurant with simple wooden tables and uncovered bricks. The fish and the freshly prepared desserts are recommended. Closed: Monday and November. **€€**

Piccolo Lago
Località Fondotoce
Via Turati 87
Tel: 0323-586792
Lovely setting overlooking the lake, this wooden chalet has a comfortable and elegant ambience. Highly acclaimed for the quality of the cuisine and well-chosen wine list.Reservations recommended. Closed: Sunday evening, Monday, 20 December–10 February. **€€€–€€€€**

LIGURIA & RIVIERA

Genoa

Antica Osteria del Bai
Via Quarto 12
Quarto dei Mille (7 km/4 miles outside Genoa)
Tel: 010-387478
Highly acclaimed, historic restaurant where Garibaldi once ate, inside a fortress overlooking the sea. Typical Genoese cuisine at one of the top restaurants in Genoa. Closed: Monday. **€€€€**

Da Rina
Mura delle Grazie 3/r
Tel: 010-2466475
Traditional trattoria in Genoa's oldest restaurant with good cooking. Fresh fish is the speciality. Closed: Monday, and August. Reserve. **€€–€€€**

Gran Gotto
Viale Brigata Bisagno 69/R
Tel: 010-564344
Near Stazione Brignole. A rustic atmosphere and regional cooking. Try the *trenette al pesto*. Closed: Saturday lunch and all day Sunday. Reserve. **€€€€**

La Bitta nella Pergola
Via Casaregis 52
Tel: 010-588543
Elegant marine atmosphere in this Michelin-starred restaurant. Regional cooking, specialising in fish. Closed: Sunday evening, Monday and August; also Sunday lunch in July. **€€€€**

Pansön dal 1790
Piazza delle Erbe 5
Tel: 010-2468903
This charming Genoese restaurant is situated in a safe but slightly dilapidated square close to Via XX Settembre. All Genoese dishes are on offer, including *pansoti al sugo di noci* (pasta with walnuts). Closed: Sunday dinner and two weeks in August. **€€€**

Zeffirino
Via XX Settembre 20
Tel: 010-591990
In the centre of the city, with modern furniture and good cuisine. Famous for the legendary *pesto alla genovese*. Reserve. **€€€**

Portofino

Da u'Batti
Vico Nuovo 17
Tel: 0185-269379
A small, intimate restaurant with a very pleasant veranda. Good seafood features strongly. Closed: Monday, December–mid January. **€€–€€€**

Taverna del Marinaio
Piazza Martiri dell'Olivetta 36
Tel: 0185-269103
Set on the harbour, this taverna's interior is elegantly shipshape. Excellent seafood. Closed: Tuesday. **€€€**

San Remo

Bacchus
Via Roma 65
Tel: 0184-530990
Well-looked-after *enoteca* with simple delicious dishes from Liguria. Recommended are the pasta and the fish dishes, such as cuttlefish. Closed: Sunday. **€€**

Paolo e Barbara
Via Roma 47
Tel: 0184-531653
Elegant, small Michelin-starred restaurant right in the heart of town. Booking essential. Closed: Wednesday and Thursday; 19–30 December; 23–29 January; 22 June–7 July. **€€€€**

Vernazza

Gambero Rosso
Piazza Marconi 7
Tel: 0187-812265
Close to the port: a small *osteria* noted for its seafood. Closed: Monday (except August) and mid-December–February. **€€€**

EMILIA ROMAGNA

Bologna

Buca San Petronio
Via de' Musei 4
Tel: 051-224589
Excellent-value restaurant set in a *palazzo* in the historical centre. Traditional, regional cooking and freshly made pasta. Outdoor dining in summer. Closed: Wednesday evening (except during holidays/festivals) and August. **€–€€**

Caffè Commercianti
Strada Maggiore 23/C
Tel: 051-266539
Well-known watering-hole for the literati and intelligentsia of Bologna, including luminaries such as Umberto Eco.

Cantina Bentivoglio
Via Mascarella 4/b
Tel: 051-265416
Set in the cellars of a *palazzo*, this atmospheric wine bar attracts a young crowd. Closed: Monday. **€€**

I Carracci
Grand Hotel Baglioni
Via Manzoni 2
Tel: 051-222049
Superb cuisine offered here in Bologna's most elegant, frescoed restaurant. Closed: Sunday in August. **€€€€**

La Pernice e La Gallina
Via dell'Abbadia,4
Tel: 051-269922
Highly acclaimed, elegant restaurant in the historical centre of Bologna. Traditional and innovative cuisine are skilfully blended to produce gourmet cuisine. Closed: Monday lunch and Sunday and for a period in August. **€€–€€€**

Pappagallo
Piazza della Mercanzia 3c
Tel: 051-231200
Very popular restaurant, not only

for its location near the two towers, but also for its Bolognese specialities. Closed: Sunday and for a period in August; also Saturday in June and July.
€€€

Price Guide

The price of a three-course meal for two with wine:
€ = under €25
€€ = €25–50
€€€ = €50–100
€€€€ = over €100

Ferrara

La Romantica
Via Ripagrande 36
Tel: 0532-765975
Classic Italian cuisine with Ferrarese dishes, too. Closed: Sunday evening, Wednesday and periods in July and August. **€€**

Modena

Fini
Rua Frati Minori 54
Tel: 059-223314
Classic, elegant, but homely, with traditional regional cuisine and one Michelin star. Try *bolliti* (boiled meat). Closed: Monday, Christmas/New Year and two weeks in August. Reserve. **€€€–€€€€**

Oreste
Piazza Roma 31
Tel: 059-243324
This traditional restaurant has a pleasant, rather "retro" atmosphere. The specialities are meat and home-made pasta. Closed: Sunday evening and Wednesday; 26 December–6 January and period in July. **€€**

Parma

Gran Caffè Cavour
Via Cavour 30b
(off Piazza Garibaldi)
The place to see and be seen, where tables spill out onto the cobblestones. Opulent interior with frescoed ceilings and sparkling chandeliers.

La Greppia
Strada Garibaldi 39/A
Tel: 0521-233686
Fresh, handmade pasta is a speciality in this small, elegant, acclaimed family-run restaurant. Excellent home-made desserts too. Closed: Monday and Tuesday, July and Christmas. **€€€**

SAN MARINO

Righi La Taverna
Piazza della Libertà 10
Tel: 0549-991196
Rustic, with highly acclaimed food. Bistro downstairs and more formal dining room above. Closed: Wednesday and 1–14 January.
€€–€€€

THE ADRIATIC

Ravenna

Antica Trattoria Al Gallo 1909
Via Maggiore 87
Tel: 0544-213775
Wonderful pergola in summer. Good, traditional local food with plenty of vegetarian options. Closed: Monday, Tuesday and Sunday evening; 20 December–10 January and Easter. Reservations advised. **€€–€€€**

Rimini

Acero Rosso
Viale Tiberio 11
Tel: 0541-53577
Refined and elegant fish restaurant, now with one Michelin star, with excellent traditional cuisine. Open daily for dinner, also for lunch on Sunday and holidays. Closed: Monday (and Sunday evening in winter), Christmas and one week in August. Reserve. **€€€–€€€€**

Lo Squero
Lungomare Tintori 7
Tel: 0541-27676
Pleasant restaurant on the promenade by the sea. Welcoming atmosphere inside is matched by plenty of seating outdoors. Closed: Tuesday in low season and November–mid-January. **€€–€€€**

Culture

Music

The famous La Scala in Milan is a must for every opera fan. Ballets and concerts are also held there. There are also some performances at the Teatro degli Arcimboldi. During the summer, parks are crowded with people enjoying a variety of outdoor cultural events sponsored by the city.

In Turin, classical music is at its peak from late August until the end of September, when *Settembre Musica*, an international music festival, featuring the best national and international performers, takes over the town.

For information on opera in Milan, see the box on La Scala *(page 380)*.

VERONA

For more than 80 years, a world-famous opera festival has been held every year – in July and August – in the big **Roman arena** (Piazza Bra, www.arena.it). The marvellous open-air acoustics and great lighting always make it a memorable occasion. Classics like *Madam Butterfly, Tosca and Turandot*, Bizet's *Carmen von Bizet* and Verdi's *Aida* are performed.

An evening at the opera in Verona is not only for opera-lovers, but is one of the major musical events in the world. But everything has its price: from €19.50 for an unreserved stone step, right at the back and high up *(Gradinata)*; from €100 for a numbered seat on the step *(Gradinata numerata)*; from €120 for a second-sector stall *(Poltrona)*; from €150 for a first-sector stall *(Poltronissima)*.

The information office is at: Arena di Verona, Piazza Bra 28, 37121 Verona, tel: 045-8051811, fax: 045-8064790.

The box office is in Via Dietro Anfiteatro 6/B, 37121 Verona. For information and bookings by phone, tel: 045-8005151, fax: 045-8013287. It is now possible to book tickets online: www.arena.it

VENICE

Venice's **La Fenice** opera house finally reopened in 2004 after being destroyed by fire in 1996.

Theatres

For information on theatre performances, ask the city's APT (Azienda Promozione Turistica) or check the local newspaper. Ticket prices vary depending on the show and venue.

In Milan, you can go to the **Piccolo Teatro**, Via Rovello 2, and its off-shoot, the **Teatro Studio**, Via Rivoli 6, as well as the new **Nuovo Piccolo Teatro** next door (booking number for all three theatres: 02-77333222).

Concert Halls

In addition to La Scala and La Fenice the following concert halls stage operas and concerts:
Parma: the Auditorium Paganini
Milan: the Auditorium di Milano
Turin: Lingotto Concert Hall

Major Opera Houses

Bologna
Teatro Comunale
Largo Resphigi 1
Tel: 051-529999
Fax: 051-529934
www.comunalebologna.it
Season events November–June.

Genoa
Teatro Carlo Felice
Passo al Teatro 4
Tel: 010-53811
Fax: 010-5381222
www.carlofelice.it
Season events October–January.

Milan
Teatro degli Arcimboldi
Viale dell'Innovazione
Tel: 02-72003744
www.teatroallascala.org

Parma
Teatro Regio
Via Garibaldi 16
Tel: 0521-218912
Fax: 0521-206156
www.teatroregioparma.org
Season events December–May.

Trieste
Teatro Comunale Giuseppe Verdi
Piazza Verdi 1
Tel: 040-6722111
Fax: 040-366300
www.teatroverdi-trieste.com
Season events December, May–July/August.

Turin
Teatro Regio
Piazza Castello 215
Tel: 011-548000
Fax: 011-8815214.
www.teatroregio.torino.it
Season events November–May.

Venice
Fondazione La Fenice
c/o Palafenice, Isola del Tronchetto, Venezia
Tel: 094-8005151 (bookings)
Fax: 041-786580
www.web.tin.it/lafenice

Verona
Fondazione Arena di Verona
Piazza Bra 28
Tel: 094-8005151 (bookings)
Fax: 045-8011566
www.arena.it
Season events June–August.

Musical Events

Aosta Organ Music Festival mid July–mid August.
Bolzano International Piano Competition Feruccio Busoni August.
Brescia Piano Festival May–June.
Cervo (Imperia) Chamber Music Festival July–August.
Gardone Riviera (Lake Garda) Drama and concerts in the open-air theatre of the Vittoriale degli Italiani (July–August).
Pavia – Concerts in the Certosa July–September; drama performances in the open air July–August.
Ravenna Festival June–July, Teatro Alighieri, Via Mariani 2, tel: 0544-32577, fax: 0544-215840. www.netgate.it/ra/festiv
San Remo is the venue for the **Italian Pop Music Festival** held at the end of February, which is extremely popular with Italians.
Stresa Musical Weeks August–September; Settimane Musicali, Palazzo dei Congressi, Via R. Bonghi 4, Stresa, Lake Maggiore, tel: 0323-31095, fax: 0323-33006.
Trieste – Operetta Festival July–August.
Turin – Settembre Musica festival takes over the town from late August until the end of September.
Urbino – Drama and art exhibitions; concerts in the Renaissance Theatre (August).

La Scala

Milan's hallowed Teatro alla Scala, tel: 02-7200 3744; reservations; www.teatroallascala.org has undergone a complete renovation. The programme is available at the La Scala website, where you can also buy tickets. Reservations open two months before the date of the performances. Most sell out on the first day. Any tickets unsold one month before the performance are available at the La Scala box office, located in the Duomo metro station opposite the ATM point (which provides information on the public-transport service in Milan). The ticket office is open from noon–6pm daily.

For information, call 02-7200 3744 between 9am and 6pm. Expect to be on hold for some time. Operators may speak some English.

Nightlife

Late Spots

Nightlife in Italy follows the American and English fashions. There are numerous nightclubs, pubs and discos where young people congregate to listen to music, dance and talk. Many of these places go in and out of popularity (or in and out of business) in the space of a few months, so there is little point in recommending them. There is nothing so out-of-date as last month's club. It is better to check details in local newspapers or listings magazines.

In recent years, Milan has been top for hip nightlife, with its rock clubs and discos, centred on the Navigli district, the canal quarter. Just turn up at night and see what is on offer. Venice is less of a city for nightlife, and most people prefer sitting in cafés and walking through the beautiful, labyrinthine streets.

Festivals

Special Events

The year is packed with special events, some linked to festivals of the Catholic Church, others to the changing seasons. Every little village in Italy has its own wonderful festivals, so take every opportunity to attend. Many are associated with the harvest (especially wine) or to local products (polenta, *prosciutto*). The remainder tend to be historical re-enactments linked to jousting or to costumed cavalcades.

Calendar

The Italians love to celebrate: whether it's a tiny parish pump affair, a spectacular, showy festival, a religious celebration or a gourmet *festa* or *sagra*, there is one somewhere in the country for every day of the year and more – and everyone is warmly welcomed.

January

1 January – New Year's Day holiday
6 January – Epiphany
Carnevale is the first 10 days before Lent, held usually in February. Meaning literally "farewell to meat" it is celebrated most spectacularly in Venice in the famous masked festivities. Other notable celebrations take place near Turin at Ivrea.
Festival of St Sebastian in Dolceacqua and Camporosso; a decorated laurel tree is carried through the town.

March/April

March/April – Easter processions take place throughout the region – notable are those on Maundy Thursday and Good Friday. Savona in Liguria is especially celebrated for its Good Friday procession.
Spring is the time of rebirth, and there are hundreds of festivities celebrating the new season's gastronomic delights, such as asparagus and artichokes.
25 April – Liberation Day – also **Festa del San Marco.** The feast day of St Mark, patron saint of Venice, is celebrated with a ceremonial Mass in the Basilica and the romantic presentation of a *bocolo* (rosebud) to women.
Lake Maggiore – San Giulio, near Stresa, holds its flower festival.

May

Festa della Sensa (Ascension Day). A re-enactment of the Marriage of Venice with the Sea; this is followed by a regatta and La Vogalonga, a marathon rowing race, a week later.
1 May – Labour Day
2 May – Palio-San Secondo, Asti. A 700-year-old ceremony with procession in 13th-century costume.
Second Sunday – Sagra del Pesce, Camogli. Huge amounts of fish are fried in supposedly the "world's largest frying pan" and distributed freely among guests and onlookers.

June

Palio delle Quattro Anitche Repubbliche Marinare (Regatta of the Four Ancient Maritime Republics). A procession of boats and a race between the four historical maritime rivals – Genoa, Venice, Pisa and Amalfi. The event rotates between the four towns: Venice in 2003, Genoa in 2004, Amalfi in 2005.
13 June – Festival of Sant'Antonio, patron saint of Padua and of lost things. Procession of the saint's relics.
24 June – Festival of St John, Genoa & Turin. Street procession and holiday to celebrate the patron saint.
29 June – Genoa. Rowing race in ancient dress.

July

International Ballet Festival, Nervi. Nervi, near Genoa.

1–3 July, Rapallo. Nostra Signora di Montallegro. Procession and firework display

Third weekend – Festa del Redentore (Festival of the Redeemer), Venice. Procession of gondolas, commemorating the end of the epidemic or plague of 1575, and fireworks. A bridge of boats is built across the Giudecca Canal to the Redentore church, built in gratitude for deliverance from the plague.

August

First Sunday – Stella Maris. Atmospheric boat procession in Camogli.

15 August – Feast of the Assumption

Second Sunday – Palio del Golfo, La Spezia. Festival on the water with regatta, rowing contest and fireworks. In **Ventimiglia, Corteo Storico** commemorates a historical event with a procession in period costumes.

23 August – San Fruttuoso, Liguria. Divers descend to the "Submerged Christ" – a bronze statue lying on the ocean bed.

The **last week of August** sees the great **Ferrara Buskers' Festival** (in Emilia Romagna).

The International Film Festival of Venice. Takes place at the Lido from late August to early September.

September

First Sunday – Historical Regatta. The finest regatta in Venice. It includes a procession up the Grand Canal led by all manner of craft containing Venetians in traditional cosumes; this is followed by gondola races.

Third Sunday – Flag Throwing Palio, Asti. Ancient festival with 800 costumed participants, historic procession and horse race.

October

First Sunday – Alba (Piedmont) has the **Fiera del Tartufo** to celebrate the prized white truffle.

4 October – Feast Day of Saint Petronio, patron saint of Bologna

First weekend – Festa dell'Uva. Wine festivals feature strongly at this time especially in **Trentino-Alto Adige and around the Lakes – for example at Bardolino.**

The San Remo motor-racing rally takes place in October.

Salone del Gusto, Turin – third week of October. One of the world's great food festivals, held at the Lingotto.

November

Festa della Madonna della Salute, Venice. A procession across the Grand Canal on floating pontoons to La Salute church in thanksgiving for the city's survival from the plague.

1 November – All Saints' Day

3 November – Feast Day of Saint Giusto, patron saint of Trieste.

December

7 December, Milan. Festival day of Milan's patron saint **Sant Ambrogio** (St Ambrose) – also the traditional opening day of the season at La Scala.

8 December – Feast of the Immaculate Conception

25 December – Christmas Day

26 December – Feast of Santo Stefano

Outdoor Activities

National Parks

Italy has some stunningly beautiful national parks (www.parks.it), including:

Parco Nazionale del Gran Paradiso

Home of the last steinbock and chamois in Italy, this Alpine park is the oldest in the country and covers 72,000 hectares (178,000 acres). Spreading over parts of Valle d'Aosta and Piedmont, it has plenty of refuges and trekking facilities, and is a magnet for nature-lovers.
Gran Paradiso Tourist Office: Località Champagne 18, Villeneuve, tel: 0165-95055.
Coyne's APT: Piazza Charnoux 36, tel: 0165-74040.

Parco Nazionale dello Stelvio

This is the biggest park in Italy (135,000 hectares/333,600 acres). It lies close to Switzerland and is rich in forests and animals. The mountains are wonderful and there are plenty of hotels.
Tel: 0342-901654 (Lombardy area), 0463-985190 (Trentino area).
www.stelviopark.it

Parco Nazionale dell'Abruzzo

Here the last brown bear in Italy lives in remote splendour in one of the highest sections of the Apennines. Visitors' Centre, Vide Santa Lucia. Tel: 0863-910405.

The Alps

If you would like to go hiking in the mountains, pick up a map showing the network of walking paths, with more than 80 overnight areas with shelters. Paths are marked with numerous red signs and distinctive small flags. Every stage calls for 5–7 hours of hiking time at an average of about 1,000 metres (3,300 ft) in altitude.

At the overnight rest areas there are shelters with double-decker bunks, essential services and a kitchen. The shelters are generally situated in inhabited localities, where it is possible to buy food, phone home, rest for a day, visit historical and ethnographic museums, chat with the inhabitants and, last but not least, eat a good meal at an inn.

An itinerary can last a month, a week or a day. From the Maritime Alps in the west to Lake Maggiore, on a route stretching for 650 km (400 miles) that spans five provinces, the hiker crosses many splendid parks, such as the Gran Paradiso, the Orsiera-Rocciavrè, the Alta Val Pesio and the Argentera.

All the areas are open to the public July–September.
For detailed information, call the **GTA Information Office**, Via Barbaroux 1, Turin, tel: 011-5624477.

Alpine Huts

The Club Alpino Italiano, Via E. Fonseca Pimentel 7, 20127 Milan, tel. 02-26141378, owns nearly 600 *rifugi* (huts) in the mountain districts and publishes a yearly book with a map and information on access, equipment and tariffs for each according to grade. The Touring Club Italiano, Corso Italia 10, 20122 Milan, tel: 02-85261, publishes information giving detailed mountain itineraries and excursion information,including huts. www.cai.it/rifugi

Sport

Spectator Sports

Football

The national sport in Italy is football. Almost every city and village has its own team. The most important national championship is **Serie A** (First Division). The winner of this competition is eligible in Europe's premier club championship, the Champions' League, against the top teams of other European nations.

The Serie A championship is played September–May, and each of the 16 teams has to play the other teams twice.

The most successful Italian football team is **Juventus FC** from Turin, followed by **AC Milan** and **Internazionale**, also from Milan. But many other cities are blessed with successful sides, including Genoa (Sampdoria), Parma, Florence and Rome (which, like Milan, has two teams – in this case Lazio and Roma).

If you would like to see a game, check the newspaper for details. Remember that it is very difficult to get tickets if the match is an important one. Ticket prices vary according to the importance of the team, the game, and the location of the seat you want. Unlike in some other European countries, matches tend to be safe, family affairs.

Motor Racing

The second passion of the Italians is represented by cars and speed. Formula One races attract people interested in the sophisticated technology and the coupling of man and car. This sport attracts mostly a TV audience because it is expensive to go around the world to see the races.

In Italy citizens support the red cars built by Ferrari. There is always a large crowd at the circuits in **Imola** (where the San Marino Grand Prix is held) and **Monza** (Italian Grand Prix). Although the car industry is centred on Turin, motor racing is based in the regions of Lombardy and Emilia Romagna.

Other Sports

Almost all other sports are enjoyed in Italy, including basketball, golf, water polo, horse racing, rugby union, rowing and sailing. In addition, the Alps, Dolomites and the Apennines provide plenty of skiing opportunities.

May is an important month for sport in Italy. The *Giro d'Italia* cycle race, a major event on the cycling circuit, is staged; the Italian Open tennis tournament is held at the Foro Italico in Rome; and equestrian sports followers enjoy their major competition of the year, which takes place in Rome's Villa Borghese gardens.

If you are interested in buying tickets for any match or event, buy the pink *Gazzetta dello Sport* newspaper, where everything under the sun about sports is listed.

Shopping

Shopping Areas

Milan

Milan is Italy's premier centre for international fashion and the nation's manufactured products. For those with expensive tastes, the most chic and elegant streets for shopping are: **Via Montenapoleone**, **Via Spiga** and **Via S. Andrea**, all near the Duomo and La Scala. These streets feature such fine stores as Krizia, Giò Moretti, Trussardi, Kenzo, Sanlorenzo, Giorgio Armani and Ferragamo, as well as Versace, Gucci, Ermenegildo Zegna, Comme des Garçons, Valentino, Dolce e Gabbana, Hermès, Chanel, Moschino, Prada, Ferre and Fendi.

Venice

The most exclusive shopping area in Venice is the **Via XXII Marzo** and the streets around **St Mark's Square**. The best local shopping areas are the Rialto Bridge and San Polo. A market is held on the **Lido** on Tuesday morning.

Bargains to shop for include shoes, clothes, gifts and fur coats.

Murano glass, hand-blown in Venice, is distinctly gaudy but a popular buy. Also, look out for colourful carnival masks, to wear or to hang up.

Bologna

Bologna is one of the leading shopping centres in Italy and is, after Milan, the second city for clothes and shoes. The classic shopping areas in the city centre are **Via Rizzoli, Via dell' Independenza, Via Ugo Bassi, Via Farini, Via Santo Stefano, Via Massimo d'Azeglio** and under the arcade of the **Pavaglione**.

Turin

Turin offers excellent opportunities for shopping, especially for fashion and antiquities. The most exclusive boutiques and finest shops are to be found under the arcades of **Piazza San Carlo**, in the **Galleria San Frederico** and along **Via Roma**. Moderate-priced shops as well as a big department store are situated in **Via Lagrange**, which runs parallel to Via Roma. Lovers of antiquities will want to explore the streets between Piazza Cavour and Via della Rocca, an especially attractive area of Turin.

Clothing Size Chart

Women's dresses:

Italian	UK	US
38	8	6
40	10	8
42	12	10
44	14	12

Men's shirts:

Italian	UK	US
36	14	14
38	15	15
41	16	16
43	17	17

Language

Language Tips

Italian is supplemented by regional dialects. In large cities and tourist centres you will find many people who speak English, French or German. In fact, due to the massive emigration over the last 100 years, you may encounter fluent speakers of foreign languages. Do not be surprised if you are addressed in a New York, Melbourne, Brussels or Bavarian accent: the speaker may have spent time working abroad.

It is well worth buying a good phrase book or dictionary, but the following will help you get started. Since this glossary is aimed at non-linguists, we have opted for the simplest options rather than the most elegant Italian.

Basic Communication

Yes *Sì*
No *No*
Thank you *Grazie*
Many thanks *Mille grazie/tante grazie/molte grazie*
You're welcome *Prego*
Alright/Okay/That's fine *Va bene*
Please *Per favore* or *per cortesia.*
Excuse me (to get attention) *Scusi* (singular), *Scusate* (plural)
Excuse me (to get through a crowd) *Permesso*
Excuse me (to attract attention of, e.g. of a waiter) *Senta!*
Excuse me (sorry) *Mi scusi*
Wait a minute! *Aspetta!*
Could you help me? (formal) *Potrebbe aiutarmi?*
Certainly *Ma certo*
Can I help you? (formal) *Posso aiutarLa?*
Can you show me...? *Può indicarmi...?*

Numbers

1	*Uno*	**10**	*Dieci*	**19**	*Diciannove*	**100**	*Cento*
2	*Due*	**11**	*Undici*	**20**	*Venti*	**200**	*Duecento*
3	*Tre*	**12**	*Dodici*	**30**	*Trenta*	**500**	*Cinquecento*
4	*Quattro*	**13**	*Tredici*	**40**	*Quaranta*	**1,000**	*Mille*
5	*Cinque*	**14**	*Quattordici*	**50**	*Cinquanta*	**2,000**	*Duemila*
6	*Sei*	**15**	*Quindici*	**60**	*Sessanta*	**5,000**	*Cinquemila*
7	*Sette*	**16**	*Sedici*	**70**	*Settanta*	**50,000**	*Cinquantamila*
8	*Otto*	**17**	*Diciassette*	**80**	*Ottanta*	**1 million**	*Un milione*
9	*Nove*	**18**	*Diciotto*	**90**	*Novanta*		

Can you help me? *Può aiutarmi, per cortesia?*
I need... *Ho bisogno di...*
I'm lost *Mi sono perso*
I'm sorry *Mi dispiace*
I don't know *Non lo so*
I don't understand *Non capisco*
Do you speak English/French/German? *Parla inglese/francese/tedesco?*
Could you speak more slowly, please? *Può parlare piú lentamente, per favore?*
Could you repeat that please? *Può ripetere, per piacere?*
slowly/quietly *piano*
here/there *qui/lá*
What? *Cosa?*
When/why/where? *Quando/perchè/dove?*
Where is the lavatory? *Dov'è il bagno?*

Greetings

Hello (Good day) *Buon giorno*
Good afternoon/evening *Buona sera*
Good night *Buona notte*
Goodbye *Arrivederci*
Hello/Hi/Goodbye (familiar) *Ciao*
Mr/Mrs/Miss *Signor/Signora/Signorina*
Pleased to meet you (formal) *Piacere di conoscerLa*
I am English/American *Sono inglese/americano*
Irish/Scottish/Welsh *irlandese/scozzese/gallese*
Canadian/Australian *canadese/australiano*
I'm here on holiday *Sono qui in vacanza*
Is it your first trip to Milan/Rome? *È il Suo primo viaggio a Milano/Roma?*
Do you like it here? (formal) *Si trova bene qui?*
How are you? (formal/informal) *Come sta/come stai?*
Fine thanks *Bene, grazie*
See you later *A più tardi*
See you soon *A presto*
Take care *Stia bene*
New acquaintances are likely to ask you:
Do you like Italy/Florence/Rome/Venice/my city? *Le piace Italia/Firenze/Roma/Venezia/la mia città?*
I like it a lot (is the correct answer) *Mi piace moltissimo.*
It's wonderful (an alternative answer) *E meravigliosa/favolosa.* (Both responses can be applied to food, beaches, the view, etc.)

Telephone Calls

the area code *il prefisso telefonico*
I'd like to make a reverse charges call *Vorrei fare una telefonata a carico del destinatario*
May I use your telephone, please? *Posso usare il telefono?*
Hello (on the telephone) *Pronto*
My name's *Mi chiamo/Sono*
Could I speak to...? *Posso parlare con...?*
Sorry, he/she isn't in *Mi dispiace, è fuori*
Can he call you back? *Può richiamarla?*
I'll try again later *Riproverò più tardi*
Can I leave a message? *Posso lasciare un messaggio?*
Please tell him I called *Gli dica, per favore, che ho telefonato*
Hold on *Un attimo, per favore*
A local call *una telefonata locale*
Can you speak up please? *Può parlare più forte, per favore?*

In the Hotel

Do you have any vacant rooms? *Avete camere libere?*
I have a reservation *Ho fatto una prenotazione*
I'd like... *Vorrei...*
a single/double room (with a double bed) *una camera singola/doppia (con letto matrimoniale)*
a room with twin beds *una camera a due letti*
a room with a bath/shower *una camera con bagno/doccia*
for one night *per una notte*
for two nights *per due notti*
We have one with a double bed *Ne abbiamo una matrimoniale*
Could you show me another room please? *Potrebbe mostrarmi un'altra camera?*
How much is it? *Quanto costa?*
on the first floor *al primo piano*
Is breakfast included? *È compresa la prima colazione?*
Is everything included? *È tutto compreso?*
half/full board *mezza pensione/pensione completa*
It's expensive *È caro*
Do you have a room with a balcony/view of the sea? *C'è una camera con balcone/con vista sul mare?*
a room overlooking the park/the street/the back *una camera con vista sul parco/che dà sulla strada/sul retro*
Is it a quiet room? *È una stanza tranquilla?*
The room is too hot/cold/noisy/small *La camera è troppo calda/fredda/rumorosa/piccola*
Can I see the room? *Posso vedere la camera?*
What time does the hotel close? *A che ora chiude l'albergo?*
I'll take it *La prendo*
big/small *grande/piccola*
What time is breakfast? *A che ora è la prima colazione?*
Please give me a call at... *Mi può chiamare alle...*
Come in! *Avanti!*
Can I have the bill, please? *Posso avere il conto, per favore*

Can you call me a taxi please? *Può chiamarmi un taxi, per favore?*
dining room *la sala da pranzo*
key *la chiave*
lift *l'ascensore*
towel *l'asciugamano*
toilet paper *la carta igienica*
pull/push *tirare/spingere*

Eating Out

DRINKS & BAR SNACKS

I'd like... *Vorrei...*
coffee *un caffè* (*espresso*: small, strong and black)
un cappuccino (with hot, frothy milk)
un caffelatte (like *café au lait* in France)
un caffè lungo (weak, often served in a tall glass)
un corretto (laced with alcohol, usually brandy or grappa)
tea *un tè*
lemon tea *un tè al limone*
herbal tea *una tisana*
hot chocolate *una cioccolata calda*
orange/lemon juice (bottled) *un succo d'arancia/di limone*
fresh orange/lemon juice *una spremuta di arancia/di limone*
orangeade *un'aranciata*
water (mineral) *acqua (minerale)*
fizzy/still mineral water *acqua minerale gasata/naturale*
a glass of mineral water *un bicchiere di acqua minerale*
with/without ice *con/senza ghiaccio*
red/white wine *vino rosso/bianco*
beer (draught) *una birra (alla spina)*
a gin and tonic *un gin tonic*
a bitter (Vermouth, etc.) *un amaro*
milk *latte*
a (half) litre *un (mezzo) litro*
bottle *una bottiglia*
ice cream *un gelato*
cone *un cono*
pastry *una pasta*
sandwich *un tramezzino*
roll *un panino*
Anything else? *Desidera qualcos'altro?*
Cheers *Salute*
Let me pay *Offro io*
That's very kind of you *Grazie, molto gentile*

IN A RESTAURANT

I'd like to book a table *Vorrei riservare un tavolo*
Have you got a table for... *Avete un tavolo per ...*
I have a reservation *Ho fatto una prenotazione*
lunch/supper *il pranzo/la cena*
We do not want a full meal *Non desideriamo un pasto completo*
Could we have another table? *Potremmo spostarci?*
I'm a vegetarian *Sono vegetariano/a*
Is there a vegetarian dish? *C'è un piatto vegetariano?*
May we have the menu? *Ci dà il menu, per favore?*
wine list *la lista dei vini*
What would you like? *Che cosa prende?*
What would you recommend? *Che cosa ci raccomanda?*
home-made *fatto in casa*
What would you like as a main course/dessert? *Che cosa prende di secondo/di dolce?*
What would you like to drink? *Che cosa desidera da bere?*
a carafe of red/white wine *una caraffa di vino rosso/bianco*
fixed-price menu *il menu a prezzo fisso*
the dish of the day *il piatto del giorno*
VAT (sales tax) *IVA*
cover charge *il coperto/pane e coperto*
That's enough; no more, thanks *Basta (così)*
The bill, please *Il conto per favore*
Is service included? *Il servizio è incluso?*
Where is the lavatory? *Dov'è il bagno?*
Keep the change *Va bene così*
I've enjoyed the meal *Mi è piaciuto molto*

Menu Decoder

ANTIPASTI (HORS D'OEUVRES)

antipasto misto **mixed hors d'oeuvres** (may include cold cuts, cheeses and roast vegetables – ask, however)
buffet freddo **cold buffet**
caponata **mixed aubergine, olives and tomatoes**

Pronunciation and Grammar Tips

Italian speakers claim that pronunciation is straightforward: you pronounce it as it is written. This is approximately true, but there are a couple of important rules for English speakers to bear in mind: *c* before *e* or *i* is pronounced "ch", e.g. *ciao, mi dispiace, la coincidenza. Ch* before *i* or *e* is pronounced as "k", e.g. *la chiesa*. Likewise, *sci* or *sce* are pronounced as in "sheep" or "shed" respectively. *Gn* in Italian is rather like the sound in "onion", while *gl* is softened to resemble the sound in "bullion".

Nouns are either masculine (*il*, plural *i*) or feminine (*la*, plural *le*). Plurals of nouns are most often formed by changing an *o* to an *i* and an *a* to an *e*, e.g. *il panino, i panini*; *la chiesa, le chiese*.

Words are generally stressed on the penultimate syllable unless an accent indicates otherwise.

Like many languages, Italian has formal and informal words for "You". In the singular, *Tu* is informal while *Lei* is more polite. Confusingly, in some parts of Italy or in some circumstances, you will also hear *Voi* used as a singular polite form. (In general, *Voi* is reserved for "You" plural, however.) For visitors, it is simplest and most respectful to use the formal form unless invited to do otherwise.

There is, of course, rather more to the language than that, but you can get a surprisingly long way towards making friends by learning how to pronounce a few basic phrases.

Bar Notices

Prezzo al tavolo/in terrazza **Price at a table/terrace** (often double what you pay standing at the bar)
Si paga alla cassa **Pay at the cash desk**
Si prende lo scontrino alla cassa **Pay at the cash desk, then take the receipt** (*lo scontrino*) **to the bar to be served.** This is common procedure.
Signori/Uomini **Gentlemen** (lavatories)
Signore/Donne **Ladies** (lavatories)

insalata caprese **tomato and mozzarella salad**
insalata di mare **seafood salad**
insalata mista/verde **mixed/ green salad**
melanzane alla parmigiana **fried or baked aubergine (with Parmesan cheese and tomato)**
mortadella/salame **salami**
pancetta **bacon**
peperonata **grilled peppers with olive oil**

PRIMI (FIRST COURSES)

Typical first courses include soup, risotto, gnocchi or numerous varieties of pasta in a wide range of sauces. Risotto and gnocchi are more commonly served in the north than in central Italy.
il brodetto **fish soup**
ii crespolini **savoury pancakes**
gli gnocchi **potato dumplings**
la minestra **soup**
il minestrone **thick vegetable soup**
pasta e fagioli **pasta and bean soup**
il prosciutto (cotto/crudo) **ham (cooked/cured)**
i supplí **rice croquettes**
i tartufi **truffles**
la zuppa **soup**

SECONDI (MAIN COURSES)

Typical main courses are fish-, seafood- or meat-based, with accompaniments *(contorni)* including vegetables that vary greatly from region to region.

La carne (meat)

allo spiedo **on the spit**
arrosto **roast meat**
ai ferri **grilled**
al forno **baked**
al girarrosto **spit-roasted**
alla griglia **grilled**
involtini **skewered veal, ham, etc.**
stagionato **hung, well-aged**
stufato **braised, stewed**
ben cotto **well-done** (steak, etc.)
al puntino **medium** (steak, etc.)
al sangue **rare** (steak, etc.)
l'agnello **lamb**
la bistecca **steak**
la bresaola **dried salted beef**
il capriolo/cervo **venison**
il carpaccio **wafer-thin raw beef**
il cinghiale **wild boar**
il coniglio **rabbit**
il controfiletto **sirloin steak**
le cotolette **cutlets**
il fagiano **pheasant**
il fegato **liver**
il filetto **fillet**
la lepre **hare**
il maiale **pork**
il manzo **beef**
l'ossobuco **shin of veal**
il pollo **chicken**
le polpette **meatballs**
il polpettone **meat loaf**
la porchetta **roast suckling pig**
la salsiccia **sausage**
il saltimbocca (alla romana) **veal escalopes with ham**
le scaloppine **escalopes**
lo stufato **stew**
il sugo **sauce**
il tacchino **turkey**
la trippa **tripe**
il vitello **veal**

Frutti di mare (seafood)

Beware the word "*surgelati*", meaning frozen rather than fresh.
affumicato **smoked**
alle brace **charcoal grilled/barbecued**
alla griglia **grilled**
fritto **fried**
ripieno **stuffed**
al vapore **steamed**
le acciughe **anchovies**
l'anguilla **eel**
l'aragosta **lobster**
il baccalà **dried salted cod**
i bianchetti **whitebait**
il branzino **sea bass**
i calamaretti **baby squid**
i calamari **squid**
la carpa **carp**
i crostacei **shellfish**
le cozze **mussels**
il fritto misto **mixed fried fish**
i gamberetti **shrimps**
i gamberi **prawns**
il granchio **crab**
il merluzzo **hake**
le moleche **soft-shelled crabs**
le ostriche **oysters**
il pesce **fish**
il pesce spada **swordfish**
la piovra **baby octopus**
il polipo **octopus**
il risotto di mare **seafood risotto**
le sarde **sardines**
le seppie **cuttlefish**
la sogliola **sole**
la triglia **red mullet**
la trota **trout**
il tonno **tuna**
le vongole **clams**

I legumi/la verdura (vegetables)

a scelta **of your choice**
ripieno **stuffed**
gli asparagi **asparagus**
la bietola **similar to spinach**
i carciofini **artichoke hearts**
il carciofo **artichoke**
le carote **carrots**
il cavolo **cabbage**
la cicoria **chicory**
la cipolla **onion**
i fagioli **beans**
i fagiolini **French (green) beans**
le fave **broad beans**
il finocchio **fennel**
i funghi **mushrooms**
l'indivia **endive/chicory**
l'insalata mista **mixed salad**
l'insalata verde **green salad**
la melanzana **aubergine**
le patate **potatoes**
le patatine fritte **chips/French fries**
i peperoni **peppers**
i piselli **peas**
i pomodori **tomatoes**
le primizie **spring vegetables**
il radicchio **red, slightly bitter lettuce**
i ravanelli **radishes**
la rughetta **rocket**
gli spinaci **spinach**
la verdura **green vegetables**

Pasta Dishes

Common Pasta Shapes: *cannelloni* (large stuffed tubes of pasta); *farfalle* (bow- or butterfly-shaped pasta); *tagliatelle* (flat noodles, similar to *fettuccine*); *tortellini* and *ravioli* (different types of stuffed pasta packets); *penne* (quill-shaped tubes, smaller than *rigatoni*).
Typical Pasta Sauces: *pomodoro* (tomato); *pesto* (with basil and pine nuts); *matriciana* (bacon and tomato); *arrabbiata* (spicy tomato); *panna* (cream); *ragù* (meat sauce); *aglio e olio* (garlic and olive oil); *burro e salvia* (butter and sage).

la zucca **pumpkin/squash**
gli zucchini **courgettes**

I DOLCI (DESSERTS)

al carrello **(desserts) from the trolley**
un semifreddo **semi-frozen dessert (many types)**
la bavarese **mousse**
la cassata **Sicilian ice cream with candied peel**
le frittelle **fritters**
un gelato (di lampone/limone) **(raspberry/lemon) ice cream**
una granita **water ice**
una macedonia di frutta **fruit salad**
il tartufo (nero) **(chocolate) ice-cream dessert**
il tiramisù **cold, creamy cheese and coffee-liqueur dessert**
la torta **cake/tart**
lo zabaglione **sweet dessert made with eggs and Marsala wine**
lo zuccotto **ice-cream liqueur**
la zuppa inglese **trifle**

La frutta (fruit)

le albicocche **apricots**
le arance **oranges**
le banane **bananas**
le ciliegie **cherries**
il cocomero **watermelon**
i fichi **figs**
le fragole **strawberries**
i frutti di bosco **forest fruits**
i lamponi **raspberries**
la mela **apple**
il melone **melon**
la pera **pear**
la pesca **peach**
il pompelmo **grapefruit**
le uve **grapes**

BASIC FOODS

l'aceto **vinegar**
l'aglio **garlic**
il burro **butter**
la focaccia **oven-baked snack**
il formaggio **cheese**
la frittata **omelette**
il grana **like parmesan cheese**
i grissini **bread sticks**
la marmellata **jam**
l'olio **oil**
il pane **bread**
il pane integrale **wholemeal bread**
il parmigiano **parmesan cheese**
il pepe **pepper**
il riso **rice**
il sale **salt**
la senape **mustard**
le uova **eggs**
lo yogurt **yoghurt**
lo zucchero **sugar**

Sightseeing

Can one visit? *Si può visitare?*
il custode **custodian**
il sacrestano **sacristan**
Suonare il campanello **ring the bell**
aperto/a **open**
chiuso/a **closed**
chiuso per la festa **closed for the festival**
chiuso per ferie **closed for the holidays**
chiuso per restauro **closed for restoration**
Is it possible to see the church? *È possibile visitare la chiesa?*
Entrata/uscita **Entrance/exit**
Where can I find the custodian/sacristan/key? *Dove posso trovare il custode/il sacrestano/la chiave?*
We have come a long way just to see... *Siamo venuti da lontano proprio per visitare...*
It is really a pity it is closed *È veramente peccato che sia chiuso*

(The last two should be tried in desperation – pleas for sympathy open some doors.)

At the Shops

What time do you open/close? *A che ora apre/chiude?*
Chiuso per ferie (typical sign) **Closed for the holidays**
Tirare/spingere (sign on doors) **Pull/push**
Entrance/exit *Entrata/uscita*
Can I help you? *Posso aiutarLa?* (formal)
What would you like? *Che cosa desidera?*
I'm just looking *Sto soltanto guardando*
How much does it cost? *Quant'è, per favore?*
How much is this? *Quanto costa?*
Do you take credit cards? *Accettate carte di credito?*
I'd like... *Vorrei...*
this one/that one *questo/quello*
I'd like that one, please *Vorrei quello lì, per cortesia*
Have you got ...? *Avete ...?*
We haven't got (any) ... *Non (ne) abbiamo...*
Can I try it on? *Posso provare?*
the size (for clothes) *la taglia*
What size do you take? *Qual'é a sua taglia?*
the size (for shoes) *il numero*
Is there/do you have...? *C'è...?*
Yes, of course *Sì, certo*
No, we don't (there isn't) *No, non c'è*
That's too expensive *È troppo caro*
Please write it down for me *Me lo scriva, per favore*
Don't you have anything cheaper? *Ha niente che costa di meno?*
It's too small/big *È troppo piccolo/grande*
brown/blue/black *marrone/blu/nero*
green/red/white/yellow *verde/rosso/bianco/giallo*
pink/grey/gold/silver *rosa/grigio/oro/argento*
No thank you, I don't like it *Grazie, ma non è di mio gusto*
I (don't) like it *(Non) mi piace*
I'll take it/I'll leave it *Lo prendo/Lo lascio*
It's a rip-off (impolite) *Sono prezzi da strozzini*
This is faulty. Can I have a replacement/refund? *C'è un difetto. Me lo potrebbe cambiare/rimborsare?*

Anything else? *Altro?*
The cash desk is over there *Si accomodi alla cassa*
Give me some of those *Mi dia alcuni di quelli lì*
a (half) kilo *un (mezzo) chilo*
100 grams *un etto*
200 grams *due etti*
more/less *più/meno*
with/without *con/senza*
a little *un pochino*
That's enough/No more *Basta così*

TYPES OF SHOPS

antique dealer *l'antiquario*
bakery/cake shop *la panetteria/pasticceria*
bank *la banca*
bookshop *la libreria*
boutique/clothes shop *il negozio di moda*
bureau de change *il cambio*
butcher *la macelleria*
chemist *la farmacia*
delicatessen *la salumeria*
department store *il grande magazzino*
dry cleaner *la tintoria*
fishmonger *la pescheria*
florist *il fioraio*
food shop *l'alimentari*
greengrocer *il fruttivendolo*
grocer *l'alimentari*
hairdresser (women) *il parrucchiere*
ice-cream parlour *la gelateria*
jeweller *il gioielliere*
leather shop *la pelletteria*
market *il mercato*
news-stand *l'edicola*
post office *l'ufficio postale*
shoe shop *il negozio di scarpe*
stationer *la cartoleria*
supermarket *il supermercato*
tobacconist *il tabaccaio* (also usually sells travel tickets, stamps, phone cards)
travel agency *l'agenzia di viaggi* (also usually books domestic and international train tickets for customers)

Travelling

airport *l'aeroporto*
arrivals/departures *arrivi/partenze*
boat *la barca*
bus *l'autobus/il pullman*
bus station *l'autostazione*
car *la macchina*
connection *la coincidenza*
ferry *il traghetto*
ferry terminal *la stazione marittima*
first/second class *la prima/seconda classe*
flight *il volo*
left-luggage office *il deposito bagagli*
motorway *l'autostrada*
no smoking *vietato fumare*
platform *il binario*
porter *il facchino*
railway station *la stazione (ferroviaria)*
return ticket *un biglietto di andata e ritorno*
single ticket *un biglietto di sola andata*
sleeping car *la carrozza letti/il vagone letto*
smokers/non-smokers *fumatori/non-fumatori*
stop *la fermata*
taxi *il taxi*
ticket office *la biglietteria*
train *il treno*
WC *la toilette*

AT THE AIRPORT

Where's the office of BA/Alitalia? *Dov'è l'ufficio della British Airways/dell'Alitalia?*
I'd like to book a flight to Venice *Vorrei prenotare un volo per Venezia*
When is the next flight to ...? *Quando parte il prossimo aereo per...?*

Conversion Charts

Metric–Imperial:
1 centimetre = 0.4 ins
1 metre = 3 ft 3 ins
1 kilometre = 0.62 miles
1 gram = 0.04 ounces
1 kilogram = 2.2 pounds
1 litre = 1.76 UK pints
Imperial–Metric:
1 inch = 2.54 centimetres
1 foot = 30 centimetres
1 ounce = 28 grams
1 pound = 0.45 kilograms
1 pint = 0.57 litres
1 UK gallon = 4.55 litres
1 US gallon = 3.78 litres

Are there any seats available? *Ci sono ancora posti liberi?*
Ha bagagli a mano? **Have you got any hand luggage?**
I'll take this hand luggage with me *Questo lo tengo come bagaglio a mano*
My suitcase has got lost *La mia valigia è andata persa*
My suitcase has been damaged *La mia valigia è rovinata*
Il volo è rimandato **The flight has been delayed**
Il volo è stato cancellato **The flight has been cancelled**
Posso metterLa sulla lista d'attesa **I can put you on the waiting list**

AT THE STATION

Can you help me please? *Mi può aiutare, per favore?*
Where can I buy tickets? *Dove posso fare i biglietti?*
at the ticket office/at the counter *alla biglietteria/allo sportello*
What time does the train leave? *A che ora parte il treno?*
What time does the train arrive? *A che ora arriva il treno?*
Can I book a seat? *Posso prenotare un posto?*
Are there any seats available? *Ci sono ancora posti liberi?*
Is this seat free/taken? *È libero/occupato questo posto?*
I'm afraid this is my seat *È il mio posto, mi dispiace*
Deve pagare un supplemento **You'll have to pay a supplement**
Do I have to change? *Devo cambiare?*
Where does it stop? *Dove si ferma?*
Bisogna cambiare a Roma **You need to change in Rome**
Which platform does the train leave from? *Da quale binario parte il treno?*
Il treno parte dal binario uno **The train leaves from platform one**
When is the next train/bus/ferry for Naples? *Quando parte il prossimo treno/pullman/traghetto per Napoli?*
How long does the crossing take? *Quanto dura la traversata?*
What time does the bus leave for Siena? *Quando parte l'autobus per Siena?*
How long will it take to get there? *Quanto tempo ci vuole per arrivare?*

Days and Dates

morning/afternoon/evening *la mattina, il pomeriggio, la sera*
yesterday/today/tomorrow *ieri/oggi/domani*
the day after tomorrow *dopodomani*
now/early/late *adesso/presto/ritardo*
a minute *un minuto*
an hour *un'ora*
half an hour *un mezz'ora*
a day *un giorno*
a week *una settimana*
Monday *lunedì*
Tuesday *martedì*
Wednesday *mercoledì*
Thursday *giovedì*
Friday *venerdì*
Saturday *sabato*
Sunday *domenica*
first *il primo/la prima*
second *il secondo/la seconda*
third *il terzo/la terza*

Will we arrive on time? *Arriveremo puntuali?*
Next stop please *La prossima fermata per favore*
Is this the right stop? *È la fermata giusta?*
Il treno è in ritardo **The train is late**
Can you tell me where to get off? *Mi può dire dove devo scendere?*

DIRECTIONS

right/left *a destra/a sinistra*
first left/second right *la prima a sinistra/la seconda a destra*
Turn to the right/left *Gira a destra/sinistra*
Go straight on *Va sempre diritto*
Go straight on until the traffic lights *Va sempre diritto fino al semaforo*
Is it far away/nearby? *È lontano/vicino?*
It's five minutes' walk *Cinque minuti a piedi*
It's 10 minutes by car *Dieci minuti con la macchina*
You can't miss it *Non può non vederlo*
opposite/next to *di fronte/accanto a*
up/down *su/giú*
traffic lights *il semaforo*
junction *l'incrocio, il bivio*
building *il palazzo*
Where is...? *Dov'è...?*
Where are...? *Dove sono...?*
Where is the nearest bank/petrol station/bus stop/hotel/garage? *Dov'è la banca/la stazione di servizio/la fermata di autobus/l'albergo/l'officina più vicino/a?*
How do I get there? *Come si può andare?* (or: *Come faccio per arrivare a...?*)
How long does it take to get to...? *Quanto tempo ci vuole per andare a...?*
Can you show me where I am on the map? *Può indicarmi sulla cartina dove mi trovo?*
You're on the wrong road *Lei è sulla strada sbagliata*

ON THE ROAD

Where can I rent a car? *Dove posso noleggiare una macchina?*
Is comprehensive insurance included? *È completamente assicurata?*
Is it insured for another driver? *È assicurata per un altro guidatore?*
By what time must I return it? *A che ora devo consegnarla?*
underground car park *il garage sotterraneo*
driving licence *la patente (di guida)*
petrol *la benzina*
petrol station/garage *la stazione di servizio*
oil *l'olio*
Fill it up please *Faccia il pieno, per favore*
lead free/unleaded/diesel *senza piombo/benzina verde/diesel*
My car won't start *La mia macchina non s'accende*
My car has broken down *La mia macchina è guasta*
How long will it take to repair? *Quanto tempo ci vorrà per la riparazione?*
The engine is overheating *Il motore si surriscalda*
Can you check the...? *Può controllare...?*
There's something wrong (with/in the)... *C'è un difetto (nel/nella/nei/nelle)...*
... **accelerator** *l'acceleratore*
... **brakes** *i freni*
... **engine** *il motore*
... **exhaust** *lo scarico/scappamento*
... **fanbelt** *la cinghia del ventilatore*
... **gearbox** *la scatola del cambio*
... **headlights** *le luci*
... **radiator** *il radiatore*
... **spark plugs** *le candele*
... **tyre(s)** *la gomma (le gomme)*
... **windscreen** *il parabrezza*

Road signs

Accendere le luci in galleria **Lights on in tunnel**
Alt **Stop**
Attenzione **Caution**
Autostrada **Motorway**
Avanti **Go/walk**

Tourist Signs

Most regions in Italy have handy signs indicating the key tourist sights in any given area:

Abbazia (Badia) **Abbey**
Basilica **Church**
Belvedere **Viewpoint**
Biblioteca **Library**
Castello **Castle**
Centro storico **Old town/historic centre**
Chiesa **Church**
Duomo/Cattedrale **Cathedral**
Fiume **River**
Giardino **Garden**
Lago **Lake**
Mercato **Market**
Monastero **Monastery**
Monumenti **Monuments**
Museo **Museum**
Parco **Park**
Pinacoteca **Art gallery**
Ponte **Bridge**
Ruderi **Ruins**
Scavi **Excavations/archaeological site**
Spiaggia **Beach**
Tempio **Temple**
Torre **Tower**
Ufficio turistico **Tourist office**

Emergencies

Help! *Aiuto!*
Stop! *Fermate!*
I've had an accident *Ho avuto un incidente*
Watch out! *Attenzione!*
Call a doctor *Per favore, chiami un medico*
... an ambulance *... un'ambulanza*
... the police *... la polizia*
... the fire brigade *... i pompieri*
Where is the telephone? *Dov'è il telefono?*
Where is the nearest hospital? *Dov'è l'ospedale più vicino?*
I would like to report a theft *Vorrei denunciare un furto*
Thank you very much for your help *Grazie dell'aiuto*

Caduta massi **Danger of falling rocks**
Casello **Toll gate**
Dare la precedenza **Give way**
Deviazione **Diversion**
Divieto di campeggio **No camping allowed**
Divieto di passaggio/Senso vietato **No entry**
Divieto di sosta/Sosta vietata **No parking**
Dogana **Customs**
Entrata **Entrance**
Galleria **Tunnel**
Guasto **Out of order** (e.g. phone box)
Incrocio **Crossroads**
Limite di velocità **Speed limit**
Non toccare **Don't touch**
Parcheggio **Parking**
Passaggio a livello **Railway crossing**
Pedaggio **Toll road**
Pericolo **Danger**
Pronto Soccorso **First aid**
Rallentare **Slow down**
Rimozione forzata **Parked cars will be towed away**
Semaforo **Traffic lights**
Senso unico **One way street**
Sentiero **Footpath**
Solo uscita **No entry**
Strada chiusa **Road closed**
Strada interrotta **Road blocked**
Strada senza uscita/Vicolo cieco **Dead end**
Tangenziale **Ring road/bypass**
Traffico di transito **Through traffic**
Uscita **Exit**
Uscita (autocarri) **Exit for lorries**
Vietato il sorpasso **No overtaking**
Vietato il transito **No thoroughfare**

Health

Is there a chemist near by? *C'è una farmacia qui vicino?*
Which chemist is open at night? *Quale farmacia fa il turno di notte?*
I don't feel well *Non mi sento bene*
I feel ill *Sto male/Mi sento male*
Where does it hurt? *Dove Le fa male?*
It hurts here *Ho dolore qui*
I suffer from... *Soffro di...*
I have a headache *Ho mal di testa*
I have a sore throat *Ho mal di gola*
I have a stomach ache *Ho mal di pancia*
Have you got something for airsickness? *Ha/Avete qualcosa contro il mal d'aria?*
Have you got something for seasickness? *Ha/Avete qualcosa contro il mal di mare?*
antiseptic cream *la crema antisettica*
sunburn *scottatura da sole*
sunburn cream *la crema antisolare*
sticking plaster *il cerotto*
tissues *i fazzoletti di carta*
toothpaste *il dentifricio*
upset-stomach pills *le pillole per male di stomaco*
insect repellent *l'insettifugo*
mosquitoes *le zanzare*
wasps *le vespe*

Further Reading

General

Across the River and into the Trees, by Ernest Hemingway.
Andreas, by Hugo von Hoffmannsthal.
The Architecture of the Italian Renaissance, by Peter Murray.
The Aspern Papers, by Henry James.
Autobiography, by Benvenuto Cellini.
Christ Stopped at Eboli, by Carlo Levi.
Le Città Invisibili, by Italo Calvino. Translated as *Invisible Cities*.
The Civilization of the Renaissance in Italy, by Jacob Burckhardt.
Death at La Fenice and other thrillers set in Venice, by Donna Leon.
Death in Venice, by Thomas Mann. (Originally *Der Tod in Venedig*.)
The Decameron, by Boccaccio.
D.H. Lawrence and Italy, by D.H. Lawrence.
The Doge, by A. Palazzeschi.
Etruscan Places, by D.H. Lawrence.
The Gallery, by John Horne Burns.
Graziella, by Alphonse de Lamartine.
Il Fuoco, by Gabriele D'Annunzio. Translated as *The Flame of Life*.
Italian Hours, by Henry James.
Italian Journey, by Johann Wolfgang von Goethe.
The Italian Painters of the Renaissance, by Bernard Berenson.
The Italian World, by John Julius Norwich.
The Italians, by Luigi Barzini.
The Last Medici, by Harold Acton.
Lives of the Artists, Vol. 1 & 2, by Giorgio Vasari.
Love and War in the Apennines, by Eric Newby.
The Love of Italy, by Jonathan Keates.
The Mafia, by Clare Sterling.
The Mediterranean Passion, by John Pemble.
Memoirs, by Giacomo Casanova. Translated into many languages.
Pictures from Italy, by Charles Dickens.

Renaissance Venice, edited by J.R. Hale.
The Rise and Fall of the House of Medici, by Christopher Hibbert.
The Stones of Florence and Venice Observed, by Mary McCarthy.
The Stones of Venice (1851–3), by John Ruskin.
The Story of San Michele, by Axel Munthe.
Those Who Walk Away, by Patricia Highsmith.
Thus Spake Bellavista, by Luciano de Crescenzo.
A Tramp Abroad, by Mark Twain.
A Venetian Bestiary, by Jan Morris.
Venetian Life, by William Dean Howells.
Venetian Red, by P.M. Passinetti.
Venice, by Jan Morris.
Venice: A Thousand Years of Culture and Civilisation, by Peter Lauritzen.
Venice and Its Lagoon, by Giulio Lorenzetti.
Venice for Pleasure, by J.G. Links.
Venice: The Greatness and the Fall, by Mark Twain.
Venice: The Rise to Empire, by John Julius Norwich.
The Wings of the Dove, by Henry James.

Other Insight Guides

Other *Insight Guides* to Italian destinations are: Italy, Southern Italy, Rome, Venice, Florence, Umbria, Tuscany, The Bay of Naples, Sicily, Sardinia and South Tyrol.

Thoroughly updated and expanded, the best-selling *Insight Guide: Rome* lifts the lid on Italy's capital.

Insight Guide: Venice is a detailed guide to this top Italian destination. Practical as well as visually stunning, it includes extensive hotel and restaurant listings.

Complementing the Insight Guides series is Insight's range of Pocket Guides. Intended for short-stay visitors, the books are itinerary based and supported by large pull-out maps. Italian destinations in the series are Venice, Rome, Florence, Milan, Sicily, Sardinia and Tuscany.

Insight Pocket Guide: Milan is the ideal guidebook to Italy's fashion capital. Perfect for a short break, it links all the main sights in easy-to-follow itineraries, which are clearly plotted on a pull-out map.

Insight's third series, Insight Compact Guides, is excellent for on-the-spot information. Titles include Tuscany, Florence, Milan, Venice, the Italian Riviera, the Italian Lakes and Rome. Supported by cross-referenced maps, photography and practical information, Insight Compact Guides are excellent and easily portable travel companions.

Feedback

We do our best to ensure the information in our books is as accurate and up-to-date as possible. The books are updated on a regular basis; however, some mistakes and omissions are inevitable, and we are ultimately reliant on our readers to put us in the picture.

We would welcome your feedback on any details related to your experiences using the book "on the road". The more details you can give us (particularly with regard to addresses, e-mails and telephone numbers), the better.

We will acknowledge all contributions, and we'll offer an Insight Guide to the best letters received.

Please write to us at:
Insight Guides
PO Box 7910
London SE1 1WE
United Kingdom
Or send e-mail to:
insight@apaguide.co.uk

ART & PHOTO CREDITS

AKG London 5, 28, 30, 39, 46, 47, 51, 53, 89R, 91, 92, 95, 229T, 259, 274, 287, 349
Apt. del Trentino 123, 127, 192T, 193T, 194
Archivio Cameraphoto Associated Press 215
Venezia/AKG London 2, 37
Matteo Bazzi/AFP/Getty Images 209
John Brunton spine, back flap top, 4BL, 61, 64, 65, 81, 94, 100/101, 104, 108, 124, 164/165, 166, 167, 174, 176, 177, 177T, 190T, 194T, 195, 231T, 244R, 249, 266, 278, 327, 336/337, 341, 347, 348, 348T, 350
Neil Buchan-Grant 14, 16, 54/55, 56/57, 58, 291, 292, 293, 294, 295, 296, 297, 304
Cavallini/Apt. del Trentino 125L
Chris Coe 275
Marco Cristofori/Corbis 73
Jerry Dennis 18, 105, 106, 208, 211, 216, 217, 218
De Ruvo/Apt. del Trentino 191
Editions d'Art Devreaux 24/25
Annabel Elston 103, 284L, 284L
The Art Archive back cover centre, 26, 27, 31, 33, 34, 35, 42, 43, 44, 48, 49, 50, 84, 87, 89L, 93, 173, 344, 345
Glyn Genin 17, 62, 63, 310/11, 312, 312, 315, 318, 319, 322, 323, 338, 339
Frances Gransden 4BR, 110
John Heseltine back flap bottom, back cover left, 32, 36, 71, 85, 86, 88, 129, 134/135, 142, 144, 145, 145T, 146, 147, 147T, 148, 149, 150, 152, 156, 172T, 180, 182, 182T, 183, 184, 184T, 185, 201, 202/203, 204, 211T, 213, 222/223, 225, 227T, 228, 229, 230, 233, 234T, 235, 235T, 236, 242, 250/251, 252, 255T, 257T, 263, 264, 264T, 265, 265T, 267, 270, 279, 282, 284T, 286, 288/ 289, 293, 302, 320/321, 325, 325T, 326, 328, 331, 331T, 332, 342
Michael Jenner front flap bottom, 2/3, 114/115, 138, 144T, 160R, 210, 219, 290, 294T, 300, 303T, 305, 306, 352
Nils Jorgensen/Rex Features 72
Daniele La Monaca/Reuters/Corbis 68
Erich Lessing/AKG London 29, 35, 121, 171
Ros Miller back cover bottom, 1, 82, 207, 210T, 212, 213T, 214, 214T, 226T, 227, 234
Anna Mockford and Nick Bonetti/APA 151, 157
Robert O'Dea/AKG London 172
Andrea Pistolesi 102
Michael Powell/Rex Features 317T
Private Archive 45, 90, 96
Mark Read back cover right, 21, 66, 75, 76/77, 117, 157T, 283, 298, 299, 300T, 301T, 303, 307T, 308, 308T, 309
Rex Features 19, 23, 72, 119, 349
Alessandra Santarelli 205
Sipa Press/Rex Features 67, 69, 78, 80
Andreas Solaro/AFP/Getty Images 22
Richard Sowersby/Rex Features 192
Survival Anglia 125R
George Taylor 120, 193, 237, 273. 273T, 275T, 276, 285
David Teuma/Getty Images 335
Topham Picturepoint 4/5, 52, 74, 97, 99, 116, 224, 231, 232, 268/269, 271, 280, 288/289, 316, 316T
Tore Gill/ACE 59

Cartographic Editor **Zoë Goodwin**
Design Consultants
Carlotta Junger, Graham Mitchener
Picture Research
Hilary Genin, Georgina Vacy-Ash

Turismo Torino 253, 255, 256, 257, 258, 260, 261
Villa Pisani 175
Bill Wassman 6/7, 8/9, 10/11, 12/13, 20, 60, 79, 98, 107, 109, 111, 118, 122, 126, 128, 130/131, 132/133, 143, 149T, 150T, 153, 154, 154T, 155, 156T, 158, 159, 160L, 161, 186/187, 188, 189, 196, 197, 198, 199, 200, 233T, 243, 244L, 248R, 277, 307, 317, 329, 330, 333, 333T, 334, 343, 345T, 346, 351
Roger Williams 178/179, 181, 238/239, 245, 246, 247, 248L, 248T, 262
Ermenegildo Zegna/Textile Valley 83

Picture Spreads

Pages 40–41
Top row left to right: AKG London, AKG London, Glyn Genin; *centre:* Erich Lessing/AKG London; *Bottom row left to right:* The Art Archive, Erich Lessing/AKG London, AKG London, AKG London
Pages 112–113
Top row left to right: Bill Wassman, John Heseltine, Apt. del Trentino, Mark Read, John Heseltine; *bottom row left to right:* Roger Wiliams, John Brunton, Bill Wassman, Mark Read, John Brunton, Roger Williams
Pages 162–163
top row left to right: John Heseltine, John Heseltine, John Heseltine; *centre:* John Heseltine; *bottom row left to right :* Blaine Harrington, Bill Wassman, Blaine Harrington
Pages 220–221
Top row left to right: National Motor Museum, Aldo Ballo; *centre:* C. Atrium Ltd; *bottom row left to right:* Zanussi, Bill Wassman, Vespa

Map Production Lovell Johns Ltd.

Index

Numbers in italics refer to photographs

a

Abbado, Claudio 99, 346
Abbazia di Pomposa 334
Abbiategrasso 226
Abetone 331, 332
Adamello-Brenta, Parco Nazionale 125, 190, 196–7
Adige Valley *see* **Trentino-Alto Adige**
Adriatic *336–8*, 339–50
  see also individual place names
AGIP 71–3
Agnelli dynasty 50, 69, *70*, 72, 74, 221, 249
Alagna 249
Alassio *298, 304*
Alba 112, 265, 266
Albenga 304–5
Alberti, Leon Battista 232, 349
Albinoni, Tommaso 93, 94
Alessandria 73, 265
Alessi 81, 82
Alfa Romeo 72, *221*
Alto Adige *see* **Trentino-Alto Adige**
Andreotti, Giulio 59
Angera 286
Antonelli, Alessandro 256
Antonioni, Michelangelo 23
Aosta 85, 246–7, *248*
  see also **Valle d'Aosta**
Apennines 123, 128, 129, 263, 331–2
Aquileia 85, 183–4
architecture 31, 82, 85–9
  see also names of architects and places
  Art Nouveau 195, 271, 303, 307
  Baroque 88, 117, 119, 120, 121
  brutalist 72, 218, 275
  classical 121
  18th-century 88
  Fascist 218, 278
  gardens 118, 119
  Gothic 86, 91
  modern 22–3
  Palladian *see* **Palladio, Andrea**
  Renaissance 86, 117, 118
  Roman 85
  Romanesque 32, 85–6
  villas 117–20, 121
Ariosto, Ludovico 43–4
Armani, Giorgio 74, 79, 80, 83, 205, 219, 220
Arona 286
art 38, 40–1, 44, 85–91
  see also names of artists
  Baroque 87–8
  Bolognese 319, 333
  cityscapes 88, 89
  18th-century 88–9, 91
  Emilian 319, 331
  Ferrarese 333
  Futurist 51, 89, 208
  Genoese 295
  genre 185
  Gothic 148
  Guggenheim Foundation 153
  Ligurian 305
  Lombard 213, 236
  Mannerist 91
  modern 151, 153, 207–8, *209*, 212, 257
  Moorish 148
  mosaics 85–6, 146, 159, 183, 184, 185, 234, 305, 344, 345, 346–7
  19th-century 89
  Pinacoteca di Brera 212–13
  prehistoric 29, 127, 128, 236–7, 301, 302
  Renaissance 86–7, 90, 118, 119–20, 148
  Rococo 88–9, 91
  sculpture 89, 217
  Venetian 40–1, 86, 87, 88–9, 90–1, 154, 210, 213, 216–17, 236, 295, 331
Arta Terme 183
Artusi, Pellegrino 103, 104
Asolo 177
Asti 112, 139, *264*, 265, 266, 278
Austria 43, 44, 46–7, 51
  Friuli-Venezia Giulia 47, 65, 139, 181, 183, 184
  Lombardy 45, 46, 47, 65, 205, 228
  Mantua 44
  Milan 45, 46, 47, 205
  Modena 46, 47
  Parma 46, 47, 326
  Pavia 228
  Piedmont 46–7
  Trentino-Alto Adige 20, *64, 65*, 66, 103, 106–7, 189, 191, 192, 193, 195, 197–201
  Trieste 103, 106, 139, 181
  Turin 65
  Veneto 47, 65, 167
  Venice 45, 46, 65, 103, 105, 161, 181
  Verona 167

b

Balla, Giacomo 89
Balzi Rossi 301–2
Bardolino 112, 128, 139, 272–3, 278
Barolo 112, 139, *260–2, 26*, 264–5, 266, 278
Bartoli, Cecilia 99
Barzini, Luigi 17, 63, 207
Bassani, Giorgio 332, 343
Bassano del Grappa 121, *164–5*, 176
Baveno *282*, 285
Bellagio *119*, 128, *270*, 281–2
Bellini, Giovanni 86, 90
  Bergamo 236
  Ferrara 90
  Milan 210, 213, 214
  Padua 90, 173
  Venice 40, 86, 90, 150, 154, 158
  Verona 90
Bellini, Vincenzo 94, 96
Belluno 177
Belotti, Giandomenico 81–2
Benetton 71, 73, 74–5, 80
Bergamo 37, 67, 88, 95, 97, 104, 128, 225, 235–6
Berlusconi, Silvio 18, 53, 68, 69, 74
Bertinotti, Fausto 20, 80
Bertolucci, Bernardo 23
Biella, Biella Valley 49, 73, 80, 83, 267
birds *see* **wildlife**
Boccadasse 297
Boccioni, Umberto 89, 213
Bocelli, Andrea 99
Bogliaco 276
Bologna *16, 17*, 18, 23, 35, 38, 60, 139, *310–11*, 313–19, 323
  Abbazia di Santo Stefano 318
  architecture 313, 314–15, 316–17, 318, 319
  art 87, 319, 333
  cafés 314
  Case Isolani 317–18
  Fascism 313, 319
  Fontana di Nettuno *313*, 314, 316
  food 104, 106, 108, 139, *312*, 313, 318, 319
  football 69
  Germany and 313, 316, 319
  immigration 49
  Museo Civico Archeologico 315
  Museo Civico Medievale 317
  Museo Giorgio Morandi 316

opera 97
Palazzo Archiginnasio 315–16
Palazzo Bevilacqua 319
Palazzo Comunale 316
Piazza del Nettuno *313*, 314, 316
Piazza Maggiore 314, *315*
Piazza Malpighi 319
Pinacoteca Nazionale 319
politics 313–14
Porta Ravegnana 317
porticoes 317
San Bartolomeo 317
San Domenico 319
San Petronio 86, 315
Santa Maria dei Servi 317
Strada Maggiore 318
Teatro Comunale 97
Università (Palazzo Poggi) 313, 318–19
Via Castiglione 318
Bolzano (Bozen) 21, *65*, 66, *102, 105*, 139, *186–7*, 198–9
Bonaparte, Napoleon 45, *113*, 212, 213, 258, 286
Bordighera 302
Bormio 237, 249
Borromeo dynasty 284, 286
Bossi, Umberto 19, 53, 68
Botticelli, Sandro 210, 217, 324
Bramantino 217
Brenta Canal/River 118, 121, 174, *175*
Brescia 22, 31, 45, 73, 93, 97, 225, 233–5
Bressanone (Brixen) 200
Brunico (Bruneck) 200
Bussana Vecchia 304
Byzantine Empire 30–1, 339, 344, 345, 346–7
see also **art**: mosaics

c

Cadenabbia 94, *116*, 117, 119
café society *2–3*, 19, *21*, 59, 63, 110–11
Aosta 247
Bologna 314
Como 280, *286*
Genoa 293, 295
Malcesine 272
Milan 110, 208, 211, 212
Milano-Marittima 347
Padua 110, 173
Pavia 228
Rimini 349
Sirmione 274
Stresa 284
Trento 191
Trieste 110, 185
Turin 110, 111, *250–1*, 255, 256, 257
Venice 110, 144, 149, *154*
Verona *56–57*, *166*, 169
Caffi, Ippolito 89
Camogli 305–6
Campione d'Italia 66, 283
Canaletto *40–1*, 89, 154, 214, 328, 331
Cannobio 286
Canova, Antonio 89, 148, 281
Caorle 175
Capo di Ponte 237
Caravaggio, Michelangelo 213, 216
Carpaccio, Vittore 40, 90, 154, 155, 213
Carrà, Carlo 208, 213
Carracci, Annibale *and* **Ludovico** 87, 319, 331
Casale Monferrato 265
Castel Beseno 194
Castel d'Avio 193
Castel l'Arquato 324–5
Castel Pergine 195
Castel Toblino 192
Castelfranco-Veneto 176
Castello di Mesola 341–3
Cattolica 339, 350
Catullus, Gaius Valerius 29, 167, 274
Cavalese 197
Cavour, Count Camillo di 20, 47, 67
Bard 244
Grinzane Cavour 265
Turin 20, 65, 111, 253, 255, 257
Cembra 196
Cernobbio 94, 280
Certosa di Pavia *4–5*, 86, 227
Cerutti 219
Cervia 347
Cervinia 249
Cervo 304
Cesena 348
Cesenatico 347–8
Chailly, Riccardo 99
Champdepraz 245
Champoluc 245, 249
Charlemagne 31, 32, 228
Charles V, Holy Roman Emperor 43, 315
Chiaravalle 227
Chioggia 340–1
Christianity 19, 20, 23, 30, 31–2, 50, 60, 85
Cinque Terre *113*, 129, *296–7*, 305, 307, 308–9
Cislano 277
Cividale del Friuli 182
climate
Bergamo 235
Cattolica 350
Ferrara 332
Lakes 112, 127, 225, 271, 278
Ligurian Riviera 300, 303
Milan *202–3*
Parma 326
Piacenza 323
Po 225–6, 323, 334
Trentino-Alto Adige 189–90, 196
Valle d'Aosta 243
Cogne 248
Colico 281
Colorno 329–30
Columbus, Christopher 22, *290*, 292, 294
Comacchio 334, 343
Communism 53, 80, 181, 313
Como 127–8, 225, 278–80, *286*
see also **Lakes**
Conegliano 113, 177
Corniglia *113*, 309
Correggio, Antonio 87, 214, 327, 328–9
Cortina d'Ampezzo 106, 176, 177, 249
Courmayeur 248, 249
Cremona 29, 32, 35, 71, 104, 128, 225, 229–30
see also **music; Stradivari**

d

D'Annunzio, Gabriele 51, 275, 287, 329
Dante Alighieri *170*, 191, 318, 331, 344, 345, 346
d'Azeglio, Massimo 65, 103
de Beauharnais, Eugène 46, 226
de Chirico, Giorgio *89*, 208, 332
della Francesca, Piero 210, 212, 213, 217, 332, 349
Desenzano 128, 271, 274
design 79, 82, 205, 211, 220–1
see also **fashion**
d'Este dynasty *26*
Certosa di Pavia 227
Ferrara 43–4, 86, 323, 332, 333, 342
Mantua 232
Mesola 341–3
Modena 43, 45, 330–1
Dolce & Gabbana 205, 211, 212, 219

Dolceacqua 302
Dolomites 123, 124–5, 126–7, *130–1*, 190, 199, 249
  see also individual place names
Domenichino 87
Domodossola 266
Donatello *172*, 173, 174
Donizetti, Gaetano 93, 95, 96, 236
Doria dynasty 43, 291, 305, 306
Dozza 334

e

earthquakes 181, 182, 304
Eco, Umberto 81, 316, *317*
economy 18, 19, 22, 49–51, 53, 68, 71–5, 80
Emilia Romagna 18, 22, 23, 35, 139, 323–34
  see also individual place names
  Adriatic 139, *336–8*, 339–50
  Agriturismo 126
  anarchism 49
  Apennines 331–2
  art 87–8, 319, 331, 333
  castles 329–30
  Communism 53, 67, 323
  economy 323
  Fascism 52, 53, 323
  fashion 80
  food 103, 104, 106, 323, 324, *327*, 335
  Gothic Line 123, 129
  opera 96
  Po Delta *see main entry*
  poverty 50
  sport 331
  walking 123, 128, 129, 331
  wines 112, 113, 334
Eraclea Mare 339
Etruscans 29, 167, 315, 343
Euganean Hills 174

f

Faenza 334
Farinelli 95
Farnese dynasty 43, 97, 323, 326, 328, 329
Fascism *49*, 52, 80, 89
  architecture 218, 278
  Bologna 313, 319
  Brescia 234
  Emilia Romagna 52, 53, 323
  Friuli-Venezia Giulia 181
  Genoa 291
  Milan 218
  Modena *48*, 335
  Nietzsche 287
  Parma 326
  Republic of Salò 53, 274
  Trentino-Alto Adige 201
  Valle d'Aosta 243, 247
fashion 74, *78*, 79–81, 82
  Milan 73, 79, 80–1, 205, 210–11, 212, 219
Fedele d'Intelvi 283
federalism *see* **politics; regionalism**
Fellini, Federico 23, 111, 349
Fénis 245
Ferragamo 74, 75
Ferrara 23, 331
  architecture 332
  art 86–7
  bicycles 332, 333
  cafés 333
  Case Romei 333
  Castello Estense 332–3
  Corso Ercole I d'Este 333
  d'Este dynasty *see main entry*
  Duomo 85, 333
  food 104, 332
  Museo Ebraico 333–4
  music 99
  Palazzina Marfisa 333
  Palazzo dei Diamante 333
  Palazzo Schifanoia 333
  Via delle Volte 333
Ferrari 22, 71, 72, *73, 220–1*, 221, 323, 330, 334
Ferre 80, 212
festivals
  chess 176
  fish 306
  flowers 301
  folk 280
  food 191, 265, 306
  music 95, 98, 99, 169, 192, 194, 197, 346
  wine 112, 192, 194
Fiat 22, 50–1, 69, 71, 72, 73, 74, 82, 221, *258*, 330
Fidenza 323, 325
films 23, 51, 153, 349, 350
Fini, Gianfranco 80
fishing
  see also **food**: fish
  Adriatic 340–1, 342, 343, 347–8
  Emilia Romagna 129, 334, 342
  Liguria 299, 300, 304, 306, 307, 308, 309, 342
Fiumalbo 331–2
flowers 120, 245, *248*, 300, 301, 303, 343
  see also **gardens; national/ regional parks, nature reserves**
Fontanellato 325
food and drink *8–9*, 63, *100–2*, 103–9, 112–13, 139
  see also **café society; restaurants**
  cheese 38, 103, 104, 105, 106, 107, 108, 109
  chocolate 19, 104, 108, 111
  coffee 73, *110*, 111
  desserts 103, 104, 105–6, 107, 108
  dumplings 103, 107, 108
  festivals 191, 192, 194, 265, 306
  fish 104, 105, 106, 108
  fritto misto 104, 108
  fruit *102*, 104, 106, 108, *128, 129*
  goulash 103, 106, 107
  honey 105
  ice cream 110
  meat 103, 104, 105, 106, 107, 108
  olive oil, olives 103, 108
  panettone 103
  Parma ham 103, 104
  Parmesan cheese (*Parmigiano*) 104, 106, 109
  pasta 65, 103, 104, 105, 106–7, 108
  pizza 65, 103, 104
  polenta 65, 103, 104, 106, 107
  poultry 104, 105
  regional 65, 103–9
  rice, risotto 38, 65, 103, 105, 106, 107, 108
  sauces 103, 104, 106, 108
  Slow Food Movement 63, 105, 108, 319
  soups 105, 106, 108
  spices 105, 106
  strangolapreti 107
  strudel 107
  truffles 107, 108
  vegetables 103, 106, 107, 108
  wines 21, 73, 108, 112–13
Forni di Sopra 183
Fra Angelico 328
Fra Galgario 88
France 43, 44, 45–6, 47
  Brescia 45
  food 103, 105, 107
  gardens 119, 120
  Genoa 46, 291
  Lakes 286
  Lombardy 46, 226
  Mantua 44
  Milan 46, 89, 212, 213
  Padua 46

Parma 326
Piedmont 65, 67, 107
Trentino-Alto Adige 194
Turin 65, 67, 103, 258
Valle d'Aosta 67, 243, 247
Venice 44, 45–6, 105, 144, 161, 181
Verona 46
Franciacorta 235, 277, 278
Frederick Barbarossa, Holy Roman Emperor 35, *41*, 228
Friuli-Venezia Giulia 31, 47, 65, 66, 112, 139, 181–5
see also individual place names

g

Gallino, Luciano 63, 73
gardens 45, 117, 118, 119–20, 125
see also **villas**
Bosco di Mesola 341
Gardone Riviera 275
Isola Bella 284–5
Isola Madre 285
Milan 212, *213*, 214
Riva del Garda *193*
Trento 192
Turin 257
Valnontey 248
Gardone Riviera 128, 274
Gargnano 271
Garibaldi, Giuseppe 22, 47, 110, 211, 225, 286, 343
Gatti, Daniele 99
Gemona del Friuli 182
Genoa (Genova) 18, 21–2, 36, 37, *288–9*, 291–7
Acquario 22, 295
architecture 291, 292–3, 294, 295
art 295
Austria and 43
banking 291, 294, 295
cafés 293, 295
centro storico 292–4
Columbus *290*, 294, 295
Doria dynasty *see main entry*
Fascism 291
food 295
France and 46, 291
hotels 293
immigrants 66
industry 49, 71
Jews 52
Loggia dei Mercanti 295
markets 295
Museo Nazionale dell'Antartide 295
opera 97
Padiglione del Mare 296
Palazzo Bianco 297
Palazzo Ducale 293
Palazzo Rosso 295
Palazzo San Giorgio 294
Palazzo Spinola 296
Piazza Mazzini *292*
Piazza San Matteo 293
Piazza Soziglia 295
politics 291–2
Porta Soprana 293–4
Porto Antico *291*, 295
restaurants 292, 295
San Donato 294
San Lorenzo 293
Santa Maria di Castello 294
Sant'Agostino (Museo di Architettura) 294
shopping *76–7*, 293
Via Garibaldi 296
Via Luccoli 297
Via XX Settembre 292
villas 117, 305
Germany *49*, 52–3
Bologna 313, 316, 319
Portofino 306
Salò 274
Trentino-Alto Adige 123, 195–6
Valle d'Aosta 243
Villa Pisani 174
Giacomini, Giuseppe 99
Gigli, Romeo 83, 219
Giorgione 87, 154, 167, 176
Giotto 86, *173*, 319, 349
Gonzaga dynasty 36, 44, 45, 97, 225, 231, 232–3
Gorizia 182
Goths 30, 32, 225, 228
Grado 181, 183
Gran Bosco della Mesola 341
Gran Paradiso, Parco Nazional del 124–5, 243, 247–8, 263
Grand Tour 45, 274
Gressoney-la-Trinité 245, 249
Gressoney-St-Jean 244
Grinzane 265
Grotte di Toirano 305
Guardi, Francesco 154
Guarini, Guarino 253, 255, 256, 257
Gucci 80, 83, 211, 219
Guercino 87–8, 319

h

Habsburgs *see* **Austria**
Hayez, Francesco 89
hotels 124
Agriturismo 124, 126
Castel Pergine 196
Cernobbio 280
Gardone Riviera 274, 275
Gargnano 274
Genoa 293
Lakes 271, 272, 274, 275, 278, 280, 282, 283–4
Levico Terme 195
Milan 212, 218
Rimini 350
Riva del Garda 272
Sirmione 274
Stresa 283–4
Trentino-Alto Adige 126, 192, 195, 196
Venice 151, 153, 340
villas 119, 177, 274, 275, 280
Huns 30, 32, 183

i

"Iceman" 29, 198–9
Il Vittoriale 275, 287
immigration 66, 69
Imola 334
industry *see* **economy**
Iseo 276
Isera 194
Isola Bella 117, 119, 120, 284–5
Isola Comacina 280
Isola Madre 119, 284, 285
Isola Pescatori 284, 285
Isolaverde 341
Isole Borromee 284–5
Isole Palmaria 309
Issime 244
Issogne 244–5
Italy, unification of *see* **Risorgimento**
Ivrea 74, 266

j

Jews 52, 53, 274
Bologna 313
Casale Monferrato 266
Ferrara 52, 104, 333–4
Genoa 52
Trieste 185
Venice 52, 160–1
Juvarra, Filippo 88, 253, 255, 257, 258

k

Kafka 271
Keates, Jonathan 309
Krizia 80, 212

l

La Perla 80
La Rocca 113
La Spezia 309
La Thuille 249
lacemaking *283*, 307
Lakes 139, 263, 271–86
 see also individual place names
 cafés 272, 274, 280, 284, *286*
 Cavedine 192
 climate 112, 127, 225, 271, 278
 Como 94, *116*, 117, 119, 127–8, 271, 277–82
 Garda 51, 53, 127, 190, 192–3, 225, 271–6, 278
 hotels 271, 272, 274, 275, 278, 280, 282, 283–4
 Iseo 112, 113, 127, 235, 271, 276–7, 278, *285*
 Kaltern *54–5*
 Ledro 193
 Lugano 271, 282–3
 Maggiore 119, 120, 127, 271, 278, 279, 283–6
 markets 276
 Nazioni 343
 Orta 286
 restaurants 277, 281, 285
 shopping 272, 274, 283
 Trentino-Alto Adige *54–5*, 125, 127, 189–90, 192–3, 195, 197, *199*
 villas 119, 120, 127–8, 271, 273, 275, 280–1, 282, 284, 286
 Viverone 266
 walking 127–8, 274, 275, 279
 water sports 190, 272
 wines 112, 272–3, 277, 278
Lancia 72
languages 66–7
 French 66, 67, 243, 299, 326
 Friulano 67
 German 31, *65*, 66, 67, 189, 195, 198, 201, 243, 244
 Ladin 67, 189
 Occitano 67
 Slovene *66*, 67
Lanzo d'Intelvi 283
Lavarone 195
Lazise 273
Lega Nord *see* **Northern League**
Legnano, Battle of 35, 68
Leonardo da Vinci 38, 214–15, 217, 328, 347
Lerici 309
Levico Terme 195
Lido di Comacchio 343
Lido di Jesolo 339–40
Lido di Spina 343
Lido di Venezia 340
Lignano Sabbiardoro 183
Liguria 23, 139, 299–309
 see also individual place names
 Agriturismo 126
 art 305
 climate 300, 303
 food 103, 104, 108, 299–300
 immigration *66*
 languages 299
 Riviera dei Fiori 120
 Riviera di Levante 305–9
 Riviera di Ponente 80, 300–305
 villas *114–15*, 117, 302, 303, 305
 walking 123, 129, 306–7, 308–9
 wines 112, *113*, 302
Limone sul Garda 276
literature 43–4, 51, 89, 177, 209–10
Livigno 249
Locarno *284*, 286
Locarsa 283
Lodi 229
Lombard League 35, 68, 232, 233
Lombardy 18, 19, 22, 35, 139, *222–4*, 225–37
 see also individual place names
 art 213, 236
 Austria and 45, 46, 47, 65, 205, 228
 economy 49–50, 73, 225
 fashion 80
 food 38, 103, 104, 107, 225, 227, 231, 232, 236
 France and 46, 226
 Longobards 19, 31, 225
 opera 96
 Parco Nazionale dello Stelvio 124, 199, 237
 regionalism 67, 68, 225, 237
 villas 117
 walking 128
 wines 112, 113, 278
Lovere 277
Lugano 283
Luino 286
Luxottica 74

m

Madonna di Campiglio 127, 196, 249
Malatesta dynasty *35*, 339, 349, 350
Malcesine 128, 272
Malles Venosta (Mals im Vischgau) 199
Manarola 309
Mandarina Duck 80
Mango 265, 266
Mantegna, Andrea *44*, 86
 Bergamo 236
 Ferrara 332
 Mantua 86, 225, 232, 233
 Milan 210, 212, 213
 Padua 173
 Venice 155
 Verona 169
Mantua (Mantova) 50, 225, 231, 232–3
 art 44, 86, 225, 232, 233
 Austria and 44
 Basilica di Sant'Andrea 44, 232
 Buonaccorsi dynasty 36
 Camera degli Sposi 86, 233
 climate 232
 food 104
 France and 44
 Gonzaga dynasty *see main entry*
 music 44, 93, 94, 97
 opera 94, 97
 Palazzo del Te 44, 233
 Palazzo Ducale 232–3
 Piazza del Broletto 232
 Piazza dell'Erbe 232
 Teatro Scientifico 97, 232
 walks 128
Manzoni, Alessandro 209–10
Marconi, Guglielmo 318–19
Marina di Ravenna 343–4
Marina Romea 343–4
Marini, Biagio 93
markets *61*
 Cesenatico 348
 Genoa 295
 Iseo 276
 Milan 216
 Rapallo 307
 Rimini 349
 San Remo 303
 Turin 255
 Venice 157–8
 Ventimiglia 301
Marostica 176
Martini, Cardinal 20, 68
Marzabotto 53
Maser *87*, 119, 177
Maserati 323, 330
Massari 150, 156
Mastroianni, Marcello 111, 349
Mattei, Enrico 71–3
Mazzini, Giuseppe 22, 110, 211, 291

Menaggio 281, 282
Merano (Meran) 199
Mestre 175
Michelangelo 214, 319
Milan 17, 18–19, 22, 30, 31, 35, 60, 139, 205–19, 225
Acquario 213
Alfa Romeo 221
Alzaia Naviglio Grande 217
architecture 205, 207, 211–12, 214, 215, 217, 218
art 38, 89, *209*, 210, 212–13, 214–15, 216–17
Austria and 45, 46, 47, 205
banks 73, 225
Basilica di San Babila 211
Basilica di San Satiro 217
Basilica di Sant'Ambrogio 214
Beccaris massacre 50
Brera quarter 212–13
Ca' Grande (Università Statale) 213
cafés 110, 208, 211, 212
canal quarter 216–18
Carbonari 46
Casa del Manzoni 209–10
Castello Sforzesco 213
Cenacolo Vinciano 214–15
Darsena 217–18
Duomo 86, *134–5, 202–4*, 207
design 79, 82, 205, 211, 220–1
economy/industry 49, 50, 53, 71, 73, 74, 205–7
Fascism 218
fashion 73, 79, 80–1, 205, 210–11, 212, 219
food 108
football 69
France and 46, 89, 212, 213
Galleria Vittorio Emanuele *138*, 208, *210*
Giardini Pubblici 211
Grattacielo Pirelli 218
hotels 212, 218
Il Quadrilatero 210–11
immigrants 66, 73, 80
La Scala 30, 93, *95*, 96, 97, 98, 99, 205, 208–9
markets 216
Museo d'Arte Contemporanea 207–8
Museo del Collezionista d'Art 214
Museo del Duomo 208
Museo della Basilica 214
Museo della Reggia 208
Museo della Scienza e della Tecnica Leonardo da Vinci 214
Museo di Storia Naturale 212
Museo Poldi-Pezzoli 209
music 30, 93, 94, 95–6
Mussolini 53
Navigli 216, 217–18
opera *see* La Scala *above*
Padiglione d'Art Contemporanea 211
Palazzo Bagetti-Valsecchi 211
Palazzo Clerici 209
Palazzo della Ragione 210
Palazzo della Stelline 215
Palazzo Reale 207–8
Parco Sempione 213
Piazza del Duomo 207, *208, 218*
Piazza della Repubblica 218
Pinacoteca Ambrosiana 216–17
Pinacoteca di Brera 212
Porta Romana 214–16
Porta Ticinese 217
restaurants 212
Risorgimento 46
San Lorenzo Maggiore *88*, 217
San Simpliciano 212
Santa Maria delle Grazie 38, 214–15, *216*
Sant'Eustorgio 217
shopping 211, 212, 218
Sforza dynasty *see main entry*
Stazione Centrale 217
Ticinese 216–17
Università Statale 214
Via Fiori Chiari 212
Via Manzoni *211*
Via Monte Napoleone 210
Villa Reale 211
Visconti dynasty *see main entry*
Milano-Marittima 347
Mincio, Parco del 128
Miramare 184
Missoni 74, 80, 219
Modena 17, 23, 29, 32, 45, 49, 60, 323, 330–1
architecture 330
Austria and 46, 47
Biblioteca Estense 330
d'Este dynasty *see main entry*
Duomo 85, 331
economy 330
Fascism *48*, 335
Ferrari *see main entry*
food 104, 335
Galleria Estense 330–1
Ghirlandina 330
music 96, 330, 335
opera 97
Palazzo Comunale 330
Palazzo Ducale 331
shopping 330
monarchy 20, *58*, 330
Umberto I 50, 244
Victor Emmanuel II 47, 49, 67, 208, 247, 253, 256
Victor Emmanuel III 52, 247–8
Monfalcone 184
Monte Bondone 191
Monte Isola 276–7
Montecchio Maggiore *118*
Monterosso 308
Monteverdi, Claudio 93, 94, 95, 97, 229, 232
Monza 117, 226
Morandi, Giorgio 208, 213, 316
Morcote 282
Moschino 79, 205, 211, 219
Movimento Nordest 68
see also **politics; regionalism**
Muggia 185
museums
Alpino Duca degli Abruzzi (Courmayeur) 248
Archaeological (Aosta) 247
Archeologico dell'Alto Adige (Bolzano) 198–9
Arte Contemporanea (Milan) 207–8
Arte e Storia Antigua Ebraica (Casale Monferrato) 266
Biblioteca Ambrosiana (Milan) 217
CAI (Trento) 124
Casa del Manzoni (Milan) 209–10
Castel Dragone (Camoglio) 306
Castello Sforzesco (Milan) 214
Ceramiche (Faenza) 334
Civico (Piacenza) 324
Civico Archeologico (Bologna) 315
Civico di Arte Antica (Turin) 255
Civico Medievale (Bologna) 317
Correr (Venice) 148
Diocesan (Bressanone) 200
Diocesan (Trento) 191
Duomo (Milan) 208
Ebraico (Ferrara) 333–4
Egizio (Turin) *256*, 257
Eremitani Musei Civici (Padua) 173
Giorgio Morandi (Bologna) 316
Jewish culture (Bologna) 313
lace (Rapallo) 307
Luigi Marzoli (Brescia) 235
Marineria (Cesenatico) 348
Musei Civici (Como) 279
Multscher (Vipiteno) 200
Natural Science (Saint Pierre) 248

naval (La Spezia) 309
Navale (Venice) 151
Navale Romano (Albenga) 305
Nazionale del Risorgimento (Turin) 256
Nazionale dell'Automobile (Turin) 57–8
Nazionale della Montagna (Turin) 124, 258
Palazzo della Pilotta (Parma) 328
Pasquale Revoltella (Trieste) 185
Pinacoteca di Brera (Milan) 212–13
Poldi-Pezzoli (Milan) 210
salt (Cervia) 347
Sant'Agostino (Museo di Architettura) (Genoa) 294
Santa Giulia Museo della Città (Brescia) 234–5
Seta (Como) 279
Storia (Pavia) 228
Stradivariano (Cremona) 230
Teatrale alla Scala (Milan) 209
Tesoro (Aosta) 247
Valle d'Aosta Furnishings (Fénis) 245
Verdi (Roncole) 325
Villa Doria (Pegli) 305

music 93–9
see also names of composers and musicians
Baroque 91, 93, 150
festivals 95, 98, 99, 169, 192, 194, 197, 346
opera 30, 35, 44, *45*, 51, 85, 93, 94–9, 208–9, 236, 326
Venetian 93–4
violins 93, 95, 230

Mussolini, Benito *48, 49*, 51–3, 174
see also **Fascism**
Alto Adige and 198, 201
Cervinia and 249
Claretta Petacci 53, 274, 275
death 53, 274
Fiat and 72
football 69
"Il Duce" 51–3
opera 96
Republic of Salò 53, 274

n

national/regional parks, nature reserves 124, 243
Gran Bosco della Mesola (reserve) 341
Mont Avic Regional Park 245
Oasi Zegna (reserve) 125
Parco del Delta del Po (reserve) 128, 129, 334, 341
Parco del Mincio (reserve) 128
Parco del Ticino (regional) 227
Parco Nazionale Adamello-Brenta 125, 190, 196–7
Parco Nazionale del Gran Paradiso 124–5, 243, 247–8, 263
Parco Nazionale delle Incisioni Rupestri 237
Parco Nazionale dello Stelvio (Stilfs) 124, 126, 199, 237
Piano di Spana (reserve) 281
Promontory of Portofino nature reserve 306–7
Riserva Naturale delle Saline di Cervia 347
Riserva Naturale di Fondo Toce 286
Sciliar national park 127
Vene di Bellochio (reserve) 343

Nervi 297, 305

Northern League 19, 22, 68, 232
see also **politics; regionalism**

o

Oasi Zegna 125
Oetzi the Iceman 29, 198–9
Olivetti 71, 74, 81, 82, 266
opera *see* **music**
Ortisei (Sant Ulrich) 200

p

Padania 53, 68

Padua 30, 37, 60, 167, 173–4
Basilica di Sant'Antonio 174
Battistero del Duomo 174
cafés 110, 173
Cappella degli Scrovegni 86, 173
Eremitani Musei Civici 173
France and 46
Orto Botanico 117, 174
Palazzo del Bo 173
Piazza delle Erbe 174
Piazza della Ragioni 174

Palladio, Andrea 87, 121
Bassano del Grappa (bridge) 121, 176
Veneto *see* villas *below*
Venice (churches) 121, 148, 156
Vicenza 171–2
villas 117, 118–19, 121, 167, 171, 176, 177

Pallanza 285
parks *see* **gardens; national parks**
Parks, Tim 17, 61, 79

Parma 23, 32, 45, 49, *60*, 323, 325–9
architecture 326, 327–8
Austria and 46, 47, 326
Baptistry *320–1*, 327
Camera di San Paolo 328
climate 326
Duomo 85, 326–7
Farnese dynasty *see main entry*
Fascism 326
food 103, 104, 106, 109, 276, *322*, 323, *326, 327*, 328, 329
football 69
France and 326
Galleria Nazionale 328
ham 103, 104, 323, *327*, 328, 329
languages 326
music 93, 96
opera 97
Palazzo Ducale 328
Palazzo della Pilotta 327–8
Parmesan cheese (*Parmigiano*) 38, 104, 106, 109, 139, 276, *322*, 323, *326*, 329
Piazza Garibaldi *329*
San Giovanni Evangelista 327
Teatro Farnese 97, 328
Teatro Regio 97, 327

Parmigianino, Francesco 23, 325, 328, 331
Passariano 181
Passo Tonale 249
Pavarotti, Luciano *22*, 23, 98, 99, 208, 330, 335
Pavia 31, 43, 71, 104, 225, 227–9
Pegli 305
Pellestrina 340
Peschiera del Garda 273
Petacci, Claretta 53, 274
Petrarch 174, 217, 318
Piacenza 29, 43, 71, 323–4
Piaggio 72, 75, *221*
Piano, Renzo 22–3, 82, 292, 295

Piedmont 18, 20, 45, 139, 263–6
see also individual place names
Austria and 46–7
food 103, 107–8, 263, *265*, 266
France and 65, 67, 107
Gran Paradiso 124–5
industry 74, 83
languages 67
Oasi Zegna 125
restaurants 264
Savoy, House of 20, 45, 46–7, 67, 88, 253, 255, 256, 257, 258, 259
secessionism 68

sports 124, 263
textiles 73, 74, 83
walking 124, 263
wines 73, 112, 113, *263*, 264–5, 266, *267*
Piermarini, Giuseppe 96
Pignotti, Luciano 23
Pinerolo 263
Pirelli 71, 218
Pisanello, Antonio 232, 236, 332
Pivetti, Veronica *and* Irene 18, 19
Po River
climate 225–6, 323, 334
Delta 128, 129, 174, 334, 341, 342
Parco del Delta del Po 128, 129, 334, 341
Piedmont 263
Valley 23, 49, 73, 104, 121, 123, 231–2, 263–4, 266, *327*, 328
politics 19, 20, 35, 49, 50, 51–3, 59–60, 67–8, 80
Polo, Marco 21
Pont-St-Martin 244
Ponte Ceresio 283
Ponte Tresa 282
Pontedilegno 249
Ponti, Giò 82, 218
Pontida 68
Pordenone 181
Porlezza 283
Porto Cassini 343
Porto Garibaldi 343
Portofino *14*, *21*, 23, 117, 129, 305, 306–7, *352*
Portogruaro 175
Portovenere 305, 309
Prada 80, 212, 219, 220
prehistory 29, 127, 128, 236–7, 301, 302, 305
Puccini, Giacomo 51, 95, 96, 97, 255

r

Raphael 212, 213, 217, 319
Rapallo 307
Ravenna 30–1, *84*, 85, 99, 323, 339, 344–7
Reggio Emilia 32, 38, 109
regionalism 17–18, 19, 20–1, 22, 23, 65–8, 103–8
religion *see* **Christianity**
Reni, Guido 87, 295, 319, 331
restaurants 20
see also **café society; food and drink**
Agriturismo 126
Bologna 319
Camogli 306
Castel Pergine 196
Cesenatico 347–8
Chioggia 341
Cinque Terre 308
Courmayeur 249
Dobbiaco 94
Franciacorta 277
Genoa 292, 295
Isola Comacina 281
Isola Pescatori 285
Marina Romea 344
Milan 212
Piedmont 264
Portovenere 309
Riccione 350
Trentino-Alto Adige 126, 192, 196
Turin 256, *257*
Venice 149, *154*, 160
Verona 167
Ricci, Sebastiano 88
Riccione 339, 350
Rimini *35*, 339, 348–50
Riomaggiore *308*, 309
Risorgimento 35, 46, 47, 49, 65, 96
Genoa 291
Lombardy 225
Musei Civici (Como) 279
Museo Nazionale del... (Turin) 256
Padua 173
Via d'Intelvi 283
Riva del Garda 192–3, 272
Riviera *see* **Liguria**: Riviera...
Roden, Claudia 65, 107, 236, 300
Rogers, Ernesto Nathan 81
Roman Empire 29–30, 85
see also individual place names
Romano, Giulio 233
Roncole Verdi 325
Rossini, Gioacchino 94, 95, 96, 97, 98
Rosso, Medardo 89
Rovereto 194
Rovigo 117, 174

s

Sabbioneta 230–1
Sacra de San Michele 263
Saint Pierre 248
St Vincent 245
Salò 53, 274
San Bernardo, Colle del Gran 243, 247
San Bernardo, Colle del Piccole 243, 248
San Daniela del Friuli 181
San Fruttuoso 306
San Marino 66, 351
San Martino di Castrozza 197
San Remo 300, 302–3
Sansovino, Jacopo 118, 148, 151
Santa Margherita Ligure 307
Santa Catarina 249
Sant'Ambrogio di Valpolicella 112, 170, 278
Santarcangelo di Romagna 350
Sarnico 277
Sarre 247–8
Sarzana *308*, 309
Sassuolo 88, 323
Savona 305
Savoy, House of *see* **monarchy; Piedmont**
Sciliar national park 127
Seborga 66
secessionism *see* **politics; regionalism**
Sestri Levante 308
Sestriere 249, 263
Severini, Gino 208
Sforza dynasty
Castel l'Arquato 324–5
Milan 38, *39*, 43, 86, 205, 215, 225, 227, 228, 229
Shelley, Percy Bysshe 225, 271, 309
shopping
Bormio 249
Campione d'Italia 283
Courmayeur 248
Cremona 230
Genoa *76–7*, 293
Milan 211, 212, 218
Modena 330
Pavia 228
Portofino 306
Rapallo 307
Riccione 339, 350
Riva del Garda 272
Sirmione 274
Susa 263
Turin 256
Venice 147, 152, 154, 157–8
Verona 167
Sigurtà 120, 273
silk 225, 278, 279
Sinopoli, Giuseppe 99
Sirmione 29, 128, 271, 273–4
Soave 112, 170, 278
society 17–23, 59–63
see also individual regions
Sottomarina 341

Sottsass, Ettore 82, 220, *221*
South Tyrol *10–11*, 18, *20*, 21, 51
  see also **Trentino-Alto Adige**
spas 194–5, 199, 274, 347
Spina 343
sports
  climbing 123, 124, 127, 190
  cycling 124, 127, 128–9, *200*, 232, *262*, 276, 332, 340, 342
  football 35, 69, 258
  golf 226, 340
  hang-gliding 176, 190, 331
  horse-riding 126, 195, 197, 331, 339
  motor-racing 334
  orienteering 123
  tennis 340
  trekking 195
  volleyball 348, 350
  walking 123–9, 190, 194, 195, 196, 197, 199, 200, 249, 274, 275, 279, 306–7, 308–9, 331, 342, 344
  water 190, 193, 195, 232, 272, 343, 348, 350
  winter 69, 106, 123, 124, 126, 127, 176, 177, 190, 195, 196, 199, 248, 249, 263, 331
Stelvio (Stilfs), Parco Nazionale dello 124, 126, 199
Strà 119, 174
Stradivari, Antonio 95, 230
Stresa 120, 283–4
Strozzi, Bernardo 295
style 71, 75, 79–82
  see also **fashion**
Südtirol *see* **South Tyrol**
Susa 263

t

Tasso, Torquato 44
Tarvisio 183
Theodoric 30–1, 85, 346
Tiepolo, Giambattista 88–9
  Bergamo 236
  Desenzano del Garda 274
  Isola Bella 285
  Milan 217
  Padua 173
  Treviso 176
  Venice 88, 90, 91, 150, 154, 156
  Vicenza 88
  Villa Pisani 119
Tintoretto, Jacopo 90, 91
  Bergamo 236
  Genoa 291
  Milan 213, 214, 295
  Modena 331
  Padua 173
  Venice *40*, 87, 90, 91, 148, 154, 158, 159–60
  Verona 170
  Vicenza 172
Titian 87, 90–1, 167
  Genoa 295
  Milan 213, 214, 217
  Padua 173, 174
  Treviso 175
  Venice 90–1, 154, 155, 158, 159
Torbole 272, *275*
Torri del Benaco 272
Toscanini, Arturo 96, 99, 328, 335
Trentino-Alto Adige *10–13*, 18, *61*, 139, *188*, 189–201
  see also individual place names
  Agriturismo 126
  Alpi di Siusi (Seiser Alm) *196*, 200
  Alto Adige 197–201
  Austria and 20, *64*, *65*, 66, 67, 103, 106–7, 189, 191, 192, 193, 195, 197–201
  castles 192, 193, 194, 196, 200
  Diocesan museums 191, 200
  Dolomites 123–4, 125, 126–7, 139, 190, 196–7, 199, 200
  Fascism 201
  festivals 192, 194, 197
  food 103, 106–7, 189, 191, 195
  France and 194
  Germany and 123, 195–6
  lakes *54–5*, 125, 127, 189–90, 192–3, 195, 197, *199*
  languages 189, 195, 198, 201
  Museo Archeologico dell'Alto Adige 198–9
  Museo Nazionale dell'Automobile 257–8
  music 94, *98*, 191, 192, 197
  Parco Nazionale Adamello-Brenta 125, 190, 196–7
  Parco Nazionale dello Stelvio (Stilfs) 124, 126, 199, 237
  Passo di Stelvio *122*, 126
  Path of Peace 123, 125–6, 194, 195
  Sciliar national park 127
  spas 194–5, 199
  sports 190, 193, 195, 196, 197, 199, 200
  Trentino 191–7
  walking *122*, 123, 125–6, 127, 190, 194, 196, 197, 199, 200
  wines 113, 192, 194, 196
Trento *113*, 124, 190–1
Treviso 37, 75, 105, 117, *174*, 175–6
Trieste 60, 184–5
  Austria and 66,103, 106, 139, 181, 184
  cafés 110, 185
  Duomo San Giusto *184*, 185
  languages 66, 67
  Piazza dell'Unità d'Italia *180*, 185
Trivero 74, 83
Tura, Cosimo 86–7
Turin 19–20, 22, 60, 88, 253–61
  architecture 253
  art 89
  Austria and 65
  Basilica di Superga 261
  Biblioteca Reale 256
  Borgo e Rocca Medioevale 259
  cafés 110, 111, 250–1, 255, 256, 257
  Church of San Lorenzo 255
  Church of the Consolata 255
  Duomo di San Giovanni 253
  Fiat *see main entry*
  food 103, 108
  football 69, 258
  France and 65, 67, 103, 258
  Galleria Civica d'Arte Moderna e Contemporanea 257
  immigrants 66, 74
  industry 49, 50–1, 71, 73
  languages 67
  Lingotto 260
  markets 255
  Mole Antonelliana 256
  Museo Civico di Arte Antica 256
  Museo Egizio 258
  Museo della Arti decorativi 257
  Museo Nazionale del Cinema 257
  Museo Nazionale del Risorgimento 256
  Museo Nazionale della Montagna 124, 258
  opera 97
  Palazzina di Caccia di Stupinigi 261
  Palazzini di Caccia di Stupinigi 88, 258
  Palazzo Città 255
  Palazzo Reale 255–6
  Parco del Valentino 257
  Piazza Carignano 256
  Piazza Carlo Felice 257
  Piazza Castello 255

Piazza della Repubblica 255
Piazza San Carlo 257
Piazza Vittorio Veneto 256
Pinacoteca Giovanni e Marella Agnelli 261
Porta Palatina 255
Reggia di Venoria Reale 261
restaurants 256, *257*
San Lorenzo *252*
Savoy, House of *see* monarchy; Piedmont
Shroud 255, 259
Superga 88, 258

u

Udine 88, 181–2
Umberto I, King 50, 244

v

Val d'Ayas *243*, 245
Val di Camonica 29, 127, 128, 236–7
Val di Senales (Schnals) 199
Valdobbiadene 113, 177
Valentino 83, *219*
Valle d'Aosta *238–9*, 243–8
see also individual place names
Archaeological Museum 247
climate 243
Fascism 243, 247
food 104, 108
France and 67, 243, 247
Germany and 243
languages 66, 67, 243, 244
Museo Alpino Duca degli Abruzzi 248
Museo de Tesoro 247
Natural Science Museum 248
skiing 69
Valle di Fassa 197
Valle di Locana 263
Valnontey 125, 248
Valpolicella *see* **Sant'Ambrogio di Valpolicella**
Valtournenche 245, 249
Varallo 267
Varenna *268–9*, 281
Varese 120, 225
Veneto, the 22, 49, 50, 139, 167–77
see also individual place names
Adriatic 339
architecture 87
art 88
Austria and 47, 65, 167
Canale Brenta 118, 121, 174, *175*
Colle Euganei 174
cycling 128–9
economy 73, 74–5, 167
food 103, 105–6
gardens 117–20
Il Sile 176
Po River Delta *see main entry*
secessionism 67, 68
villas 117–20, 121, 167, 174, 176, 177
walking 128, 129
wines 112, 113, 170, 176, 177
Venezia Giulia *see* **Friuli-Venezia Giulia**
Venice 18, 21, 32, 50, *59*, 60, *142*, 143–63
Accademia 154
Agnadello, Battle of 43, 44
architecture 121, 143–63
Arsenale 149, 150–1
art 40–1, 86, 87, 88–9, 90–1, 150, 151, 154, 210, 213, 216–17, 236, 295, 331
Austria and 45, 46, 65, 103, 105, 161, 181
bars (*bàcari*) 156, 157, 340
Basilica di San Marco *29*, 85, *86*, 144–5
Biennale 151
Burano 159
Ca' Dario 153
Ca' d'Oro 155
Ca' Rezzonico 91, *152*, 154
cafés 110, *111*, 144, 149, *154*
Campanile 147
Campo dei Mori 160
Campo San Pantalon 158
Campo San Polo 158
Campo Santa Maria Formosa 152
Campo Santa Maria Margherita 157
Campo Santo Stefano 149
Cannaregio 159–60
carnival *156*, 162–3
casino 155
Castello 149–52
Chioggia 340–1
Doges 32, 37, *40–1*, *146*, 147–8, 150, 152, 158
Dorsoduro 155–7
floods 144, 340
Fondaco dei Turchi 155
Fondamente Nuove 159
food 103, 104–5, 106, *107*, 108, 157
France and 44, 45–6, 105, 144, 161, 181
Frari, Santa Maria Gloriosa dei 90–1, 151, 158
Galleria dell'Accademia 154
Gesuati 156
Gesuiti 159
Ghetto 160, 161
Giudecca 156
gondolas *6–7*, *143*, *150*, *159*
Grand Canal *150*, 152–5
Harry's Bar 110–11, 148
hotels 151, 153
I Carmini 156
Il Redentore 156
Jews 52, 160–1
La Fenice *94*, 96–7, 149
La Pietà 91, 150
La Salute 152–3
lagoon 144, 340, 341
Libreria Sansoviniana 148
Lido di Jesolo 339–40
Lido di Venezia 340
Madonna del'Orto 91, 159
markets 157–8
Mercerie 147
Murano *81*, 159
Museo Correr 148
Museo Navale 151
music 44, *45*, 93–4
opera 44, *45*, 93–4, 96–7
Palazzo Contarini del Bovolo *85*, 149
Palazzo Ducale *40*, *146*, 147–8
Palazzo Pisani Gritti 154
Palazzo Vendramin-Calergi 155
Palazzo Venier (Guggenheim) 153
Pellestrina 340
Pescheria 158
Piazza San Marco 143–4
Ponte dei Sospiri 150
Ponte di Rialto *33*, 155
Punta della Dogana 152
Republic 21, 36–7, 40–1, 43, 44, 45, 46
restaurants 149, *154*, 160
Rialto *33*, 154, 157–8
Riva degli Schiavoni 149, 150
San Francesco della Vigna 151
San Giorgio degli Schiavoni 150
San Giorgio Maggiore *132–3*, 148, *149*
San Marco 143–7
San Nicolò dei Mendicoli 156
San Polo 157–8
San Sebastiano 156
San Trovaso 156
San Zaccaria 90, 150
San Zanipolo 152
Santa Croce 157–8
Santa Maria dei Miracoli 159

Santo Stefano 149
Scuola Grande di San Rocco 91, 158
secessionism 68, 147
shopping 147, 152, 154, 157–8
Torcello 85–6, 159
Torre dell'Orologio 147
Venetian League 68
villas 117–18, 119, 121, *154*
Zattere 156
Ventimiglia 300, 301
Venzone 182
Verbania 286
Vercelli 108, 266
Verdi, Giuseppe 35, 93, 95–6, 97, 98–9, 110, 208–9, 325–6
Vernazza *296–7*, 308
Verona 31, 35–6, 37, *56–7*, 60, 167–71
architecture 169, 170
Arena *30*, 85, 97, 98, *99*, 168
Austria and 167
cafés *56–7*, 169
Casa di Giulietta 169
Castel San Pietro 170
Castelvecchio 169
Duomo 169
Festival 98, 169
food 106
France and *100–1*, 46
Giardini Giusti 117, *120*, 170
music 85, 93
opera 85, 97, 98, *99*, 169
Piazza Bra 167–9
Piazza dei Signori 169
Piazza del Erbe 169
restaurants 167
Romeo and Juliet 167, 169–70
San Fermo Maggiore 170
San Giorgio in Braida 170
San Zeno Maggiore 85, 169
Sant'Anastasia 169
Santo Stefano 170
shopping 167
Teatro Filarmonico 97
Teatro Romano 170
Tomba di Giulietta 170
Torre dei Lamberti 169
Vinltaly 112, 170
Veronese, Paolo 118
Bergamo 236
Genoa 295
Milan 213
Modena 331
Venice 148, 154, 156
Verona 167, 170
Vicenza 172
Villa Barbaro *87*, 119
Versace, Donatella *and* Gianni 73, 80, 83, 205, 211, 219, 278, 279
Vespa *75*, 81, *221*
Vicenza 167, 171–2
architecture 171–2
art 88
Gallerie di Palazzo Leoni Montanari 173
gardens 120
Roman remains 171
Teatro Olimpico 97, *171*, 172
villas 117, 118–19, 120, 121, 171, 172
Victor Emmanuel II, King 47, 49, 67, 208, 247, 253, 256
Vigevano 227
Vignola *331*
villas 45, 117–20, 121
see also **Palladio, Andrea**
Arvedi 119
Balbianello 280–1
Barbaro *87*, 119, *154*, 177
Carlotta 117, 119, *280*, 281
Cicogna Mozzoni 120
Cordelina *119*
d'Este 280
Doria 305
Durazzo 307
Emo 119, 176
Feltrinelli 274
Fiordaliso 274, 275
Hanbury *114–15*, *117*, 302
Isola Bella 117, 119, 120, 284–5
Isola Madre 119, 285
Malcontenta (Foscari) 119, *121*, 175
Manin 181
Melzi *271*, 282
Monastero 281
Olmo 127–8, 279
Pallavicini 120, 283, 305
Pisani 119, 175
Reale 226
Romara 274
Rotonda (Capra) 118–19, 121, 171, 172
Sandi 177
Saraceno 119, 177
Serbelloni *119*, 282
Taranto 286
Trissino Marzotto 120
Valmarano ai Nani 177
Vipiteno (Sterzing) 200
Virgil *28*, 30
Visconti, Luciano 153
Visconti dynasty
Castel l'Arquato 324–5
Milan 38, 86, 205, 207, 225, 227, 228, 229
Vivaldi, Antonio *92*, 93, 94, 150
Volta, Alessandro 278–9

W

walking *see* **sport**
wildlife
see also **national/regional parks, nature reserves**
badgers 125
bears 125, 196–7, 232
birds 124, 125, 126, 128, 129, 183, 190, 243, 307, 342, 343
butterflies 245
chamois 124, 125, 126, 190, 199
deer 125, 126, 190, 196, 341
ermines 243
foxes 125, 196
hares 125, 129
ibex 124–5, 126, 243
lizards 129, 307
marmots 124, 125, 126, 129, 190, 196, 243
mouflons 190
otters 128
stoats 125
toads 342
turtles 128
wine *see* **food and drink**
World Wars 51, 52–3, 123, 125–6, 194, 195

Z

Zegna, Ermenegildo 74, 80, 83, 125, 211

HotelClub

£15 OFF

Join the Club!

Earn Rewards, Get Discounts, Stay Free,
Only with HotelClub!
Across 20,000 Hotels in 97 Countries

INSIGHT GUIDES

Register with

HotelClub.com

and get £15!

At ***HotelClub.com***, we reward our Members with discounts and free stays in their favourite hotels. As a Member, every booking made by you through ***HotelClub.com*** will earn you Member Dollars.

When you register, we will credit your account with ***£15*** which you can use for your next booking! The equivalent of ***£15*** will be credited in US$ to your Member account (as ***HotelClub Member Dollars***). All you need to do is log on to ***www.HotelClub.com/insightguides***. Complete your details, including the Membership Number and Password located on the back of the ***HotelClub.com*** card.

Over 2.2 million Members already use Member Dollars to pay for all or part of their hotel bookings. Join now and start spending Member Dollars whenever and wherever you want – you are not restricted to specific hotels or dates!

With great savings of up to 60% on over 20,000 hotels across 97 countries, you are sure to find the perfect location for business or pleasure. Happy travels from ***HotelClub.com!***

www.insightguides.com